OneStream Foundation Handbook

[Second Edition]

The Architect Factory

Edited by Peter Fugere and Chul Smith

OneStream Press

Disclaimer

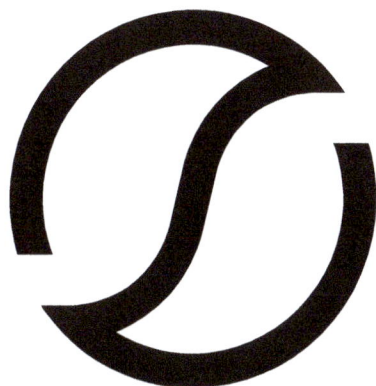

50% OFF VOUCHER

Certification

Validate your technical competence and gain industry recognition with OneStream Software.

In purchasing this book, you are eligible to claim a 50% discount on the OneStream Lead Architect Certification Exam.

To request your voucher, open a case with Credentialing via the ServiceNow Support Portal (https://onestreamsoftware.service-now.com/). Include proof of purchase that contains your name and address, the book title, date of purchase, and proof of payment.

 onestream

About the Authors

Peter Fugere. Recognized as a leader within the consulting community, Peter has been working to deliver world-class Corporate Performance Management (CPM) solutions for the past 20 years. He has worked with Oracle Hyperion Financial Management, Oracle Hyperion Planning, Oracle EPM Cloud Financial Consolidation and Close, Oracle Hyperion Financial Data Quality Management, Hyperion Enterprise, Upstream, SAP BPC (Business Planning and Consolidation) before leaving Oracle in 2012 to help build the OneStream consulting practice.

This work is dedicated to my wife, Courtney. I could not have wished for a better friend and companion. Her support, faith, and love keep me going.

Greg Bankston. A veteran of the consulting community, Greg started working with CPM solutions in the late nineties before moving into consulting with Hyperion Solutions. With exposure to multiple project management methodologies over the last 20 years, during which he has managed well over a hundred projects, Greg has developed a keen sense of where risks typically lie on projects, how to avoid them, and the quickest methods to ensure efficient success.

My chapter is dedicated to my wife, Clara. She left her country, a flourishing career as an architect, her family, friends, and everything she knew to start a new life with me. She is the strongest and bravest woman that I've ever known, and I owe the amazing life that we have together to her.

Eric Osmanski. Eric is a CPA who joined the OneStream Software services organization in 2014 to deliver revolutionary Corporate Performance Management (CPM) solutions. He is currently an Architect focusing on the design, development, and maintenance of OneStream applications for OneStream's largest and most complex customers.

My chapter is dedicated to my wife, Marisa.

Jonathan Golembiewski. Jon Golembiewski is a Senior Architect on the OneStream Services team. Jon joined OneStream in 2013 as one of the first members of the Services Team. Jon's experience stretches across both Consolidation and Planning projects. He has worked on projects in over 20 countries, including OneStream's first customers in South Africa, Australia, Finland, and Norway. Jon has also helped build and deliver training for both customers and consultants. He has lived in Amsterdam and currently resides in Pittsburgh, Pennsylvania.

I'd like to thank my parents, Dave and Sandra, for giving everything they could to me. I could have never achieved success without you.

John Von Allmen. John Von Allmen is a CPA who has experience in Financial Reporting, Data Integration, and Consolidation Software. He worked for UpStream Software and Hyperion Solutions and then founded DataFusion Consulting. John has served many different roles at OneStream as a founder, from Consultant to Pre-Sales and Chief Financial Officer. He served as Chief Financial Officer until October 2019 and is currently a Vice President in the Architect Factory of OneStream Software.

This work is dedicated to my wife Elizabeth and my son Jack.

Todd Allen. Todd Allen has been with OneStream since it acquired its first customer. He has 20+ years of software industry experience in a variety of arenas, including traceability systems on factory floors, healthcare solutions, software startups, and implementation consulting services. Along with his peers, he carries a deep passion for customer success and exceeding the status quo..!

This work is dedicated to my family (Wife – Betsy, Son – Jack, and Daughter – Savannah). Thanks for being patient, understanding, and supportive of our OneStream journey.

Nick Kroppe. Nick has a deep passion for enabling implementation consultants and customers, which he has been doing for over five years in his role at OneStream. Nick started out his OneStream career as an implementation consultant and has since grown into a technical guru focused on enabling the OneStream community. Nick currently works as the North America Remote Consulting Support Manager, and has worked with over 250+ customers in his OneStream career.

Nick dedicates his contribution to this book to his family and to all his colleagues that have helped him along the way in developing both as a OneStream professional and a better individual.

Chul Smith. Chul has over 25 years of accounting, finance and IT experience using, maintaining, implementing and supporting consolidation and finance systems as both client and consultant. In 2006, he moved from corporate consolidations in Minneapolis, MN, to HFM consulting in Paris, France. In 2007, he relocated to London, England where he spent the next four years consulting with a small Swedish IBM Cognos Controller consultancy. The use of Controller across Europe expanded his work experience to nine countries in multiple industries.

His 2012 United States homecoming triggered his return to HFM & FDM as a freelance consultant with projects in New York City, Montreal, and Sherbrooke, Quebec. He began working with OneStream in 2013 and a year later, was hired to join their services team. Today, he's a Distinguished Architect within OneStream's Strategic Customer Advisory team.

Chul holds a Bachelor of Science in Accounting from the University of Minnesota – Carlson School of Management and a non-practicing CPA license in the state of Minnesota.

Jody Di Giovanni. Jody Di Giovanni is the Director of Remote Consulting Support at OneStream Software, where she leads a team of highly skilled OneStream Remote Support Consultants that focus on customers' post-go-live success and implementation build items. Jody came to OneStream in 2015 with experience in Accounting and Financial Systems, including one of the first OneStream implementations.

A huge thank you to my three beautiful and ever-supportive kids for their love, patience, and smiles that continue to inspire me every day. A shout-out to my RCS team, who amaze me day in and day out with your skills, and who are such an amazing group to work with. And last, but not least, thank you Tony, for teaching me not only OneStream, but to be a better person.

Jacqui Slone. Jacqui is the Director of Training at OneStream Software. In 2013, she began working at OneStream as a technical writer and from there moved over to the training department. She has spent most of her time at OneStream delivering training and developing course content for customers, partners, and employees. In 2019, she became the Director of Training and leads a global team of content developers and trainers.

I am forever grateful to the OneStreamers who opened the door and took a chance on the high school English teacher. You were always patient and made time for me even though I know you didn't have either to spare. A big thank you to my family who always go above and beyond to support me even when I don't deserve it. To the OneStream Training Department, thank you for your dedication, passion, and the incredible contribution you make each day. Lastly, thank you Starbucks Iced Coffee, for supporting me through each workday and work night.

Nick Blazosky. Nick joined OneStream in 2017 after spending his entire career in CPM consulting. He is proud to be one of the original members of the North American Pre-Sales team, and is currently configuring GolfStream and the vertical demo applications as the leader of the Demo Engineering Team. Nick lives with his wife and daughter in San Antonio, Texas.

This book is dedicated to all the mentors I've had along the way in the CPM space. If you have the chance to inspire and lift up young people starting their careers, I hope you can. First, I want to thank Tad Bowen for introducing me to Hyperion, giving me my first job in consulting, and for his continued guidance to this day. Thank you to my Marketsphere friends. I would be lost if it wasn't for the great friendship and mentorship of Janie Villarreal and Satish Masina during my time in Houston and Darren Garett, who would let me ask all the "stupid" questions I wanted after work, trail running at the Umstead State Park. To the folks from my time at TopDown Consulting – Paul Hoch, Steve Davis, and Ricardo ("El Jefe") Musquiz – I learned so much from your examples, it's hard to put into words how thankful I was to work with the best in the business. It'd be hard to imagine my life without Tucker Pease, who I met at TDC and who vouched for me at OneStream. I owe Tucker so much as a mentor, constant source of encouragement, and friend. To Bill Lovelace, for taking a chance and bringing me into Pre-Sales, despite me coming from a consulting background and losing my laptop the first week on the job. Finally, to Roy Googin, who I instantly befriended, day one, drinking gin and talking about OneStream. Roy has been my mentor and friend at OneStream: a confidant and sounding board all-in-one. To everyone else who helped, listened, inspired, and challenged me, I wish I could list you all, but know that you are all appreciated.

Andy Moore. Andy works as the Director of Partner Enablement in North America, focusing his efforts on enabling colleagues, partners, and customers. Andy's OneStream experience stretches over 5+ years with experience on over 100+ customers. Andy's focus is not in just one area of OneStream but across the entire platform, focusing on providing companies with holistic designs that create value, enable growth, and which provide successful business transformations.

I'd like to dedicate my work in this book to my fiancé Kristen, my colleagues, friends, and family for continuously coaching, supporting, and believing in me, which has given me the drive to get to this point! I look forward to continuing my work at OneStream and giving back to the community that helped me get to where I am today.

Sam Richards. Sam joined the OneStream Software services organization in 2016 as a senior consultant when he decided to leave the world of corporate reporting. He has over ten years of experience in the Finance/IT field, and is currently an Architect at OneStream, focusing on the design and development of some of its largest and most complex customers.

I wouldn't be able to accomplish what I have without the love and support of my wife, Candace Richards, and children Kinslee and Everly.

Terry Shea. Terry Shea is the Vice President of Analytic and Integration Solutions at OneStream. A well-known expert in the EPM space, Terry has over 20 years' experience developing data integration and analysis solutions for hundreds of organizations of all sizes and across all industries, including some of the largest multi-national companies in the world. Terry is currently part of a team charged with developing OneStream expertise throughout the company/partner/customer ecosystem.

Dedicated to my wife and kids: Lauren, Kiera, Fiona, Dylan, and Meghan.

Shawn Stalker. Shawn Stalker joined OneStream in 2013 and serves as the Vice President of MarketPlace Development. Shawn has worked in the Corporate Performance Management (CPM) area for over 20 years, maintaining, implementing, and supporting consolidation and financial systems. He has worked on products such as Oracle Hyperion Essbase, Oracle Hyperion Financial Management, and OutlookSoft, before joining UpStream Software in 2006, where he helped to build their development and QA teams. Shawn worked at UpStream through acquisitions by Hyperion and then Oracle prior to joining OneStream, where he helped start the QA and MarketPlace teams.

To my children Nola, Keira, and Gavin, who will inherit this world and make it a better place.

Jeff Jones. Jeff joined OneStream Software in 2014 as a technical support engineer and currently serves as the Vice President of Customer Support. Since joining OneStream Software, he has been heavily involved in many large customer projects assisting with environment sizing and application performance tuning. His mission is to continue to strive for 100% customer success and to continue to provide the highest level of support to the OneStream customer base.

This work is dedicated to my wife, Erin. Her love and support are what keep me reaching my career goals and enjoying life.

Tony Dimitrie. Tony joined OneStream Software in January 2012 as employee #10. Tony dedicated his first year to OneStream's first customer and did whatever was needed in order to make the partnership a success. This soon transitioned into being a Subject Matter Expert for customer implementations led by partners. Tony started the Implementation Support department, which can be identified as Remote Consulting Support (RCS) today. Tony has a wealth of OneStream product and organizational knowledge, which helps serve Tony in his current role as Vice President of Training & RCS.

To Jody, who drives me to be better each day, and my friends and family who have put up with my s*!t for years.

Errata

Despite best efforts, mistakes can sometimes creep into books. If you spot a mistake, please feel free to email us at errata@onestreampress.com (with the book title in the subject line).

The errata page for this book is hosted at *www.onestreampress.com/OneStreamFH2*

Table of Contents

Chapter 8: Rules and Calculations   211

Chapter 14: Performance Tuning   387

Foreword

The Journey

The picture below was created by Bob Powers' son, Kyle Powers, and it tells the story of how Bob and I have been sharing the dream of creating the OneStream platform.

We used this graphic to try to explain to prospects why we thought we deserved a chance at their business. Read on if you want a little color on how we presumed the most-admired companies in the world should give OneStream a chance.

The *OneStream Foundation Handbook* represents a huge sense of pride and accomplishment for me. You are probably wondering why I would make this statement. After all, I did not write the book; a group of super-smart and dedicated people (OneStreamers, as we like to call them) did the hard work. To understand why this book feels like such an accomplishment, and source of pride for me, we need to go all the way back to the 1990s when I first started working with first-generation CPM products (IMRS Micro Control and Hyperion Enterprise).

I spent the first ten years of my career working as an accountant and financial analyst in some large global corporations. I had hopes and aspirations of becoming a CFO at one of these prestigious companies. However, at the same time, I was writing and selling custom business software as a side interest. I still remember the day (in June 1993) that I was introduced to a Lotus 1-2-3 Add-in (yes, I said Lotus 1-2-3!) that connected my spreadsheet to my analytic application and which allowed me to submit my intercompany matching updates to our corporate headquarters. This Add-in allowed me to work on budgets, create financial statements, and use my spreadsheet skills to interact with a larger data universe (I was blown away).

Fast-forward a few years, and IMRS Micro Control had become Hyperion Enterprise. At this time, I found myself in charge of a worldwide Hyperion Enterprise deployment at a massive global manufacturing company (we had 80 deployments of Hyperion Enterprise around the world). This job was quite a challenge – the company really relied on Hyperion Enterprise – but every time the business changed, we had to update all 80 instances of the application. (This was crazy hard, time-consuming, and incredibly stressful.) There had to be a better way to manage this system and deliver the application to Users around the world. There was. The answer was Citrix. Citrix allowed us to deploy the application in a single instance and centralized fashion. From my perspective, this change created the foundation of the Modern CPM platform. Having a centralized

1

global information system with the agility to model changing business scenarios, support external statutory reporting, and provide a flexible planning system, became an expectation and a requirement for the office of the CFO.

In the late 1990s, after Citrix and web application development technologies took hold as a foundation technology for deploying enterprise software, a new set of challenges came into focus. The centralization of critical business systems drove higher data volumes, higher User concurrency, and increased the complexities related to data integration. In January of 2000, Craig Colby, Jeff DeGrieck, and I founded a company called UpStream Software. Our goal was to reduce the growing cost and complexity of collecting and validating the source data that was required to feed Hyperion Enterprise. This was a niche strategy, but we felt good about the opportunity because Hyperion was a market leader. The UpStream company was ultimately acquired by Hyperion in 2007, and is now known as Financial Data Quality Management (FDM).

UpStream is an important part of this story for a lot of reasons. First, it taught me and the other founders how to be entrepreneurs, and let us build a company that had an extreme focus on the customer. This is critical because we knew what we were trying to accomplish, and all our energy went into achieving the goal of creating a transparent and Workflow-driven approach to loading data. Second, the UpStream journey introduced us to the people who would go on to form the foundation of OneStream's thought leadership team and partner community. Third, UpStream provided broad exposure to all of the different CPM application technologies that were emerging in the early 2000s. Our focus at UpStream was to provide smart connectors that let us remote control any CPM engine that had an open API. This meant that with each integration we built, we gained a fresh perspective on the strengths and weaknesses of each of the different products in the market. We were gaining a deep understanding of where the CPM market could go.

So, why is this book such a source of pride? Stay with me a little longer; I promise I will tie this all together for you. I mentioned that UpStream introduced us to key members of the CPM community, and that statement *cannot be emphasized enough*. I did not know it at the time, but UpStream created an intersection of technologies, ideas, people, and relationships that would enable a group of us to think beyond the niche ideas of UpStream into the grander vision that underpins OneStream software.

In November 2000, Craig and I flew to Stamford, Connecticut, for an engineering meeting between UpStream and Hyperion. UpStream was a partner that was tightly integrating with Hyperion's CPM products, and we were gaining a little market recognition. Hyperion engineering and product management had some early interest in what we were doing with UpStream WebLink, because data loading and data quality was always a big customer pain point. Nothing came out of this meeting in terms of a business relationship, but the meeting introduced me to Bob Powers – the engineer that was working on the next generation analytic engine that Hyperion was developing to replace Hyperion Enterprise.

Bob attended the meeting, asked a few questions, and stopped me as we exited the meeting and said, "Really impressive product... are you thinking about integrating with Hyperion Financial Management (HFM)? That is our next generation product that I am working on."

I immediately liked Bob; he was super-smart and humble. I was eager to build a connector to HFM, and I was excited about having a direct relationship with the lead engineer. From 2001-2006, life was a blur; UpStream was growing 90-100% a year, and we were building integrations to all of Hyperion's products and some competing products (Comshare and OutlookSoft). In 2003, we settled in and became an exclusive partner to Hyperion, and the UpStream engineering team and I started working a lot closer with Bob and Hyperion's engineering team at this time. We collaborated on tighter engine integration, product UI consistency, performance, and overall technology advancement.

Bob and I were forming a mutual respect for each other's engineering skills, and we liked collaborating. Then, in 2006, Hyperion came to me and said, "We have been dating long enough. We would like to purchase UpStream and make you part of the family." After careful consideration, we felt this was the best outcome for all stakeholders since the company was really built for – and targeted towards – Hyperion's products and community. UpStream became Hyperion FDM in mid-2006, and we started to really integrate UpStream's engine technology into the Hyperion product suite. Bob and I began to work more closely together, and we often talked about what a next-generation CPM product could be.

Almost there… the OneStream dream is about to take shape!

In 2007, acquisitions became prevalent in the CPM space, and in a matter of months, all the pillar companies were scooped up by larger enterprise software companies. In mid-2007, Oracle acquired Hyperion, then quickly after that SAP acquired Business Objects, and IBM acquired Cognos. Then, just like that, the standalone CPM market was gone. At this time, Bob and I both stepped away from the CPM market. Bob went on to become the CTO of a SaaS company, and I took some time off so that I could spend more time with my family.

Bob and I kept in touch over the next few years, but we were both busy living our lives as we watched the financial crisis rage around us (what a crazy time). Around 2009, I started getting bored, and I was looking for a new challenge. Jeff DeGrieck, Craig Colby, and I began to think about our next company. We initially focused on XBRL as a potential market opportunity. Bob and I talked about this, but he was not that interested since his true passion was centered on in-memory analytic engines and not statutory reporting. I also had a real passion for engineering complex analytic software, but I just didn't think there was room in the market to compete against Oracle, SAP, and IBM. I felt that we should just focus on an adjacent/complementary product space such as XBRL.

Here is where it all comes together. In late 2009, Jeff DeGrieck, Craig Colby, and I went to Washington DC to attend an XBRL conference. Within four hours of attending the conference, we were at the bar mourning the death of our 'next' company idea. It only took us a few sessions and a few interviews with existing players in the market to realize there was no way to build a meaningful business in the XBRL space. We ate lots of good food, drank too much, and goofed around in the capital for a few days, and then returned home. After that conference, we had a choice. Do nothing and look for other business interests or follow what we know and believe in our passion for CPM. It was hard for us to legitimately say to each other, let's build an application to take on the big dogs (Oracle, SAP, and IBM).

In 2010, OneStream was born. It started with a call to Bob, where we discussed the potential to create a unified platform that encompassed the capabilities of all the products that we had seen in the evolving CPM space. This space had expanded over the years to go way beyond Financial Planning and Reporting to now include solutions such as Account Reconciliations, Financial Close Management, and many other domain-centric products for the office of finance.

I remember being on the phone with Bob and pacing around my front yard when we came to the conclusion that we would embark on a software architecture and coding journey that would be the equivalent of two people trying to eat an elephant for dinner. We discussed the idea that we needed to build a platform that could basically replace the 15 or so different CPM products with a single unified platform. The name OneStream comes from the idea that these 15 products needed to become one platform with infinite Extensibility. This started another blurry phase in my life as both Bob and I went into coding overdrive. We literally divided up the engines that needed to be coded, and just set out coding until we had the foundation of a product.

In 2011, we began to have some core CPM capabilities in place, and it was time to get Craig Colby and other key people like Jeff DeGrieck, Eric Davidson, Terry Shea, Matt Baranowski, Todd Allen, John Von Allmen, Tony Dimitrie, Shawn Stalker, and Todd Newman involved to formally launch the product. This was a massive product that would require a lot of testing and validation before we could sell it to a customer. The 2010-2012 years were really focused on R&D and technical validation; the engines had to be solid, and the data had to be right. We managed to get our first customers in 2012 and began the long process of building an operational company.

The next task was to get a group of industry and product experts to join our team and drive us towards product implementation success. We went after Peter Fugere, who I had met way back in the early days of HFM (he wrote the book on HFM). Next, John Von Allmen said we should go after Steve Mebius (he architected the Hyperion GE implementation). Steve was a big fan of Jon Golembiewski, so we hired him too. Tony Dimitrie knew Jerri McConnell, who knew Eric Osmanski, and the list of Rockstars grew. At the same time, we were heads down on guaranteeing success at our first customer – Federal Mogul – and we were working with Jody Di Giovanni, a

Foreword

OneStream evangelist, and she eventually joined our team. Each time we added a key team member, they led us to other key people, and many of them have come together to share their deep knowledge of OneStream as authors of this book (Shawn Stalker, Jon Golembiewski, Eric Osmanski, Jody Di Giovanni, Jacqui Slone, Chul Smith, Nick Kroppe, Jeff Jones, Andy Moore, Sam Richards, Nick Blazosky, Greg Bankston).

Here is where the pride and personal gratification starts. Just like UpStream, we started a business with a passion for our product and a commitment to our customers (our mission has always been to create fanatical customer success). The combination of a great product and great people has let us attract the best and brightest people from the CPM community. The one thing that I have always known is that if we created a great product and we could attract the best people in the CPM industry, there would be no stopping us. When I look at the names of the authors and contributors to this book, I see a list of people that have given a lot of time, energy, and late nights to help OneStream develop as a company. I am humbled by their commitment to making OneStream a great company.

Each Rockstar that joins OneStream helps us attract and hire the next Rockstar. I have only talked about this phenomenon from the product and services side of this business, but this pattern of relationships and friendships repeats itself in every part of our company. This is the true magic of OneStream.

Tom Shea, Co-Founder and CEO OneStream Software

1

Introduction

Originally written by Peter Fugere, updated by Chul Smith

Welcome to the OneStream Foundation Handbook. We hope this book will serve not only as a guide to help you become certified, but also act as a reference as you build your career implementing and supporting OneStream.

This book is meant to be part of your library, but not your only reference; indeed, it is not an administrator's guide. Administrator guides answer the 'how' of settings in OneStream, but this book answers the 'why'.

For example, if you need to know where the settings are for the intercompany (IC) member, so you can map data to it for your intercompany accounts, this book will not be all that helpful to you. That information is well-documented in the OneStream Documentation (click the ? in the application) and Resources section of OneStream Community website. But those places do not tell you *how* other people are using the IC member to simplify the close, how they integrate it with other features, plus any tips for making the close easier and more auditable. If you need to understand *why*, then I think the following pages in this book will help.

The good news, moving forward, is that there really could not be a more qualified team to bring this information to you. Not only has the team writing this book pioneered many of the approaches detailed, they have also been working exclusively with OneStream longer than anyone else. They have decades of experience with Corporate Performance Management (CPM) systems, and have worked with products from SAP, Oracle, and other suites.

What is OneStream?

OneStream Software is a powerful platform that performs all the critical roles one would desire from a world-class Corporate Performance Management (CPM) solution. At its core is a powerful budget and forecasting, consolidation, financial data quality, and management reporting solution. This platform includes solutions like Account Reconciliation, Task Management, People Planning, and Compliance solutions.

OneStream, as mentioned above, really is a *platform*. A technology platform is a set or group of technologies or applications on which other technologies or applications are developed. A great example of this is Visual Basic. On that technology, all kinds of applications and solutions have been created; from simple macros in Excel to more complex database automation programs. OneStream allows developers to write software on our software, and that defines a true platform.

We talk a lot about extensibility. Extensibility means the ability to be extended or stretched. Really, it is a software engineering and design principle that considers the ability and level of effort required to implement new functionality, and which facilitates enhancements without impacting the existing functionality. It is a powerful concept. OneStream is extensible in several ways, which all need to be considered when forging designs. They include dimensions, workflow, cubes, and applications. The Solution Exchange also allows for extensibility. Extensibility allows OneStream to do everything it does.

The OneStream Solution Exchange has fully functioning applications, sample dimensions, and application starter kits. OneStream develops some of them while others have been created by our partner network and those in the OneStream Community. A couple of OneStream-developed examples include People Planning and Capital Planning. People Planning manages all employee and vendor-related details, including compensation benefits and travel expenses; this makes it easier to add new employees and their training plans. Capital Planning manages all capital assets and related expenses, including depreciation and insurance. Customers can get information about the impact capital planning decisions have on business-wide financial results. We won't get too far into each of these solutions in this book, but we will cover the foundational concepts that will allow you to design for, and consider, the implications of adding anything from the Solution Exchange.

The other concept we will spend some time on, in this book, is the concept and principles of **relational blending**. This is a powerful concept that is based on the simple fact that *not everything belongs in a cube data model*. Other products will force virtually everything into a cube if they are based on multidimensional models. It's the old cliché, 'When you're a hammer, every problem looks like a nail.' In OneStream, we have a full toolbox. When you want to use a cube, a relational table, or something in between, you can (and should). Because of the platform, users will not have issues around the timing of data and the integration of multiple systems. This is a game-changer.

OneStream is more than just a CPM product. It includes XP&A, financial signaling/steering, and account reconciliation, to name a few. It holds a lot of power and flexibility. We will cover our proven methodology in this book, plus explain how you can benefit from the system and work off an effective blueprint. One thing we have a lot of pride about (here at OneStream) is having so many clients willing to be a reference. Many companies use OneStream with fantastic results. Many people use the platform to make their close and budget cycle smoother and improve the work they are doing. The key is obvious: there is a right way to put this tool in place. This book shares the right approach, and the tips that will save you hours – maybe days – of frustration and pain.

Contents

This book is not just written for people who want to implement OneStream for the first time, although the flow of the book does follow the lifecycle of design and implementation. Before you even get the product in your company, you will likely need to build a case for buying the tool. This book will help you to understand the three differentiators that OneStream offers, and help you unlock the full value of a project.

Chapter 2, *Methodology and the Project* by Greg Bankston (updated by Greg Bankston), covers multiple areas when planning for, and beginning, your implementation. We cover things such as requirements gathering, design considerations, choosing a partner, and testing methodologies.

We also discuss the importance of defining scope, and creating a timeline, as well as supporting your application after the project team has moved on. We even tackle the tough topic of project management, particularly regarding why a project manager is critical, along with understanding different methodologies, such as Waterfall and Agile.

Finally, we discuss the overarching challenges of managing your implementation. What critical elements do you have to balance during the course of a project in order to achieve success? What are the trade-offs involved in them? How can you mitigate risk along the way?

At the end of Chapter 2, you should have a solid understanding of how to best position yourself and your implementation for success, and how to handle obstacles as they arise. Experience has shown that challenges always come up, so it's best to be ready for them!

Chapter 3, *Design* by Peter Fugere (updated by Chul Smith), will cover the critical steps when making sure a project gets off on the right foot. This chapter explains how to utilize cubes and extensibility to have a good design. This chapter will start to explain key objectives and provide the foundation for beginning your design. You should leave this chapter with a good understanding of what OneStream is capable of.

Then, the chapter will cover key drivers to help identify the goal when embarking upon a project using OneStream, plus the team that should be assembled. The key to having a good project will be starting the first two phases correctly from Chapter 2, thus providing a strong foundation for your project. The design part of this chapter will cover the fundamentals of dimensions, and some key considerations when designing them.

The main aim of this chapter is to explain how you might get better use from the product, by making some simple updates to the design. It will cover many of the tips and techniques you will need to have a great implementation, which will allow the later chapters to go into deeper detail. There is no 'secret sauce' to having a great project. There are some simple guiding principles that – when followed – ensure success. In fact, almost every successful consulting company uses quite similar processes and approaches. The key is simplifying the transfer of ownership and ensuring high-speed end-user adoption.

Chapter 4, *Consolidation* by Eric Osmanski (updated by Nick Bolinger), will cover the concepts and approach for building what many consider to be one of the two pillars of CPM. Consolidation is much more than aggregating data. Global enterprises are tasked with solving complex consolidation challenges every day – often with legacy tools or spreadsheets that are inflexible, create manual work, and unreliable. As an organization grows and becomes more sophisticated, these tools are no longer able to meet the business's requirements. In this chapter, we cover the most common challenges and the various solutions OneStream's unified platform can provide, always keeping in mind the balance between maintenance, user experience, and performance.

Chapter 5, *Planning* by Jonathan Golembiewski (updated by Jonathan Golembiewski), takes his years of experience implementing planning, and explains some of the most important design considerations. Easily the most common use of OneStream, planning (with the detailed requirements that today's companies require) is anything but easy. The volumes of data, the complexity of calculations, and the need for flexibility make OneStream just about a necessity.

Chapter 6, *Data Integration* by John Von Allmen (updated by Joakim Kulan), covers the fundamentals of gathering data from disparate source systems and serving it to the OneStream database in a way that provides transparency, auditability, and security.

Chapter 7, *Workflow* by Todd Allen (updated by Chul Smith), will cover what the workflow is. Why do we have workflow? And where does one start!? Great questions. For folks who are new to OneStream, workflow is one of the more powerful portions of the tool. We consider it the backbone of the system. It defines *who* does *what*, *when*, and *how*.

In this area of the platform, we can import basically any kind of data. Then transform it, validate it, calculate it, automate it, and perform analysis on it. We can even certify it. Those are just some highlights, as workflow has so much to offer. Take the journey with us through the history and evolution of OneStream workflow!

Chapter 8, *Rules and Calculations* by Nick Kroppe and Chul Smith, breaks down the intricacies of writing rules. If these calculations were easy, most products could do them. They don't. OneStream expertly handles the most difficult and sophisticated aspects of consolidation and planning, from translation, eliminations, and contributions – and why we do what we do in OneStream – it is all covered here.

Chapter 9, *Security* by Jody Di Giovanni (updated by Bobby Doyon), provides a unique perspective on security, not just from the standpoint of implementation, but from the author's world of experience in support. Jody sees the impact of bad design practices and the rework required to fix them. Jody's views and guidance are truly matchless and invaluable, and she will explain the foundational principles for building security that can last for the lifetime of your implementation.

Chapter 10, *Reporting* by Jacqui Slone and Chul Smith (updated by Chul Smith), covers reporting fundamentals. A system is only as good as the reports you create. In this chapter, you'll learn how to deliver quality reports that perform to their peak.

Chapter 11, *Excel and Spreadsheet Reporting* by Nick Blazosky (updated by Nick Blazosky), covers all the things you can do with OneStream in Excel. Quick Views, Cube Views, Table Views, Excel, and Spreadsheet. With so many options, which one should you choose and why? This chapter familiarizes readers with the various ad-hoc reporting methods and how to use them. By the end of this chapter, the reader should be an expert in the various means by which to create ad-hoc reports.

Chapter 12, *Analytic Blend* by Andy Moore, Sam Richards, and Terry Shea (updated by Chul Smith), discusses OneStream's unmatched ability to 'blend' validated financial data, highly dimensional operational data, and detailed transactional data in one platform for comprehensive, controlled, and consumable analysis and visualization. You will be able to combine financial, operational, and transactional data in a single dashboard for all-inclusive visualization and analysis. Allow your finance team to maintain one source of truth for data, extending access to business managers and executives with confidence. And eliminate data latency and unnecessary replication of financial data for analysis, while retaining security, intelligence, workflow, governance, and audit trails. Phew!

Chapter 13 sees Shawn Stalker (updated by Shawn Stalker) cover the *Introduction to the Solution Exchange*. It includes a brief history and how it was created, then delves into the Solution Exchange's relationship with the platform development team, development processes, how we differ, and how we work together. Shawn then covers what is in the Solution Exchange, before diving into environment considerations, solution upgrading, and customization.

Chapter 14, *Performance Tuning* by Jeff Jones and Tony Dimitrie, covers how to tune and optimize your application. Again, we have two experts – who are responsible for supporting many of our client applications – sharing their experiences. Not only do they give examples, but they explain *why* and *how* to resolve numerous issues.

The Life Cycle of Data and its History

It all starts when someone buys something. It could be anything – a book, a car, or a coffee. This simple transaction, done millions and billions of times, is the start of a chain of events that drives the reporting of a business. The cashier enters that transaction into a cash register, or more likely today, a computer. All kinds of information are captured: the item bought, date and time, location of the sale, the price, and probably more.

That single transaction record gets moved to a larger database. More detail of the transaction is identified and tagged to the data. In what region did this sale take place? What reporting period is it? Lots more detail is captured.

But how does that data become something meaningful that explains what is happening in the business? And the real question that more and more companies ask is how that single data point contributes to something that is *actionable*.

In the late 1970s, IBM and Oracle developed the first SQL databases based on Edgar Codd's research on the System R database. Computers were large, bulky, and expensive, and the ones available for less than a few thousand bucks were only for enthusiasts. But over the next 20 years, the price and other restrictions would fall. Companies built large databases (at that time) of all kinds of information, but the reporting fell short. The large transaction volumes made the types of summary viewing slow and difficult.

The large databases recorded these transactions in sales databases, inventory systems, and general ledgers. The data across all of them was often not consistent, though.

More broadly, key systems like the general ledger are often considered the 'book of record'. This book of record is the single truth that should be used across the business – because those are the numbers that are externally reported.

However, businesses do not report transactions; they report balances or subtotals of the transactions. Furthermore, the types of calculations that need to be done on the data are not things that lend themselves to be done on transactional data. Accounting rules requiring translation and eliminations are complicated enough to reconcile on a summary level, but useless on the transactional level. Business processes, like forecasting and budgeting that add dimensions and slices of data, are done at a level above transactional data.

So, while the large SQL databases captured transactional data as part of a business process, used to run the business, more agile databases were needed to support decision-making. A special type of database for this was called OLAP. By the 1990s, many companies were developing all kinds of such agile OLAP databases, for all kinds of different functions in the business. Consolidation, tax provisioning, budgeting, capital planning, cash forecasting, and human resource systems were all springing up. Helping companies undertake these different business reporting endeavors became known as Corporate Performance Management (CPM).

By the early 2000s, there was an opportunity for the larger players to consolidate all these functions at different companies and bundle them as 'suites'. While they could address many business issues, and help with reporting, the management of these systems proved costly and difficult – to say the least.

The other thing happening in the early 2000s was that many new vendors began to offer new reporting called Business Intelligence (BI). Most BI projects then were managed by the IT department, and they looked to leverage the Extract, Transform, and Load (ETL) tools and Online Analytical Processing (OLAP) software that companies had in place. There was a natural overlap with CPM suites, and many of them began to offer BI as part of the CPM offering.

By the late 2000s, new companies sprung up that even broke the individual processes into several databases. Disconnected planning, for example, doubled down on creating applications spread across organizations. While it gave smaller groups more of a voice in creating plans, a quick Google search will reveal how it created a lot of infighting.

And while all that was happening, in the offices of the CFOs, the costs of supporting massive transactional databases, maintaining the software to keep them in sync, and the dozens of business vendors each offering an application was getting ridiculous. I was on a CPM project for a health provider in Michigan in 2011, and we had a project manager, seven product-specific experts, and an infrastructure consultant on the team. We completed a design and installation for one client, and the cost was over $100,000. We did not even start building anything for them! Costs were getting out of control, which brought pressure and scrutiny on projects that made them more difficult to manage and deliver.

By the early 2010s, the team at OneStream had an idea that – in hindsight – seems so obvious, but which was truly revolutionary. If we could deliver a platform that could do all the things mentioned above, the support, complexity, and difficulty of maintaining all these CPM databases would be drastically reduced. The suite was created from different products, all using different technology at different times, by different companies. This platform would be a single set of software that could do everything CPM was defined by, but which could grow and evolve with the business. This platform would defy disconnected planning, but still allow everyone to have specific applications and requirements. It was a game-changer.

Why Use the OneStream Platform?

OneStream looks at our platform as having three main functions. They are CPM (corporate performance management), operational data/OKRs, and AI/ML. These groupings give different types of insight into your business at different times. I like to describe it as if you're driving a car. CPM is like looking in your rear-view mirrors – the information you are getting is in the past. Even Budget data, by the time it is approved, is dated. This data is often required by law and regulations, and includes Actual, Budget, and Forecast data.

Operational data is like looking at your car's dashboard. You can see the immediate feedback of metrics that tell you how to steer your business. These are often defined as OKRs or metrics in a business. Units sold, new hires; these are small data sets updated very frequently. And while having this information allows you to react quickly, these data sets don't help you long term.

Machine learning used in planning on-time series data is like seeing out your windshield and down the road. The constant, immediate, and accurate forecasts give more information about where you want to take your company.

This Foundation book will focus on CPM and its purpose. Companies that spent millions on data warehouses found the reporting from these systems wanting, and needed better solutions. OneStream is built for consolidations and planning; it is ready to do basic work on day one.

For example, intercompany reconciliations can be a challenge without a CPM tool. You can't use Excel reliably anymore. The fact that OneStream has an out-of-the-box report that allows users to view not only the accounts they have going out, but what other people *in other legal entities* have booked against those amounts, helps the people who are booking those transactions to be proactive.

I like to say CPM tools change the conversation. Instead of people explaining to someone else that there is 'an issue' – each person can see for themselves what the issue is, and more importantly, proactively work to resolve said issue. Instead of, "Did you know your intercompany doesn't balance," the conversation would be, "Yes, I saw the issue, and we think we know what booking caused it. We will have an update in the next couple of hours." This saves time in the reporting process. It makes people more productive.

Flexibility

OneStream, with its Extensible Dimensionality, allows for simple and complex changes to structures. You can have an account as a base member for the Budget, but be a parent for Actuals – or vice versa. The ability of rules to recognize the different structures, and parents and values within system accounts, allows OneStream to aggregate data in a variety of ways. You can design accounts and User Defined dimensions to give tremendous flexibility and handle all kinds of unforeseen changes.

You can load the data one time, and consolidate it in as many ways as you need with different structures and parents. Each parent-child relationship allows for the separate storage of elimination and proportional data. Also, each entity has four separate places where journals can be posted to the system, including parent members. All in all, OneStream provides a means to handle anything that comes your way as your reporting structure changes.

Accountability

OneStream records just about everything that users and administrators do. You can also see key tasks your users are doing and when, and there are audit logs that record how the data changes and who is making those changes.

Workflow with security makes it easier for end-users to navigate the system, and harder for someone to make a mistake. OneStream records date and time stamps, and also records user IDs whilst authenticating them with a variety of commonly-used network security databases. These measures ensure the system is secure and data is safe.

Mergers and Acquisitions

The front end of OneStream benefits from the decades of knowledge our founders have accumulated whilst working with Fortune 100 companies on data integration.

Acquisitions can sometimes prove to be a struggle to integrate to a corporate standard. Consider how every company has a different chart of accounts and structure to their databases. Even companies that work in the same business might have quite different accounts and naming conventions. How do you bring together all these systems into one common chart of accounts? OneStream! An auditable and secure source for all of your data.

Speak Better to Your Data

Not only does OneStream offer one place for reporting data – including consolidation, budgets, and forecasts – it brings together tax provisioning, account reconciliations, leaseholding reporting, and much more. The ability to have all this data in one system speeds up reporting, and ensures that there is little chance the numbers will be out of sync. Instead of reconciling data, people on your team can do things like analyze KPIs or key differences. They won't be spending their time making sure every report reconciles, and each report reconciles to each other.

In turn, workflow's ability to report on all tasks gives visibility into what is driving the time people take to submit. This improves the opportunities to see what is really happening in the business, leading to smarter decisions.

Validating the Data

In this book, we are going to explain how to take advantage of certification and confirmation rules to allow for many types of data to come together and reconcile. Text and document attachments allow OneStream to become the book of record for all your financial close-related documents.

Costs – Rising Audit Fees

Because OneStream has set the standard for data integration and reconciliation, integrations with other systems lead to a platform that is easier to audit; you will find all your data in one place. This improves transparency without sacrificing any security.

OneStream reports provide basic reporting for journals and intercompany data, which makes the system much faster to audit and understand. With OneStream, you can reduce and replace manual control procedures with automated and preventative controls that ultimately reduce your processing and auditing costs. This includes tasks like eliminations and allocations, plus common or repetitive validations within the system.

Leading Practices

The goal of this book is to provide a way for our community to build a system – for our mutual clients – that lives up to the promise of OneStream. There will be reasons why you might not follow every prescribed approach or detail here in this book, but knowledge is power, and you should consider the pros and cons of doing so. Moreover, you should explain these pros and cons to any client. They might be willing to live with something, knowing they are getting a benefit.

Conclusion

In this chapter, we covered the history of OneStream and what defined it. We also laid out the critical parts to a project, and aligned them with the chapters that are to follow. With this knowledge, you are ready to begin your project. That project may be a new set of reports, adding a cash flow, or a full implementation – now you are ready.

Closing each chapter, the authors have included a photo and short story about something that makes them proud to work at OneStream. We thought it would be fun to share *our* journey with our readers. This is mine.

Epilogue

In 2013, I was managing a consulting team doing implementations.

My last book about implementation practices had been released in 2011, but even in two short years, it was clear that there had been a seismic shift in the landscape of Corporate Performance Management (CPM) software. (The biggest change being the movement of products to the cloud.)

The team recognized this shift, and that new products needed to be considered if we were to maintain growth. Alongside other trips, I headed out to Michigan to look at a brand-new startup company called OneStream Software.

I knew all the people there; anyone who worked on Hyperion would know them. The team from Data Fusion was the top group of data integration consultants in the field, and included Eric Davidson (a product manager since 2001), Craig Colby (one of the owners of UpStream), Bob Powers (Vice President of software development for Hyperion and the inventor of Hyperion Financial Management), and Tom Shea the founder and inventor of UpStream (later rebranded as FDMEE). Like many people in the space, I got to meet and work with all these people. It was clear that there was something special happening at OneStream.

As I did my research, I needed to know if the company had *more* than some well-known leaders, and if a real product existed. I came with a couple of senior managers from my team for a training session and demo. The three of us heading to the OneStream headquarters had worked on hundreds of applications; we would know the limitations very quickly, and if the product was viable.

Chapter 1

We met in a small office on Main Street in Rochester. It was clear this company was just starting out, but the product left us impressed. This was a *platform*; it was an approach unlike anything else in this space. The highlight came at the end when Eric Davidson offered to upgrade the server while we watched. I politely explained we had to catch a flight in three hours. Eric finished the upgrade in seven minutes! The three of us at the meeting left enthralled.

Since that time, most of the consultants I have worked with on other products have migrated to OneStream. All of them have realized what I did during that week of training. The OneStream platform is a powerful tool that does more to meet the needs of a client than any other single product.

It is going on twelve years for me working on projects and helping companies use OneStream. One of the greatest pleasures of my working career has been in helping to build the team in the photo on the next page. I consider myself truly lucky to have worked with so many amazing consultants.

We have an amazing team, and they are as responsible as anything for this company's success. These people deliver our projects. A big part of our success has been our unusually high reference rate; at OneStream, we honestly believe every client will be a reference. Indeed, OneStream is well-known for giving prospective clients our entire client list to call as references. That is truly remarkable in software. Often, our competitors can only give one or two.

To maintain our growth, it was obvious to the team at OneStream that we needed to get more information about our best practices out to the community. This book should help you take your design and implementation game to another level.

In this book, you will find chapters written by experts with decades of combined experience, working on the largest and most complex companies in the world. I hope this will serve as your guide to help us deliver on more and more successes!

2
Methodology and the Project

Originally written by Greg Bankston, updated by Greg Bankston

Over the course of this chapter, we will delve into the myriad considerations to keep in mind when beginning an implementation of OneStream Software. We will discuss requirements gathering, along with design considerations, testing methodologies, and the different types of training that can be leveraged.

We will also cover important topics around defining scope, creating a timeline, and supporting your application after the implementation is done. Equally importantly, we will discuss project management in general, along with why a project manager is essential. Of particular interest to many will be discussions on different methodologies, such as Waterfall and Agile.

Of course, before any implementation can begin, the formalities have to be handled. That means a scoping session (or perhaps a few) is required to reach an understanding of the goals and deliverables of the project, as well as the conclusion of contract negotiations between the implementer and the customer.

Once the **statement** of **work** is created and executed between all parties, the project is officially funded and approved at all levels. By this time, there should be project managers for the implementer, as well as the customer, already identified; together, they will drive the project going forward until its completion.

Requirements Gathering

The project manager will drive the project after the statement of work is executed and will get things started with a **project kick-off meeting** that officially communicates the project initiation to key stakeholders, introduces the team, disseminates timelines, sets expectations, and generally gets the ball rolling. For OneStream Services and most OneStream implementation partners, this meeting is immediately followed by the **requirements gathering workshop**.

Gathering the requirements of the system is truly where it all begins. Before a developer can write a single line of code, they must have a design that they are working towards. However, before a design even begins to take shape, there must be a common understanding between the implementation team and the key business stakeholders defining the desired business outcomes… in plain English, what the system is expected to do when it's live.

Think of a custom home – a construction worker doesn't just show up and start pouring concrete for the foundation and throwing up drywall. Before that happens, an architect draws up a set of plans that details every line of wiring, every pipe in the plumbing, and every light switch and fixture.

Before that architect can produce that first draft of plans, there has to be an understanding of what that home is expected to look like when it's finished. How many square feet? How many bedrooms? Bathrooms? Garages (attached or detached), pool, and so on. Once that understanding is reached about the end-vision, only then can a design begin to take shape. And it's only then – once the foundations of the design are in place – that a developer can begin to build the metadata, and the rest of the system can take shape from there.

It's important to emphasize that a totally complete design is not required to start. Back to the custom home example, you don't have to know what kind of ceiling fans you want in the living room or what kind of carpet you want in the bedrooms on Day One. You can decide that later. However, if you decide you want another bedroom once the foundations have been poured and the framing is up, you're likely in for a world of extra cost and hassle as the builder tears things down and starts over.

What NOT To Do...

It may seem obvious, but we sometimes need to remind customers that OneStream is a software company and not a process advisory firm.

While implementing the software, OneStream Services or other implementation partners can provide guidance based on experience, but OneStream Software limits its focus solely to the tool itself. There are other consulting firms, including multiple OneStream implementation partners, that can not only implement the software, but also ensure the process is engineered for optimal efficiency. That said, we have seen things that drive better (or worse) results when implementing the software.

When I wrote the first edition of this chapter a few years ago, I called out the "Lift & Shift" implementation approach as an example of what not to do. (To many experienced OneStream professionals, it's typically called "Lift & S##t" because that's what the customer ends up within their OneStream application.) It's something that we still see today, at times, and it consistently causes issues when expanding the platform to address other business problems.

A Lift & Shift is where the customer wants to take a legacy system (typically Oracle Hyperion, SAP's BPC, Anaplan, Longview, etc.), lift its dimension design, actual metadata (hierarchies, chart of accounts, etc.), shift it over, and 'drop' it into a OneStream application. While it sounds like a simple approach that is appealing at the outset, it exacerbates problems, many of which may be unknown at the time.

The primary problem with the Lift & Shift approach is that it leverages a legacy design that was created almost 20 years (or more) ago, creating self-imposed "tool limitation"; it immediately 'hamstrings' OneStream with those limitations. When this happens, the customer has essentially cheated themselves out of a significant portion of the latest advances in technology that make OneStream the leading CPM software tool available. Without fail, the customer later complains that they aren't getting everything they originally expected from OneStream, and it all comes back to the Lift & Shift approach to the design.

While it's fine (even advisable) to review what is contained within a legacy system, by no means does OneStream advocate replicating what was done before. Rather, use this new implementation to improve upon what was done previously. Identify pain points within a legacy system that OneStream can resolve as the requirements are captured and the design begins to take shape.

With all that in mind, let's take a closer look at what is essential to understand and document during requirements gathering.

> **Critical:** Do NOT do a "Lift & Shift" approach when implementing OneStream. It will put immense limitations on the design and future expansion of the platform.

Foundational Elements

Regardless of whether the first phase is primarily focused on consolidations or FP&A functionality, the primary goal is to build a foundation for the application to enable further expansion and use of the platform.

The primary requirement, before a single meeting is held about requirements, is to ensure that there is proper participation and availability of key stakeholders (both business and IT, as well as others) and subject matter experts, and that the discussions are initiated by an executive sponsor. Implementations can quickly go awry when key stakeholders are not represented or aligned, or they have no clear vision established at the executive level.

Many key areas of an initial implementation are closely intertwined and must balance against one another. A balance must be found and is primarily done based on how the information is to be utilized. What specific reporting need will be satisfied? What business decision or desired outcome will be achieved with the information?

It is critical to remember that these decisions will have long-reaching implications. If the right level of detail isn't loaded into Stage, then there could be an impact on Reconciliation Account Manager, as well as drill-back capabilities. The way data is calculated – stored vs. dynamically – is a significant driver of consolidation and Cube View rendering times. Metadata and dimension layouts can impact Data Unit sizes and affect almost everything within the application.

Keep these various elements in mind while designing the foundation and lean on seasoned OneStream architects to find the proper balance among them.

Reporting Perspectives

What other reporting perspectives might be required for consolidating the financial results or reporting to management?

Obviously, some form of entity structure will be required, and there is usually more than one such structure, also known as alternate hierarchies. The most common version is considered a legal or company code hierarchy that would match the company's legal structure required for reporting to regulatory agencies. However, there could be other hierarchies of the entity structure that may be required as well, such as: geographical or regional, cost center, department, business unit or business area or management structure.

Management reporting is where the rulebook gets thrown out the window. Beyond the common EBITDA line, there can be no end to the custom requirements put forth by management in order to drive the business successfully.

Rarely, if ever, does management reporting align with generally accepted accounting principles. Obviously, this is because management has one set of numbers to report to external stakeholders, but they need an entirely different perspective of the business in order to make operational and strategic decisions.

OneStream can accommodate essentially all management reporting needs. The challenge is going to be getting a solid understanding of what those needs are likely to be in the system. As with everything else, the best place to start is with reports currently in use by the management team to make their daily business decisions.

In many cases, it can be as simple as an alternate hierarchy within the Entity dimension or perhaps an alternate rollup of specific accounts. On the opposite end of the spectrum, the management team may need a dashboard of specific KPIs, which require data not found in your primary data sources. This might require a different means of getting data into the system, as well as creating custom Cube Views or dashboards to present the information to the management team.

Chart of Accounts

There are numerous elements to consider when crafting the chart of accounts within OneStream.

The level of detail required may vary on whether the data is for Actuals or Budget. If account reconciliations are required in the future, make sure to allow for appropriate levels of detail and mappings to assist with that solution when it's time. For that matter, look to see if there are already other **account reconciliation tools** in use. If so, it may be beneficial to load the deepest level of detailed data into OneStream and then map the summary level required for reporting to the cube. (More to come on this during design chapters.)

Beyond the entity structure, what other reporting perspectives will be needed, whether now or in the future? (See **stubbed dimensions** for specifics). Do any of the financial reports contain customer-level data? Would this information be useful while compiling management discussion and analysis reporting? What about product-level details or data for segment reporting?

Data

The driving questions that will guide the entire project are – *what data is presented on these reports*, and *how is it used*? One has to review the reports closely to understand the types of data, validate that the data is available, as well as the level of detail required, in order for OneStream to eventually produce these reports.

Are the reports limited to Actual results only? To what level are the results reported? Are they by period or only by quarter? What other levels of data are also included in these reports? Is there department-level data reflected as well? What about channel or product? Is Budget or Forecast data presented? If so, is it at a monthly or weekly level? Maybe it's a rolling forecast or an annual plan that is used to compare Actuals against.

One critical element to consider is prior years of historical Actuals – how many years of historical Actuals will be required in OneStream once the system is live and in use on a regular basis? Most publicly traded companies that report to regulatory agencies require at least three years of historical Actuals in the system. Some prefer additional years of history as well, while some private companies do not even require that much and can only get by with one or two years of history.

Regardless of how much history is involved, one consistent risk that I have observed on…

EVERY.

SINGLE.

PROJECT.

…is the underestimation of the amount of time needed to validate the historical Actuals in OneStream compared to what was previously reported.

Unfortunately, there is no simple rule of thumb to apply in this situation. There are simply too many variables in play that will drive the time required. For example, how complex is the mapping from the old system to OneStream? How many resources are available to assist with the validation effort? Were there any 'offline top-sides' (e.g., adjustments made outside the legacy system prior to reporting that were never captured within the data)? In this case, specifically, validating the data will prove to be very difficult indeed.

> **Tip:** The data on the reports drives everything! What is it? Where did it come from? How will it be used elsewhere?

Calculated Data

The approach to calculating data is worth touching upon, yet it all comes down to the way the data is to be leveraged and the density of the base-level data. There are two primary methods of calculating data within OneStream – stored and dynamic.

When storing data, the system is physically writing the data into cells into the database. That means that the data is calculated once and doesn't need to be recalculated unless it's source data changes. When stored data is called upon for a report, it is simply queried from the cells in which it's stored and presented in the reporting layer.

For dynamic data, however, the approach is the opposite. It only calls the source data into memory when needed (for example, on a Cube View variance calculation) and processes the algorithm at that time. It does so every single time the calculation is called for during a business process.

Let's take each of those approaches to their extreme points:

- Store everything – consolidation times will soar, as will storage requirements. Reporting times will be blindingly fast, but only as long as the data doesn't change.

- Dynamically calculate everything – consolidation times will be next to nothing, but the time required to produce a simple financial statement with a few ratios and variances will be exorbitant.

There's a balance between the amount of data and how it's stored vs. performance vs. reporting requirements, and as is typically the case, every customer and application may be different. Each deserves its own analysis and deliberate approach to deliver the best user experience for calculations and reporting functions.

To be fair, the development of the ultimate solution may require more than one iteration, changing some formulas from stored to dynamic and vice versa until that proper balance is found.

Foreign Currency

Unless the company is 100% owned and operated within a single country, there is a high probability that some form of foreign currency will be needed within OneStream.

Will local currency be loaded into OneStream along with exchange rates and translated into reporting currencies, or will it be loaded into OneStream translated into the reporting currency from the general ledger? If the former, where will the foreign exchange rates originate? Is there a reporting requirement for constant currency analysis where the current year's results are translated against last year's rates?

Consolidations

Implementations involving consolidations of Actual financial results typically have scope that is better understood and more refined from the outset. That's because consolidations are usually crafted to satisfy internal management and external regulatory agency reporting requirements. Simply put – the rules for consolidations are already in place by regulatory agencies and generally accepted accounting principles (US GAAP or IFRS).

The most common (and effective) method to truly understand the core requirements of a consolidation system is to begin with the end in mind by looking at the reports produced by the legacy (or current) system. Typically, these involve an income statement (or profit & loss statement), a balance sheet, and a cash flow statement. Upon reviewing these documents, many requirements should immediately become apparent.

Complex Ownerships

If a company is not 100% owned, or all of its subsidiaries have NCIs (non-controlling interests), there will likely be **complex** or **custom consolidations** involved. OneStream has seen some customers create a customized **"equity control"** solution, which typically handles all ownerships between legal entities using forms, dashboards, customized business rules, etc.

For example, if Entity A has a joint venture with Entity B for Subsidiary C, then the consolidations will likely be pretty simple. Depending upon whether the equity method is used, or if OneStream actually needs to calculate a percentage of assets and liabilities, the calculations are still going to be fairly straightforward.

Where it gets dicey is when Entity A owns 20% of Entity B, which owns 37% of Entity A, yet Entity C owns 15% of Entities A and B. If they were done in Excel, for example, consolidating the legal entities would be difficult because the ownership calculations would want to create a 'circular reference.' Building this inside of OneStream is typically the best approach, so long as only the ownership percentages or shares change.

Intercompany Activity

What level of intercompany activity is tracked today? Is intercompany activity only eliminated at the first common parent? Is transaction matching required?

Intercompany activity is a simple requirement to address when the source data has both sides of the transaction (the company code and its intercompany partner), and the mappings are straightforward. The most important thing to understand for intercompany activity is the level at which it's eliminated and the quality of the source data.

What about **intracompany** or **intersegment** activity? While rare, some customers have required the ability to eliminate activity within a single legal entity, but across departments or business areas. That requires a bit more effort during design, but it is definitely something that should be captured as a requirement from the outset.

I once helped manage an implementation on a legacy product at a company that had an enormous amount of intracompany and intersegment activity. One business unit sold a lot of product to another business unit, and the results had to be corrected accordingly. But the Entity dimension was already in use for legal entities and the business units were treated as departments in another dimension. The architect at the time came up with the brilliant idea of using the Entity dimension to create an alternate hierarchy for departments and using the Entity dimension to automatically eliminate the intracompany activity.

Today, OneStream allows for multiple Entity dimensions or can even create a separate cube to handle these types of reporting requirements during design. However, the main thing to remember is to surface the need as early as possible, so that it can be incorporated into the design from the beginning.

An interesting footnote is that architect works at OneStream today and continues to deliver simple but elegant solutions for OneStream customers.

Cash Flow Statement(s)

Cash flows are a challenge for almost everyone. I'll let the rest of the team discuss (further into the book) their experiences, but almost every project that I've been involved with has faced trouble with the cash flow statement. If not in building it, then in tying it out versus prior reported versions.

When capturing requirements on cash flows, the first question to ask is whether it will be by direct or indirect method. What other formats will be produced as well – free cash flow? Is there a specific version of the cash flow statement for internal management versus external? Is the external version solely for GAAP, or is there one required for other reporting purposes, such as bank covenants?

Statistical Accounts

Accounts within OneStream are a wide-open playing field. Beyond what is loaded from the general ledger, OneStream can calculate an endless variety of metrics and allocations as needed. For example, the customer may need calculations for accounts payable, days sales outstanding, accounts receivable turnover, liquidity ratios, EBITDA, or a variety of other statistical or metric calculations.

The most efficient way to capture these requirements is to pore over the most recent reports and pull out those metrics that are commonly used, before creating an inventory of them (along with the logic, point of view, and source data), which can then be passed along to the development team during requirements and design discussions. They can raise any questions or delve into details that they find unusual.

Allocations

Allocations are what I consider to be statistical calculations on steroids. They are found within a consolidations implementation and even more so during Financial Planning and Analysis solutions. They can seem monstrous when first broached, but once they are fully understood and documented, it becomes a matter of coding and testing them.

As with statistical calculations, the most efficient way to capture requirements is to fully understand the logic upfront. What is the process around the allocations? Are they using the Step method, where costs get allocated based on a sequential process?

What is the basis for allocating the costs? Is it an operational data value, like machine hours? If so, where will that data come from, and how will it be loaded? Will cost be allocated based on headcount? If so, will the human resources system allow for access to the database to pull that data into OneStream, or will security requirements require the HR system to export specific data that OneStream will then import from a separate location, such as an FTP folder?

Allocations can definitely be handled efficiently in OneStream, but the development team should be asking these types of questions during requirements in order to understand what challenges await them during design.

Planning

Much like management reporting, there are no rules in **Financial Planning and Analysis** (FP&A) projects, where the rulebook gets thrown out the window.

Budgeting and forecasting other types of analysis are at the discretion of each company. A company may decide to use zero-based budgeting, or it may decide that a driver-based budget is more appropriate. Business leadership may also decide to use a rolling forecast of either 12, 18, 24, or 36 months. This is especially true when the business model is so complex that it takes so much time and effort to create a budget that half the year has passed by, and it is no longer relevant. Or, perhaps the industry involved is so volatile that only six months can be reliably predicted at any given point, and beyond that is truly a waste of resources. In either case, it likely makes sense to eliminate the budget completely and focus resources on a rolling forecast that is timelier and provides better accuracy.

In the end, it all comes down to what the business leadership team feels is the most accurate way to gauge and anticipate future business.

Financial Planning Areas

What financial components are typically planned, and at what level?

For example, a pharmaceutical company started their budget by seeding the top 10,000 SKUs at the product level, then moved out into the various functional areas of the company.

Is the workforce planned in detail? Is it by role or by person? Are specific details – such as FUTA, SUTA, and fringe benefits – planned by each person? How are transfers in and out handled in the planning process today?

Are projects currently planned in great detail? Some larger Oil & Gas companies will plan each and every property or region down to the lowest level of detail, including generators, pump heads, and other significant expenditures.

Does the company plan financial statements besides the normal income, balance sheet, and cash flow statements? Are the detailed plans by department or cost center? Again, the starting point should be what reports are currently used to drive operational business decisions. When looking at them, determine what data is on those reports. Where did it come from, and does it add accuracy or value to the process of making business decisions?

Products and Scenarios

There are many other areas to consider when it comes to executing the planning process.

For example, is there a need to plan on product detail or profitability level? If so, at what level of detail does the product or profitability analysis go down to? Is it down to the SKU level? Or only the product category or class level?

For that matter, what kinds of scenarios will be required throughout the planning process? Will there be multiple Forecast scenarios? Multiple versions for each Forecast? Will they be saved for future analysis to compare the accuracy of the Forecasts versus Actual results? All of these requirements will drive the design in one particular direction or another. For example, say that you want to plan on a weekly basis, and there could be multiple versions for each Forecast. That will likely drive the use of OneStream's weekly time profile or User Defined dimensions for the weeks along with scenario versions to avoid data explosion in one Scenario dimension. There will be more to come on that in the design chapters.

Planning Models

Because of the many different types of disparate data involved, it could easily make sense to break a planning process into multiple cubes. You might have one cube specifically for physical net sales, another for eCommerce sales, another for SG&A, etc., especially if each of those operational areas goes into great detail within the Accounts or Entity dimensions. One company has over three dozen models that they replicated within OneStream for their long-range plan. This had to be split into multiple cubes based on common dimensions, which then rolled up into a corporate-level cube for reporting. It was a tremendous amount of work, but they were ecstatic to get out of the world of Excel.

It is critical to get a comprehensive understanding of all the different types of data and reporting requirements involved throughout the planning process(es). If this is actually done thoroughly, it will provide for a much better long-term design and maximize the opportunity for future growth within the application.

Operational/Financial Signaling

Operational and financial signaling is available with OneStream's analytic services capabilities. Using Analytic Blend, customers can leverage the multidimensional aspects of the cube with governed data, along with millions of lines of transactional and operational detail.

This type of capability allows customers to create signaling solutions in almost real-time (daily, weekly, etc.) with things like working capital, cash, sales pacing, KPIs, etc. It can also apply financial intelligence to financial and non-financial data. The use of financial hierarchies within the data model allows for a consistent presentation and structure to the data.

Solution Exchange Solutions

OneStream Solution Exchange has too many downloadable solutions to mention here. The main thing to remember is that Solution Exchange is a key differentiator for OneStream in the CPM industry. It is truly what allows OneStream to be called a platform, since *it allows software to be written on top of the OneStream software.* No other CPM software can make that claim.

Solution Exchange is the interchange between customers and the solutions offered by OneStream, its partners, and other customers and acts similarly to your smartphone's application store. Solutions developed by OneStream or others are made available on the Solution Exchange once they've passed OneStream's quality control standards.

While the top Solution Exchange downloads fluctuate from one month to another, the best approach is to discuss the options with your implementation partner for immediate or future needs.

> **Tip:** Remember, design with future Solution Exchange options in mind to maximize the return on investment.

Solution Exchange (not all-inclusive)

Several solutions have been – and will continue to be – developed, maintained, and supported by OneStream. The primary purpose of the Solution Exchange remains to deliver unique and cutting-edge solutions, particularly Sensible Machine Learning (SML), to address the ever-evolving challenges faced by our customers. Some of the more popular ones are OneStream Financial Close, Application Control Manager, System Diagnostics, Analytic Blend, Relational Blending (such as Planning for Thing, Capital, Cash, People, and Projects, as well as Compliance Reporting), and Task Manager.

OneStream Financial Close

Along with consolidations, reconciling between what was reported to stakeholders and the source data has become a more stringent requirement over the past 20 years. The market has exploded over that time with different software packages produced by other companies specifically to address the challenge of reconciling accounts of all types.

For some customers, this may not be such a major issue because they are only dealing with a few hundred accounts. However, a vast number of companies in the world today deal with literally tens or hundreds of thousands of accounts that require reconciliations on a regular basis, sometimes monthly or quarterly. It's these companies that start looking at software packages to help them streamline and maximize efficiencies in their reconciliation process and relieve the burden within their accounting departments.

For OneStream, OneStream Financial Close is a natural fit because it is a collection of solutions to maximize efficiencies within the close cycle. In particular, OneStream's Account Reconciliations solution drives tremendous gains in the time to close. To maximize future flexibility, it is a common practice to load all of the trial balance source data to the **Stage,** a key differentiator in OneStream's platform versus other limited applications. In essence, it should be loaded exactly as it appears within the general ledger. Then, the data is simply mapped via transformation rules to reflect what needs to be reported to stakeholders. While a company might have 10 revenue accounts on their P&L, they might have hundreds in their general ledger. Load *all* of the data into Stage and map it with transformation rules to only show the 10 accounts in the cube. Of course, all of that will be covered further in later design chapters.

As for requirements considerations for reconciliations, one of the first things to think about is whether there should be a centrally controlled process or if it will be decentralized to lower-level business units and only reviewed/managed at the corporate level for the final steps.

Additional considerations would include what currencies are reconciled for source data as well as reporting data, and whether accounts can contain different currencies. How many reconcilers are there going to be, and how often will reconciliations be performed? Where will the sub-ledger data come from, and will it be within OneStream? At what levels are the reconciliations to be required? At the company level? Perhaps at the department or cost center level?

These are the types of questions that will need to be answered when considering the use of account reconciliations for OneStream.

Task Manager

Before beginning to implement Task Manager, the best starting point is to document all of the processes that you will want to manage within Task Manager at the detailed level. You'll want to have each task documented on a step-by-step level for the task name, frequency, start time, duration, location, task action, conditional formatting requirements, preparer and approver (and/or group), etc.

Are there any task dependencies that you will want to include within Task Manager? Are they inside OneStream, or will they need to be sourced from another system? Is there a need to integrate with other systems to import data or export task statuses? What kind of security will be required for the tasks, their status, and their owners?

Task Manager is a typically straightforward solution to implement. For OneStream Services, we typically allow three to six weeks for installation, configuration, and knowledge transfer to the customer. After that, the customer has all of the knowledge required to continue building out Task Manager for future needs.

Partner-developed Solutions

Several solutions are developed, maintained, and supported by top-tier OneStream partners and undergo the same quality control reviews as OneStream-developed solutions. They are priced and sold as separate add-on solutions to the OneStream platform. When a customer finds one of these solutions of interest, they can contact that partner directly from within that solution. Once they work out licensing agreements, they will receive a license key from OneStream that will allow them to download or unlock the solution.

Other Solutions

These solutions are developed by OneStream, partners, or customers and are shared across the breadth of the OneStream community. There is no cost associated with these solutions, and they are supported by a moderated OneStream Community forum. These solutions are typically focused on blueprints, utilities, and other productivity solutions. Some examples include:

- CPM Blueprint
- ESG Blueprint
- Data Schedule Manager
- Hierarchy Validation Tool
- Extensibility Relationship Analysis

The CPM Blueprint

One key solution found on the Solution Exchange was actually developed by OneStream but made available as a tool for immediate use and a reference application. As mentioned elsewhere, a well-designed application is the foundation for OneStream to be set up for future expansion into other functional use cases and provide further return on investment with the software.

The CPM Blueprint was initiated when Tom Shea connected with customers to hear their feedback about how to further improve the platform. He learned that there was an opportunity to provide sound design guidance from the outset that both customers and partners can leverage when implementing OneStream.

Seven OneStream Distinguished Architects pulled together to craft the CPM Blueprint, which leverages best practices and uses insights gained from hundreds of prior implementations. The includes multiple benefits "out-of-the-box", including:

- Proper use of extensibility
- Workflows for financial reporting and management reporting
- Cube Views for Budget, as well as row and column templates
- Business rules for a variety of needs:
  - Custom calculations for budgeting and forecasting (with data management steps)
  - Data Quality No Calculate Event Handler for workflow steps
  - Workflow approval/rejection automated emails
  - Journal Event Handler for segregation of duties
  - Parse business rules
  - Batch file load rule w/automated email with mapping errors
  - Scenarios for constant currency analysis
  - Confirmation rules for legal reporting
    - Out of balance
    - Rollforward checks
    - Override checks
    - Retained earnings check

CPM Blueprint has been tested and proven in the field. For customers that have essentially standard requirements, the CPM Blueprint can dramatically accelerate time to value for their implementation. Even for those with highly unusual customer requirements and business processes, the CPM Blueprint is still a valuable tool to leverage for knowledge and learning.

It's important to point out that no company or partner can create a standard accelerator that every single customer can leverage against their unique business processes and metadata. But OneStream has provided a blueprint as a reference for design guidance, while also making it easy to add/subtract/modify for a customer's specific requirements.

Designing your OneStream Application

Many people, even those accustomed to legacy systems, still don't understand that a good design isn't just about creating good-looking reports. They miss the opportunity to allow for future growth, or they don't consider their stakeholders' current expectations that will be transferred to any new system, particularly OneStream.

Goals of the Design

As previously stated, it's impossible to overemphasize the criticality of gathering solid requirements for your OneStream implementation because they will feed directly into – and drive – all design decisions. Even before diving into the details, you need to start by identifying the ultimate goals of the OneStream application beyond any functional requirements. Beyond the types of reports OneStream will need to produce, or the KPIs that need to be calculated, what other design implications need to be addressed as you're uncovering requirements?

For example – will it be a global application that has to fit maintenance within a specific timeframe? Are there process windows or service level agreements (SLAs) that have to be met for the business on a regular basis, such as source data loads during month-end close that have to be completed within a one-hour time frame or by a certain time of the day? Do the stakeholders already know of an exorbitant amount of data that might pose a challenge to the application, such as saving dozens of versions of a Forecast for FP&A? These are all high-level goals that should be determined even before detailed functional requirements.

Application Sizing

The size of the application will be driven by many subjective and objective factors, which will be covered in later design chapters. However, you can determine early on if there are potential concerns to address during the design.

One example is the number of members within dimensions, particularly the Entity dimension. A large Entity dimension will – in turn – drive a very large Data Unit. This will have an impact on calculations, data management jobs, etc. A large User Defined dimension, such as products or customers, could also require considerations on the size of the application.

Overall, once you begin to see very large volumes of data and very high member counts within dimensions – yet these dimensions are not all consistently used across functional areas of the company – consider breaking up an application that might grow too large now (rather than later) into multiple, smaller applications.

> **Tip:** An application design goal is to *plan ahead* for anticipated growth.

A case-in-point: an extremely large retail company has global operations, with bricks-and-mortar stores, outlets, internet sales, and international business operations. Data volumes were expected to be millions of records per period just for the bricks-and-mortar stores. Putting all of that data with drastically differing dimensions across the different divisions would, in all likelihood, create future application sizing issues. Knowing this requirement early-on, the implementation team split the application footprint into multiple applications rather than one very large one at the outset, preventing a future rebuild in a year or two.

Application sizing also provides additional flexibility to manage the cloud or hardware resources by application. Even though it will still be a single environment, such as production, having separate applications opens up additional settings for better segregation of resources at the application level. Be sure to check out the chapter on Design, where sizing and the factors that impact it are discussed in more detail.

Application Performance

Another common design goal for the application revolves around processing times. As mentioned earlier, you need to look at the business processes supported, as well as any SLA requirements imposed by the business users or IT.

A common process time requirement is where the financial reporting team needs data loaded within one hour of its availability from the source general ledger. This is a critical goal to know prior to going into design. That alone could drive the decision to use multiple cubes, extensibility, or both.

Along the same lines, if the business users are accustomed to a processing time today based upon a legacy system – such as running a data management job to create a new Forecast scenario – knowing that existing expectation of time is also critical prior to going into design.

> **Tip:** An application design goal is to *know your stakeholder's expectations on process times* prior to going into design.

Data Modelling

With OneStream, the key concept to understand is its power around ways of importing, processing, and analyzing data.

In the early days of CPM, there might be multiple use cases to solve with a CPM tool, whether it was consolidations, FP&A, data analysis, BI, etc. The problem was that they typically required a lot of data integration work to keep everything aligned, homogenized, and current. Consequently, there was a strong tendency to put as much as possible into a single model (cube, application, etc.).

OneStream eliminates the burden of integrating all of that disparate data. *It's all in a single platform.* Now the question is – what data model makes the most sense to use?

Think of it this way – a data model is a tool. Like all tools, each type of data model is best used under specific circumstances, with its own advantages and disadvantages. Just like you wouldn't use a screwdriver to change a tire on a car in the middle of the Daytona 500, you wouldn't want to use the wrong kind of model to process and analyze a particular type of data. Just as it's critical to pick the right tool for the job, you must choose the correct type of data model for the use case under consideration.

For example, it wouldn't be ideal to try and shove 50,000 people into a cube dimension. That type of data is best stored in a register, with summarized and relevant data shared into a cube. Conversely, it doesn't make sense to attempt a multitude of financially intelligent calculations with time series (MTD, QTD, YTD) within a register when that can much more easily be accomplished within a cube.

You can mix and match data models as necessary for what fits the use case, volumes, and data type(s) involved. Just as a customer went through a selection process to determine that OneStream was the ideal CPM platform for their needs, it's worth careful consideration to select the proper data model given the specific set of circumstances.

I'm not exaggerating in the least when I say that there has never been a platform like OneStream on the CPM market. Ever. It hands over a set of tools that any NASCAR pit crew would drool over, so make sure to use the right tool for the job at hand.

Task Automation

Throughout the requirements-gathering exercise, the implementation team should be driving the questions around which components of the process can be automated versus those that should be performed manually.

One example is when initiating a new Forecast scenario – it should not require a manual step to actualize the new Forecast scenario by copying all the Actuals for every period up through the most current period. That step is likely an automated task performed after-hours, so it is ready for the business users when they sit down at their desks the next morning.

There are literally dozens of tasks that can be automated within OneStream. They can be anything from data management jobs to copying a dataset from one source point of view (POV) to another, or importing data from source general ledgers, or even exporting data out of OneStream back into a data warehouse.

In the first edition of the Foundation Handbook, I mentioned having joked on numerous occasions that OneStream can probably even automate a customer's coffee maker for them if they can find one that accepts the right commands. Apparently, Nicolas Argenta took that as a literal challenge and posted on OneStream Community explaining how he was able to do exactly that – get OneStream to make his coffee. As a fellow coffee fiend, I applaud his efforts and success. (His post can be found here… https://community.onestreamsoftware.com/blog/blog/how-to-make-coffee-with-onestream/4206)

Now that OneStream can make my coffee, I'm wondering what else it can do in the kitchen? Since I'm from Texas, I can't help but wonder if it could start my WIFI-enabled smoker and set the temperature for a brisket or ribs.

Task and Data Audit

One of OneStream's strengths revolves around its ability to capture audit information throughout the application. Essentially, almost any task and any change of data can be recorded for analysis later.

As an example, perhaps this system suddenly experiences a drastic degradation in performance for no obvious reason. Because of task audit information, the administrator can look to see what was happening at that point in time, on what server, who initiated the job, and if it was conflicting with other jobs.

If one particular job is running for an exorbitant amount of time, logging will enable the administrator to trace a particular business rule that is taking too long to execute. Once isolated, the administrator can optimize this business rule, thereby improving performance times.

Another scenario could involve upper management asking why a particular number changed in the Forecast. Data audit capabilities will permit the administrator to explain that a specific finance manager added 2% to the number on Wednesday evening.

The best recommendation for task and data audit is to consider prior questions and scenarios that require significant effort to research. While it is possible to go too far with task and data audit information (which would involve filling the logs too quickly or possibly degrading performance if too intensive), strive to find a balance between capturing enough information versus too much.

Backups and Logs

> **Note:** this section is primarily for legacy customers still deployed with their own on-premise environments. OneStream is currently offered only as a SaaS solution, and on-premise instances will no longer be supported as of December 31, 2027. At the time of publication, OneStream's support policy is found at https://www.onestream.com/wp-content/uploads/Sunset-Policy-November-2023-.pdf

OneStream has a multitude of options when it comes to backups and logs. For an on-premise environment, customers should discuss disaster recovery plans with their IT department. They should also discuss backup requirements from a business perspective for any risk of catastrophic system corruption during business-critical cycles.

For cloud environments, such as Azure, backups are typically available on a minute-by-minute basis. Again, it would simply be a discussion with the customer's IT group as to what those settings should be within the cloud environment.

Regarding logs, it is a best practice to keep logs at the proper level of detail to provide meaningful information to troubleshoot an issue, but not so much detail that the logs fill up too quickly and require too much maintenance.

Ludovic DePaz wrote a very informative blog on OneStream Community called "Log like a champ with OneStream." [https://community.onestreamsoftware.com/blog/blog/log-like-a-champ-with-onestream/29056] In that post, Ludovic explains how, when there's a lot of development effort underway with multiple coders, consider logging to a flat file rather than an error log. This prevents clogging up the main error log with debugging messages.

Ludovic followed that post with another one titled, "Log Like a Champ with JSON" [https://community.onestreamsoftware.com/blog/blog/log-like-a-champ-with-json/32255]. That post takes logging another step further by logging non-string objects as strings. Using JSON functionality, Ludovic explains in that article how to log almost anything… "This technique is not limited to Lists; you can log literally anything: a DimPk, a MemberInfo, and even Databuffers look good with JSON (although they have their own `.LogDataBuffer` method, which might be preferable most of the time)."

Another requirement is to consider whether those logs should be sent to administrators upon a critical failure. For example, when OneStream is attempting an automated data load, but another maintenance job is still running and locks up the tables that OneStream is trying to access, it might be a good idea to send an email notification with the log attached to administrators, so that they can investigate the issue prior to business users discovering that the data load failed.

Testing Methodology and Analysis

Over the past 20 years, the biggest mistake that I see customers make on an all-too-frequent basis is when they don't allow sufficient time to properly test what they've just built.

A salty project manager told me early in my career that I should allow an equal amount of time for testing as I did for the build. So, if it took three months to build an application, I should allocate an additional three months to properly test it from end-to-end.

When dealing with tight timelines and very limited budgets, that's a tough stance to maintain. For whatever reason, customers will be willing to spend exorbitant amounts of time and effort testing an ERP, a Point-of-Sale system, or a data warehouse, but they feel like an application responsible for reporting the financial results to their external stakeholders or managing the operations of their business should be rolled out with minimal testing.

We at OneStream cannot stress enough the need for good, solid, and thorough testing, as outlined in this section of the chapter.

Unit Testing

Unit testing comprises of the initial test by the developer before a development object is turned over for further testing. In this instance, it could be validating a calculation that provides the same results as an Excel model when given the same sample data. It could also be something along the lines of an end-user report that matches a mock-up provided in Excel or PowerPoint.

Every object developed should be unit-tested by the builder before it's utilized in further development and testing. To do otherwise will cause delays and rework because errors and issues will be found later down the development path.

Integration / System Testing

Integration or system testing involves a complete end-to-end test that starts with the source data system producing the initial data – sometimes in the form of a flat file or triggering a data load in OneStream – which would then be integrated into OneStream. It might also include producing outputs to other systems as required, such as final consolidated Actuals or the latest driver-based Forecast to be loaded back into a data warehouse.

On multiple occasions, I have seen customers and partners strive to reach a targeted date for system integration testing before the critical development objects were completed. In the vast majority of these cases, it resulted in a halfhearted system integration test with poor results, which misled the implementation team and stakeholders into a false sense of security. Again, it goes back to the concept of allowing enough time for good, thorough, proper testing, and the analysis of the results.

> **Tip:** You drive the timeline. Don't let the timeline drive you. Be realistic with the timeline. Delays happen, and schedules might have to be shifted accordingly. Find the balance between holding on to a challenging timeline (when it's still achievable) versus adjusting it when it's not.

Data Validation

There is no hard data to back this up, but my estimation is that 8 out of 10 projects hit delays when it comes to validating historical data.

It is such a common risk to the project that OneStream Services specifically includes a risk warning in all its statements of work when engaging with customers.

Over the last 20 years, I have heard multiple metrics bandied about for how much time to allow for historical data conversion. In one instance, it was one week for each period of historical data, yet for another situation, it became one month. In the end, there is no hard and fast rule. It simply comes down to the amount of data involved, the complexity of changes between the original chart of accounts and dimensionality compared to the new versions in OneStream, and the integrity of the historical data compared to what was actually reported at that time.

The integrity of historical data can often be the most challenging aspect of the data conversion process. Many years ago, I spent six months guiding a customer through validating one year of historical Actuals. The challenge was because, even though they had their data in a CPM system at the time, they had no governance on 'pencil in' entries prior to reporting their financial results. These 'pencil-ins' were last-minute changes to the financial results dictated by the management team just prior to publishing their reports. Consequently, there were a lot of adjustments that were sitting in an Excel file on someone's laptop that never made it into the CPM system. Obviously, when my customer merged with another company, it made it very difficult to import the historical data from their system into the other company's system without creating major discrepancies.

Some critical things to remember when it comes to data validation:

- Data reconciliation helps you build the tools you need to support users.
    - The effort that comes with data validation drives a higher level of comfort and self-sufficiency with OneStream.
- It will uncover EVERY data issue, whether you want it to or not.
- It is where most projects have cost overruns, stall, and struggle.
- More data – more problems…
    - The more history you load, the more problems you will uncover.
- As issues go down, complexity goes up.
    - Most common issues (mappings, hierarchy changes) are resolved early on in the first few periods validated, leaving the more difficult items for research.
- Documentation for Audit.
    - Be sure to confer with Audit to know what documentation they require prior to getting started.

Bottom line – be realistic and pragmatic when estimating how much time data conversion is likely going to require. If not, simply be ready to adjust your timeline once you get into that part of the project.

> **Tip**: Remember, *design* with the end in mind!

Centralized Data Validation

Each implementation's process could be a bit different at the detailed level, but it usually comes down to the simple fact of comparing old data (from the legacy system or source general ledger) against new data (what's in OneStream).

Whether it is better to have a centralized validation process (where corporate does all of the work) or a decentralized validation process (i.e., the field or business units do a significant portion of the work) is open to discussion. There are advantages and disadvantages to both approaches, and it simply depends upon the corporate culture, the various workloads already on the resources, and the demands of the project timeline. In either case, the process is essentially the same but merely distributed across different workgroups.

Assuming the OneStream configuration is compatible, a common approach is to create data extracts for raw year-to-date (YTD) historical data. OneStream transformation rules within OneStream would map the historical data from the source system into the newly created dimensional values within the OneStream application.

Once imported, passed through the transformation rules, and then finally loaded into OneStream, the validation process would begin.

Reconciliation spreadsheets are the primary tool used to support the data validation process by facilitating the comparison of data between the source (the current consolidation system or the manual spreadsheets) and OneStream. Each workbook would contain at least three tabs as follows:

- Tab 1 should contain the historical data from the source system.
- Tab 2 will pull loaded data from OneStream using the Excel add-in.
- Tab 3 will compare the results of the first two tabs and calculate any differences.

A **test results tracker** spreadsheet will be maintained to log any reconciling differences identified during the data validation process. For each reconciling difference, several details should be documented, such as a description of the difference, the name of the individual who identified the difference, a description of the final resolution, how it was resolved, etc.

A **validation tracker** should be used to monitor the progress of the data conversion team by providing an overview of the status (loaded, validated, approved) for each entity/time period/ scenario/dept ID/product, etc., combination that is being reconciled/reviewed. This Excel spreadsheet would be used to track the validation process and ensure that progress is being made.

The summarized process regarding historical data would look something like:

- Extract and load the general ledger data to OneStream.
- Validate OneStream against the current legacy system.
- Load data from other systems or manual spreadsheets to OneStream, segregating this data on different UD members to keep it distinct from the general ledger data.
- Validate OneStream against the Excel spreadsheets.

The process regarding go-forward data would be:

- Extract and load the general ledger data extracted from the general ledger to OneStream.
- Validate OneStream against the current legacy system.
- Book any adjustments necessary in the consolidation system and repeat.

Reports and/or outlines may also be used to facilitate reconciliation and validation.

The following diagram would represent the data flow:

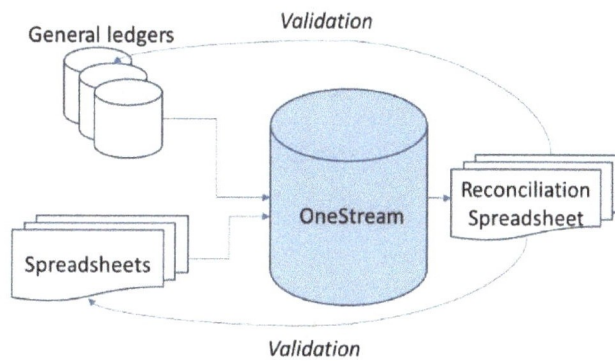

Figure 2.1

Role	Responsibilities
OneStream Application Administrator	• Provides approach and methodology for data conversion. • Manages the overall documentation of the data conversion process and applicable results (planning, progress tracking, data conversion resource management, etc.). • Completes data loads. • Manages the creation of reconciliation spreadsheets. • Coordinates the creation and testing of mapping tables from source systems to OneStream.
OneStream Project Team	• Builds/runs reconciliation spreadsheets. • Performs initial spot reconciliation using sample reports provided by OneStream. • Supports the reconciliation/validation processes by researching any questions raised by OneStream testers. • Updates test results trackers with issues.
Data Conversion Coordinator	• Creates a list of end-users who need to be included and ensures security access is granted and computers are updated as needed. • Tracks results and progress. • Escalates any issues found when needed. • Ensures data conversion effort continues to progress.

Figure 2.2

Validation Steps

The following table shows a typical data validation process:

Step	Description	Action / Decision	Tool	Responsible
1	Load data to OneStream	Go to Step 2	OneStream	Administration & Support
2	Update validation tracker to indicate 'loaded' status	Go to Step 3	Validation Tracker	Administration & Support
3	Run calculations/consolidations in OneStream	Go to Step 4	OneStream	Project Team
4	Refresh reconciliation spreadsheet(s)	Go to Step 5	Reconciliation Spreadsheet(s)	Project Team
5	*Reconciling differences?*	*If yes, go to Step 6. If no, go to Step 10*		*Project Team*
6	Determine the nature of reconciling difference(s) and document it/them in the validation tracker		Validation Tracker, OneStream	Project Team
6a	*Extract issue?*	*If yes, go to Step 1. If no, go to Step 6b*		*Project Team*
6b	*Mapping issue?*	*If yes, go to Step 3. If no, go to Step 6c*		*Project Team*
6c	*Application configuration?*	*If yes, communicate to Administration & Support; Administration & Support go to Step 7. If no, investigate, document, and go to Step 2*		*Project Team*
7	Assess if change is required to metadata / business rules	Go to Step 8	Validation Tracker	OneStream; transition to Administration & Support

Step	Description	Action / Decision	Tool	Responsible
8	Complete change request form and communicate to Application Team	Go to Step 9	Change Request Form	Administration & Support
9	Update metadata / business rule (App Team)	Go to Step 2	Metadata (DRM; OneStream) or Rules (OneStream)	OneStream; transition to Administration & Support
10	Document resolution in validation tracker (if applicable). Update validation tracker to indicate 'closed' status	Go to Step 11	Validation Tracker	Administration & Support
11	Update validation tracker to indicate 'validated' status	Go to Step 12	Validation Tracker	Administration & Support
12	Obtain signoff from a designated approver	Go to Step 13	Email	Administration & Support
13	Update validation tracker to indicate 'sign off' status	Go to Step 14	Validation Tracker	Administration & Support
14	Extract / save final versions of data extracts, mappings, and loaded data		OneStream	Administration & Support

Figure 2.3

When a period is ready for signoff, the conversion owner(s) should follow up with the designated approver(s) to obtain a signature signifying that sign-off has been completed.

When signoff has been completed by the designated approver(s), the validation tracker should be updated to reflect the 'signed-off' status of the data.

When signoff is completed, the final data extract, mapping tables, and converted data that have been loaded into OneStream must be saved as a final version. Additionally, the entity should be locked.

Pro Forma

The use of a **pro forma period** is similar in concept to a placeholder for pro forma reporting.

For example, in the case of acquisitions, there might only be a partial year's worth of data available from the date of the transaction. Yet, you need to see how the company would have looked if the acquisition had occurred on the first day of the fiscal year.

In that case, you would load only the Actual results from the data of the acquisition into the Actuals scenario. That would prevent skewing the reporting for Actuals in the future. However, you could then create an alternate pro forma scenario or a pro forma member into a data type dimension if you have one to hold the extra data prior to the acquisition date. That would allow for a more meaningful analysis, as if the acquired company had been in place for the full year.

Without naming the companies involved, I once had a customer conduct a divestiture on an outdated technology, which is unfortunately still on the market today.

Due to secrecy, they could not even tell us the name, so we just called it "SpinCo" for "Spin Off Company". We then spent months separating all of their data and functionality from the existing (multiple) applications. We also created a pro forma scenario to start tracking their data separately from the remainder of the company to give the Board and Executive Management the ability to see the ultimate results of the divestiture as it occurred.

Validating pro forma data would follow the same process as any other dataset, such as Actuals.

Local Currency Trial Balance

Usually, the first dataset to be validated is the local-currency trial balance. That's because it is the most pristine form of data available within both systems.

The reconciliation workbook would have the trial balance at the base level of accounts and base level of User Defined dimensions by business unit or entity for the legacy system, another worksheet for the new OneStream data, and a variance worksheet to show the differences.

Work through the first two or three periods of data to confirm that the mappings between the source system and OneStream are correct, and data is valid at the lowest levels.

Beyond mapping differences, variances are most certainly going to originate because of 'pencil-in' entries, or other data adjustments that never made it back into the original source data. Once the initial two or three periods have been completed, the root causes of these variances will typically either be corrected (such as a mapping update), or they will repeat themselves later in future periods and be easily found. Consequently, the later periods will usually be easier to validate because of known variances. Only truly new variance issues will arise in future periods.

Once the data is validated at the base (lowest) level, move on to the parent levels of accounts and User Defined dimensions. There will likely be differences in subtotals, and Excel could be a useful tool to find common levels of sub-accounts between the source and OneStream hierarchies. Again, once those first two or three periods are identified, and the validation spreadsheets are set up, the following periods should be easier.

Be prepared that there will be adjustments and entries to correct the base level and parent level data. Accounts or entities move between hierarchies over time. Key metrics or calculations could have been changed over time, as well. It's guaranteed that some kind of entries will be required.

The important thing, however, is to maintain focus on how OneStream should be built and configured for future use. Don't go to great lengths trying to rebuild history within OneStream. It's called history because that's exactly what it is – history.

Once the local currency trial balance has been validated, moving on to the translated trial balance becomes a much easier effort.

Translated Trial Balance

Once the local currency trial balance has been completely validated, the translated trial balance should be straightforward, assuming absolutely nothing has changed in the translation methodology. But what if it has?

More challenges could arise when validating translated trial balances, however. Accounting principle or hierarchical structure changes could make validating historical translated data impractical because the variances are too numerous and sporadic. In this situation, it could be simpler to load translated balances for historical data. This should make the data much easier to reconcile.

However, since you're putting in OneStream, this could be an ideal time to take advantage of a different translation methodology. This leads us to flows.

Flows

Flows are where you would expect to see differences with translations. US GAAP and IFRS follow the same general principals wherein balance sheet accounts are translated using the end of the period rate (month, quarter, year, etc.), but non-balance sheet accounts – such as P&L and cash flow accounts – would translate at the periodic rate. While OneStream can translate using both methods as needed, not all legacy systems can do so, and it could create variances accordingly.

It is essential to validate the flows themselves before attempting to validate a complex statement of cash flows. It will be much simpler to conduct some rudimentary validations for accounts payable, accounts receivable, etc., in an isolated manner than to configure a complex cash flow statement and then sort out from where an error originates.

Adjustments

Adjustments will occur. Simply be ready for them and *definitely document them*. They could occur for a number of reasons.

In many cases, it's a one-off adjustment to align with a 'pencil-in' adjustment that was made to financial statements before reporting the results but which, for whatever reason, never made it back into the source system.

There could also be what are considered **period 13 adjustments**, final year-end adjustments that are not attributable to a specific period within the fiscal year but are required before officially closing the books. Because some source systems do not have a dedicated period 13, these adjustments are typically offline.

Along the same lines, many accounts are translated at the end of the year rate, so the next year's opening balance has to use the same value. Other accounts use historical spot rates for translations, such as dividends declared. These would all require adjustments to ensure the data ties as it should.

Eliminations

Intercompany and ownership eliminations could pose unique challenges because of company restructures over time. Acquisitions, divestitures, joint ventures, and other organizational changes could all drive elimination variances.

KPIs

Key performance indicators could reveal variances for a variety of reasons – the most common of which are changes to a chart of accounts. In a legacy system, a KPI such as EBIT (Earnings Before Income and Taxes) might have changed due to reclassifications above or below the net income line on the income statement. Perhaps KPI calculations used two years ago were recently deemed irrelevant and are no longer in use. Or maybe the algorithm was altered at some point.

Allocations

Allocations could reflect variances due to the same reasons as KPIs. Perhaps source data or mappings have changed, or perhaps the algorithms were modified.

During development, the allocations would have been unit-tested based on sample data or historical data. One method to validate allocations in a detailed manner is to create a separate spreadsheet specifically for allocations that compares manually allocated amounts (created by using source data and Excel functionality) against OneStream results. In this approach, if there is a variance, it would be easier to trace because all of the data elements feeding into OneStream would be easily visible within the manually calculated formulas.

Chapter 2

Go-Forward Actual Results

Because the go-forward Actuals won't actually have any historical perspective for comparison, the best way to validate them is via parallel testing (covered later in this chapter). In this approach, the OneStream-created results are compared to similar results for the same period produced by the legacy system. Known variances at the detailed level would be accounted for due to prior data validation efforts and known differences between the two systems. Any remaining unexplained variances would then be investigated for resolution.

Centralized vs. Decentralized

As previously mentioned, data validation can be performed via a centralized or decentralized approach. One thing to consider for each approach is the level of knowledge expected by different workgroups.

For example, if field users need to be comfortable within OneStream, they should be involved in data validation. That's because working within the system – e.g., multiple cycles through working within the application, going in and out of OneStream, investigating variances, troubleshooting calculations – will create a comfort level thanks to familiarity with the tool.

Conversely, if the field users are going to have minimal involvement with OneStream and only put data into the system with a form, yet corporate users are going to be heavily dependent upon OneStream and need to be intimately knowledgeable on its functionality, then a centralized approach would make more sense.

Either way – consider the primary groups of users that will need the most training, and leverage these resources for data validation. While tedious and time-consuming, it's difficult to underestimate just how much benefit the hard work of data validation brings through hands-on training.

One other consideration when determining a centralized versus decentralized process is the corporate culture in play. Is it more corporately focused, where most decisions are driven by the main office and pushed out to the various business units? Or are the business units and field users more accustomed to various levels of autonomy? Does the corporate accounting office have a significant degree of trust towards the field users who will be validating their data? These are all factors that need to be considered when selecting the most efficient and appropriate process for data validation.

Rollforwards in Local Currency for Current Year

Rollforwards in the local currency should be simple to validate. You're simply looking at the prior period balance sheet versus the current period and validating the difference at the local currency level.

This can be addressed with a separate workbook in Excel with those calculations. Since there's no foreign exchange in play, the calculations should be very straightforward.

Budget & Forecast

Budget and Forecast numbers can be validated in the same manner as Actuals. However, because they're not typically at the same level of detail as Actual results, a separate Excel workbook may be required to address the different levels of detail for the charts of accounts.

Alternate Exchange Rate Scenarios

Alternate exchange rate scenarios use other exchange rates to see the results in different currencies. In the United States, they're called **constant dollar** scenarios.

The main purpose is to remove any foreign currency impact from the financial results, thus leaving true operational and economically driven activity, and not skewing the results due to fluctuations in currency rates.

For those new to the concept, an example of this is a company that has operations in a country with a volatile currency. Reporting Venezuelan operations has been a challenge over the last few years because it is difficult to discern what results were because of the company's performance versus intense fluctuation in the Bolivar in recent times. By using an alternate exchange rate scenario, you can put all of the local currencies into a common currency and view the results without any foreign exchange impact.

Validating these scenarios leverages an Excel workbook once more. Using an Excel sheet to capture the results in local currency and another to calculate them in the common currency (USD or EURO, for example), you compare the results of the calculated common currency versus the OneStream calculated results. The main concern is to use the same exchange rate methodology and exchange rates in both sets of calculations to remove any variances.

Validation of Outbound Data Integrations with Other Systems

Outbound data integrations for other systems require some 'out-of-the-box' thinking, as there is no one-size-fits-all approach.

The main concept is to get to the appropriate level of detail being exported before comparing it to a similar level of detail from a legacy system or data created offline.

For example, if post-consolidated Actual results are exported back into a company's data warehouse for other reporting needs, use Excel worksheets to compare against a legacy system's results. The challenge will be getting to a true comparison since, as with historical data, the legacy system will have differences in hierarchies, mappings, etc.

User Acceptance Testing

User acceptance testing (UAT) gives end-users and stakeholders their first comprehensive opportunity to work with the system. UAT scripts should be representative of normal activities that occur during the business process, such as importing data, validating data within a system, running reports, putting in adjustment entries, etc. The primary goal of UAT is to ensure the application meets all the functional requirements of the end-users and provides them with the opportunity to provide feedback prior to deployment.

The UAT test group should be users who will use the system on an ongoing basis, with the required functional knowledge. They should have expertise and be in the best position to determine if the application satisfies the functional requirements.

UAT scripts ensure consistency with the testing, and confirmation by the business users that they would satisfy the functional requirement. Once completed, they would also serve as documentation for what was tested, considered acceptable, and made ready for deployment.

Defects or issues are captured in an issue log and remediated after UAT is complete but prior to deployment. Any issues that are considered out of scope or future enhancements should be prioritized for future development and included in a subsequent release.

One common delivery method for UAT is to conduct it in a war room setting, meaning a conference room where everyone is going through scripts together, allowing the development team to answer questions as needed.

Before UAT begins, the development team should clearly identify and document the entry criteria, dependencies, and exit criteria.

The following entry criteria need to be satisfied to begin testing:

- Successful completion and sign-off of previous test cycles (unit test and SIT). This includes the finalization of any remediation activities.

- If performance testing was done, this test cycle has been completed successfully.

- The testers have been identified, contacted, trained, and informed of their roles and responsibilities for the test cycle.

- Test conditions, scenarios, data requirements, and test scripts (with detailed expected results) have been finalized, cross-validated against requirements, and agreed to by project management.

- Test cycle control schedule (including the test script execution schedule) has been completed, approved, and communicated to the test team.

- There is a clear cutoff of application development and data import/validation before UAT begins.

- Historical data has been validated through the period(s) to be used in UAT.

- All reports that OneStream is responsible for building have been completed and unit-tested. (Recall that only a representative list of reports was tested during SIT.)

- Strictly enforced change control process to track and assess the impacts of changes to application development and data import/validation versus UAT conditions.

- A representative set of access IDs and passwords for testers have been setup, validated, and communicated.

- Required infrastructure is in place and ready to support test analysts (e.g., desktops, printers, etc.).

- Fully-defined, trained, and approved issue management process.

- Access to test scripts has been granted to all relevant users.

- All required test documentation has been loaded into appropriate project folders or testing software.

- Identification of a POV to use for testing (cube, scenario, time, entities).

Tests should follow the expected activities that users will perform during a business process, which could include performing the following tasks:

- Update metadata.

- Update Member Formulas and business rules.

- Create a test user per Workflow Profile and confirm the user's functionality.

- Run Cube Views, forms, and reports.

- Perform data import, validate, and load.

- Input data on a form.

- Run reports.

- Open journal period in OneStream.

- Create, approve, and post journal entries.

- Run a journal report.

- Run an intercompany matching report.

- Process the cube to calculate, translate, and consolidate data in OneStream (i.e., run calculations) and test the results of calculations.

- View data using Excel (Cube Views, Quick Views).

The following is a sample test plan for UAT:

Task Name	Work	Resource Names	Start	Finish
User Acceptance Testing Activities				
Develop UAT scripts				
• Create & submit UAT scripts				
• Review UAT scripts				
• Modify UAT scripts based on feedback				
• Finalize UAT scripts				
• Approve UAT scripts				
Create dashboard for UAT status reporting				
Test execution plan				
• Create test execution plan				
Execute UAT				
• Execute test scripts				
• Log any defects in issues log				
• Record results of tests w/screenshots				
• Compile & triage defects from testers				
• Conduct triage meetings				
Re-test defect fixes				
• Re-test defect fixes (regression testing)				
• Log defect fixes				

Task Name	Work	Resource Names	Start	Finish
Finalize test execution & test results				
Sign-off on UAT results				
• Update & review traceability matrix				
• Review traceability matrix				
• Approve traceability matrix updates				

Figure 2.4

Roles and Responsibilities

Below are the roles and responsibilities of the team members:

Role	Responsibilities
Customer	Write, review, and approve UAT scripts and define expected results. Timely update status of issues within the issues log. Coordinate setup of user IDs/security access. OneStream assist as needed. Manage test effort. Coordinate internal / external dependencies. Sign-off on test script results once testers complete work. Review and approve updated traceability matrix. Sign off on QA acceptance report.
Testers Project Team, Business Users	Review and approve test scripts. Execute test scripts as directed. Identify and compare Actual results to expected results. Log issues observed or encountered and provide daily defect list to test coordinator for status tracking. Update status of issues retested. Communicate any problems or recommendations to customer team. Assist other testers as appropriate. Complete all required documentation. Sign-off on test scripts once completed.

Role	Responsibilities
OneStream	Provide guidance for the creation of UAT scripts and definition of expected results.
	Participate in UAT 'war room' to explain tests and facilitate a more coordinated execution of tests.
	Resolve assigned issues and report status to test coordinator.
	Re-test and regression test defect fixes of the application.
	Complete all required documentation.
	Communicate any problems or recommendations to customer.
	Update traceability matrix and distribute for review & approval.
Test Coordinator	Create UAT plan.
	Run UAT war room.
	Create QA acceptance report.
	Document defect status updates.
	Support UAT by tracking status, defects, and resolutions.
Project Manager	Oversee and assist customer team in all aspects of test effort.
	Provide updates in status and escalation of issues to customer's management team as needed.
Technical Support	Support environments (servers, network connectivity, etc.).
	Create backups.

Figure 2.5

Exit criteria define the successful conclusion of the test cycle. The exit criteria include:

- Each data integration should achieve a minimum level of accuracy versus expected results.
- Performing allowed tasks in each Workflow Profile should achieve a minimum level of accuracy versus expected results.
- Completed test scripts with notes.
- Source files and screenshots providing proof of testing and results.
- Test scripts related to resolved issues have been retested, and results have been updated.
- All planned test conditions and scenarios have been executed or determined to not be on the critical path.
- All issues have been documented and assigned.
- Issues that have been prioritized at critical and high-severity levels have been resolved or have a defined action plan for resolution.
- Changes to procedures due to workarounds, etc., have been identified, and process documentation has been updated.
- Test scripts and cycle close memorandum have sign-off, completed by the OneStream testers, customer reviewers and test coordinator, and project manager.

Load Testing

Since many customers do not require load testing, it's not commonly included in estimates for implementations unless specifically stated as a requirement. Be sure to discuss during scoping and estimation discussions to ensure that sufficient time, resources, and budget are allotted to satisfy the requirement.

Due to proprietary coding within the OneStream engine, commonly used load testing products such as LoadRunner are incompatible and cannot be used for OneStream implementations.

Early in the OneStream days, there was a free solution available called Load Test Suite, which replicates a typical end-user process. However, it was only available to on-premise customers and was never an option for SaaS customers. Now that OneStream is only offered as a SaaS solution, new customers will need to get creative on how to improvise their load test activities.

The most efficient way to address load testing within OneStream is to identify the points during the process when the maximum level of activity occurs. There could be moments during the process where 100 people are running reports, all while a consolidation is scheduled to execute. Identify those heavy loads on the system and then attempt to replicate them during a test session with real people as much as possible.

If getting a group of testers together that would be large enough to replicate a live situation is not an option, the next best (and actually the most accurate) option is to use parallel tests to measure and tune performance. Since OneStream is a SaaS solution, customers can log a case with Support to request a temporary scale-up of resources for the parallel test. After the test is complete, the customer can work with Support and OneStream diagnostic reports to review levels of activity and stresses on the system. The OneStream instance can then be tuned accordingly.

When considering load testing, be sure to have realistic targets set from the beginning. Define success beforehand in order to understand what is achieved.

Parallel Testing

Users perform tests necessary to take the system live. They continue to operate primarily in the legacy system, performing their normal activities, but then repeat the same activities in the new system. Results between the two systems are tied out, and any defects are noted. Scripts are not used for parallel testing.

Entry Criteria / Dependencies

The following entry criteria need to be satisfied to begin testing:

- Successful completion and sign-off of previous test cycles (unit test, SIT, and UAT).
- The testers have been identified, contacted, trained, and informed of their roles and responsibilities for the test cycle.
- Test conditions, scenarios, data requirements, and test scripts (with detailed expected results) have been finalized, cross-validated against requirements, and agreed to by project management.
- Test cycle control schedule (including a schedule of test script execution) has been completed, approved, and communicated to the test team.
- Clear cutoff of application data validation activities.
- Strictly enforced change control process to track and assess impacts of application changes versus test conditions.
- All data integrations have been built and tested.
- All historical data has been loaded into the application.
- The customer has completed the validation of all historical data.
- All reports have been completed, tested, and signed-off.

- All users have been trained.
- Security testing has been completed, and 100% of end-users are able to login with appropriate rights.
- All users who normally work on the close should have valid IDs and passwords; this information should be communicated in advance, and users should verify that they are able to login.
- Required infrastructure is in place and ready to support test analysts (e.g., desktops, printers, etc.).
- Identification of a POV to use for testing (cube, scenario, time, entities).
- Fully defined, trained, and approved issue management process.
- All required test documentation has been created.

Datasets and Flow Models

Parallel testing requires that a full data load (all entities) be loaded to effectively simulate an anticipated real close.

Test Plan

A sample test plan is as follows:

Task Name	Resource Initials	Work	Start	Finish
IMPLEMENTATION PHASE				
Execute deployment plan				
Create go-live readiness checklist (OneStream to provide)				
Create cut-over plan (OneStream to provide)				
Create parallel testing readiness checklist (OneStream to provide)				
Implementation communication to key stakeholders				
Conduct parallel #1				
Execute parallel 1				
Track and manage parallel 1 results				
Conduct parallel #2				
Execute parallel 2				
Track and manage parallel 2 results				
Conduct parallel #3				

Task Name	Resource Initials	Work	Start	Finish
Execute parallel 3				
Track and manage parallel 3 results				
Compile parallel test execution results				
Go live decision				

Figure 2.6

Roles and Responsibilities

Role	Responsibilities
Customer	Timely update status of issues to issues log. Manage test effort. Perform initial triage; if issue requires assistance from OneStream, communicate any issues assigned to OneStream and manage triage.
Testers Project Team, Business Users	Resolve assigned issues and report status to test coordinator. Complete all required documentation. Communicate any problems or recommendations to customer.
OneStream	Resolve assigned issues and report status to customer. Complete all required documentation. Communicate any problems or recommendations to customer.
Project Manager	Oversee and assist customer team in all aspects of the test effort. Provide updates in status and escalation of issues to customer's management team as needed.
Technical Support	Support environment (servers, network connectivity, etc.). Create backups.

Figure 2.7

Success / Exit Criteria

Exit criteria define the successful conclusion of the test cycle. The exit criteria include:

- Each data integration should achieve 100% accuracy versus expected results.
- Performing allowed tasks in each Workflow Profile should achieve 100% accuracy versus expected results.
- Test scripts related to resolved issues have been retested, and results have been updated.
- All planned test conditions and scenarios have been executed or determined to not be on the critical path.

- All issues have been documented and assigned.

- Issues that have been prioritized at critical and high-severity levels have been resolved or have a defined action plan for resolution.

- Changes to procedures due to workarounds, etc., have been identified, and process documentation has been updated.

- Test scripts and cycle close memorandum have sign-off completed by testers, customer team, and project management.

After parallel tests have been successfully completed, the system can go live. For a month after go-live, OneStream will provide post-implementation support to ensure the success of the go-live.

Training and System Documentation

Training

Training is just as important (if not more so) than the other phases of the project. Even if the design is beautiful, the build of the system went perfectly, and all of the testing was flawless, none of it matters if the users can't leverage, or refuse to adopt, the application. The key to ensuring that they do so is training.

Types and Delivery

There are multiple ways to deliver training, which can be outlined below:

- **Custom training** – the customer administrators would teach all training classes, regardless of user type. OneStream Services or the partner would be present and available to answer questions with which the customer administrator needed help.

- **Train-the-trainer** – where OneStream Services or the partner would teach customer administrators or super-users to be the trainers for the broader end-user community.

  Documentation would be produced as needed, as a part of the initial training phases. Typically, the first training class is for training the administrators and the super-users on the system, as well as teaching them how to convey the information to the user community. This is by far the most common approach seen on OneStream projects, due to its low-cost approach.

- **Combined UAT/training** – a time and cost savings approach that would combine user acceptance testing with training. The rationale is that on certain projects, the same end-users required for UAT will also be the ones that require the training. It's an easy way to save at least a week, perhaps more, on the project timeline when you combine UAT and training into a single session, not to mention cost savings as well. Lastly, it is also much easier on end-user schedules because they don't have to help with separate sessions for UAT and then training.

Given the advances in today's technology with online meeting services, all of these training approaches could potentially be performed entirely remotely. However, there is tremendous value in having the users in a single room with trainers and administrators walking around and assisting them as they have questions or encounter an issue. While potentially more challenging logistically, it is typically a more efficient and value-added approach.

Audience Determines the Approach

As previously discussed, the audience is (or should be) the ultimate driver for which type of training is most practical.

For intensely intricate systems that involve unsophisticated end-users, a custom training class led by the consulting team could be a more practical approach, especially if the company administrators and super-users are not comfortable and confident with their teaching abilities and knowledge of the system.

Conversely, more straightforward applications with knowledgeable and sophisticated end-users should likely leverage a train-the-trainer approach. Why spend the additional time, money, and energy to create custom classes if the company administrators and super-users can convey the knowledge to the end-user community?

If time is of the essence and cost is a driving factor, then consider combining UAT with training. This is especially true if people have a difficult time pulling away from their day jobs. It will prove easier to get everyone into a room for a single session of a few days than hoping to coordinate everyone's schedules for several separate UAT and training sessions.

> **Tip:** Tailor the training to the audience.

System Documentation

System documentation can vary depending on the implementation partner and the requirements of the application. OneStream Services, for example, delivers an administrator guide at a minimum. There could be other forms of documentation, such as training documentation, rules documentation within the application, data integration documentation, etc.

The main thing to remember is that customers should have sufficient documentation from the implementation partner to be self-sufficient after the project is over. This should be discussed prior to the beginning of the project. Customers should also be sure to get the documentation required prior to implementation as partner consultants move on to other projects. It's extremely difficult to come back six months after the project is over to write documentation that was forgotten or not needed at the time. It might also be almost impossible if the consultant involved has left the implementation partner altogether.

Managing the Implementation

Identify Your Team

Once the software selection process is complete, and the obvious answer reveals itself to be OneStream, the next step is to choose who will help implement the software.

Choosing an implementation partner, as well as the internal company team, are the most critical decisions once the software has been selected. Consequently, each deserves a little further discussion about them.

Choosing a Partner

In the beginning, when OneStream was just emerging onto the market, implementation partners were not as plentiful. Now that OneStream has become a market leader in the CPM space, there are literally dozens of partners available for consideration. But what should you keep in mind when looking at your implementation partner candidates?

To be clear – OneStream places an extremely high value on its partner community. Accordingly, we have made a tremendous investment in the creation of support infrastructure for our partner community. As a member of management for OneStream Services, I can say with confidence – and intimate knowledge – that we have a phenomenal group of partners and any customer of OneStream should feel confident in whichever partner they choose.

Regardless of whether it may be OneStream Services or another partner under consideration, you will want to look at various factors to base your decision upon:

- **Partner Certification Level** – the higher the certification (Diamond, Platinum, Gold, Silver), the greater the experience and track record of successful projects. However, this successful reputation may come at a premium price.

- **Professional Certifications** – implementation partners will include various professionals within their consulting ranks, such as CPAs, PMPs, MBAs, etc. Seeing professionals within their implementation team shows a willingness by the partner to invest in quality talent within their organization. Since the first edition of this book, multiple levels of OneStream certifications have been made available as well. Look for the number and level of certifications when considering a partner.

- **OneStream Practice** – a reputable partner will have a dedicated practice of consultants specifically for OneStream. By practice, I mean more than two or three consultants. While there may be very small partners within the community, their smaller size limits their flexibility when resource constraints arise.

- **Industry Experience** – the better partners will come to the table with a breadth of experience and knowledge across multiple industries. That is simply the nature of the consulting world. Projects will invariably involve retail, services, manufacturing, and a host of other industries. It is specifically for this experience and knowledge that most customers will choose a particular implementation partner.

- **Strength of Team** – you are choosing a partner to be a trusted advisor, not just do whatever they are told. Your partner should be ready, willing, and able to tell you if something you want is a bad idea. They should also be able to give you alternatives. Do yourself and your company a favor – listen to them.

Along with choosing the best partner for their company, the executive sponsor has one more critical job – making sure that the key stakeholders *listen to that partner.* Just as a customer knows their business inside and out, an implementation partner knows the best way to take advantage of the cutting-edge technology found within OneStream.

When they recommend a model or approach, it's because that's the best way to get the most out of the system's capabilities. It may require some minor modifications to a current process to get the best out of OneStream's capabilities, but if it meets the desired business outcome, that is the thing to remember. There have been multiple implementations that were stalled because a customer did not listen to their implementer and forced them to configure the OneStream application in a particular way, only to experience the poor performance about which the partner warned them and the solution had to be rebuilt accordingly.

OneStream Software can certainly offer some suggestions for implementation partners as a part of the software sales cycle. Yet, it is ultimately the customer's responsibility to make the decision, based upon their comfort level and assessment of each partner. Be sure to give the decision the consideration that it's due.

Administrator

Just as with the implementation partner, choosing the company's administrator for OneStream is a critical decision – actually more so – since the implementation partner will only be on the project until the system is in production. The administrator, however, will remain in place for the foreseeable future and be responsible for the maintenance and future growth of the OneStream platform. Obviously, this role is critical for the future of OneStream in each of its customers and there are a few things worth mentioning when choosing one.

- **Technical Aptitude** – this doesn't mean that the candidate can program in seven coding languages and understand how IBM's Watson performs its magic. Rather, the candidate can program in VB.NET, C#, or has the ability to learn to do so.

- **Business Acumen** – conversely, the candidate does not have to be a CPA. However, it will be very helpful for the administrator to understand the difference between an income statement and a balance sheet. Also, how does a cash flow statement work? Do they understand when an accountant says that last year's net income doesn't roll to retained earnings correctly? Will they understand the drivers needed in the system to calculate net sales for next year's budget? It is not an easy skill set to find.

- **Problem-solving** – an administrator will also require an analytical mindset that can troubleshoot problems in a structured manner. Invariably, issues will arise: a mapping change is required that was not communicated before data was loaded, a new account was added in the source general ledger but not to OneStream, an end-user is frustrated because they cannot understand where data in the system originated. These are only a few examples that an administrator will chase down when they are responsible for the platform. They will have to have the proper mindset and attitude in order to do so.

Finding a solid administrator requires an investment in training and a patient attitude. They cannot be expected to become OneStream experts in a one-week training course. Identify the administrator before the project begins and send them to proper training *prior* to the requirements and design phase. This will allow them to have maximum exposure to the consulting team, as well as the decisions made for the system they will support in the future.

> **Tip:** Be sure to allocate enough administrator resources. Always have a backup and invest in the admins with certified training.

Define the Scope

A properly defined scope (the body of work to be constructed) is one of the core elements of a successful project. There are multiple factors to be considered when determining the scope prior to the start of the project.

Back to the house analogy – you don't sign a contract for a builder to show up on Monday and begin to pour the foundations, build the walls, add the roof, and pave the driveway. Before all that happens, a general understanding regarding the size of the house, the number of rooms, if it will have an attached or detached garage, and a finished basement, along with a host of other decisions, needs to be made.

For a OneStream project, there should be an understanding of what will be built, even if at a high level initially. Is this going to be a consolidation system to help close the financial books and report to investors? Or maybe a Financial Planning & Analysis system to create next year's Budget and weekly Forecasts? Perhaps an account reconciliation tool or a solution to help plan at the resource level? Should it be all of the above? Let's dig into that...

Roadmaps

Roadmaps are multi-phased initiatives that lay out a vision for a longer-term program. Rather than a ready-fire-aim approach, where the first phase might be a consolidation solution, potentially followed by a planning solution (but not sure whether it will be a Budget or Forecast), a roadmap actually reviews the business environment and determines a phased approach.

A classic approach with the roadmap is for an implementation partner to look at all of the business processes and their current states. Afterward, the team will then listen to future business objectives and goals to craft a future state of recommended processes across the functional areas. Finally, a gap analysis will show what will be required to move from the current state to the future state. This gap analysis will become the program.

> **Tip:** OneStream has evolved to be more than solely a CPM tool. It is truly a platform where developers can write custom software on top of the OneStream platform. Therefore, leverage a roadmap from the outset to maximize the future functionality and scalability of the foundation.

Roadmaps can give business leaders an idea of what they're signing up for, the resource requirements for the duration, an estimated cost, and a specific set of milestones to show progress along the way. Because the team begins the first phase with the future vision in mind, they also minimize the risk of rework because a future requirement was not considered. By having the end state in mind, the implementation team has as much information as possible to properly design the system for future growth and scalability.

Implementation Size vs. Complexity

There are multiple constraints on a project with inverse relationships. This means as one side increases, the other side has to decrease. One such example is with implementation size versus complexity.

There have been countless occasions in the past where a customer wishes to implement a highly complex, very robust, and powerful solution that could include 4, 5, 6, or more solutions within the application. Yet, once that scope has been properly estimated, and they see the size of the implementation, sticker shock sets in.

The bottom line (literally) is that with complexity comes more effort. If a customer already has a well-staffed and highly-skilled OneStream department within their organization, a lot of that effort can be assumed by that team. However, that is rarely the case. Consequently, if the work is to be done, it will have to be done by the consulting team.

If budget is a deciding factor (and it usually is), keep the complexity of the solution in check as scope is defined. Doing so will likely prevent instances of sticker shock later down the road.

Timeline vs. Functionality

There have been multiple instances over the years of the customer who wants to do everything under the sun within the first phase. In essence, they want to 'boil the ocean.' If the implementation partner doesn't put on the brakes, the project team will – for lack of better wording – bite off more than it can chew.

When considering scope, *keep it reasonable*. Don't start a project expecting to achieve a consolidation solution, a budget solution, account reconciliations, and People Planning, where each of those solutions is infinitely complex and requires significant resources.

For example, if the timeline available is only four months, it is simply not enough time to put in an extravagant driver-based budget, with planning at the resource level, along with capital planning, as well as cash planning. The timeline is simply too tight.

Instead, focus on what functionality can be delivered within those four months based on the priority communicated by the stakeholders. Perhaps for this budget cycle, start with only the driver-based budget. Another option would be to allow input forms for budget numbers at the base level, which can then be aggregated, and use the extra time to implement cash planning.

In the end, the balance must be maintained between what functionality can be reasonably designed, built, and tested within the time allotted.

Stakeholder Involvement

The ultimate key to any successful implementation is managing expectations, especially those of stakeholders.

Stakeholders are the ultimate customer, not just for the consulting team, but for the customer implementation team as well. Within the customer's organization, the stakeholders are the ones who will ultimately decide if OneStream satisfies their needs.

One of the worst things that can happen on a project is for the team to reach UAT, only to be told by the stakeholders afterward that the system will meet none of their actual needs. The only real way this can happen is if the stakeholders were kept in the dark during the build and test phases. Yet, without their involvement on a regular basis, how can anyone be sure that the project is going to meet their needs at the end?

For OneStream Services, we regularly leverage what we call conference room pilots. These are typically for a couple of hours every three weeks or so. They serve as an opportunity to hold checkpoint meetings with the stakeholders to ensure the implementation team is on the right track, and that the stakeholders continue to feel that the system will meet their needs in the end.

The adage that we often hear is: "Involve the stakeholders early and often." Over the course of many years, and multiple projects, I have never seen that fail to be successful.

The Holy Triad – Scope, Time, and Resources (Budget, People)

The balance that every project manager in the project team strives for is between three equally important components on every project.

- **Time** – the overall project schedule
- **Resources** – people or funding
- **Scope** – the solution to be built and the work to be performed

The challenge is that if one is increased too much, the other two will begin to suffer.

For example, increasing scope (multiple solutions within a single phase) will either require more time or more resources to achieve those results. By adding the additional work in scope, there is a corresponding need for either more time or more resources to get the work done.

From another angle, what if resources were suddenly to become scarce? Say, two key people left the project team. If the timeline doesn't change, and no other resources can replace the departing people, then the scope will have to be reduced. It is not realistic to expect a smaller team to deliver the same amount of work within the same timeframe than what was originally expected. If someone were to attempt to force the smaller team to achieve the same results on the original schedule, the most likely outcome will be a substandard work product, or the team will simply implode.

Always seek a balance between the resources available (either funding or people), time, and scope. In the middle, as shown in the diagram below, is where you will find the best quality.

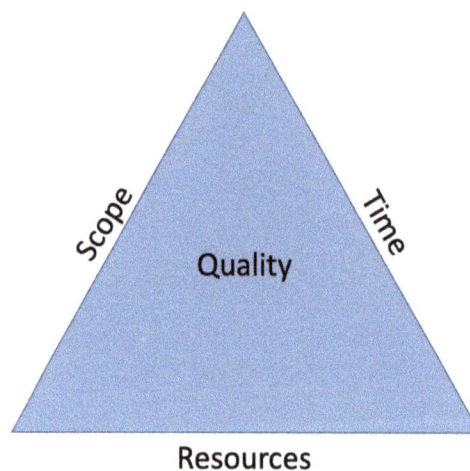

Figure 2.8

Create a Timeline

A case in point for balancing the holy triad is when it comes to creating a timeline. The timeline can either be driven by scope and resources, or it can drive scope and resources itself.

If scope is the most important factor and resources are fixed, then the timeline will have to be flexible accordingly. However, if the timeline is fixed (for example, an upcoming annual budget cycle in four months), as are resources, then the scope has to be flexible.

The question to be asked before the project even begins is – is there a specific timeline driving the project? If so, then your timeline is fixed, and you then determine what scope can be achieved within the timeline with the available resources. If there is no fixed timeline, then scope can become the primary driver.

Requirements and Design

The requirements and design phase can take as little as one week or as much as three months (or maybe even more). It all depends upon the complexity of the solution within the scope.

I was speaking with Mel Lenhardt once about requirements and design, and he put it perfectly. In essence, he said there is both a science and an art to building an application. I would wholeheartedly agree.

The science is related to those items that have to be confirmed and documented during requirements and design meetings. Things such as:

- Dimensionality
- Extensibility
- Metadata structures
- Workflows
- Data (inbound and outbound)
- Future roadmap items

All of the above, if they should change significantly halfway through the build, would require significant rework.

> **Tip:** That conversation is what drove me and a couple of coworkers to create a methodology that is a hybrid of Waterfall and Agile called Waterline. See page 53.

For example, imagine the application has been built, data has been loaded, and the team is working on Cube Views when suddenly a new requirement surfaces to add an entirely new dimension to the application and the cube. Of course, it can be done, but there will be a lot of rework entailed to rebuild data sources, reimport data, rework the workflows, etc. Get a firm understanding of those items early on to prevent rework later in the project.

Items that do not necessarily require confirmation from the outset fall more into the presentation area – "The Art" as my friend Mel would put it. These would include:

- Cube Views
- Dashboards
- Forms
- Some calculations

These types of presentation items can certainly be defined at a high level but do not require a detailed understanding beyond the data that would appear on them.

In summary, it is common to 'rush' the requirements and design discussions, especially if the timeline is fixed and things seemingly start off a bit late. However, a safer approach is to allow *extra* time instead to ensure all topics can be thoroughly discussed, key decisions made, and everything documented prior to writing one line of code. If the requirement and design are completed early, then it becomes a pleasant surprise, and now there's extra time to move into the build. This is a much better situation to handle than the alternatives.

Build

The build itself (creating the app and metadata, creating data sources and importing data, creating Cube Views, etc.) can vary drastically by project. It depends upon a number of factors, such as:

- The number of alternate hierarchies
- Data sources and their complexities
- Calculations and/or allocations

- The number of workflows and their associated steps
- The number of Cube Views and dashboards
- Security and other items

Volume and complexity will both add time to any of the items above. The challenge is to strike the right balance between them to optimize each one.

Of course, all of this could be a very large body of work that will require significant effort. However, with sufficient resources (people), the work can be divided up, and the timeline accelerated.

Test

There are two distinct areas that are commonly reduced when the budget begins to tighten: project management and the test phase.

A safe approach to most projects is to allocate and budget the same amount of time and effort for testing that was estimated for the build phase. Consequently, if it requires three months to build an application, plan for three months for testing. This would include data conversion and validation (covered earlier), SIT (system integration testing), user acceptance testing, parallel testing, potentially performance testing, as well as remediation time for any issues uncovered during the various tests. If that time is ultimately not needed, then the project will finish early and under budget. That's better than the alternative.

Keep in mind, the more testing performed, the more errors and issues that can be resolved prior to the end-user community using the system. This will drastically preserve integrity in this system for the user community and increase system adoption.

Rollout

In order to estimate the amount of time required for rollout, you need to consider the efforts required for migration, the amount of training required, and the logistics involved. These three items are the primary efforts during the rollout phase.

For example, with training, how many users will require training? If you break those users into groups of 10 or 12 per class, how many classes will that require? How many trainers will be available? Are they all in a single country, or will global travel be required – which will need to be scheduled? How much and what type of training documentation will be used (which requires time to create)? All of these questions will drive the training portion of the rollout phase.

When it comes to migrations, this is heavily dependent upon the customer's corporate and IT policies. Many customers have rigid and formal policies around testing, certifications, and approvals, as well as intricate deployment processes that must be followed before an application is considered in production. Other customers can consider an application in production simply by changing the name of the application.

We have seen some projects with a three-week roll-out phase – two weeks for training and one week for migration. On the other extreme, there have been projects with three months due to extensive training with multiple classes across several countries, as well as complex and rigid migration policies. Like everything else with a complex project, there is no easy answer. All of the factors mentioned above must be considered when creating a timeline for the rollout phase.

Planning to Support Your Application

Great. Awesome. You are now live on OneStream. Yet, how will you maintain it and troubleshoot issues as they arise going forward? Let's look at some options.

Center of Excellence Model

The Center of Excellence (CoE) model involves a team of core individuals – from various functional areas – managed under a centralized model that is dedicated to the support of the OneStream application.

This team could be comprised of representatives from finance, accounting, IT, and audit, as well as any other functional areas that would be directly impacted by the OneStream application.

The reason that this model can be so effective is because it revolves around a core team that is dedicated to supporting OneStream as their primary responsibility rather than doing it on a part-time basis. Because they are focused solely on supporting OneStream, they will provide thought leadership and best practices across the enterprise.

They can also provide a better ROI by performing research and development to understand how to best maximize the value of OneStream. For example, the CoE will immediately understand and recommend using OneStream when an account reconciliation tool is needed, rather than investing in a separate SaaS offering that will cost the company additional money.

IT Support

Other companies prefer to focus on their support solely through the IT organization. This may be a good approach, depending upon the resources available within IT. The challenge with a pure IT support model is that it is heavy on the technical skill set and light on the business knowledge. Stakeholders will have difficulty explaining the requirements to a code-oriented developer. Make no mistake – a developer with technical skills is essential for the support of OneStream. However, there also has to be some element of business knowledge as well. If that skill set can truly be provided from within the IT functional area, then this support model has a good chance of success.

Admin/Functional Support

An administrator model is seen most frequently at OneStream. The administrator will attend training prior to the start of the project in order to take full advantage of knowledge sharing and learning opportunities during the requirements and design sessions.

As covered previously in this chapter, an administrator should have equal amounts of technical skills and business acumen. As the implementation is underway, they will be learning and absorbing knowledge from the development team that will become essential after the application is live.

For smaller customers – and many larger ones – the administrator model is the most practical approach to supporting OneStream in the future.

Managing the Project

In my opinion, formed over the last 20-odd years, project management is often the most underappreciated aspect of project implementation. During the project estimate, as the business stakeholders want more, the scope increases, and the cost goes up, the initial place that people look to cut costs is within the project manager role. Time and time again, I have seen this come back around later in the project to create more issues and cost more money than if the project manager role had been left intact and someone was truly in charge at the outset to minimize risk and address issues as they arose.

Why Use a Project Manager At All?

Whenever I'm asked to justify the need for project management, even in a part-time capacity for a smaller project, I typically use a sports analogy. You constantly see professional NFL teams spend millions of dollars on a head coach, and MLB teams will do something similar for a Manager of their club. While they're not out there on the field – carrying the ball or swinging the bat – they are considered critical to the success of the team. They identify where the game is at risk by anticipating their opponents' moves, changing players out when they're tired or underperforming, and capitalizing on opportunities when they present themselves.

Project managers do the same thing for their teams. A good project manager will see a delay coming days or weeks ahead of time because the circumstances that cause it will formulate well before it actually happens. Developers are typically hyper-focused on writing a complex piece of code (a calculation, transformation logic, or an integration connection) or resolving a performance issue, and are rarely able to look beyond the most immediate deliverable that they're trying to complete.

A good project manager will also manage scope creep – one of the most common threats to successful completion and an intact budget. It's truly amazing how frequently a project with a specific set of deliverables will go off track because a business stakeholder asks for just one more report book, or an additional integration.

Early on in my career, I learned that lesson the hard way because – as I was building an Essbase Financial Reporting Cube – a key business stakeholder came by and asked me if I could include one more reporting element, which wasn't in the original requirements and design discussions. After looking it over, I realized that it would require an entirely new dimension to the model. Once added, however, it caused the database to explode and performance to go down the tubes. I then spent the entire weekend (for free) rebuilding the application back to where it was prior to adding the new dimension. In the end, I lost a full week of the timeline and gave up my own personal time because I didn't want to simply say, "No, I'm sorry. It's out of scope." That was a hard lesson to learn.

To summarize, it's hard to imagine the New England Patriots without Bill Belichick (which I'm sure Peter Fugere will appreciate). While it's hard to picture the Yankees from the early 2000s with Mariano Rivera, it's just as strange to picture them without Joe Torre. Now, tell me again why you don't think a project manager is needed.

Managing Risk and Change

Be honest. Risk is inevitable, as is change. And it typically comes with its own bad news. I have an expression that I picked up years ago that says, "Bad news doesn't get better with time."

When something on the project goes awry (and it invariably will), it is critical to communicate to the appropriate parties as soon as possible, after all of the facts are available, and put a mitigation plan in place to address it.

The worst moments on a project are when an issue is brought to the management team that has been a risk for weeks, perhaps months, but never communicated. On top of having to deal with the issue itself, there is the added layer of frustration that comes with the sudden knowledge of, "I could have prevented this had I only known about it sooner." It's not an enjoyable situation in which to be.

Finally, as the tone of the preceding paragraphs suggests, *be realistic* when it comes to risk. There is a 100% chance that things will go wrong. Count on it. The best thing any project leadership team can do is anticipate those risks, plan for them, and keep a very close eye on them.

Effective Communication

The common element throughout most of this chapter centers around the essential need for communication.

Defining scope? Gathering requirements? Managing risk? They all require solid communication.

Throughout the project, ensure that stakeholders and developers alike understand that they have a voice and should use it to convey their ideas, uncertainties, and concerns. If they don't, they will hesitate to clarify a requirement until it's about to be tested, or they won't mention a risk they anticipate because they don't want to cause problems.

For more formal styles of communication, there are numerous tools, theories, and methodologies available to consider. Yet, things can be simplified to as little as a weekly status report, a project financials report, and a project plan. With those three items, you can manage almost any project.

A quick word on project financials – be sure to include a forecast, also known as an **estimate-to-complete**. It's shocking how many Fortune 500 companies, who have immense formal processes and policies in place, don't ask for – or pay attention to – a project forecast. They monitor Actuals closely, looking at burn reports, timesheets, and run rates, but they have no idea if they have enough budget to get them through project completion.

Ensure your OneStream implementation tracks the forecast at the resource level and by week. That will surface any anticipated overages immediately when someone is working 50 hours per week for two months, or a key resource is extended for six weeks.

Methodology Type – Agile vs. Waterfall

Waterfall versus Agile. Agile versus Waterfall. This is the discussion that has gone on for years and will likely continue for more to come. So, which one is best for a OneStream project? In the classic answer of a consultant – it depends.

Most fans of Agile will admit that it is not necessarily the best methodology when the requirements are known, the design is firmly locked down, and there's little risk of them changing. This is the type of implementation where the Waterfall methodology is at its best.

Conversely, Waterfall is not an ideal approach when the requirements are not fully understood, or the design is highly subject to change. In all fairness, this is where Agile shows its strengths.

However, Agile cannot be leveraged in its most classic sense, where requirements are at a conceptual level and the details are refined in the middle of a sprint. The reason is that if a fundamental requirement is discovered in a sprint late in the project, such as adding a new dimension, or changing what data is loaded at the base level, it will likely set the project back drastically.

As mentioned in the section on requirements and the design timeline, it is essential to get the 'science' requirements locked down and the design as fully complete as possible. Once those pieces are reasonably final, the subsequent phases of the project can proceed in an Agile manner. In fact, OneStream is on the verge of creating its own version of Agile for future projects, and it may be in use by the time this book goes to print.

After the publication of the first edition of the Foundations Handbook, the Waterfall vs. Agile debate struck much closer to home and drove the creation of something entirely new for OneStream's implementation approach.

Why Not Both? – OneStream's Waterline Methodology

We hear the question a lot… Waterfall or Agile? It's like Chevy vs. Ford or BMW vs. Mercedes for Europe. The two methodologies are typically positioned against each other. Well, why not both? What if one could take the best parts of each and leverage them at the right times for the project?

There are various hybrid methodologies available, but none seemed to meet the specific challenges of changing or undefined requirements for OneStream during certain parts of the implementation. Therefore, we created Waterline – a hybrid of Waterfall and Agile specifically tailored to OneStream implementations.

In 2022, I had just finished the bulk of a customer's OneStream implementation that included multiple cubes and extremely complex designs. The customer was adamant that we use Agile, which we did, only to find that the key business stakeholders didn't fully grasp what functionality they needed the system to provide or the new types of reporting that OneStream could provide.

During various sprints, we had to rebuild some cubes multiple times because of changes to core elements of the design. The key business stakeholders would look at the latest sprint and then realize that they needed (or wanted) a new level of reporting that required a new dimension or to completely rebuild the metadata.

One particular cube had to be rebuilt more than five times before it was approved by the business stakeholders.

Obviously, all of the rebuilding effort was wasted time and money. It literally added weeks to the timeline and tens of thousands of dollars to the budget. It was the catalyst that drove me and two coworkers to create a new hybrid methodology called Waterline.

Gaia Kaldor and I met early on in 2022 to come up with a way to prevent the rework that a pure Agile methodology has the tendency to create. As previously mentioned, the main risk with Agile is that it doesn't lock down detailed requirements for the application as a whole from the outset. There could be a new requirement in sprint 7 that no one discussed or knew about in sprint 1.

Our conclusion was to take the requirements and design portion of Waterfall and leverage those stages to lock down the essential elements of the application. Once those are confirmed and finalized, the project could move to an Agile approach to create stories for the non-essential elements that wouldn't create rework. We named this new methodology Waterline.

We chose Waterline because it represented building a beautiful ship on which to sail around the world. As the ship is under construction, it's critical that everything that lies below the water is locked up tight and will stand the test of time. If not, when the ship is launched from dry dock, it'll immediately take on water and have to be put back into dry dock for expensive and time-consuming repairs.

Items on the ship that were above the waterline, aren't as critical early on. It doesn't really matter what color of paint will be used in the staterooms, what will be on the menu in the dining halls, or what size of pool tables will be in the recreation rooms. None of those items would force the ship back into dry dock and undergo intensive rework.

We used the graphics below to explain it to coworkers, customers, and prospects.

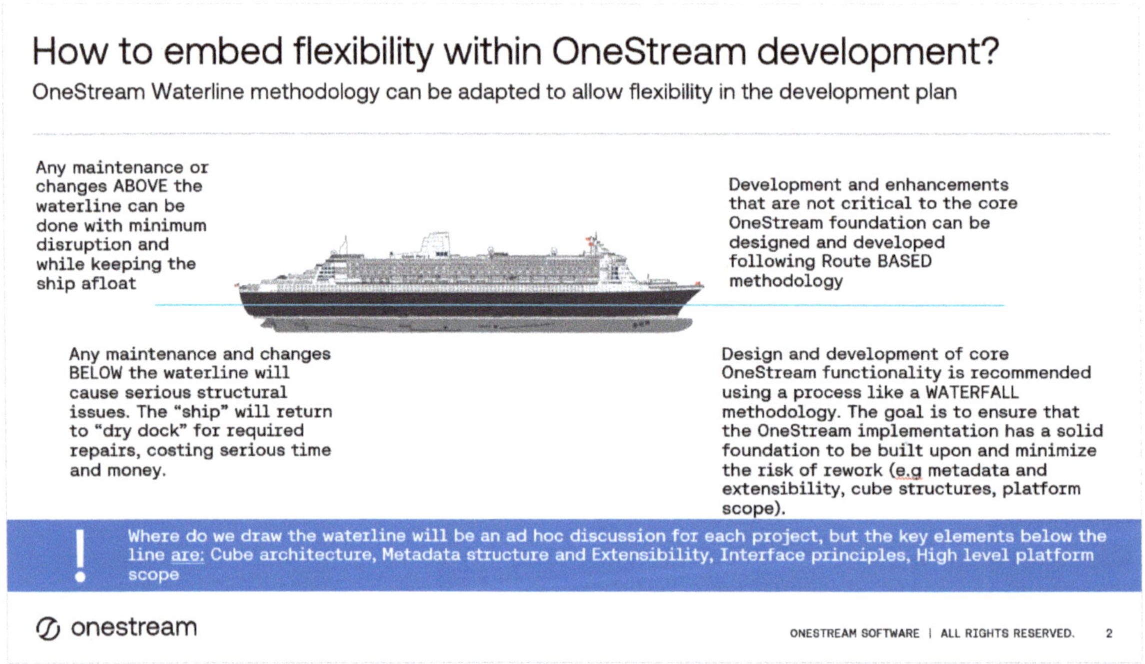

How to embed flexibility within OneStream development?
OneStream Waterline methodology can be adapted to allow flexibility in the development plan

Any maintenance or changes ABOVE the waterline can be done with minimum disruption and while keeping the ship afloat

Development and enhancements that are not critical to the core OneStream foundation can be designed and developed following Route BASED methodology

Any maintenance and changes BELOW the waterline will cause serious structural issues. The "ship" will return to "dry dock" for required repairs, costing serious time and money.

Design and development of core OneStream functionality is recommended using a process like a WATERFALL methodology. The goal is to ensure that the OneStream implementation has a solid foundation to be built upon and minimize the risk of rework (e.g metadata and extensibility, cube structures, platform scope).

! Where do we draw the waterline will be an ad hoc discussion for each project, but the key elements below the line are: Cube architecture, Metadata structure and Extensibility, Interface principles, High level platform scope

⍟ onestream

ONESTREAM SOFTWARE | ALL RIGHTS RESERVED. 2

Figure 2.9

Below the waterline would involve reviewing current and anticipated reporting requirements to understand the data models, dimensions, and metadata involved to meet them. Security and other factors that might require separate cubes or foundational elements to the application should also be reviewed and finalized.

Above the waterline items like reports, dashboards, detailed build of security, input forms, etc., would move into an Agile-style mode of delivery with sprints. If a key stakeholder doesn't like a font or header on a report, that won't create catastrophic rework and fits nicely into a future sprint.

The graph below reflects the approach when considering above vs. below the waterline.

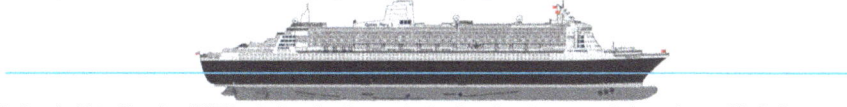

Figure 2.10

Overall, leverage experienced OneStream architects if considering any form of Agile. Consider what should be above vs. below the waterline.

When presenting Waterline as an option for an implementation methodology, I typically wrap it up with the question to the customer... "Do you want the Queen Mary, or do you want the Titanic?"

Reach out to your implementation partner if more information on Waterline is needed.

Plan for Success

There are several key areas that can be addressed before the beginning of the project that will drastically increase the chances of success.

Train Early

Have your administrator and, ideally, a backup person, attend training just prior to the start of the project.

This will allow them to take what they learned in class and understand how the implementation team might address their specific requirements during the design sessions. It will also allow them to assist key stakeholders in explaining a requirement in the clearest terms for the implementation team to truly understand it.

Document Processes Prior to Kick-Off

Processes that are not documented in advance will require significantly more discussion during requirements and design meetings. It's truly eye-opening when a simple forecast process can take a half-day or more to explain to the implementation team. Even worse is when the customer cannot agree amongst themselves what the process is or even should be.

Documenting these processes before the start of the project will prevent that confusion and maximize the efficiency of the requirements in design discussions.

Staffing Before, During, and After Project Kick-off

There will be a heavier demand for key stakeholders' time before and during the project initiation, specifically for requirements and design discussions.

Key stakeholders should be heavily involved in documenting the processes before the project begins, as previously discussed. They should also plan to participate significantly in the requirements and design discussions. This doesn't mean they will be in the meetings all day and every day. For example, financial planning & analysis stakeholders do not necessarily need to attend the discussions that center around consolidated reporting. Conversely, financial accounting stakeholders do not need to attend the discussions focused on the budgeting and forecasting processes. Manage their expectations – upfront – regarding how much they'll be needed.

Beyond the requirements and design discussions, there should be periodic meetings to showcase and confirm progress with the stakeholders. They will also participate during user acceptance testing and any parallel tests. It will likely seem like a rollercoaster ride when it comes to the demands on their schedule, but without their participation, there is no assurance that the system will meet their needs.

Quality Assurance

Few things are as painful as moving into a system integration test or user acceptance test, only to find that the development completed was sub-par and doesn't work properly. When this happens, rework is necessary, timelines suffer, and there are some very tense discussions between the implementation team and customer management.

Continuous Process

Quality assurance should be a never-ending process. Someone on the team, usually an architect, would be responsible for reviewing the work of other project team members. Anything found to be substandard should be sent back to that developer for rework. In this way, throughout the build phase, mistakes are uncovered during open testing and caught before they have a chance to reach the end-user community.

Minimize Rework

Project leadership on the implementation team should be checking the work of the development team early when they first begin working on a deliverable. For example, rather than waiting until 20 Cube Views are completed, the architect should review the initial two or three to ensure they meet standards. The same approach would be appropriate for workflows, security, business rules, data integrations, etc.

Change Management

Promoting the understanding that change is coming, and is a good thing, is no easy task. The vast majority of people are comfortable in their everyday lives with what they're doing and the tools they have, so they will need some encouragement to make the switch.

Promote User Adoption

The primary goal of change management is to ease the end-user's anxiety about moving to a new system.

Throughout the project, make every effort to regularly communicate with the end-user community regarding the status of the project, the progress that has been completed, and the new and exciting features that they will receive.

Encourage feedback and questions wherever possible, and leverage executive management to voice similar encouragement when appropriate. Hearing the CEO or President of the company indicate that this new OneStream system is going to make their lives better, and their jobs easier, can truly go a long way toward easing their worries.

Tools to Use

There are numerous tools to assist with change management. Some, but not all, include:

- Town Hall meetings
- Newsletters
- Videogram messages
- Lunch and Learns

The implementation partner should have some ideas and suggestions as well. Be sure to get their input at the beginning of the project to have a change management approach enabled from the outset.

Conclusion

This chapter covered the essentials to be considered before, during, and after the project begins. This includes a multitude of things to contemplate when determining the initial scope of the project. It also stresses things to keep in mind when choosing your implementation partner and administrator, along with critical items that will help you plan for success. There are many things to be wary of when going through requirements and design, as well as testing what was built, and validating the data (remember, it'll take longer than you think), not to mention training options and supporting your application after it's live.

One final, parting thought. After spending 25 years in this industry and the vast majority of those within Services to implement software, I can state unequivocally that *a poorly implemented first phase will prove immensely costly to the customer. User adoption will waiver, and the ability to take further advantage of the solutions available to the platform will evaporate.* As mentioned earlier, customers should be diligent and judicious in their selection of an implementation partner. Then, LISTEN TO THEM.

Conversely, partners MUST BE CONSULTATIVE to customers. Just because a customer is accustomed to a particular process does not make it imperative to negatively impact the OneStream design. The customer needs to understand that they're going down a bad path and prevented from doing so. Partners MUST HAVE the gumption to tell a customer that they are wrong and why (nicely, of course).

I would like to give special thanks to Gaia Kaldor who, along with George Celentano, was my partner in creating Waterline, as well as her valuable help in updating this chapter for the revised version of the handbook. She's a consummate professional and always willing to lean in to help.

Epilogue

I realized that I had made the right decision in joining OneStream while at my first Services Summit in October 2016. The excitement of what lay ahead was palpable amongst the team. The energy was unique – even better than 'the good ol' days' of Hyperion Solutions. It truly felt like family. Years later, I can emphatically say that it still feels that way.

To top it off, we held an event at The New Orleans School of Cooking, with Chef Kevin Belton, where we all learned to make authentic Cajun dishes. I still cook the jambalaya several times a year because of this event.

3
Design and Build

Originally written by Peter Fugere, updated by Chul Smith

The design is the most important part of the project. It sets you up for an easy build and ensures testing will go as smoothly as possible.

The ability to design separates the consultants who can only lead a project from the ones who proudly wear the label architect. It's understanding the product, being able to think critically about the business process, and directing the conversation. Nothing will replace the experience of having design meetings and answering questions; however, this chapter should give you a foundation from which to start.

In this chapter, I will explain the critical questions you will need to ask during design, the impact of those decisions, and the core concepts that impact the performance of the OneStream solution. The second purpose of this chapter is to talk about the build. Not where to click, but *why* we set up our applications the way we do.

Design

The ability to do solid and well-performing design is what separates the best consultants from the pack. In my years of doing this work, I have coached dozens of consultants, many of whom have gone on to become very senior and valuable members of our team. They all have a few traits in common. Just like when you take golf lessons and see what the pros are doing and copy that, I think it's valuable to see what the best design people are doing and consider how to incorporate their approaches into yours.

First, all great consultants follow a structured strategy. They have a tested and proven agenda. They all have some humility – they do not know everything. The client will know their business better than you do, and you hopefully know OneStream better than they do. The design process should be collaborative. This means being okay with having peers review your work. And I cannot emphasize this enough – *ask questions*! The best consultants will workshop with their clients. This includes having a prototype. You can start this by having a shell of the existing application or mock-ups of your first pass of the dimensions. The visual of the mock-up will go miles toward explaining the concepts.

The design session should be a time to generate solutions with the client. This is the first chance you get to explain how OneStream works, and it is as educational for the client as it is for you (the consultant) driving the design. The best design meetings I was ever part of were an interactive back and forth, driving out the details of the business process.

Importantly, the design meeting should *include the project stakeholders*. Of course, there are often topics that do not apply to everyone. That might mean not everyone is in the room for every topic. Nonetheless, I cannot tell you how many times someone who was just casually involved with the project has brought something insightful to the design. So, if it is reasonable to do so, I encourage larger participation.

Not everyone who is in the room will have attended administrator training. A good technical overview will explain key concepts and set terms for people so they can follow along. I have found when people do not understand one topic, they will *not always ask*! Instead, they will sit quietly and wonder, "What does that mean?" Meanwhile, you will have moved forward ten topics. It can save you a lot of time – plus improve the quality of your design – if you spend the time at the beginning of the session covering the basics of OneStream. It is also strongly recommended that the client administrators attend product training prior to the meeting so that they understand the features and functions of the product(s) being implemented.

I like to say that, during *requirements*, I listen 90% of the time, but during *design* I will be talking 90% of the time. Design is a chance to explain the product and timeline to your client, "This is what I heard; this is when it will be done; this is who will do it," and most importantly, "This is *why* we will do it this way." If you ask a client to make any decisions, the answer you should be expecting should be something that would be fine either way: not a decision on performance and design. You should never ask if they want better performance; assume they do. As the expert, you should understand and be able to articulate the impact of any choices being made.

The following items should be available for review during the design meeting:

- Proposed, detailed chart of accounts (in Word or Excel)
- Proposed, detailed custom dimension structures
- Excel listing of all calculated values and any conditions
- Complete list of all reports and executive decks (including visualizations or charts), prioritized, along with a soft copy of each
- Decisions on any open items from the analysis phase
- Sample data files from each data source
- List of every user, including user ID, domain, and name

A good design meeting should move into reviewing and discussing the client's reporting and analytical needs. I like to start by looking at the reports that we will be building. In those reports, you have almost everything you need. You can see the dimensions and the calculations and get a sense of the data volumes you will need. It is a great place to start. But as with any good discussion, you need to have an objective. That objective is creating an application that is:

- Going to perform well
- Meets all reporting needs
- Is scalable for new needs and data volumes
- Considers future functionality on the client's roadmap
- Maintainable

The design meeting will help accomplish a plan to meet these goals. It should be considered the final discussion. In fact, even if you worked for weeks to nail down the most detailed design, the business is evolving and growing (hopefully), and – as such – the reporting requirements likely will too.

I was once part of a project that followed a strict waterfall approach. We spent several weeks detailing each report and calculation – we had it all nailed down. Then, four weeks into build, they acquired a new company!

Too short can be a problem, too. You need to have enough time to flush things out. One or two weeks seems to work very well for most clients. However, this should get longer if there are many stakeholders, multiple solutions, complex data issues, and/or multiple consulting teams.

> **Tip:** Three balanced pillars support an application design:
>
> 1. End-user experience: Meeting the client's reporting/analytical needs while ensuring usability with speed of adoption.
>
> 2. Performance: Maintaining reasonable processing times (e.g., retrievals, calculations, etc.) throughout the application.
>
> 3. Administration: Simplifying application maintenance where possible.

Client's Reporting/Analytical Needs

A good design agenda dives into detail about the client's business process. Even if you covered this during the requirements meeting, it is still good to go back over and change the focus of the discussion to *how* you will meet the requirements in the new system. I would encourage the client to listen to the playback of what was heard. It is not uncommon for people to skip over that part of a design document. The benefits of having a thoughtful review should never be minimized. Then, the conversation can turn toward the timeline, design topics, and team resources (skills and availability).

The place we often start **troubleshooting** a project is design. Every project should have a detailed design document. This document should be clear and explain the decisions made. There is often a lot of boilerplate that makes its way into these documents, and I think it is because people feel they need to justify the cost of the document and the writing of it to the client. But I have found that the extra boilerplate creates a document that is just too unwieldy to consume. If you review your design with a client and they are not challenging and asking questions, you have not met your goal. They either do not understand or did not read the document. If you still feel compelled to write a lot of nonsense or copy something from the Admin Guide into your design document, then I would recommend boiling the design down to a couple of PowerPoint slides and taking the time to review it with the client.

> **Tip:** *Keep processing times* (retrievals, calculations, maintenance) *reasonable.* Be careful that you do not create a separate dimension for every single view/slice the client wants, as it could result in many dimensions and database explosion. You need to understand the limitations of what you are putting in each cube, when to use the relational blending, and the limitations of today's hardware and database connections. That means understanding the Data Unit, and the benefits of blending the relational tables. We will cover that later in this chapter.

So, what is a reasonable processing time? This depends on the client's expectations. Consolidations for a single month of more than 10 minutes, or a full year of over 30 minutes, are both normally a red flag. However, each client may expect different results. If they are using a system now, it is especially important to get those metrics from them. An hour might be fine if it's half as long as it takes in the older system. You will want to set the expectation early that we cannot estimate calculation times without loading a representative dataset into the database and running calculations.

I strongly encourage planning a time for a review of performance *as early as possible* during the build when you have that representative dataset. If you find the performance is not as expected, then you will have time to fix it. You need to avoid waiting until the project is about to go live to find out the performance times are not good. One final note on processing times is to *never use the desired processing times as a success factor of the project*. There are times when you will want to automate a process or possibly add something that is not done in the current process. These are valid reasons why it might take longer. Having time as a metric will mean having to explain why things take longer than expected.

> **Tip:** *Speed of Adoption.* The ability of end-users to incorporate the tool is the adoption speed. The faster they can incorporate OneStream into their jobs, the better! The design of an application is not to show how smart you are, or to create something the client cannot maintain, and I always ask myself, "Is the performance gain here worth the added support and complexity?" Indeed, I have a friend who likes to say, "My car can go 120 miles per hour, but that doesn't mean I should go 120 miles per hour." The same thing is true with a good design. You should have a reason for doing something in the application. The best consultants understand why.

Overly complex dimensionality could put the ability of users to understand the application at risk. I will often look at the existing system and ask how comfortable the users are with known dimensionality. If – across the organization – many users are already comfortable with the dimensions and naming, you may want to leverage that as a starting point. For example, if two-thirds of users have been using the numbers and labels of the general ledger system for reporting, you should consider using that as a basis for your design. Not only will those users become instantly familiar with the structure, but account reconciliation will be much faster since people will intuitively know where to find their data. In fact, when a large group sources their data from that dimension, even the users who do not will benefit. They are often accustomed to relating to those dimensions. And the project team will likely find mappings that already exist. That being said, customers who take a rigid approach to their dimensionality without being open to modifying them to best fit OneStream, sacrifice functionality and benefits that our software provides.

Another mistake people make (which slows down the speed of adoption) is too many dimensions or having **cross dimensions**. It is already difficult for many users to conceptualize 18 dimensions.

But when they must think about multiple dimensions for the same type, they will be confused. Sometimes people want to see data by source, and we call this a **Type dimension**. OneStream also has an **Origin dimension** *that identifies if data was loaded or manually entered.* The Type and Origin dimensions have to be combined to get the right data view, and can be confusing. While it is not uncommon, and I will tell you it is not wrong – you should clearly explain the cost of using a dimension like this. Maybe consider limiting where it is used.

Another consideration for dimensions includes stacking. **Stacking dimensions** is combining multiple types of dimensions into a single dimension. An example is combining product and market in one dimension. It will work well and will not impact performance but may confuse the end-user, especially if they are unrelated.

Think about what dimensions can be reused and which cannot. You could and *should* consider combining something like product type and product, but you should not be combining location and tax jurisdiction. The product dimensions are related; when combined, they simplify the reporting and updating of metadata. Location and jurisdiction are likely not really the same and – if they are – may not be in the future. Dimensions that already exist should not be replicated.

Dimension names and content that do not represent intuitive business views can confuse the user. They will need to think about having different custom members for each account.

Forms and Excel spreadsheets should look, as much as possible, like the existing documents used. Where possible, you should consider using existing spreadsheets for certain types of forms. The more familiar the documents look, the more comfortable the end-users will be.

Rules are a valuable and powerful tool in OneStream. However, each rule will require the server to do something, and it can add up! A friend once said the best rule file is an empty one. Okay, he was joking, but to be fair, it requires no maintenance and is the fastest to calculate. So, maybe not completely joking. The best advice I can give you is to keep your rule file simple, and only include the rules that you need. Limit when and where the rules run by limiting the scope of the rules.

Use the formula for **Calculation Drilldown** for as many calculations as possible. One recommendation I would make is not only including the inputs for the cell, but adding cells that help with analysis, too. Remember that you can drill down on all the accounts that appear. For example, you could include the revenue account when showing the change in depreciation for cash flow. So, while the movement on the balance sheet should equal what is on the cash flow, it could help an end-user to see the expense line to ensure the statements flow correctly all the way through.

Use the **Documents** folder to store documents for the end-user. This includes all training materials that were presented. I also include things like the close calendar and, if available, the account glossary. Not every company has a proper portal or SharePoint web page for their team. The documents folder can distribute the documents that help end-users. I very often create a sample Excel template for end-users to use to create their own Excel add-in spreadsheets. It accelerates the use of the Excel tool if they have a reliable starting point that already works. It takes a lot of the guesswork out of using this tool.

The last comment I will make about helping increase your speed of adoption is to record short training videos. These can be embedded directly into the Workflow for each step a user must complete! You could have specialized videos by domain, finance function, or even language! Having dozens of videos by language could be difficult to manage for the administrator, though. So, you could identify a troubled group that has issues, either local training or employee turnover, and give that group some extra help with a specialized video to help keep them on track.

Designing and Building Your Model

I explained the goals of the design meeting. The part of the design that people struggle most with is organizing the dimensions in a way that will yield objectives defined in the design. Being able to break down those dimensions – thinking of both present and future needs – is really the goal. There are some performance guidelines you need to think about that I will get into later in the chapter. Let us break down the steps of a good design.

Gather All Dimension Types

I suggest gathering all the reports. All the information you will need exists within those reports. The dimensions, data sources, and rules can be gleaned off those reports. And from the client's perspective, if that report comes out fast, reliable, and accurate, then 'how' that happens almost does not matter.

Review the Detail of each Dimension to Ensure it Meets Reporting Needs

Each dimension you identify may not be fully represented in the report. Discuss the dimensions to ensure you understand the full detail that needs to be captured. Often, it helps to have the dimensions electronically so you can display them and discuss the detail. For example, one report may have the cost of sales accounts broken out by department. I would ask if they also break out operating expenses by department. If they do not, then is that something they want to do? This point is critical to discussing the dimensions; just because they do not look at something now does not mean they do not want to.

Clients always ask, "What other people are doing?" That can be a frustrating question to ask a consultant because you may have only been engaged on the project for a couple of weeks as you start to design. Often, what the client really means is, "What could we be doing better?" The easiest thing is to help see what dimensions they are not fully utilizing. If they have department detail down all expense lines, why not consider that for future use? Ask them the question. In almost every project I have been part of, I have been able to help our application add detail that had not been there before.

There is a balancing act here. While we do not want to find the project falling into the morass of a business process reengineering effort, we want to use the software in the most efficient way. So, it is proper and smart to challenge statements like, "This is the way we've always done it." I will take the time to explain that the most efficient companies will adapt processes to get faster or better results. But, again, limited to the context of small changes determined by the software.

It should be said that the goal is not to automate inefficiency. We do not want to take a bad process and fold it into a design. Otherwise, you will still have the same problems, just with the new tool.

Group the Dimensions to Identify Cubes

As you organize your dimensions into cubes, you will see dimensions that share all or part of their hierarchy. Product groups could be a summary or parent level of product name. In that case, you could have a dimension type of product group, and product name could be another group that rolls up to product group.

Product Group

Product Names

This is the dimension extensibility. People often make a critical error here: use extensible dimensions! I will explain more of the performance benefits when discussing our performance guidelines later.

You should analyze all dimensions for this overlap. You can consider both functionality and purpose. We often call that looking at the dimensions horizontally and vertically. This just means consider the dimensions changing by scenario (Actual, Budget, and Forecast) and by User Defined (business function). You may need to consider the dimensions changing by entity as well.

Then you can group your dimensions by 'cube'. I know, I put cube in quotes because – at this point – you do not know if they will really be cube or Scenario Type. You will also have to consider your options for cube design.

It's important for the implementation team to determine the best data model for the data set. You've got dimensions, but maybe the data is better suited in a relational data model rather than a multidimensional cube data model. Sometimes, it's a coin flip, but there are times where application performance will suffer if the data is in a suboptimal model.

Consider Future Solutions and Ensure Your Design Considers Other Dimensions Needed

A good design will discuss future use. Not only use of the dimensions (as said earlier) but of future solutions. If the application will ever add the Tax Provisioning solution, it makes sense to review the dimensional model to ensure there is no duplication of dimensions. For example, you may have locations identified as a dimension. You may think that jurisdiction in the tax solution is a duplicate. It may or may not be. You may be able to share this dimension. You should be familiar enough with the tax solution to know jurisdiction is not the same as location. I would not expect anyone to know what every dimension does in every Solution Exchange solution. So, after you have gathered your dimensions, and discussed a roadmap of future plans, compare any dimension you have identified with those future solutions. They are documented and will give you an explanation.

This point also applies to extensibility. We sometimes advise our design leads to "stub out dimensions." What that means is to ask what dimensions they are not using now, which they should consider or want to add later. They may have sales detail and plan to report on this by regional manager, but they don't have the detail in the ledger. It is something they want to add, but it will not be available for the current project. I would add the dimension type at a minimum and then – as detail is added or refined – update the dimension. The reason is that if you change the dimension type on a given cube, you will have to reload and reconcile the data again. No one wants to do that. Avoid that by making the plan upfront.

Create Foundation of Workflow – Begin Refining the Workflow for each Cube within the Parameters of the Requirements

The workflow is one of those things that can be hard to design out-of-the-gate. It is incredibly powerful if used right. So much so that we dedicated a whole chapter to this topic. However, for the design, it is helpful to set up a basic workflow. Once you have shown it to your stakeholders, you can refine it and add to it. Remember that workflows are defined by each cube.

Identify and Plan All Data Flows into OneStream and Between Solutions within OneStream

One other benefit of gathering reports is you can ask, "Where does this data come from?" for each of them. You will have data from ledgers, data marts, and Excel sheets. You will want to plan for getting data into the application as soon as possible for not only will it help you create a prototype, it will help to identify missing or incorrect data more quickly.

Create Rules Inventory – Identify All Rules to be Built

Having a full list of all rules will not only make sure you don't miss anything, but it will also help you identify and plan to utilize the rule passes optimally. You can learn more about the rule passes in the Rules chapter.

Create Report Inventory – Identify All Reports to be Built

You do not want to miss any reports, so having a full list will help. I always break down the reports to the group that is 'must-have'. Then, the reports that are 'like to have'. The tedious changes of formatting can add more time than you might expect. I have seen people propose doing the reporting as a mock-up in Excel first. It does not save you any time! It takes just as long in Excel as it does in Cube View Editor to write a report.

Plan for Training End-Users

Each of the documentations you write will build on each other throughout the project. The requirements help with design, which helps with project documents, which helps with test cases, which helps with user acceptance testing, which helps with training, and then end-user guides. You should be thinking of training out-of-the-gate. What is the process that gets those reports populated? If you keep going back to those reports and break down the steps that get them completed, you will ultimately get to the goal.

Okay, now you have a good design document. You have discussed all the dimensions the client thinks they need. You have the requirements. How do you transform that into a design which you can have some confidence will perform well? Well, you will need to decide what dimensions will hold what, and decide on the cube and application set-up. There are only two major guiding principles that you will need to follow (Data Unit and data volumes). If you do, you can be sure the application will perform quickly and reliably. While there are other things to consider, these two will be the source of most issues.

Data Volumes and Design

To fully understand the design of cubes, I must provide a little background. One of the most important considerations when building a OneStream application is the potential size of the Data Units that the system will create, as well as the number of Data Units in the application.

What Makes OneStream Unique

What makes OneStream a different tool from standard analytic engines is that OneStream mixes reporting performance with updating performance. Consider databases with large volumes of transactional data. These databases need to store everything, and these OLTP (online transaction processing) databases have simple queries, large data volumes, and are made to process transactions. Performance is based on the ability to find data and recall it as it is needed for reporting.

By contrast, OLAP (online analytic processing) databases are built to optimize the reading process. OLAP databases will do more complex queries and smaller volumes. A database that relies on the ability to pull data from stored tables has limitations. And a database that relies on in-memory processing completely has limitations as well.

OneStream combines reporting performance with updating performance, and the part of the technology that makes this possible is the Data Unit. Firstly, it is designed around common reporting dimensions that define almost all financial reporting, things like the scenario, time, and entity. Users tend to look at data by this point of view (POV). Secondly, by residing in-memory, the changes in updating performance are instant. This is extremely effective for financial reporting. When you consider updating performance, you are thinking of the Data Unit. OneStream's core engine combines the storage of the relational and dynamic properties of a multidimensional tool.

Data Units

To understand how OneStream performs many of its tasks and operations – including logic execution, consolidation, and data cache – it is critical to understand the concept of Data Units. A Data Unit represents the constituent of work for loading, clearing, calculating, storing, and locking data within the OneStream multidimensional engine. A Data Unit is also something that shares some common point of view (POV) information. OneStream can deliver three different levels of Data Unit granularity. As this relates to design, I will address level 1 (for other levels, please refer to the OneStream Design and Reference Guide).[1]

Data Unit – Level 1

This is the largest unit of work within the system and is mostly thought of as entity, scenario, and time. Users of financial analytic systems typically think about clearing, loading, calculating, and locking combinations of entity, scenario, and time.

Members of the level 1 Data Unit:

- Cube
- Consolidation
- Entity
- Scenario
- Parent
- Time

These level 1 dimensions define the Data Unit, and it consists of the stored data records for the above combination of dimensional intersections. When you reference any combination of these dimensions, a **Data Unit** is created in the server's memory. The server calculates parent members of account, flow, and User Defined – dynamically – and generates a small cube of this data. The greater the size of the Data Unit, the larger the strain placed on the system.

You can estimate the size of a Data Unit by multiplying the number of members in the account and User Defined dimensions to determine all possible intersections. Thus, an application with many accounts (for example, 10,000) and large custom dimensions (Custom 1 has 10,000 members, Custom 2 has 7,500 members, and so on) will result in potentially exceptionally large Data Units. You will then need to evaluate the data to determine the quantity of stored records for each Data Unit. This needs to be evaluated for both base and parent-level entities as they are handled the same by the system.

I like to explain the Data Unit like a page in a workbook. It is easier to see.

---

[1] Data Units, OneStream Design and Reference Guide, OneStream Software, 2016 – Reference to this document will be used throughout this chapter.

◢	A	B	C	D	E	F	G	H	I	J	K	L	M	N
1	Consolidation													
2	Entity													
3	Scenario													
4	Parent													
5	Time													
6	View													
7	Origin													
8		Account	Flow	IC	UD1	UD2	UD3	UD4	UD5	UD6	UD7	UD8		Data
9		Sales	None	None	100	abc	P100	GA200	None	None	None	None		1,000
10		Sales	None	None	101	abc	P101	GA201	None	None	None	None		500
11		Sales	None	None	102	abc	P102	GA202	None	None	None	None		750
12		Sales	None	None	103	abc	P103	GA203	None	None	None	None		333
13		Sales	None	None	104	abc	P104	GA204	None	None	None	None		2,000
14		Sales	None	None	105	abc	P105	GA205	None	None	None	None		1,005
15														

Figure 3.1

Here is an example of a Data Unit, with each record a single row in a spreadsheet. Each record and loadable dimension has a data value. None of the parent members are shown in the rows. If you wrote a rule to loop over each of these records in the Data Unit (represented as a row, above), you would only run the rule six times. This thinking helps the rules in OneStream be 'data-driven'. That means the volume of data will dictate what and when rules run. This can be a very efficient way to design an application.

You can't beat factorial math here. Adding one dimension can create millions or more intersections of data. Adding a dimension for the existing six records with only four members could increase that Data Unit from 6 to 24.

The size and number of Data Units are what you are trying to manage. A cube with exceptionally large User Defined dimensions – populated with a lot of data – will have large Data Units. A cube with everything pushed into the Entity dimension will have much smaller, but many more, Data Units. If the processor is spending all its time creating and managing these Data Units, because they are either big or numerous, it does not have capacity for anything else.

OneStream treats a zero as data, so it is strongly recommended to avoid loading or calculating cells with zero 'hard coded' values. Dense account or custom dimensions will result in slower performance as the application server must process and aggregate many records resulting in performance degradation. I would be careful with allocation rules; while they will not populate the database with a lot of zeros, they could populate the database with **near-zero data**. I define near-zero data as data that is not zero, but numerically insignificant. If I have a bad rule that creates thousands of cells with fractions of a penny, the number will not increase the accuracy of the financial data but can slow the system down. Near-zero data adds no value and will slow performance.

Data Unit Statistics	
Point Of View	
Cube	Houston
Entity	Houston
Parent	
Consolidation	USD
Scenario	Actual
Time	2022M3
General	
Total Number of Stored Records	12560
NODATA Status	
Number of NODATA Cells	17
Number of Zero Cells	5398
Number of Real Cells	7145
Number of Derived Cells	0
Storage Type	
Number of No Activity Cells	17
Number of Input Cells	0
Number of Journal Cells	0
Number of Consolidated Cells	3409
Number of Translated Cells	0
Number of Calculated Cells	9134

Figure 3.2

OneStream will provide detail on the data that is zero in the **Data Unit statistics**. This is available by right-clicking on a cell in a grid (see Figure 3.2) or within the **System Diagnostics** Solution Exchange solution. The number of zeros should be monitored closely, and if they either spike significantly or increase above 10% of the data, they should be addressed. You will need to identify the source of the zeros and resolve it.

It is important to note that the period is part of the Data Unit. So, if you loaded data in each month, and did not load data in the subsequent months, the system will generate either a year-to-date or periodic zero. While this is not real data, you will see that number if you loop over the cells of the Data Unit in your rules. Stored calculations also add cells of data that could require processing.

Stored Data versus Calculated-On-the-Fly Data

The OneStream application server is a hybrid transactional and multidimensional Engine. Some of the information is persisted in the relational data store, and some of its data is only calculated within the Data Unit and stored in RAM on the application server when specifically requested by a user.

OneStream does not provide any administrative options for configuring what information is stored and what is calculated on-the-fly. We will talk about which dimensions are sparse later in this chapter. All base-level information for dimensions, calculated numbers, line-item detail, text, and journal information is stored and persisted in the relational database. All parent levels of accounts, intercompany partner (IC), and all custom dimensions, are calculated when a requested Data Unit is created.

For example, an end-user opens a form with cost of sales for a given department, market, and channel. The Data Unit is retrieved from the relational database, created, and then stored in RAM, and then the number is sent to fulfill the request. If the user then selects another account and the members of the level 1 Data Unit cube have not changed, then that number is already stored in RAM and is sent to fulfill the request. If the user then changes the account to total expense, the

Data Unit in memory will have already aggregated the parent-level values. The hierarchy in the Data Unit stores the total and any other intermediate totals for the product dimension in RAM. As other users request the data from the members of the level 1 Data Unit cube, the Data Unit will remain in memory.

Data Volumes

If you find you have a data issue, it will be important to get some details on where the issue is. Data volumes vary widely by application. To get some actionable analysis on your data, your volumes should be measured in the following manners to be of relevance:

- **Input level data for one year** – this is measured by extracting all of the base-level entities (choose the [Base] hierarchy), all base-level accounts ([Base] hierarchy as well), for all base periods, for the densest year/scenario combination. This metric indicates the complete volume of data loaded into the application for that year/scenario. It is important, primarily, as a baseline for the other data metrics.

- **Calculated base-level data for one year** – performs all the same selections as above, but this time *includes calculated data* (check the Include Calculated Data). Note that this assumes the application has been fully consolidated, or at the very least that all base entities have been calculated and have an OK calc status.

- **Consolidated base-level data for one year** – performs the same selections as in 2 (above) with one important distinction: *only choose the primary top entity in the application*. The reason for this is to attempt to measure the densest dataset in the application.

- **Consolidated base-level data for one single period** – performs the same selections as in 3 (above), except this time *selects only the last period in the year*. This is the simplest way to measure the maximum number of records in each Data Unit by counting all the unique combinations of account/User Defined/IC members that have been loaded to, or calculated during, the consolidation process. This set of unique base combinations provides the definition of total base records, which will be discussed in several cases below.

What we are looking for in this exercise is to establish the data explosion from rules, as well as the largest Data Unit size. Seeing patterns in the data will give you clues to find the issue – a rule, an error on data loading, or some other problem.

While hardware can help lessen the impact, Data Units over 2 million records are significantly slower. One should consider the cost of hardware and the required time of consolidation when choosing to have these large volumes of Data Units. With OneStream extensibility, you are likely better off creating a new cube or leveraging the relational store (either Analytic Blend or custom SQL table) than trying to fit too much data in one cube.

Data Unit – Interdimensional Irrelevance and Database Sparsity

When building your application, you add User Defined dimensions, and the data resides at these intersections. When you create your first pass, there will be many intersections that normally would not make sense. These intersections are often left blank or have no data. We call these intersections of blank data **interdimensional irrelevance**. You would never use the Intercompany dimension on accounts like deferred tax assets. It is uncommon. So, you can – and should – prevent the accidental use of those accounts and limit the database sparsity.

Why do you care if there are used cells in the dimensions? Because of the Data Unit. As those intersections get populated, either intentionally or unintentionally, then the performance of the system will degrade. This can happen either slowly, as is often the case with loading zeros, or suddenly, as is often the case with a bad rule causing data explosion.

So, why would you allow all intersections to be open at all? When migrating an existing application, you will find it significantly easier to allow input at all intersections. Over time, the data may have changed, or the quality improved, but going forward you may want to explore incorrect combinations of data to identify and resolve these issues. If you are about to work through a full data reconciliation effort as part of a project, it would be good to limit the intersections (even at least somewhat) to ensure you are resolving as much as you reasonably can. If the data quality of the history is poor, this may be a much greater effort than you realize.

The first way to manage what dimensions are open is by using **constraints** on the dimensions. You can limit what User Defined dimensions are used by account and by entity. This is a powerful feature that many designs don't fully utilize. I worked on an application with a single, large-product dimension, extended down from group to part numbers. Obviously, you do not want this dimension for all entities. But for reporting, have a way to capture the group at the parent entities, and each entity has its own part numbers. Since entities shared part numbers, simply adding dimension types would not work. A single dimension type would need to exist in multiple types, and that is not allowed. So, I added only two types – the group and part number. The part number rolled up to groups. I then created some smaller alternate roll-ups of the part numbers needed by entity. Then, using constraints, I limited which part numbers were available by entity. Not only did this limit the ability to load bad data, but it also ensured the parent entity's Data Unit would perform as well as possible.

Another issue is **database sparsity**. This is where data is only sparsely used across dimensions. For example, one customer member will only be populated with one product member and this occurrence is consistent across all customers and products. You often see this when people think they will have more detail than exists. They want a dimension for the whole P&L, but only a subset of expense accounts really uses it. The risks are the same as per interdimensional irrelevance. Somehow, these empty data intersections will get mistakenly populated. And when they do, it will not likely be during a low point; often, these issues come up during a close and will become a critical issue. Your design can easily avoid this. Start by combining dimensions when it makes sense. If only a handful of accounts use a dimension, and within that dimension there are only one or two members – I would ask if we really need that detail in the cube. Or can we combine it into the Account dimension? Or can we leave the detail in the Stage and drill back to it? Another option is to just assign the User Defined to only the accounts that will be using them. A detailed look at the data will tell you the correct accounts to use. Any of these approaches would protect the Data Unit.

Selecting Valid Account Combinations for Budget and Forecast

Earlier in the chapter, we talked about limiting the intersections of data to prevent data explosion and other issues. It is possible that you want more dimensions available in one scenario and not for another. You could want to leave the Actuals history wide open and have only limited restrictions.

Often, the ledger manages the valid account strings, and you will not be worried about invalid Account and User Defined dimension combinations getting loaded into the application. If you also consider the historical data could have changed, or is not high quality, restricting the combinations for all the history could be more work than you are prepared to take on. However, you need to think long and hard about leaving it that wide open for Budget and Forecast. This is especially true if people are loading data via Excel. They could create all kinds of invalid account strings completely by mistake. In those cases, you have three options for managing this. You could use the constraints but know those will only vary by cube. The next option is to create a simple conditional input rule; these rules are very flexible and powerful. The third option is using the rules, but also using an input template or administrative cube. You can flag the intersections you want to turn on or off in the administration cube. It could be as simple as loading a '1' to those intersections, then have the rule loop over those intersections.

Data Unit – Performance

As you can gather from this section, the Data Unit design is important. If any single Data Unit gets to 1 million intersections of data and the Data Unit grows, you will see an increasing impact on performance. The largest Data Units should never be above 2-3 million intersections.

Early systems (before OneStream) were designed for 5,000 records per entity. The next generation started at 10,000 and could not consolidate with more than 100,000. The sweet spot for OneStream is between 250,000 and 500,000 records. As you increase above that number, the performance will deteriorate at an increasing rate. The processor speed becomes more critical at that point. The higher the frequency of the processors, the faster they can create these Data Units.

As you build the application, if you find Data Units this size, you should consider a couple of issues. Firstly, you should look to see if you can break up the entity or cube to spread out the data. Secondly, you should explain the impact on performance. You will have some idea if you are doing a prototype. If you have not, then I would consider building one. This is an issue that is easily managed if you have performance data; avoid the surprises! Set the expectation with the client.

I have had clients who think a two-minute consolidation is exceptionally long, and others who are amazed we can do the consolidation in less than a couple of hours. They have different expectations based on the data volumes and calculations and the systems they have used before. If you can explain that on each occasion you 'give up some time, for some benefit', you will help them understand how the entire process is improving, and hopefully they will be happy with whatever times the system generates.

One last note on Data Units as it relates to new features such as dynamic attribute dimensions. Now that you understand the dynamic nature of the Data Unit, it should be obvious that adding members can create millions of aggregation points that can impact performance. Dynamic attribute dimensions can create an explosion of intersections. If you are creating trillions of cells of calculations, expect this to slow reporting and Excel. Consider this impact and test changes in terms of impact as you move forward.

Cube Design

Once the dimensions are considered, you will need to group them into cubes. Cube is just a concept of the data dimensional model grouping. A cube is an organizational structure that holds data in OneStream. Each must contain the 18 dimension types you have defined. And if you have not determined a dimension type for a dimension? Then the cube will use the default type and the member None. A major consideration for designing cube grouping is understanding that workflow and security are driven from the cube. So, I typically look at the purpose of the data and group the dimensions appropriately.

A wrinkle in the cube design is understanding the capability of Scenario Types. You can change the Data Unit dimensions by each scenario within a given cube. So, you can override the default for Account, Flow, and the User Defined dimensions in a scenario. This is a great option for scenarios that will report in similar workflows, but which need different dimensions. Actual and Budget data are probably the most common use of this. You would give the Actual scenario the Actual type, and Budget the Budget type. Then, within the cube setting, change the dimension as needed. The administrator guide does a great job explaining the details.

Let's look at an example. During design, the client asks for consolidation, budget, tax provisioning, and sustainability data. For the Actual data, each data submitter must also update the Forecast and Budget data. Well, Actual scenario is a great case for using the Scenario Type. The workflow will be the same for the end-users because they only need to change scenarios. Your reports, rules and dimension can be changed conditionally by Scenario Type. The reporting is easier, too, simply because you do not have to change cubes. The fewer choices the end-user must make, the better.

However, the sustainability cube would likely have different end-users, limited common data, different security, and ultimately a different workflow. Sustainability data is likely collected from plant managers or different users than those who control the financial systems. Data is unlikely to be financial in nature and will also not be subject to blackout restrictions and controls. This sustainability scenario is probably better served by being its own cube (and, at a minimum, its own Scenario Type). All these differences will give the client more flexibility to make changes.

Determining the Dimensions in the Database

I always recommend rethinking the idea of having users select multiple dimensions for the same dimension type. In other words, one conceptual dimension to one dimension type. I would not put rollforwards in User Defined 1, and cash flow movements in User Defined 2. Both are rollforward adjustments, but for different accounts, and are related. I would think carefully about having adjustments broken out in one dimension, and a data source in another. Firstly, not only does this confuse the end-users, but it makes reporting more difficult and creates an inflexible application. It undermines the benefit of extensible dimensions. You could create a relationship between dimension types and use them in other ways for future applications.

Another example of this is when people want to put accounting function as the Account dimension and break accounts across Account and User Defined (UD), by placing operating expense accounts in the User Defined dimension. I'll define function here to be like a department; for example, accounting, sales, legal, etc. Accounts in this example are natural accounts, like salary, bonus, etc. The other choice is to put all of the natural accounts in the Account dimension, and function in the User Defined dimension. The first thing to understand is that both options provide the exact same detail. There is no benefit for either with respect to level of detail. So why would I choose one over the other? There are some questions to ask. What does the client currently use? Do they only use function? If this is the driver of reporting – and the users mostly expect it – then having the dimensions split won't confuse the end-users, just the opposite.

Another question to ask here is if a functional income statement is used for other scenarios. If end-users never break out expenses for Budget and Forecast beyond that function, asking them to add a natural account might be a non-starter. The point here is that while there is no clear right or wrong approach, there are guiding principles that will help you understand the right choice for any design. It is never okay to just let the client decide without this context. This was a simple choice for adding function. Both options provided the same reporting detail, but one of the choices will meet their needs, based on how they are using the dimensions for other scenarios.

So how do I begin my mapping of these dimensions for cubes? I often go right up to the whiteboard and start breaking it down. I create an application and design matrix. The following table (Figure 3.3) demonstrates which dimension (and dimension detail where necessary) is included in each application by cube. I take the time to review this alongside the design team, and try to find a consensus that it will meet our reporting needs.

Dimensions	Cube 1 (Financial Data)		Cube 2 (Planning)		Cube 3 (Subsidiary)	
Scenario Type	Actual	Budget	Budget	Forecast	Actual	Budget
Time Periods	X	X	X	X	X	X
Years	X	X	X	X	X	X
Scenarios	X	X	X	X	X	X
Flow	X	X	X	X	X	X
Accounts	IFRS	Detailed	Only salary relevant	Detailed	Mgt COA	Mgt COA
Entities	X	X	X	X	X	X
UD1 Products	-	X	X	X	-	X

Dimensions	Cube 1 (Financial Data)		Cube 2 (Planning)		Cube 3 (Subsidiary)	
UD2 Projects	-	X	X	-	X	X

Figure 3.3

'Unspecified' Dimension Members

In the case where specific data points do not exist across one or more dimensions (e.g., balance sheet account detail does not exist across the product and customer Dimensions), use None members in each of these dimensions to designate a placeholder member to contain the data. As the detail becomes available later, you can either break out the history to the new members or start breaking out the detail at a go-forward point. This approach is easy to add later, and will not require reloading, and hence reconsolidating and reconciling the database again.

Cube Integration

Often, you will have to move data between the applications. Fortunately, OneStream gives us some great options. You will have the ability to connect the cubes by creating **linked cubes** via the Entity dimension. Conversely, you could use rules to copy data. You can even update the workflow to pull data from one cube to another using rules. Then, you can drill on the data by using the formula for Calculation Drilldown to specify how a user can drill. The rule is simple, too. All of this is covered in the Rules chapter of this book.

You can also use OneStream as a data source. Why would you want to do that? Because you could summarize or remap data and allow people to drill from one cube to another with the benefit of the mapping. If data is being transformed, it would be helpful for users to see this in the system. Since it is how other data sources are mapped, it can be a great way for the user to copy the data, as they will be familiar with it.

You need to be careful if you create too many copies of the data. This is important to understand… *cubes can reference other cubes*. You do not want to copy data unnecessarily. Also, copying data creates timing differences. By using a rule to copy at a parent level, and drilling to the detail in another cube, data synchronization will be faster, and you have mitigated the timing difference.

Intercompany Across Cubes

If you find an opportunity to break an application by cube for business channel or region, you should know you will have intercompany partners (IC) available for all entities available in each cube. And if you do not need to share the IC across all cubes, you should know they will be available! So, in the latter case, please consider using conditional input rules to limit people making the mistake of choosing the wrong IC member.

Cube Design Options

There are a few design options, and each has advantages and disadvantages to the application design. The first three are typically for financial data designs.

Monolithic Cube

This cube type is good for extremely small and simple designs for specialty use or very small data sets with no possibility for extensive expansion. It does not make use of extensibility and, therefore, is not often recommended for an application of any size or significance. In this design, you would likely make use of the Scenario Types. This is also a popular choice for 'lift & shift' applications because the assumption is this design is temporary and will be replaced. When it is replaced, the extensible option can be implemented.

Super Cube – Linked Cubes

This is the cube example used in the **GolfStream** application. There is a parent/top cube, and its dimensions are at a higher level of detail to the cubes that roll up to it. There is only one level from the parent/top to detail cubes. You can have several detail cubes, and each can have different dimension detail. This is the most common design as it makes the best use of extensibility, is the most common way to manage Data Unit sizes in the parent/top cube, and allows for the greatest flexibility later.

Paired Cubes

Paired cubes are combinations of cubes that allow for some special situations. The most common use of this design manages **split** and **shared entities**. Split entities are where the same entity can exist in multiple cubes. Shared entities are where the users can load to the same entity in multiple cubes. Since dimension members can only exist in one cube, there needs to be a common Entity dimension that has all entities in every cube. That would be assigned to all cubes.

For each cube, there will be a second dimension that has its hierarchy but uses the base members of the first Entity dimension as its base members. For each cube in the original design, you would create two cubes. All dimensions must be the same except for the Entity dimension. One cube has the base entity's dimension; the second has the hierarchy dimension. Then the cubes must be linked by making the cube with all base entities the child of the other. This effectively creates a base cube with all entities for its parent. Users would only ever be in the parent cube, so they do not see all entities. While this will not remove the need to copy the data, all data could be copied by a data management job rule. The linking of cubes must then be done by rules.

Specialty Cubes

Specialty cubes are basically monolithic cubes but are much more limited in purpose. They would be used as administrator cubes (driver cubes, overrides, or equity control) or specialty apps (process control). The benefit of putting these cubes as standalone is simplicity of security. They can easily be separated from the rest of the application.

Some Other Cube Design Considerations

You might ask, "How many cubes can I have? This seems like a lot." Having more cubes will not slow the application. You should not worry about adding cubes. Remember to think of the process as the end-user. A high number of cubes will mean more maintenance, but it should not be a deterrent. The gains in performance – while hard to estimate – will justify the needed support.

Always consider the roadmap. How will the cube design fit with the long-term solutions? Not many people look to OneStream to have only one solution. The benefit of a platform is the ability to leverage multiple solutions. You will do yourself a big favor by ensuring your design considers the dimensions and cube designs of future applications. Even if you don't have dimensions that could be overlapping or duplicative, you will need to consider the data integration between these cubes and solutions.

Determine if you will 'stub out' dimensions for future use. It is for the same reason as above… no one usually buys a platform for one solution – especially if the first project goes well – they will see other uses for OneStream very quickly. When you create a dimension type, even if it only has the default 'None' member, you make it as simple as adding new members when it is time to add detail.

Make all Cube Views as dynamic as possible. We haven't spent much time on reporting in this chapter; however, it is another major design consideration. If you have used extensibility properly, you will find that dynamic references to the metadata will give you reports that require very little updating as the dimensions change. That means a single report can be used across the application, and as the company grows. You will find an incredibly happy administrator who only has a fraction of the reports to maintain.

ALWAYS leverage extensibility.

When Should I Use Extensibility?

I just said, always! All applications should be designed for extensibility, or at the very least, you should have a particularly good reason for not doing it. One of the biggest complaints of customers that have had the solution longer than a year or so is they wished they thought more carefully about the future. Extensibility gives you the advantage of flexibility. It will also help if you find yourself with a performance issue; specifically, the use of multiple cubes and creating breaks in dimensions when possible. To understand why, remember what the Data Unit, and a good Data Unit design, is.

Benefits to the client in multiple ways:

1. Performance

2. Flexibility – the multiple cube approach gives clients the possibility to make changes to the design for new dimensions, added models, or performance changes.

The application will perform better when using extensibility. When you watch consolidation times by entity, you will see the base entities moving very quickly, and as the consolidation moves up to the top, it slows down significantly. There are two primary reasons for this; first, for each child entity below a parent, the processor uses a processor thread to aggregate that data. At the base of the hierarchy are many child entities, and so many threads can be used. At the top parent, there may only be a couple of child entities, so only a couple of threads can be used. Second, the dataset for parent entities is naturally denser as the data consolidates at the higher levels. By using extensibility, you can design smaller Data Units for the parent entities. This dramatically improves consolidation times.

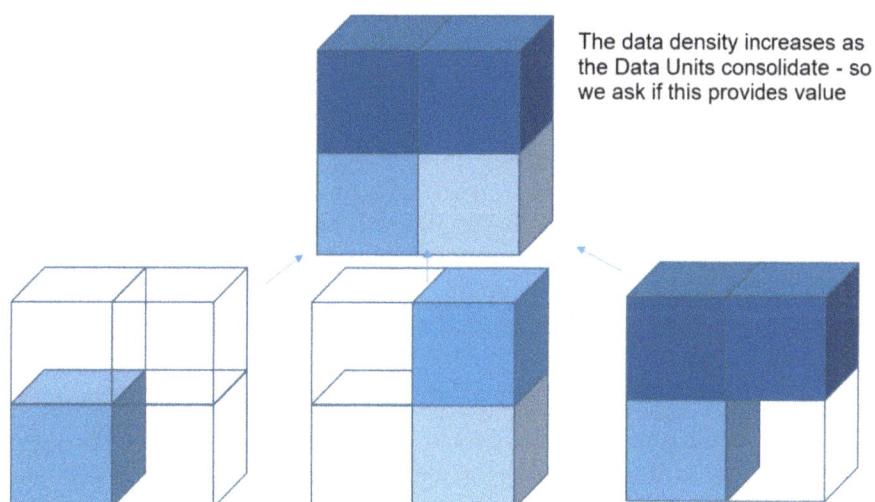

The data density increases as the Data Units consolidate - so we ask if this provides value

Figure 3.4

In the example above, each cube represents a Data Unit. The three base units are not completely full for every possible intersection. Because they do not have overlap, the Data Unit for the parent entity is completely full and would perform the slowest. So, we ask ourselves here if there is anything to be gained by aggregating the detail to that parent Data Unit. Can we get the same reports from the child Data Units?

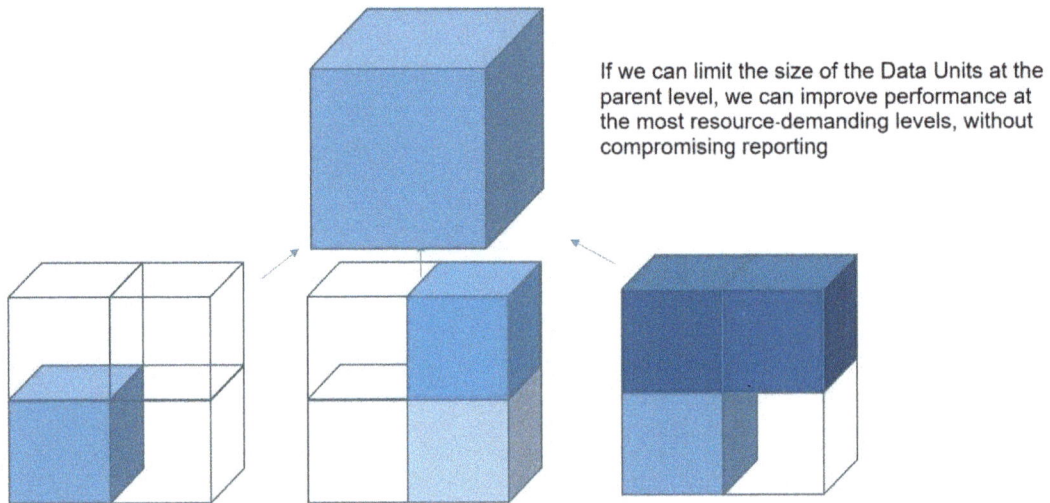

If we can limit the size of the Data Units at the parent level, we can improve performance at the most resource-demanding levels, without compromising reporting

Figure 3.5

With many members in UD, there is an opportunity for invalid data cells to get populated. This could be from poorly-written rules that allowed for the population of those members, or allowed end-users to load zeros. By limiting the available cells by base cube, you can minimize this risk.

Typical symptoms of application design problems, or memory configuration problems, are almost certainly due to a server that is too busy swapping Data Units in and out of memory. Customers may – at times – attempt to stop or 'kill' a running report by ending the execution of the client, restarting the client, and launching another report. This action, however, does not stop the server from pursuing its query, but instead results in an even longer queue of activity requested of the already overloaded OneStream server.

Another reason to use extensibility is that it allows for flexibility by giving a way to add dimensions or new members more easily without impacting the entire user base. You must remember that changing the dimensions on the cube will require dropping the tables for the cube and creating a complete rebuild. This is especially problematic if the data is Actuals, as all the history of loading and workflow sign-off could be lost. This would mean the data will likely need to be reconciled all over again, and this will require some significant re-work.

Relational and Analytic Services Design

Since so many clients are now pushing the envelope of what should be in a CPM system, they want access to more detail across more systems. The thing is, not everything needs to be in a cube. Data (especially the data that is more transactional in nature) does not fit well in a cube concept. This is true because data does not always fit nicely into hierarchies. Take employee compensation, for example. Employees, when looking at an extremely specific point in time, could fit into a hierarchical structure, but not over any normal stretch of time. Employees can transfer between departments, resources are shared between departments and varying percentages of their time, or just flat out quit. In those cases, the data is just as well served in a flat table. We offer that as an option in OneStream, and we call it **Analytic Services**.

Now, we have a whole chapter on Analytic Blend (Chapter 12) in this book, so I am only going to say what is important as it relates to cube design. I would encourage you to read that chapter to understand the various options and consider how they will impact your design.

There are a couple of differences between the concepts of Analytic Services and Analytic Blend, although both involve SQL tables that can handle large volumes of data. We are talking millions of records, so this is great for detail that you might need (but do not want to see) in the cube.

Analytic Services is an umbrella term for the broad range of analytic capabilities in OneStream, ranging from financial consolidation to data aggregation to transaction analysis. The ability to support all *three types of data models in one platform is ground-breaking.* It intelligently brings together CPM, financial analytics, BI, operational, and other transaction-level data for comprehensive analysis and visualization directly within OneStream.

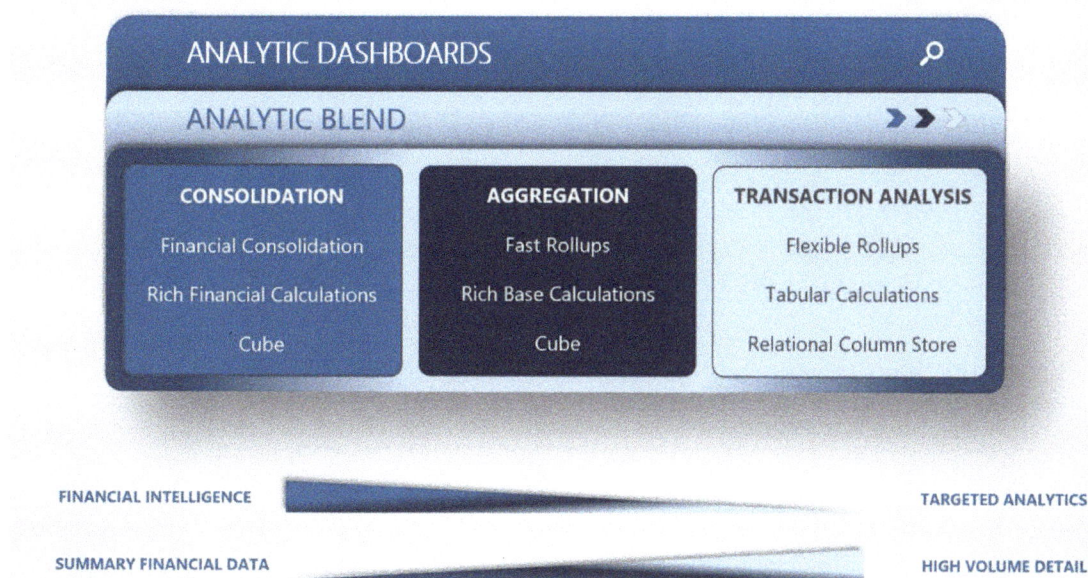

Figure 3.6

Analytic Services expands OneStream's *unified platform* across a broad range of data and analysis requirements. It bridges the gap between the full cube and the blend tables. The cube can have an extremely specific (even down to a single cell) level of data in a calculation. Analytic Blend has only the most basic calculations. There is no aggregation of the type you would expect from a cube.

Another use of Analytic Services is for certain Solution Exchange solutions, where it serves as the database. The **OneStream People Planning** solution leverages its own table. However, there are limited calculations that you would use here. If you need to do calculations, you might consider doing them on the load of data. You can add new fields and do some calculations on the load.

Analytic Blend is the concept of using a SQL table to house all the transitional data records. The advantage of copying the data here is that you can accumulate the details from a variety of sources. You can always drill to the source if you have a direct connection. It might not be possible to drill to the source data, though. You may have a licensing issue, or there are too many sources.

With Analytic Blend, you can have aggregations based on the metadata the cube uses. These aggregations will need to run at a specified time, possibly overnight. They are not as dynamic as the cube. Cubes can run consolidations at any time, and the Data Units from the cube aggregate every time they are called. You might have to consider using multiple tables to get the dimension views you want, while all those views might fit in a single cube. But the volume of data is far more than you would put into a cube.

You can report on the blend tables with the dashboards in OneStream.

This example is a case of using the right tool for the right job. One final note on the blend options. Your design should – as much as possible – ensure that blend options are transparent to the end-users. By that, I mean build your reports and process so users do not have to select cubes, and as few other dimensions in the POV as possible.

Extensible Applications

Why might you need the application to be extensible, you ask? With the options for so many cubes and relational tables, is this not overkill? Well, there are times when you need to have this option if the current database and its connection is simply not big enough. In other words, there is a database limitation. A second example might be when the business process does not support a single application. Private companies sometimes have requirements where an application has sensitive data that not everyone will have access to. Such data could exist in its own application, and still take advantage of common metadata and workflow. Extensible applications allow you to mitigate the risk from the current limitations of today's hardware.

A vast majority of OneStream customers use a single production application, which gives the following benefits:

- Create a scalable platform that can unify financial processes in a single application.
    - Consolidations
    - Planning
    - Transactional Analysis (Analytic Blend)
- Eliminate redundant maintenance caused by multiple product solutions.
- Eliminate the need to support multiple technology platforms.
- Provide an extensible development environment within the platform.
- Solve domain-specific business problems with reliable Solution Exchange solutions.
- Unify analytic and relational solutions under a common platform.

All of these are possible when standard, non-exotic hardware is not required. As soon as the limitations of today's hardware become a restriction, you are limited by the simple physics of the volume of data. This is when you might need to consider an extensible application design.

It is important to understand what an application is. OneStream can have one installation with multiple applications. There are some common components in an application, and they are held in the framework.

OneStream has a single framework for each installation. The framework database holds the following:

- Common structures required by applications controlled by the framework.
    - Users
    - Groups
    - Application definitions
    - Error logs
    - Activity logs
    - System-level dashboards

Each application will house components (it needs a set of tables), and the dataset is a collection of the following:

- Analytic metadata
- Workflow definitions
- Integration definitions
- Data quality definitions
- Staging data
- Analytic data
- Analytic Blend data
- Dashboard visualization
- Solution Exchange solutions (Apps)

- Custom 'customer-driven Solution Exchange solutions (Apps)
- Application resource utilization

An installation has a web tier, an application tier, and a database tier. Good designs will consider the impact on, and limitations of, the hardware for each tier. As data is calculated, especially when the volume of data is high, we need to consider following:

- All cubes must fit in memory (managed cache).

- All Stage transformations must fit in memory (burst cache).

- All metadata must fit in memory (managed cache).

- All workflow must fit in memory (managed cache).

- All dashboards and Solution Exchange solution definitions must fit in memory (managed cache).

- All framework definitions (users & groups) must fit in memory (managed cache).

The database also needs considerations to be made for these large data volumes:

- All metadata must fit in the application database.

- All Stage and analytic data must fit in the application database.

- All metadata and data must be backed up and restored together.

Large applications can create stress on the hardware. Sometimes, it does not even seem large, but when you consider the complexity of 18 dimensions, the dataset can get large quickly. For example, if one only used ten members in ten of the possible 18 dimensions – that is ten to the tenth power, or ten billion records (10,000,000,000). OneStream can handle many multiples beyond ten in each of the dimensions. Even average-sized applications can have thousands of members.

Large applications have other considerations. Even a backup and restore can be problematic. Not only will the size create a long processing time for the SQL database, but being selective about what to back up can be difficult. Exceptionally large applications can take longer to initialize, as everything is loaded into memory. Once again, the hardware is a limitation.

Required data caching must often manage much more data – even though the user for the given task might not be concerned with the full set of data. The size of Data Units becomes more difficult to manage as well, since more data is available. Data Units are the small arrays of data calculated and stored in memory. They are combinations of account, IC, flow, and the UD members. The more of those members that are populated, the more that need to be calculated and stored in memory. Larger applications put more pressure on the RAM, as they will have more and larger Data Units. This does not necessarily help the user with reporting, and they are likely working only in a subset of that data.

These larger Data Units also require more IO to the database, and since the server will provide added pressure on RAM, there could also be more caching of data. Which all finally leads to the most constrained resource we have, which is the connection to the database. We need a SQL database because we require transactional reliability. It is not practical or reasonable to build a monster database. However, as the hardware does evolve and grow, the OneStream software will be able to take advantage of many of those hardware gains. This is also true in the cloud. While OneStream has no *scale up* limitations, it can use all application server processors and all application server memory.

OneStream also has no *scale out* limitations. XScale supports 1-N application BOT servers (batch workload servers), and XScale supports 1-N application general call servers (UI/reporting servers). However, the hardware available is, by definition, a scale out limitation. The database *scaled up* eventually hits a limit and cannot meet application server demand. The network *scaled up* eventually hits a limit and cannot meet application server demand.

The cloud also has limitations. The architecture of the cloud is:

- Redundancy focused

- High-availability focused

- Reliability over exotic performance

Servers are treated as expendable; not something that you name and take care of. Cloud servers are created and destroyed as needed, and you cannot have exotic hardware in this architecture. Size and speed are limited compared with what is available. Azure *limits* will ultimately define how far a single application can be pushed.

Having looked at the background, we can now look at the Data Unit and size of the database to determine how big the server needs to be. While there are no absolutes, we look at applications with Data Units of 2 million, and data record loads of 10 million as red flags. We also look in those applications for heavy multi-threading operations like consolidation and data loading.

Breaking the solution into multiple applications provides the solution to this problem of scalability. Using the **Rest API** from OneStream will allow you to keep the data, metadata, and workflows in sync. These functions will allow you to link many of the features, like updating the workflow across applications, on the same instance of OneStream.

This is just another way OneStream is scalable. And with the addition of this option, you can see how OneStream is infinitely scalable. There really is no limit; even current hardware doesn't stop you.

Design Example

Problem

At a medium-sized company, we created a single cube. During our performance test for our prototype, we found the consolidation times were excessively long. It was taking 45 minutes for what should have been a reasonable dataset. Using the data analysis described in this chapter, we found two issues. The first was that the UD1 dimension had extraordinarily little overlap across the leaf entities. The second was calculated data for allocations was generating a large volume of detail that was not reported.

The sum of these issues created the poor performance, with so many members in UD1 and some poor rules that allowed for the population of those members. In addition, existing data volumes at the top entity in UD1 were too dense. Typical application design problems, or memory configuration problems, are almost certainly due to a server that is too busy swapping Data Units in and out of memory. As mentioned above, customers may – at times – attempt to stop, or 'kill', a running report by ending the execution of the client, restarting the client, and launching another report. This action, however, does not stop the server from pursuing its query, but instead results in an even longer queue of activity requested from the already overloaded OneStream server.

Resolution

Let's tackle the second issue first. By adding some control of scope, you can limit where the rule runs. Then, you can decide if you need to consolidate all the data from the allocation. You can measure the impact of the rule by running the calculation with and without the rule. A detailed review of the rule usually leads to performance improvement. See the Rules chapter for more detail.

By using the power of cubes more effectively in the design, we can avoid this issue completely. Here is a great example of why you should avoid the single cube design approach. Let's start by breaking up the UD1 by group:

Corp – corporate summary cost centers, by group

Hist – historical cost centers no longer active

CC1 – logical grouping of cost centers

CC2… and so on…

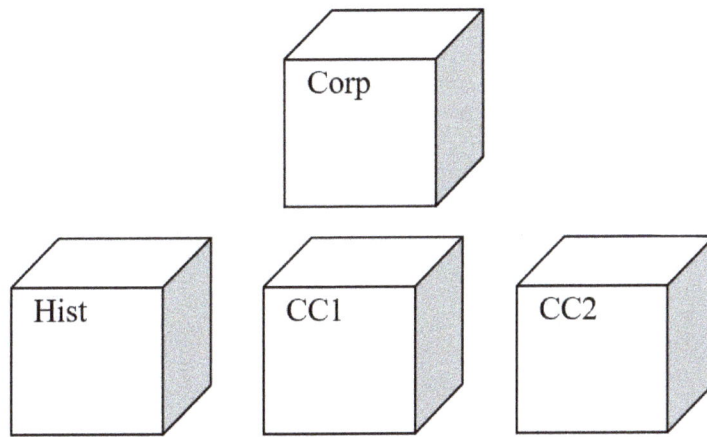

Figure 3.7

Each cube would now only have the cost centers required for each entity. Not only does this solve performance issues, but it will simplify navigation for each user as they will only see the cost centers they need by entity. Each Data Unit queried will be smaller and perform faster. The more we can break down the cost center dimension, the better.

An example that is commonly used for larger projects is having two cubes, a 'detailed cube' and a 'summary cube'. The detailed cube would have large dimensions in accounts and User Defined dimensions. The summary cube would have fewer members in the accounts and User Defined dimensions. However, the data would be naturally sparser in the detailed cube. The summary cube would be denser with data. This yields all the reporting detail and maximizes the performance of the data as it aggregates.

What Makes an Application Large?

People may be concerned about how big their application is getting, with all the cubes and tables, so I want to give some context. Each option below has a cost and benefit.

- Look for Data Units that exceed 1 million records. While OneStream can handle much higher volumes, these are large enough to warrant inspection and review of the design.

- More cubes could create integration points but – as per our example – is likely the best design.

- More dimensions – less is better where possible, but reports should consider ensuring that requirements are met.

- The database structure depends on a client's reporting/analytical needs.

Some guidelines for numbers of members are as follows:

Dimension	Small Application	Medium Application	Large Application
Accounts – members	500 or less	5000 or less	20,000 or less
Accounts – levels	<5	<8	<12
Custom 1	<100	<10,000	<100,000
Custom 2	<100	<10,000	<100,000
Custom 3	<100	<10,000	<10,000
Custom 4	<100	<10,000	<10,000
Entities	<1000	<10,000	<50,000

Figure 3.8

Chapter 3

Prototyping a Design

Introduction and Purpose

Following the design, a prototype can be created based on available data, metadata, and report specifications (possibly in a follow-up visit). This is not meant to be a full build, but more of a quick build (2-3 days tops) based on available information. The prototype can then be updated based on client feedback and available metadata, etc. – it is not meant to be a throw-away application.

Now that you have identified where your dimensions will go, you need to start building the application. The sooner you can start testing your assumptions about the data volumes and dimensions, the sooner you can be assured that performance will be acceptable. I would plan for the time needed to do a prototype. This will give you some real advantages. You can:

1. Validate the expected performance.

2. Begin to benchmark expected times for tasks.

3. Validate the design will meet the reporting needs with your client.

4. Refine your design by having a working example for complex topics like workflow.

Let us talk about that last point. Workflow is incredibly powerful and will give the users of OneStream some incredible information over time. You cannot only manage the data loading and audit experience, but you can identify where bottlenecks are in the close process over time.

Planning users often do not see the value of a workflow. This is especially true if they are coming from a legacy system that does not have this type of functionality. But workflow can help manage the user experience so that often confusing steps – like selecting the correct point of view – are completely automated. The topic can be difficult to design because it's so flexible. Having a working example to demo to end-users will help refine the experience. Often, there is not a specific step for this in a project plan, and that is okay, but I would recommend planning on short meetings during the build to show functionality and confirm the design. This will allow stakeholders and users, who are new to planning, to see the initial results of the design. Seeing the outline content, and sample reports/business rules, solidifies the design discussions and validates that the client's needs are being met.

Workflow Design

Overview

The workflow is a critical part of the design but is very difficult for people to conceptualize. The focus here needs to be on the *process*, and not the entities or structure. Often, people coming from other tools are hung up on the idea of the hierarchy they need to follow. This is a great use of the prototype, as a picture tells a thousand words.

Considerations for Workflows

- When you promote a parent level, its children must be promoted.

- Security must be added for each level.

- Determine here who can enter journals, parent entities, or base entities.

- Using the training dashboards is strongly recommended.

Confirmation Rules

- What are the most common checks they perform on the data?

- What checks do they use now?

- Do they want to have thresholds on the data?

- Group these by warning and error – then by submitter and approver.

- Basically, any validation that someone does visually on a report or in a "check" cell formula in Excel would be a great candidate for a confirmation rule.

Certification Rules

- Do they need Sarbanes–Oxley questions addressed?
- Group these by warning and error – then by submitter and approver.

Data Loading and Considerations for Partitioning

One client was loading data by month for a large dataset. The dataset was about 8 million records. The IT group pushed back on grouping the load by entity; they said it was not possible. Since we were seeding data for the Forecast, it would be easy to load a single file for a given month to an 'admin' location. This could run overnight, so performance would not be too bad. When we added a new scenario, we were loading different months at the same time. Effectively, the file was being portioned by period.

Since we were loading data to the same entities just for different periods, we created an issue where the system could not figure out the zero for missing data or how to clear data it should not have. Moreover, this was a bad design.

We went back and created a load file by entity group. Not only were we able to resolve the data loading problem, we had a more scalable design. Firstly, if there was a change, we could load a subset of the entities instead of all of them (this was much faster). Secondly, since we grouped by entity, we could have a greater number of smaller partitions, which allowed us to utilize more threads on the load.

Dimension Types

Overview

Before you build the cubes, you will need to determine the dimensions required for each cube. Dimensions could have relationships by each dimension type. For example, the accounts you might need for a subsidiary could inherit the accounts from the corporate standard.

Considerations for Each Dimension

Take the time to think about each of the following. Avoid duplicating dimensions.

- Description/purpose
- Number of members
- Naming conventions (duplicates within dimension)
    - Use prefixes or suffixes with numeric member names to eliminate potential duplicate member names in two or more dimensions or where numbers are used as member names. For example, subsidiary dimension: `1100_Service for Service Revenue`, and maybe in the corporate dimension: `1000_Revenue`.
    - I have a strong preference to always use the dimension labels that your customer is most comfortable with. This will help with the speed of adoption!
    - If they aren't sure, then ask what data source represents the largest set to load. If half of the data is coming from one ledger, for example, then that should be the label of the base members in that dimension. Not only is the mapping a simple `* = *`, the data reconciliation for half of the data is much easier. You will be able to line up the dimensions in a sheet and just go down the list quickly.
    - For parent accounts, consider that OneStream allows you to use labels and descriptions for report headers. Using labels and descriptions also applies when searching for members. Labels that are too long will mean more work when writing rules. I find rules that have `A#Sales * A#Percent = A#PctSales` much easier to read than `A#1000 * A#7999 = A#19999`.

  o Consider having a way to identify which accounts are calculated, or parents, by using the labels.

  o At the end of the day, I always ask, "Okay, what will be most familiar and easiest for your end-users?"

Top Customs

Each dimension should have a top. This will help when you want to create your reports. I like a top dimension that is simple and quick to write yet identifies the dimension I am referencing. For example, UD1Top.

Calculation Efficiency

Utilize dynamic calculations where possible. Remember, dynamic calculations will not be referenced during consolidation. However, too much of a good thing can be bad! Consider these calculations being run every time the cell is called. Excessive use will hurt performance.

Dimension Design

Time Periods/Years Dimensions - Implications

Time Dimension Types

The Time dimension should require the least discussion.

Without mentioning who was running the project, I was part of a meeting that scheduled four hours to discuss the Time dimension. After I said, "Can we all agree there are 12 months in a year?" we really had nothing else to talk about. I know, sometimes there is a thirteenth period. But that would not have been as funny a story.

Seriously, though, this dimension is simple. You may need a thirteenth period. If so, add it. You might be okay with an adjustment member in a User Defined dimension, though. I will say, regarding the thirteenth period, that if you are adding it only to duplicate what is in the ledger, you might be adding complexity for no gain. The reason the thirteenth period exists in a ledger is often to roll the income statement into the balance sheet and add year-end adjustments. Both of those reasons are not valid in OneStream.

You can have fiscal calendars that are different than the traditional calendar. For those calendars that start with months other than January, you simply change the labels. Period one then becomes March. This is also how to manage different fiscal calendars in OneStream. It is not complicated.

You will just need to do some thinking about the Time dimension when you do your mapping. First, pull periodic data from your source, then know that period one is March in your source cube, and period one is January in your destination.

Time Dimensions: Questions and Considerations

• Will data need to be entered, reported, or analyzed by week?

• What is the fiscal calendar (fiscal year-end)?

• How many years of data will be loaded and maintained?

• Is data loaded in a YTD or monthly (periodic) format?

  o Financial reporting apps with general ledger sources are typically YTD.

  o Budget and Forecast are typically periodic.

  o Other apps could typically have monthly data loaded (e.g., salary, CapEx).

• How often is data loaded?

• What are the necessary reporting frequencies – MTD, QTD, and YTD?

- Are there any calculations or views of data that would require spanning across years? (e.g., rolling forecast).

  o Define them and how they are used.

  o Do these spanning views affect only a few accounts or many accounts?

One last thing to mention is that throughout this book, the authors may use the terms "periodic" and "MTD" interchangeably. In most applications where the Time dimension is monthly, this is true. However, if your application was set up using a weekly Time dimension, these terms differ in only the scenarios that use weekly time. Periodic would be defined as weekly data. MTD means you're viewing the weeks of data that have been loaded to date. For example, if you're in the third week of the month, the periodic view would give you only data for week 3, whereas the MTD view would give you the data for weeks 1 through 3.

Scenario Dimension

Scenarios require thinking about the process, use of data, and workflow. Typically, you will start with Actuals, but you can truly start with any scenario of data. Since you need Actuals for Forecast... that will drive the decision. I will honestly say, however, that I have seen projects start just about everywhere, and they are successful.

Consider breaking out scenarios for versioning, and full years of data.

Scenario Dimension Considerations

- Create Scenarios dimension groups in your application to separate each plan cycle with their own review cycles.

- Scenarios can be grouped by Scenario Type – this allows for the following:

  o Different dimensions (except scenario and entity)

  o Varied workflows

  o Grouping of rules using Scenario Types

- Assigning access might determine additional views to control user access (e.g., Actual is read-only).

- Different exchange rate tables can be applied to respective scenarios; do you need multiple scenarios, or will one do?

- The time range property allows you to:

  o Determine start and end year, start and end period of the workflow

  o Determine valid periods for data entry

  o Periods outside the range are read-only

    ▪ Define specific variances needed.

  o Which members and type of variance ($, %)

  o Will expense reporting be used; some clients don't always want it

A period is missing data when a subsequent period has data, but a prior period has none. During processing, missing data is always considered zero. Zero View for Adj and Zero View for Nonadj determines if zeros appear as a periodic or YTD value. This ensures that derived data, based on zero values, remains the same in both data views in grids and reporting details. This only applies to account types of income, expense, and flow.

If the View is	And Zero View is	Then the Value is
YTD	YTD	Each period following the last period that contains data is zero.
YTD	Periodic	Each period is the YTD value, even if it contains data.
Periodic	YTD	The first period that does not contain data is a number that cancels all previous periods' values. The value for all periods following that period is zero.
Periodic	Periodic	Each period that does not contain data is zero.

Figure 3.9

This sometimes causes confusion for future months when zero is loaded. Let us say you load 100 in January and 200 YTD for February. The rates are probably going to be different for each month – so just assume it is .9 for January, and .95 for February, and 1 in March. If you load nothing for the month of March, local currency YTD will be zero. But there will be an amount periodic. It will be the reverse of the prior month's YTD value. This can be more confusing when you consider it because – if the rate changed – there is a residual foreign exchange amount for each account. But I assure you, the software is correct. Go ahead and do the math!

Entity Dimension

Entities are special dimension members, especially in OneStream. They are not only important from a reporting structure, they are the basis of intercompany members, the drivers for foreign currency translations, and drive the workflow design. Entity will also have an impact on ownership and security. Special care should go into reviewing this dimension.

Overview

You can consider legal entity for Actuals. You could also look to create an entity for each location or responsibility center that submits a plan for approval. The entity, in effect, does not have to be the same for scenario, but then you will need to consider how to move data between scenarios.

Each entity has a base currency; if no base currency is defined, use the application currency.

Entity/Organization Dimension Considerations

- Will multiple organizational structures exist (legal, management, regional)?

- Typically, legal entity should be the base member in this dimension – this is the member that should be flagged for intercompany. Intercompany partners that are parent entities will cause issues in the event of a reorganization.

- Are department and/or cost center details specific to one entity (entity dim roll-up), or is detail common to all entities (separate User Defined dimension)?

Entity/Org Dimension Considerations

Typically, flag only base entities as IC partners; this will simplify reorganizations and restructuring of the entity hierarchy.

- The Entity dimension does not 'extend' like others – please refer to the OneStream Design and Reference Guide.

- For each business unit that is going to have different Entity dimensionality, they need their own Entity dimension type, which gets assigned to its own cube.

- Using relationships, insert entities from other Entity dimensions into your main Entity dimension to tie all the dimensions and cubes together.

- Relationships are used for creating multiple hierarchies.

- Parent entities always store data.

- Entity constraints & defaults
    o Entity defaults can be used to 'tag' an entity similar to an attribute.
        ▪ Best practice is to choose dimensions with few members, for performance reasons.
    o Constraints lock in selections for the User Defined dimensions to only those selected values as valid values for input and calculations.

Account Dimension

Overview

The Account dimension will require a bit more effort. You need to consider the different accounts by group, and level of detail, and when they will be used.

- Use accounts to specify the information that you want to gather from a source's systems and planners.

- Account types define the time balance and variance reporting properties.

There are applications that do not make use of account type functionality. I would only use this option when the legacy system uses that convention. Otherwise, you will find issues. The preferred approach is the 'positive as normal' design, utilizing account types. The goal is to build an application that supports reporting presentations consistent with public filings. Public filings should present financial statements as positive amounts across the income statement and balance sheet, standardizing data collection. There are exceptions to this rule by line item, such as when presenting 'non-operating income' balances.

The data is loaded and presented as (+); however, the account attribute manages the debit/credit nature of the data to correctly aggregate amounts through the hierarchy. Additionally, revenue and expense accounts are 'flow type', which then allows frequency views such as YTD and periodic.

	Debit	Credit
Revenue		X
Expense	X	
Asset	X	
Liability		X

Figure 3.10

The impact of not using the account types correctly causes issues with Cube Views and reports. **Sign flipping** is required for external reporting, which is not normally necessary. The journal module becomes difficult to read and then requires custom intercompany reports. Data entry may need to be explained since people will need to know debit vs. credit and positive vs. negative sign flips, depending on the setup. All these workarounds may be acceptable if already done in a legacy system, but it could cause a lot of unnecessary confusion.

Typical Structures

I would review the structure the client presents. Some typical structures and related questions include:

- Profit and loss (P&L)
    - Non-financial reporting apps might have a subset of the entire P&L (e.g., gross margin).
    - Expense reporting settings, as necessary.
    - What sign (+ or -) should be used for contra accounts.
        - Balance Sheet
    - Expense reporting settings as necessary, usually up to the client – typically liability and equity Accounts.
    - Out of balance account to balance the balance sheet.
    - Currency translation adjustment (CTA) account to derive the effect of differences in currency rates.
    - Retained earnings ending balance flow.
- Cash Flow
    - Are changes in balance sheet calculated based on prior month, prior year-end, and/or prior quarter-end?
    - Need client's definition of cash flow formulas
- Statistics, metrics, analysis
    - Need client's definition of statistic formulas.
    - Do not store percent or ratios. Store the numerator and denominator instead. The percent or ratio should be a dynamic account type and rule.
    - Have 'input only' measures for percentages or ratios that are input.
- Unit, rate, and dollar calculations
    - Usually involve 'activity driver' relationships within the accounts dim.

Account Dimension Questions and Considerations

With a financial reporting application, I would also consider the level of account detail necessary.

Do you have the correct level of detail? If an application includes Actual and Budget data, the Budget data typically exists at a higher level of detail than Actual for some accounts, and maybe more detail for others. Analyze the combinations of accounts and User Defined dimensions to get the right mix.

I would ask if adjustments to the data are made in the application, and will these adjustments need to exist separately from the data loaded. Take our example, from before, of a period thirteen; maybe you should consider a User Defined member for capturing these adjustments.

For intercompany accounts, group them by eliminating members and create a plug (suspense) account for each combination.

Flow

Overview

Every application should have a Flow dimension. A basic Flow dimension will not only provide a basis for cash flow, it will give a currency translation proof by providing a calculated foreign exchange amount for every line item on the balance sheet. The standard and complex Flow dimensions are in the Solution Exchange, and are a good place to start. It is expected you will customize this dimension.

If there is any dimension where people struggle to understand functionality, it is the flow. So, while I have avoided spending too much time explaining anything that is already discussed in the administrator guide, I am going to explain a little more of what the features and financial intelligence for flow do.

Switch Sign

Depending on the account type, this property would be set to `True` to switch the sign of data for the Flow member, or set to `False` to keep the sign as is. Let us say users enter data as a positive, and expect the number to decrease the total, like a contra account. This setting manages this, which is easier to do than manually updating every form and Excel sheet.

Switch Type

This option switches the type of data based on the account attribute; for example, setting an asset to an expense. This is useful when treating rollforward accounts as income statement accounts in the balance sheet.

Flow Processing

These settings are used for dollar override values. They are used less frequently, as this override will only work in the base entity the data is loaded. However, it is a nice feature for smaller applications and will reduce the number of rules written. To be used, an account must be flagged as `True` by using the setting `UseAltInputCurrencyInFlow`. (Except for `IsAlternateInputCurrencyforAllAcounts`.) The Flow dimension can hold both values of a dollar override, and the settings differ based on how this setting is used.

Flow Processing Type

Is Alternate Input Currency

This indicates a dollar override. You would set this for the override member.

Is Alternate Input Currency for All Accounts

This indicates that all accounts will be able to use this alternate currency. You would use this if you had an alternate currency for all accounts. Unlike other systems, OneStream will allow you to enter multiple currencies for a single entity.

Translate using Alternate Input Currency, Input Local

This will override the translated value with the amount inputted at the local currency level.

Translate using Alternate Input Currency, Derive Local

This will override the translated value and change the local currency value to be derived, based on what the local currency rate would be. This setting probably should not be used in a trial balance unless accounting for the out of balance condition that might result.

Alternate Input Currency

This setting contains a list of all available currencies to put in for the source value override. If this Flow member has a USD override, then it should be set to USD. If the override is a EUR override, then it should be set to EUR. Typically, this is the default currency of the application, but can also be used in instances of functional currency.

Source Member for Alternate Input Currency

Define the actual Flow member to override the value for the current Flow member.

Flow Dimension Considerations

- Will you be loading ending balances or activity for the balance sheet?

- Where will you load data for the P&L?

- Will you be using the default override functionality of OneStream?

Other User Defined Dimension Considerations

The User Defined dimensions are very flexible.

Overview

- Determine what other views of data are needed for the accounts and entities.

- Use constraints to limit intersections that are not in use.

User Defined Considerations

- Define specific detail level and each generation group/roll-up.

- Alternate hierarchies will require maintenance and data validation.

Dynamic Components

Finally, consider the impact of any dynamic components. There is a performance impact to every option added to the design. Only add what you need. Dynamic components, while they're immensely powerful, could cause any larger application to struggle.

Conclusion

It is not a coincidence that I have said – multiple times in this chapter – that the design is the most important part of the project. It is critical, but it is not impossible if you follow some simple guidelines. Understand Data Unit and performance considerations. Data Units that are not too small, and not too big, perform best. Know the ways that OneStream is extensible, and leverage that to create an application that performs well.

To conduct the design meeting, start with all the requirements and review the reports you intend to develop. Then do the following:

- Gather all dimension types.

- Review the detail of each dimension to ensure it meets the reporting needs.

- Group the dimensions to identify cubes.

- Consider future solutions and ensure your design considers other dimensions needed.

- Create the foundation of workflow. Begin refining the workflow for each cube within the parameters of the requirements.

- Identify and plan all data flows into OneStream and between solutions within OneStream.

- Create a rules inventory – identify all rules to be built.

- Create a report inventory – identify all reports to be built.

- Plan for training end-users.

- Gather the dimensions, define the data model(s) depending on any differing data sets and present a design that encompasses cubes and or blend options.

- Ask the client to review and sign off on the design.

- Then, if time and budget allow, build a prototype.

If you do these steps, you have significantly reduced the risk of a bad design.

Epilogue

I had been with OneStream for three months, sitting with Tom Shea, Bob Powers, and Craig Colby, and a prospect from Sweden, Hein Scholten (great guy, by the way).

At that meeting, Hein told us, "This is all nice what you promise, but I need to know you can deliver." So, we agreed to a large proof of concept.

The next thing I know, we were taking on our biggest competitor's most complex project in Europe.

Looking back, it was very audacious of us. I was commuting from Boston to Copenhagen. We had some of the first designs for a project of this size. We met in a castle in Denmark, and in Times Square, New York.

The first picture is from our design meeting at Kokkedal Slot, Hørsholm, Denmark. The second is Tom presenting before that meeting in 2013.

4

Consolidation

Originally written by Eric Osmanski, updated by Nick Bolinger

In today's economic environment, organizations are faced with more pressure during the financial close process than ever before. The pressures to lead decision-making processes require the financial close to be fast and agile, and for organizations to have confidence in the financial statements.

Yet, it is amazing how many organizations are leading their business with manual spreadsheets and legacy applications. Closing the books with these tools comes with countless inefficiencies we hear every day – manual and redundant efforts, lack of consistency, inflexibility, and little confidence in reported numbers, among others. Either teams are stuck in the process of 'making it work' or there is one person who has built a convoluted series of workbooks that no one else understands or uses. In these situations, most of the financial close is spent generating the financial statements rather than analyzing the financial statements.

In this chapter, we will discuss some key consolidation concepts and dive deeper into the complex challenges that organizations face, and how we provide solutions for them in OneStream.

Key Consolidation Concepts

Before going into detail on particular consolidation topics, it is important to outline some key consolidation concepts. These concepts lay the groundwork for the implementation and will help you determine the best methods for application design.

The consolidation concepts outlined in this section are not meant to be a comprehensive or complete guide to the accounting guidelines, but rather an overview. Accounting standards evolve over time, and the appropriate standards should always be reviewed in detail.

Consolidation Methods

Consolidation methods are used in order to properly calculate the values that are consolidated from an entity to its parent. These are the values written to the share and elimination members within OneStream's Consolidation dimension.

Share is the proportionate value that is being consolidated into its parent, and the **elimination member** is the amount being removed while being consolidated into its parent. The consolidation method that is used is determined by whether the parent entity has control of the subsidiary. When a parent entity has control – regardless of ownership percent – it must consolidate the subsidiary; if not, other non-consolidating methods are used.

Consolidating

The consolidation of entities has differences based on the accounting guidelines.

Under U.S. GAAP as of 2024, there are two consolidation models – the **variable interest entity model** (VIE) and the **voting interest model**.

The VIE model is applied first and was designed to accommodate situations in which control is demonstrated in ways other than through voting interests. Under the VIE model, an entity is consolidated when the parent entity has significant power over the activities of the VIE and has significant economic exposure to the gains or losses of the VIE. Consolidation under the VIE model also has different measurement, presentation, and disclosure requirements that need to be considered. If the conditions to consolidate under the VIE model do not apply, or if it is an exception to the VIE model, then the voting interest model would then be applied.

Under the voting interest model, full consolidation is used when a parent entity has a controlling financial interest, and the percentage ownership of the subsidiary is greater than or equal to 50%. Under this method, the financial statements of the subsidiary are consolidated into the parent.

Whether a parent entity is required to present consolidated financial statements under IFRS is based on its control of the investee. Control is defined as when a parent entity has power over the investee, has rights to returns due to its involvement, and can influence its returns from the investee based on its power. When all three control elements are present, the financial statements of the subsidiary are consolidated into the parent.

The parent company records the amount owned as an investment in the subsidiary, and the subsidiary records the same amount in equity. All intracompany transactions – including the investment and equity – are eliminated during consolidation so that the values are not overstated. If ownership is less than 100%, the parent company will record in equity, and on the income statement, the non-controlling interest in the subsidiary, which is equal to the subsidiary's equity at the percentage *not* owned by the parent.

Non-Consolidating

Under the voting interest model, the **equity method** is used when the percentage ownership of the investee is between 20 and 50%, and the investor has significant influence. The balances of the investee are not consolidated under the equity method. Instead, the investor records an investment on the balance sheet equal to its ownership share of the investee's equity balance. For each period, the investor increases (or decreases) its investment by its ownership share of the investee's net income (loss), known as **equity pickup**. The ownership share of net income (loss) is also recorded on the investor's income statement separately.

Under the voting interest model, the **cost method** is used when the percentage ownership of the investee is less than 20%, and the investor has little or no influence. Under this method, the investee's trial balance is not consolidated, and the investor records an investment at **cost** instead. No equity pickup occurs, like in the equity method, and the only entries made are when dividends are received.

Investment entities are an exemption under IFRS and do not consolidate their subsidiaries when they meet the investment services, business purpose, and fair value management conditions. Under this exemption, the investee's financial statements are not consolidated, and the investment entity measures their investment in the investee at fair value through profit and loss.

Translation Methods

Companies that consolidate foreign entities' results must translate their functional currency financial statements into the reporting currency, according to the guidance set forth in accounting standards. Companies require consolidated financial statement results in various currencies due to external reporting, statutory reporting, management reporting, or other analysis requirements. When this is attempted using Excel spreadsheets, or a legacy application, the task of collecting, translating, and consolidating all of the entities in the organization is time-consuming, costly and, in many cases, inaccurate! OneStream has the ability to streamline this process through its consolidation engine, which allows for automatic translation into any currency.

Translation of the financial statements from functional to reporting currency is accomplished by using various exchange rates to convert each financial statement line item, in accordance with the following:

- Revenues and expenses translated at the average rate for the period.

- Assets and liabilities translated at the closing rate at the end of the reporting period (balance sheet date).

- Equity, except for retained earnings, translated at the historical exchange rate at the time of the transaction.
- Retained earnings translated at a weighted average rate for the year.

The above are generally the ways that balances are translated under U.S. GAAP and IFRS, but other translation methods may be appropriate in cases such as, but not limited to, remeasurement, hyperinflationary, or temporal.

Periodic Method

Income and expense financial statement line items are translated at the average rate for the period using the periodic method. The periodic method takes the functional currency period movement and multiplies that by the period's average rate. The translated value is then added to the prior period's translated YTD value to calculate the YTD translated value.

Direct Method

Asset and liability financial statement line items are translated at the closing rate, at the end of the reporting period, using the direct method. The direct method takes the functional currency YTD balance at the end of the reporting period and multiplies that by the closing rate.

Cube

When beginning to design and build your OneStream application, the cube plays a fundamental role – it determines how the data will be translated and consolidated according to the consolidation algorithm type and FX rates settings. The algorithm types are closely related to the various methods previously discussed, so an understanding of each type and how they interact with the application is imperative.

Consolidation Algorithm Types

When a consolidation is executed in OneStream, data is moved up the Entity and Consolidation dimensions (see Figure 4.1). The consolidation algorithm type on the cube specifies how the share and elimination members will be treated, and each is explained below.

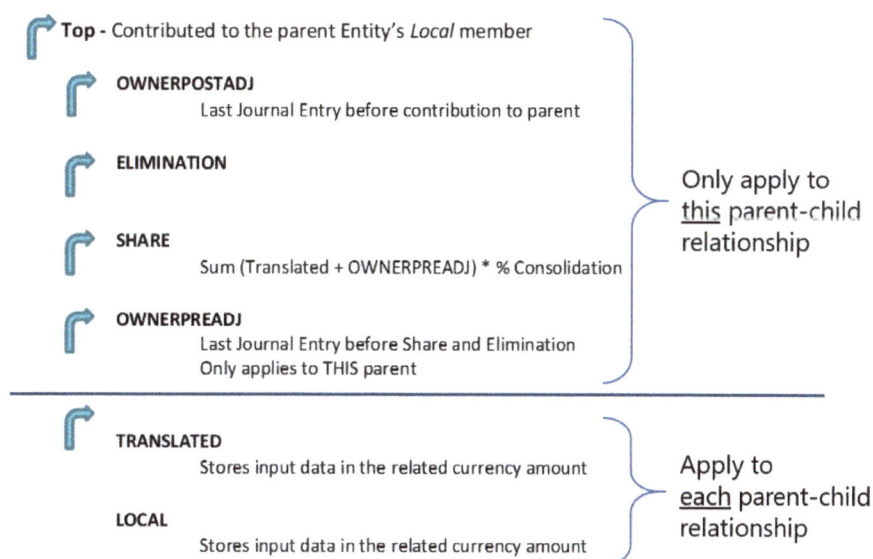

Figure 4.1

Standard

Standard (calc-on-the-fly share and hierarchy elimination) is the most commonly used consolidation algorithm type. This cube setting calculates an entity's share amount dynamically (the value does not get stored in the OneStream database). Share is a Consolidation dimension member defined for a specific parent/child relationship and is calculated as an entity's *translated balances + owner pre-adj journals * percent consolidation*. Eliminations under standard are calculated using OneStream's built-in algorithms.

Stored Share

The stored share consolidation algorithm type stores the amounts for share rather than calculating them dynamically as in standard. However, the eliminations under stored share are still calculated as in standard, using OneStream's built-in algorithms.

This consolidation algorithm type may be used when you have the need for different logic in calculating share than is performed in standard (defined above). An example of this would be if you had a minority interest calculation, where the share contribution cannot be driven from the percent consolidation.

When the stored share consolidation algorithm type is used, the rules to calculate the value need to be written under the finance function type Calculate (or CustomCalculate).

```
Case Is = FinanceFunctionType.Calculate
            Select Case api.FunctionType
                Case Is = FinanceFunctionType.Calculate

                    If api.Pov.Cons.Name.XFEqualsIgnoreCase("Share") Then
                        CalcMinInt(si, api, args)
                    End If

            End Select

            Return Nothing
        Catch ex As Exception
            Throw ErrorHandler.LogWrite(si, New XFException(si, ex))
        End Try
    End Function

#Region "Share Rules"
        Private Sub CalcMinInt(ByVal si As SessionInfo, ByVal api As FinanceRulesApi, ByVal args As FinanceRulesArgs)
            Try
                'Constants used in calcs
                Const All_None = ":F#EndBal:I#None:U1#Loc_000:U2#None:U3#Input:U4#Input:U5#None"
                Const All_Top = ":F#Top:I#Top:U1#Loc_ALL:U2#AllDepts:U3#USGAAP_PreEquity:U4#wAlloc:U5#None"

                Dim entity As String = api.Pov.Entity.Name
                Dim entityId As Integer = api.Pov.Entity.MemberId

                'Grabs the current calculated entity's ownership % and type
                Dim pOwn As Decimal = api.Entity.PercentOwnership(entityId)
                Dim ownType As Integer = api.Entity.OwnershipType(entityId)

                'Performs the calculation based on the ownership type of the entity
                Select Case ownType      'Ownership Type:
                    Case Is = 1000       'Full Consolidation
                        api.ExecuteDefaultShare()
                    Case Is = 2000       'Holding
                        api.ExecuteDefaultShare()
                    Case Is = 4000       'Equity
                        api.ExecuteDefaultShare()
                    Case Is = 7000       'Non-controlling Interest
                        api.Data.Calculate("A#808000:O#Elimination:C#Share:V#Periodic" & All_None & " = " & _
                        "A#NETINC:O#BeforeElim:C#Local:V#Periodic" & All_Top & " * ((100 - " & pOwn & ") * .01)")

                        api.Data.Calculate("A#310000:O#Elimination:C#Share:V#YTD" & All_None & " = " & _
                        "A#310000:O#Elimination:C#Share:V#YTD:T#POVPriorYearM12" & All_None & " " & _
                        "+ A#808000:O#Elimination:C#Share:V#YTD" & All_None & "")

                        api.Data.Calculate("A#CYNI:O#Elimination:C#Share:V#YTD" & All_None & " = " & _
                        "- A#310000:O#Elimination:C#Share:V#YTD" & All_None)

                    Case Else
                        api.ExecuteDefaultShare()
                End Select
            Catch ex As Exception
                Throw ErrorHandler.LogWrite(si, New XFException(si, ex))
            End Try
        End Sub
```

Org-By-Period Elimination

The org-by-period elimination consolidation algorithm type uses the calc-on-the-fly share – as in standard – but has unique elimination considerations. When determining if the data cell's IC member is a descendant of the entity being consolidated, this consolidation algorithm type considers the position of the entity in the hierarchy and also checks the percent consolidation for every relationship down the hierarchy. If percent consolidation is zero for the particular relationship, the IC member is determined *not* to be a descendant of the entity.

In comparison, the standard elimination (hierarchy elimination) only considers the position of the member in the Entity dimension hierarchy. Standard elimination is the default approach and does not consider percent consolidation.

Stored Share and Org-By-Period Elimination

The stored share and org-by-period elimination consolidation algorithm type is a combination of the two settings which have been explained above.

Custom

The custom consolidation algorithm type allows for the ability to calculate share and elimination data intersections using logic within a business rule. This is often used when you have custom eliminations that are different from OneStream's built-in algorithm and org-by-period elimination logic. This could be due to having custom eliminations within a User Defined dimension or wanting to write eliminations to unique and specific data intersections.

```vb
Case Is = FinanceFunctionType.ConsolidateShare
Case Is = FinanceFunctionType.ConsolidateElimination

Private Sub CalcElim(ByVal si As SessionInfo, ByVal api As FinanceRulesApi, ByVal args As FinanceRulesArgs)
    Try
        'Determine accounts to process
        Dim entDimID As Integer = api.Pov.Entity.DimTypeID
        Dim entityPK As DimPk = api.Pov.EntityDim.DimPk
        Dim parentID As Integer = api.Pov.Parent.MemberID
        Dim icDimID As Integer = api.Pov.IC.DimTypeId
        Dim ud5CalcElim As Integer = api.Members.GetMemberId(dimtype.UD5.Id,"CalcElim")

        'Read the source data from the Translated and OwnerPreAdj consolidation members
        Dim destinationInfo As ExpressionDestinationInfo = api.Data.GetExpressionDestinationInfo("")
        Dim sourceDataBuffer As DataBuffer = api.Data.GetDataBufferForCustomElimCalculation(False,True,True)

        'Eliminate the intercompany data using Data Source member 'CalcElim'
        If Not sourceDataBuffer Is Nothing Then
            Dim resultDataBuffer As DataBuffer = New DataBuffer()
            For Each cell As DataBufferCell In sourceDataBuffer.DataBufferCells.Values
                Dim icMemberID As Integer = cell.DataBufferCellPk.ICId
                Dim icName As String = api.Members.GetMemberName(icDimID,icMemberID)
                Dim entICID As Integer = api.Members.GetMemberId(entDimID,icName)

                Dim isDescendant As Boolean = api.Members.IsDescendant(entityPK,parentID,entICID,Nothing)
                If isDescendant Then
                    If (Not cell.CellStatus.IsNoData) Then
                        'Change the data source member to CalcElim
                        Dim elimCell As New DataBufferCell(cell)
                        elimCell.CellAmount = elimCell.CellAmount * -1
                        elimCell.DataBufferCellPk.UD5Id = ud5CalcElim
                        resultDataBuffer.SetCell(api.DBConnApp.SI,elimCell,True)
                    End If
                End If
            Next

            'Store the results for the Share Consolidation member that is currently being executed
            api.Data.SetDataBuffer(resultDataBuffer,destinationInfo)
        End If
    Catch ex As Exception
        Throw ErrorHandler.LogWrite(si, New XFException(si, ex))
    End Try
End Sub
```

Performance Considerations

When determining what consolidation algorithm type settings are needed for the application, it is also important to be aware of performance implications. Under the standard consolidation algorithm type, OneStream does not store share because it is dynamically calculated on the fly. When turning on any of the above consolidation algorithm types which store share, there will be performance implications in doing so.

When storing share, the consolidation engine has to perform the custom logic written in the business rule and write the records to the database; the size of each Data Unit will become larger as a result of the additional records.

Elimination records are stored in the database under all consolidation algorithm types. When turning on custom eliminations, performance implications will depend largely upon the rule design. Additional records may be written to the database and the engine may spend more time within the custom elimination logic than it would with OneStream's built-in algorithms.

Translation Algorithm Types

Standard

Standard is the most commonly used translation algorithm type. This cube setting takes an entity's local currency values and translates them based on the FX rate types (average, closing, etc.) and FX rule types (periodic, direct) assigned to the scenario.

Standard Using Business Rules for FX Rates

Standard using business rules for FX rates is similar to standard but allows the ability to use a business rule to specify translation rates for any given intersection. Any intersections not specified in the business rule will translate based on the standard translation logic. This is commonly used during the translation of Forecast, Constant Currency, and other such scenarios.

It is also commonly used when the rate needed for translation already exists in the FX rate table but in another rate type/time, or the rate needs to be determined dynamically. For example, consider needing to translate the Actual scenario at the current year's Budget rates. In this case, all of the Actual data needs to be translated based on rates which already exist in the FX rate table. By using a business rule, we can dynamically determine what the year we need to translate is based on, without having to copy rates that have already been entered to another rate type. This reduces administrator maintenance by eliminating the need to copy or enter duplicate rates within the system.

```
Select Case api.FunctionType

    Case Is = FinanceFunctionType.FxRate

    Dim scenarioType As String = api.Scenario.GetScenarioType(api.Pov.Scenario.MemberId).Name
    Dim strAccountType As String = api.Account.GetAccountType(api.Pov.Account.memberid).Name 'Account Type
    Dim strRateType As String
    Dim numNoInputPeriods As Integer = api.Scenario.GetWorkflowNumNoInputTimePeriods(api.Pov.Scenario.MemberId)
    Dim curMonth As Integer = api.Time.GetPeriodNumFromId(api.Pov.Time.MemberId) 'Current month being processed
    Dim curYear As Integer = api.Time.GetYearFromId(api.Pov.Time.MemberId) 'Current year being processed

    'Run of Actual at Budget Rate Scenarios
    If scenarioType.XFEqualsIgnoreCase("Actual") And api.Pov.Scenario.Name.XFContainsIgnoreCase("BudgetRate") Then

        If strAccountType = "Revenue" Or strAccountType = "Expense" Then

            'ActualAt2021BudgetRate
            Dim year As String = Mid(api.Pov.Scenario.Name, 9, 4)
            Dim timeName As String = year & "M" & curMonth
            Dim timeID As Integer = api.Time.GetIdFromName(timeName)     'Time period ID of the Budget Rate year

            strRateType = "BudgetRate"
            Dim rate As Decimal = api.FxRates.GetCalculatedFxRate(strRateType, timeID, args.FxRateArgs.SourceCurrencyId, args.FxRateArgs.DestCurrencyId)
            Return New FxRateResult(False, rate, FXRuleType.Periodic)

        End If

    End If  'If scenarioType.XFEqualsIgnoreCase("Actual") And api.Pov.Scenario.Name.XFContainsIgnoreCase("BudgetRate") Then
```

Custom

Custom translation logic is rarely used but allows for the ability to calculate the translated values for all intersections within a business rule. The system is flexible to modify to custom unique methods that are not common, nor out-of-the-box.

FX Rates

Setting the cube default currency and translation method (rule type) used for revenue, expense, asset, and liability account types is done on the Cube Properties (see Figure 4.2).

FX Rates	
Default Currency	USD
Rate Type For Revenues And Expenses	AverageRate
Rule Type For Revenues And Expenses	Periodic
Rate Type For Assets And Liabilities	ClosingRate
Rule Type For Assets And Liabilities	Direct

Figure 4.2

These settings apply to all scenarios within the cube, unless the cube settings are overridden on the Scenario properties by marking Use Cube FX Settings to False and modifying the rate and/or rule type (see Figure 4.3).

FX Rates	
Use Cube FX Settings	False
Rate Type For Revenues And Expenses	AverageRate_Budget
Rule Type For Revenues And Expenses	Periodic
Rate Type For Assets And Liabilities	ClosingRate_Budget
Rule Type For Assets And Liabilities	Direct
Constant Year For FX Rates	(Not Used)

Figure 4.3

OneStream uses the FX rates entered in order to translate an entity into the currency of its immediate parent. This means that if a GBP entity has an immediate parent of USD, OneStream will translate the GBP entity to USD during translation and consolidation. If the currency of the immediate parent is the same, then OneStream will not translate the results of the entity. If an entity requires translation to a currency other than its immediate parent, that translation currency could be set on the entity using the Auto Translation Currencies setting or an alternate hierarchy developed (refer to the parent currencies section for a breakdown of the pros and cons related to each of these approaches).

During translation, if the rate is not specifically entered in the FX rate table, OneStream will use the process of triangulation in order to determine the rate based on the Default Currency of the application. What that means is, if the default currency of the application is USD and the GBP/USD and EUR/USD rates are entered, OneStream will derive the GBP/EUR or EUR/GBP rate based on the other rates entered (see Figure 4.4). Triangulation will only occur if the rates provided include the default currency. For example, if the default currency is USD and the rates entered are for GBP/JPY and EUR/JPY, OneStream will not derive the GBP/EUR or EUR/GBP rate.

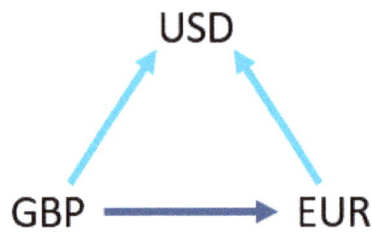

Figure 4.4

Entity

Many of the accounting complexities that occur within the Entity dimension are due to the translation and consolidation of data up the entity hierarchy. As such, the Entity dimension is a key dimension that requires scrutiny in the design phase of any implementation. Several design considerations and entity properties are available to use to help facilitate and streamline the consolidation.

Relationship Settings

Relationship settings on the Entity members which can vary by Scenario Type and time (see Figure 4.5) are used to help consolidation based on various consolidation methods; each is explained in more detail below.

Figure 4.5

Percent Consolidation

Percent consolidation is used to define the percentage of the entity which is consolidated into its immediate parent. This setting, by default, will take all account balances and multiply them by the percentage entered to determine the contribution to its immediate parent during consolidation.

It can also be referenced in business rules – for example, if custom logic needs to occur based on whether the entity's percent consolidation is greater or less than a certain value.

```
Dim dValue As Decimal = api.Entity.PercentConsolidation(entityId,
parentId, varyByScenarioTypeId, varyByTimeId)
```

Percent Ownership

Percent ownership is a setting that has no effect on consolidation by itself. This setting can be used to enter ownership percentages, which can then be referenced in business rules developed to perform various consolidation methods. For example, the percent ownership is often referenced in calculating minority interest on the consolidation member share (refer to the stored share section).

```
Dim dValue As Decimal = api.Entity.PercentOwnership(entityId,
parentId, varyByScenarioTypeId, varyByTimeId)
```

Ownership Type

Ownership type is a setting that has no effect on consolidation by itself. OneStream pre-populates this setting with four options (full consolidation, holding, equity, non-controlling interest), and five custom options (custom 1–5), which then can be referenced in business rules developed to perform various consolidation methods (refer to the stored share section).

```
Dim objOwnershipType As OwnershipType =
api.Entity.OwnershipType(entityId, parentId, varyByScenarioTypeId,
varyByTimeId)
```

Intercompany Eliminations

Intercompany elimination is the process by which balances held between entities under a common parent are removed during consolidation, with any discrepancies being held in a plug (balancing) account.

OneStream utilizes a combination of the entity, account, and IC members in order to eliminate intercompany balances. When two entities are consolidated into a common parent, OneStream creates a balanced entry for each intercompany account. The intercompany balance is reversed, and the offsetting value is booked into the designated plug account. When both entities have matching values, the debits and credits within the plug account will net to 0. If the balances between the two entities do not match, the plug account will hold the difference between their intercompany balances.

Figure 4.6 displays how the intercompany elimination process works in OneStream. As Houston Heights and South Houston get consolidated in the parent entity Houston, their balances with each other are eliminated and the offset amount is booked to the plug account. When the plug account is netted, there is a difference of 100 remaining at Houston.

		IC Receivables	IC Payables	IC Rec-Pay Plug
South Houston	⊟ Ending Balance	0.00	700.00	
	Elimination		-700.00	700.00
Houston Heights	⊟ Ending Balance	800.00	0.00	
	Elimination	-800.00		-800.00
Houston	⊟ Ending Balance	0.00	0.00	-100.00

Figure 4.6

Settings

In order for the intercompany eliminations to execute properly in OneStream, several settings need to be applied:

The **IsIC Entity** property on the entity must be set to True. This signifies that the entity can engage in intercompany activity and is then automatically added as a member in the IC dimension. If an entity is a member in the IC dimension, then it could be selected as a valid IC partner. This setting should be applied to the lowest level of intercompany activity available.

The **IsIC Account** property on the account must be set to Conditional or True. When the IC account is set to Conditional, an intercompany balance in this account can be with all IC partners except themselves. It can also be with the IC member none, which represents third-party balances and does not eliminate during consolidation. When this setting is True, the IC partner on intercompany balances can be the same as the entity.

Accounts requiring balances to be eliminated *must* have a plug account assigned. If the account does not have a plug account assigned, regardless of the IsIC account property, the balances in this account will not eliminate during consolidation.

Plug accounts are used to hold the offset value during the intercompany elimination process and should be reserved for that purpose only. They should not have data loaded to them, and the Allow Input setting should be marked False to prevent the entry of data to these accounts.

Plug accounts should have the setting IsIC Account marked as True so that the values held in this account are visible by intercompany partners; this helps with the reconciliation process.

Parent Currencies

Parent entities are typically set up so they all have the same currency – the reporting currency of the application. A common request from customers is to have the ability to see parent entities in multiple currencies through the consolidation. There are two primary approaches that can be implemented so that you can achieve this – **alternate hierarchies** or through the **auto translation currencies** setting on the entity.

Alternate Hierarchy

If an entity requires translation to a currency other than that of its immediate parent, a common approach is to create an alternate hierarchy, where each hierarchy has unique parent entity names and are assigned a different currency. For example, if the primary entity hierarchy has parent entity ABC in USD, but you also need to see that rollup in EUR, the approach would be to create a new structure with the parent name ABC_EUR (or anything unique) and assign it a currency of EUR. All of its descendants would be shared from the primary hierarchy.

This approach comes with its own set of pros and cons. The benefit of using this approach is its simplicity – only a new parent needs to be created, and everything which has been designed and implemented for the application should stay the same.

The disadvantages to this approach, however, are added maintenance and a potentially more confusing user experience. The administrator will have another hierarchy (or hierarchies) to maintain, users will have to make sure they are consolidating all hierarchies, and users will also have to make sure they select the appropriate entity (based on the currency they would like to view) in reporting.

Auto Translation Currencies

OneStream allows for the ability to specify multiple currencies for an entity to translate to, through its Auto Translation Currencies property on the entity (see Figure 4.7).

⊟ Vary By Scenario Type	
Equity Pickup	
Sibling Consolidation Pass	(Use Default)
Sibling Repeat Calculation Pass	(Use Default)
Auto Translation Currencies	GBP, USD

Figure 4.7

While an entity already translates into the currency of its immediate parent, this allows for translation into other currencies automatically when a translation occurs. Now, instead of maintaining multiple hierarchies with various different parent currencies, maintenance is moved to an entity property only when a new currency translation is needed or can be removed. Users do not have to change entities depending on the currency and, instead, can toggle based on OneStream's Consolidation dimension, which holds the application currencies.

With this approach, however, there are things to contemplate and certain design considerations that need to be made prior to any implementation.

Limitations

- Currencies in the Auto Translation Currency property are not the consolidated total of its children.

  - For example, if there are two base entities with an auto translation currency of CAD, and the parent has no auto translation currency, you cannot view the parent in CAD. The parent must also have an auto translation currency on it, and will translate on the fly, independently of the base entities.

  - This means that it also does not consider account overrides on the children entities. New overrides will have to be entered for the parent entity as well.

Things to Consider

- Rule modifications

  - Rules that run in translated currencies must be opened up to also run on parent entities.

  - Custom eliminations may be needed on balances not translated using the standard FX rates (e.g., historical overrides).

- Overrides

  - Users will need to input overrides into all of the currencies specified in the Auto Translation Currencies property for that entity.

  - Input on parent entities is limited to the Origin of `AdjInput`, so forms, rules, and account Adjustment Type settings will have to be configured appropriately.

- Performance

  - Consolidation times will be negatively impacted, and will depend largely on the rules, how many currencies, entities, etc.

Tips

- Only assign auto translation currencies to entities that are required to translate to an alternate currency (a currency other than its local currency and that of its immediate parent).

- If the parent entity is assigned the currency you want to translate to, the auto translation currency should not be applied.

  - e.g., I have a parent entity of AUD with a direct parent of USD; a USD auto translation currency should not be applied to the AUD entity.

- Parent entities required to be viewed in their local currency and other currencies should be assigned their local currency, when applicable.

  - e.g., I have two SGD base entities which roll up to a parent. The parent needs to be in SGD and USD. The parent should be assigned a local currency of SGD. This reduces the number of overrides required.

Using this approach does come with things to consider, primarily translation and consolidation rule modifications, but the approach has been used with many customers. When deciding which approach to use, choose a balance between maintenance, performance, and user experience; decide which approach gives the best mix for the customer.

Parent Adjustments

Parent adjustments are a common requirement across many companies – the ability to make a top side entry that is reflected in the parent entity but which is not booked to a specific base entity.

There are two common ways of handling such adjustments – through the use of OneStream's Origin dimension or through adjustment entities. Either approach can be successful, but the pros and cons relating to user experience and maintenance must be weighed up with the customer.

Origin

OneStream's Origin dimensions allow for the easy input and tracking of adjustments made to base and parent entities (see Figure 4.8). Journal/adjustment data is entered into the `AdjInput` Origin dimension and when it is translated or consolidated, the data moves into the `AdjConsolidated` member. This allows for the differentiation of adjustments when looking at a parent entity; all of the consolidated adjustments from child entities are in the `AdjConsolidated` member, and any adjustment being made directly to the parent entity can be inputted to `AdjInput`.

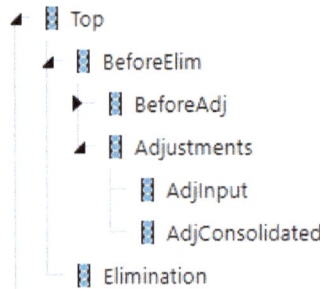

Figure 4.8

With this method of entering parent adjustments, there are pros and cons; it comes down to knowing the customer, and the user community that is going to be using the data.

On the one hand, this is a seamless way of inputting adjustments – there is no additional build that needs to occur in order to do so; indeed, the system was designed to be utilized in this manner.

On the other hand, some customers may find this to be a difficult way to find the data. When looking at any analysis which is not by Origin, it may appear as if the sum of the parts do not equal the total (see Figure 4.9).

	Jan 2022
US Clubs	10,000.00
Houston	11,000.00
Houston Heights	5,000.00
South Houston	6,000.00

	Jan 2022		
	AdjInput	AdjConsolidated	Top
US Clubs	-1,000.00	11,000.00	10,000.00
Houston		11,000.00	11,000.00
Houston Heights	5,000.00		5,000.00
South Houston	6,000.00		6,000.00

Figure 4.9

Adjustment Entities

Another common approach to making parent entity adjustments is the creation of adjustment entities (see Figure 4.10). Under this method, new entities are created as a child of the parent, typically with a suffix Adj and assigned the same currency as the parent. Any adjustments which would need to be booked at the parent entity are now booked into the new adjustment entity.

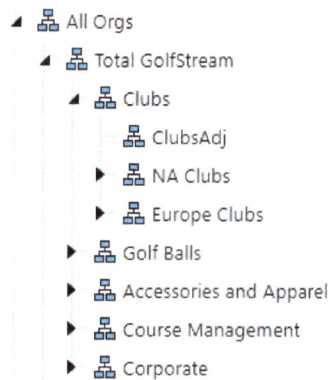

```
▲  🖧 All Orgs
    ▲  🖧 Total GolfStream
        ▲  🖧 Clubs
               🖧 ClubsAdj
            ▶  🖧 NA Clubs
            ▶  🖧 Europe Clubs
        ▶  🖧 Golf Balls
        ▶  🖧 Accessories and Apparel
        ▶  🖧 Course Management
        ▶  🖧 Corporate
```

Figure 4.10

This approach's benefits come from its visibility and simplicity – the purpose of these entities is clear, and it is easy for a user to find the data. A user can drill down on a parent entity, and the data is in its own entity, isolated from other entities. Also, the entirety of the Origin dimension becomes available, which means that a user can load data through the import member, enter data through the forms member, or load a journal to the AdjInput member within this entity.

However, many users may not prefer this approach because it adds additional build and maintenance. Any time a new parent is added to the application, a new adjustment entity potentially has to be added. Other users may dislike this approach because the entity is not a true entity in their structure.

Equity Pickup

Equity Pickup is the process of revaluing the investments of an investor to reflect the current value of its proportionate share of the investee's equity balance. OneStream allows for the automation of these entries – including layered ownership models – by entering ownership percentages, defining the calculation sequence, and developing a rule to generate the entries.

```
If (Not api.Entity.HasChildren) And (api.Cons.IsLocalCurrencyForEntity) Then 'Base Entities and Local Currency
    Dim destinationInfo As ExpressionDestinationInfo = api.Data.GetExpressionDestinationInfo("")
    'Get a data buffer of all ownership percentages
    Dim pShOwn As DataBuffer = api.Data.GetDataBufferUsingFormula("RemoveZeros" & _
    "(Cb#Golfstream:S#Actual:A#PShOwn:V#YTD:O#BeforeAdj:U1#None:U2#None:U3#None:U4#None:U5#None:U6#None:U7#None:U8#None)",,False)

    If pShOwn.DataBufferCells.Count > 0 Then
        Dim resultDataBuffer As DataBuffer = New DataBuffer()
        For Each cell As DataBufferCell In pShOwn.DataBufferCells.Values

            'in Golfstream:      account 17800 = investment account on balance sheet
                          '      account 65000 = income from subsidiary account on P&L
                          '      account 69000 = net income

            'Get the investees NI
            Dim investeeNI As Decimal = api.Data.GetDataCell("E#[" & cell.DataBufferCellPk.GetICName(api) & "]" & _
            ":A#69000:V#YTD:O#Top:I#Top:U1#Top:U2#Top:U3#Top:U4#Top:U5#DataSource:U6#None:U7#None:U8#None").CellAmount

            If investeeNI <> 0.00 Then   'If the investees NI is not 0
                Dim resultCell17800 As New DataBufferCell(cell)
                resultCell17800.DataBufferCellPk.AccountId = api.Members.GetMember(DimType.Account.Id, "17800").MemberId
                resultCell17800.DataBufferCellPk.OriginId = DimConstants.Import
                resultCell17800.DataBufferCellPk.FlowId = api.Members.GetMember(DimType.Flow.Id, "EndBal").MemberId
                resultCell17800.DataBufferCellPk.ICId = cell.DataBufferCellPk.ICId
                resultCell17800.DataBufferCellPk.UD5Id = api.Members.GetMember(DimType.UD5.Id, "CalcEPU").MemberId

                'Calculate the change in investment as the ownership % * the investee NI
                resultCell17800.CellAmount = cell.CellAmount * investeeNI
                resultDataBuffer.SetCell(si, resultCell17800, True)

                Dim resultCell65000 As New DataBufferCell(cell)
                resultCell65000.DataBufferCellPk.AccountId = api.Members.GetMember(DimType.Account.Id, "65000").MemberId
                resultCell65000.DataBufferCellPk.OriginId = DimConstants.Import
                resultCell65000.DataBufferCellPk.FlowId = api.Members.GetMember(DimType.Flow.Id, "None").MemberId
                resultCell65000.DataBufferCellPk.ICId = cell.DataBufferCellPk.ICId
                resultCell17800.DataBufferCellPk.ICId = cell.DataBufferCellPk.ICId
                resultCell17800.DataBufferCellPk.UD5Id = api.Members.GetMember(DimType.UD5.Id, "CalcEPU").MemberId

                'Calculate the investor NI as the ownership % * the investee NI
                resultCell65000.CellAmount = cell.CellAmount * investeeNI
                resultDataBuffer.SetCell(si, resultCell17800, True)
            End If
        Next

        api.Data.SetDataBuffer(resultDataBuffer,destinationInfo)

    End If
End If
```

Ownership Percentages

Ownership percentages must be entered for each investor and investee relationship. A form is created in OneStream where these percentages are entered for each relationship using the entity (investor) and intercompany partner (investee) (see Figure 4.11).

	Galleria	Downtown Houston	South Houston	Houston Heights
South Houston				
Galleria				
Houston Heights			100%	
Downtown Houston	100%			100%

Figure 4.11

A form is typically used to enter ownership percentages because the percentage consolidation / percentage ownership settings on Entity members do not permit designation of the investee. In the case where the holding company has multiple investments, or an investee is split owned, having the ability to designate the investee is required. In situations such as this, a new account is typically created to store the percent ownership, and the ownership percentages are entered through a form.

Calculation and Consolidation Passes

A layered ownership structure often exists for a company, as seen in the above screenshot – Houston Heights has investments in South Houston, and Downtown Houston has investments in Galleria and Houston Heights. In this case, Houston Heights needs to be calculated first in order to properly reflect its balances prior to calculating Downtown Houston.

Instead of leaving this up to the user to ensure entities are calculated in the correct sequence, OneStream provides the ability to specify what the sequence is for sibling entities using the Sibling Consolidation Pass setting (see Figure 4.12).

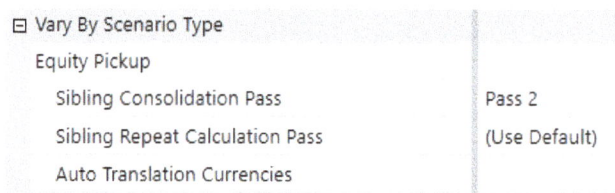

Figure 4.12

In this example, Houston Heights would be set to Pass 2 (Pass 1 is the default for all entities), and Downtown Houston would be set to Pass 3 to ensure that Downtown Houston is only calculated and consolidated after Houston Heights.

Org-By-Period

Reorganization of entity structures may occur for a number of reasons – mergers, acquisitions, disposals – and in some cases, they can be frequent within a company. When organizational structures change, having the ability for the current structure to coexist with past structures is critical. This allows a company to easily have consistent and reliable comparability while reducing the maintenance burden of multiple hierarchies.

When entities move parents during the year, an entity's balances must be reported based on the percentage contributed to each parent in that reporting period. For example, consider if an entity consolidated under Parent A 100% through March and then a reorganization occurred where the entity then consolidated under Parent B 100% from April forward (see Figures 4.13 and 4.14).

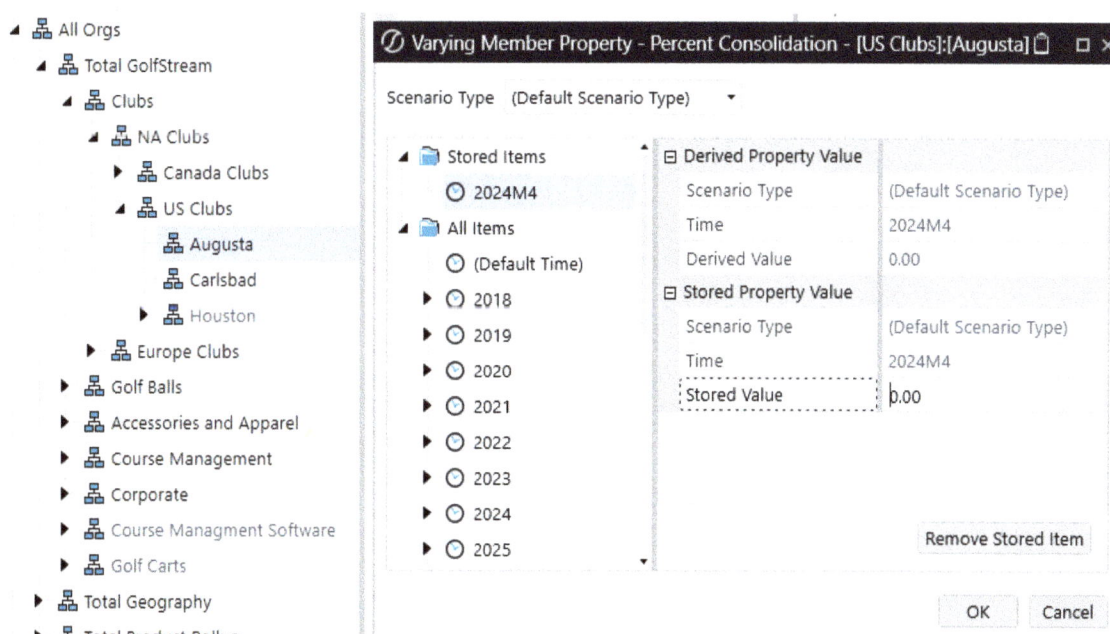

Figure 4.13

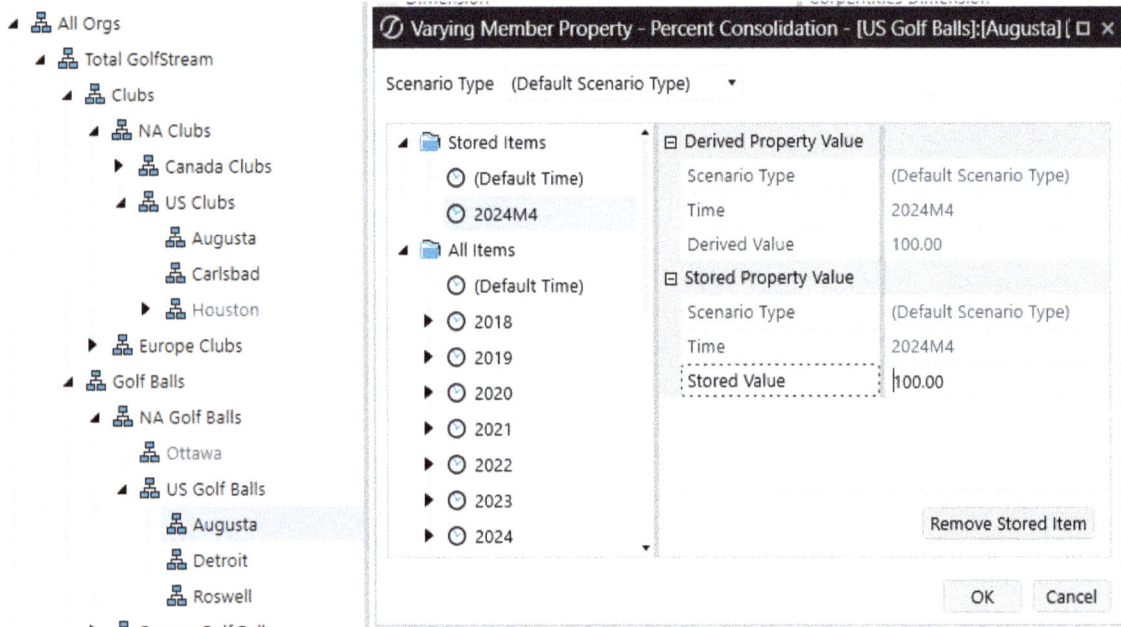

Figure 4.14

Beginning in April, only the entity's balances in the month of April can be consolidated to Parent B. Consolidating on a YTD basis would overcontribute the entity's balances to Parent B.

This is accomplished in OneStream with a few settings. The percent consolidation on the entity, which can vary by time period, must be set and the consolidation view of the scenario must be set to periodic. These settings tell OneStream what percentage of the entity consolidates into each parent and to consolidate on a monthly basis, instead of moving its YTD balances. Additionally, eliminations need to consider an entity's place in the hierarchy but also the percent consolidation for the relationship. OneStream has built-in logic to accommodate this and is explained further in the Org-By-Period Eliminations section above.

Considerations

When implementing periodic consolidation, it is important to understand how eliminations are calculated. All of the data in the data record tables is stored YTD, which includes the elimination member. If no data is loaded for an IC member, then the YTD will be stored as 0, and the periodic number will be derived as the reversal of the previous month's YTD balance (see Figure 4.15).

		Month 1		Month 2		Month 3		Month 4		Month 5	
		Periodic	YTD	Periodic	YTD	Periodic	YTD	Periodic	YTD	Periodic	YTD
Top	⊞ Top							185.00	185.00	0.00	185.00
Elimination	⊞ Top	-50.00	-50.00	-60.00	-110.00	-75.00	-185.00	185.00	0.00	0.00	0.00
Share	⊞ Top	50.00	50.00	60.00	110.00	75.00	185.00	0.00	185.00	0.00	185.00
Translated	⊞ Top	100.00	100.00	100.00	200.00	100.00	300.00	0.00	300.00	0.00	300.00
Local	⊟ Top	100.00	100.00	100.00	200.00	100.00	300.00	0.00	300.00	0.00	300.00
	With IC Partner	100.00	100.00	100.00	200.00	100.00	300.00	0.00	300.00	0.00	300.00

Figure 4.15

However, in the case of org-by-period, when an entity moves within the hierarchy (and thus the IC balance goes to 0), the elimination should still live on within the parent it occurred in. In order to accommodate this, formulas will need to be written to pull forward the elimination YTD when no data is loaded to an IC member.

Flow

The Flow dimension is a customizable OneStream dimension that is used to facilitate other complexities that come along with the financial consolidation – capturing historical FX rate overrides, calculating beginning balances, activity, and FX impacts, as well as cash flow rollforwards and the cash flow statement.

Each of these items plays an important role in financial consolidation; in this section, we dig deeper into some of the key design considerations of the Flow dimension.

Periodic vs. YTD Data Loads

When loading trial balance and other information into your application, there are two primary ways – **periodic** (monthly activity) or **YTD** balances. While YTD is more common, there are situations where the source ERP cannot extract YTD balances, and periodic balances must be loaded. Either data load can be accommodated in OneStream with certain setups.

An important consideration is that ERPs loading periodic data need checks to make sure prior period adjustments have been included, whereas YTD data loads would inherently include the prior period adjustments.

YTD

When loading YTD balances into OneStream, the flow setup (Figure 4.16) becomes straightforward. The YTD ending balance of each account is loaded directly to a base member within the ending balance hierarchy (EndBalLoad). The base members within beginning balance, activity, and FX are calculated based on the ending balance which is loaded.

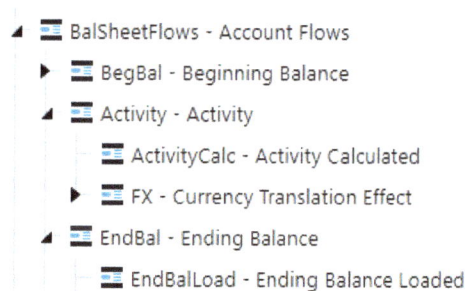

Figure 4.16

Within this hierarchy, only the ending balance (EndBal) should aggregate to the top of the dimension. Since this balance is provided directly, a user can pull the local currency ending balance without any other calculations needing to be run.

Alternatively, as in periodic data loads, if any of the other members (BegBal, Activity) are aggregated to the top of the dimension, it would also require a calculation (since these are calculated members) to be run in order to populate the members.

YTD balance loads within the Actual scenario are the most common across companies because it provides a simple structure, it is easily understood, includes prior period adjustments, and does not require any calculations (for loaded accounts) to view YTD balances on a local currency basis.

Periodic

When loading periodic balances into OneStream, certain items must be considered.

First, the scenario member's No Data Zero View settings should be set to Periodic. Since periodic balances are being loaded, this setting tells OS how it should handle a balance when it is not loaded in the period. This means that when a balance is not loaded in the current period, OS will treat that as a periodic (monthly) 0, which results in the current period YTD being equal to the previous period YTD balance.

The Flow dimension hierarchy (see Figure 4.17) design becomes crucial when loading periodic balances, where the difference in setup (versus YTD) is explained further below.

- **Balance sheet activity** – this needs to be a separate member from the monthly activity being loaded for the income statement because the balance sheet activity Flow member requires the switch type setting to be set to True (and the income statement activity should have this setting as False). This allows for balance sheet activity to be translated at the average rate.

- **Ending balance** – the ending balance of your balance sheet accounts becomes an aggregated total of *Beginning Balance + Activity + FX* (in a YTD load, since the ending balance is provided, it becomes the only aggregated member). The income statement activity member and the stat account input member (EndBalInput) can be aggregated as well.

- A calculation would need to be run in order to provide YTD local currency ending balances because the aggregated ending balance relies on the calculated beginning balance.

```
▲ ▣ EndBal - Ending Balance
    ▶ ▣ BegBal - Beginning Balance
    ▲ ▣ Activity - Total Activity - FX Inclusive
          ▣ ActivityBalSheetLoad - Balance Sheet Activity - Loaded
       ▶ ▣ FX - Total FX
          ▣ ActivityIncStmtLoad - Income Statement Activity - Loaded
          ▣ EndBalInput - Input Ending Balance
```

Figure 4.17

Loading data as periodic comes with one distinct advantage over a YTD load, and that is the number of records requiring to be loaded each period can be significantly reduced than when compared to YTD. Periodic data loads only require the user to load account balances that have activity. A YTD data load has to load any account balance, whether or not it has activity in the current period (as long as it still has an ending balance in the current period).

However, a periodic approach to loading data is not as common because its downsides include: a more complicated hierarchical structure, it requires movements to be separated for balance sheet and income statement accounts, it requires solutioning related to prior period adjustments, and it requires calculations (for loaded accounts) to view YTD balances on a local currency basis.

Historical Overrides

As the financial statements are translated from an entity's functional currency to the currency of its immediate parent, certain accounts – such as equity – must be translated using the spot rates at each specific transaction date. There are two primary ways to account for this using OneStream: using historical exchange rates or using historical values (both of which are discussed below).

Using Historical Exchange Rates

One method of translating accounts at historical exchange rates is to enter the specific spot rate at the transaction date. Transactions occur throughout time at various rates, and each specific transaction must be translated accordingly. Entering historical exchange rates is not done often by companies because it requires either transactional data with the associated rates to be stored in OneStream or a calculation of the weighted average rate to be applied to the balance. This is difficult because transactional level detail is not typically stored in a OneStream cube, and the maintenance of the various rates in the system can be overwhelming.

Using Historical Values

The method used more often by companies is entering the translated value of the balance. This requires account balances which are already loaded from the trial balance, and the user to load the translated value either through a file or data entry form. OneStream has functionality built into the platform to easily facilitate this method.

Out-of-the-Box: Account and Flow Member Configuration

When configuring OneStream to override the translation of an account using entered balances, using the out-of-the-box approach comes with benefits and limitations. The main benefit of this approach is not having to write or maintain any rules, as all of the settings needed are properties on the Account and Flow dimension members.

However, using this approach for historical rate overrides does come with limitations. Since the Flow member where you load your ending balance can only refer to a single currency override, multiple Flow members by currency will be needed (a member for each override currency). Also, it does not carry forward the override from period to period, so overrides will need to be entered each period or a rule written to pull the value forward into the next period. Additionally, the override values are by individual intersection, but many times, users want to enter the total override because there are too many intersections within an account. In this case, a rule would need to be written to accommodate how the total override is spread to the individual intersections.

With multiple currency overrides, if having the ability to pull forward override values or not doing intersection-based overrides is a requirement, then it may be better to go with a custom override approach, as discussed below.

Custom Override: Account and Flow Member Configuration

Another method used in OneStream for historical override values is to develop custom rules. This method is used when more advanced override functionality is required. Some examples of this may include the customer wanting to pull forward override values, having the ability to enter a single value for the total account balance (and have it allocated to all of the intersections of the account), or simplifying the metadata when entering various currency value overrides.

For the configuration of this method, all accounts which will use a historical value override will have a unique **text field identifier**.

In the Flow dimension, the historical override value will be entered into a member. A formula can be written to pull forward the override value so it only has to be adjusted when there is a new transaction.

```
If (Not api.Entity.HasChildren()) Then
    If api.Cons.IsLocalCurrencyforEntity() Then
        api.Data.Calculate("F#USDOverrideInput:O#Import = RemoveNoData(F#USDOverrideInput:T#POVPrior1:O#BeforeAdj)")
    End If
End If
```

On the member where the historical override will be entered, the flow processing type should be set to Is Alternate Input Currency For All Accounts. This will make the translated intersection of the historical override member invalid. Since the historical override member has the translated value entered to it, the balance does not require translation and this setting will avoid these unnecessary data values.

On the Flow dimension member where the local currency balances were loaded, a formula is written to take the historical override value from the associated Flow member and write it to the translated value of the account (if the account has the unique text field identifier). Within this formula, custom logic can be applied.

```
Dim foreignCurrency As String = api.Pov.Cons.Name

If (api.Cons.IsForeignCurrencyForEntity()) And (Not api.Entity.HasChildren()) Then

    Select Case foreignCurrency
    Case "USD"
        api.data.Calculate("F#EndBal = Eval(F#USDOverrideInput:C#Local)", AddressOf OnEvalDataBuffer)

    Case "AUD"
        api.data.Calculate("F#EndBal = Eval(F#AUDOverrideInput:C#Local)", AddressOf OnEvalDataBuffer)

    End Select

End If

    Formula Footer
    Helper Functions Header
Private Sub OnEvalDataBuffer(ByVal api As FinanceRulesApi, ByVal evalName As String, ByVal eventArgs As EvalDataBufferEventArgs)...
```

This approach may seem daunting, but the rules applied to these members are customer-agnostic in most cases, and there isn't a need to change or re-write them on every implementation. The flexibility and ease of use for the user outweigh the perceived downside of requiring rules. An example of the outlined configuration above along with the described Member Formulas can be found in the CPM Blueprint on the Solution Exchange.

FX and CTA

CTA, or cumulative translation adjustment, is the calculation of the cumulative balance sheet exposure as a result of the difference in translation rates for each reporting period and is reported in OCI. At each reporting period date, balance sheet accounts are either translated at the closing rate, historical exchange rate, or weighted average rate, which results in changes attributable only to the differences in these rates. For example, a functional currency balance could not change from period to period, but the reporting currency balance could, due to the exchange rate used.

CTA reported on the balance sheet is the summation of the FX for each individual balance sheet account. Calculation of FX is comprised of two major components:

- FX on the opening balance, calculated as the change in the current closing rate and the closing rate at prior year-end.

- FX on the current movement, calculated as the change in the current closing rate and the current average rate.

FX exposure is important for a company to understand in order to analyze pure account movements. Changes in balances on the surface may appear as a positive or negative change in cash, but analyzing the FX proves what the true effect on cash inflows or outflows was. Why is this important? Take accounts receivable, for example. If the balance in accounts receivable went down from period to period, it may appear as though the company is collecting cash. If you are able to break down the A/R account into its pure activity versus FX exposure, you can analyze just how much, if any, the company collected.

With the OneStream Flow dimension, the calculation and reporting of FX and CTA are simplified. FX members are created and attached to each balance sheet account, with rules (as outlined above) to calculate the components of FX (see Figure 4.18). This allows a user to report and analyze every account by its FX exposure.

FX - Currency Translation Effect
    FXOpen - FX Opening Balance
    FXCurMovement - FX Movement

Figure 4.18

As part of a company's audit, they are often asked to provide proof of the calculation of the translation adjustment in CTA. This is no longer a disconnected, separate process to calculate a proof and make sure it reconciles to the CTA balance. The FX by account can be totaled and moved to the CTA account so that the calculation of CTA is the proof. If the calculation of FX by account is not correct, the balance sheet won't balance in the translated currency.

Cash Flow

The cash flow statement analyzes the cash inflows and outflows of the business in order to understand its financial performance, including its ability to pay down existing and future debts, to reinvest funds for growth, and its sustainability during economic hardships. Overall, the cash flow statement explains the period's activity in cash in detail. What were the proceeds from the sale of PP&E or investments? Did the company incur debt over this period through borrowings? What was the change in working capital? Whether cash increases or decreases during a period, a business needs to understand why and what is causing it in order to determine any course of action.

Companies often struggle with the collection of detailed balance sheet and income statement activity information in order to support the cash flow statement and the required level of analysis. Rarely is this information readily available or complete in a database to integrate with. More often than not, the detailed information to support the cash flow is pieced together by a group of accountants and manually entered. Within OneStream, the Flow dimension plays a vital role in capturing the changes in balance sheet accounts and collecting detailed rollforward information.

Rollforwards

Rollforwards are a record of the activity in the account, explaining how the account balance went from its beginning balance to its ending balance. When a trial balance is loaded into OneStream, it typically only includes the periodic or YTD balances. This allows for the calculation of the balance sheet account movements, but not always the required level of movement detail. The trial balance does not detail the purchases or disposals of PP&E, borrowings or payments of debt, or impairments of goodwill during the period, for example. All of the movement in the account for each period needs to be fully explained, or there is a component of cash inflows or outflows that is incomplete. This would throw the cash flow statement out of balance.

Cash flow rollforwards are created within OneStream to capture this information, whether through an import process or manual entry. If loading some or all of this information through an import file, it is a mapping exercise as the data gets loaded. If it is captured through manual data entry, forms are created for the user to easily enter and see whether they are explaining all of the activity.

Flow Configuration

Within OneStream's Flow dimension, rollforwards are designed and built based on the detailed movement information being captured (see Figure 4.19).

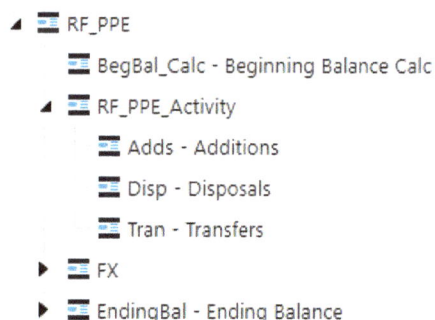

Figure 4.19

In real time, a user will be able to see how much activity needs to be explained on the account through the use of aggregation weights. The Flow members `BegBal_Calc`, `RF_PPE_Activity`, and `FX` will use an aggregation weight of `-1`, while `EndingBal` will use an aggregation weight of

1. By doing so, OneStream's on-the-fly aggregation will net these members and allow the 'Check Sum' (RF_PPE member) to be updated as the user is entering the activity (see Figure 4.20).

	Begin Balance	+ Additions	- Disposals	+/- Transfers	= End Balance	Check Sum	Comments:
16000 - Machinery & Equipment at cost		116,049.57	8,168.00		116,049.57	8,168.00	
16100 - Land at cost							
16200 - Buildings at cost							
16300 - Hardware at cost							
16400 - Software at cost							
16500 - Leasehold at cost		9,993.69			9,993.69	0.00	
16600 - Furniture at cost		11,825.10			11,825.10	0.00	
16700 - Other at cost							
16800 - Accum Depreciation		73,979.17			73,979.17	0.00	
16999 - Net PP&E		63,889.19	8,168.00		63,889.19	8,168.00	

Figure 4.20

Switch Type

Flow dimension members use the account type to determine their behavior (what FX rate to use to translate, and whether the account has a periodic and YTD value), but there is an ability to easily change the behavior for specific Flow members through the Switch Type setting. For purposes of rollforwards, the activity members are attached to balance sheet accounts but need to translate at the period's average rate. Like income statement accounts, the activity in these accounts happened throughout the period and translation by the average rate is appropriate. By adjusting the Switch Type setting to True, the activity members are now treated like income statement accounts, including the translation (see Figure 4.21).

⊟ Settings	
Formula Type	(Not Used)
Allow Input	True
Is Consolidated	Conditional (True if no Formula Type (default))
Switch Sign	False
Switch Type	True

Figure 4.21

Cash Flow Hierarchy Configuration

The cash flow statement metadata structure is typically created in the Account, Flow, or a UD dimension, but of the three options, a UD dimension provides the greatest reporting and analysis benefits.

Companies often reconcile their cash flow statement through a **CF worksheet** or **proof**, where balance sheet accounts or groupings are in the columns, and the cash flow statement is in the rows. This allows for a matrix to make sure that the activity of each balance sheet account is properly accounted for in the cash flow statement. If the CF statement is built in the Account dimension, this is harder to accomplish because the matrix becomes account by account. Formulas are then needed, which may lead to hardcoded cells within the worksheet. If the CF statement is instead built in the Flow dimension, the creation of the matrix worksheet becomes Flow by account, which allows it to be built dynamically. Additionally, moving the cash flow statement metadata to a User Defined dimension instead of Flow (see Figure 4.22) allows for the same matrix view but also gives the user additional visibility into the flow intersections. This configuration creates the optimal view into one's cash flow.

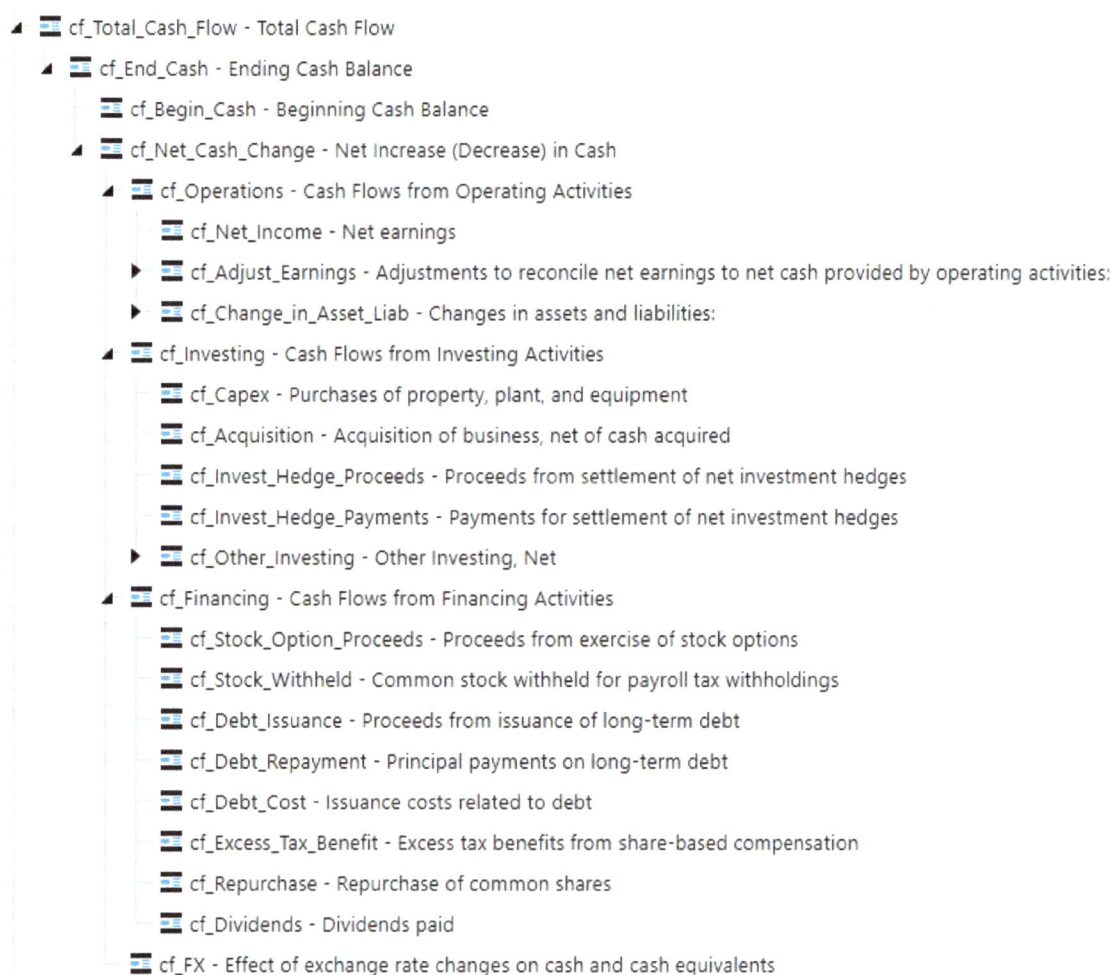

- ▲ cf_Total_Cash_Flow - Total Cash Flow
  - ▲ cf_End_Cash - Ending Cash Balance
    - cf_Begin_Cash - Beginning Cash Balance
    - ▲ cf_Net_Cash_Change - Net Increase (Decrease) in Cash
      - ▲ cf_Operations - Cash Flows from Operating Activities
        - cf_Net_Income - Net earnings
        - ▶ cf_Adjust_Earnings - Adjustments to reconcile net earnings to net cash provided by operating activities:
        - ▶ cf_Change_in_Asset_Liab - Changes in assets and liabilities:
      - ▲ cf_Investing - Cash Flows from Investing Activities
        - cf_Capex - Purchases of property, plant, and equipment
        - cf_Acquisition - Acquisition of business, net of cash acquired
        - cf_Invest_Hedge_Proceeds - Proceeds from settlement of net investment hedges
        - cf_Invest_Hedge_Payments - Payments for settlement of net investment hedges
        - ▶ cf_Other_Investing - Other Investing, Net
      - ▲ cf_Financing - Cash Flows from Financing Activities
        - cf_Stock_Option_Proceeds - Proceeds from exercise of stock options
        - cf_Stock_Withheld - Common stock withheld for payroll tax withholdings
        - cf_Debt_Issuance - Proceeds from issuance of long-term debt
        - cf_Debt_Repayment - Principal payments on long-term debt
        - cf_Debt_Cost - Issuance costs related to debt
        - cf_Excess_Tax_Benefit - Excess tax benefits from share-based compensation
        - cf_Repurchase - Repurchase of common shares
        - cf_Dividends - Dividends paid
    - cf_FX - Effect of exchange rate changes on cash and cash equivalents

Figure 4.22

Calculation Approach

There are various ways to calculate the cash flow statement in OneStream – Member Formulas or business rules are two of the most common approaches in the past. However, using Member Formulas or business rules to calculate each line in the cash flow statement is rules-intensive and isn't appropriate for all levels of administrators to maintain. With each modification of the cash flow statement, the administrator has to go into a formula and make the adjustment within the code. This isn't bad for an administrator familiar with writing and modifying rules, but it can be challenging for others without this background.

A hybrid approach of business rules with **text field tagging** allows for a dynamic and metadata-focused approach, which is easy for an administrator of any level to maintain and users to understand.

Text Field

Using this approach, balance sheet accounts and select income statement accounts (when necessary) are tagged with a text field. The text field on these accounts includes the source Flow dimension movement, target cash flow statement line item, and appropriate signage in which they are mapped to (see Figure 4.23). Additional splits of the mapping are designated with a | (pipe) character. In the example shown, FX flow movements for the account with this text field are mapped to a separate cash flow statement line.

115

Vary By Scenario Type And Time	
General	
In Use	True
Formula	
Formula For Calculation Drill Down	
Adjustment Type	Journals
Text	
Text 1	Activity_Excl_FX:CF_ChgAR:-1|FX:CF_FX:-1

Figure 4.23

A standard cash flow rule is written to take all the data in the account/flow intersections which have an appropriate text field and push it to the specified cash flow statement line items. With any change to a mapping, the administrator only has to modify text fields on metadata, which can also vary by Scenario Type and/or time. The code is dynamic in reading the text fields so no updates are needed to any code. All users have visibility into how the cash flow statement is calculated by looking at the properties of any member, and reports can be written to display this mapping as well. There are no more questions on where the number came from or sifting through long rule files to determine how line items were calculated. An example of the configuration outlined above can be found in the CPM Blueprint on the Solution Exchange.

Other Consolidation Topics

Discontinued Operations

Discontinued operations is a component of a company's business that has been divested, shut down, or disposed of. When these disposals meet the criteria outlined by financial accounting standards, they must be reported separately from continuing operations on the balance sheet, income statement, and cash flow statement. The presentation of these amounts separately must begin in the first period the discontinued operation is classified as held for sale, and for all comparative periods. Reclassification of these balances allows users to properly evaluate a company's continuing or ongoing operations.

User Defined Dimension

This method accomplishes discontinued operations requirements by creating a new member (e.g., DiscOps), within a User Defined dimension. If the application is already using a dimension to track the source or adjustment type of data, it can be included there. This allows the user the flexibility to toggle to pre-disc ops balances, the disc ops reclassified balances, and balances net of disc ops throughout the entity hierarchy (see Figure 4.24).

Figure 4.24

To calculate the reclassification, we need to be able to appropriately identify what has been discontinued and how to reclassify its amounts. An example would be if an entity was discontinued (this can also be segments, product lines, etc.). In this case, we need to identify that the entity has been discontinued, which is usually done through a text field on the entity. Next, we need to identify where the account balances are going to be reclassed to, so they can be presented separately. Each account will have a text field which is equal to the discontinued account which its balances will be reclassed to (see Figures 4.25 and 4.26).

▲ IS54999 - Intangible Expense	General	
IS52100 - Intang. Amort - Trademarks/Tradenames	In Use	True
IS52200 - Intang. Amort - Patents	Formula	
IS52300 - Intang. Amort - Customer Lists/Contracts	Formula For Calculation Drill Down	
IS52350 - Intang. Amort - Customer Relationships	Adjustment Type	Journals
IS52400 - Intang. Amort - Non-Compete Agreements	Text	
IS52500 - Intang. Amort - Licenses	Text 1	
IS52600 - Intang. Amort - Technology	Text 2	
IS52900 - Intang. Amort - Other	Text 3	
	Text 4	IS89211

Figure 4.25

Name	IS89211
⊟ Descriptions	
Default Description	(Income) Loss from Discontinued Operations

Figure 4.26

A rule is written which takes all of the data from entities (or other dimension members) with the appropriate disc ops text field identifier, and in the accounts with an appropriate text field, and pushes it to the discontinued account/disc ops UD member. An offsetting value is written against the account holding the balance/disc ops UD member, so the entry is balanced. With any change to a mapping, the administrator only has to modify text fields on metadata, which can vary by Scenario Type and/or time. The code is dynamic in reading the text fields, so no updates are needed to any code. Users have visibility into how disc ops is calculated by looking at the properties of any member, and reports can be written to display this mapping as well. There are no more questions on where the number came from or sifting through long rule files to determine how line items were calculated.

Acquisitions

An acquisition is when a company purchases a majority of another company's shares or assets and has control over the business decisions of the acquired organization. A company can acquire another company for many reasons, whether it is part of the company's growth strategy, diversification by entering into a new market, or to reduce competition, amongst many others.

Acquisition accounting occurs outside of OneStream, but the question becomes how do we integrate this new company into our existing application? There can be several areas of the application that need to be updated, including metadata, integrations, and workflows. These are all of the areas expected when a new dataset needs to be integrated.

Beginning Balances

It's also more likely than not that the acquisition occurred during the year, so beginning balances need to be properly reflected for rollforwards and cash flow purposes. How does the beginning balance sheet get entered and picked up properly? With OneStream's dedicated Flow dimension, this becomes a straightforward process. A member is created in the Flow dimension (e.g., `BegBal_Inp`), where a user will import or manually enter the beginning balance sheet to. The beginning balance member (e.g., `BegBal_Calc`) will first look to see if a beginning balance sheet was entered and, if so, use those values; if not, it will use the prior year-end (see Figure 4.27).

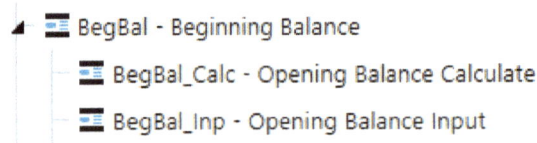

Figure 4.27

Pro forma

Pro forma financial statements are essentially what-if scenarios – reports used to gain insight into what the business may have looked like in the past, or what it will look like in the future based on certain assumptions or hypothetical events. Pro forma financial statements typically come up when integrating acquisitions and wanting the ability to see what the financial statements would have looked like if the company was acquired from the beginning of the year (or even in prior years). To produce pro forma financial statements in OneStream, there are two common approaches – using a User Defined dimension or a separate scenario.

User Defined Dimension

This method accomplishes pro forma requirements by creating a new member (e.g., `Pro forma`), within a User Defined dimension. The application may already have a dimension that tracks the source of all data which may be used. This allows data to be loaded to the existing dimension members while all pro forma data (pre-acquisition periods) would get loaded to the new `ProformaAdj` member, as pro forma data will not be split out by source (see Figure 4.28). The pro forma member would only be selected on reports as needed.

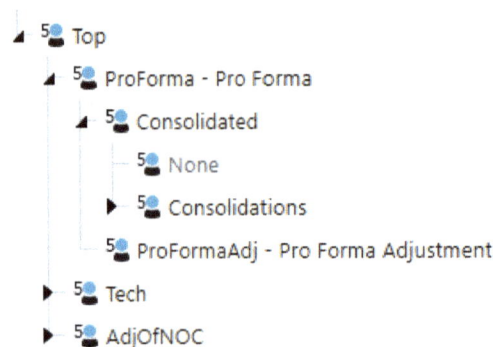

Figure 4.28

This has some key advantages over the scenario approach, in that there is never the need to copy or move data, which means no further development work, the data is always current, and no reconciliation is required.

Scenario

This method accomplishes the pro forma requirements by creating a new scenario (e.g., `Proforma`) within the Scenario dimension. This allows data to be loaded to the Actual scenario, while all pro forma data (pre-acquisition periods) would get loaded to the new pro forma scenario. After the Actual periods are closed within the Actual scenario, a process would occur that would copy the data to the pro forma scenario, with the result being that the Actual scenario holds all post-acquisition periods, while the pro forma scenario holds all the pre- and post-acquisition data.

As mentioned above, because this approach requires copying and moving data, there is potentially more development work in the form of copy rules or jobs. This approach also introduces data latency, and with any movement of data, there is a certain level of reconciliation which would be required.

Constant Currency

As global companies are analyzing their financials, it is important to understand the performance of the company without the impact and unpredictability of fluctuating exchange rates. Constant currency analysis is the translation of the financial statements at fixed exchange rates in order to eliminate the effects of exchange rates. To perform constant currency analysis, all periods of the financial statements are translated at a constant rate for accurate comparability. This analysis is often used to compare how the company is doing against its budgeted or forecasted numbers, or how the company is trending in key areas. The fluctuations in exchange rates could be masking trends, whether favorable or unfavorable, which would otherwise be identifiable. Departments or employees are often measured on key performance figures, and without stripping out exchange rate effects, the results could be skewed and be measured unfairly. There are several ways to accomplish constant currency analysis in OneStream, and the common approaches are discussed below.

Scenario Settings

Translating a scenario at another year's rates is available using scenario setting Constant Year For FX Rates (see Figure 4.29).

⊟ FX Rates	
Use Cube FX Settings	False
Rate Type For Revenues And Expenses	AverageRate_Budget
Rule Type For Revenues And Expenses	Periodic
Rate Type For Assets And Liabilities	ClosingRate_Budget
Rule Type For Assets And Liabilities	Direct
Constant Year For FX Rates	2022

Figure 4.29

When applying this setting, OneStream will use the rates from the year specified to translate the values within the scenario. What this means is that if 2021 results are being translated with the settings above, January 2021 will be translated at January 2020 rates, February 2021 will be translated at February 2020 rates, and so on.

Translation Rules

Utilizing translation rules allows for more flexibility when calculating constant currency. While the Constant Year For FX Rates only allows all data within the Constant Currency scenario to be translated at a single year's rates, using translation rules allows for each year within the Constant Currency scenario to act independently.

As an example, a company may want its Forecast translated at Budget rates. Using translation rules, each subsequent year of the Forecast can be translated at the corresponding Budget rates for the year, without the creation of new scenarios.

User Defined

Using this approach, a member is created with a formula that will translate the local currency results at the rate specified (see Figure 4.30). The translation at the constant currency rate happens at the same time the normal financial results are being translated.

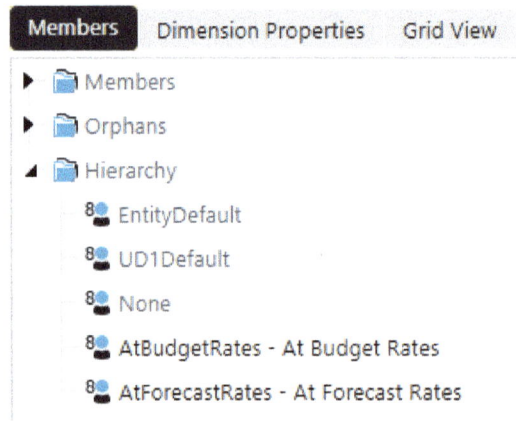

Figure 4.30

This means there is no data latency, and analysis on the constant currency rate can be done simultaneously during the close. It also means another scenario isn't required, so source data does not move, and no level of validation has to occur. However, Data Unit size must be considered. With this approach, the data within the Data Unit (cube, entity, parent, consolidation, scenario, and time) may be doubled, tripled, etc., depending on how many constant currency rates are needed. Since calculations occur against the Data Unit, increasing the Data Unit size will increase the calculation and consolidation time.

This approach may be appropriate for applications that have low record counts in the Data Unit or which analyze constant currency regularly during the close cycle.

Scenario

Using a separate scenario provides the same flexibility to translate each period at any rate while reducing the Data Unit size. Using this approach, a scenario is created for each constant currency rate required (see Figure 4.31). Data is copied from the source scenario to the Constant Currency scenario and translated at the constant currency rate.

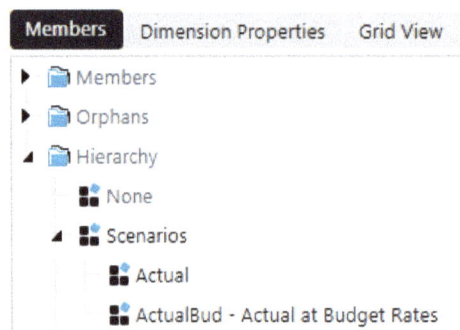

Figure 4.31

This approach reduces the Data Unit size because it creates a new Data Unit and the calculation performance of the Constant Currency scenario acts independently of the source scenario. However, whenever data is moved, there is a level of reconciliation that has to occur to ensure the data is copied correctly.

This approach may be appropriate for applications with high record counts or companies that only analyze this data at particular times later in the close cycle. Copying and translating the data can be scheduled or user-driven and not increase calculation overhead during the close. Hybrid scenarios can also be utilized to aid with the data copying process.

Conclusion

In OneStream, there are several options you may have at your disposal to solve many of an organization's complex problems and – in many instances – there isn't a single solution that works for every customer. When weighing solution options, it is imperative to keep a balance of maintenance, user experience, and performance in mind. The balance between these three key aspects is rarely the same from customer to customer, but knowing the administrator and the user community will help in understanding the right balance.

I hope this chapter helped you understand many of the fundamental consolidation concepts and solutions in OneStream so that you may have options to strike the perfect balance with your customers.

Epilogue

One of my favorite memories thus far with OneStream was in 2017, when 20 OneStreamers decided to run the Tough Mudder in my hometown of Buffalo, NY. Through our participation, we raised money for a great charity: the Navy-Marine Corp Relief Society (NMCRS).

All of the employees from the Detroit area traveled down together on a bus, and several others flew in from other states around the country. On the morning of the run, it started raining consistently and – little did we know – it would be up and down the slopes of the ski resort it was being held on. The course conditions made it even more challenging, and I can't say that everyone finished the course but we had a lot of laughs throughout the 10 miles and several hours we were out there. It was a team event where we were able to raise money for a great cause and everyone could have fun outside of the office together.

5
Planning

Originally written by Jonathan Golembiewski, updated by Jonathan Golembiewski

When I embarked on my first Planning project, I had been at OneStream for almost two years. In that time, I had mostly worked on consolidation projects as those were the type of projects we focused on in the early days. This project would be the very first complex, driver-based planning solution that would be implemented in OneStream. It was also the first implementation of People Planning (which would become the basis of the Specialty Planning suite of Solution Exchange solutions).

While I didn't have a lot of planning experience, I did have a solid grasp of the vast capabilities of the OneStream platform. I would since come to learn these capabilities could solve just about any planning problem you could imagine.

In the end, the first planning project at OneStream was a success, and we were able to implement a very elegant solution (thanks to the help of numerous colleagues and a very patient customer). Since that first project, OneStream has implemented hundreds of unique planning solutions across companies of varying sizes and complexity. This is a testament to the 'Power of the Platform' and how OneStream is constantly adapting and improving to meet the needs of the market.

Designing Planning Solutions in OneStream

The OneStream platform offers a unique set of tools to handle the complex planning requirements of large corporations. Retail, manufacturing, and service industries have vastly different business models and will, therefore, have vastly different ways of producing their financial plans. It is also common for one company to have a variety of business models operating under the same umbrella.

Further, financial planning does not happen in isolation from other financial processes such as consolidation. Often, Actual data is used as the basis of financial plans. Imagine a CFO asking an analyst, in June, for a report that gives the projected end of year results. This report would need to blend data from both Actual historical data with data from the annual budget or forecast. Further, there is tremendous value in having financial data that is comparable across scenarios. For example, a CFO wants to see how the most recent period's financial results compared with the plan for every product in a department. If there isn't a commonality between these two datasets, this report would be cumbersome, if not impossible, to produce.

This is where OneStream shines. It was built upon the idea that all these financial processes belong in the same product, and accomplishing this can create tremendous value for the office of the CFO. OneStream's Extensible Dimensionality allows the data that supports these processes to live within the same cube without having to sacrifice specific planning requirements and complexities. Plan data can be prepared at more or less detail than Actual data while still holding a common point for reporting.

Another unique aspect of financial planning is the variety of methodologies and sources of data that can be drawn from to assemble a company-wide financial plan. Data is often sourced from transactional databases, payroll systems, or production data warehouses. OneStream's robust data integration engine can bring this data into the application so it can be enriched and used across various planning processes. This feature is also important in explaining the 'why'. Having the data living in one tool gives tremendous value when combined with OneStream's robust reporting and analytical tools. After all, financial projections are only useful if they can be used to make informed business decisions.

The founders of OneStream set out to create a platform that can bring everything together into a connected enterprise-wide plan. Accomplishing this is a paradigm shift in the industry. My goal for this chapter is primarily to get you – the reader – to think about planning more broadly in the context of other business processes. When implementing planning in OneStream, you should be thinking about the big picture as much as the fine details. I will try to put the key concepts in the context of the bigger picture and never as isolated processes.

Approach to this Chapter

The goal for this chapter is to create a common framework for how to approach planning projects in OneStream. I will focus specifically on how to design and utilize OneStream's robust set of tools most effectively for your customers.

As we move through the sections of this chapter, I will first try to establish a foundation of the basic concepts in financial planning. I think it's important to understand the underlying business processes that companies use to produce their plans before tackling the more technical elements. I will start by identifying the various types of planning processes you are likely to encounter, and the methodologies used to create them. From there, I will explain how we can leverage OneStream's unique capabilities to build a unified solution that encompasses all these financial processes and methodologies.

Along the way, I will also give tips and techniques that can be employed to build planning tools in OneStream. These are mostly meant to be a nudge in the right direction and not hard and fast rules. Anybody who has spent time in a Financial Planning & Analysis department, or has experience implementing planning CPM solutions, knows that the first rule of planning is that there is no 'one way of doing things'. Even companies within the same industry can have vastly different approaches to creating their financial plans. At OneStream's annual Splash Conference, where OneStream consultants and customers gather from all over the world, many conversations can be heard describing different ways of implementing similar planning solutions.

There are always several ways of getting to the same result, and this is especially true of a product with the robustness and flexibility of OneStream. For consultants or users of other planning tools, it is highly likely that you will encounter planning challenges that you've never seen before. That being said, 'out-of-the-box' thinking is not only encouraged but necessary.

This is not to say there aren't industry trends, patterns, and common techniques that can and should be followed. This chapter will attempt to provide a basic framework, common language, and tips and techniques for tackling planning projects in OneStream.

Further, every design decision should be weighed against two important benchmarks – performance and maintenance. You can build the greatest, most-accurate planning solution with every bell and whistle imaginable, but if it requires a 10-person team of data scientists, IT experts, and system administrators to maintain, you haven't created much value for your client. Similarly, you can create a highly-detailed plan that tracks profitability for every SKU in the company's product catalog, but if it takes hours to generate a simple report because the performance is poor, it will not be very useful to the Executive Team. As such, these two standards should be at the back of every consultant's mind when making any design decision. Unfortunately, both metrics can sometimes be difficult to measure. One customer's perception of poor performance could be vastly different to another's. It's important to establish benchmarks and set expectations early in the project.

As a final thought, I will note that it's impossible to cover every possible design nuance and that consultants, working jointly with FP&A team members, should do their best to weigh the pros and cons of all possible solutions before coming to a decision. I hope that by the end of this chapter, you are armed with better knowledge to tackle the variety of situations you are bound to encounter.

What is Planning?

Let's start by defining what planning is, as it's a rather broad term that can mean a lot of different things. In the context of OneStream and this chapter, I am more specifically referring to financial planning. Traditionally, financial planning refers to the projection of a company's future financial position. All companies need to create financial projections to make business decisions, decide how to invest capital, and provide guidance to investors. Companies strive to create accurate financial projections in the shortest amount of time possible. This dynamic is why most companies look to a powerful tool like OneStream to achieve this goal.

Financial planning is typically used to drive financial decisions. This type of planning is more closely related to the Actual data reporting requirements, as financial plans are periodically measured against Actuals. Supporting data structures are typically multidimensional with semifrequent updates to metadata. Financial intelligence and data aggregation are necessary against these structures as well. The preparation of financial plans requires heavy interaction with end-users, and calculations derive most of the data.

OneStream is also positioned to handle other, more detailed planning processes outside of traditional financial planning.

Specialty Planning

Specialty planning refers to planning that focuses on a specific area within the financial plan. The level of detail used to generate specialty plans is generally much greater, but will ultimately feed into (and relate back to) the greater financial plan. The data structure within specialty planning is highly detailed and transient in nature – changing frequently. Users will need to interact with this data moderately and execute stored calculations against the data. Sophisticated financial intelligence and aggregations will usually not take place in specialty planning. An example of specialty planning would be **People Planning**. A detailed people plan could provide insight into hiring decisions or highlight differences between supply and demand.

Operational Planning

Operational planning refers to highly detailed datasets that provide key information and metrics between financial periods to help drive financial decisions. It provides real-time financial information to guide the business on shorter timeframes – such as daily or weekly. Operational planning data is not interacted with, or modified, by end-users. Simple calculations and aggregations can be performed.

The majority of this chapter will focus on financial planning, but we will make several references to specialty planning and operational planning as well. The Analytic Blend Chapter (12) goes into much greater detail around how to design and implement operational planning.

Designing & Building Planning in OneStream

Classifying Planning Projects

Planning projects can take many shapes and forms. It's important to understand, upfront, what kind of planning project you will be undertaking.

We can classify planning projects based on the following criteria:

- **Stand-alone** – this is the first implementation of OneStream at the customer, and planning is the first phase. The biggest thing to keep in mind for these project types is to make sure the solution is set up to accommodate future phases.

- **Phase 2 (or later)** – there is an existing implementation that is already live, and planning will be a subsequent phase. For example, consolidation is already live, and now planning is being implemented. For these project types, prior phase solutions should be carefully reviewed, as many existing elements can be leveraged for planning.

- **Combined** – planning is being implemented alongside consolidation (or another solution). Combined solutions may have separate project teams dedicated to each solution. Communication between both phases is key as there will be many areas of overlap. For these types of projects, it often makes sense to hold at least some of the design sessions together with both groups.

A Note on Actuals

The vast majority of OneStream customers fall into the latter two categories of projects and have implemented consolidation or Actuals before (or in parallel to) planning. There are several reasons for this. First, Actuals are often used as the basis or source for the plan. Second, most companies need to produce variance reports that compare the plan against Actuals. I don't think I can remember having ever implemented a planning solution in OneStream where Actuals didn't need to be considered!

If you think about it, this makes sense. Financial planning should align to financial consolidation and reporting. However, you should never assume this is the case. Later in this chapter, we will outline how to analyze this and come to the right decision on how to integrate planning data alongside Actual data.

Planning Design Principles

In Chapter 3, Peter described the fundamentals of a OneStream design session. The same principles he explained will apply here, and I will seek to expand on them as they specifically relate to planning.

A planning design typically occurs over several meetings. Depending on the size and scope of the project, it may stretch over several weeks. It's important to establish clear goals for the meetings and agree on what the outputs will be.

Below are some basic principles that should be followed for every planning design:

- Strive for standardization

- Avoid replicating manual processes

- Consider future phases

Design Approach

The basic premise I use for planning designs is to focus on the business processes first, before moving into technical design elements. There will likely be non-technical people in the room and certainly people who don't know OneStream. By focusing on the business processes and using familiar terms initially, you will set the stage for an easier transition into the more technical OneStream-specific topics. To this point, there should be two main focal points in the design meetings.

The **business process design** is a description of the inputs and tasks performed by the planners to produce the company's financial Plans. The BPD will focus on the business side of things. It's not meant to be technical or OneStream-specific. The BPD is 'solution agnostic', meaning that it should be the same if you were designing a solution in Excel rather than with OneStream.

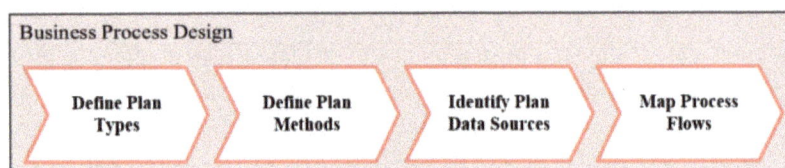

Figure 5.1

The **technical design** describes the specifics of how the solution will be built and configured to meet the requirements of the business process design. This is where OneStream-specific terms and elements will be referenced. It is also what will become the blueprint for building the solution.

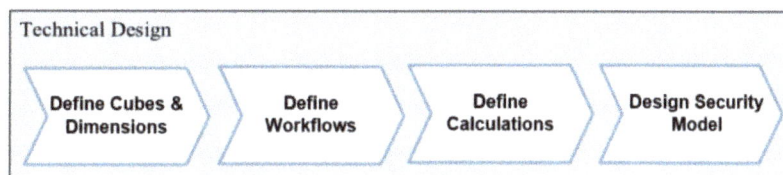

Figure 5.2

The coming sections of this chapter will break down these two aspects of the design into greater detail.

Business Process Design

As mentioned above, the business process design (BPD) should be the starting point for the planning design. The goal for the BPD is to create a bridge from functional to technical. To do that, we will start by defining some basic planning terms. Some readers may find this rudimentary, but I'd suggest skimming through this section to at least get familiar with the vocabulary I will be using. As with most professional topics, there is a lot of interchangeable jargon, so this will at least get everyone on the same page. I also think it helps to use more generic terms in design sessions when there may be non-technical people in the room. After all, part of being a consultant is being able to effectively translate functional terms to technical software.

Plan Types

Just like the wall of deodorant varieties at the drugstore, there are many different types of financial plans. Let's think of our own personal budgets. You probably have a monthly budget of how much you will earn, spend, and save. You have fixed costs such as rent and utilities, and variable costs such as meals and entertainment. You also likely have a longer-term financial plan for planning larger purchases or preparing for retirement. Without these plans, it would be very difficult to make personal financial decisions.

Businesses are no different and often have numerous financial plans that are used to drive business decisions. We can define a *plan type* as a financial plan that shares a common preparation process, duration, scope, and level of detail. The below sections will define and describe several plan types, commonly seen within the industry.

Budget

Most companies prepare an annual budget as a one-time exercise before the start of the next fiscal year. The preparation cycle for the budget is usually longer than for other planning processes and can occur over several months, often going through several iterations. The budget can be at a different level of detail than other planning processes and is often used as the basis for subsequent forecasting cycles.

Forecast

Forecasts are usually prepared periodically throughout the fiscal year and are meant to quickly capture changes in a company's business. A forecast usually occurs at a higher frequency, often monthly, and sometimes quarterly or weekly. The scope of a forecast is also defined by the number of periods forecasted. The most common forecast is 'year-to-go' (YTG), in which Actual data is blended with Forecasted data to create a projection for the current year only. In this case, the number of periods forecasted is variable as the company operates throughout the year.

A **rolling forecast** refers to a forecast that always spans a constant number of periods. A 12-month rolling forecast will always project 12 months from the current month.

Long-Range

Long-range plans typically span over multiple years and are updated less frequently than other plan types. They will often be prepared at a higher level within Account or reporting dimensions. For example, a long-range plan may only project results of total company sales instead of breaking down sales across individual products like in the Forecast or Budget.

Operational

An operational plan is typically a highly-detailed plan that is often specific to a department or section of the company. Operational planning often uses detailed driver or transactional data as the basis for creating the plan.

Planning Time

Once you've established your plan types, the next step is to collect information related to the timing, duration, and other time-related information, which will have downstream configuration effects relating to scenario properties, data seeding logic, and workflow settings. The information covered in this section is typically collected in a design session or scoping call.

Preparation Cycles

How often is this type of plan created? Once a month? Once a year? How long does each cycle take? A day, a week, three months?

Each plan type will have a preparation cycle, which is how often this plan type is prepared. A budget may be prepared once a year, while a detailed forecast might be prepared each month. It's also important to understand how long each cycle lasts. The annual budget may be prepared over a period of three months, while the preparation of the monthly forecast is much quicker, lasting only three days.

Input Frequency

Input frequency refers to the time unit of the plan data (e.g., monthly or quarterly). A budget would likely be prepared as 12 units of monthly data. It could also be prepared as four units of quarterly figures, or 52 units of weekly figures. A long-range plan could be five units of yearly figures.

Plan Duration

Plan duration is the number of time units that the plan consists of. A yearly budget with a monthly input frequency would have a plan duration of 12 months.

The plan duration will mostly control the workflow settings in the Scenario dimension.

Plan Input View

The plan input view refers to how the plan data will be entered into the system. This can either be year-to-date (YTD) or periodic. Periodic will refer to the input frequency (e.g., week-to-date for weekly, month-to-date for monthly, quarter-to-date for quarterly, and so on).

It's important to note that OneStream always stores data as YTD, so this setting is mostly dependent on how the data will be *entered* into the system. A good way to approach this is by looking at how a user will be typing numbers into a form, or how the data will be imported from external data sources. In general, users are most comfortable entering periodic data (e.g., they would enter month-to-date numbers into a scenario with a monthly input frequency). It is also possible to have different input views between adjustments and imports.

Plan Methods

There are a lot of ways you can derive a financial plan or a budget. Let's go back to our personal budget, and think about how we might plan our monthly dining and entertainment expenses.

One place to start would be to look at our average monthly expenditures over the past 12 months. This would probably be pretty accurate but would fail to capture monthly spikes due to special occasions, such as holidays or anniversaries. Alternatively, we could determine the number of 'nights out' we are planning for each month and then multiply that by an average dinner bill. As you can quickly see, there are a lot of different ways to create a financial plan.

There is a common joke amongst planning consultants that "The numbers are just made up anyway." But try telling that to a CFO when he asks how you got to a particular number for projected sales for a product! Being able to explain the basis of financial projections is an essential requirement of any planning tool.

During the design session or scoping call, it is important to identify what plan methods will be a part of the overall solution. The next sections will cover planning methodologies commonly seen within the industry and give an introduction as to how they should be tackled in OneStream. We'll use an example of salary costs to illustrate the application of each planning method.

Driver-Based Planning

Driver-based planning describes a financial plan that is derived from two or more driver inputs. A simple example of a driver-based sales plan is *price per unit * quantity of units sold.*

Often, one driver input is used as an input in many calculations. The same quantity driver can be used in the cost of sales calculation as well as form the basis for warranty costs. As such, a company can get a sense for the sensitivity it may have to one particular driver or assumption. This allows the system to do the work and can greatly reduce the burden on the end-users.

Driver-based planning can also give organizations powerful analytic options. Changing the value of one driver can have impacts across the entire income statement and balance sheet. Imagine a supply chain disruption that delays the shipment of a specific product. A forecast can be quickly adjusted by changing one or two inputs and recalculating a plan.

Further, driver data is often sourced from other systems or entered by sales and manufacturing teams. It is important to identify these sources and compare their level of detail to that of the reporting cubes. Depending on what you uncover, the driver data may fit better in its own cube or may lack the detail necessary to support the reporting requirements.

In a driver-based plan for salary costs, we need to first define our drivers. In this example, we will use headcount as our quantity and average salary as the price. We might have managers enter headcount for their respective departments each month. We could also have managers enter average salary, or we could calculate within the system using historical data. Either way, the result will be a simple formula:

*headcount * average salary = salary expense*

This method gives insight into projected salary costs by allowing visibility into the drivers that were used. For example, an analyst can say, "Salary costs increased by 20% due to the hiring of five employees" and reference the headcount driver trend.

Driver-based plans will make heavy use of the OneStream calculation engine. I will walk through several examples of driver-based calculations in OneStream later in this chapter.

Factor-Based Planning

Factor-based planning refers to the use of either historical or existing data as the basis for a financial plan. A growth factor (often a percentage) is then applied to extrapolate financial data over the duration of the plan.

In a factor-based plan for salary costs, we would use the last 12-month average salary cost as the starting point. A growth factor of 20% would be entered by a department manager, and the salary costs would be extrapolated to create the plan.

Factor-based planning has an advantage in that it can be produced quickly; however, it will typically fall short on accuracy as the adage "Historical results do not predict future performance" can be applied. As such, the use of factor-based planning is usually limited within organizations or reserved for long-range plan types, where the level of detail is much higher and there is a greater level of uncertainty.

I will walk through several examples of factor-based calculations in OneStream, later in this chapter.

Zero-Based Planning

Perhaps the antithesis to factor-based planning, zero-based planning refers to planning in which each expense must be detailed and justified for each planning period. This method of planning typically focuses on the operating expenses section of a company's income statement. Historical data or drivers are purposely ignored as the process for producing a zero-based budget starts from zero each period.

A zero-based approach to salary costs may involve a manager justifying each existing position within their department and making a business case for any planned new hires over the planning periods. Supporting detail could be provided as either text explanations or the attachment of supporting files.

Zero-based planning has the advantage that it forces each expenditure to be justified. Explanations, attachments, or line item detail is often required to support each expense. Cost-cutting initiatives within an organization will often drive heavier use of this methodology for producing financial plans.

This type of planning puts more responsibility on the planner to provide details and defend each line item. OneStream has several tools available that can support zero-based planning.

- Data cell annotations

- Data cell attachments

- Cell detail

These tools can be used to collect textual information or categorize costs. This information can then be shown on reports or drilled into from Cube Views or Excel Quick Views. Refer to the Data Integration Chapter for more information on these features.

Transaction-Based Planning

Operational plan types generally fall into the category of transaction-based planning in that the data used as the basis for the plan is much more detailed and transactional in nature. This can be thought of as a type of driver-based planning in which the drivers are loaded or inputted as a list, and can have various attributes associated with them. The amount of detail captured is much greater than for traditional driver-based planning processes. This creates a very specific set of requirements that need to be considered at implementation time, so we have carved it out as its own plan type.

Transaction-based planning can put a much higher strain on an organization's finance teams due to the highly detailed nature of the data. Detailed lists of items with attributes must be verified, maintained, and updated throughout the planning processes. However, accuracy and insight into the financial data are benefits that often outweigh the drawbacks.

OneStream's blend engine provides powerful tools for this type of planning. In turn, the Solution Exchange has several 'specialty planning' solutions specifically designed to solve this type of planning requirement.

To plan salary costs using a transaction-based approach, we will start at the same place we did for our driver-based approach. Let's take our *headcount * average salary = salary expense* equation and go one step further to each individual employee. So, instead of one number for headcount and one number for average salary, we will create a list of all employees with their respective individual salaries. We can also collect additional attributes about each employee, such as salary, bonus percentage, merit increase month, and training costs. Planned new hires or terminations would then be integrated during each planning cycle. Calculations would be run against the list of employees to produce the detailed salary cost, which would be transformed and loaded into the cube at an aggregated 'total employee' level.

It will likely take longer for end-users to prepare this plan in relation to the driver-based method, but from an analytic point of view, you have the ability to go deeper than just FTEs and are able to gain valuable insight into the details of each employee, and how they contributed to the overall salary cost expense.

Plan Data Sources

For all plan methods and types, data from a variety of sources will be required to produce financial plans. These data sources will need to be identified and integrated into the build.

Below are some examples of common data sources:

- Historical data (Actuals)
- Production data
- Production schedules
- Hiring plans
- Salary tables
- Labor Union agreements
- Sales projections

Once you've identified each data source, you should also collect some additional information about each of the data sources. The method of inputting into the system, the person responsible for the input, and the format of the data will be very helpful. You won't always be able to find this out in the design phase, but you'll need to know it eventually, so find out as early as possible. If you can get samples of the files, even better.

Data Source:	Method of Entry	Format	Person Responsible
Historical Data	Copy from OneStream	Business Rule	OS Admin
Production Data	Import	CSV	OS Admin
Production Schedules	Input	n/a	Cost Center Manager
Payroll Data	Import	CSV	HR Manager
Salary Tables	Input	n/a	HR Manager
Labor Union Agreements	Input	n/a	HR Manager
Sales Projections	Import	Excel	Sales Manager

Figure 5.3

During the BPD phase, we will just create an inventory of the data sources with some basic information. Later, in the technical design, we will determine *how* and *where* we will integrate each data source in OneStream.

Plan Process Flow

Understanding the detailed process behind how each plan type is prepared is crucial. By now, we've already collected a lot of information about each plan type – we know the plan methods, preparation cycles, and data sources that are needed. Now it's time to fill in the gaps and lay it out into a process flow of what happens, when it happens, and who does it. It's good to focus on cause and effect, and the timing of certain tasks. Try to get information on cut-off times or dates in the process.

Next is an example of a plan process flow:

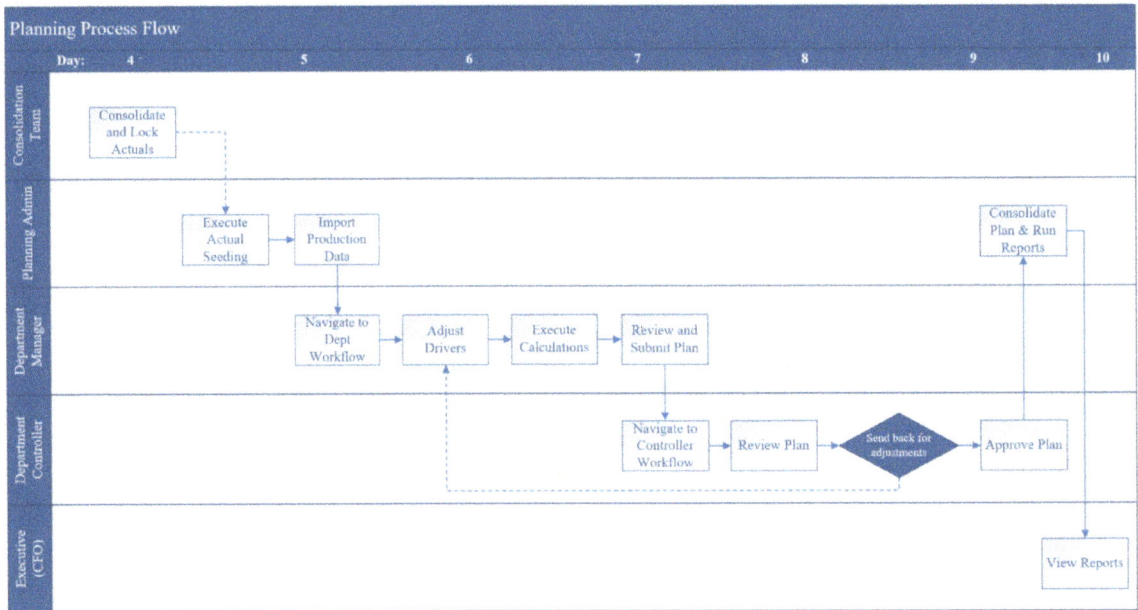

Figure 5.4

The plan process flow brings everything from the BPD together and will identify any gaps or areas that need to be investigated in more detail. It is also a good idea to scrutinize the process and identify areas that can be automated or redefined.

Later in this chapter, we will expand on this concept by translating the process flow to OneStream's workflow mechanism.

Conclusion

It's best to start planning design sessions by focusing on the underlying business processes instead of the technical details. If you've done a good job here, the rest of the design and build will be much easier. Let the business processes drive the software… not the other way around. In the next sections, we will discuss how we can now take the business process design and transform it into a technical design.

Technical Design and Build

Once you've completed the business process design, you will be in a great position to start the technical design. For all the nerds reading (which I assume is the majority of the audience for this book), you can rest easy because we are finally getting to the technical stuff.

The technical design is when we determine *where* our data is going to go, *what* calculations we need to build, and *how* users are going to interact with the solution. We will use the information collected from the business process design to guide us. The basic components of the technical design are shown below. We will break each of these down in the next sections.

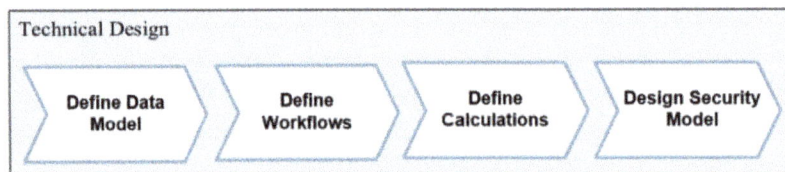

Figure 5.5

Defining the Data Model

The data model refers to how all the data related to the plan is organized in OneStream. This includes data imports, user inputs, and data that is derived from calculations.

It's important to consider all the above options when designing the overall data model. Not all data should, or needs to, reside in the cubes.

The final picture of your data model will largely depend on the plan types, methods, and plan data sources identified in the business process design. The goal of this part of the design is to create a data model that meets the reporting needs of the organization while performing well and requiring the least amount of maintenance.

Picking the Right Tool for the Job

The first key to success in designing your data model is to align each set of data to the appropriate tool in OneStream. The OneStream platform offers a lot of ways data can be stored, calculated, and analyzed.

- Cubes
- Relational tables (includes specialty planning)
- Staging tables
- Analytic Blend

Cubes are great at storing, consolidating, and giving fast access to summary data. They are not designed, however, to hold large volumes of transactional data. Putting unnecessary or misplaced data in the cube can lead to performance issues. If you wanted to use a cube to retrieve all potential voters in the US, you'd likely have dimensions for state, county, and party registration, but would stop short of creating individual voter names within a dimension as it would be millions of members. Further, storing this data in a cube would be cumbersome to maintain and cause performance issues. Think about how often you'd have to add a new member to the voter dimension! Instead, the data can remain in staging tables where it can be drilled into from the cube. Analytic Blend can also be used for analytical purposes.

To review, data in the cube should:

- Require financial intelligence
- Require stored aggregations and consolidation
- Require complex calculations
- Require the ability for users to both read and write
- Not be transactional in nature
- Not have frequently changing or transient metadata
- Not be textual in nature

If a dataset doesn't meet these requirements, it can probably be better stored elsewhere without sacrificing analytic value.

Perhaps equally as important as determining what data goes into your cubes is understanding what data *does not* belong in the cube. Throughout a planning implementation, you are likely to need a variety of data types to support the plan. Keeping this data outside of the cube can drastically improve overall performance and user experience without compromising functionality.

Some examples of data types that you may need to support your planning solutions but which can remain outside the cube:

- Production dates
- Vacation and holiday schedules
- Invoice detail

- Text attributes

- Transactional data

- Transient data

In other CPM tools, it was assumed that this data would need to reside in the same place as the financial data if it was needed in calculations or reports. This was mostly because there were limited alternative options. If it couldn't go into the cube, then it needed to remain outside of the system in an Excel spreadsheet, Access database, or a third-party tool. OneStream has unique capabilities, however, to store data outside the cube while being totally accessible to users in reports, forms, and business rules. In the next sections, we'll discuss the various options we have in OneStream to store these types of data.

How the data is ultimately used will largely determine where it should reside in OneStream. Understanding reporting needs, whether users need write access to edit it, and how it needs to be reported will be important factors in your decision.

Cubes and Dimensions

We will start the data model discussion with cubes. Although cube data is stored in a relational database, it best services a multidimensional data model. It has a powerful consolidation, aggregation, and calculation engine, along with robust financial intelligence and reporting tools. All cube and dimension designs should leverage extensibility to the greatest extent possible. Extensibility will give your cubes ultimate flexibility and optimize performance.

By using extensibility, you will significantly reduce the build-time of the project and the maintenance going forward. Perhaps more importantly, extensibility can have a tremendous impact on business processes and how companies produce their financial plans. In my experience, when implementing planning solutions for large organizations, most companies start with a very disjointed planning landscape. Various teams within their organizations use a variety of methods and tools to get their financial plans. Then, there is another separate team that must cobble everything together to get it on a report. I have seen 20MB Excel files that crash half the time you try to open them. The maintenance burden and margin for error is just too high. Extensibility is the tool that can help solve these problems. It's an opportunity to standardize dimensions, calculations, and data. In planning design sessions, I try to push organizations into standardizing as much as possible.

Before we dive into the details of how we can use extensibility, we need to define a few other items. We'll first define our Scenario Types and scenarios, then we'll determine the inventory of reporting dimensions we need to support the reporting for each plan type. From there, we will look at the unique properties of the Entity dimension and determine which dimension we should assign as our entity. After that, we will assign the rest of our dimensions in a matrix. Last, but certainly not least, we will determine our cubes and circle back to extensibility.

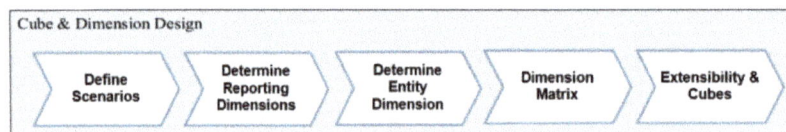

Figure 5.6

Scenarios

The Scenario dimension is a logical starting point when designing cubes and dimensions, as they will need to be clearly defined before considering extensibility.

Beyond extensibility, there is a lot of flexibility around Scenario built into other areas of the OneStream platform as well. Member properties, calculations, and workflow can all have different settings by Scenario Type. Because of this, designing the Scenario dimension first usually makes sense, as it will have implications for almost every other design element.

To determine the number of scenarios you will need to create to support all planning processes – plan types are a great place to start. It is usually easy for an organization to tell you all the plan types they produce. It's rarely a good idea to ask, "How many planning scenarios do you have?", however, as you are likely to draw confusion, especially if the customer does not have experience with other CPM solutions. Rather, framing the question around plan types will prompt them to describe their normal business processes, which can then be translated into the number of scenarios and Scenario Types.

Scenario Types

Scenario Types are a way to group scenarios that will share common dimensions, properties, and calculations. Dimension member properties, workflow, and calculations are a few examples of behavior that can vary by Scenario Type.

Plan types will generally translate directly to Scenario Types. It's really that simple. If you've identified your plan types in the BPD and collected all the relevant information about them, you've probably already identified your Scenario Types as well. The next step will be to determine the scenario members for each one.

> **Note:** Extending cubes by Scenario Type is referred to as **horizontal extensibility,** which will be discussed at length later in this section.

Naming Conventions

Once you've defined your Scenario Types, it's time to create the individual scenario members for each one; you'll want to give some thought to the naming conventions.

I always hate naming things in OneStream. It's one of the few things that you generally don't change once you've started loading data. So, once you've picked a name, you're stuck with it. I think it's a good idea to create some general guidelines for scenario names and then try to stick to them as closely as possible. Something like `PlanFrequency_PlanDuration_PlanningType`, e.g., `Yearly_12Month_Forecast`, could work for 90% of your scenarios.

In general, planning scenarios that do not span across multiple years can, and should, be reused for subsequent planning cycles. For example, the same Budget scenario that was used for 2020 can be used again in 2021. When the plan duration of a scenario does span across multiple years, it is typically best practice to create 'year-specific' scenarios by appending the year to the scenario name, e.g., `Budget_2020`, `Budget_2021`. This is because there will likely be data overlap in planning cycles from year to year. If the 2020 budget has an 18-month plan duration, there will already be data in the first six months of 2021 when the 2021 budget cycle starts. It is certainly possible to clear the data before starting the 2021 budget, but other elements such as audit logs and workflow statuses will be more cumbersome to reset. A general rule of thumb is that if a plan duration spans across multiple years, a scenario member should be created per year.

Scenario versions (which are covered in a later section) should also be considered.

Input Frequencies

Input frequency is a technical setting on scenario members that defines how the data will be entered within the Time dimension. The input frequencies that OneStream supports are illustrated below:

Chapter 5

Yearly: Year is the lowest level of granularity and accepts input.

	2024	2025	2026	2027	2028
Operating Result					
Sales	15,000,000.00	19,050,000.00	21,717,000.00	24,757,380.00	28,223,413.20
Growth		25.00%	12.00%	12.00%	12.00%
Consolidated Gross Margin	6,750,000.00	8,572,500.00	9,772,650.00	11,140,821.00	12,700,535.94
Gross Margin Rate	45.00%	45.00%	45.00%	45.00%	45.00%

Monthly: Choose the number of planning periods and locked actual periods.

	2024M1	2024M2	2024M3	2024M4	2024M5	2024M6	2024M7	2024M8	2024M9	2024M10	2024M11	2024M12
Operating Result												
Sales	406,040.10	422,526.96	552,365.75	462,111.51	480,875.09	628,643.75	529,926.00	547,280.71	715,455.22	598,522.85	622,856.50	814,254.78
Growth	1.00%	1.00%	1.00%	1.00%	1.00%	1.00%	1.00%	1.00%	1.00%	1.00%	1.00%	1.00%
Consolidated Gross Margin	182,718.05	184,545.23	186,390.68	188,254.58	190,137.13	192,038.50	193,958.89	195,898.48	197,857.46	199,836.06	201,834.40	203,852.74
Gross Margin Rate	45.00%	45.00%	45.00%	45.00%	45.00%	45.00%	45.00%	45.00%	45.00%	45.00%	45.00%	45.00%

Mixed: Apply a mix for longer planning periods. The first year is monthly, then it becomes yearly. Months and years both accept input.

	2024M1	2024M2	2024M3	2024M4	2024M5	2024M6	2024M7	2024M8	2024M9	2024M10	2024M11	2024M12	2025	2026	2027	2028
Operating Result																
Sales	406,040.10	422,526.96	552,365.75	462,111.51	480,875.09	628,643.75	529,926.00	547,280.71	715,455.22	598,522.85	622,856.50	814,254.78	5,802,574.68	6,538,341.15	7,367,402.81	8,301,589.48
Growth	1.00%	1.00%	1.00%	1.00%	1.00%	1.00%	1.00%	1.00%	1.00%	1.00%	1.00%	1.00%	12.68%	12.68%	12.68%	12.68%
Consolidated Gross Margin	182,718.05	184,545.23	186,390.68	188,254.58	190,137.13	192,038.50	193,958.89	195,898.48	197,857.46	199,836.06	201,834.40	203,852.74	2,611,158.61	2,942,253.52	3,315,331.26	3,735,715.27
Gross Margin Rate	45.00%	45.00%	45.00%	45.00%	45.00%	45.00%	45.00%	45.00%	45.00%	45.00%	45.00%	45.00%	45.00%	45.00%	45.00%	45.00%

Weekly: The maximum granularity is weeks. The distribution of weeks among months and the number of days per week can be configured.

	2024W1	2024W2	2024W3	2024W4	2024W5	2024W6	2024W7	2024W8	2024W9	2024W10	2024W11	2024W12	2024W13	2024W14	2024W15	2024W16
Operating Result																
Sales	100,000.00	101,000.00	102,000.00	103,000.00	104,000.00	105,000.00	106,000.00	107,000.00	108,000.00	109,000.00	110,000.00	111,000.00	112,000.00	113,000.00	114,000.00	115,000.00
Growth	1.00%	1.00%	1.00%	1.00%	1.00%	1.00%	1.00%	1.00%	1.00%	1.00%	1.00%	1.00%	1.00%	1.00%	1.00%	1.00%
Consolidated Gross Margin	45,000.00	46,000.00	47,000.00	48,000.00	49,000.00	50,000.00	51,000.00	52,000.00	53,000.00	54,000.00	55,000.00	56,000.00	57,000.00	58,000.00	59,000.00	60,000.00
Gross Margin Rate	45.00%	45.00%	45.00%	45.00%	45.00%	45.00%	45.00%	45.00%	45.00%	45.00%	45.00%	45.00%	45.00%	45.00%	45.00%	45.00%

Figure 5.7

Examples

Scenario members can be configured for a nearly infinite number of plan types. We can't cover every possibility in this chapter, so we'll go through some common examples of plan types and how to apply the various scenario properties. This should give you a pretty good idea of what each property does and how you can apply them to your unique requirements.

Example 1: Yearly Budget

Plan Type: Budget

Preparation Cycle: Once a year

Input Frequency: Monthly

Plan Duration: 12 months

Plan Input View: Periodic (month-to-date)

⊟ Workflow	
Use In Workflow	True
Workflow Tracking Frequency	Yearly
Workflow Time	
Workflow Start Time	
Workflow End Time	
Number Of No Input Periods Per Workflow Unit	0
⊟ Settings	
Scenario Type	Budget
Input Frequency (Vary By Year)	Monthly
Use Input Frequency Data In Lower Frequencies	False
Default View	Periodic
Retain Next Period Data Using Default View	False
Input View For Adjustments	Periodic
Use Input View For Adj In Calculations	False
No Data Zero View For Adjustments	Periodic
No Data Zero View For NonAdjustments	Periodic
Consolidation View	Periodic
Formula	
Formula For Calculation Drill Down	
Clear Calculated Data During Calc	False
Use Two Pass Elimination	False
Allow Input Into the Aggregated Consolidation Member	False

Figure 5.8

We set the Workflow Tracking Frequency to Yearly, which means this scenario will be prepared once a year. The plan duration of 12 months means we won't span across years, and we can 'reuse' this scenario every year.

Example 2: 12-Month YTG Forecast

Plan Type: Forecast

Preparation Cycle: Once a month

Input Frequency: Monthly

Plan Duration: Variable

Plan Input View: Periodic (month-to-date)

For this example, we will end up with 12 scenarios since the preparation cycle is once a month. The naming convention for our scenarios will be Forecast_MX, where X represents the month number.

Scenario Name	Plan Months	Actual Months
Forecast_M1	12	0
Forecast_M2	11	1
Forecast_M3	10	2
Forecast_M4	9	3
Forecast_M5	8	4
Forecast_M6	7	5
Forecast_M7	6	6
Forecast_M8	5	7
Forecast_M9	4	8
Forecast_M10	3	9
Forecast_M11	2	10
Forecast_M12	1	11

Figure 5.9

General	
Dimension Type	Scenario Dimension Type
Dimension	Scenarios Dimension
Member Dimension	Scenarios Dimension
Id	1048664
Name	Forecast_M3
⊞ Descriptions	
⊞ Security	
⊟ Workflow	
Use In Workflow	True
Workflow Tracking Frequency	All Time Periods
Workflow Time	
Workflow Start Time	
Workflow End Time	
Number Of No Input Periods Per Workflow Unit	2
⊟ Settings	
Scenario Type	Forecast
Input Frequency (Vary By Year)	Monthly
Use Input Frequency Data In Lower Frequencies	False
Default View	Periodic
Retain Next Period Data Using Default View	True
Input View For Adjustments	Periodic
Use Input View For Adj In Calculations	False
No Data Zero View For Adjustments	Periodic
No Data Zero View For NonAdjustments	Periodic
Consolidation View	Periodic
Formula	
Formula For Calculation Drill Down	
Clear Calculated Data During Calc	False
Use Two Pass Elimination	False
Allow Input Into the Aggregated Consolidation Member	False

Figure 5.10

For our year-to-go (YTG) forecast, the number of forecasted months will vary from month to month as Actual data is reported.

It's important to point out the use of All Time Periods as the Workflow Tracking Frequency. Since this scenario does not span across multiple years, it can be reused in subsequent years. This means we want to make all time periods available to this scenario and not restrict it to a range. Also, notice the use of No Input Periods. Since this example is for Forecast_M3, the first two months would be populated with Actual data via a seeding rule. Setting the No Input Periods to 2 will remove the risk of users changing already reported historical data. It will also have the added benefit of disabling those columns for input on forms.

Example 3: 12-Month Rolling Forecast

Plan Type: Forecast

Preparation Cycle: Once a month

Input Frequency: Monthly

Plan Duration: 12 months

Plan Input View: Periodic (month-to-date)

The main distinction between a rolling forecast and our YTG forecast example is the fixed plan duration in the rolling forecast. In a rolling forecast, the same number of periods is forecasted *regardless* of what period of the year it is.

Below are the scenario settings.

General	
Dimension Type	Scenario Dimension Type
Dimension	Scenarios Dimension
Member Dimension	Scenarios Dimension
Id	1048665
Name	RollingForecast_2025M3
⊞ Descriptions	
⊞ Security	
Workflow	
Use In Workflow	True
Workflow Tracking Frequency	Range
Workflow Time	2025M3
Workflow Start Time	2025M1
Workflow End Time	2026M2
Number Of No Input Periods Per Workflow Unit	2
Settings	
Scenario Type	Forecast
Input Frequency (Vary By Year)	Monthly
Use Input Frequency Data In Lower Frequencies	False
Default View	Periodic
Retain Next Period Data Using Default View	True
Input View For Adjustments	Periodic
Use Input View For Adj In Calculations	False
No Data Zero View For Adjustments	Periodic
No Data Zero View For NonAdjustments	Periodic
Consolidation View	Periodic
Formula	
Formula For Calculation Drill Down	
Clear Calculated Data During Calc	False
Use Two Pass Elimination	False
Allow Input Into the Aggregated Consolidation Member	False

Figure 5.11

Since scenarios for this plan type will cross over multiple years, the naming convention is `RollingForecast_YearMonthNumber`. Also, note the difference in the workflow settings. A tracking frequency of Range is used with a start time of 2025M1 and an end-time of 2026M2 for a total of 14 months (two months of Actual data and 12 months of Forecast data). I will also point out that using a range should include months back to M1 in order to get a full-year view in reports. In 2026, a new rolling Forecast scenario will be created since there will be an overlap of periods.

Example 4: Five-Year Long Range Plan

Plan Type: Long term

Preparation Cycle: Once a year

Input Frequency: Monthly in the first year, yearly in years 2-5

Plan Duration: Five years

Plan Input View: Periodic (month-to-date & year-to-date)

For our five-year plan, we'll need to include the year in the scenario name since we are spanning across multiple years. I like to use the year in which the plan is being prepared. I have also seen the final year of the plan used.

General	
Dimension Type	Scenario Dimension Type
Dimension	Scenarios Dimension
Member Dimension	Scenarios Dimension
Id	1048666
Name	2025_5YearPlan
⊞ Descriptions	
⊞ Security	
⊟ Workflow	
Use In Workflow	True
Workflow Tracking Frequency	All Time Periods
Workflow Time	
Workflow Start Time	
Workflow End Time	
Number Of No Input Periods Per Workflow Unit	0
⊟ Settings	
Scenario Type	LongTerm
Input Frequency (Vary By Year)	(+1 Item) Monthly
Use Input Frequency Data In Lower Frequencies	False
Default View	Periodic
Retain Next Period Data Using Default View	True
Input View For Adjustments	Periodic
Use Input View For Adj In Calculations	False
No Data Zero View For Adjustments	Periodic
No Data Zero View For NonAdjustments	Periodic
Consolidation View	Periodic
Formula	
Formula For Calculation Drill Down	
Clear Calculated Data During Calc	False
Use Two Pass Elimination	False
Allow Input Into the Aggregated Consolidation Member	False

Figure 5.12

The Input Frequency can vary by year, so it is set as Monthly in the first year and Yearly from 2026 onwards.

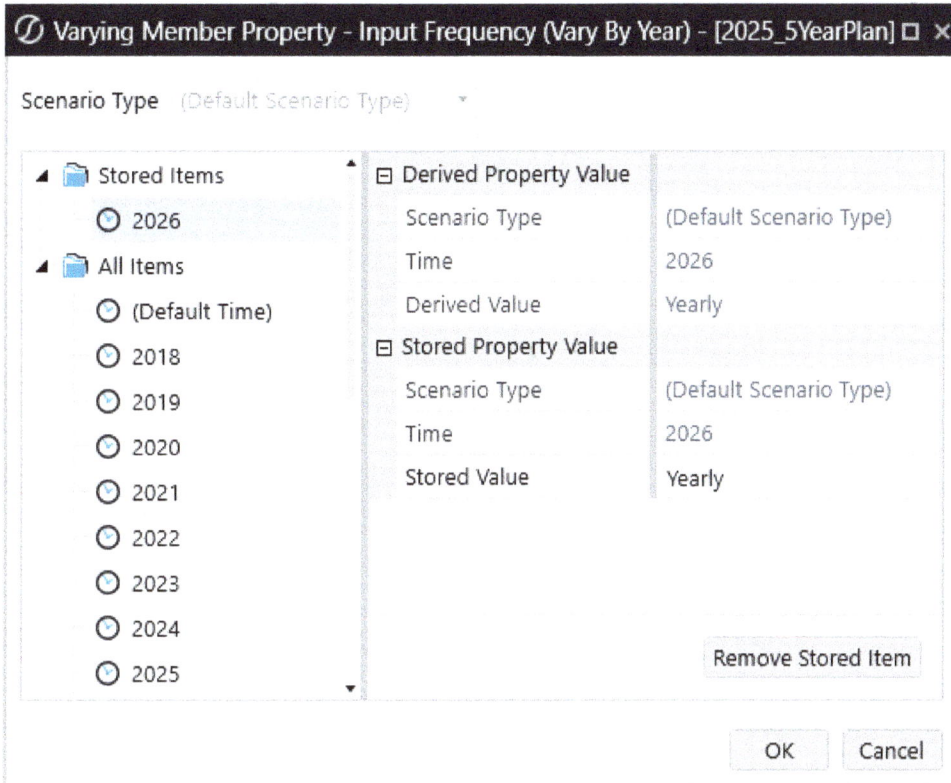

Figure 5.13

Versions

During a planning cycle, there may be a requirement to track the changes made at certain points in the cycle either to monitor accuracy, or to present significant changes in the plan to management. Versions will typically relate to the same plan type (e.g., Budget Version 1, Budget Version 2, etc.). Creating the storage point will allow for easy reporting and trend analysis of the different versions.

There are generally two ways to handle planning versions within OneStream, with one being the recommended method. The first involves the creation of additional scenario members to track each version. The 'baseline' or **version 0** scenario can be cloned and copied quickly and potentially reused in subsequent cycles. A good technique for naming conventions is to use a suffix appended to the end of the related scenario. For example, V1, V2, V3, etc., would be appended to Budget with an underscore to create Budget_V1, Budget_V2, and Budget_V3 scenario members. This suffix can then be parsed out and referenced in business rules, reports, and dashboard menus to streamline the user experience when toggling between versions.

It is likely that data will need to be copied from the baseline scenario into each version, rather than starting each version from scratch. For this, a scenario formula can be utilized, using the suffix to dynamically pull data from the prior version.

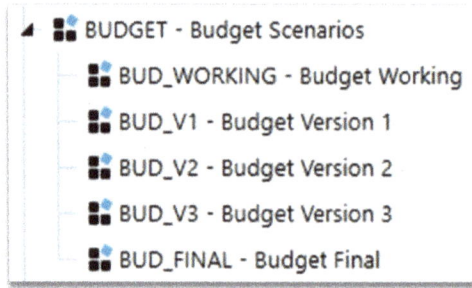

Figure 5.14

The second option would be to track versions within the same scenario using a UD dimension.

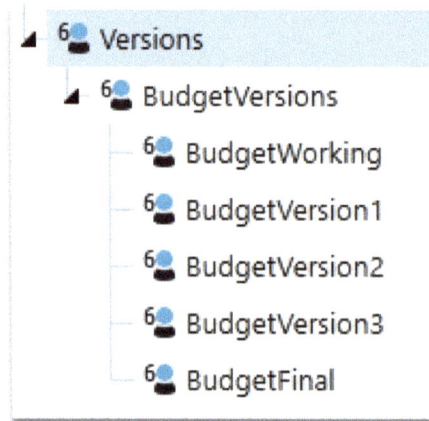

Figure 5.15

The recommended method for versioning is to use scenarios, but there may be instances where the UD method makes sense. The driver for making the decision between the two options comes down to dimension availability, performance, and process requirements. If you have used all 8 UD dimensions or plan to use them in the future, then using a UD for versions is not an option. From a performance standpoint, adding scenario versions will have no effect on the performance of other scenarios since you are creating an additional Data Unit. Creating additional UD members and copying data to them could significantly increase the size of the Data Unit and slow down aggregations, calculations, and reports. Also, since the UD dimensions are outside the Workflow Unit, they cannot be locked down without assigning the version UD as a channel. If another UD dimension is assigned as the channel dimension, then the option to lock down channels would be lost.

There are, however, a few benefits to taking the UD dimension approach. First, version data may not need to be copied from version to version since it can be aggregated within the scenario in the UD dimension member hierarchy. Second, the UD dimension members can be re-used and applied to ALL scenarios that need versions. This means that there won't be a need to create additional versions for each Scenario Type that needs them.

In addition to the technical setup, the process of *how* versions are used should be considered. If users will be working across multiple dimensions, the process should offer clear cut-off points as to when they should stop working in one version and move to the next. Another approach is to create a 'live' scenario, where users will always work, and have an admin copy data off to each version. Again, setting and communicating the cut-off points is key, and the process should be clear and well-defined before discussing the technical set up.

What-if Scenarios

What-if scenarios are similar to versions in that they will likely have data copied into them and then be modified (based on new assumptions). When creating what-if scenarios, the same principles as versions should be applied.

It's important to note that there is no 'out-of-the-box' functionality for what-if scenario analysis. OneStream simply provides the ability to create new scenarios, copy data, and leverage the same properties and assumptions as existing scenarios.

While simple things like overlaying a high-level adjustment to a what-if scenario are possible with minimal incremental development, there are no inherent 'what-if' capabilities unless they are built. For example, if a driver-based planning methodology is used to create the budget, then the Budget What If scenario would be created with the same Scenario Type and would use the same methodology. A user could change a driver value and recalculate the plan, but could not calculate a new plan by applying a factor instead. This, of course, can be built, but it should be treated as a new 'plan type' and designed from beginning to end as such.

It is also important to note that OneStream has addressed what-if scenarios with a Solution Exchange tool that can be quickly configured and deployed.

Scenario Analysis 1-2-3 affords users the ability to quickly create and iterate through several what-if scenarios utilizing different driver-based rules in order to efficiently analyze different outcomes. The solution allows for the creation and management of multiple rules and the execution of calculation jobs and scenarios. The solution also includes built-in reporting capabilities to compare results across scenarios.

It is likely that additional what-if solutions and capabilities will be addressed within the Solution Exchange or with platform updates in the future.

Determine Reporting Dimensions

Now that we've defined our Scenario Types and scenarios, we'll need to figure out what dimensions will need to be supported for reporting. Each Scenario Type should be looked at separately as they could require different dimensions or levels of detail within the same dimension. The best place to start is by scrubbing through reports or looking at legacy system configurations. You should also consider Actuals in this exercise, as Actual data is likely to be shown alongside planning in many reports. If there is an Actuals or consolidation cube in OneStream already, then this should be easy.

After you have a complete inventory of dimensions, the next step is to look for commonalities between them. Often, the personnel responsible for one plan type are completely different from one another, and they may use different names to describe the same dimension. For example, the team that prepares the budget may use a dimension called 'Department' while the forecast team uses 'Division'. After a bit of questioning, you might determine these are the same thing. This may be the first time these processes have existed in the same tool. This is the chance to align and standardize the processes. You will also find dimensions that are unique to a plan type.

Also, note any technical dimensions that are uncovered. **Technical dimensions** are dimensions that don't provide any analytic or reporting value but can provide support for a technical process. An example would be a data source dimension, which could allow data to be cleared only for one data source in the loading process.

After identifying all the dimensions, I like to lay them out in a matrix so that it is easy to see which dimensions are relevant for each plan type.

Dimensions	Plan Type			
	Actual	Strategic Plan	Budget	Forecast
Accounts	X	X	X	X
Legal Entity	X	X	X	
Product	X	X	X	X
Cost Center	X		X	X
Department	X		X	X
Data Source (technical)	X	X	X	X

Figure 5.16

The data model is now starting to take shape, and we can start to see some commonalities and differences with dimensions across the plan types.

Determine Entity Dimension

A note on consolidation: The next few sections will make mention of the consolidation process and Actuals reporting. Consolidation is often viewed as the antithesis to planning. Consolidation is reporting history, while planning is reporting the future. Consolidation has strict accounting and legal rules that all companies must follow, while planning employs a variety of methodologies at the behest of the individual planner.

It is unlikely any of your plan types will have statutory consolidation or GAAP reporting requirements; if they do, they will likely be very minimal. However, if any of your plan type requirements include any of the below, then using the same Entity dimension as your consolidation cube is probably a requirement instead of an option.

- Intercompany eliminations

- Currency overrides

- Percent ownership

- Joint venture or equity method accounting

If you've determined that you need one or more of these in planning (again, a rare case), then have a good read through the Consolidation Chapter (4). I would also suggest leveraging existing consolidation functionality that has already been built to the best extent possible.

Once you've defined all the reporting dimensions, you'll need to start assigning them to one of the dimension types in OneStream. The first dimension that should be assigned is the Entity dimension.

It's vital not to understate the importance of the Entity dimension selection as it is crucial for a variety of functions inside OneStream. Here is a brief summary of the functions that the Entity dimension controls across the product.

- **Extensibility** – extensible cubes require a common Entity dimension. If you want to extend a cube by Scenario Type, sharing an Entity dimension is a requirement.

- **Calculations and consolidations** – entity is part of the *Data Unit*. Calculations and consolidations in OneStream run for all data in a Data Unit. Data Units also process in parallel, so spreading data across more Data Units will generally perform faster than the same data volume in fewer Data Units. See Chapter 14 for a more in-depth analysis of cube size and sparsity, and the impact on performance.

- **Translation** – the currency of the financial data loaded to the cube is designated in the Entity dimension. Data is translated from entity currency to parent currency.

> **Note:** there are special functions within the Flow dimension that allow multi-currency input within an entity.

- **Reporting** – the Entity dimension determines data storage points. Data stored in more entities will require less dynamic processing when generating reports, resulting in better-performing reports.

- **Workflow** – entity is part of the Workflow Unit that controls the data loading, locking, and clearing mechanisms.

- **Security** – security that is entity-driven requires much less maintenance than security at the Account-level dimensions.

Given how much functionality is dependent on the Entity dimension, it is important that you make the right selection. There is a lot to consider, and there will likely be tradeoffs. Each potential Entity dimension candidate should be weighed against all the factors listed above. The next sections will outline some guidelines and considerations for determining the Entity dimension assignment in your cube(s).

Align the Entity Dimension Across Scenario Types as Much as Possible

The first question you should ask yourself is if it is feasible to use the same Entity dimension for all Scenario Types. It is highly likely that showing Actual and planning data side by side on the same reports is a customer requirement. Sharing an entity is the easiest way to make that possible with minimal maintenance or additional build work.

Sharing an entity does have consequences and assumes there is enough similarity between the data in the Scenario Types to warrant it. Sometimes Scenario Types are just fundamentally different in their reporting, collection process, and data structure, and sharing an entity will do more harm than good. Let's explore what we should look out for when considering an Entity dimension for a planning Scenario Type. We will assume we have an existing consolidation cube using Legal entity as the Entity dimension, and we are considering using Legal entity for planning.

Submission Process and Workflow

Sharing an Entity dimension assumes at least some similarity in how the data is entered into the system across Scenario Types. Let's say the general process of our consolidation scenario is that a user submits a trial balance for a Legal entity, enters some data into a form, then validates and certifies the data. We can easily see that this submission process is driven by Legal entity. Now, let's say our budget process is driven by department. Budgets are entered by department managers for an entire department across many Legal entities. OneStream's workflow is flexible enough to handle this situation, but there are a few things to keep in mind.

First, you'll need to use a **workflow suffix** to vary the workflow structure by Scenario Type.

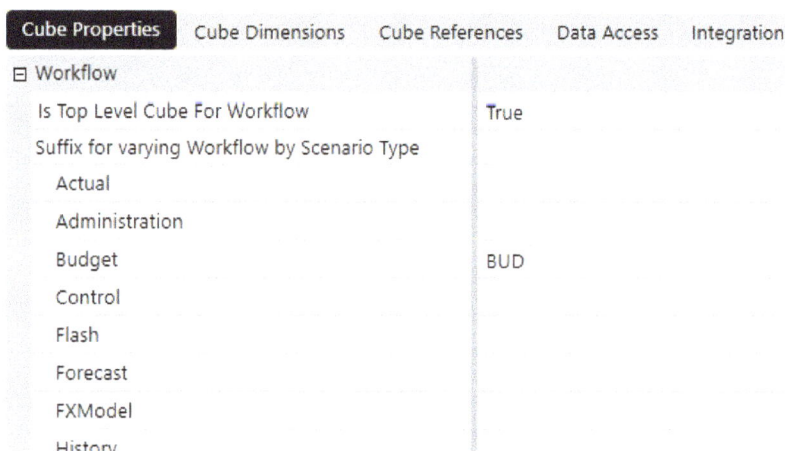

Figure 5.17

Entering data across multiple entities in one workflow breaks up the **Workflow Unit**, which means you'll have to take special care with how data is imported and locked. If locking or importing data by department is a requirement, the use of **workflow channels** will need to be employed to break the Workflow Unit. Note that only one UD dimension can be assigned to a workflow channel and this setting is made at the *application level*. This means that if two Scenario Types need a different dimension as the channel, only one dimension can be used as a channel, and the other will have to use a different entity.

If data locking is not a requirement, and data importing is not needed or done centrally, this won't be a big deal.

Refer to Chapter 7 for more information about workflow design.

Performance

When I talk about performance, I am specifically referring to two things:

- **Consolidation and calculation performance** – how quickly OneStream is able to process and store data within Data Units.

- **Reporting performance** – how quickly OneStream is able to derive and display cube data on reports or data queries.

A key driver of performance is Data Unit size and sparsity. Remember that entity is part of the Data Unit, so the choice for Entity dimension will have a direct impact on these two things.

Using the same Entity dimension across Scenario Types could result in vastly different Data Unit size and sparsity between them. This could be due to a Scenario Type using more dimensions or the same dimension but at a greater level of detail. When considering an Entity dimension, the number of data records within Data Units should be estimated as best as possible to get an idea for performance. If the number of data records is large (>500k records), you should consider a different dimension as the Entity to create less data record volume and sparsity.

Data Copying

Scenario Types that do not share an Entity dimension will pose a challenge if the data needs to reside on the same reports, or if one is used as a source for the other. Getting the data to a point of symmetry will require data copying to transpose data from one cube to another. In some cases, this can be complex and have a performance impact.

Let's look at our consolidation cube with Legal entity as the entity, and our planning cube with Department as entity. Requirements dictate that we need to show data from both cubes on the same report. This wouldn't be possible without some additional work. First, we'll need to assume that Department exists in the consolidation cube as UD dimension. Next, we'll need to copy the data from one cube into the other. One way to do it would be to create an 'Actual' scenario in the planning cube, and write a rule to copy the data from the consolidation cube into the planning cube. The rule would transpose the Department UD dimension from the consolidation cube into the Entity dimension of the planning cube. Note that intercompany detail would need to be ignored to make this work.

Data copying is a trade-off for having cubes with different Entity dimensions. While each cube may perform better overall, the data copying is an added step in the process.

Translation

Currency translation happens in the Entity dimension. If currency translation is part of your planning requirements, and you've designated a different entity than Actuals, you will have to take special consideration to set up the currency translation correctly.

To illustrate this, let's look at an example of a company that has a consolidation cube with currency translation based on the functional currency of the Legal entity. For planning, Department is used as the Entity dimension with department managers entering a budget for a single department spanning across multiple currencies.

This design is possible by using the **alternate input currency** functionality within the Flow dimension. Each Department entity would be designated with the reporting currency, and currency input would be controlled within the Flow. All data would be translated back to the entity's currency during the Data Unit Calculation Sequence.

Conclusion on Entity Dimension

We've covered quite a bit regarding the Entity dimension, and I hope you leave this section less confused than when you entered it. The major takeaways from this section should be understanding the functions of the Entity dimension in OneStream and ensuring you spend the proper time determining the Entity dimension(s) needed for each Plan Type.

To summarize what we've covered, I think everything boils down to these main points:

- Align your entities across financial processes as much as possible so that extensibility can be leveraged.

- Give adequate consideration to data volumes and sparsity (by Data Unit) early in the build and assign the Entity dimension to plan types accordingly.

- Get data into the cube as early as possible and monitor performance. If performance is acceptable, then don't second-guess your decision.

- Understand requirements around data submitting, loading, and locking for each plan type.

- If performance is unacceptable, there are several considerations to make for picking the right Entity dimension. Weigh the pros and cons of each, discuss with relevant stakeholders, and decide. Refer to the Performance Tuning Chapter for a more in-depth discussion of how to analyze and troubleshoot performance issues.

Sometimes, a particular Entity dimension just won't fit for some plan types, and that's perfectly fine. Don't force a square peg into a round hole. It's better to have optimally performing standalone cubes than one extended cube that performs poorly for some Scenario Types. There are a lot of factors to consider, and there will often be trade-offs. One choice for the Entity dimension might streamline reporting but create longer-running calculations or aggregations or make the security model more complex.

Let me offer a personal anecdote from a project where I was the architect for a large driver-based planning implementation. We created a driver cube to hold all the drivers used in the calculations.

In the reporting cube, `Business Unit` was used as the Entity dimension as it was the driver of intercompany eliminations and workflow. Since the driver data was not related to any one business unit, there didn't seem to be an obvious choice for Entity. We ended up loading all the driver data into one Entity called `Global`. When we loaded the data in, we had more than a million data records in the Global Entity for one month. This was a perfect example of a 'large, sparse Data Unit'. The cube performed horribly. Data loads, calculations, and reports all took much longer than was tolerable. We knew right away; we made a mistake in our Entity dimension choice. After looking at data volumes and which dimension would create the densest Data Units, we ended up pivoting Account as the entity, which was somewhat counter-intuitive to traditional thinking. Performance was almost night and day. Learn from my mistake and give the proper attention to the Entity dimension upfront, so you can prevent a major headache later.

Refine your Dimension Matrix

Now that we've determined what to use for the Entity dimension across our Scenario Types, we can refine our dimension matrix a bit more. First, we can now assign dimension types to our dimensions. Next, we can look at each dimension and determine the level of detail each Scenario Type needs. Some dimensions can use higher or lower levels of detail depending on the needs of that Scenario Type.

Dimension Type	Dimension	Scenario Type			
		Actual	Plan	Budget	Forecast
Entity	Legal Entity	x	x	x	
Entity	Cost Center				x
Account	SummaryAccounts	x	x		
	Detail Accounts			x	x
UD1	Product Family	x	x		
	Product Type			x	
	Product				x
UD2	Cost Center			x	
UD3	Department			x	x
UD4	Data Source (technical)	x	x	x	x

Figure 5.18

Our data model is almost there! The last steps will be to apply extensibility and assign our dimensions to cubes.

Cubes and Extensibility

Now that we've set up scenarios, picked the right Entity dimension, and defined the reporting dimensions, we can now determine how those dimensions will be assigned to cubes.

I started this section by talking about extensibility and how important it is, but then veered off a bit. The ultimate number of cubes we will need will depend on how we use extensibility. We'll start by defining the different types of extensibility we have.

Types of Extensibility

As Peter mentioned in Chapter 4, there are two types of extensibility – **horizontal** and **vertical extensibility**.

Horizontal extensibility refers to the concept of sharing, inheriting, and extending dimensions across financial processes or **Scenario Types**. Horizontal extensibility does not require the creation of multiple cubes. When using horizontal extensibility, each Scenario Type can have its own level of reporting detail while still retaining a point of commonality through inherited dimensions.

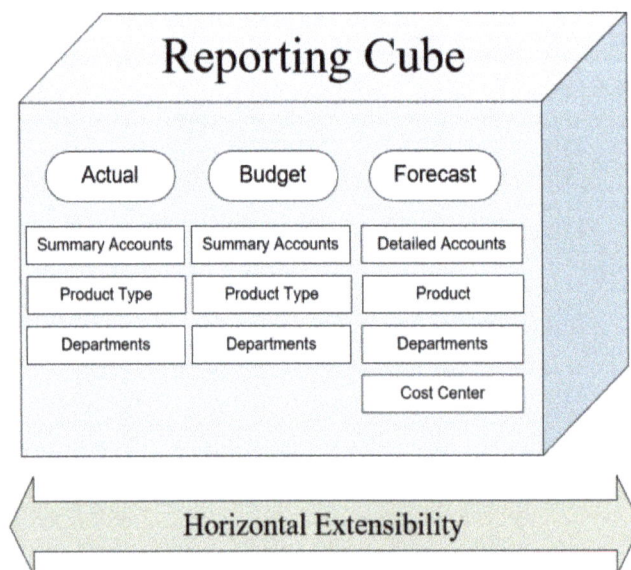

Figure 5.19

Horizontal extensibility takes place within the same cube, with all Scenario Types sharing the same Entity dimension. Accounts, flows, and UD dimensions can be assigned differently for each Scenario Type.

Vertical extensibility refers to sharing and extending dimensions by *entities.* It requires breaking the entity hierarchy apart into multiple cubes. A master cube will contain the full entity hierarchy and consolidate data from the sub-cubes. Each sub-cube can have its own dimensions or levels of detail within the same dimension. This allows for both a better-performing and more flexible cube design.

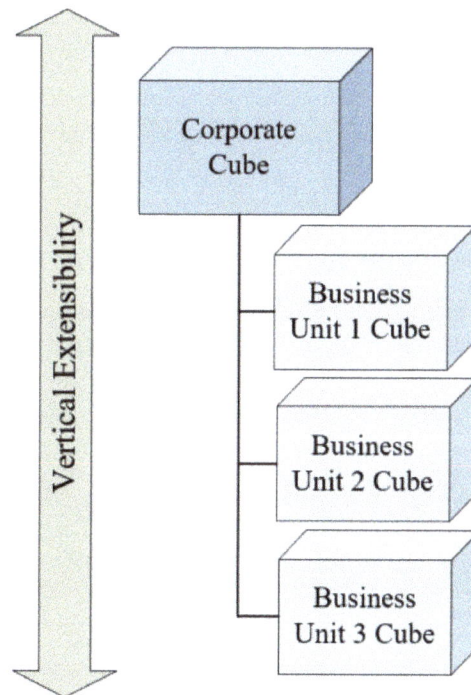

Figure 5.20

Each business unit has its own Entity dimension, which is inherited in the corporate cubes Entity dimension. Accounts, flows, and UD dimensions can be assigned differently for each BU cube.

> **Note**: In each type of extensibility, both the Entity and Scenario dimension must be shared.

How to Apply Extensibility

Now that you understand the different types of extensibility, a lightbulb hopefully went off when I described horizontal extensibility. This type of extensibility allows you to extend cubes by Scenario Type, which suits planning perfectly since several plan types will typically exist. Let's look at some common situations and how cubes and extensibility can be applied differently.

Example 1: One Cube – Extended by Scenario Type

For this example, we have all Scenario Types using the same Entity dimension, which means we only need one cube extended by Scenario Type.

149

Dimension Type	Dimension	Cube: Reporting			
	Scenario Type:	Actual	Plan	Budget	Forecast
Entity	Legal Entity	x	x	x	x
Account	SummaryAccounts	x	x		
	Detail Accounts			x	x
UD1	Product Family	x	x		
	Product Type			x	
	Product				x
UD2	Cost Center			x	
UD3	Department			x	x
UD4	Data Source (technical)	x	x	x	x

Figure 5.21

In this situation, each Scenario Type is free to use different dimensions or different levels of the same dimension. This provides each Scenario Type with maximum flexibility and easy reporting by creating commonality within all dimensions.

Example 2: Separate Cubes – Consolidation & Planning Cube

For this example, we've determined that all our planning Scenario Types will use a different Entity dimension than consolidation, due to differences in process and high data volumes. This will require two cubes – one for consolidation and one for planning. The planning cube can still make use of horizontal extensibility to assign different dimensions and dimension levels by planning Scenario Type.

Also, notice the Actual Scenario Type being used in the planning cube. This is an optional step that will allow data to be copied from the consolidation cube so that it aligns with the planning cube. By doing this, the planning cube can use the Actual data for calculation or provide variance reporting.

Dimension Type	Dimension	Cube: Consolidation	Cube: Planning			
	Scenario Type:	Actual	Actual	Plan	Budget	Forecast
Entity	Legal Entity	x				
Entity	Cost Center		x	x	x	x
Account	SummaryAccounts	x	x	x		
	Detail Accounts				x	x
UD1	Product Family	x	x	x		
	Product Type				x	
	Product					x
UD2	Cost Center				x	
UD3	Department				x	x
UD4	Data Source (technical)	x	x	x	x	x

⇧

Actual Scenario Type created in planning cube to align data between cubes.

Figure 5.22

Example 3: Hybrid

In this example, we have one planning Scenario Type that shares an entity with the consolidation cube, while the rest of the planning scenarios use cost center. Both cubes will use horizontal extensibility to extend dimensions to different Scenario Types. The Actual Scenario Type is being used in the planning cube here, just like the last example.

Dimension Type	Dimension	Consolidation		Planning		
		Actual	Plan	Actual	Budget	Forecast
Entity	Legal Entity	x	x			
Entity	Cost Center			x	x	x
Account	SummaryAccounts	x	x	x		
	Detail Accounts				x	x
UD1	Product Family	x	x	x		
	Product Type				x	
	Product					x
UD2	Cost Center				x	
UD3	Department				x	x
UD4	Data Source (technical)	x	x	x	x	x

Figure 5.23

Conclusion on Extensibility

Extensibility should always be a part of your cube design. Depending on the requirements you've uncovered during the BPD, there are a few ways it can be applied effectively. Carefully look at each Scenario Type and identify the similarities and differences between them. Then, use extensibility to bring them together in a unified model.

Specialty Cubes

You will likely encounter datasets that need to go into the cube for analytic reasons or where the data is needed in other cubes for calculations. These can sometimes be referred to as specialty cubes. Some examples are:

- Driver data cubes
- Labor reporting cubes
- Profitability cubes

These cubes can still use leverage extensibility and shared dimensions with other cubes if needed, and should be scrutinized with the same principles for optimizing performance and maintenance.

Specialty Planning Solutions

Let's go back to my first planning project, where we deployed People Planning for the first time. The requirement was to calculate employee-related costs using individual attributes for salary, bonus, and benefit categories. To accomplish this, we needed somewhere to store this information. We also needed to run complex calculations against the data to derive the plan.

We could have created a cube with an employee dimension and imported the payroll data to the cube. This was certainly possible but was likely to be a bad idea for several reasons. Over time, this dimension would grow larger and larger as the company hired new employees. Employees who left the company would remain in the cube as they would have data associated with them.

Data structures like this – that are constantly changing, or which are dependent on a point in time – are a good example of **transient data**. This type of data poses a challenge if kept inside the cube due to the constant maintenance that is required to keep the dimensions and members up to date. Performance will also suffer as the cube becomes larger and sparser. Over time, more and more members would be created only to be eventually deprecated.

This data is much better served in a relational table. The data can be collected in a transactional register, where it can be summarized and mapped to a cube. Specialty planning solutions also have a powerful calculation engine that can perform complex logic and math expressions on the transactional data.

Specialty planning should be your go-to tool for requirements like the one above. There are numerous other use cases for specialty planning solutions:

- Asset planning
- Project planning
- Cash planning
- Travel planning
- Sales planning

The use of these solutions should be identified early in the project as they have additional configuration considerations and will influence how cubes are structured.

Staging Tables

Data is staged in the OneStream data integration suite before it is summarized, transformed, and loaded into the cube. The staging tables are designed to hold the raw data from transactional source systems. Staging tables have columns for all 18 dimensions available in the cube, and 40 additional attribute columns. These attribute columns can be used to store detail that can be drilled into from reports.

Say, for example, we are loading sales data, by product, from an external system into our planning cube. The source file contains a field that indicates whether a product has been discontinued. This information has little analytic value, so we may choose not to load it into the cube. However, it still might be useful to know which products are discontinued so that we don't calculate a sales forecast for them. By mapping the data to an attribute column in Stage, we can still easily perform lookups on the staging table in our rules.

A key limitation is that entries into these tables can only be made through the import workflow steps. Users cannot make manual entries into staging tables or edit them through dashboards. For this requirement, it is best to use a custom SQL table.

Chapter 6 on Data Integration goes in-depth on this topic.

Custom SQL Tables

The OneStream database architecture consists of dozens of SQL tables. Most configurations, settings, and mapping tables are stored in SQL tables. Most solutions available in the Solution Exchange use custom SQL tables as well. In addition to the pre-installed tables, additional tables can be created to store custom datasets. When creating custom SQL tables, make sure to consult the client's database administrator and adhere to SQL best practices.

The benefits of SQL tables are that they can be completely customized for the specific dataset you need. You can create a table with two columns or 40, and give each column its own name and data type. Data can be loaded into the tables through Excel using a standard OneStream import template. Table data can also be referenced in business rules using several API and BRAPI functions.

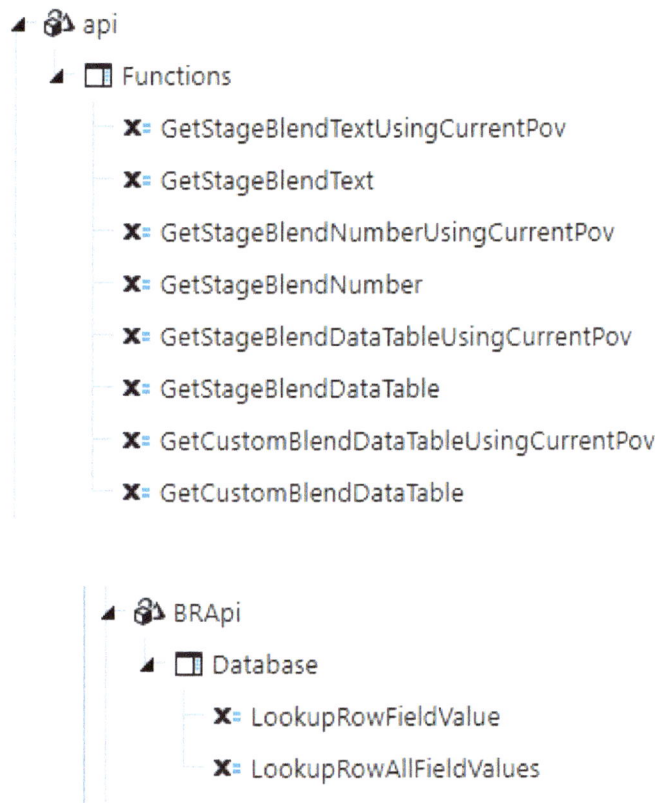

Figure 5.24

Another benefit to custom tables is that they can be integrated into workflows and exposed to users so they can add rows or edit the tables.

Let's take our discontinued product example from before. Instead of the discontinued product information being available in the import file, it needs to be inputted into the system by the product manager. In this case, staging tables will not work as they are read-only and can only be populated via data imports. Instead, we can create a custom SQL table with columns for product name and status. Additional columns could be added to collect other information, such as discontinuation date or reason. Custom SQL tables can be embedded into workflows seamlessly using dashboards.

If a custom SQL table is used in workflow, you should make the table dynamic by adding workflow point of view columns to the table. These can be hidden from the user, and the table can be automatically copied from period to period if needed.

Figure 5.25

A `Where` clause can be used to filter the table to the user's current Workflow POV.

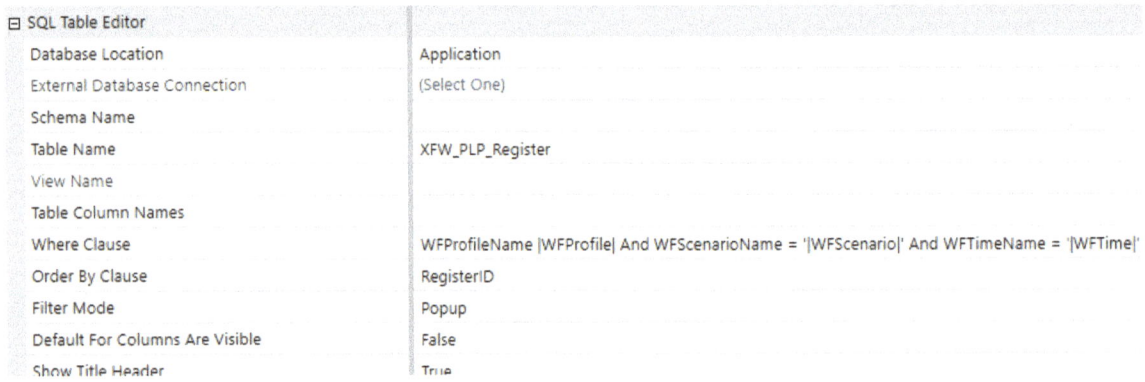

SQL Table Editor	
Database Location	Application
External Database Connection	(Select One)
Schema Name	
Table Name	XFW_PLP_Register
View Name	
Table Column Names	
Where Clause	WFProfileName |WFProfile| And WFScenarioName = '|WFScenario|' And WFTimeName = '|WFTime|'
Order By Clause	RegisterID
Filter Mode	Popup
Default For Columns Are Visible	False
Show Title Header	True

Figure 5.26

Analytic Blend

Analytic Blend is an aggregate storage model designed to support large data volumes that are often transactional in nature. Simple calculations and fast aggregations can be performed on Analytic Blend data. Analytic Blend also has powerful and robust reporting and data visualization tools. A key limitation of Analytic Blend is that it is read-only, so users cannot adjust or make inputs to the data.

If you have a dataset that needs one or more of the above, then you should strongly consider using the Analytic Blend solution.

Refer to Chapter 12 for more detail on how this tool can be used.

Conclusion on Data Model

OneStream is a tool that can handle just about any type of financial planning that takes place within an organization. More and more data is becoming available to FP&A departments, and that data is being used to create more accurate financial plans. This can make plans more intelligent but also poses technical challenges for planning software. During an implementation, it's important to identify *all the data* that is required for the creation of the plan.

Below is a summary of the benefits of each tool.

Tool:	Cube	Staging Tables	Specialty Planning	BI Blend	Custom SQL Table
Data Importing, Transforming & Validation	X	X		X	
Complex Calculation Engine	X		X		
Complex Consolidation Engine	X				
Simple Calculations			X	X	
Simple Aggregations		X		X	
Ability for Manual Entry	X				X
Varies by Workflow	X		X		X
Advanced Reporting	X			X	
Data Visualization Tools	X			X	
Suitable for Large, Sparse Data Sets		X	X	X	X

Figure 5.27

Business Rules and Calculations

Just about every planning solution will need calculations. Luckily, OneStream has a powerful calculation engine that can handle calculations of the highest complexity. Chapter 8 covers business rules basics, so please refer to that chapter for explanations of basic concepts and syntax.

Depending on which plan methods are employed within your solution, you may end up with a large volume of calculations. If you're not careful, you can easily create a monstrosity that is cumbersome to manage and maintain. As stated in the introduction to this chapter, performance and maintenance are the two key benchmarks that you should be constantly thinking about. Nowhere is this more important than when writing calculations. This section will talk you through how to best organize your calculations so that they perform well and are maintainable by the customer.

Determine Rule Types

While OneStream's calculation engine has a common framework, API function library, and syntax, you can break calculations down into their functional objective for organizational purposes. Below are some groupings that can be used:

- **Seeding rules** – rules that move data from one cube or scenario to another within OneStream. For example, copying Actual data to the Actual months of the Forecast.

- **Planning rules** – rules that support the creation of the plan. These can be further broken down into driver-based calculations, allocations, and factor-based calculations.

- **Reporting rules** – dynamic calculations that support reporting, such as ratio or KPIs.

Custom Calculate versus Calculate

When building your cube calculations, you have the option to use two finance function types – calculate or custom calculate. On the surface, the difference can seem subtle but – fundamentally – the difference is quite large.

```
Case Is = FinanceFunctionType.Calculate
    'api.Data.Calculate("A#Profit = A#Sales - A#Costs")

Case Is = FinanceFunctionType.CustomCalculate
    'If args.CustomCalculateArgs.FunctionName.XFEqualsIgnoreCase("Test") Then
    'api.Data.Calculate("A#Profit = A#Sales - A#Costs")
    'End If
```

Custom calculate was actually added to the product as a direct response to the needs of planning projects. It is recommended that custom calculate rules be the default finance function type used on planning projects that have a large volume of calculations, as they will generally perform much better if built and used correctly.

First, a Bit of History

Way back in 2015, OneStream had started implementing more and more planning solutions. Many customers that started with consolidation were exploring ways to extend and expand the software. A large hospital operator had been using OneStream for consolidation and was in the midst of designing their planning solution. For consolidation, each hospital would submit a trial balance, then calculate and consolidate the entire hospital (Hospital was designated as the Entity dimension). Their budgeting process followed a slightly different process where department managers would enter budget drivers for an entire department within the hospital and then calculate results for that department.

Since Budget and Actuals used the same Entity dimension (Hospital), each time a department manager executed a calculation, it would run all Member Formulas and business rules for that entity regardless of the department. This was wreaking havoc within the budget process as department managers were seeing calculated figures before they even calculated, not to mention that performance was suffering given that department managers were constantly running calculations on top of each other.

To remedy this problem, the custom calculate function was added. This now allowed calculations to run at a more granular level than the Data Unit. Department managers could now execute a calculation for only their departments instead of having to run all calculations for an entity. This is a testament to OneStream's dedication to the continual evolution of the product to meet customers' needs.

What Exactly is the Difference?

The **calculate function type** runs within the Data Unit Calculation Sequence (DUCS). All the steps in the DUCS are executed each time a calculation or consolidation is run for a Data Unit. This means all Member Formulas, formula passes, and business rules will run on every calculation instance. The DUCS is built into the calculation and consolidation engine and is very useful in preserving data quality by organizing many calculation functions, such as clearing data and writing to members within the Consolidation dimension. However, it can be a bit 'heavy-handed' when it comes to planning, where there will likely be a larger volume of highly detailed calculations.

The **custom calculate function type** allows calculations to take place *outside* the Data Unit Calculation Sequence. Calculations can be built to be more specific to the exact view of data that a user is working with. A user can calculate sales for five departments without executing any other calculations in the cube.

Using Custom Calculate Rules

There are a few things you need to make sure you do when you use custom calculate rules. DUCS takes care of a lot of things behind the scenes that you'll now have to make sure to include in each custom calculate rule.

Data Clearing

A **clear data script** should be added at the top of every custom calculate rule so that all previously calculated data is cleared before re-calculating. If you fail to include this, you could end up with data from a previous calculation 'stuck' in your cube, which could become very difficult to find and remedy.

```
api.Data.ClearCalculatedData(True,True,True,True,"A#SalaryExpense")
```

It's important to align your clear data script with your calculation script so that the data being cleared aligns directly to the data being calculated.

Durable Data

The *is Durable Data* option should be used so that OneStream does not clear the data during DUCS. At some point, the cube will get consolidated and the DUCS will run; when it does, all calculated data will be cleared, assuming the Clear Calculated Data property on the scenario is set to True. OneStream does not treat all calculated data the same. The data that results from a calculation can be set as durable, which will protect it from being cleared during a consolidation.

```
Api.Data.Calculate("A#SalaryExpense = RemoveZeros(A#FTE * A#AverageSalary)",True)
      ▲ 1 of 3 ▼  ⓞ  Sub DataApi.Calculate(formula As String, isDurableCalculatedData As Boolean)
```

Linking to Workflow

You'll want to give some thought as to where and how custom calculate rules are launched since they won't be executed as part of the standard calculation/consolidation algorithm. Custom calculate functions can be executed from two places:

- Data management steps and sequences

- Dashboard buttons

Either of these two components should be linked to a user's workflow so the calculation can be executed within the natural flow of the process.

Using Parameters & POV Members

Another very useful aspect of the custom calculate function is the ability to pass user-controlled parameters into the rule via name-value pairs or `API.Pov`. This can add a lot of flexibility to your rules and give users more control over what is calculated. It can also help reduce maintenance and the overall volume of code needed in a build.

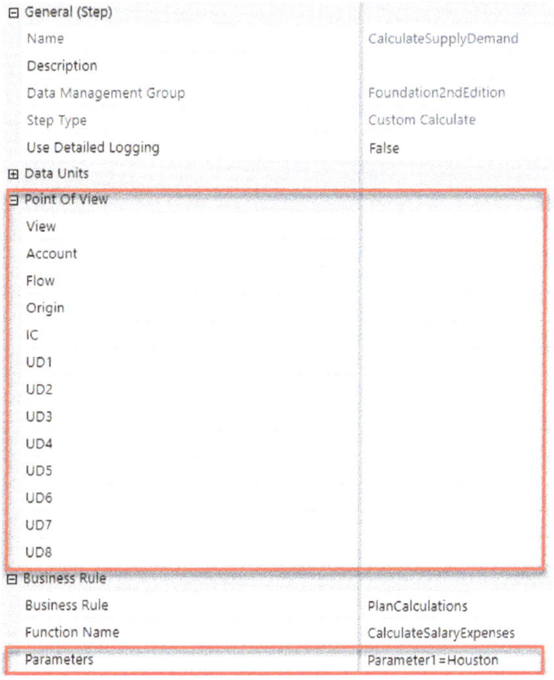

General (Step)	
Name	CalculateSupplyDemand
Description	
Data Management Group	Foundation2ndEdition
Step Type	Custom Calculate
Use Detailed Logging	False
Data Units	
Point Of View	
View	
Account	
Flow	
Origin	
IC	
UD1	
UD2	
UD3	
UD4	
UD5	
UD6	
UD7	
UD8	
Business Rule	
Business Rule	PlanCalculations
Function Name	CalculateSalaryExpenses
Parameters	Parameter1=Houston

Figure 5.28

Calculation Examples

The OneStream Financial Rules and Calculations Handbook should be referred to for a detailed breakdown of the finance engine and how to write calculations. This section will give some basic examples of planning rules that should give you a strong arsenal of knowledge for writing calculations in your planning project. These examples will expand upon the fundamentals covered in Chapter 8 to planning-specific use cases.

Below are a few assumptions to note about the examples:

- `RemoveZeros` is used to 'clean up' our data buffers by ensuring that any cells that have no data or zeros are removed. Using `RemoveZeros` for all rules is a good practice.

- It is assumed that we are following best practice and only running calculations at base-level entities and the local consolidation member.

Chapter 5

Driver-Based Planning Calculations

Api.Data.Calculate

`Api.Data.Calculate` is the most fundamental function for writing calculations in OneStream. It is very powerful at performing math functions on data within a multidimensional model. One simple `Api.Data.Calculate` rule can produce hundreds of thousands of data cells.

Let's start with a simple example of what a typical driver-based calculation might look like using `Api.Data.Calculate`. We'll again use salary expense as our example. The drivers used to calculate `Salary Expense` are FTEs (full-time employees) and average salary expense. The formula is simply FTE multiplied by average salary.

```
api.Data.Calculate("A#SalaryExpense = RemoveZeros(A#FTE * A#AverageSalary)")
```

The above calculation is making use of the `Api.Data.Calculate` function. This function is fundamental in nearly all OneStream calculations as it allows for the simple arithmetic of two or more data buffers. Remember from the Rules Chapter that a data buffer is just a group of data cells. Since the `Api.Data.Calculate` function allows us to multiply/divide/add/subtract groups of cells, we can create a lot of output cells with one simple calculation. We can visualize what our `Api.Data.Calculate` function is doing by looking at the data within the input data buffers.

`A#FTE`:

	FTE
Selling	
Sales	30.00
Marketing	25.00
Advertising	10.00
Manufacturing	
Material Management	20.00
Logistics	10.00
Production	15.00
Quality Management	8.00
Distribution	4.00
Engineering	12.00
Purchasing	2.00

Figure 5.29

`A#AverageSalary`:

	Average Salary
Selling	
Sales	60,000.00
Marketing	75,000.00
Advertising	70,000.00
Manufacturing	
Material Management	
Logistics	
Production	
Quality Management	
Distribution	
Engineering	
Purchasing	

Figure 5.30

The first thing you probably noticed is that our manufacturing departments are lacking values for average salary. This will be cleared up in the next example. For now, let's look at the output data buffer:

A#SalaryExpense:

	FTE	Average Salary	Salary Expense
Selling			
Sales	30.00	60,000.00	1,800,000.00
Marketing	25.00	75,000.00	1,875,000.00
Advertising	10.00	70,000.00	700,000.00
Manufacturing			
Material Management	20.00		
Logistics	10.00		
Production	15.00		
Quality Management	8.00		
Distribution	4.00		
Engineering	12.00		
Purchasing	2.00		

Figure 5.31

The output of our calculation created three new data cells. We can see no output values were calculated for our manufacturing departments since one of the input data buffers did not have cells in those members. In a real cube, you will likely have many more cells in your output data buffers, generating hundreds or thousands of new records in the database. You can quickly start to see the power of the Api.Data.Calculate function.

Rarely will a calculation be that simple, so let's add a few complexities. Let's address our manufacturing departments, which will use a different logic to calculate average salary. The manufacturing departments will use an average hourly wage instead of salary, and we will also need the number of working hours in each month.

To handle this requirement, we will need to include a **filter** in our calculation script. The new salary calculation will look like this:

```
api.Data.Calculate("A#SalaryExpense = RemoveZeros((A#FTE * A#AverageSalary)" _
    & " + A#AverageSalesCommission)",,"U1#Sales.Base")
api.Data.Calculate("A#SalaryExpense = RemoveZeros((A#FTE * A#AverageHourlyWage * A#WorkingHours)" _
    & " + A#AverageSalesCommission)",,"U1#Manufacturing.Base")
```

We can now separate our calculation into two distinct Api.Data.Calculate functions, using a filter to make each calculation only run for specific departments. The filter removes cells from the result data buffer cells, narrowing the scope of the calculation.

Next, let's add another dimension to our model – cost center. We want our salary expense to have cost center detail; however, average salary data is not available for each cost center. We do have cost center detail for headcount, though.

We will discover in Chapter 8 that data buffers must be balanced (have the same dimension details) to perform math functions on them, so our formulas, as written above, will not work unless we use the **MultiplyUnbalanced** function. The 'unbalanced' functions in OneStream give an easy way to perform math functions on data buffers that have different levels of detail. Let's now re-write our calculations using the MultiplyUnbalanced function.

```
api.Data.Calculate("A#SalaryExpense = MultiplyUnbalanced(RemoveZeros((A#FTE * A#AverageSalary:U2#NoCostCenter, U2#NoCostCenter)" _
    & "+ A#AverageSalesCommission)",,"U1#Sales.Base")
api.Data.Calculate("A#SalaryExpense = MultiplyUnbalanced(RemoveZeros((A#FTE * A#AverageHourlyWage:U2#NoCostCenter * A#WorkingHours, U2#NoCostCenter)" _
    & "+ A#AverageSalesCommission)",,"U1#Manufacturing.Base")
```

Since the average salary account lacks cost center detail, we know that all data will be on the `NoCostCenter` member. That member gets concatenated to the average salary account and then specified in the third argument of the `MultiplyUnbalanced` function. The resulting salary expense account will now contain cost center detail as the result data buffer inherits the detail of the unbalanced buffer.

Eval Function

The **Eval** function allows for the evaluation of individual data cells in a data buffer. This function is extremely useful for calculations that require more complex logic, and is a back pocket necessity for every planning consultant.

For example, you may need to check a cell value and apply different logic depending on the value. Or you may need to perform a lookup in a relational table based on the dimensionality of an individual cell. This type of **cell information** cannot be accessed with an `Api.Data.Calculate` function.

When using Eval, the cells from that data buffer can be looped through in a sub-function and manipulated.

To illustrate the Eval function, let's add one more complexity to our calculation requirement. We want to calculate overtime based on the headcount compared to FTE. If our FTE value is greater than the headcount value, then we can assume we will need to pay some overtime. Our formula written in plain English would be:

```
Overtime Expense = (FTE / Headcount) * Average Overtime Wage
```

You will notice that we need to put a condition in here somewhere to only run this calculation if the `(FTE / Headcount)` expression is greater than 1. This isn't possible using the filter function. To accomplish this, we will need to analyze the amount of each data cell in the data buffer. For this, we will need to use the Eval function.

In our case, we need to evaluate the resulting data buffer of `(FTE / Headcount)`. We can apply the `Eval` this way:

```
api.Data.Calculate("A#OvertimeExpense = RemoveZeros(Eval(A#FTE / A#Headcount) * A#AverageOvertimeWage)", AddressOf OnEvalDataBuffer)
```

The expression `(A#FTE / A#Headcount)` is wrapped in the `Eval` function. The sub-function is referenced in the last argument of the `Api.Data.Calculate` function. The sub-function will filter the result cells of the expression and then execute the rest of the formula. The sub-function is shown below.

```
Private Sub OnEvalDataBuffer(ByVal api As FinanceRulesApi, ByVal evalName As String, ByVal eventArgs As EvalDataBufferEventArgs)

    Dim resultCells As New Dictionary(Of DataBufferCellPk, DataBufferCell)
    For Each sourceCell As DataBufferCell In eventArgs.DataBuffer1.DataBufferCells.Values
        'Filter the list of cell to only cells with an amount > 1
        If sourceCell.CellAmount > 1 Then
            'Add this dataCell to the new list
            resultCells(sourceCell.DataBufferCellPk) = sourceCell
        End If
    Next
    'Assign the new list of DataCells to the result.
    'The final list of resultCells is what will be assigned to the Api.Data.Calculate
    eventArgs.DataBufferResult.DataBufferCells = resultCells
End Sub
```

The `Eval` sub-function executes a loop through all of the result cells and then applies logic to them. In this case, we are checking whether the amount is greater than 1. Only if the condition is true are the cells then included.

Calculation Drilldown

Also covered in Chapter 8, data that is the result of a formula can be drilled into so that users can see the details of calculation logic. It is a good idea to always use Calculation Drilldown formulas for all calculations, but it's worth making special note of this feature here because of the heavy use of calculations in driver-based planning.

Let's look at an example of a Calculation Drilldown formula for our driver-based `Api.Data.Calculate` example from before:

Formula

```
api.Data.Calculate("A#SalaryExpense = RemoveZeros(A#FTE * A#AverageSalary)")

Dim result As New DrillDownFormulaResult()
result.Explanation = "Formula Definition: FTE * Average Salary"
result.SourceDataCells.Add("A#FTE")
result.SourceDataCells.Add("A#AverageSalary")
Return result
```

We can see that the drilldown formula is written so that the formula definition is displayed along with the inputs to the calculation. This will give the user visibility into the data that was used to derive the calculation result.

Factor-Based Planning Calculations

Like driver-based planning, factor-based planning will mostly be derived via calculations. The general process is that a user will input a factor or growth rate, which is then multiplied against data from another scenario, like Actuals.

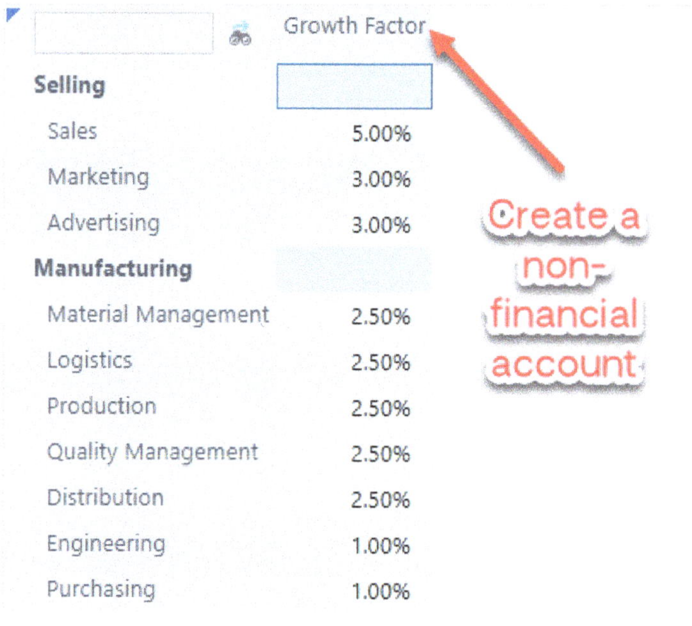

Figure 5.32

The growth factor can then be applied to all accounts via an `Api.Data.Calculate` function in the scenario formula.

```
api.Data.Calculate("S#FactorBasedForecast = MultiplyUnbalanced(S#Actual * S#POV:T#POVYearM1:A#GrowthFactor, A#GrowthFactor)")
```

Since the growth factor is constant for all months the users will input on, we could also extrapolate the plan based on the trailing 12-month average of the last Actual month.

Data Seeding

Data seeding is the process of copying data from one scenario to another and is likely to be an important part of your planning solution. Some plan types will require data from historical periods to arrive at a full-year view. Remember our YTG rolling forecast example where Actual and Forecast data is blended to derive an end-of-year financial projection.

Scenario:	Forecast_M3											
Plan Period:	1	2	3	4	5	6	7	8	9	10	11	12
Data:	Actual	Actual	Forecast	Forecast	Forecast	Forecast	Forecast	Forecast	Forecast	Forecast	Forecast	Forecast

Scenario:	Forecast_M4											
Plan Period:	1	2	3	4	5	6	7	8	9	10	11	12
Data:	Actual	Actual	Actual	Forecast	Forecast	Forecast	Forecast	Forecast	Forecast	Forecast	Forecast	Forecast

Figure 5.33

Some plan types may also use data from other scenarios as a baseline. Data from one scenario can be used as a starting point or as the basis for a factor-based plan. If using versions for a plan type, data from the prior version will need to be copied into the current version.

We've established that data seeding is important, so let's now discuss the different tools available in OneStream and how to use them.

Data Copying Methods

There are several ways to copy data between scenarios. We will make mention of the two most prevalently used methods, although one is certainly used more than the other.

Data Management

The first method involves using a Copy Data data management step.

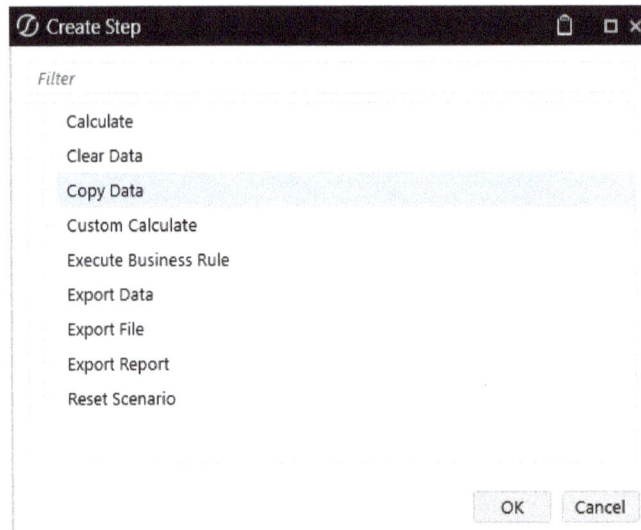

Figure 5.34

In a Copy Data step, source and destination Data Units can be specified, and there are options for copying forms, imported, or adjustment data.

⊟ General (Step)	
Name	Clubs Copy Scenario
Description		
Data Management Group	Foundation2ndEdition
Step Type	Copy Data
Use Detailed Logging	False
⊟ Source Data Units	
Source Cube	CFDrivers
Source Entity Filter	E#[Houston Heights]
Source Scenario	Budget
Source Time Filter	T#2024.Base
Source View	
⊟ Destination Data Units	
Destination Cube	CFDrivers
Destination Entity Filter	E#[Houston Heights]
Destination Scenario	Budget_V2
Destination Time Filter	T#2024.Base
Destination View	
⊟ Origin	
Copy Imported Data	True
Copy Forms Data	True
Copy Adjustment Data	True

Figure 5.35

The data management step can be executed within a sequence from a dashboard or integrated into a user's workflow, so that it executes at the proper time in the plan process. It's important to note that copying data in this way also copies audit information, which will likely run slower than the second method. Due to performance and lack of flexibility, this is not the most widely used method.

Seeding Using Custom Calculate Finance Business Rules

The second method involves using a custom calculate finance business rule.

Data can be copied quickly and easily within the OneStream calculation engine. We've already gone through several examples of writing finance rules, and we can apply the same principles to our seeding rules. Let's start with the `Api.Data.Calculate` function. Below is a simple example of a scenario copy rule using `Api.Data.Calculate`:

```
api.Data.Calculate("S#Budget_V2 = S#Budget_V1")
```

That's it! That's all it takes to copy all the data from one scenario to another. Integrating logic to only copy certain entities, accounts, or time can make your seeding rules much more complex, so you'll likely need the full arsenal of business rule writing skills you've learned in this book.

Location of Seeding Rules

In general, seeding rules should run as a custom calculate finance rule. A few sections ago, I described the differences between custom calculate and Data Unit Calculation Sequence calculations. Since seeding rules typically copy data that does not change, they will only need to be run once, or when the source data has changed, which will likely not be often. Seeding rules that run in the DUCS will run every time a calculation and consolidation is executed, resulting in unnecessary clearing and re-copying of the same data and suboptimal performance. The custom calculate rule can be linked to a dashboard and executed centrally by an admin or by each user and their respective set of entities. Remember to use the DurableData = True and always include a ClearCalculateData script!

What's in a Name?

In the Scenario section, we touched on naming conventions for scenario members. Data seeding should also be considered when naming scenarios. In many cases, the period, year, or version will be included in the scenario name and can be parsed out in your rule. Let's look at the seeding rule for our YTG forecast scenarios. For this plan type, our scenario names include the current month number (e.g., Forecast_M2, Forecast_M3, etc.). Let's say we want to copy the previous month's forecast into the current forecast. Here is how the seeding rule might look.

```
32
33    '--------------------------------------------------------------------------
34    ' Helper method used to seed forecast with blended data based on the forecast month
35    '--------------------------------------------------------------------------
36    If (api.Cons.IsLocalCurrencyforEntity() And Not api.Entity.HasChildren()) Then
37
38        'Various useful Time Period-related information
39        Dim curFcstYear As Integer                          'The 4 digit year based on current forecast scenario
40        Dim ne1FcstYear As Integer                          'The year after the curFcstYear
41        Dim curFcstMonth As Integer                         'The 2 digit month based on current forecast scenario
42        Dim curYear As Integer                              'The year that is currently being processed
43        Dim curMonth As Integer                             'The month that is currently being processed
44        Dim ne1FcstMonth As Integer                         'The month after curFcstMonth
45        Dim ne2FcstMonth As Integer                         'The month after ne1FcstMonth
46        Dim srcScenario As String                           'Source scenario for Forecast months
47        Dim curScenario As String = api.Pov.Scenario.Name   'Forecast scenario being calculated
48        Dim curTime As String = api.Pov.Time.Name           'Time period being calculated
49
50        'Parse the current Month and Year based on POV Time period
51        curMonth = Mid(curTime,InStr(curTime,"M")+1,2)
52        curYear = left(curTime,4)
53
54        'Parse the Forecast Month and Year based on Scenario Name
55        curFcstYear = api.scenario.GetWorkflowStartTime.ToString.substring(0,4)
56        ne1FcstYear = curFcstYear + 1
57        curFcstMonth = Mid(curScenario,InStr(curScenario,"M")+1,2)
58        ne1FcstMonth = curFcstMonth + 1
59        ne2FcstMonth = curFcstMonth + 2
60
61        'Determine source Scenario - for January, use the budget; for all other months, use the prior forecast
62        If curFcstMonth = 1 Then
63            srcScenario = "BudgetV1"
64        Else
65            srcScenario = "Fcast" & "M" & curFcstMonth - 1
66        End If
67
68        api.Data.Calculate("S#[" & curScenario & "]:O#Import = S#[" & srcScenario & "]:O#Top")
69
```

In line 57, we can parse out the month name from the scenario name using standard VB.NET (or C#) functions. From here, we can do some simple math to determine the prior month's scenario. Since there is no Forecast_M0, we have a special condition to set the source scenario to BudgetV1 when the current scenario is Forecast_M1.

Use Scenario Text Properties!

Like naming conventions, scenario text properties can be used to store information that can be used in seeding rule logic.

```
api.Scenario.Text(api.Pov.Scenario.MemberId, 1)
```

Text properties can provide more flexibility in that they can be easily changed by an administrator.

To give an example, let's look at an example budget preparation cycle. Users will start preparing the budget in September and go through several iterations before finalizing in late October. Beginning balances for balance sheet accounts are being pulled from the most recently closed month of Actuals. From the start of the budget cycle to the end, another month will be closed. Storing the most recently closed Actual month in a text property allows the administrator to easily update the beginning balance logic without having to touch any code.

Remove the Guesswork!

OneStream's dashboard tool can create slick interfaces that give users drop-down menus, selection boxes, and input screens. While this flexibility can be extremely useful elsewhere in your build, I would try to avoid it when it comes to seeding rules. Seeding logic should be predetermined to the greatest extent possible. This removes any room for user error.

Imagine a CFO looking at a plan that was derived from baseline data seeded from another scenario. It may not be clear what the user selected as the baseline scenario, or it could have changed from version to version. If strict seeding logic is agreed upon – upfront – it can be cleverly programmed into the seeding rules so that you always have a predictable outcome.

Copying between Extended Scenarios

If you are using extended cubes and dimensions across Scenario Types, you will likely need to copy data from a cube or scenario that uses different dimensionality. The `ConvertDataBufferExtendedMembers` function is designed to convert data from an extended cube or scenario to the dimensionality of the destination cube.

```
'Convert dimensionality
Dim destinationInfo As ExpressionDestinationInfo = api.Data.GetExpressionDestinationInfo("")
Dim sourceDataBuffer As DataBuffer = api.Data.GetDataBuffer(DataApiScriptMethodType.Calculate, "" _
    & "Cb#AnotherCube:S#AnotherScenario", destinationInfo)
Dim convertedDataBuffer As DataBuffer = api.Data.ConvertDataBufferExtendedMembers("AnotherCube","" _
    & "AnotherScenario", sourceDataBuffer)
api.Data.SetDataBuffer(convertedDataBuffer, destinationInfo)
```

Conclusion on Seeding Rules

In general, you should strive to build your seeding rules with the intention that they should never have to be touched unless new plan types are added, or there are material changes in the data seeding methodology of existing plan types. Using the tips and techniques above can help create rules that both perform well and require minimal maintenance over time.

Workflow

Workflow is the last section in this chapter because it brings everything we've covered so far together in one place for users. We refer to 'that place' as a **Workflow Profile**, and each user will navigate to one before doing almost anything in OneStream. Workflow is so important, in fact, that there is an entire chapter in this book dedicated to it. Chapter 7 covers the fundamentals and basics of workflow design, so this section will mostly focus on planning-specific considerations. Let's quickly review the main goals of workflow:

- To protect the end-user from analytic model complexities

- Manage and audit data collection

- Manage and enforce data quality, certification, and locking

- Manage and intelligently coordinate the data consolidation and calculation process

- Deliver reports and analytic tools

- Create a standardized end-user experience

Designing Workflow for Planning

In contrast to financial processes like consolidation, which can require stringent controls and audit requirements, planning processes are mostly liberated from those constraints. This isn't necessarily always the case but, generally, you have a lot more flexibility with how planning workflows are designed. I have seen planning Workflow Profile structures range from dozens of profiles organized into a hierarchy to just one universal workflow that all users access and navigate like a web page.

Now that I've left you more confused than you started, let's go through how to approach a planning workflow design. A planning workflow design should consist of three things:

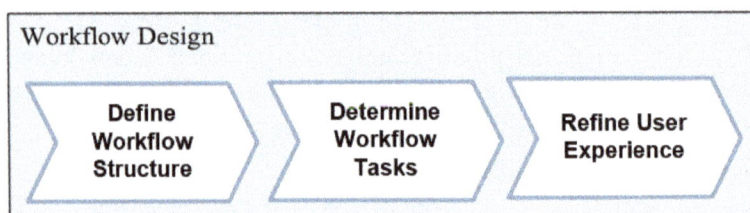

Figure 5.36

Your ultimate workflow design will depend on what kind of user experience the customer wants for its users. Find out what users are used to, from tools they have used in the past. This is where you will go back to the plan process flows defined in the BPD to use as your starting point.

Determine Workflow Profile Structure

A workflow structure refers to how Workflow Profiles are organized. A workflow structure can organize profiles in a hierarchy with various levels of review points, or have them laid out in a flat list. A Workflow Profile structure also serves technical purposes with how data importing, clearing, and locking behaves. Below are some requirements that will influence your Workflow Profile structure design.

Data Importing to the Cube

Data imports require some special workflow considerations due to how OneStream clears and loads data into the cube. Entities can be assigned to workflows, which restrict data imports to that entity from other workflows. Additionally, data generally cannot be loaded to the same entity from multiple Workflow Profiles without the use of workflow channels. This ties back to the section where we discussed how the workflow plays a role in Entity dimension selection.

Data Locking Requirements

An important requirement that relates to workflow structure is if, and how, data needs to be locked. Most of the time, this isn't very important since planning data isn't subject to the same audit requirements as Actual data. However, if you fall into the exception, you must give careful thought to your workflow structure. This also relates to the Entity dimension, as data is locked for an *entire* entity (ignoring workflow channel usage), so you typically want a Workflow Profile per Workflow Unit if possible.

Consider a process for Actuals in which there are 25 legal entities. Each user submits data for a legal entity and locks the workflow (and, by definition, the entity). For the budget, department managers submit budgets across multiple legal entities. Since department drives the budget workflows, the requirement is to lock each department. Workflow channels would need to be used to lock only certain departments within the entity. This is possible in OneStream using workflow channels, but only one UD dimension can be used as the channel. This is also an *application* setting, which means it cannot be set per cube or Scenario Type.

Another option would be to 'lock' the data outside the standard workflow mechanism using **conditional input business rules** assigned to the cube. This option can certainly work well in some situations, but additional maintenance should be considered.

Determine User Types

Identifying user types will help drive the workflow design by helping to provide context for a structure. Different user types will interact differently with the solution, and users within the same type will be completing many of the same tasks. Some general classifications of user types:

- **Data preparers** – users are generally interacting with data by importing files, typing numbers, and running calculations. They will also do some review and analysis.

- **Data reviewers** – users that are primarily responsible for some or all of reviewing, approving, and locking data.

- **Plan administrators** – users that execute central tasks such as opening scenarios, seeding data, or importing central files.

Extensible Workflows

Workflow Profile structures can be shared across Scenario Types with the underlying tasks associated with that profile specific to the scenario. If the budget submission process follows closely to Actual, you can leverage the same structure. If not, extensible workflows can be used.

Extensible workflow essentially gives you the ability to create a completely different set of Workflow Profiles specific to a Scenario Type. This creates a fundamental separation between the different processes for both the end-user and administrator.

Determine Workflow Tasks

For every Workflow Profile identified, you will need to determine each task that a user needs to complete. Hopefully, a light is going off because this should sound familiar. We already started to uncover this during the *plan process flow* exercise in the BPD. Starting with the plan process flow, you can distill things down to individual tasks that a user needs to complete. Next, try to understand the order in which each of those tasks needs to be completed, and if there need to be reviews or sign-off points within the process. These will all need to be presented to the user at some point within the workflow.

Refine the User Experience

There are thousands of books written on user experience theories and techniques. I simply do not have the expertise or the page space to explore this in great detail, so I will only make a few points here.

The most important thing to remember is that OneStream gives you a framework for building just about any type of user experience you can come up with. You can build strict, linear processes that carefully guide a user from task to task. You could also venture to the other end of the spectrum, where users work in a freeform Workspace, navigating haphazardly back and forth between tasks.

Make sure you allocate enough time in the project to go through several iterations of the user experience design. Start with something basic and have users test it, collect feedback, and refine. In most cases, users do not know what they want until they see something and start to use it.

Using Dashboards

Many workflow types in OneStream are designed to fit a linear process (e.g., a user imports a file, validates the data, then loads and processes the cube before finally certifying the workflow). While some planning processes will fit that mold, it is more common to have a planning process that is circular (e.g., a user inputs drivers, calculates costs, runs a report, changes a driver, recalculates, and repeats multiple times before finally certifying the data).

For these types of processes, OneStream's robust dashboarding tool is available. Dashboards give users more of the 'web page' experience. Using dashboards, you can create and tailor the user experience to exact specifications. You can put data entry screens, reports, and buttons to execute tasks all on the same screen.

Standardize as Much as Possible

"If you try to make everyone happy, you'll make nobody happy."

While dashboards are tremendously powerful in creating tailored user experiences, they will also require additional build time and maintenance (remember our rule from before). Creating a dashboard specific to every user's wishes will create a maintenance nightmare. Spend time early in the project standardizing dashboards as much as possible.

To address this exact point, OneStream has several solutions (found on the Solution Exchange) that can be easily installed and configured into any application.

- **Actor Workspaces** – these are pre-built dashboards geared towards specific user types that can be configured for your specifications. They can be set as a user's home screen or linked to a workflow. These dashboards pull properties from user properties and security so that the dashboard is relevant to each user.

- **Data Entry 123** – the Data Entry 123 Solution is a contextual development environment for creating data entry forms. The framework provides a simple design paradigm that facilitates quick form building. This centralized approach helps standardize the look and feel across forms while easing the change management process of forms, selectors, and calculations.

I highly recommend leveraging these solutions as they can significantly reduce development time and reduce maintenance.

Conclusion

OneStream is a dynamic software platform that was designed to support all corporate financial planning processes. FP&A teams have more data available at their fingertips than ever before. This puts a lot of strain on the chosen planning tool. If you're not careful, you can easily get lost in the maze of design. I hope that after reading this chapter, you have a better knowledge foundation to draw from when you are designing your next planning solution in OneStream.

Epilogue

OneStream opened our global headquarters in Rochester, Michigan, in 2015. It reflects our "Work Hard, Play Hard" mentality.

6
Data Integration

Originally written by John Von Allmen, updated by Joakim Kulan

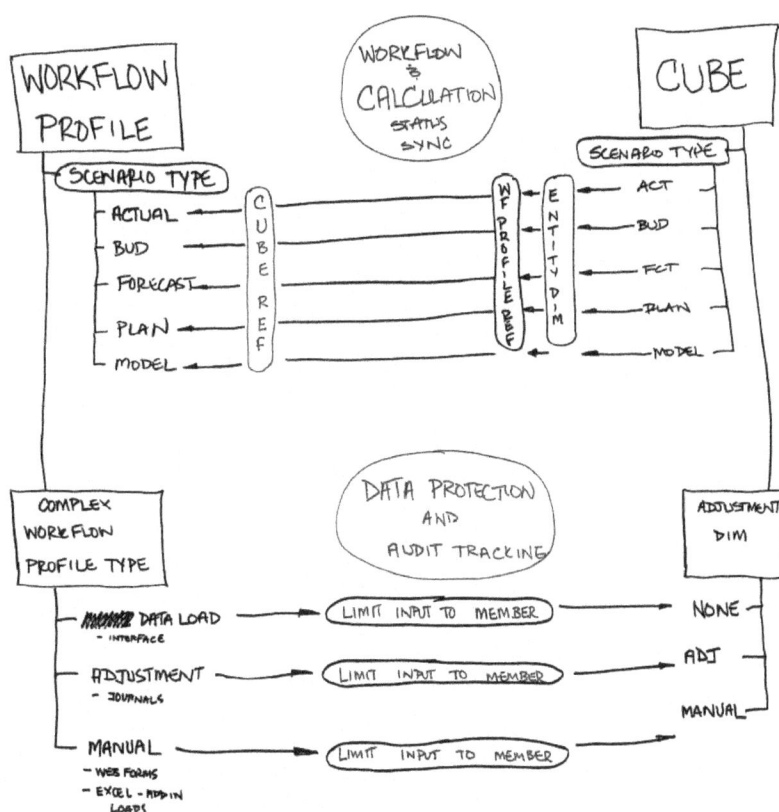

The ability to consume data from any data source, and load or integrate data into software, is probably the biggest problem most software companies do *not* consider when creating an application. Most software packages usually only have one way to load a data file, or force a specific format (in order to get a file into the system, or a separate product), and there is usually only one way to get the data out in order to reuse the data. That concept really changes with the use of OneStream. With OneStream, you receive a very powerful toolbox to help manage and coordinate all your data.

You will learn in this chapter that there are many different options to get data into the OneStream system, and that you can reuse and leverage both the source and target data that was created by OneStream. This chapter will not cover using the data parser and business rules, but cover the concepts of how to get and use the data into OneStream. OneStream has a wide variety of tools to load and map any dataset, and there is virtually no limitation on the type of data that can be consumed and analyzed or reported in OneStream.

Not only does OneStream help coordinate disparate data sources, but it becomes a data source itself to reuse and repurpose data for other processes such as account reconciliation or other reporting or analysis needs. MarketPlace solutions (found on the Solution Exchange) such as People Planning, allow you to collect data for planning and place it into tables consistently, instead of having hundreds of different Excel files doing different functions. Account reconciliation (RCM inside OFC) allows you to use the same data for the trial balances to do the reconciliations. Analytic Blend allows for collecting much more granular data inside OneStream as well, in a relational table, with ties to the cube metadata and power to do aggregations and advanced data transformation. Then, to help report on this data, there are some really powerful FDX (Fast Data eXtract) APIs available to use. OneStream becomes a complete ecosystem of data.

Data Quality

The creators of OneStream have been at the forefront of data quality since the early 2000s. UpStream Software was created by OneStream's founder, Tom Shea, to load Hyperion Enterprise and provide an audit trail and mapping tool. UpStream gave everyone a consistent, repeatable process to load data, and provided gratification in the form of a digital 'fish' when they completed a step. You may ask, why a fish? Because the data flows upstream from the local general ledgers to corporate, just like a fish swims upstream.

UpStream was also a tool for both accountants and complex integrators. While other ETL tools required consultants and others to rebuild the same basic platform repeatedly to get data into systems, UpStream already had the workflow process done, and the steps were easy for basic accountants and administrators who wanted to bring up new datasets quickly. There were products from Hyperion that would take a file and map it and prepare output, but – in that process – you lost all visibility as to what the output data used as its mapping rule, and how many line items were summed into the final amount.

In 2006, with over 300 successful customers and the need for an audit trail – required by auditors and customers – Hyperion purchased UpStream Software and rebranded it Financial Data Quality Management (FDM). The main problem FDM was tasked with solving was the moving of data between Actual and Forecast. How do you take data from Hyperion Financial Management (HFM) and move it into Essbase, and take data from Essbase and move it back into HFM? This disconnect was part of the problem that OneStream wanted to solve and *has* solved with one platform of OneStream. You can use extensibility to have different levels, and metadata in Actual and Forecast, and have everything in one product. You no longer have to group and maintain two different products with two different metadata structures.

Early in 2010, when building the platform from the ground up, the data quality process was reimagined. With years of experience, consistent problems could be solved easily by using settings and making them part of out-of-the-box functionality for a basic administrator to use and consume data files. The common tasks that required scripting engine assistance were reimagined to be solved with settings.

The power of a scripting engine still exists, and is still used as a solution to solve the most complex problems. Most of the problems were solved because data resided in one system and didn't have to go back and forth between separate consolidation and planning systems.

Staging (Data Quality Engine)

All of the data being loaded into OneStream starts out in a file, in a system, or in a database table.

The challenge is to get that data out of disparate sources and into one common system. The data parsing engine of OneStream consumes the data from the source files and systems, and places the data into staging tables. The staging tables have the consumed source data, the mapping used, and the target dimension. These tables are the basis of the audit trail and the drill back. The data is cleansed to be in a consistent format for consumption by the cube, or used in other areas of the product, such as reporting.

When FEMA gets ready to help people after a natural disaster, they have staging areas – places they work from to coordinate and manage the response. OneStream does the same thing by having a staging area, which we will refer to throughout this chapter as **Stage**.

The source data that is prepared and staged, and outputted in this system, can be reused in any format to solve any complex data problem. The aggregation of the source data can then be reused for another purpose. One process needs data aggregated one way, but the financial or planning dataset needs the same data aggregated in a different way. It's the same data, just looked at in a different slice.

Through every stage of data consumption, there is a complete log and audit trail that satisfies the completeness objectives of any audit system.

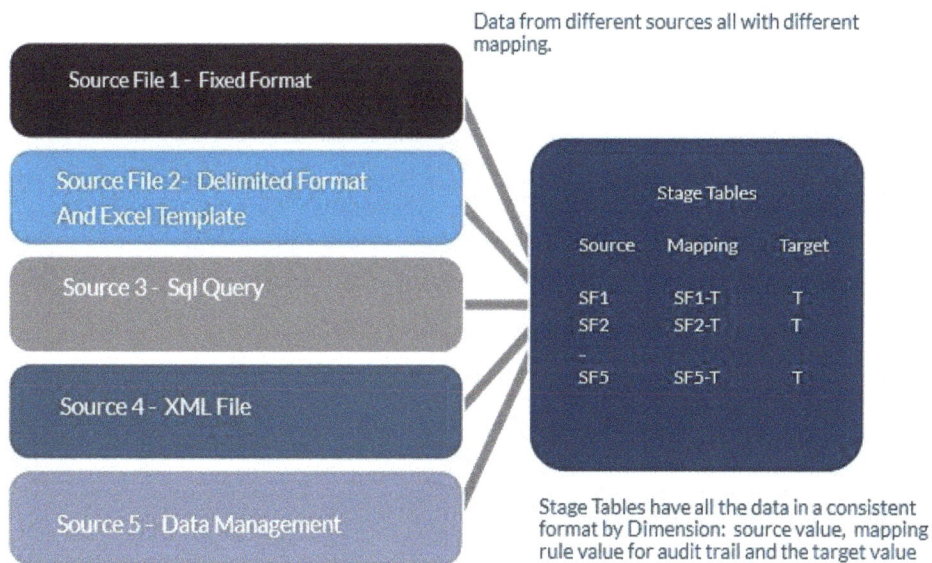

Figure 6.1

Non-Stage Data Tables

Not every record of data gets processed through the mapping engine. There are a number of datasets for other solutions that are kept outside the cube in data tables created by solutions such as People Planning or Analytic Blend. (It is an option to design a process where OneStream can write to and from the data quality engine.) Data collection tables are just database tables that are created to consume data. Excel files can be set up to load these datasets as well. This process is built into solutions, and they will come with predefined Excel templates for loading the data. There is no mapping of these items except for the type of data matching to the column. The same theory applies to staging as we create areas to prepare data for use as a consistent data structure.

Direct Loads (Non-Stage)

When loading data into the financial cube that requires less audit trail, such as forecasting data, flash data, data used for *what if* purposes or whatever the use case might be, you can opt to load data through all the standard engines as a normal import, less the overhead of storing source information in the Stage tables. Yes, this will not give you full audit capabilities, so should not be used for regular monthly reporting, but it will allow you to load data quicker into the cube from the source.

Origin Dimension

In order to understand how data is consumed by a OneStream cube, it is necessary to understand the **Origin dimension**. The Origin dimension is the way OneStream segments the data for each entity – into separate buckets – by three types of dataset. This dimension combines the concepts of data protection and data layering and isolation. The Origin dimension acts as a barrier to protect how data is loaded in different forms. Data loaded through import does *not* write over data in the form's Origin member by isolating the three groups.

- **Import** – data imported from a flat file or query or an Excel template.

- **Forms** – data inputted manually or via an Excel template or an Excel add-in.

- **Journal Entries** – OneStream journal entries that can be inputted manually, used as templates, or loaded through Excel.

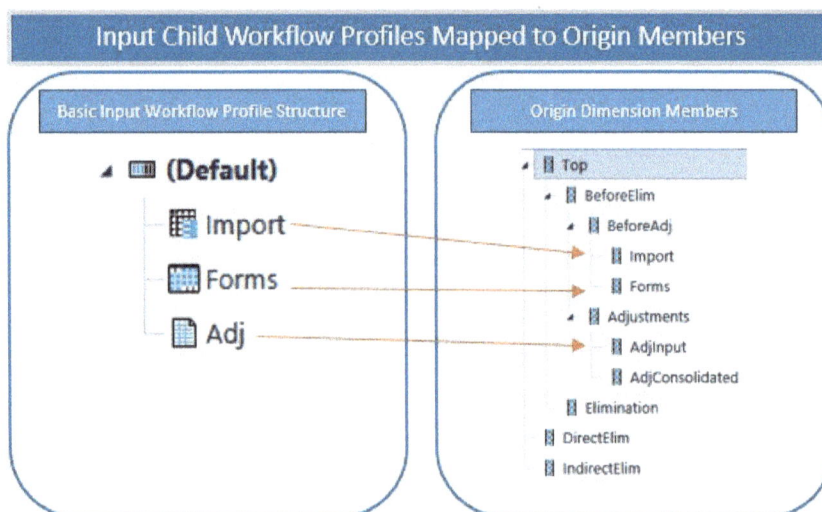

Figure 6.2

Assembling the Data Sources and Considerations

For any OneStream project, it is extremely important to understand that data needs to complete the project's objectives in the design document. Analysis of the data sources is required to make sure they can provide the data that the cube design requires. As the model of the cube is designed, the cube should be at least 90% complete before mapping and work on the data integration begins (e.g., the work in the Stage should not begin until the prior work is substantially done). That's not to say there will not be changes. There are always changes to a model! Your job is to minimize these changes with a thoughtful and thorough design process.

After the design document is complete, there are four major considerations when starting the data integration project.

Inventory Files and Sources

Inventory files and sources are typically part of the project where a lot of the unknowns reside:

- How does each group prepare the data?

- How much of it is a system?

- How much is collected manually?

In managing a project, the pitfalls are in the details. It is extremely important to put together an inventory and get as much information as possible from all parties. Samples of the data files, the queries, and the data itself, for example. It is important to understand the analytic model to make sure the data provided can satisfy the objectives of the reporting cube. The inventory should contain ledger information, type of data, and responsible party. The customer must give you the file or the query to prepare the data. You can typically find some economies of data sources and mapping in this exercise. Do the ledgers across the company use the same account numbering scheme? Are the output formats the same structure? A company grown by acquisition typically has a wide variety of data sources that don't match up.

The most important field of any data source is the **amount**. When reviewing a dataset, the amount is the most important field in any file format that is used and will determine if a record is accepted or rejected. Amount(s) can be in a single column (tabbed format) or a matrix format. OneStream can easily read either type of file – out-of-the-box – without business rules.

Single Column (Tabbed)

Sales Product	Amount
Golf Club	1,000
Golf Shirt	1,500
Golf Balls	100
Golf Bags	800

Figure 6.3

Matrix Format

Products	Store A	Store B	Store C	Store D
Product A	23	45	31	25
Product B	87	23	55	38
Product C	64	56	62	26
Product D	37	32	91	8
Product E	93	35	54	43

Figure 6.4

OneStream can use any file produced by a system. There is generally no reason to pay a programmer to pull data into a specific file format for OneStream.

OneStream is not just limited to files; the more common practice now is a direct connection to pull data in real time. The ability to load from a direct connection is more accurate because you can refresh by just pushing a button. The file is limited to the last time the file was run. If changes are made, the file must be rerun and then reloaded, but with a direct connection, the consumption is instantaneous. OneStream is a pull system and will pull data from databases, etc. *We do not allow for a push of data to our data tables*.

There are many different types of data to be loaded in OneStream. The dataset should be complete for the subject the system intends to analyze. Sometimes, a trial balance might not be a complete dataset that includes all the data needed to generate a cash flow statement. An example of a deficiency in a trial balance might include fixed assets which are not detailed in the trial balance. The transactional detail could be loaded, or an input form could be used to separate the detail of the account – showing additions, disposals, and transfers.

Examples of data sources which are included but which are not inclusive:

- Trial balances or trial balance by department
- Income statements by department or geography
- Accounts payable detail
- Accounts receivable detail
- Fixed asset details
- Forecast
- Vendors
- Sales by region or product
- Products by SKU#

> **Tip:** Source files or trial balances should be in the natural sign of debit and credits.

- Makes it very clear what value is a debit and a credit
- The file balances to zero and can be easily proven with a rule
- Can use a derivative translation rule or a balance account in OneStream to test mapping for signs equaling zero

Historical Data

The second major data integration consideration with any project is that historical data is always an unknown and a challenge to reconcile. As part of the inventory, it's important to know how the data is going to be loaded (e.g., which method or data source).

- Where is that data source coming from?
- How much history is going to be reconciled?

Two years of historical data is typical in an implementation project when working with only a few sources and a straightforward mapping. As I have learned – over and over again – there are many special 'one-time' cases. You need your customer's involvement and participation in this to tie out the data. This is a good task for the customer to focus on, and take responsibility for, as they know their data and results better than a consultant.

A common issue is that the customer has their normal day-to-day job, and *your* needs can get in the way. Ask your customer to provide dedicated resources for this process; work as a team but make the customer responsible for approving and reviewing the data tie out. You will probably need to leverage OneStream Excel templates in a lot of these exercises to compare and tie out data.

How Much Data?

The third major data integration consideration in any project is a balancing act on how much data is in the ledger and how much data is in the cube.

This requires discipline by the designer of the cube not to recreate everything that is in every ledger system. The cube should be summarizing data and should not be a data warehouse of every possible product combination. There is the capability to drill back to a source system. If you have set up a direct connection, then it can drill back to the source items and see what makes up a number.

Customers tend to want to make a data warehouse out of a cube, but there is no need to make a cube a data warehouse. If everything has one-to-one mapping, that might be a clue that the ledger is being fully replicated. There isn't a need to replicate the ledger or every single ledger the customer owns. OneStream is not a general ledger system. There are alternative solutions, including drill back or Analytic Blend reporting, so that the cube is not overburdened as a data warehouse. OneStream can report off data that is not contained in its ecosystem. It can create a data adaptor and pull that information into a report for presentation purposes.

Performance of the Data Load

The fourth major data integration consideration is the volume of data and tuning behind processing times and mapping. What works best for the data file, mapping, and scripting is sometimes a bit trial and error. Loading 2,000 records with mapping is different to loading 1 million records with mapping.

There are several things to consider when looking at performance.

The Quality of the Data File or Query

Sometimes, the query is a stored procedure, which is probably very tight; and sometimes the query might be a manual query that is not as efficient. We have seen queries that try to do math in the query, and they may (or may not) be the answer. There might be economies in massaging the query to become more efficient.

The Complexity of the Mapping Rules

This will be covered in more detail later in the chapter when mapping processing costs are discussed.

Spreading the Data Load

With large data record sets, it might make sense to separate the data into smaller chunks of data. One data load with 1 million records could take ten minutes because it's a sequential data load. The parser is sequential, but by breaking it up, the parser can be used by multiple data load and workflow processes. The same data could be loaded in two minutes by breaking it up into five separate groups of records. Splitting the data by business units (entities in OneStream) is the most common approach here.

Working through the Problems

Both data sources and the mapping process, during any build, involve an element of trial and error.

The first item to concentrate on is getting the data read. For that, you need a basic map. The `Import` function on the workflow does both imports and mapping. This requires a data source and a mapping. The basic transformation map for view, scenario, and time, and a transformation rule profile with at least the dimensions being loaded from the data format having a blank profile for all the other dimensions being used, is required before a data file can be loaded.

It's okay not to do all the mapping at first. Reading data sources and mapping go together, but once you get the data source working, it's easy to modify the data source to become tighter.

Look at the data that is being imported into the Stage. If you have a 10-digit string account number, such as `2300028932`, where `23000` is the account, `28` is the geography, `932` is the product. If you only need the account information to map, it might be good to only take the first five digits and make the mapping easy as a one-to-one.

But if the dimension needs the other information, it also might be good to break the dimension up and add separators such as `23000_28_932`. This will allow some flexibility with wild card mapping.

Maybe the geography isn't needed, though, and `23000*_9*` gets mapped to a specific account. The separators can help the mapping by saying every account with `23000` and a product `9` goes to a specific account.

Sometimes, you just have to root around and try things out to see how data and mapping are structured, and the number of records. These combinations change all the time during build. Look to make things easy but adaptable for the future. An alternative solution could be to use a **composite mapping rule** that looks to the source of the product dimension or as a lookup table. Those solutions may make sense based on the volume and complexity of data. There is always more than one way to solve a problem.

Large datasets that contain more than 1 million records may require some adjustment to the Workflow Profile setting:

- Cache Page Size set to 500

- Cache Pages In Memory Limit set to 2000. This combination allows more cache pages to be processed in memory. You may have to adjust settings to find the right combination based on hardware availability.

- Cache Page Rule Breakout Interval set to 0. This setting can increase performance by determining if all the transformation rules have been satisfied within a cached page, thus stopping further transformations happening in that cycle by not having to continue through the remaining transformation rules. Default is 0, meaning all transformation rules will be evaluated for all records in all cached pages.

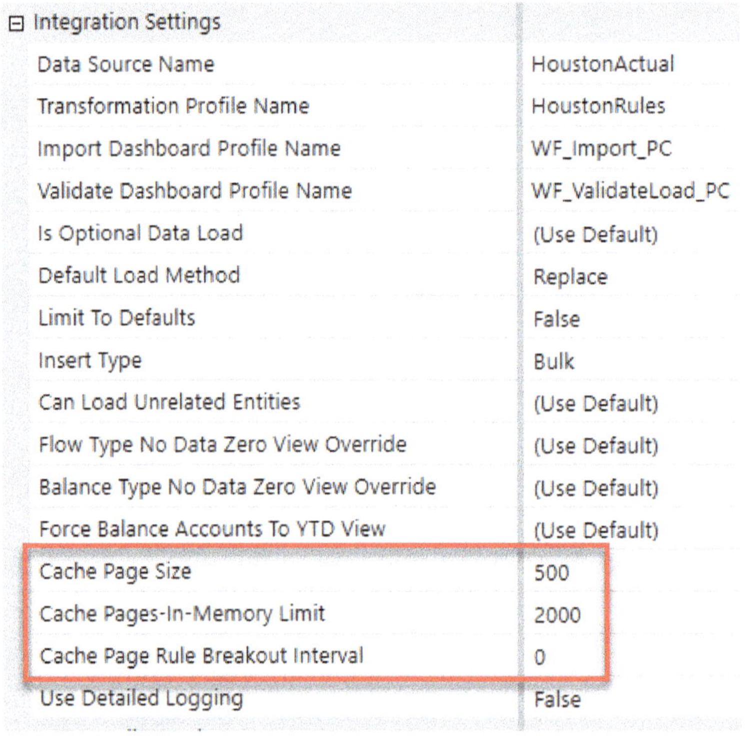

Integration Settings	
Data Source Name	HoustonActual
Transformation Profile Name	HoustonRules
Import Dashboard Profile Name	WF_Import_PC
Validate Dashboard Profile Name	WF_ValidateLoad_PC
Is Optional Data Load	(Use Default)
Default Load Method	Replace
Limit To Defaults	False
Insert Type	Bulk
Can Load Unrelated Entities	(Use Default)
Flow Type No Data Zero View Override	(Use Default)
Balance Type No Data Zero View Override	(Use Default)
Force Balance Accounts To YTD View	(Use Default)
Cache Page Size	500
Cache Pages-In-Memory Limit	2000
Cache Page Rule Breakout Interval	0
Use Detailed Logging	False

Figure 6.5

Data Load Basics of Analytic Blend

All the data resides in OneStream and can be used (or be reported) by a data blend.

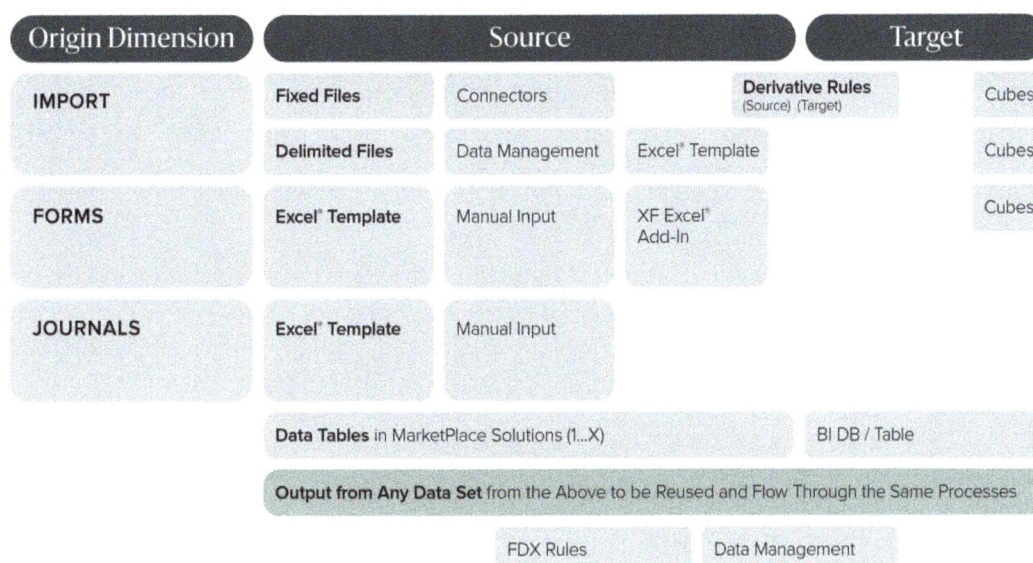

Origin Dimension	Source				Target
IMPORT	Fixed Files	Connectors		Derivative Rules (Source) (Target)	Cubes
	Delimited Files	Data Management	Excel® Template		Cubes
FORMS	Excel® Template	Manual Input	XF Excel® Add-In		Cubes
JOURNALS	Excel® Template	Manual Input			

Data Tables in MarketPlace Solutions (1...X)		BI DB / Table

Output from Any Data Set from the Above to be Reused and Flow Through the Same Processes

FDX Rules	Data Management

Figure 6.6

The table above is a snapshot of the entire ecosystem, and how to get and reuse data in OneStream. Each Origin dimension has its option to load data.

Data Source Types

- **Fixed files** – standard repeatable data files that have text items in specific segments of information in the file.

- **Delimited files** – files that have data separated by items such as a comma, semi-colon, or another character.

- **Connectors** – format that connects to a database, an ODBC connection, or consumes a file prepared by a connection (such as XML) from a Rest API.

- **Data management export sequences** – format that pulls data from other areas of OneStream. For example, pulls data from a MarketPlace solution or another cube.

- **Excel template** – this could be a manual input or a link to one or more spreadsheets. Can be used for imports, forms, or journals.

- **Manual input** – creates a form for data to be inputted manually. This form can be downloaded from a form in Excel and inputted.

- **Excel add-in** – this could be a manual input or a link to one or more spreadsheets; it uses formulas to load to specific data cells.

- **Derivative rules** – creates additional records that can be used for checking a trial balance, creating offsets or allocations. The rules can be done on source data or target data after mapping.

- **OneStream cubes** – data prepared in the cube for consolidation and eliminations, which can be extracted and reused.

- **MarketPlace solutions** – data in these add-on platform solutions can be extracted and put into a OneStream cube.

- **DB Tables** – specific tables set up for Analytic Blend.

The OneStream ecosystem embraces all this data, which can be reused and consumed for other projects and other purposes. Indeed, there is no limit to the data that can be used and reused in the ecosystem!

Data Parser and Business Rules

A complete book could be written detailing data parser uses and the unlimited extended capability of business rules, but this book will leave that to the training classes and a future book. The data parser in OneStream changes based on what type of flat file is being used. Whether fixed or delimited, it has out-of-the-box capabilities to do tabbed and matrix data loads without business rule scripts.

Business rules allow a full scripting engine to complete complex tasks in the dataset that cannot be done out-of-the-box. The next few pages will summarize the types of formats.

Fixed Files

Fixed files typically have some sort of header(s), have data spaced out over the file, and are generally easy on the eyes. It's usually a system report of some kind that is created in the source system and printed to a file. Business rules can be applied to complex fixed files to extend the capabilities of OneStream software.

```
Run Control ID:   Report_Catalog
Report:  Trial_Balance
Language: English
Date Produced:                                                       02/01/2020    13:42:54
Version:  Final
Org:  Manchester Bags


Account              Div  Period      Currency Description                     YTD Balance      Active
10015-000-54-00-000  110  2020-01     GBP      BANK - WELLS FARGO LP DISBU      383,244.00   Y
10030-000-54-00-000  110  2020-01     GBP      BANK - CHASE DEPOSIT           1,001,256.31   Y
10035-000-54-00-000  110  2020-01     GBP      BANK - WELLS FARGO LP DEPOS - H  753,451.40   Y
11000-000-54-00-000  110  2020-01     GBP      TRADE A/R- CONTROL            18,146,938.23   Y
11100-000-54-00-000  110  2020-01     GBP      A/R ACCRUAL                      289,822.35   Y
11111-000-54-00-000  110  2020-01     GBP      TRADE RECEIVABLES CONTRA DRV    -427,785.00   Y
11520-000-54-00-000  110  2020-01     GBP      A/P VOIDED CHECKS                  9,103.26   Y
11900-000-54-00-000  110  2020-01     GBP      ALLOW DOUBTFUL ACCT              -56,407.49   Y
12200-000-54-00-000  110  2020-01     GBP      WIP MATERIAL - FWD                 2,583.00   Y
12200-000-54-00-000  110  2020-01     GBP      WIP MATERIAL - NYL                 2,841.82   Y
12200-000-54-00-000  110  2020-01     GBP      WIP MATERIAL - GEN             1,932,528.33   Y
12300-000-54-00-000  110  2020-01     GBP      FINISHED GOODS - FWD           6,161,404.27   Y
12300-000-54-00-000  110  2020-01     GBP      FINISHED GOODS - FWD           4,648,159.76   Y
```

Figure 6.7

Delimited Files

Delimited files are just data separated by a character. Be careful that the delimiter does not have a use/function in a field, though. Sometimes, a customer name or an account name could be using a comma or one of the other delimiters in the name. Take a company name like New Company, Inc. The data field could have a comma and a period in it, and if used as a delimiter, it can throw off the entire file.

Take the numbers in the following example. This comma-delimited file was probably generated by an Excel file, as the numbers are set in double quotations. The parsing engine of OneStream can recognize this, and there won't be an issue with the additional commas inside the double quotation marks. OneStream will read them as amounts. Common file reading problems are addressed in a lot of OneStream's out-of-the-box functionality, and business rules applied to complex, delimited files can extend the capability of the software.

```
* * * Top of File * * *
Amount,Entity,Cons,Scenario,Time,View,Account,Flow,Sub1,Product
"108,000.00",Frankfurt,Local,Actual,2020M1,YTD,54199,None,Direct,None
"112,000.00",Frankfurt,Local,Actual,2020M1,YTD,50300,None,Direct,None
"105,000.00",Frankfurt,Local,Actual,2020M1,YTD,54199,None,Indirect,None
"103,000.00",Frankfurt,Local,Actual,2020M1,YTD,50300,None,Indirect,None
"110,000.00",Frankfurt,Local,Actual,2020M1,YTD,60999,None,None,Woods
"90,000.00",Frankfurt,Local,Actual,2020M1,YTD,60999,None,None,Putters
"55,000.00",Frankfurt,Local,Actual,2020M1,YTD,43000,None,Engineering,None
"42,000.00",Frankfurt,Local,Actual,2020M1,YTD,43000,None,Quality,None
"32,000.00",Frankfurt,Local,Actual,2020M1,YTD,43000,None,Production,None
"150,000.00",Frankfurt,Local,Actual,2020M1,YTD,10999,EndBal,None,None
"125,000.00",Frankfurt,Local,Actual,2020M1,YTD,11999,EndBal,None,None
"110,000.00",Frankfurt,Local,Actual,2020M1,YTD,16000,EndBal,None,None
"112,000.00",Frankfurt,Local,Actual,2020M1,YTD,17100,EndBal,None,None
"110,000.00",Frankfurt,Local,Actual,2020M1,YTD,20999,EndBal,None,None
"175,000.00",Frankfurt,Local,Actual,2020M1,YTD,23000,EndBal,None,None
"106,000.00",Frankfurt,Local,Actual,2020M1,YTD,24300,EndBal,None,None
"115,000.00",Frankfurt,Local,Actual,2020M1,YTD,27999,EndBal,None,None
6,Frankfurt,Local,Actual,2020M1,YTD,Headcount,EndBal,Engineering,None
7,Frankfurt,Local,Actual,2020M1,YTD,Headcount,EndBal,Quality,None
55,Frankfurt,Local,Actual,2020M1,YTD,Headcount,EndBal,Production,None
* * * End of File * * *
```

Figure 6.8

Connectors

Connectors are used to connect to database tables with SQL queries. ODBC connections, XML files, Webservice API's, and a host of other possibilities are applicable. Below is a brief sample of some data from a QuickBooks trial balance. These formats require the use of business rule scripts. The use of business rules can read any dataset, and consume it based on fields.

Figure 6.9

Data Management

Data management jobs are internal OneStream processes that can pull data as a source from another area of the product, such as a cube (plus data that was calculated within the cube), by creating data management profile steps and sequences.

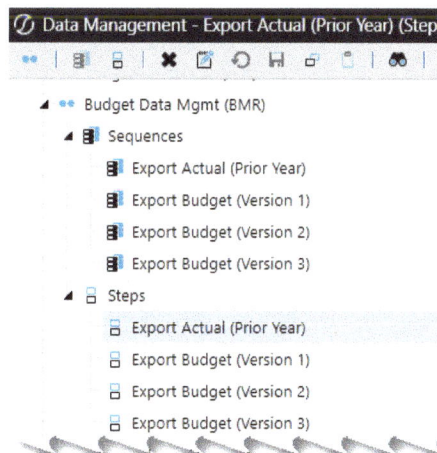

Figure 6.10

Additional Data Input Sources

Excel Templates

For a lot of companies, Excel is the software that captures and collects a lot (if not most) data. Excel is familiar to just about everyone, and users can easily prepare data in spreadsheets. Data can be consumed by placing information into a template with header tags and a range name, and then be loaded through a workflow. The data source must set the Allow Dynamic Excel Loads property to True in order to import Excel data to the Stage. But, based on the table, data can be loaded to other members of the Origin dimension. Excel files can have multiple range names in a file and multiple tables.

The column headings can be done one time on a top row and applied across all the records.

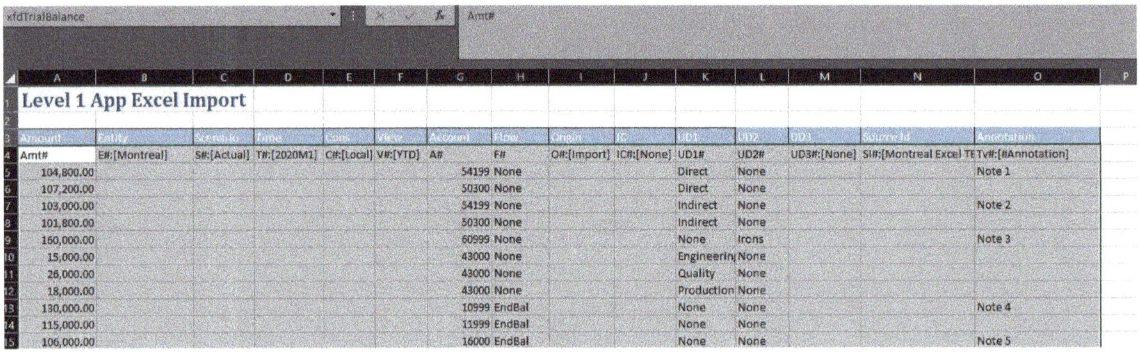
xfdTrialBalance | Amt#

Level 1 App Excel Import

Amount	Entity	Scenario	Time	Cons	View	Account	Flow	Origin	IC	UD1	UD2	UD3	Source Id	Annotation
Amt#	E#:[Montreal]	S#:[Actual]	T#:[2020M1]	C#:[Local]	V#:[YTD]	A#	F#	O#:[Import]	IC#:[None]	UD1#	UD2#	UD3#:[None]	SI#:[Montreal Excel TE	Tv#:[#Annotation]
104,800.00						54199	None			Direct	None			Note 1
107,200.00						50300	None			Direct	None			
103,000.00						54199	None			Indirect	None			Note 2
101,800.00						50300	None			Indirect	None			
160,000.00						60999	None			None	Irons			Note 3
15,000.00						43000	None			Engineerin(	None			
26,000.00						43000	None			Quality	None			
18,000.00						43000	None			Production	None			
130,000.00						10999	EndBal			None	None			Note 4
115,000.00						11999	EndBal			None	None			
106,000.00						16000	EndBal			None	None			Note 5

Figure 6.11

The Excel format is set up with tags on the first line and range names. The range names have specific meanings.

XFD	Data load to Stage
XFF	Form data
XFJ	Journal data
XFC	Cell details

Figure 6.12

Forms

Forms are used for manual inputs. Sometimes, some information is not included in the source data or needs some detail. The example shown here is just for headcount. The creation of forms and their use in workflow will be discussed in another chapter.

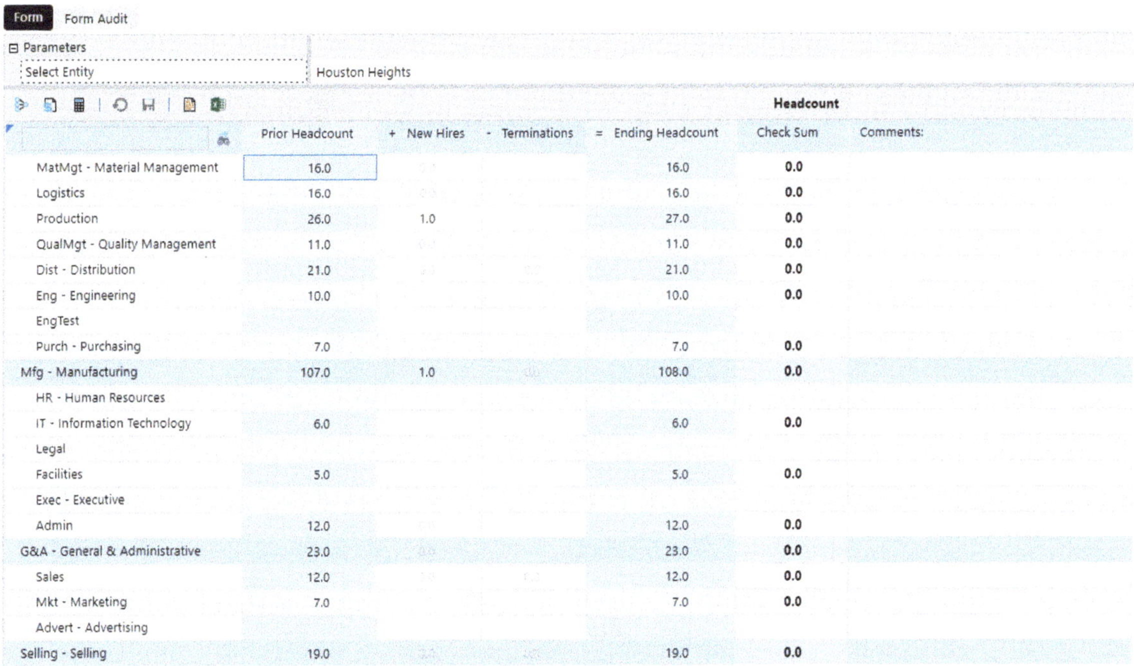

Figure 6.13

Adjustments (Journal Entries)

One best practice is to put all journal entries into the source system and reload, but in some cases, the ability to have journal entries in the system aids tasks like consolidating entries that have no ledger home.

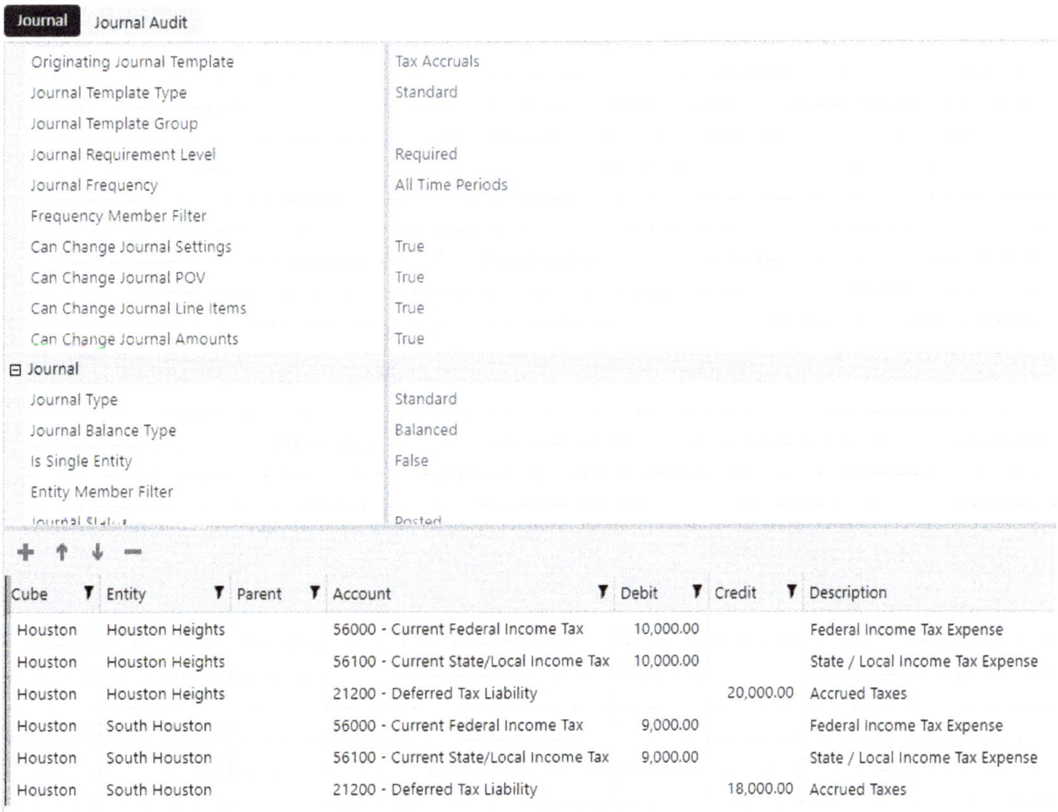

Figure 6.14

Workflow Data Protection and Layering

The concepts of layering and data protection are used in OneStream to separate and close off data areas from one another. Reloading a Data Unit is typically based on entity, as an entity is usually the main way that data is loaded into a cube.

A number of concepts, such as workflow, data sources, and Origin dimension, come together in this diagram to show how they all work together. Data (in the import dimension) is isolated from the forms and the journals.

Data in the import dimension can be isolated and protected by the source ID and/or the workflow channel. The workflow channel can use an account-level dimension member – such as product – to help separate the Data Unit into an isolated data load.

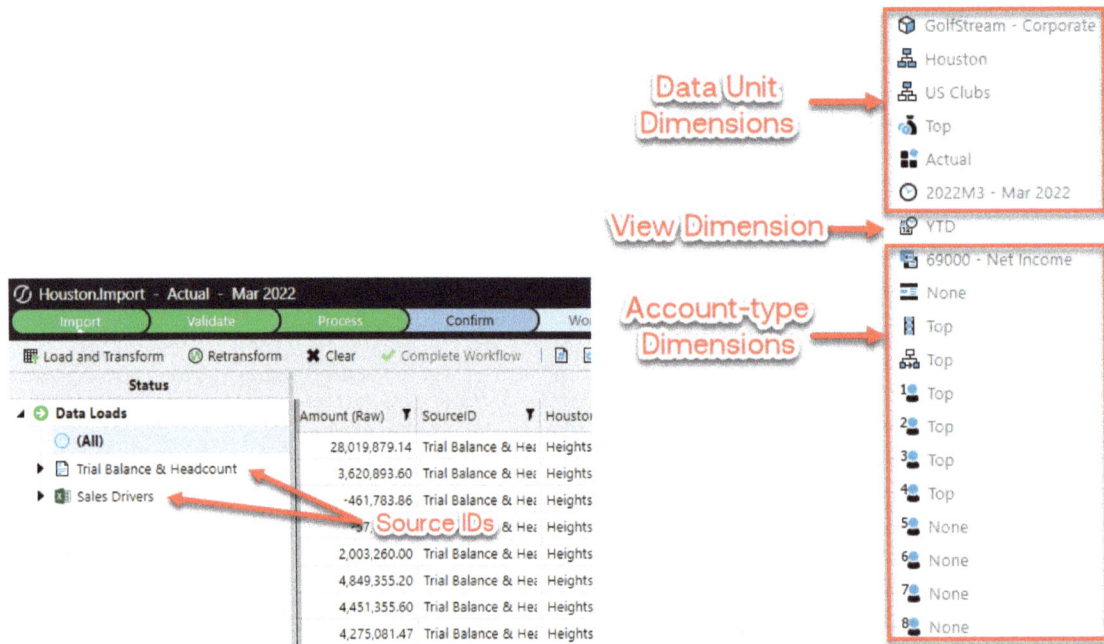

Figure 6.15

The **source ID** is a field in the data source that allows a field to be tagged to determine how to reload data. The workflow channel can be another tool used to parse, based on one of the account-level dimension members. At one company, each plant produced more than one product and had different finance people for each product (and they planned separately). The Workflow Chapter will cover the use of the workflow channel, adding another layer of data protection.

A commonly reused source ID is the name of the data file. The next figure is an example of a snippet editor that can be added to the system from the MarketPlace, and which can extend the capabilities of the business rules with pre-written code snippets.

```
'----------------------------------------------------------------------------------------------
'Reference Code:    XFR_GetFilenameForSourceID
'
'Description:       Gets the file name being processed, strips off the unique indentifier that XF
'                   adds to the file name and returns the origninal source file name.
'
'Usage:             Parser business rule intended to be used on the SourceID field in a data source.
'
'Created By:        Tom Shea
'Date Created:      2-01-2013
'----------------------------------------------------------------------------------------------
Public Function Main(ByVal si As SessionInfo, ByVal globals As BRGlobals, ByVal api As ParserDimension, ByVal args As ParserArgs) As Object
    Try

        'Get the filename and strip off the Unique ID suffix if it exists
        If api.Parser.Transformer.FileInfo.SourceFileName.Contains("_") Then
            'Split filename into segments (Parse by "_" character)
            Dim segments As List(Of String) = StringHelper.SplitString(api.Parser.Transformer.FileInfo.SourceFileName, "_",
                & StageConstants.ParserDefaults.DefaultQuoteCharacter)

            'Create a string builder object and then loop over the segments and put the file name back together
            'but skip the last segment which is the Unique ID suffix.  We use a string builder rather than concatenating
            'with the "&" because string builders are much faster.
            Dim segName as new System.Text.StringBuilder
            For seg as Integer = 0 to segments.Count - 2
                segName.Append(segments(seg))
                If seg < (segments.Count-2) Then segName.Append("_")
            next

            'Return the contents of the string builder as a string
            return segName.ToString
        Else
            'File name does not contain "_" just return it
            Return api.Parser.Transformer.FileInfo.SourceFileName
        End if

    Catch ex As Exception
        Throw ErrorHandler.LogWrite(si, New XFException(si, ex))
    End Try
End Function
```

Figure 6.16

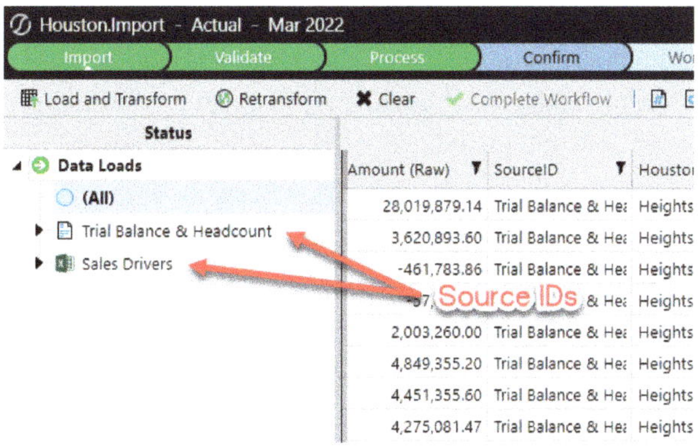

Figure 6.17

This figure shows how a single entity in a workflow can be carved up to reload and segment data for the entity. The Origin dimension creates a separation of data.

Data reloading can be separated by different source IDs in one workflow and have multiple channels.

Origin by Layer of Data Protection

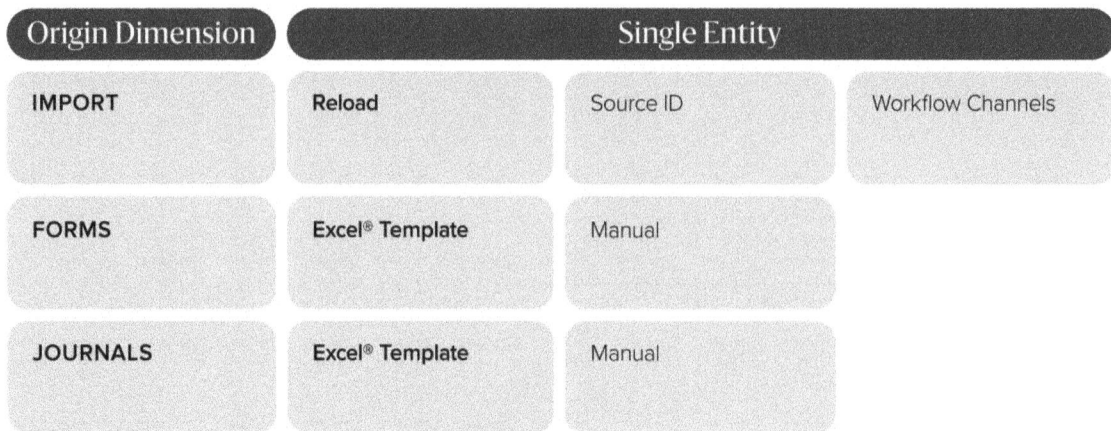

Origin Dimension	Single Entity		
IMPORT	Reload	Source ID	Workflow Channels
FORMS	Excel® Template	Manual	
JOURNALS	Excel® Template	Manual	

Figure 6.18

Organizing and Naming Convention

With data sources, business rules, translation rules, form templates, and journal templates, it is important to think about naming conventions thoroughly. Make any naming convention consistent and understandable. Use prefixes or suffixes. Because this platform can create cubes and share dimensions from the library, certain parts can be reused and placed in a profile and used again and again.

A data source based on a ledger system can be reused if it's the same ledger and format. The same format can be reused multiple times instead of creating one by entity, or the same query could be used by having a dynamic change based on some workflow variables that will substitute variables into the query to pull differently based on workflow. We can use substitution text strings in the workflow to change how a query gets used.

⊟ Substitution Text Settings	
Text 1	QBOSLLC
Text 2	Accrual
Text 3	
Text 4	

Figure 6.19

There are also some global transformation rules that can easily be reused. The dimension rules for scenario, time, and view should be named as global because they can be reused over multiple cubes. These three dimensions can only have one-to-one mapping. So, make it simple, if you can, and only have one group for each one if they don't overlap with different strings. The mapping is usually a simple actual to actual. Be careful about dimension mapping, though; if there is mapping that can be reused, then name it accordingly so you can add it to more than one profile.

You can rename certain items without penalty. As you continue to build your application, and want to keep consistency in your naming convention as well as naming convention changes, you can modify some of the items easily to adapt to your naming convention. It's important to understand what each piece of the puzzle is.

Item	Rename/Locked	Naming Example
Data Sources	Rename	Entity (Michigan), Workflow (Cleveland Plant), General Ledger (SAP, Sage, etc.)
Transformation Dimensions	Rename	Global Scenario A_Sage A_Cleveland
Transformation Rule Profiles	Rename	Entity (Michigan), Workflow (Cleveland Plant), General Ledger (SAP, Sage, etc.)
Parser Business Rules	Locked (could change name and recreate but would have to be reattached)	XFR_Sage_Account XFR_Cleveland_Product
Form Template Groups	Rename	Data Entry (Data Entry)
Form Template Profiles	Rename	DE_GL
Forms	Rename (v8.0 and newer)	A_AR, B_PPE, C_LTDebt
Journal Template Groups	Rename	JE_Elimination
Journal Template Profiles	Rename	JE_EntityA
Journals	Rename (v8.0 and newer)	JE_IntercoElim

Figure 6.20

Attributes

There are 13 mappable dimensions, but there are also extra fields to assist in capturing other source data that can be used for other purposes. These include label dimensions, 20 attribute dimensions, and 12 attribute value dimensions. These fields can be activated on the cube and used for collecting source data; while not important for the data cube, they could be used to analyze and report on records such as SKU numbers or product numbers.

Business Rules

Business rules enhance the ability to read a file. If a file can be read without them, don't use them unless they benefit the mapping process. Business rules might be used to carve up a string, or join strings together when combining items for mapping. Use a – or _ to separate items.

Transformation Rules

Transformation rules are rules that map a source member to a specific target value. There are different types of transformation rules and usage examples.

Think about data and needs before mapping begins. Usually, mapping is provided by a group that doesn't have mapping expertise but who can get lucky if the users have experience or proper training. Typically, there are economies that can be gained by reviewing the types of mapping and figuring out the best use of mapping. The following table is just a recap of the different types of mapping available.

Derivatives are additional rules that can be used to create records as check figures or supplementary records for mapping. Some examples include: a sum of all records to make sure the trial balance balances, testing the sign of a record or records, and the allocation or creation of offsets. Using derivatives is only one way of allocation; there are other allocation methods that can be done at the target.

Transformation Rule Type	Definition	Example
Source Derivative	Applied logic & math to inbound source data	Does trial balance equal zero? Does an asset go negative and need to be reclassed as a liability?
One-to-One	Explicitly mapped members (Scenario, Time, and View can only use these rules)	Actual -> Actual 05/31/2021 -> 2021M5 Monthly -> MTD 23099 -> 23000
Composite	Supports mapping 'slices' of members such as a product	A#51000: UD2#H* to the UD1 member of sales
Range	Map a range of accounts from A to Z to = target.	Map accounts 21230~21239 to 20300
List	Map a delimited list of accounts to one account	Map accounts 41137;42642;42688 to account 60100
Mask	Wildcard mapping that takes the place of one character (?) or multiple characters (*)	Map accounts that start with 86 (as 86*) to 41000 or *84*7* to 41000 Account starts with any one character, then 86 (as ?86*) to 42800 Any account to any account if there is a match: * to * Mask rules run less efficiently due to use of? or embedded asterisks (e.g., *84*7*)

Transformation Rule Type	Definition	Example
Target Derivative	Applied logic & math to post-transformed Stage data	Does an aggregated mapped total need to be mapped differently because it is positive or negative?
BlendUnit All Derivative	Applied logic & math to post transformed Blend partitioned page data (Non-Stage)	Executes for ALL BlendUnit pages (base or parent)
BlendUnit Base Derivative	Applied logic & math to post transformed Blend partitioned page data (Non-Stage)	Executes for base BlendUnit pages only
BlendUnit Parent Derivative	Applied logic & math to post transformed Blend partitioned page data (Non-Stage)	Executes for parent BlendUnit pages only

Figure 6.21

Transformation Performance

This information is taken directly from our training materials as it is the best summary of the costs of mapping. Each type of mapping rule has a cost, and small trial balances don't have a significant issue with time. The more records, the more time they take to map.

Understanding the economics of these different rules is important. Just because something is in the red doesn't make it bad. Question marks cost a lot of processing power. They should be limited, but there might be times they make sense; if they cause the data load to take longer, it might be time to consider other mapping alternatives.

Using question marks on both sides would be extremely costly as the data has to be carved up and put back together.

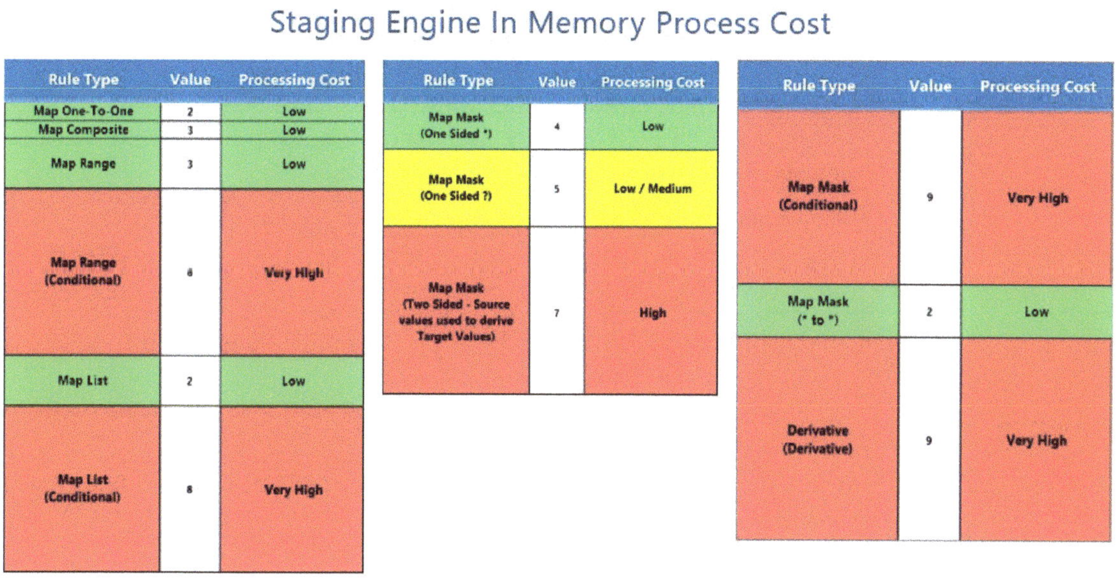

Staging Engine In Memory Process Cost

Rule Type	Value	Processing Cost
Map One-To-One	2	Low
Map Composite	3	Low
Map Range	3	Low
Map Range (Conditional)	8	Very High
Map List	2	Low
Map List (Conditional)	8	Very High

Rule Type	Value	Processing Cost
Map Mask (One Sided *)	4	Low
Map Mask (One Sided ?)	5	Low / Medium
Map Mask (Two Sided - Source values used to derive Target Values)	7	High

Rule Type	Value	Processing Cost
Map Mask (Conditional)	9	Very High
Map Mask (* to *)	2	Low
Derivative (Derivative)	9	Very High

Figure 6.22

187

Rule Type	Processing
Map One-To-One	Simple update pass through to the database.
Map Range	Simple update pass through to the database.
Map Range (Conditional)	Uses a lot of data transfer and memory utilization. Required to return a record set with all dim fields back to the app server to perform conditional mapping.
Map List	Simple update pass through to the database.
Map List (Conditional)	Uses a lot of data transfer and memory utilization. Required to return a record set with all dim fields back to the app server to perform conditional mapping. Keep LIST least restrictive. Break list into multiple, smaller lists for optimal memory utilization and faster rules processing.
Map Mask *	Use one-sided * for low processing overhead. Simple update pass through to the database.
Map Mask ?	Simple update pass through to the database. Use one-sided ? for low/medium processing overhead. Masking queries must use table scans which can hurt performance on large record volumes. Keep total number of ? to a minimum. More ? causes longer time for database engine to process the mask.
Map Mask * to *	Processes very quickly. Simple update pass through to the database.
Map Mask (Conditional)	Uses a lot of data transfer and memory utilization. Required to return a record set with all dim fields back to the app server to perform conditional mapping. Keep Mask criteria restrictive. Limit each query to a small chunk. Example: 1*, 2*, A*, B*
Derivative	Uses a lot of data transfer and memory utilization. Required to return a record set with all dim fields back to the app server to perform conditional mapping. Executes a SQL Statement that pulls ALL dimension fields from worktable with a LIKE clause as main criteria and passes records back to the application server. Required for the application server to derive the calculated rows. New records are inserted into the worktable one by one.

Figure 6.23

ODBC Connectors and Rest API

With ledgers moving to the cloud, there are a lot of products out there that can be used to connect to cloud-based software and ledger systems directly. I have been able to connect to multiple products using ODBC connectors by third parties – for QuickBooks and other products – from vendors, including QODBC and CData.

These products do take some knowledge of SQL and some time to set up, but once set up, they work on demand. They also require some knowledge of the product and tables and stored procedures. I found them to be useful but more complicated than using a REST API. However, with our Azure cloud offering, this becomes more problematic from a security point of view and is not available to customers hosting in Azure.

Most cloud products have a REST API, which allows you to directly connect with the product, albeit with some barriers (e.g., IDs and passwords) that are needed at a nominal cost. There are several REST APIs that have samples. Some of those ledgers or source systems include Sage Intacct, Salesforce, Workday, SAP, Dynamics AX, and Hubspot. Some software providers ask you to buy the developer license in order to get the necessary credentials and their protections for your data; not just anyone can get to them. Credentials are typically needed to get back data in an XML format before it can be read and parsed in a connection business rule.

Smart Integration Connector (SIC)

When either the ODBC connector or REST API service are not exposed publicly, meaning the OneStream environment cannot get to them directly, you will need to leverage the Smart Integration Connector (SIC), which is a solution that uses a local agent (SIC Gateway) to be installed inside the customer's network and then leverages Azure Relay technology to communicate with OneStream. More information can be found in the product documentation or by attending one of our training sessions for SIC.

Automation with Batch Process

OneStream has the ability to fully process files through the workflow by using batch processing. Files can be prepared with a naming convention that can be used to auto load. By dropping a file into the `Harvest` directory, and with a specified interval, batch files can be loaded into OneStream. This works well for fixed, delimited, and Excel files. Blank files can be created for connector-based data sources and the data management export sequences.

Field Layout:

```
File ID-WorkflowProfileName-ScenarioName-TimeName-LoadMethod.txt
```

File Name Example:

```
1TB-Detroit;Import-Actual-2011M1-R.txt
```

Conclusion

Data Integration is the foundation of all the data that can be reported through OneStream. Managing data, and deciding upon the level and detail of data, is a large part of any design. Don't unnecessarily populate the system with data you don't need; use OneStream to analyze all the data you have. If you need to investigate, you can drill back to larger data sources and warehouses. You can get any data into this system, and roll it up and report on it in many different ways. Controlled, organized data should be your primary focus when building the platform.

Epilogue

This photo is from September 13, 2011, when the original team was performing the first implementation of OneStream. The group was discussing metadata design for the application, and mapping from the legacy source system of Hyperion Enterprise to consume the historical data and the dimension mapping from Enterprise to OneStream.

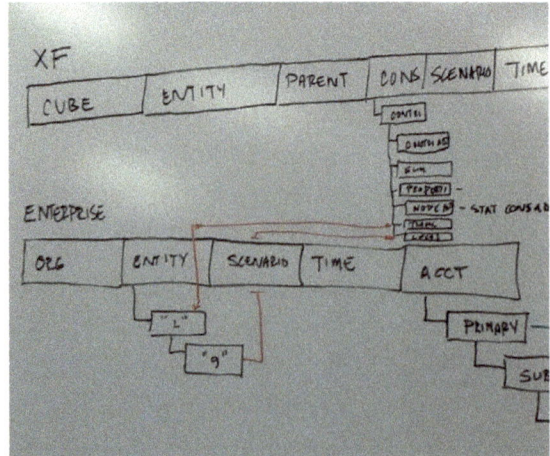

Our first customer wanted 14 years of data reconciled, and *that was extreme*. But it allowed the customer to retire its legacy system forever, and allowed us to test the system with the volume of data. The funny thing is that, as a consultant, I loaded and reconciled their prior system 14 years before that. The *same* data was reconciled twice, by the same person, 14 years apart.

This second photo is from our May 2017 Splash Conference. It was a big moment when we arrived and saw our name – up in lights – at the Hard Rock Hotel.

It was also one of those moments, as a startup, when you just have to laugh. We had just reached 100 employees, 75+ of whom were coming from different parts of the world, and all the corporate credit cards were being rejected for each US-based employee (as the pre-payment authorizations were being charged to a casino!). I had to call our bank to make sure they knew people were going to be staying there, and to authorize the charges!

7
Workflow

Originally written by Todd Allen, updated by Chul Smith

Introduction

Workflow is an extraordinarily strong orchestration engine within OneStream's **Corporate Performance Management** (CPM), one that was created by the pioneers of the CPM industry.

Workflow in OneStream is a process tool that takes into account how many of our clients' employees will need to enter data at different times, in possibly different time zones, in hundreds of locations, for all the varied business processes that make up their business. While other companies claim to have a workflow, none can compare to the power and flexibility of OneStream's offering.

Workflow is one of the more powerful components to OneStream, and pretty much every chapter in this book has a touchpoint that is either tied to, leads with, or ends with workflow. It is the backbone of the platform.

When a user logs into the system, OneStream's workflow guides them to make sure they complete all the steps necessary within their process. Not only does workflow guide users, but it tracks their individual progress, which can be reviewed later. Imagine if you could look back on the past year of closing and evaluate who needed more time and who closed quickly. Could you cut a day from your close? Maybe you need to move quickly to update an older general ledger system? This is valuable, actionable data.

Transparency is typically important for our clients, and we have created one system (data loading/analytic engine) that solves multiple business problems across multiple business units (extensibility). Workflow is set up based on the different tasks involved in budgeting versus those for Actuals; tasks required in forecasting versus those in planning. When developing OneStream, we knew that our software had to be flexible for these situations, especially during the loading and feeding of data, and we learned early on that one size does not fit all. Not every user is going to remember everything all the time, either. With these complexities, we needed to figure out how to protect the end-user.

This chapter will give you some history into workflow's origin, design basics, and some key considerations to ensure a successful project.

Workflow Review

At some point, you will have inevitably seen a demonstration of OneStream. I am sure you will remember the picture below (Figure 7.1). Consider how data is sourced in three ways: data input, a journal, or manual data entry. Data loading is either a file, an Excel spreadsheet, or sourced from a database (e.g., general ledger).

That data feed then goes to the Stage table for transformation and mapping. These tables, journals, and forms are all fed into the cube, which is our financial model. The design of said cube is what drives reporting and performance. Then, you can report on the data using Cube Views, reports, or Excel. Each of these steps – by the end-users – is a step in your workflow! This is repeated for each site, such that Site 1 and Site 2 can work concurrently on their data.

Workflow ensures that users follow the steps needed for your process. It tracks when they complete each step successfully.

OneStream Application

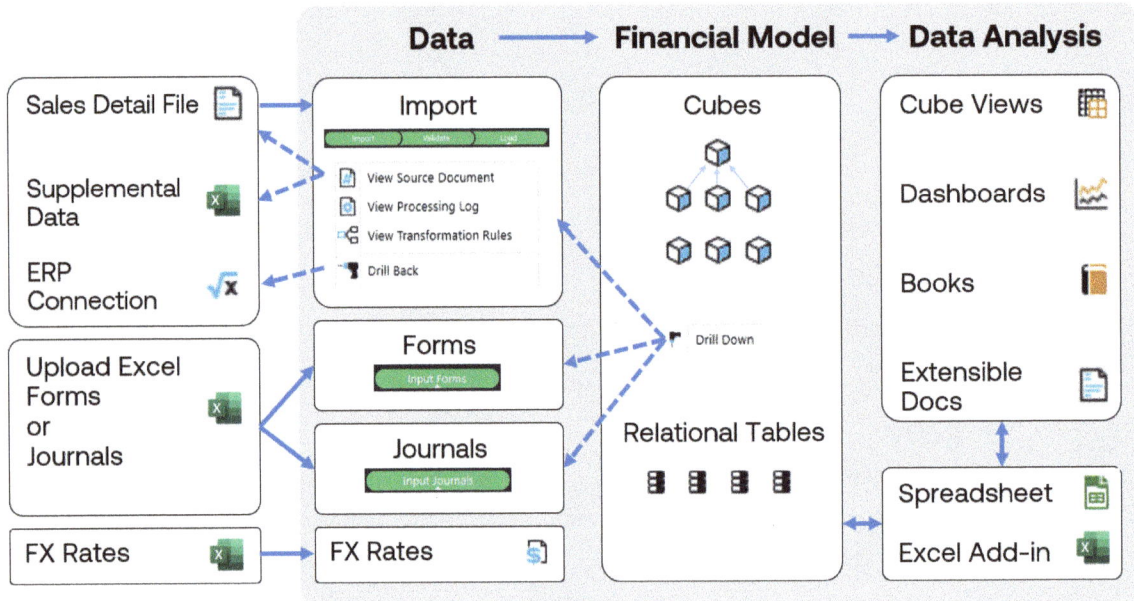

Figure 7.1

Workflow Evolving

The genesis of workflow was originally three concepts:

- Responsibility Hierarchy
- Transparency to process
- Strict Sign-off & Control

When we started building the concepts of workflow, we began with the most complex and strict financial process – the month-end close of Actuals. Those first passes at workflow had struggles, though, and we recognized that the typical certification process could be a bit too restrictive. Not every process was as restrictive as month-end Actual reporting. We needed better ideas, which would be more accommodating. As such, we continued to develop other solutions like Workspace.

Workspace is a completely customized workflow, to match the business process, which allowed us to loosen up restrictions and progress into large-scale, complex, planning-type projects, and custom solutions. Planning process controls vary wildly and require a much less restrictive process.

As we continued to develop our foundational concepts around workflows, we found performance and automation started to become a bigger issue to address in larger implementations. In these types of projects, all data would be loaded centrally under a single **Review Workflow Profile**. Below is a diagram of the workflow inputs.

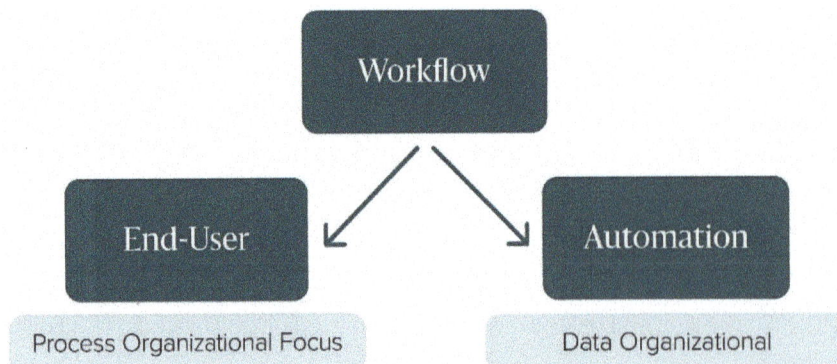

Figure 7.2

We conceptualized the workflow inputs as two sources of activities: end-user and automation. Each of these sources drives the workflow process.

End-User (Hierarchical/Responsibility)

End-users will be driving the workflow. The structure you build will guide these users and their approvals. The approvals are parent members of the base inputs. This forms a hierarchy.

The workflow hierarchy should align with your organization and process structure. Following this logic, data loading and certification exist in a hierarchical manner. Someone submits the data, someone above them reviews it, and so on. Dependencies are all inherent to the Workflow Profile hierarchy, and the workflow can ultimately roll up to the corporate headquarters. The structure of the hierarchy is pleasing to the eye but can be challenging from the administrator's perspective because there could potentially be so many review points. Plus, you may end up adding additional profiles that do not really add any value outside of the visual structure.

Automation (Lights Out, a Popular Choice)

We suggest prototyping an automated workflow early, and first running things manually to iron out all the wrinkles. You will also need to plan for kickouts or mapping issues. With an end-user, someone is watching the load, but with an automated feed, no one is checking as it is loading. It could be running overnight! You need to consider where and how you store data loading errors so the process can continue, but also have a process for the customer to perform analysis on items the next business day. Once this runs like a well-oiled machine, then you can go to a completely automated model.

This option is exceptionally clean. You can have a review profile with your data loading items from source systems. Examples are a single ERP data load, or siblings of ERPs, or centralized loading. This is quite easy and simple to configure.

When creating automatic feeds, be sure to plan them out with room to grow, and make sure you consider future acquisitions. You can stub out a section for future reference and should also consider loading your data through connectors in a lights-out fashion. All of this can be accommodated through a combination of workflow, data management, connector business rule(s), and data integration.

Please note that a lights-out process in OneStream is not a secret black box. It still uses the same mechanics as a manual process, including all the auditability. All the drilldown and functionality will be there, too.

Or Hybrid of the Above

Like most solutions, the best answer to many a problem is not one or the other, but a mix of both. With respect to performance and data structures, this is the next evolution. Larger applications require more data, and hence there is a hunger for more performance and the desire for lights out processing. For this, we need to design the data import accordingly. With automation, we may need to load a single ERP, which can be massive through a single import. This could be run overnight or done during off-hours, but if the process needs to be timely, we need to look at how best to break this up.

The cost of calculations is in the reprocessing. If transformations (mappings) change, we have to run against the whole dataset, and that means reloading everything. Remember, we are loading a dataset and creating the links to drill back to the source data... either to the Stage table or to source data.

Chapter 7

Data Volumes and Performance

Loading to the Stage

Good design is critical to good performance. For a good design, we need to understand the mechanics of workflow, and how we translate data to disk. We also need to think about data structure and automation. The two most important ways we can impact performance are through parallel processing and partitioning. Parallel processing is the primary way to improve the performance of data loading and to get the data into the analytic model. In a nutshell, it means concurrent loads of data happening at the same time. Partitioning is how we break up the data file coming in.

We want to keep the partitioning to manageable groups. Ultimately, the amount of performance and throughput you can apply to a workflow process comes down to the efficiency of the data structures. We do not want to overload the application server with too much data being sent to the database. We have hardware limitations that restrict how much data can move in a timely fashion. This could cause system conflicts and backups, and will make a bad situation worse. If we understand how the data is stored on the disk, however, we can maximize concurrency in these large batch processes through parallel processing.

We are often dealing with large files (several million records). For this, let us consider large as 1 million rows. Can we process a million-row file? Of course! But what if we need to reprocess (remap) or perform this on a more regular basis? That million could be tens of millions or more as it is loaded multiple times.

We should study that 1 million row file and see how we can parse the file for efficiency. Parsing means breaking it up into multiple files. What if we could break it into four files? Now, we can process four 250k files in parallel. And if we must reprocess, it will take a quarter of the time. This is where understanding data structures will give you the insight needed for the most performant workflows.

If we chose months to break up the rows, we would have no more than 12. If we chose entity, we could have as many as we have entities (hundreds or more). We could group the entities, too. Therefore, we should *never* partition by months (period). One million divided by 12 will create larger groups than one million divided by 100 entities. So, each group runs faster, and more can run at the same time – or in parallel. Finally, if we have a change, we can load that entity (or entity group) without having to load everything.

The OneStream **partition** is created using an algorithm that breaks up the GUID (identification field as a 16-byte integer) to look at the first 4 bytes. This breaks up the single bucket of data and spreads it to the 250 tables in SQL. The OneStream application does this automatically.

Workflow Clusters

We will want to create a workflow hierarchy which then puts data into a **workflow cluster**.

A workflow cluster primary key (PK) aligns to a data storage index when using business rules (specifically the BRAPI); we always refer to the workflow PK cluster.

The following is an example from the GolfStream application (The OneStream reference application):

- Workflow GUID (Houston)
- Scenario Id (Actual)
- Time Id (2020M1)

All this data will be co-located together. So, how do we know how it is stored in the SQL database? If we look at SQL Server, we see just one table, but SQL Server sees 250 tables. It uses the workflow cluster PK GUID and takes the first four bytes as direction as to where it needs to go into the 250 tables, based on an algorithm we have built in our system. We did this so we do not fight and compete against each other. We may be loading 1,000 entities across all these structures at the

194

same time, and if all the data went into a single partition there could be locking opportunities. If one user is loading while another user is loading or deleting, there could be conflict with each other, which causes locking, too. So why is partitioning so important in the staging area? Clustered index!

Note: Each time we create a new workflow, the system automatically creates a GUID for that workflow. Our Stage tables all use the same partitioning and data structures.

Let us go back to that original diagram (Figure 7.1). When a workflow is created for data loads, it is configured to receive data from the outside world, but we do not know if we're receiving valid accounts, entities, etc. We do not even have a primary key, and we still haven't mapped anything yet. We simply need to ingest the unknown data.

Then, we need to clean the data and distill it down to something that is good enough to send over to the analytic engine. We only know two dimensions – Scenario and Time – but with them, we now know we can put that bucket of data into the clustered index. It could be ten rows; it could be 1 million rows. We do not know much more than that. So, let us think about the difference between the analytic cube and data loading processing. Let's explain the contrasts below.

We break this up by two important concepts:

- **Bucket** – Stage engine data loading
- **Cell** – Analytic engine – distinct cell by a primary key

Work in the Stage area is done by bucket. Buckets are dealt with in their entirety and cannot be broken down like cells; therefore, we do not want to create a bucket that is too big. If there is one problem, then the whole bucket must be emptied and refilled. If we can break this up by multiple buckets, it is more efficient.

Buckets can be broken up by workflow, scenario, and time, all of which are the WF **cluster index**. Buckets reside inside a partition. I could be loading Plan and Actuals at the same time, within the same partition, and this is more efficient because I can work with large loads of data, and SQL can manage accordingly.

Let's take a moment to define what **paging** means for a computer operating system. In computer operating systems, paging is a memory management scheme by which a computer stores and retrieves data from secondary storage or use in main memory. In this scheme, the operating system retrieves data from secondary storage in same-sized blocks called **pages**. Paging is an important part of virtual memory implementations in modern operating systems, using secondary storage to let programs exceed the size of available physical memory.

In the following diagram, the data records (individual lines of the file) are moved to the tables in SQL databases, as shown by the database icon. Within each of the SQL databases, you can identify a single cell of data by scenario.

Workflow Hierarchy

Data Load

ERP_A	Group 1
	Group 2
	Group 3

ERP_B	Group 1
	Group 2
	Group 3

Equals - WFCluster Pk

WFKey (GUID)	Scenario	Time
5DE84C38-E0EF-4653-BEFF-0913B0235E93	0	2011005000
572D947B-FAC1-4753-831B-0AF8832A1C0D	10	2011005000
D76EDB33-8680-4E08-9A79-1179059F033C	30	2011004000
35CAE6FB-2D68-45AA-A055-17C882FAFBBB	0	0
8AA77EE2-2557-46C2-8770-1E95789A0C7E	10	10
56984C20-A766-40DC-8941-21FD4632CAE9	30	30

SQL Concurrency

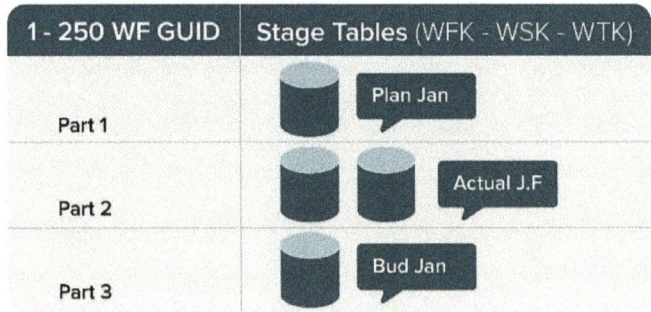

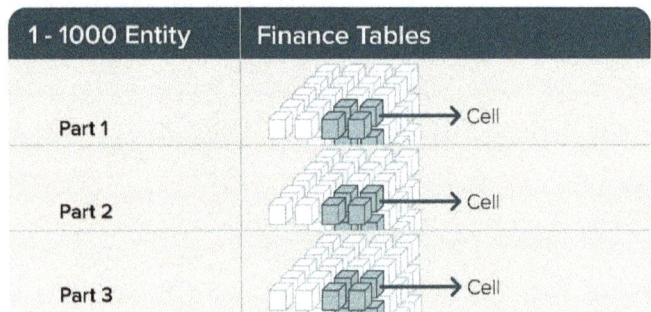

1 - 250 WF GUID	Stage Tables (WFK - WSK - WTK)
Part 1	Plan Jan
Part 2	Actual J.F
Part 3	Bud Jan

Turns buckets of data into cells…

SQL Concurrency

1 - 1000 Entity	Finance Tables
Part 1	→ Cell
Part 2	→ Cell
Part 3	→ Cell

Figure 7.3

Buckets function at the page level. The page is by scenario and by entity. The cell concept, by comparison, is quite different – each cell is one single number or record. When I update a cell in something like Excel, I am updating that single cell, as opposed to a set of data, which is more like a bucket. That bucket will update all records.

As the data loading process continues, I perform my mapping and I am now ready to send data back to the SQL Server. We grab the GUID, the Scenario ID (Actual), and Time ID (2020M1) – and with these three pieces and rows of data, the data moves to SQL. There is a function we have written inside SQL Server to read the first 4 bytes (as mentioned) and figure out how this equates to an integer between 0 and 250. This balances very well across the 250 partitions. You do not have to think about it; it's all done by OneStream.

If you're curious about your application's partitions, there's a report called **Stage Data Partition Statistics** found under the Application Analysis report group within the Standard Application Reports solution (which can be downloaded from the Solution Exchange).

This report will show how many workflows are in the system and if any of them share the same partition. (You will want to monitor if any of the workflows are overlapping.) Partitioning is all about isolating buckets! Why? If you go back in time, remember it was Site 1 loading, Site 2 loading, etc. By default, it broke up the buckets into their own partitions.

If we need to break up a bucket, how do we do that? Easy, the answer is always *by entity*. You look at the existing dataset. If we have a smaller 500k row file, this really should be no problem, but a planning load could be 12 million rows, so this may need some attention. 122 million records will cause issues for the connection to SQL to process things quickly. The Stage partition is configured into buckets (1 to 250 tables). The analytic engine is by cell. 1 to 1000 (each year has 1k tables).

Loading from the Stage to the Cube

Now that we have loaded the data into the Stage, and transformed it, it's time to load the cube. We now turn the buckets within the Stage into cells within the cube.

We need to map to the cube that will break up the data by Data Unit, so we start with the entity. The cube says okay, I see the bucket; how many entities do you have? I see you have 10 entities… I will go ahead and load those in parallel. This way, I can get super-high throughput. This is how the data structures are aligned.

What did we learn? Always partition by entity. There is an inherent relationship between workflow and entity, which aligns all the way through the data structures. Then, we always recommend loading time in sequential order. Start with January, then February, and so on.

In the example below, we start with the outside data and trace its movement to the cube.

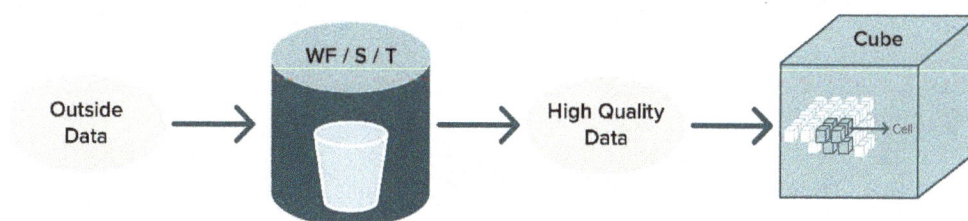

Figure 7.4

In the above diagram, you will see how this flow of data comes together.

- **Stage engine** – Outside data is fed to the Stage engine. This is loaded by clustered index, always updates the whole bucket, deletes the whole bucket, etc.
- **Analytic engine** – Focused by a primary key.
- **Load cube** – Breaks out the buckets of data into cells of data.

Remember, the database is designed to meet reporting requirements, and we need to make sure the data gets there as efficiently as possible.

There is not always a single design metric for a well-performing workflow, but around one million rows per location is efficient. If larger than that, additional analysis should be performed, and this is where you can apply the concepts from above.

End-User Use Case

With one client, we needed to replace an existing consolidation tool, so we were gathering requirements, and one of the first topics of discussion was workflow. The process when designing workflow is to define who does what tasks, when they do it, and how they will be processed.

The design started by finalizing the financial model, including the metadata structures, and we were soon ready to talk about data loading processes. We spent more time on data gathering and reviewing design than traditional implementations because we had to make sure we captured all the real-world situations in the newly completed workflow section of OneStream. This client was a Tier 1 automotive supplier with hundreds of locations all over the globe and with a roadmap of acquisitions that needed to be considered as part of the design.

This is a great use case for working through the workflow thought process. So, where did we start? Having the financial model defined was important. The discussion then turned to moving the data from the source to the reporting definition. We needed to be flexible, as we all knew there would always be some last-minute changes, but the core design needed to be in place, so we had a consistent process to the target cube.

When we designed the cube, we took the time to understand our end-user audience. Who does what, and why are they doing it? What are the review levels? What is the process? These questions may seem overwhelming to answer, but it's a perfect time to review the process and potentially weed out any bad habits. From here, we broke the audience up into groups.

The first group was the data loaders who were involved in loading data, the type of data loaded, and the frequency of the loads. This included single sites that loaded a single file, as well as shared service centers that loaded many entities.

I mentioned that the financial model needs to be in place; well, that also means the entity structure. This plays a critical role in the workflow design. Not that the workflow design must match the financial entity structure; it is just that we must understand the entities that we need to load to. Each entity needs to be accounted for in our workflow design.

Our initial whiteboards started off by breaking the groups up by region. Based on the regions, we defined the data loaders and reviewers. A driving factor for this was that we wanted to keep the data loading responsible to an individual. Multiple folks loading to the same entity could be problematic without proper coordination. The entity is a key to the loading process in terms of merging and replacing data. Take the time to understand who is loading to that entity and that there isn't any cross-loading. We took the approach of having a single owner (with a proxy as a backup) as a driving factor. This made the design very straightforward. This approach of having a single entity by location or user source is critical to avoid users overwriting each other's data as they load. The last user to update the database would have only their changes in the system.

This approach also helps with the security design. Each entity will be given a security group, and that group can be used for the workflow. This is a very simple approach. The user has access to an entity in reporting and data loading, all from the same security group. Sometimes, a **shared service** center may decide to break out into their own consolidated group, which adds to these security classes.

You'll want to review the size and frequency of your files. For example, in the shared service scenario, you could have a rather large file that was being loaded many times during the first couple of days of the close. They would be reloading the whole bucket of data unless the file is broken out. Do we keep it as one large file, or do we take the time to break it up? If we break it up, there will be more integration mechanics that we'll need to build/configure – different transformation rules, etc. From our testing, this would save time, but it wouldn't be enough for long-term maintenance.

This client wanted one data source and one transformation set of rules. Our decision was to keep the large data file load as it was. The alternative would have been a more granular workflow structure. The shared service section also had a different set of reviewers as shared service only mapped and loaded the data; if there were any mapping issues, they would address them, but all the validations were performed by local controllers.

Initial Workflow

After numerous whiteboarding sessions, we were at a point where we could stub out an initial workflow. As mentioned in the opening chapter, it was time to build out what we heard. In our case, we built out one of each of the groups and did a roadshow. We did this for two reasons. The first was to make sure we were able to translate what we captured during our requirements into a usable flow for them. Secondly, the roadshow was an early form of training. Looking back, user acceptance training was pretty much seamless, and we attribute some of that to the early roadshows.

To complete the data loading, we had to address historical data for which we created a dedicated location. Typically, people call it 'admin' or 'history' and allow access to it by administrators only. Since we were defining what entities would be assigned to their respective workflows, we turned to the ability to load unrelated entities on for the historical loads. This allowed us to load to all entities. One mistake people often make here is allowing the historical data and current end-user data to load to the same time periods. You do not want to do that. When data is loaded, it is often done as 'replace'. This, again, creates a situation where people are loading data and overwriting each other's submissions. In this case of loading historical data, we would recommend having two separate workflow locations to load to the same entities. One for end-users going forward, and the aforementioned one for administrators for history. Since each group does not have an overlapping time period, this should avoid overwriting each other's data. If they do load to the same periods, you will need to add workflow channels to your design.

Once we configured the data source and transformation rules, we were able to successfully populate our new application. In our example, there were 11 or 12 years of historical data.

Up and Running

Now, we had a working application. Once the data was loaded, we began to test things like rules and the speed of reports. We were able to see if account settings like Type were issued correctly. Having a dataset that is representative of the Actual data used is critical. The sooner this is loaded, the better, for you are able to identify issues sooner.

With the workflow structure in place, it was time to understand what type of data the users were going to load. We broke that section up by file loading (import child), data entry (forms child), and journals (adjustment child). Each location would originally have the ability for all three areas to be loaded. As this was early in the design, we were also thinking about how we were going to create our generic **workflow templates**. Knowing we had many sites, the workflow templates were going to save us time during the build phase. The templates let you define all the settings once, then apply them to new workflow locations many times. It is faster than checking each box for each location.

For the file loading, we needed to understand the types of files, sizes of the files, any direct connectors, MTD or YTD, supplemental data, headcount data, etc. Only direct data loading and a generic journal were chosen. The source system would need to make the update, and trial balances would be reloaded. We were big fans of that decision. We now had a workflow structure, rough security shell, and had figured out all the different source systems feeding OneStream. In parallel to the workflow design, we worked on the data sources and transformation rules. These items linked into the workflow configuration.

The one item that was incredibly labor-intensive was the transformation rules section. As part of the processing steps in OneStream, we have a **validate** step (using the transformation rules) to ensure every piece of information is mapped accordingly.

> **Note:** Do not underestimate the time it will take to validate your mapping rules. For more information on data integration, please refer to Chapter 6. People often ask if consultants can help with this part of the process, but *you want* the end-users to do this work as it will help them understand the mapping later.

As part of workflow, we can define what type of scenario you want the end-user to load to. (Actual, Budget, etc.) In a consolidation project, you load to Actual, but in our case, we took a slightly different approach. We loaded to a scenario we had created called `Actual_Test`. In the background, meanwhile, the admins were loading the present production data to Actual. This way – during our parallels – we could validate that the two matched. (Back to the point, earlier, of vetting out your transformation rules.) During the parallels, we had Cube Views to compare the differences (to make matters more seamless for the end-users). You may find you could use a temporary scenario for holding data, too.

Intercompany was another prerequisite that needed to be configured in the financial metadata model before we could configure it in OneStream's workflow. Intercompany elimination is the process of canceling out account balances for intercompany partners for intercompany accounts (receivable/payable), with any unresolved balance being placed in a plug account.

Intercompany eliminations occur once the values roll up to a common parent. All this exchange can happen within the respective parties visually in workflow. Once the data has been loaded, the parties can see what their differences are, and even exchange communication through the product. There are also intercompany reports that come with a standard install. For all the intercompany configuration details (Figure 7.5), refer to our Design and Reference guide. This is also important to configure in your workflow templates, as there are a few steps in setting this up.

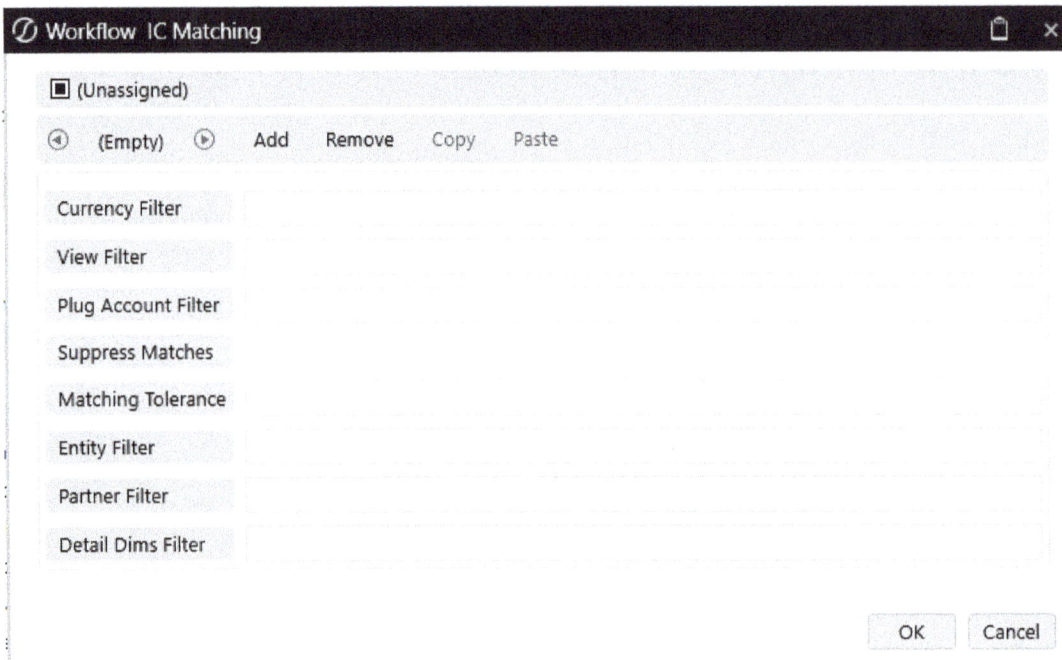

Figure 7.5

Back to our example, where – as we continue our journey through the workflow design – it was time to understand what type of calculations we needed to perform on the newly-imported data. The goal was to define each body of the workflow and ensure they did not overlap with each other. Another reason we perform calculations is that – in the event you do move forward with confirmation rules – the data will need to be calculated/consolidated to have accurate rules. This is a critical item to understand, as you don't want your audience constantly stepping over each other and impacting your hardware with inefficient consolidations.

Every workflow design, including Workspace-type designs, needs to thoroughly review the consolidation/calculation paths. In our case, we limited who had consolidation authority. Only administrators and specified super-users had access to perform the final consolidations. All others had the ability to calculate their respective datasets. Here is another advantage to OneStream's workflow – you calculate your datasets as you roll to the top and have the administrator carry out (or automate) a data management job to perform the final consolidations. Without putting in guidelines/restrictions, folks would have been stepping over each other.

Another requirement, as part of the workflow design, was to reproduce validation checks (about 15 of them) that corporate performed (based on the respective sites' data that was loaded). We call them **confirmation rules**, and they have their own section in workflow. They allow administrators to build out different validation checks to confirm pretty much anything they want before signing off on the data. They can be as simple as checking that a trial balance balances. These validations can create a warning or stop the process, depending upon the severity you choose. We chose to have a standard set of validations that everyone would perform. This included ones that would stop the process. (Saving corporate tons of hours.)

As part of our UAT, we discovered that certain corporate accounts needed the ability to adjust once it was 'pencils down' for the sites. A function called **central input** was created. This central input allows data to be loaded for all entities from just one person, like you may see for a shared service center. In our case, we created forms for the adjustments. As a designer, you'll want to ask questions surrounding what type of data will need to be adjusted. OneStream can accommodate central loading for forms or journal adjustments.

OneStream also provides complete transparency to both the owner of the entity (workflow) and to the corporate adjuster. The owner of the location being loaded to will see another workflow child with a gray checkmark. That workflow child can be clicked on to see what user/date/time the adjustment was made. When using central input, you need to have **channels** configured. This will prevent people from overwriting each other's data. For additional details, and how to configure this, please refer to OneStream Navigator.

Now that we had the data loading processes in good working order, next up was to tackle the reviewer process. This was the next step in the process hierarchy. We looked at this across two different paths – controller and finance director review. The single-site locations were very easy as we had created reviewers for their regions, and they aligned nicely with data loading sites. The challenge was more on the shared service side. For the shared service loaded entities, we created separate review Workflow Profiles and came up with something we called **named dependents**. The product gives us the flexibility to assign folks to review entities that they didn't directly load on (which, in some cases, covered mixed entities). For example, if the entities were mixed over multiple data loading sites, the data loaders would see this dependency of each of them in their workflow view.

Another way to look at this is as follows. Let us say Site A has Entity 1, 2, and 3, and Site B has Entity 4, 5, and 6. One of the reviewers is responsible for Entity 1, 2, and 6. Named dependents gave us the functionality to solve that requirement across sites.

The last step for the reviewers was the ability to certify. As we rolled this out, we defined a list of questions that soon became very cumbersome and ultimately turned into our one-click **quick certification** option.

With the data being successfully loaded, and the parallels complete, it was time to move on to the next phase: budget and then forecast. We got the whiteboard back out and reviewed the process through the budget and forecast lens. We quickly discovered it had a different audience with different timing. This was a challenge. We already had the entity assigned to specific workflows along with the appropriate security. We had also made the decision to have only one primary person responsible for that site, which meant one cube root. To further complicate things, we would have a different audience than the shared service loading audience. Adding a suffix (FST for forecast, for example) for workflow – by varying Type – gave us the functionality and flexibility to break out our new group into their own workflows. Furthermore, it gave us the ability to open forms for their data updates.

This is a key part of any design considerations – what are the pros and cons of breaking out workflows based on Scenario Type? As stated throughout, make sure you understand the landscape of your data, and where its final resting place will be. For example, if I'm an Actual person, do I ever need to see Budget and Forecast? This is where we can break up the process by Scenario Type. Note that each Scenario Type can take on its own look and feel. For example, under the Budget Scenario, Actual person(s) may only see a full-year time period, with forms, dashboards, or even Workspaces. Access to these Scenarios can also be managed through security.

Be aware of the volume of workflows, as you do not want to add any unnecessary overhead. As we progressed through the final phase of the project, we created 600+ workflows.

Workflow Items for Planning Type Projects

Typically, a consolidation project will have a more defined data loading structure than a planning-type implementation. For the consolidation, you'll want to define an owner and proxy, as this will be the best way to control who does what and when. For planning-type projects, you may want to consider something we call a **Workspace**. This can literally be a blank canvas. If you're not interested in the standard workflow setup, you can set up the home page as a Workspace and have folks land here.

- A Workspace is a dashboard that can be used to complete workflow processes or be a user's home screen.

- Workspaces are commonly used with some of our Solution Exchange Solutions, such as: People Planning, OneStream Financial Close, Task Manager, or Actor Workspaces.

- All the dashboard's components provide the behaviors and actions necessary to successfully complete this part of the workflow.

Please refer to Planning, in Chapter 5 of this book, for additional details.

Periods

Another thing to consider during the build of the workflow is when each period will be completed. Will the end-user do all periods at once, or will they be done month by month? Will they do periods randomly during the year? You must determine the periods to be completed and ensure the configuration will accommodate the process.

Structure

As nice as it looked on paper, our initial structure for the automotive parts organization was too rigid. Rigid from the perspective that it was not overly forgiving from a certify/locking viewpoint.

Many folks had performed their data loading, validations, and even answered their certify questions, but were reluctant to click the final certify. The reason for that was it would automatically lock the workflow. If they had to make any last-minute changes, they would have to ask the administrators to unlock them. When it was the last day of data loading, the administrators would go through and lock workflows because many of them were still open. I know this does not sound like a problem, but the locking needed to be performed in a surgical way. This meant that just the data loading would be locked while reviewers stayed open.

After a couple of closes, we flattened the list to make the locking process cleaner and smoother by simply taking out the unnecessary hierarchy steps. They were there for structure only and really did not add any value.

The next item I cannot emphasize enough – consolidations! As you map your workflows, make sure you do the same with your calculation definitions. This is another important step in the overall design to ensure data is being consolidated/calculated at the appropriate time. We cover some of the benefits later in this chapter. Ultimately, you will be creating an administrator dashboard or Cube View for user communities to manage all consolidations moving forward. As part of your design, make sure you do not have them stepping all over themselves.

Scenario Types map out the big picture. We strongly suggest you map out your Scenario Types and even build what you can as best you can. Understanding what data goes where is a critical step to define in the beginning. By building what you can, you will make changes easier later.

Naming Conventions

As part of any strategy, you need to define your data loaders and the reviewers. Even if you are limited, and are loading from a single ERP, make sure to have a common naming convention that can readily expand as you grow. Consider new acquisitions, retired sites, etc. These naming conventions also play a major role in your security model. Any future reporting, or even simple searches in your grids, can be narrowed down by meaningful suffixes or prefixes.

Another key consideration to highlight (we did not need this during our first project, but it is something you should be familiar with) is **workflow channels**. Here is another workflow design decision. These alternate workflow channels can be attached to non-trial balance accounts and applicable workflows so that these items can be locked at an earlier or later time than trial balance-related workflows. Do I need to incorporate workflow channels to facilitate data locking at a more granular level? If yes, do I want to do it by account and User Defined? Or do I want to perform this by UD? You will want to review this upfront as – most of the time – it's an afterthought. Why now? Because if you are using a UD for these, that dimension cannot be assigned by cube, Scenario Type, etc. In other words, that UD is the *only one that can be used for workflow channels* for the entire application.

Workflow Design

Our example use case was an amazing journey as we developed, configured, and learned how best to apply workflow to an exceptionally large organization. We defined who did what, when, and how, from end to end.

We learned a ton during that first implementation, which filtered through into creating an incredibly robust portion of the OneStream tool. Everything starts with a plan, but as you learn along the way, you adjust.

You need to start with your end-users. Understand the entire process they will go through and incorporate that as the basic workflow. You then need to provide the reports and forms that will support those tasks. Add process steps to trigger calculations/consolidations. Add confirmation and certify checks. Add training support. You want the end-users to own this process of loading data. By pushing the work to the field, all data loading can be performed by the field sites, and they can address any validation issues locally as they are closer to their datasets. Once the data has been cleansed and successfully loaded, we can have the appropriate folks review and certify the data. Finally, it's important to understand – as a project team – the overall flow of the calculations and consolidations that are triggered throughout this process. This way, everyone can clearly understand the status of their data and who can see what during each step.

More broadly, creative solutions are great, but consider how you document them and how they can be easily supported by the local administrator's group. While on that subject, it's good to define a local COE (center of excellence) at your customer base. A center of excellence is a group or single admin who can centrally support the solution. This also includes your super-users, who will help teach the community the benefits of OneStream and how they work.

Of course, administrators will have full access to the system, but you will also be building out a section just for these same individuals. Items such as access to consolidation grids, shortcuts to FX rates, WF status reports, etc. Basically, do not lose sight of administrators.

To make the full workflow experience best for your end-users, you could have a combination of OnePlace, defined workflows, or even a Workspace home page.

> **Note:** Unless you have a defined home page, everyone will navigate through OnePlace.

One option to consider when designing your workflow is to consider the combination and order of the process steps. For example:

- Data loading, validations, and certify = workflow
- Data consumption & review = OnePlace using Cube Views & dashboards, or a home Workspace, or guided reporting, or Task Manager

We covered a lot in our project example. Discussing each of these steps and the related options will be confusing, especially to a client who is seeing the flexibility for the first time. I would again recommend building a prototype to walk them through the design. For discussion purposes, I would list out the steps as follows:

- Document review process to build hierarchy
- Identify all data sources
- Create admin location for historical
- Determine the parsing of the data for end-user data
- Determine the number of load formats and mapping rules required
- Breaks load up by input, forms, and adjustments
- Do you need central inputs? Then configure channels
- For each location:
  - Determine the calculations needed for each step
  - Consider which and how calculations (in addition to consolidations) may need to be triggered
  - Reports needed
  - Training needed
  - Confirmation rules
  - Certification rules
- Configure locking and certification of data

Automation Use Case

Let's look at another client example – a large retail company with a file size of about 6 million rows. At that level, we made a design decision to break this up by entity. We broke out some of the larger entities into their own workflows, and grouped the smaller ones to their own workflows. You can apply this same concept on different ERPs; break out the systems into their own locations.

From here, we automated the data loads into batches. This allowed us to load multiple locations at once. In this case, we were able to use the parallel API batch loading.

Here is an example of the rule:

```
BRApi.Utilities.ExecuteFileHarvestBatchParallel(si, fixedScenario,
systemTime, valTransform, valIntersect, loadCube, processCube,
confirm, autoCertify, ParallelCount)
```

We used a level of eight parallel processes in this case. (Please note there is an art, not a science, with parallel processing.) Tons of testing was performed for us to settle on eight. We started low, at four, and continued up until we saw the servers being overwhelmed. Pay particular attention to the database server. This has been mentioned before; you should always be testing and validating all your assumptions. Prototyping is a great way to validate.

Data Loading and Considerations for Partitioning

In another example, a client was loading data by month for a large dataset. The dataset was about 8 million records. The IT group pushed back on grouping the load by entity; they said it was not possible. Since we were seeding data for the forecast, it would be easy to load a single file for a given month to an 'admin' location. This could be run overnight, so performance would not be too bad. When we added a new scenario, we were loading different months at the same time.

Effectively, the file was being portioned by period. Since we were loading data to the same entities – just for different periods – we created an issue where the system could overwrite data in the wrong periods, going against the core methodology of accounting standards. Period 1, then Period 2, etc., in sequential order.

Moreover, this was a bad design. We went back and created a load file by entity group. Not only were we able to resolve the data loading problem, but we also had a more scalable design. Firstly, if there was a change, we were able to load a subset of the entities instead of all of them. (This is much faster.) Secondly, since we grouped by entity, we were able to have a greater number of smaller partitions, which allowed us to utilize more threads on the load. This allowed us to successfully load the file.

Workflow Items for Analytic Blend

All of the conversation so far has been focused on our OneStream Stage engine and the data quality engine, which then feeds the finance engine.

There is another engine that hasn't been covered yet, however, called the **blend engine**. You may have heard the term Analytic Blend within the community. From a workflow perspective, we should touch on a few points. Workflow is a conduit to Analytic Blend processing, using the same features as data sources and transformation rules. In this case, you're just loading, using the blend engine and not the Stage engine. So, from a configuration perspective, you are configuring for Analytic Blend.

For a complete description and detailed overview of this functionality, please refer to the Analytic Blend Chapter (13) of this book.

Tips and Tricks

It is all about sharing. This section is more of a reference to help prevent some of those future 'gotchas' that you may encounter. Here is a list of some of the more common ones for your reading pleasure.

- You should understand the relationship workflow has with the **analytic data cube**. The Origin dimension plays a key role between the two engines. The input children are mapped directly to origin members in the analytic cube to create a control mechanism between the workflow hierarchy and the cube. This linkage enables the workflow engine to control importing, form data entry, journal (adjustment) data entry, and data locking processes for one or more entities. This is an important concept to understand. For further information, please refer to the Design and Reference Guide.

- **Workflow source ID** – this can be an important concept, depending on the complexity of your customer's loading process. This defines which file is loaded (if multiple) and will only reload that one – based on source ID – if it is a recurring theme.

- **Workflow Profile parent definitions** – important to consider if you're thinking of parallel loading as part of your design; now is a good time to separate each of your entities by its own parent. Yes, this could be a bit of work, but the initial labor of the configuration will pay off in the long run. (More details on parallel options are below.)

- **Intercompany (IC) configuration** – this is a derived dimension in OneStream and ties to metadata configurations within the Account dimension.

  o Journals posted to an entity that are not in the entity's currency will not show up on the IC matching report.

- o The IC matching report will look off if you use a balancing account rather than two different accounts (like an IC Payable/Receivable).

- o The IC matching report uses the plug account to identify the associated IC accounts and evaluates the IC detail on the identified accounts.

- o The IC matching report is not secured by the user.

- o The user does not need view access to the IC partner to see the partner's IC balances alongside their entities.

- o Translates on-the-fly where indicated.

- o Historical/override accounts will not reflect the override amounts if the entity hasn't yet been translated.

- o Matching tolerance assigned is simply a number; it does not translate. In other words, if the tolerance is 100, then it's 100 in all currencies (100 USD, 100 EUR, 100 GBP, etc.)

- o Be cautious when using a linked cube design.

- We covered **workflow calculations** lightly, earlier, but you should be aware of the additional functionality they offer:

- o You can define what type of calculation, translation, or consolidation you want to perform and trigger them throughout the process.

- o Auto-assign entities through assigned entities and loaded entities options.

- o Run consolidations across multiple hierarchies and scenarios.

- o Control which entities are tested by confirmation rules.

- o Launch data management sequences as a step.

- **Workflow text fields** – this gives a creative workflow designer the ability to perform advanced tasks, involving items such as reporting parameters, forms parameters, and import parameters. Note: you must click on the Scenario Type to see these properties.

- o Using **WFText properties** can personalize and restrict inputs (e.g., connector SQL Where clause) and reporting, amongst other uses.

- o If Workflow Profiles happen to be named in a certain way, |WFProfile| could be used to substitute the Workflow Profile name instead.

- **Workflow business rules and Event Handlers** – think of these as the added value steps that you may need, but which aren't configured to automatically happen. Business rules and Event Handlers give you a window to stop the process, perform your scripted added value, and then return to your normal processing to complete the task. They are available as part of the workflow configuration (and are covered in other sections of this book).

- Load the **signs** as you report them, and let the product do the rest. You need to consider this when altering signs outside the natural mapping process in OneStream. This could cause issues down the road with Solution Exchange solutions such as OneStream Financial Close.

- **Solution Exchange OneStream Financial Close**:

- o A design consideration is whether the initial load to Actual was from something like a central import or individual workflows. You want to be aware of where we get the data from.

- o Need YTD source data in Stage.

- o Journals and forms go directly into the cube. Since Stage is bypassed, journals and forms are not part of OneStream Financial Close or transaction matching.

- o Talk to your customer upfront to let them know that journals and forms are not part of OneStream Financial Close and transaction matching.

- **Solution Exchange Specialty Planning** – from the design, spend time assessing the pros and cons of one workflow doing all the work, or breaking the work up into multiple workflows. Take the time to understand the responsibilities of the end-users, such as who should just load to the register versus the final load to the cube. (Consider the Workflow Profile suffix for lights-out processing, and calculate a plan before completing workflow. You can refer to the Navigator and OneStream Community for further details.)

- **Solution Exchange Task Manager** – this is another solution that can be defined as a front end to workflow to help extend the experience. This solution tracks items like consolidation and aggregations, workflow statuses, and assigned tasks grouped by close dates with charts to view the progress of upcoming and overdue tasks.

- **Solution Exchange Process Control Manager**. Here are some highlights you may want to consider.

  o Which workflow users/security groups can input data or complete review steps?

  o Which scenario/periods can be modified?

  o Which Origin dimension input channels can modify data?

  o Which accounts can be modified based on their related phase?

- **Closed workflow** – okay, so someone was creative and closed a workflow; what do I do now? First, let's check to see who may have done this. In OnePlace, go to the top workflow for the scenario and year that was closed. Click on the Audit for details. To stop this, go to the workflow screen to the top cube root and change all the dropdowns under the Security section to Administrators, except for Access Group.

Workflow Performance Considerations

As part of your design, you will want to understand the order of operations from your community. For example, if you are implementing a consolidation project and have a large end-user community that loads data for the first couple of days of the close – make sure you have the appropriate Stage servers defined to handle the load.

Once the data loading is complete, the focus is then on transitions to data consumption; you can utilize your same Stage servers as general servers (multipurpose an existing server) to maximize the use of your hardware. This configuration is what we typically configure out-of-the-box, but it's up to you to fully understand the audience and the timing of their actions to make sure the hardware is being fully utilized. Please refer to the Performance section of the book for more details on the breakdown of the OneStream server types. You can also work with our Customer Support to ensure your hardware configuration is optimal.

Another decision that the customer makes is whether to embed consolidate/calculate or force consolidate/force calculate into the workflow process.

Consolidate/calculate checks the cell status for each period in the year from which it was triggered. It runs for any periods that need it, up to and including the period from which it was triggered. Most workflow processes using consolidate/calculate are generally the most efficient for your end-users. The process doesn't run excessively and therefore minimizes wait time.

In this case, it's important to embed calculation definitions throughout most workflow processes. This is especially true with planning implementations. It's an underutilized benefit of the workflow and reduces the time reviewers and corporate consolidations must wait to get consolidated data.

Force consolidate/force calculate runs for each period in the year, up to and including the period from which it was triggered. The difference here is that it does NOT check cell status. This means that the engine runs for every entity in the hierarchy from which it was triggered. This often results in excessive and unnecessary processing on entities that don't need it. Due to this, it often takes more time, forcing the users to wait longer for the job to finish throughout the year.

There are a couple of considerations to weigh up when deciding between the two. First, because consolidate/calculate checks the cell status, the engine may not recognize changes that have been made since the last consolidate/calculate for when that Data Unit was run (e.g., FX rates or Member Formulas). Second, in applications with extremely large Data Units, generally far exceeding the recommended maximum size, force consolidate/force calculate *could* be faster than consolidate/calculate because the engine doesn't check the calc status of every cell. The sacrifice made is that consolidations and calculations will be run excessively and redundantly, which could put stress on the system and/or create an unacceptable user experience. Also, be cautious of any business rules or Member Formulas that have changed over time and ensure that they contain a time condition directly in the rule or by Time and/or Scenario Type on Member Formulas.

Another item that comes up periodically is the discussion around running workflows in parallel. Here are some things you will want to consider.

- You can consider loading workflows in parallel if the entities do not overlap.

- Or you can consider breaking out each entity with its own parent, to not have one parent with all the entities below it.

- You can also consider loading multiple periods if you load each period, respectively. For example, load Jan in parallel, before loading Feb, etc. DO NOT OVERLAP entities by time.

- Managing sibling imports for parallel processing. If this is considered, please refer to the OneStream Design and Reference Guide – Section: Load Overlapped Siblings for the 'Load Overlapped Siblings' toggle flag. Note: this is only available on version 6.1.1 and newer.

- You can break a large file down by entities, and filter by using a business rule.

- It is possible to use workflow channels to further break down a blend process; for example, it is possible to load multiple cost centers for the same entity and process them at the same time.

One Last Thing

Some closing thoughts on good practices that can help ensure project success.

- Understand what calculations/consolidations should run, when they need to run, how they're triggered and, if necessary, who will trigger them. Whiteboard and document the full process.

- Assign scenario suffixes at the start of the build.

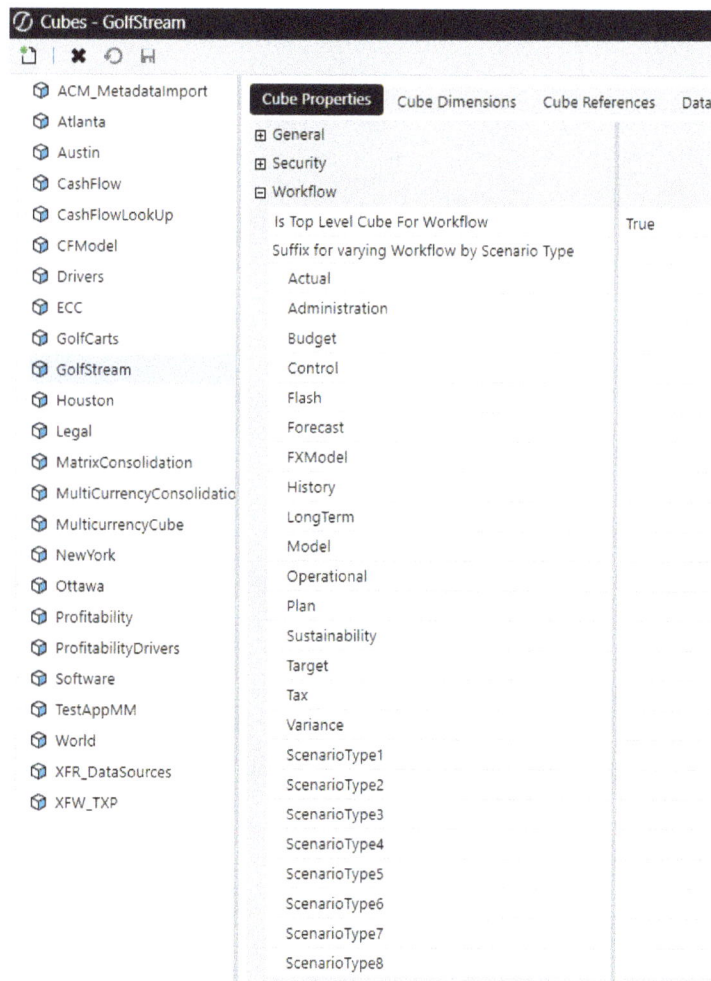

Figure 7.6

- Pick a naming convention for security groups and stick with it! More about this in the Security Chapter (Chapter 9).

- Do not modify the default workflow (aside from assigning security groups)!

- Build a 'Do Not Use' workflow structure; add the default WF profile.

- Workflow locking versus closing workflow (I do not recommend closing workflows for general use; only close for discontinued operations that will never be used again). Why you ask: here is a snippet from the Design and Reference Guide… The workflow engine will take a snapshot of the current workflow hierarchy structure being managed from the workflow being closed. This also means the workflow hierarchy is not accessed from memory (cache), as would be the case with a workflow in an open state. A closed workflow must be read from the database rather than memory because it is considered a point-in-time snapshot stored in a historical table. This is a performance penalty noticed when reading the entire closed workflow hierarchy for a scenario and time. Workflow hierarchies should only be closed if major changes are being made to the workflow hierarchy and the structure of a cube and historical hierarchy relationships need to be preserved.

- If you do have to modify many workflows, do not forget the Grid View option under the Cube Root Workflow Profile. You can pivot this table to see exactly what you need to see. This can save tons of time.

Fun fact: The gray bar next to the amount field in the import/validate/load screens can be moved to lock your view while scrolling to the right.

Conclusion

As you can see, workflow is an integral part of the overall implementation. To further support our 100% satisfaction, we need to make sure the end-user experience is pleasurable and clear. This should include a leave-behind of materials, such as admin guides, so the customer is able to maintain OneStream long-term.

In this chapter, we covered the history of OneStream workflow and the benefits it provides. You are armed with the knowledge to build out an amazing process that will help your community navigate to the right step at the right time.

Epilogue

In closing, there are so many proud milestones that I've experienced at OneStream, but there is one that still stands out: Splash Chicago on the Navy Pier.

We typically get to any venue early, just to help with any last-minute preparations. As we were getting ready in Chicago, I remember thinking, 'Wow, this is big!'

Once the event started, we looked at each other and said, "We've made it!" Not only was every seat full, but we also had folks standing around the outline of the facility. So proud.

8

Rules and Calculations

Originally written by Nick Kroppe and Chul Smith, updated by Nick Kroppe and Chul Smith

Rules and calculations influence almost every area of the OneStream platform and are a pivotal skill to develop over the course of any OneStream career. Taking the time and effort to learn them enables you to develop new skillsets that will tremendously empower you throughout an implementation. Every OneStream rule writer will likely state the same thing – there are few more satisfying feelings in the OneStream world than writing a perfect business rule or calculation for the first time. Reading this chapter is your first step to becoming a rules and calculations expert!

In this chapter, we'll focus on sharpening your understanding of rules and calculations by exploring the scope of business rules and the purpose they serve. We'll also review the fundamentals and main considerations of how rules and calculations should be designed and implemented. Finally, we'll take a deep dive through the calculation engine and review must-know business rule best practices and syntax tips we've learned across the past decade.

Let's begin our journey by taking a stroll through the scope of OneStream rules, and discuss how best to apply them in a OneStream application.

Rules Scope and How to Apply Them in an Application

The goal of this section is to review the different types of rules within the platform, introduce their purpose, and discuss how they're triggered. OneStream rules can be broken out into two different categories: business rules and Member Formulas. We'll discuss each one and then finish by highlighting their use cases.

OneStream Programming Language Options

Although you may have noticed that the screenshots of example code presented throughout this book are in VB.NET, OneStream has recently expanded its coding language options. In addition to VB.NET, consultants and administrators now have the option to develop business rules using C#. However, it's worth noting that currently, the option to develop in C# is only available in business rules, while Member Formulas and other areas in the product that support code require VB.NET. Given the choice of coding language for business rules, which one is better, preferred, or recommended for your application? The answer ultimately lies with the customer.

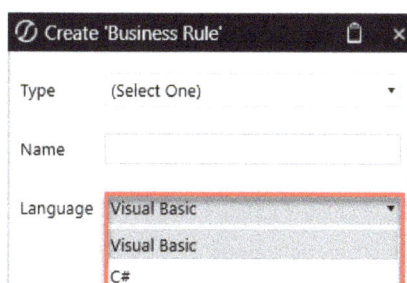

Figure 8.1

There are numerous comparisons of these languages on the web, so I won't go into those arguments here. It's important that the customer decides which coding language they want to use to develop custom business rules within their OneStream application. Some customers have internal resources who are very competent in using VB.NET or C#, which will drive their decision. Customers who must hire to fill the administrator role will likely encounter more candidates with C# experience. Furthermore, OneStream plans for new releases via the Solution Exchange to be written in C#. However, most candidates and former consultants with extensive OneStream experience will have written most of their rules using VB.NET.

I've heard some coders say, "VB.NET is a dead language, and it will be retired soon." Although I can't speak to the validity of that statement, I'm able to say that OneStream successfully navigated Microsoft's sunsetting of Silverlight in 2021 and currently has no plans to retire the use of VB.NET in the OneStream platform. Either way, I suggest language consistency when developing custom business rules in an application.

Types of OneStream Business Rules

The way OneStream business rules are organized and grouped within the platform is driven by their purpose and how they are applied in an application. The different types of rules in the OneStream business rule library are listed below.

1. Finance
2. Parser
3. Connector
4. Smart integration function
5. Conditional rule
6. Derivative rule
7. Cube View Extender
8. Dashboard dataset
9. Dashboard Extender
10. Dashboard XFBR string
11. Extensibility rules
12. Spreadsheet

Finance Rules

Understanding finance rules and their fundamentals is a logical place to begin our business rule learning path because of their flexibility, versatility, and familiarity among many applications. We use finance business rules for many different purposes within the platform.

The **finance function type** describes and groups the different use cases of a finance rule; they include financial calculations, member lists, custom translations, complex ownership and elimination logic, conditional input, on-demand rules, and much more. From this statement alone, it's clear that this type of rule does it all and will likely be a major factor in your application.

Although the use cases and flexibility of a finance rule often seem to be limitless, the implementation of a finance rule is satisfyingly simple and consistent. During the rule design, you must first decide its purpose and how you want it to be triggered. This will lead to your decision on what finance function type (remember, this is the use case) you'll use to write your logic.

In the figure below, you can see a visual of the most popular finance function types, which are what I often refer to as *use cases for a finance business rule*. At the end of the day, the finance function type case statement, in which you place your code, correlates with the purpose of your logic and controls how the code will be triggered in a OneStream application.

```
23              Select Case api.FunctionType
24
25                  Case Is = FinanceFunctionType.MemberListHeaders
26
27                  Case Is = FinanceFunctionType.MemberList
28
29                  Case Is = FinanceFunctionType.DataCell
30
31                  Case Is = FinanceFunctionType.FxRate
32
33                  Case Is = FinanceFunctionType.Calculate
34
35                  Case Is = FinanceFunctionType.ConditionalInput
36
37                  Case Is = FinanceFunctionType.CustomCalculate
38
39                  Case Is = FinanceFunctionType.Translate
40
41                  Case Is = FinanceFunctionType.ConsolidateShare
42
43                  Case Is = FinanceFunctionType.ConsolidateElimination
44
45              End Select
```

Figure 8.2

We use the cube and the financial events that occur in a cube – such as a calculation, consolidation, or the rendering of a report – to act as the natural triggering mechanism for the finance business rule. You do this by attaching the rule to a cube.

Keep in mind that there are a few exceptions to attaching the finance rule to the cube to trigger it. The use of finance function types, such as member list and data cell, are not required to be attached to the cube and can instead be triggered directly from a Cube View row or column, while the finance function type confirmation can be triggered from a confirmation rule.

Parser Rules

Business rules are leveraged and called directly from data sources in OneStream. These types of integration rules enable you to use code along with OneStream's staging engine to effectively parse incoming data during an import event. Use cases for a parser business rule include integration efforts such as parsing the debit and credit field values from a source GL file, character trimming and concatenating, and the common use case of deriving a source ID from a source file name. A parser business rule can be called directly from a data source dimension by setting the Logical Operator to Business Rule and defining the logical expression value as the parser business rule name you wish to apply to the data source dimension.

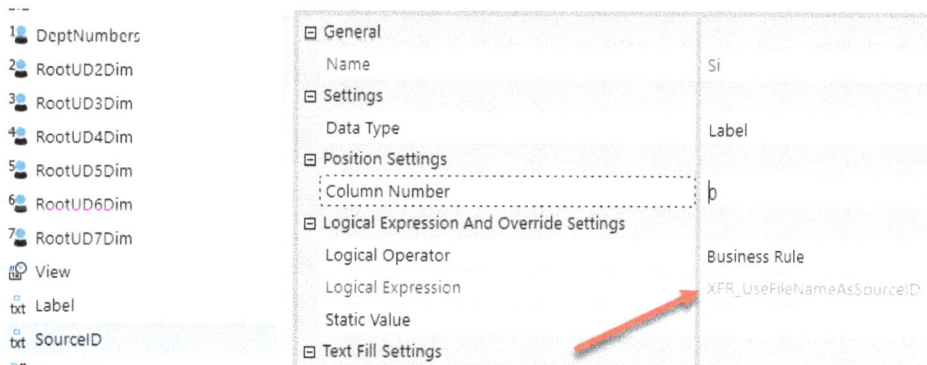

Figure 8.3

213

Connector Rules

A connector business rule can be used to facilitate integration efforts to pull data out of an external database, data warehouse, or OneStream ancillary table, and into a workflow. Although not required for integrations that pull data out of an ancillary table, a connector rule typically leverages an external connection that is configured on the application server, which enables the connector to pull data from an external system. A connector rule can be attached directly to a connector data source and is triggered when a user clicks import in a workflow. Lastly, a connector rule can also be used to enable detailed sub-ledger drill back functionality, which enriches a user's data investigation and analysis in OneStream.

In a connector business rule, there are four specific ConnectorActionTypes that correlate with a connector's capability and use cases, listed in the code below. The GetFieldList action type defines the field names that will be returned in the source data table. It's triggered when the Stage engine reads the configured data source upon an import event.

Secondly, the GetData action type is used to process (query) the incoming source data, whilst the GetDrillbackTypes action type helps enable you to design custom drill back to additional detail that may reside in an external database or data warehouse. Lastly, the GetDrillBack action type formally handles the drill back processing to retrieve the drill detail and present it in a specific display.

```
Select Case args.ActionType
    'return the field name list
    Case Is = ConnectorActionTypes.GetFieldList

    'process the query to retrieve the source data
    Case Is = ConnectorActionTypes.GetData

    'Return the list of Drill Types (Options) to present to the end user
    Case Is = ConnectorActionTypes.GetDrillBackTypes

    'Process the specific Drill-Back type
    Case Is = ConnectorActionTypes.GetDrillBack

End Select
```

Figure 8.4

Smart Integration Function Rules

A smart integration function rule is a new type of business rule originally released in platform version 7.2 as a private preview. It later became more widely used in 7.4 and hit generally available release status in platform version 8.0 and upwards. This type of business rule may be used to execute remote functions in support of Smart Integration Connector-facilitated integrations that are written in connector or extender business rules.

The goals for Smart Integration Connector are to establish all required data source connections without VPN and establish residency and management of data source connections solely in your network.

With Smart Integration Connector, you can:

- Securely establish connectivity between OneStream Cloud and data sources in your network without a VPN connection.

- Create and manage network data source integration using OneStream administration interfaces.

- Locally manage database credentials and ancillary files.

Ultimately, smart integration function rules enable you to code and centrally store remote functions that need to be called from other business rules, such as a connector business rule to facilitate integrations that pull or push data from OneStream.

Conditional Rules

A conditional rule can be used to conditionally map an incoming source value to a target value by leveraging coding logic. A common use case for a conditional rule would be to dynamically set the target value based on the transformed target or source member for a particular Stage dimension. This technique uses the `Args.GetTarget()` or `Args.GetSource()` arguments as shown next.

```
'retrieve the incoming record's target account value
Dim targetAccount As String = args.GetTarget(StageConstants.MasterDimensionTokens.Account)
'retrieve the incoming record's source U1 value
Dim sourceU1 As String = args.GetSource(StageConstants.MasterDimensionTokens.U1)
```

Figure 8.5

Some other conditional rule use cases include leveraging the metadata properties of a target dimension member to determine the mapping for a value in another Stage dimension. For example, you can use a conditional rule to map source UD1 members to specific UD1 targets depending on whether or not the Stage record is being mapped to an intercompany account. The conditional business rules can be as dynamic and flexible as you need them to be, depending on the complexity of the mapping requirement. However, keep in mind that this type of mapping technique is very intensive from a processing and performance perspective.

A conditional business rule can ultimately be applied to an individual transformation rule, including composite, range, list, and mask transformation rules, and is triggered when the transformation fires during an import event.

Derivative Rules

A derivative business rule generally completes two main tasks in OneStream. First, it can derive or add a record to Stage, then set the resulting record's amount via a calculation. This derived record can be temporary – which means the record does not get transformed and can be used for check rule validations. This is what we refer to as an **interim-derived record** in Stage. Alternatively, this derived record can be final – which means the record can then be transformed and loaded into the financial cube.

Lastly, a derivative business rule can be used to enable pass or fail data validation checks, or **check rules,** which can be used to enforce specific data validation logic during the validate step of a workflow. For example, a derivative rule can facilitate a data validation check that will ensure the trial balance is in balance before allowing a user to complete the validate step.

Ultimately, a derivative business rule is attached to a derivative transformation rule in the logical operator setting. It can then be triggered upon import, when deriving records in Stage, as well as upon the validate step when used as a derivative check rule.

Cube View Extender Rules

Cube View Extender business rules can be used in an implementation to highly customize and format Cube View PDF reports. If you need to implement specific formatting for a Cube View in PDF format that is not available with standard Cube View formatting settings, a Cube View Extender may be a good option for you.

These rules have the ability to format any individual item on a PDF report, such as a logo, page number, title, header font, word wrapping, font color, cell value, and much more. The ability to individually format a Cube View PDF report with a Cube View Extender rule is nearly limitless.

These business rules are applied and triggered directly on a Cube View by setting the Custom Report Task property to Execute Cube View Extender Business Rule and by setting the business rule property to the name of your Cube View Extender business rule.

> **Note:** An extremely important item to note is the logic and formatting that a Cube View Extender business rule facilitates can only be applied and triggered when the Cube View runs as a PDF report. Your logic will not, and cannot, fire when the Cube View runs as a data explorer grid.

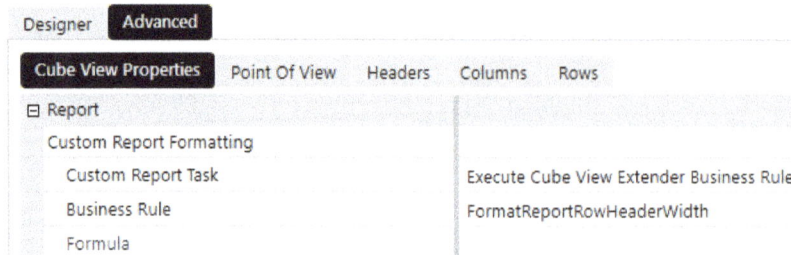

Figure 8.6

Dashboard Dataset Rules

Dashboard dataset rules are a personal favorite of mine and can be used to create custom datasets and data tables for advanced parameters, reports, and dashboards. If you can master the dashboard dataset rule technique, you'll be able to deliver on nearly any custom reporting request during your OneStream career.

Dashboard dataset rules enable you to execute SQL queries, Method queries, and OneStream BRAPIs to tailor customized datasets using the power, conditional logic, and flexibility of coding. This means that this type of rule can be used to execute custom SQL queries to query data from the OneStream application database, framework database, or even an external data warehouse. Perhaps the most powerful use case of the dashboard dataset rule is its ability to leverage OneStream BRAPIs to build data tables from scratch, or massage and customize data tables on the fly that may be originally produced by a SQL query or Method query.

Now that we understand the basics of the use cases for a dashboard dataset rule, let's discuss how they are applied in an application. A dashboard dataset rule can be called in two main ways. First, they can be called directly in a data adapter to enable dashboard reporting.

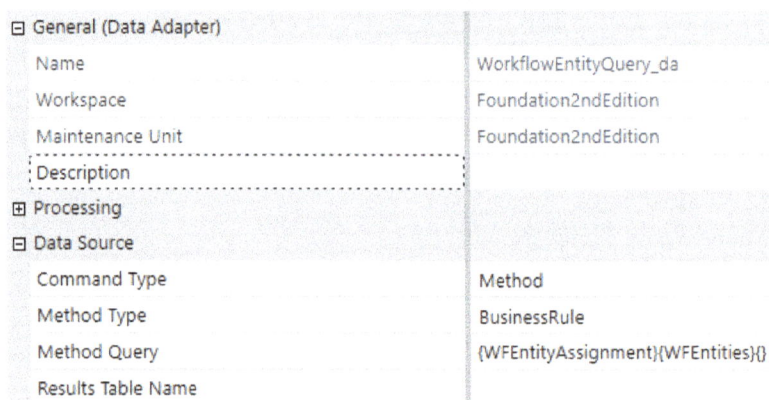

Figure 8.7

Second, they can be called in a bound list parameter to create a custom list of selections to present to a user in a parameter or dashboard component.

General (Parameter)	
Name	CustomTimeDescs
Workspace	Foundation2ndEdition
Maintenance Unit	Foundation2ndEdition
Description	
User Prompt	
Sort Order	0
Data Source	
Parameter Type	Bound List
Default Value	
Result Format String Type	Default
Result Custom Format String	
Command Type	Method
Method Type	BusinessRule
Method Query	{CustomTimeDescriptionHelper}{CustomTime}{TimeMemberFilter=T#Root.base, TimeProfile=TestCustom}
Results Table Name	ResultTable
Display Member	TimeNameAndDesc
Value Member	TimeName

Figure 8.8

If you need to create a custom data table to source a parameter or query a OneStream database table or external table to source a report, a dashboard dataset rule should be your go-to option.

Dashboard Extender Rules

Dashboard Extender business rules can be used to create highly customized interactive dashboards, including the facilitation of task-driven dashboard clicks. If you are tasked with building advanced interactive dashboards for a client, knowing the ins and outs of Dashboard Extenders will be invaluable to the construction and functionality of your dashboards.

These rules provide tools to explore the art of the possible, taking your dashboarding abilities to the next level. Some common use cases for a Dashboard Extender include designing button click actions that send emails to OneStream users, the execution and triggering of a OneStream workflow process (such as an import event or workflow status update), as well as the presentation of a custom message to a user.

There are three main ways to apply and trigger a Dashboard Extender business rule; we call this the Dashboard Extender function type (or use case). As you can see in the figure below, there are three Dashboard Extender function types: LoadDashboard, ComponentSelectionChanged, and SQLTableEditorSaveDate, all of which are triggered differently.

LoadDashboard triggers when a dashboard attempts to render, ComponentSelectionChanged triggers when a dashboard component such as a button or combo box is clicked, and SQLTableEditorSaveData triggers upon clicking save in a SQL table editor component. The trigger method drives where you need to write your rule. For example, if you want your code to fire upon a user clicking or selecting something, you would write your rule within the ComponentSelectionChanged function type.

```
23          Select Case args.FunctionType
24
25              Case Is = DashboardExtenderFunctionType.LoadDashboard
26
27              Case Is = DashboardExtenderFunctionType.ComponentSelectionChanged
28
29              Case Is = DashboardExtenderFunctionType.SqlTableEditorSaveData
30
31          End Select
```

Figure 8.9

217

When it comes to applying Dashboard Extender business rules, you can first apply the rule directly to a dashboard. However, the Dashboard Extender can only be triggered on a main dashboard and cannot be applied and triggered in dashboards that are nested within a main dashboard. Secondly, you can call a Dashboard Extender on almost any dashboard component, such as a button, combo box, chart, Cube View, grid view, and more. Lastly, a Dashboard Extender can be called directly on a SQL table editor dashboard component to enable custom logic when a user clicks save in a SQL table editor component.

Dashboard XFBR String Rules

I'm fanatical that consultants and administrators who have no coding experience in VB.NET, C#, or any other programming language should start with dashboard XFBR string rules. Why? These incredibly flexible rules can be found and used virtually everywhere in an application. Noobs don't need to worry about understanding Data Units, data buffers, balanced or unbalanced dimensionality, or data explosion – the rules simply return text that is based on logic. The rule writers will learn simple functions, syntax, and logic. They'll figure out common calls like how to get the name of a dimension or Workflow Profile or user. It's the best starting point for someone who will progress on to writing finance business rules and Member Formulas.

What do I mean by they can be "used virtually everywhere in the application?" Well, the statement speaks for itself – they can be used nearly anywhere an application is expecting text; this includes report books, formatting properties, headers or row/column names in Cube Views, and any component in dashboards. Again, the rules return text that is based on logic.

Some common use cases of implementing a dashboard XFBR string rule include dynamically setting a Cube View POV member, formatting a Cube View or dashboard, setting a Cube View row or column's Member Filter, setting a Cube View's row or column shared template, setting a parameter's default value, and pulling data cell amounts from a cube to be used to facilitate a Specialty Planning calculation. The key word or theme here is *dynamic*. The impact this business rule has across the platform minimizes maintenance.

For example, your report contains three columns: Actual, Current Forecast, and Prior Forecast. The current month is March. You named your Forecasts: Jan_FC, Feb_FC, Mar_FC, etc. So, when you want to report on March, your Current Forecast is Mar_FC and your Prior Forecast is Feb_FC. Moving on to April, Apr_FC becomes Current, and Mar_FC becomes Prior. To prevent the user from having to select all three columns, you can prompt the user to select only the current month which would give you the correct Actual and Current Forecast columns. How does OneStream know the Prior Forecast without user input? There's some simple logic that needs to happen. You could write an XFBR string rule to use the month that the user selected and – based on that selection – return the correct Prior Forecast.

If you want to improve and enhance the end-user experience, and it can be supported by conditional logic, a dashboard XFBR string business rule will become your best friend and go-to solution.

Extensibility Rules

Extensibility rules might just be the most underutilized type of business rule in OneStream. There are two main types of extensibility business rules, which we classify as **Extender rules** and **Event Handler rules**.

Extender business rules are mainly used to facilitate the execution of custom automated tasks. Common use cases include automating the import of source GL data in a workflow, file management tasks such as picking up or placing a file on an FTP server, and the export of custom datasets to a CSV file (or other file types) to then be stored in a specific file location.

The unique part about Extender rules is they're one of only two types of business rule that can be called directly from a data management step. We often see these two components working together in a fully automated solution and, thus, you'll want to consider an Extender business rule as a vehicle for you to write logic that enables automated tasks in OneStream.

The second type of extensibility rule is an Event Handler business rule. The first time you see the power and capability of an Event Handler rule in action, you will probably lose your mind and be blown away! OK, I'm exaggerating – these rules can't compete with seeing an English bulldog riding a skateboard through a 30-person leg tunnel. [Google it.]

Event Handler business rules can be used to trigger custom tasks or processes in an application when a specific event occurs in the platform. Some powerful use cases include writing an Event Handler to seed a scenario upon a process cube workflow event, sending an email to application admins when an import fails in a workflow, emailing a journal approver when a journal is submitted, emailing a specific user when a workflow is certified, and auto-creating members in the dimension library upon an import event.

In addition, an Event Handler rule can be used to block specific processes from occurring, such as preventing a user from locking or certifying a workflow and, in general, throwing custom error messages to a user upon a specific event occurring in an application.

You're probably wondering how Event Handler business rules are called within an application. These rules are the only type of rule that do not need to be called from another artifact to be triggered. OneStream has an event engine built within the platform that listens for when specific events occur and subsequently triggers the code you wrote in that type of Event Handler.

There are seven different types of Event Handler rules:

1. Transformation Event Handler

2. Journal Event Handler

3. Data Quality Event Handler

4. Data Management Event Handler

5. Forms Event Handler

6. Workflow Event Handler

7. WCF Event Handler

The event you use to trigger your custom code determines what type of Event Handler business rule to use and how to write the logic within it.

Within each individual Event Handler business rule, you can access specific sub-events in which you will write your logic. **BR event operation types** are specific events that happen in an application. For example, within a Transformation Event Handler business rule, you can write code to intercept many different transformation events such as import, validate, load cube, and clear Stage data sub-events. The sub-events that you can leverage to execute custom logic can be found within the event listing section of the OneStream API guide, and we'll talk more about Event Handler design tips and tricks later in this chapter.

Spreadsheet Rules

A Spreadsheet business rule enables users to read or write to database tables that exist in the OneStream application within the Spreadsheet tool.

The table view data presented in Spreadsheet can originate from any OneStream database table, such as a Solution Exchange solution ancillary table or a custom data table created on-the-fly using code.

This type of extremely powerful business rule enables users to perform read/write actions and analysis on ancillary table data using a familiar reporting interface. Common use cases for a Spreadsheet rule include designing a report that enables users to analyze Specialty Planning register data, a report that allows users to modify, add, and remove data from a Specialty Planning register, or a report that presents a custom data table – all presented within the Spreadsheet tool. This is yet another powerful reporting option when it comes to reporting on data that originates from a custom data table or OneStream database table.

As you've probably guessed, a Spreadsheet business rule can only be applied and triggered directly on a Spreadsheet file by creating a table view definition.

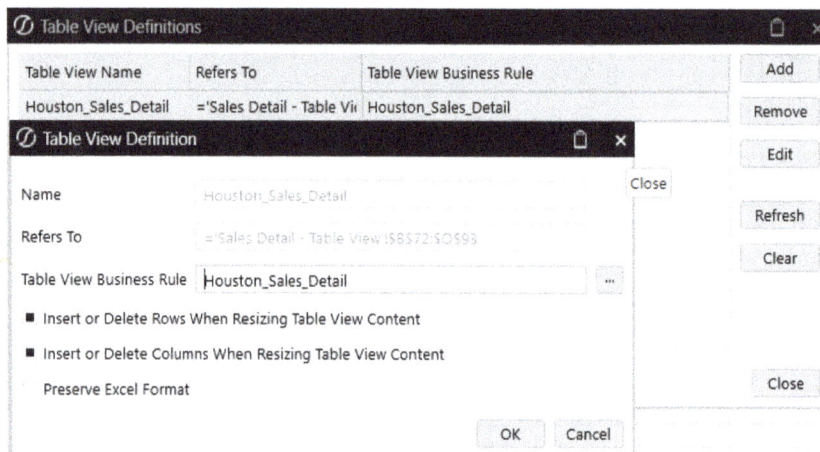

Figure 8.10

Member Formulas and Calculation Drilldown

As I mentioned earlier, Member Formulas make up the second category of rules in OneStream. This means we not only have the ability to write calculations in individual business rules, but we also have the option to write calculations directly on dimension members. The Member Formula calculation can result in stored calculated data point(s) that reside in the cube or dynamically calculated data, i.e., calculated on-the-fly, and presented in a report. In this section, we'll introduce the basic concepts of Member Formulas and Calculation Drilldown, talk about how they're triggered, and end by comparing the differences between writing calculations directly on a member and writing calculations in a business rule.

In addition to facilitating calculations, Member Formulas enable you to write a Calculation Drilldown formula to present a user with drilldown detail for calculated data. The Calculation Drilldown feature can also be used to give the user insight into how a particular result was calculated by exposing the inputs of the calculation formula. You can write Member Formulas and Calculation Drilldown formulas on Scenario, Flow, Account, and UD1-UD8 dimension members.

When comparing the execution behavior of a stored Member Formula versus a dynamic calculation, the differences are twofold. Member Formulas written as stored calculations can be triggered upon a calculation, consolidation, or translation event, while dynamic calculation Member Formulas are triggered and calculated when called in a report.

Lastly, a Calculation Drilldown formula triggers when a user drills down on a dimension member that contains a formula for Calculation Drilldown (see the next figure). This is often used to expose the member's calculation inputs, which allows the user to see exactly how OneStream amounted to the result of the calculation.

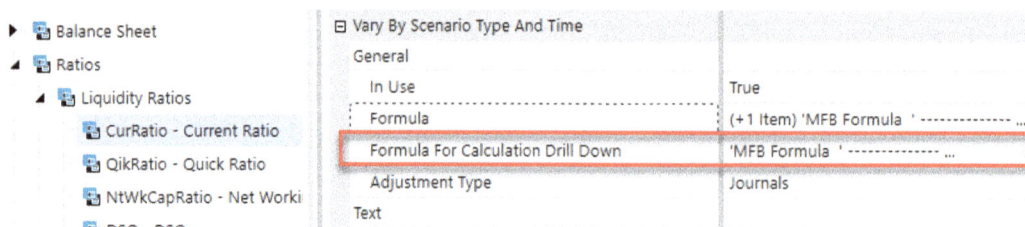

Figure 8.11

Business Rules versus Member Formulas

When designing a OneStream calculation, there are a handful of fundamental considerations to think about when ultimately choosing which type of OneStream rule best suits the requirements of a client's calculation. These concepts can be split into four different categories: 1. purpose, 2. flexibility & maintenance, 3. execution requirements, and 4. performance.

Keep in mind the goal of this section is not to steer you towards writing calculations as a Member Formula or as a business rule, but instead to compare the two approaches and discuss the differences so that you can pick the best approach for your specific calculations.

Purpose

Clearly understanding the *purpose* of rule requirements is critical when choosing whether to design a client's calculation in a finance business rule or directly on a member in a Member Formula. There are specific rule purposes such as custom translation, share, and consolidation logic, that will need to reside in a finance rule. Your experience with other CPM tools may have you questioning why OneStream would even create Member Formulas if they're doing the same thing as a business rule. This thought is completely valid, and I'll expand on the advantages and disadvantages of using them.

Flexibility & Maintenance

The flexibility and ease of maintenance of Member Formulas versus business rules is more complex than you may initially think. The benefits of Member Formulas in a consolidation implementation are often a drawback when using them in a planning implementation. Let's explore further.

When written properly, Member Formulas run specifically to that particular member. No more sifting through thousands of lines of code to find a particular formula!

Member Formulas can vary by Scenario Type and/or time without the need to write code. The Member Formula stores all of these variations directly on the member via properties, through which the administrator can carry out maintenance using drop-down menus. For example, you'll likely encounter a client who wants a member calculation to change as of a certain date, or to calculate things differently between an Actual scenario and a Forecast scenario. Again, the Member Formula accommodates this out-of-the-box, without needing to write additional lines of code.

Calculated members are then all assigned one of 16 formula passes that fire according to DUCS (more on that in the next section). This allows the admin to order them as needed, and those calculated members – dependent on other calculated members – can fire sequentially. I'll revisit this in the performance section.

To summarize, Member Formulas allow the administrator to easily find related code, minimize coding by time and Scenario Type, and assign formula passes for sequential calculations. These convenience factors sound great and are a big plus, especially after go-live, when we leave the client, as administrators generally don't have the skill sets to maintain the rules at our level. However, with the positives come the potential drawbacks.

Due to the formula being held at the dimension member level, if a calculation is the same for many members, the administrator may replicate the same code over and over for each individual member. If the administrator needs to change the code, that person needs to go to each member to change each formula one-by-one. This not only takes time but also increases the risk that the administrator will miss updating some of them.

The formula passes assigned to the members cannot vary by Scenario Type or time. In other words, if you have a Member Formula currently firing on pass three for Actual, but need it to fire on pass five for Budget, you can't write a Member Formula that will satisfy both requirements – at least one calculation would need to go in a business rule. A third way of describing this is that a member can only be assigned one formula pass. If the formula pass is three, it's three for all Scenario Types and time.

Again, consultants and administrators address these drawbacks by putting some types of calculations in a business rule. As a very general rule of thumb, calculations for consolidation or Actual data, use more Member Formulas, while calculations for planning or forecasting data use business rules. Why?

Actual data is generally sourced from ERPs, and the calculations are very specific to the individual members. Prior year retained earnings is a very specific calculation and ends up on a very specific member. Current year retained earnings is the same. Key KPIs can be described similarly, too – DSO, DPO, % of sales, % of gross profit, as examples.

On the other hand, planning data often uses Actual data as a calculation input, and the calculations may span over very large groups of members within a given dimension. For example, Jon mentioned three types of planning methodologies – driver-based, factor-based, and zero-based planning. The results of each of those methodologies are multiplying drivers for large groups of accounts. All sales accounts might be price * quantity. No one wants to go into each of the sales accounts to write the same formula on each individual account. If the customer multiplies prior year Actuals by a growth factor, you'd have the same headache. So, calculations of this nature are generally written in a business rule and NOT on Member Formulas.

Execution Requirements

The next consideration when choosing to write your calculations in a Member Formula versus a business rule is how you'll trigger the calculation. Again, both execute every time a Data Unit calculates or consolidates. If this is your requirement, your choice may remain as a toss-up. However, if you only want the calculation to execute on-demand by a user, consider using the custom calculate finance business rule. These types of rules are far more common in planning implementations and are often triggered by an end-user during their data submission process. These rules have the ability to run individually as well as separately from the standard business rules and Member Formulas that execute during a calculation or consolidation event.

During the design of workflow, it's important to understand what the end-user will be doing at every step during the process. For example, let's say a user calculates a group of accounts in the fourth step of their data submission process. They don't subsequently modify any of the source data in the calculations, and the remaining steps in that user's process, therefore, should not re-calculate those accounts. Granted, if they do re-calculate, the results won't change, and no harm, no foul. My argument is why re-calculate if the results won't change? By re-calculating over and over, they need to wait for the engine to do things it's already done with no additional benefit.

Performance

The performance difference between Member Formulas and business rules – out-of-the-box – favors Member Formulas. OneStream multi-threads Member Formulas for each dimension within a specific formula pass during the calculation sequence. In other words, all accounts with Member Formulas on the same formula pass fire simultaneously. This point of efficiency is built into the OneStream engine with no additional coding.

On the other hand, business rules execute as they're written. If you write five calculations in a business rule, OneStream will execute them in the order in which they appear in the rule. Change the five calculations to hundreds, and you'll experience a considerable difference in performance between writing the calculations as Member Formulas versus within a single business rule.

This fact somewhat puts the option of using Member Formulas far ahead of using business rules, but the design considerations drive out which option better suits and addresses the requirements.

Writing calculations in business rules isn't a bad thing to do – in fact, it's probably necessary. Good consultants and coders develop logic to address some of the 'downfalls' of writing calculations in business rules. These include calculating only the intersections that are required to be calculated (e.g., at base entity and local currency only), using data buffers effectively, and building triggers into the workflow for the calculations to execute once rather than multiple times throughout the process. I would expect to find a balance of both Member Formulas and business rules in any application that's been configured to address requirements for multiple processes.

Must-Know Financial Calculation Concepts

Now that you've acquired a solid foundation of rules knowledge – including a high-level understanding of their use cases and how they're triggered in an application – understanding the platform's calculation engine will be pivotal in taking your financial rules knowledge to the next level. When designing financial rules and calculations in OneStream, you must have a deep understanding of **DUCS**… and I'm not talking about Ernie's favorite bathtime toy.

In the OneStream world, we refer to the OneStream calculation sequence as the **Data Unit Calculation Sequence** or DUCS for short. When I talk about truly understanding DUCS, I mean knowing what the heck happens behind the scenes when you run a calculate or force calculate in the platform. Understanding the precise order of when calculations and rules fire during a calculation process is a must-know concept during your rules journey!

Along with an understanding of the calculation sequence, it is equally as important to begin to train your mind to think of financial calculations in units of Data Units and data buffers. Understanding both concepts will provide you with the tools and skills to write functional and, most importantly, performant financial rules in an implementation.

OneStream Calculation Sequence

As we discussed earlier in this chapter, a financial calculation that gets triggered during a cube calculation event can be written in a variety of different places, including in a finance business rule, and directly on a member as a stored Member Formula. Furthermore, in a OneStream application, you'll likely have multiple members in different dimensions that have Member Formulas. You may even have calculations that have dependencies on others, meaning a calculated member's formula may refer to the results of *another* calculated member.

As you can begin to see, there is the potential for many calculations to fire during a calculation event, including Member Formulas and up to eight unique finance business rules that may be assigned to a cube. However, not to worry, there is a method to the calculation engine's madness. The platform's calculation engine is a master of precision as it fires rules in a very methodical manner and precise order. Understanding the order behind the scenes will enable you to design your financial rules in the right place, to fire at the right time, as well as take advantage of the engine's ability to multi-thread calculations as much as possible.

When a calculation event occurs in the system, the finance engine handles the event by executing the following calculation sequence:

- Clear previously calculated data (based on cell storage type – will not clear durable data). Note: OneStream will only perform this action if the calculated scenario has its Clear Calculated Data During Calc setting set to True

- Run scenario Member Formula

- Perform reverse translations by calculating Flow members from other alternate currency input Flow members

- Execute business rules 1 and 2 (as assigned to cube)

- Execute formula passes 1 through 4 (account formulas, then flow formulas, then UD1 formulas, UD2, … UD8)

- Execute business rules 3 and 4 (as assigned to cube)

- Execute formula passes 5 through 8 (account formulas, then flow formulas, then UD1 formulas, UD2, … UD8)

- Execute business rules 5 and 6 (as assigned to cube)

- Execute formula passes 9 through 12 (account formulas, then flow formulas, then UD1 formulas, UD2, … UD8)

- Execute business rules 7 and 8 (as assigned to cube)

- Execute formula passes 13 through 16 (account formulas, then flow formulas, then UD1 formulas, UD2, ... UD8)

It is also very important to note that the calculation sequence can fire multiple times at varying levels of the Consolidation dimension when consolidating a parent-level entity. The calculation sequence, as described above, can trigger up to seven times during a single consolidation or force consolidate event based on the following intervals:

Levels of consolidation for each entity (up to seven calculate operations).

- **Calculate** local currency

- Translate local currency to parent's default currency (i.e., `C#Translated`)

- **Calculate** translated currency

- **Calculate** `OwnerPreAdj`

- Perform the default or custom share functions (if default, share is calc-on-the-fly. If custom consolidation, **calculate** share)

- Execute default or custom elimination functions (including populating `O#Elimination`), then **calculate** elimination

- **Calculate** `OwnerPostAdj`

- Combine the data from top consolidation member from each child entity to insert data in the parent entity's local consolidation member

- Step 9 is to **calculate** parent entity's local currency consolidation member

Because individual calculations can be triggered at many different stages of the calculation and consolidation sequence(s), designing your financial rules to fire at the appropriate times is absolutely critical to a well-performing application. The golden nugget to keep in mind here is you only want your rules to fire *when they are needed to execute* – this methodical and purposeful mindset will promote well-performing calculation and consolidation processing times in a OneStream application.

Calculations Start with the Data Unit

Now that you understand when financial rules can be triggered, you're likely wondering how to control if and when a rule fires during a calculation and consolidation sequence. In this section, we'll explain how Data Units drive the design and the execution behavior of your financial calculations.

An important concept to understand when it comes to the finance engine is that every calculation and consolidation event in OneStream is driven by the Data Unit for which the financial event is run (triggered).

The Data Unit is ultimately the subset of data that will be calculated or consolidated. Data Unit dimensions are defined by cube, scenario, time, entity, parent, and consolidation member. When performing a calculation or consolidation in OneStream, the finance engine is simply not aware of the non-Data Unit dimensions (Account, Flow, Origin, IC, UD1-UD8) set in your point of view. Instead, the finance engine is purely focused on – and tied to – the Data Unit dimensions.

When designing calculations in a finance business rule or Member Formula, it is extremely important to determine and control *when* a rule will execute during a calculation sequence by defining the specific levels of the Data Unit – such as the consolidation and entity – for which the rule will fire. It's often strongly suggested to implement Data Unit **If conditions** – to control when a rule should execute during a calculation sequence. For example, many times a financial calculation is only required to execute on specific Data Units such as on base entity and local currency Data Units. Refer to the following code for a common best practice Data Unit `If` condition – that controls a calculation to run for base entities and local currency.

```
'execute for base entities and local currency
If ((Not api.Entity.HasChildren()) And (api.Cons.IsLocalCurrencyForEntity())) Then

End If
```

Figure 8.12

> **Note:** If your calculation is required to fire for specific Data Units and – thus – you have the use for Data Unit `If` conditions, it is best practice to insert the necessary Data Unit `If` conditions as early as possible in your logic, towards the top of your rule. This will ensure all variable declarations and proceeding code is only triggered for Data Units that meet the `If` statement calculation criteria. This promotes better performance as you will have designed your code to avoid processing code for Data Units that are not required to be calculated.

As we discussed earlier in this chapter, during a consolidation event, it is possible for a single formula to calculate up to seven different times at varying levels of the Consolidation dimension for a given entity. By implementing Data Unit conditions in your financial rules, you can prevent your Member Formulas and finance rules from firing unnecessarily *at all levels* of the Consolidation and Entity dimension – such as at parent entities, foreign currencies, or relationship-type consolidation levels.

Learning to Think of Calculations in Units of Data Buffers

Now that we understand the importance of Data Units and how they drive the financial events that occur in OneStream, the next step in our finance rules journey will be to learn how to think of the inputs (sources) and outputs (results) of our calculations in units called **data buffers**.

In the OneStream world, a data buffer is a term used to describe a 'slice' or subset of data that exists within a given Data Unit. A data buffer can be a collection of cells that refer to both the input (source) and output (result) of a financial calculation. In reality, it is important to note that a Data Unit is, in fact, a data buffer itself – it's a large collection of cells. The data buffers we're discussing in this section relate to breaking down Data Units into smaller data buffers.

When designing a stored calculation in a finance business rule or Member Formula, a calculation

is often the result of math that is performed on a collection of data cells (DatabufferA + DatabufferB) that result in multiple output/result cells being calculated.

The collection of data cells in the source, and the result of calculations that are associated with specific dimensionality within a Data Unit, are what we describe as a data buffer. To better visualize the meaning of a data buffer and further understand how they're an important piece of OneStream calculations, let's review a basic calculation example together.

In the example calculation, below, we have defined the inputs (source) and output (result) of our calculation as such: Result = A + B. Please note that screenshots of code often use line breaks to fit the code within the page margins.

```
'run for base entities and local currency
If ((Not api.Entity.HasChildren()) And (api.Cons.IsLocalCurrencyForEntity())) Then
    'result = databufferA + dataBufferB
    api.Data.Calculate("A#DatabufferResult:O#Import:F#EndBal = " & _
    "A#DatabufferA:O#Top:F#EndBal + A#DatabufferB:O#Top:F#EndBal")
End If
```

Figure 8.13

Notice that our rule begins with Data Unit `If` conditions to ensure the rule only fires for base entities and local currency as we'll let the consolidation engine naturally handle the consolidation of the data up the Consolidation and Entity dimensions (rather than unnecessarily calculating these data points).

Next, it is important to understand that the source of the calculation (`databuffer A + databuffer B`) consists of two different subsets of dimensionality, which are both unique data buffers that are comprised of a collection of unique data cells. Because we've defined only three dimensions within each source data buffer (Account, Origin, Flow), there is a possibility for multiple cells to exist within each slice of dimensionality. For example, in the `SourceDatabufferA` account at `O#Top:F#EndBal`, there could be many data cells that exist in this dimensionality across the UD1-UD8 dimensions. The same concept applies to the `SourceDatabufferB` account at `O#Top:F#EndBal` where many data cells could exist in undefined dimensions as well.

It is important to understand that unless you have defined all 12 account-type dimensions (Account, Flow, Origin, IC, UD1-UD8) in the result and source of your formula, you will be performing math on data buffers, and the result is a data buffer that may contain a collection of cells produced by the calculation.

Now that you understand the definition of a data buffer, and how we use them when writing calculations in OneStream, we'll review our top must-know stored calculation best practices.

Stored Calculation Techniques and Best Practices

In this section, we'll introduce commonly used API functions that are utilized in the majority of the calculations in OneStream and review our stored calculation best practices and performance considerations.

Stored Calculations Using Api.Data.Calculate

The `api.Data.Calculate` function is by far the most popular API and technique to use in calculating financial cube data in OneStream… and for a good reason! The API is a straightforward function where you specify a source and result of your calculation. The function also allows you to utilize optional arguments to further control the precision and efficiency of the calculation.

It is critical to understand that all stored calculations, including those that are facilitated by an `api.Data.Calculate` function, will run on all Account-type dimensions of the result and source Data Units of the calculation. In the earlier example, listed again below, although the calculate API only has the Account, Origin, and Flow dimensions specified in the source and target of the calculation, the formula will process and calculate for all the dimensions that are not specified, such as the Intercompany and User Defined dimensions.

```
'run for base entities and local currency
If ((Not api.Entity.HasChildren()) And (api.Cons.IsLocalCurrencyForEntity())) Then
    'result = databufferA + dataBufferB
    api.Data.Calculate("A#DatabufferResult:O#Import:F#EndBal = " & _
    "A#DatabufferA:O#Top:F#EndBal + A#DatabufferB:O#Top:F#EndBal")
End If
```

Figure 8.14

In fact, any dimension not specified on the left and right-hand side of the equals sign in the calculate function will run for all members within the dimension. For example, the calculation outlined previously will query and potentially write cells to any of the dimension members in the IC and User Defined dimensions that contain data in the source data buffer. This is an extremely important concept to understand when writing stored calculations, and we'll talk more about it later in this section.

An `api.Data.Calculate` function is what we refer to as an **overloaded API function** in OneStream. This function can be used in three different formats depending on the complexity and requirements of the calculation. Let's review each of them below.

Three different versions of `api.Data.Calculate` – bold arguments are required, while the nonbolded arguments are optional.

```
api.Data.Calculate(|)
  ▲ 1 of 3 ▼  ☺ Sub DataApi.Calculate(formula As String, Optional accountFilter As String, Optional flowFilter As String, Optional originFilter As
                String, Optional icFilter As String, Optional ud1Filter As String, Optional ud2Filter As String, Optional ud3Filter As String, Optional
                ud4Filter As String, Optional ud5Filter As String, Optional ud6Filter As String, Optional ud7Filter As String, Optional ud8Filter As
                String, Optional onEvalDataBuffer As EvalDataBufferDelegate, Optional userState As Object, Optional isDurableCalculatedData As Boolean)
```

Figure 8.15

1. **Formula with Durable Calculated Data** – typically used when writing a simple calculation that requires the calculated data to be stored as durable data.

   - `api.Data.Calculate(`**`Formula as String, IsDurableCalculatedData as Boolean`**`)`

2. **Formula As String with Eval and User State** – typically used when writing a calculation that leverages an Eval, which enables the rule writer to evaluate the individual source cells of a data buffer to conditionally process data cells for a calculation.

   - `api.Data.Calculate(`**`Formula as String, onEvalDataBuffer as EvalDataBufferDelegate,`** `UserState as Object)`

```
'run for base entities and local currency
If ((Not api.Entity.HasChildren()) And (api.Cons.IsLocalCurrencyForEntity())) Then
    'evaluate the cells in the source data buffer and conditionally write the cells to the result buffer
    api.Data.Calculate("A#DatabufferResult:O#Import:F#EndBal = Eval(A#DatabufferA:O#Top:F#EndBal)", AddressOf onEvalDataBuffer)
End If


Private Sub OnEvalDataBuffer(ByVal api As FinanceRulesApi, ByVal evalName As String, ByVal eventArgs As EvalDataBufferEventArgs)
    'best practice to clear out the result buffer first
    EventArgs.DataBufferResult.DataBufferCells.Clear()
    'start looping through the dictionary of source cells
    For Each sourceCell As DataBufferCell In eventArgs.DataBuffer1.DataBufferCells.Values
        'filter out cells that are NoData cells
        If (Not sourceCell.CellStatus.IsNoData) Then
            'filter out cells that have an amount equal to or less than 1
            If sourceCell.CellAmount > 1.0 Then
                'create a copy of the source cell - we'll use this to set a new dynamic cell amount
                Dim resultCell As New DataBufferCell(sourceCell)
                'add 5 to the existing cell amount
                resultCell.CellAmount = Decimal.Add(sourceCell.CellAmount, 5.0)
                'add the cell to the result data buffer
                eventArgs.DataBufferResult.SetCell(api.SI, resultCell)
            End If
        End If
    Next
End Sub
```

Figure 8.16

3. **Formula with Account-Type Dimension Filtering, Eval, User State, and Durable Calculated Data** – this is the most commonly used instance of the `api.Data.Calculate` function and allows for the most flexibility in either simple or complex calculations. This instance only requires a formula argument and can leverage the filtering arguments. We'll discuss the details and importance of filtering in an `api.Data.Calculate` later on in this chapter.

- api.Data.Calculate(**Formula as string**, accountFilter as String, flowFilter as String, originFilter as String, icFilter as String, ud1Filter as String, ud2Filter as String, ud3Filter as String, ud4Filter as String, ud5Filter as String, ud6Filter as String, ud7Filter as String, ud8Filter as String, onEvalDataBuffer as EvalDataBufferDelegate, UserState as Object,IsDurableCalculatedData as Boolean)

```
'run for base entities and local currency
If ((Not api.Entity.HasChildren()) And (api.Cons.IsLocalCurrencyForEntity())) Then
    'perform the data buffer math and only calculate cells for specific members in the UD1 and UD3 dimensions
    api.Data.Calculate("A#DatabufferResult:O#Import:F#EndBal = " & _
    "A#DatabufferA:O#Top:F#EndBal + A#DatabufferB:O#Top:F#EndBal",,,,,"U1#Services.base",,,"U3#Americas.base")
End If
```

Figure 8.17

Ultimately, the version of the calculate API function you use varies, based on the situation and complexity of the requirements. Personal choice also plays a factor. In the upcoming sections, we'll focus on the performance considerations which will lead to the use of the filtering arguments found in the third api.Data.Calculate example above.

Stored Calculations Using Get/Set Data Buffer

In addition to the api.Data.Calculate function, the Get/Set data buffer functions are another leading calculation technique that uses data buffer math to calculate result cells for your calculations. The choice to use one of these calculation functions is based on the rule writer's personal preference, as there is not necessarily a firm best practice recommendation. That being said, for complex calculations that require conditional cell-by-cell processing, I personally prefer the flexibility and precision that the Get/Set data buffer approach offers. We'll dive into the fundamentals and abilities of the Get/Set data buffer functions together throughout this section.

As mentioned earlier, the Get/Set data buffer technique enables you to perform data buffer math and is similar to the api.Data.Calculate function in theory. The technique can be split into three fundamental pieces.

1. GetExpressionDestinationInfo – used to define the result's dimensionality, aka the result data buffer, or the target dimensionality to which the calculation will be written.

   - Api.Data.GetExpressionDestinationInfo(**destDataBufferScript** as String)

```
'define the destination - aka the result data buffer of where the data will be saved
Dim destination As ExpressionDestinationInfo = api.Data.GetExpressionDestinationInfo("A#DatabufferResult:O#Import:F#EndBal:I#None")
```

Figure 8.18

2. GetDataBuffer – Overloaded function used to retrieve a source data buffer that is used as an input to a calculation, or the source data buffer. This is equivalent to the right-hand side of the equals sign in an api.Data.Calculate function. (Required arguments in bold.)

   - Api.Data.GetDataBuffer(**scriptMethodType** as DataApiScriptMethodType, **sourceDataBufferScript** as String, **expressionDestinationInfo** as ExpressionDestinationInfo)

   - Api.Data.GetDataBuffer(**scriptMethodType** as

```
DataApiScriptMethodType, sourceDataBufferScript as String,
changeIDsToCommonIfNotUsingAll as Boolean,
expressionDestinationInfo as ExpressionDestinationInfo)
```

- Api.Data.GetDataBuffer(**scriptMethodType** as

```
DataApiScriptMethodType, sourceDataBufferScript as String,
changeIDsToCommonIfNotUsingAll as Boolean,
includeUDAttributeMembersWhenUsingAll as Boolean,
expressionDestinationInfo as ExpressionDestinationInfo)
```

```
'retrieve souce data buffer A
Dim dataBufferA As DataBuffer = api.Data.GetDataBuffer(DataApiScriptMethodType.Calculate, "A#DatabufferA:O#Top:F#EndBal:I#None", destinationInfo)
```

Figure 8.19

3. SetDataBuffer – Used to save a data buffer (collection of cells) to a result destination. This is equivalent to the left-hand side of the equals sign in an api.Data.Calculate function. This API ultimately saves the calculated data. (Required arguments in bold.)

- Api.Data.SetDataBuffer(**dataBuffer as DataBuffer, expressionDestinationInfo as ExpressionDestinationInfo,** accountFilter as String, flowFilter as String, originFilter as String, icfilter as String, accountFilter as String, ud1Filter as String, ud2Filter as String, ud3Filter as String, ud4Filter as String, ud5Filter as String, ud6Filter as String, ud7Filter as String, ud8Filter as String, isDurableCalculatedData as Boolean)

```
'save the source data buffer A to the destination - this saves the calculated data cells
api.Data.SetDataBuffer(dataBufferA, destination)
```

Figure 8.20

With the Get/Set data buffer technique, you can retrieve source data buffers, perform data buffer math, and write a collection of cells to specific result dimensionality (a result data buffer). When it comes to retrieving the source data buffer(s) that make up the source of the calculation, there is another powerful API you can use to retrieve data buffers and perform data buffer math to facilitate the source of your calculation. The GetDataBufferUsingFormula API function works much like the GetDataBuffer API; however, the former provides additional flexibility and performance tuning by enabling you to define Account-type dimension filtering syntax to further home in on the source cells that are required for your calculation.

Let's review the GetDataBufferUsingFormula API below.

1. GetDataBufferUsingFormula – overloaded function used to retrieve the source data buffer(s) of a calculation. This API provides you with the ability to perform data buffer math within one API function and enables you to filter down the source data buffer with the FilterMembers syntax. Note that within the FilterMembers syntax, the specific ordering of the dimension filters does not matter. (Required arguments in bold.)

- Api.Data.GetDataBufferUsingFormula(**formula as String,** scriptMethodType as DataApiScriptMethodType, changeIDsToCommonIfNotUsingAll as Boolean, includeUDAttributeMembersWhenUsingAll as Boolean, expressionDestinationInfo as ExpressionDestinationInfo, onEvalDataBuffer as EvalDataBufferDelegate, userState as Object)

```
Dim sourceDataBuffer As New DataBuffer()
sourceDataBuffer = api.Data.GetDataBufferUsingFormula("A#DatabufferA:O#Top:F#EndBal:I#None + A#DatabufferB:O#Top:F#EndBal:I#None")
```

Figure 8.21

- Api.Data.GetDataBufferUsingFormula(**formula** as String,
  scriptMethodType as DataApiScriptMethodType,
  changeIDsToCommonIfNotUsingAll as Boolean,
  includeUDAttributeMembersWhenUsingAll as Boolean,
  expressionDestinationInfo as ExpressionDestinationInfo,
  onEvalDataBuffer as EvalDataBufferDelegate, userState as
  Object)

```
Dim sourceDataBuffer As New DataBuffer()
sourceDataBuffer = api.Data.GetDataBufferUsingFormula("A#DatabufferA:O#Top:F#EndBal:I#None + " & _
"A#DatabufferB:O#Top:F#EndBal:I#None", DataApiScriptMethodType.Calculate, False, destination)
```

Figure 8.22

> **Syntax notes:** ordering of the Account-type dimension filters does not matter. When using one dimension filter, square brackets [] are not required around the filter. When using more than one dimension filter, square brackets are required to be wrapped around each individual dimension filter. It's good practice to get into the habit of wrapping square brackets around each filter.

```
'define the result dimensionality - the result data buffer
Dim destination As ExpressionDestinationInfo = api.Data.GetExpressionDestinationInfo("A#DatabufferResult:O#Import:F#EndBal:I#None")
'use GetDataBufferUsingFormula to perform data buffer math and filter down the calculation to fire for specific members in UD1 and UD3
Dim sourceDataBuffer As DataBuffer = api.Data.GetDataBufferUsingFormula("FilterMembers(A#DatabufferA:O#Top:F#EndBal:I#None + " & _
"A#DatabufferB:O#Top:F#EndBal:I#None,[U1#Services.base],[U3#Americas.base])", DataApiScriptMethodType.Calculate, False, destination)
'save the data buffer math calculated cells to the result buffer
api.Data.SetDataBuffer(sourceDataBuffer, destination)
```

Figure 8.23

Lastly, another convenience that the Get/Set data buffer technique offers is ease and performance when it comes to cell-by-cell processing. By utilizing a GetDataBuffer API function in your calculation, you query a collection of data cells in memory and now have convenient access to the data cells in the form of a **data buffer cell dictionary**. With this data buffer cell dictionary object, you can now loop very efficiently through the data buffer cells, evaluate, and conditionally process the source cells based on their cell amount, cell status, and dimensionality. In addition, you not only have the power and flexibility to conditionally include or exclude the source cells that are potential inputs for your calculation, but you also have the ability to dynamically set the result calculated cells' cell status, cell amount, and result dimensionality.

In the example below, you'll find an advanced example of a financial calculation that uses the Get/Set data buffer technique to conditionally process the source cells of a calculation by cell status while dynamically setting the result calculated cell dimensionality.

```
'run for base entities and local currency
If ((Not api.Entity.HasChildren()) And (api.Cons.IsLocalCurrencyForEntity())) Then
    'retrieve a data buffer of data cells for F#EndBal at U1#Top for base balance sheet accounts
    'and dynamically set the result cell UD1 based on the account text 1 property
    Dim sourceBuffer As DataBuffer = api.Data.GetDataBufferUsingFormula("FilterMembers(F#EndBal:U1#Top,[A#[Balance Sheet].base])")
    If (Not sourceBuffer Is Nothing) Then
        'define the static destination dimensionality
        Dim destination As ExpressionDestinationInfo = api.Data.GetExpressionDestinationInfo("F#EndBal")
        Dim textOne As String = String.Empty
        Dim resultBuffer As New DataBuffer()
        'loop through the dictionary of source data buffer data cells
        For Each sourceCell In sourceBuffer.DataBufferCells.Values
            'filter out no data cells
            If (Not sourceCell.CellStatus.IsNoData) Then
                'retrieve the cell's account text 1 property
                textOne = api.UD1.Text(api.Pov.Account.MemberId, 1)
                'ensure an account text 1 value is set
                If (Not textOne = String.Empty) Then
                    'make a copy of the original source cell
                    Dim resultCell As New DataBufferCell(sourceCell)
                    'dynamically set the result cell UD1 dimensionality to the account text one property
                    resultCell.DataBufferCellPk.UD1Id = api.Members.GetMemberId(DimTypeId.UD1, textOne)
                    'add the result cell to the result buffer
                    resultBuffer.SetCell(si, resultCell, True)
                End If 'end text one check
            End If 'end cell status check
        Next 'end data buffer cell loop
        'save the result cells to the result destination
        api.Data.SetDataBuffer(resultBuffer, destination)
    End If 'end data buffer check
End If 'end base entity/local currency check
```

Figure 8.24

Now that we've learned the fundamentals of using data buffer functions to facilitate calculations, let's further discuss our best practice performance considerations and the tips that you'll need to write efficient financial rules in OneStream, which will keep your application healthy and your customers happy!

Stored Calculation Performance Considerations & Tips

When writing calculations, the efficiency of the calculation is nearly as important as the ability to calculate the correct cell values. You might smirk at that statement at first, but throughout your OneStream journey, you will find that inefficient calculations can cripple an application's performance, especially when working with large data models. In this section, we'll outline our key considerations and tips to enable you to write performant calculations and promote sound consolidation performance.

One of the fundamental laws when writing performant calculations is to always – and I mean *always* – avoid nesting a calculation within a member list loop. All too often, I see rules that initialize a member list, such as a list of accounts, then loop through the list and ultimately execute a calculation via an `api.Data.Calculate` within the loop. These types of calculations have the potential to derail the calculation and consolidation performance of an application, especially in large data models. This is due to the inefficiency of looping through a list in code and iteratively executing a calculation over and over for each member in the list; this becomes an awfully slow approach to performing a calculation for a subset of members. In a situation like this, if the member list consists of hundreds or thousands of members, the art of looping through these members and performing a calculation one by one will take an eternity in terms of code processing time.

Have a look at the code below as an example of what NOT to do when writing a calculation. In general, avoid executing a calculation within a member list loop – at all costs!

```
'BAD Performance Example
'run For base entities And local currency
If ((Not api.Entity.HasChildren()) And (api.Cons.IsLocalCurrencyForEntity())) Then
    'get a list of base balance sheet accounts
    Dim balanceSheetList As List(Of Member) = api.Members.GetMembersUsingFilter(api.Pov.AccountDim.DimPk, "A#[Balance Sheet].base")
    If (Not balanceSheetList Is Nothing) Then
        'loop through the accounts
        For Each bsAccount As Member In balanceSheetList
            'perform a calculation for each balance sheet account
            api.Data.Calculate("A#[" & bsAccount.Name & "]:F#EndBal:U1#None = A#[" & bsAccount.Name & "]:F#EndBal:U1#Top")
        Next 'end account loop
    End If 'end member list check
End If 'end base entity/local check
```

Figure 8.25

The inefficient calculation in the code above could easily be avoided and optimized by taking advantage of our ability to implement filtering in an api.Data.Calculate or GetDataBufferUsingFormula function.

In the code above, the logic is essentially written in a way that filters the calculation to specifically run for base balance sheet accounts. This same concept of filtering can be applied but in a much more efficient manner by leveraging the techniques in the example shown below. Utilizing filter arguments in an api.Data.Calculate or the FilterMembers syntax in an api.Data.GetDataBufferUsingFormula function are two great ways to filter down your calculations to fire on specific Account-type dimension members. This filtering technique will assist you in avoiding member list loops and limit the number of cells the calculation is required to evaluate and calculate. Filtering is a fundamental approach to writing efficient calculations in OneStream.

```
'Better performance using GetDataBufferUsingFormula FilterMembers
'run For base entities And local currency
If ((Not api.Entity.HasChildren()) And (api.Cons.IsLocalCurrencyForEntity())) Then
    'perform a calculation on all base balance sheet accounts by using FilterMembers
    Dim destination As ExpressionDestinationInfo = api.Data.GetExpressionDestinationInfo("F#EndBal:U1#None")
    Dim sourceBuffer As DataBuffer = api.Data.GetDataBufferUsingFormula("FilterMembers(F#EndBal:U1#Top, [A#[Balance Sheet].base])")
    api.Data.SetDataBuffer(sourceBuffer, destination)
End If 'end base entity/local check

'Better performance using api.Data.Calculate filtering
'run For base entities And local currency
If ((Not api.Entity.HasChildren()) And (api.Cons.IsLocalCurrencyForEntity())) Then
    'perform a calculation on all base balance sheet accounts by using a filter
    api.Data.Calculate("F#EndBal:U1#None = F#EndBal:U1#Top","A#[Balance Sheet].base")
End If 'end base entity/local check
```

Figure 8.26

When implementing filtering in an api.Data.Calculate function, there are several syntax tips worth noting. The ordering of the dimension filters is specifically important, and empty placeholders are required for the filters that are between the optional/unused arguments and the used arguments. For example, you may utilize a UD2 filter and not require the use of additional filters or additional arguments in the calculate function. In this situation, your filter would look like the example below:

```
'run for base entities and local currency
If ((Not api.Entity.HasChildren()) And (api.Cons.IsLocalCurrencyForEntity())) Then
    api.Data.Calculate("F#EndBal:U1#None = F#EndBal:U1#Top",,,,,,"U2#Irons.base")
End If
```

Figure 8.27

The same concept applies when using multiple filters or a filter argument and another argument such as an Eval. Empty placeholders are required when implementing multiple arguments that have unused arguments between them. However, if additional optional arguments are not used after the last used argument in the function, the proceeding arguments (filters, Eval, etc.) are not required.

```
''run For base entities And local currency
If ((Not api.Entity.HasChildren()) And (api.Cons.IsLocalCurrencyForEntity())) Then
    api.Data.Calculate("F#EndBal:U1#None = F#EndBal:U1#Top",,,,,,"U2#Irons.base,U2#Clubs.base",,"U4#CustomerSegmentA.base")
End If 'end base entity/local check
```

Figure 8.28

Also, it is important to note that all instances of filtering in an `api.Data.Calculate` and `api.DataGetDataBufferUsing` formula can use any standard OneStream Member Filter syntax and valid Member Expansion. The general rule of thumb is that if you can use a specific Member Filter or expansion in a Cube View, you can use it as a filter in a calculation.

Lastly, in regards to filtering syntax, the `FilterMembers` syntax is unique and is specified differently than the filtering defined in an `api.Data.Calculate` function. When implementing one Account-type dimension filter, square brackets around the filter are not required, and the ordering of the filters does not matter. However, it is my recommendation to get into the habit of using brackets because you will need them when using multiple filters. See the examples below for visuals of filtering within an `api.Data.GetDataBufferUsingFormula` function.

```
'one filter
Dim sourceBuffer As DataBuffer = api.Data.GetDataBufferUsingFormula("FilterMembers(F#EndBal:U1#Top, [A#[Balance Sheet].base])")

'two filters - different dimensions
Dim sourceBuffer As DataBuffer = api.Data.GetDataBufferUsingFormula("FilterMembers(F#EndBal:U1#Top, [A#[Balance Sheet].base], [U2#Irons.base])")

'two filters - same dimension
Dim sourceBuffer As DataBuffer = api.Data.GetDataBufferUsingFormula("FilterMembers(F#EndBal:U1#Top, [U2#Clubs.base], [U2#Irons.base])")
```

Figure 8.29

In addition to implementing filtering in your stored calculations, the `RemoveNoData` and `RemoveZeros` syntax enable you to write your calculations to avoid processing source cells that are no data cells, or data cells that are equal to zero. Keep in mind, in specific situations, a no data cell or zero cell may need to be evaluated and even written to the database as a calculated value. However, in many cases, you may not have the requirement to calculate these types of cells.

The Remove Zeros function is designed to filter out cells that are equal to zero as well as cells that have a cell status of No Data, while the Remove No Data function will simply filter out no data cells. A rule of thumb is to avoid using the Remove Zeros syntax when writing a calculation to a periodic view member, which often occurs indirectly when the scenario being calculated has a default view property set to periodic.

Periodic calculations often require zeros to be evaluated and written as derived data to the database. However, in YTD calculations, zero cells and no data cells are often not required to be calculated, and can be avoided by leveraging the Remove Zeros or Remove No Data functions, respectively. At the end of the day, implementing remove functions in your stored calculations can eliminate the wasted processing of cells that are not required to be calculated, as well as limit the writing of unnecessary cells to the database. Both functions can reduce calculation times and improve overall consolidation performance.

See the code below for syntax examples on how to introduce the Remove Zeros and Remove No Data functions into your stored calculations.

```
If currMonth = 1 Then
    api.Data.Calculate("F#BegBalCalc = RemoveZeros(F#None:T#POVPriorYearM12)","A#[Balance Sheet].base")
Else
    api.Data.Calculate("F#BegBalCalc = RemoveZeros(F#BegBalCalc:T#POVPrior1)","A#[Balance Sheet].base")
End If

If currMonth = 1 Then
    api.Data.Calculate("F#BegBalCalc = RemoveNoData(F#None:T#POVPriorYearM12)","A#[Balance Sheet].base")
Else
    api.Data.Calculate("F#BegBalCalc = RemoveNoData(F#BegBalCalc:T#POVPrior1)","A#[Balance Sheet].base")
End If
```

Figure 8.30

Another very helpful performance tip – when writing stored calculations – is to leverage formula variables to effectively cache reused data buffers in memory. This allows the finance rule or Member Formula to refer to a data buffer in multiple calculations that require the same source data buffer. For example, if you have a requirement to perform two calculations and each calculation requires data buffer math that uses a commonly shared input, the use of formula variables will enable you to retrieve and cache the data buffer in memory once, and refer to this data buffer in each calculation.

The idea here is that if a data buffer is going to be used in multiple calculations within the same rule, why query the same data buffer more than once when we have the ability to query, cache it in memory once, and refer to it as many times as we need throughout the rule. The example below contains an example of using formula variables to set a data buffer variable in memory and refer to it in two different stored calculations. Note that the syntax used to refer to a formula variable is the variable name you assign to the object and a prefix of a dollar sign, e.g., $DataBufferVariable.

```
'run for base entities and local currency
If ((Not api.Entity.HasChildren()) And (api.Cons.IsLocalCurrencyForEntity())) Then
    'retrieve the commonly shared data buffer in memory
    Dim sourceBuffer As DataBuffer = api.Data.GetDataBufferUsingFormula("A#DataBufferA:O#Top:F#EndBal:I#None")
    'set a formula variable for the data buffer so that we can refer to the data buffer in multiple calculations
    api.Data.FormulaVariables.SetDataBufferVariable("SourceBufferA", sourceBuffer, True)
    api.Data.Calculate("A#DataBufferResult1:O#Import:F#EndBal:I#None = $SourceBufferA", ,,,,"U1#Services.base")
    api.Data.Calculate("A#DataBufferResult2:O#Import:F#EndBal:I#None = $SourceBufferA + A#DataBufferB:O#Top:F#EndBal:I#None",,,,,"U1#Mfg.base")
End If
```

Figure 8.31

A more advanced derivation of this can be applied by using GetFilteredDataBuffer. Since we are talking about foundational knowledge in this book, I won't go into a detailed explanation of the function. However, to give you a high-level summary, you basically create and use a dictionary to filter, or get a subset of, a data buffer that you previously brought into memory, and use it in your calculation. Like using a data buffer variable, it prevents you from having to query an additional data buffer since it's already in memory.

Lastly, another must-know and strongly recommended stored calculation best practice is to avoid using BRAPIs in finance business rules and Member Formulas when an equivalent API is available.

The use of BRAPIs in finance rules should be avoided when possible due to OneStream potentially needing to open a connection to the database when executing a BRAPI function from the finance engine. In an application with a lot of entities, where multi-threading occurs on a regular basis during a calculation process, the BRAPI calls found in a finance rule or stored Member Formula can open additional database connections for *each* entity and *each* rule where a BRAPI is present. If unnecessary BRAPI functions are scattered regularly across many different finance rules and Member Formulas, this could result in an error message during a consolidation that states: max connection pool reached and can ultimately cause **database deadlocks** to occur during consolidations.

When a database deadlock occurs during a consolidation, a CPU thread is required to wait until another database connection is available, which results in a calculation slowing to a halt and causing poor calculation performance. In general, avoid the use of BRAPIs in a finance rule and stored Member Formula when equivalent APIs are available.

In this section, we've learned the ins and outs of stored calculations, including an overview of the fundamental stored calculation API functions, and reviewed our OneStream stored calculation best practices and performance tips. In the upcoming sections, we'll review business rule design tips and use cases to further understand how rules are designed and used in an implementation.

Calculate versus Custom Calculate

You know *what* OneStream needs to calculate, so now think about *when* it should calculate.

As highlighted previously, the process holds as much importance in OneStream as the calculations and consolidations. I think we all agree that running a top-of-the-house consolidation each time a user wants to see the result of a calculation on one entity is overkill. Using that concept, running all calculations for an entity each time a user wants to see the result of a specific calculation on that entity is equally as redundant. This is where you evaluate if you're going to use the calculate or custom calculate function in your business rule.

Back to the task at hand – when should my calculation fire? The answer is fairly straightforward; if you want it to calculate every single time OneStream calculates or consolidates a Data Unit (based on the given entity's calc status), you would use the calculate function. On the other hand, if you want to run a calculation at a specific point in time (i.e., on-demand) and not over and over and over, you would use OneStream's custom calculate function. This can save a lot of time during the processing of any cube(s), thus enriching the end-user experience.

Jon went into detail, previously, and gave a few examples when considering using them during a planning implementation. On the consolidation side, I've most commonly seen them used for more complex allocation rules. For example, generally speaking, allocations only need to run if the data that's being allocated has been loaded. Hopefully, your rule skips the allocation section in the rule if there's no source data anyway; but, if you wrote it in a custom calculate function, you can have the end-user trigger it when they want to (or even better, bake it into their process, so it runs automatically when it needs to run).

Designing Member Lists

The member list functions in finance business rules don't necessarily require a whole lot of forethought. Many lists can be called by simply using filters in your Cube Views or business rules, but sometimes you want more sophisticated lists. GolfStream provides a number of custom lists. The two most common that I've used are an alphabetized member list and a ranked member list (e.g., by descending sales for the top 20 customers).

Basically, you'll want to use a member list rule any time you want to add logic to a list that goes beyond what the `where` clause can handle in your Member Filter – listing your dimension members in a particular order being the most common.

Designing Translation Rules

Foreign currency translation is common to the majority of OneStream customers. These translation rules allow flexibility and ease the maintenance of the multiple rates at which data may need to be translated.

As you already know, when you set up a scenario, it asks if you want to use the cube FX settings or not. Should you not use the cube settings, it asks for the rule and rate types for that particular scenario. Rethink the common, knee-jerk reaction to set up new rate types for each of your scenarios!

Let's talk about a Forecast scenario as an example. The months that are being copied from the Actual scenario are generally translated using the Actual rates. The rest of the year holds Forecast data, and that rate will be different – it could be the Budget rate, the most recent average rate, or the most recent closing rate (maybe it even has its own rate). In any case, I ask the simple question – are the rates you need to use already in the system? In our Forecast example, the answer is yes for the Actual months and – depending on the requirement – could be yes for the Forecast months. If you set up a new Forecast set of Forecast rates, then the administrator (or whoever maintains the rates) would need to enter the Actual rates in two different rate types – the one the Actual scenario uses, and the one the Forecast scenario uses. Instead, we can use these business rules to return the rate we want to use from *any* rate type, as well as change the rule type on any account type.

To do this, you'll create a finance business rule and use the `FxRate` function. This function simply analyzes the period and scenario it's processing during translation and – based on the logic written – goes and grabs the rate from where it's located in the system. For our Forecast example, the Actual months would use the rate found in the Actual scenario rate type for the period and account that's being translated. The Forecast months would use a different rate – let's say it's the most recent closing rate – using the same business rule logic.

Again, all the rule is doing is returning a rate from a rate type, a cube intersection, or it can calculate a rate for you and use it during translation.

In addition to the rate, these rules can also change the rule type on accounts. For example, most US customers translate assets and liabilities using the direct method (i.e., YTD balance multiplied by a rate), and revenue and expense using the periodic method (i.e., periodic Jan balance multiplied by Jan rate, plus periodic Feb balance multiplied by Feb rate, plus, etc.). There are exceptions to this; for example, when a customer wants to translate non-cash assets using the periodic method while the rest of the balance sheet uses the direct method. When this has been the case, I have needed to create a rule to change the rule type when translating these exceptions.

Overall, it's important to ask questions to determine how many different rates and rate types will be used across the various scenarios while minimizing the maintenance required for all of them. If the rate already exists, use these rules to tell OneStream where to find it and how to translate it.

Sometimes, customers have much more complex translation requirements – ones that may not be solved using OneStream's out-of-the-box translation functionality. I've seen customers use either a UD or the Flow dimension and the translated amounts reside in the local consolidation member. In such a case, they needed to pair this with a translate rule. These types of currency requirements are rare, but we do have several customers who have used this method for their currency analysis reporting.

Designing Consolidation Rules

OneStream's standard engine addresses most customers' consolidation requirements, but what do you do when it doesn't? There are standard settings on entity relationships that tell OneStream ownership and consolidation percentages and ownership type. You can use these settings to drive your consolidation rules. Turning on **custom consolidation** does impact application performance, so keep this in mind when determining if it's required. If your customer just has a handful of entities that can be handled using the standard consolidation, it's better to use it than to write a bunch of rules. My philosophy is that *the best business rule is no business rule*.

What's the best way to determine if you can use OneStream's consolidation engine, or if you're going to write custom consolidation rules? The first thing to remember is that OneStream utilizes multi-threading – it analyzes all Data Units that it can process at the same time in parallel threads. This can be an issue if you need to process certain base entities sequentially. You're able to set this sequence using the **sibling consolidation pass**, so it's not a definitive reason to write custom consolidation rules.

A second example might be that a customer has a non-controlling interest balance. Again, by itself, it's not enough information to drive the decision. Do they load it, calculate it, or book a journal entry? How do they want to handle it going forward? Do they want to see the subsidiary with (or without) NCI, or both? Additional questions to ask should address if they have consolidating or non-consolidating subsidiaries. These answers start to paint the picture and drive you down one path or the other.

An alternative to using the entity relationship settings is to use an **equity control cube**. That standalone cube uses the entity/intercompany intersection to hold the percentages in ownership. This may be the solution in circumstances where you may have layered ownership.

Customers sometimes want eliminations to happen on a UD member so they can see layers of the data as it eliminates. Granted, this could be a training topic as the elimination layer already exists on the consolidation and origin members. If the customer wants to see different types of eliminations, then using a UD would satisfy that requirement. Either way, UD members can be easier for end-users to comprehend, so the customer may prefer it in their reporting.

No Input Rules

No input rules (or conditional no input rules) allow you to protect specific intersections from being imported to via a workflow or modified via forms and XFSetCell. This obviously works in conjunction with the OneStream security model to provide an environment where people can only change the data to which they have write access. The end-users subjected to no input rules still have access to view that data.

Granted, data access security (aka slice security) can be employed as an additional layer of security to lock down cubes at a more granular level of detail than just the Data Unit. Sometimes, though, you may not want to complicate your overall security model for just a few intersections. This would be a perfect solution, given the users are allowed to view data but not change it. These rules check to see if the user trying to modify data belongs (or doesn't belong) to a specific security group. Based on this, it will either allow the user to save the data or not, throwing an error notifying the user of a security limitation. Again, your logic can run these rules based on anything that's available within the APIs or BRAPIs.

Designing Dynamic Calculations and Member Formulas

Where do you start when determining what type of Member Formula you should write? You must determine a couple of things: 1. Will the calculated data need to be aggregated, consolidated, or translated? 2. Will the calculated data feed another database, application, or data warehouse? If the answer is yes to either of those questions, the calculation will likely be a stored Member Formula.

Because dynamic calculations aren't stored, they don't aggregate, consolidate, or translate and aren't available for extraction via data management or SQL queries. If you didn't initially discuss this with the customer, and you're well into your build, you're not completely out of luck. You can rewrite a majority of the calculations fairly easily as a stored calculation, or you can get creative by providing a Cube View or Quick View of the data, which will run the calculation and use that as your data source to feed your downstream database.

OK, OneStream doesn't need to aggregate, consolidate, or translate the resulting calculation and won't source the data to any other systems – so do you go dynamic or stored? Performance is the second consideration. Since dynamic calculations run when they're called, the user waits until those calculations complete, and the Cube View renders. Stored calculations run when the cube calculates or consolidates. Once that data is stored, OneStream doesn't process any calculations when the Cube View renders; it simply retrieves data. So, it may depend on the volume of dynamic calculations, along with their complexity found on a Cube View – does it take a while to render (e.g., over five seconds)? If it does, you may want to think about changing those to stored calculations.

You've deduced that performance doesn't cause any issues on either end, so – again – do you go dynamic or stored? The complexity of the calculation can factor into the decision. I like to break calculations down into different types – percentages, sums/differences, and quotients/products. I break percentages out from the rest because they generally aren't aggregated and need to be calculated at base and parent levels. Dynamic calculations fit this type of situation perfectly. They're also easier to write because you don't need to think about Data Units or any aspects of the

OneStream calculation engine. Any dimensions omitted from the code use the members from the Cube View.

Next, I analyze the sums and differences to see if it's possible for these to be handled using an alternate hierarchy. Again, my philosophy is the best business rule is no business rule. Yes, it's an additional hierarchy to maintain for the administrator, but if I think about future changes, I ask if that person would be more comfortable modifying a hierarchy or business rule.

Finally, the quotient/products are pretty straightforward and extremely common, especially in allocations and driver-based planning models. These rules are more complex in nature and require more thought. These types of rules commonly use data buffers and unbalanced math, so it could be possible that writing Member Formulas on every member isn't the best solution.

Now that you've decided to write a stored calculation, OneStream recommends following some best practices to ensure performant execution. Start by writing the rule to fire at only base entities and local currency. The consolidation engine takes it from there. If you end up needing it to fire at the parents as well as the base entities, then you can always change it. Second, place importance on the precision of your calculation. You want your rule to fire when it absolutely has to execute and perhaps for specific intersections. For example, you need to write a calculation for an account on three specific UD members. Focus on writing your rule to only fire for the three UD members rather than running it for all of them – pretty straightforward. These two tips will ensure your application calculates, consolidates, and translates with maximum efficiency.

I previously mentioned that end-users can drill down on calculated members to see the components of the calculation. Unfortunately, administrators and/or consultants must write the Member Formulas for Calculation Drilldown separately from the calculation Member Formula, which means there are two formulas to be written. Member Formulas for Calculation Drilldown also work for those calculations that are written on a calculate or custom calculate business rule instead of directly on the member. End-users find great value in this feature, so it's important that you write these throughout the build. It's easiest to just write them upon completion of the Member Formula or business rules.

A final reminder that often frustrated me when I wrote these during my early OneStream days – don't forget to change the formula type on your member! I can't tell you how many times I wrote a Member Formula that didn't calculate due to not changing that property to a valid formula pass.

Also, remember that your dynamic calculation members need to be specified as `DynamicCalc` on both the formula type and account type.

One more tip when troubleshooting your stored calculations. If the formula result differs from what you expect, change your formula type to **formula pass 16**. This ensures that the result calculates last during the calculation sequence. I've encountered numerous times where my Member Formula was correct, but a different rule somewhere in the application overwrote my calculation.

Seeding Rule Best Practices

I can't name an implementation where I didn't need to write a seeding rule. These rules provide a starting point in a process by copying existing OneStream data to a new cube or scenario. There are a few ways you can achieve this, some better than others, but they're all available depending on the customer's business requirements.

When thinking about seeding rules, it's generally a one-time exercise that establishes a starting point for a given process. That dataset, unless broken down, can be very large; the larger the dataset, the longer it takes (naturally) for OneStream to process it.

It's important to discuss the customer's vision for the process. As a first step, will one user trigger the process for the entire company, or will individual end-users seed their own data as they start their process? Will the source data change during the forecast process, or will it be locked down to any changes? These two answers give you different ways of thinking about how you're going to integrate this step into the process, as well as how you write your business rule.

To answer the first question, let's assume the customer wants one user to seed the data for the entire company. You know this may take some time due to the large dataset, so maybe it's something that is scheduled to run overnight while no one is working in the system. What if there are a number of international users who will still be working in OneStream during the process? Just another thing to accommodate. Hopefully, the source data remains static as the international users are working in other sections of the application.

The alternative to one giant load would be to break it down into smaller datasets by allowing end-users to seed their own data as the first step in their process. This way, end-users must wait for *their* data to be seeded, rather than the entire company's data, to begin their work. Going a step further, one method that has recently gained traction among customers has been using Event Handler rules to seed all Forecast scenarios once the month has been closed. This technique isn't more performant than seeding the entire scenario at once, however the end-user *perceives* that it is. In both methods, the same volume of data is seeded to the Forecast scenario and takes the same amount of total time. By using Event Handler rules, the end-user only waits for a month of data to be seeded because the other months have already been copied when they weren't waiting for it.

Once seeded, the process has started, and the end-users have their starting point. In a perfect world, there's no need to run the seeding rule again. Since we're all imperfect, I believe we can agree that both methods need to be flexible enough to perform the seeding process multiple times if needed. However, you want to avoid running the seeding rule during every calculation or consolidation – no one wants to wait for that every time. Therefore, you should write these rules as custom calculations and possibly durable data. Users can trigger the rule via dashboard or data management on demand – regardless of whether it's one giant dataset or multiple smaller datasets.

The next step you'll want to do is determine how you want to tell OneStream how many months to seed. Some customers use the Global POV for this. Others embed the selection in the dashboard or mechanism where the user triggers the business rule. You could also base this on the specific scenario setting, no input periods, as a third option. This also goes back to the vision that the customer may have as to how they want to complete the seeding process.

The last dataset will seed the remaining Forecast months – it doesn't matter if it's a yearly Forecast or a rolling Forecast that spans years; you still need to know if those months need to contain data or not.

To reinforce the takeaways from the seeding rule process, the size of the dataset (and therefore its processing time) and the desired process will drive how best to configure the seeding rules.

That's all fine and good when the dimensions haven't been extended, but what happens if you're dealing with extended dimensions between your source and target? You need to use a data buffer along with the API to convert the extended members to the target dimensions. This only works if your target is at a higher level than your source. If your target is at a lower level than your source, OneStream doesn't know how to distribute or allocate that high-level number across the lower levels so you must define it in your rule.

One last request I've seen from customers is **seeding commentary** or **consolidating commentary** that's been stored in the system. OneStream stores comments, annotations, and variance explanations differently than data – in fact, it doesn't even consider it data. These are stored at specific metadata intersections, and they stay there. They don't consolidate or translate as it doesn't really make sense. Imagine consolidating a bunch of variance commentary to a parent entity – you'd see "due to increasing fuel prices, volumes lower than expected, Covid furlough." Again, it doesn't make a lot of sense. However, there are customers who still see value in 'consolidating' these – like if they want to view all of the comments in one dashboard without having to find each intersection. In that case, there's a dynamic calc that you can use to show them on reports. But I digress… we're talking about seeding comments, not consolidating them.

Seeding comments require you to write a custom calculate rule to get the data cell annotations and set them on the target intersections. This rule also requires a SQL query to pull from the `DataAttachment` table (again, OneStream doesn't consider it data). You would then trigger the rule using a data management job (or dashboard button, or process cube that triggers the data management job). This isn't a very common request, but it does pop up from time to time and, yes, like most requests, OneStream can do it.

Dashboard Dataset Rules

When you have the requirement to build a custom report or bound list parameter that uses a data adapter to create a custom dataset that will be viewed in a OneStream dashboard component – such as a grid view, report, chart, combo box, BI viewer, etc. – designing the dataset in a dashboard dataset rule should be your first preference due to a dashboard dataset rule's performance and overall flexibility.

Throughout my OneStream career, I've most commonly used the dashboard dataset rule technique to avoid having to write complex and inefficient SQL joins against multiple OneStream database tables to create a custom dataset or data table for a report or parameter. After seeing years' worth of one-off customer reporting requests, you'll often find a client may request a custom dataset that will require an intense SQL join on two to three OneStream database tables to produce the required data. The most common driver for performing a SQL join, for a custom dataset, is when you are looking to retrieve the name of a dimension member, workflow, property, or other OneStream artifact in which the name and ID or key exists in different OneStream database tables. Before you fall deeper into the complexity, poor performance, and dilemma of an intensive SQL query using joins, let's first think of the power that a dashboard dataset rule has to offer. Within a dashboard dataset rule, you have the power and flexibility to craft a truly custom dataset/data table using the power of OneStream BRAPIs. Let's have a look at the following custom report request below.

Let's say we have a client that has a custom reporting request to create a grid view report that displays information relating to the Workflow Profile to which an entity is assigned within a given cube root Workflow Profile structure. When considering how to retrieve the required dataset, you might have a quick look through the application database tables. Here, you'll find that the Workflow Profile entity assignment information exists in the table called `WorkflowProfileEntities`. However, you'll find the initially deflating fact that the data in the table itself is stored using IDs and keys, both of which are meaningless information to the end-users that will be running the report.

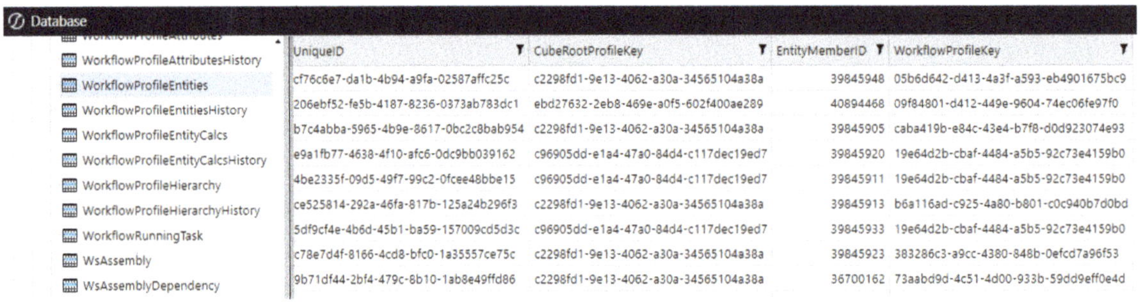

UniqueID	CubeRootProfileKey	EntityMemberID	WorkflowProfileKey
cf76c6e7-da1b-4b94-a9fa-02587affc25c	c2298fd1-9e13-4062-a30a-34565104a38a	39845948	05b6d642-d413-4a3f-a593-eb4901675bc9
206ebf52-fe5b-4187-8236-0373ab783dc1	ebd27632-2eb8-469e-a0f5-602f400ae289	40894468	09f84801-d412-449e-9604-74ec06fe97f0
b7c4abba-5965-4b9e-8617-0bc2c8bab954	c2298fd1-9e13-4062-a30a-34565104a38a	39845905	caba419b-e84c-43e4-b7f8-d0d923074e93
e9a1fb77-4638-4f10-afc6-0dc9bb039162	c96905dd-e1a4-47a0-84d4-c117dec19ed7	39845920	19e64d2b-cbaf-4484-a5b5-92c73e4159b0
4be2335f-09d5-49f7-99c2-0fcee48bbe15	c96905dd-e1a4-47a0-84d4-c117dec19ed7	39845911	19e64d2b-cbaf-4484-a5b5-92c73e4159b0
ce525814-292a-46fa-817b-125a24b296f3	c2298fd1-9e13-4062-a30a-34565104a38a	39845913	b6a116ad-c925-4a80-b801-c0c940b7d0bd
5df9cf4e-4b6d-45b1-ba59-157009cd5d3c	c96905dd-e1a4-47a0-84d4-c117dec19ed7	39845933	19e64d2b-cbaf-4484-a5b5-92c73e4159b0
c78e7d4f-8166-4cd8-bfc0-1a35557ce75c	c2298fd1-9e13-4062-a30a-34565104a38a	39845923	383286c3-a9cc-4380-848b-0efcd7a96f53
9b71df44-2bf4-479c-8b10-1ab8e49ffd86	c2298fd1-9e13-4062-a30a-34565104a38a	36700162	73aabd9d-4c51-4d00-933b-59dd9eff0e4d

Figure 8.32

When you find yourself in a situation like this, avoid listening to that little devil on your shoulder egging you on to create a data adapter that performs intensive SQL joins on multiple OneStream tables, such as the `Member` and `WorkflowProfileHierarchy` tables to source the Entity member name and Workflow Profile name fields. Instead, think of using a much more flexible and performant dashboard dataset rule to go after this missing information.

With the use of a dashboard dataset rule, you can design a rule that creates a starting data table by performing a Select * on the `WorkflowProfileEntities` table. From there, we can then massage the starting data table by creating and populating three additional fields in our amended data table. We'll ultimately use the power of coding and the OneStream BRAPIs to derive and populate new fields that will contain the entity name, workflow, and cube root profile name information we were originally lacking by converting the IDs and keys to meaningful names.

Leveraging OneStream BRAPIs in a dashboard dataset rule to query and derive the missing information is a huge performance saver that will help you avoid writing intensive SQL queries to source the same information. Let's review the code below as an example of how we can design a dashboard dataset rule to tailor a custom dataset that presents the workflow entity assignment information using the Entity member and Workflow Profile names.

```
19  Namespace OneStream.BusinessRule.DashboardDataSet.WFEntityAssignment
20      '----------------------------------------------------------------------------------------------
21          'Reference Code:        WF Entity Assignment
22          '
23          'Description:           Used to create a custom data table of workflow entity assignment info
24          '
25          'Use Examples:          To be called by a data adapter and presented in a Grid View or Report
26          '
27          'Created By:            Nick Kroppe
28          '
29          'Date Created:          12/16/2019
30      '----------------------------------------------------------------------------------------------
31      Public Class MainClass
32          Public Function Main(ByVal si As SessionInfo, ByVal globals As BRGlobals, ByVal api As Object, ByVal args As DashboardDataSetArgs) As Object
33              Try
34                  Select Case args.FunctionType
35
36                      Case Is = DashboardDataSetFunctionType.GetDataSetNames
37                          Dim names As New List(Of String)()
38                          names.Add("WFEntities")
39                          Return names
40
41                      Case Is = DashboardDataSetFunctionType.GetDataSet
42                          If args.DataSetName.XFEqualsIgnoreCase("WFEntities") Then
43                              'declare an empty data table
44                              Dim dt As New DataTable()
45                              'declare the starting SQL query
46                              Dim sql As New Text.StringBuilder()
47                              sql.AppendLine("SELECT * ")
48                              sql.AppendLine("FROM WorkflowProfileEntities ")
49                              sql.AppendLine("WITH (NOLOCK)")
50                              'Open DB connection and execute the SQL query
51                              Using dbConnApp As DbConnInfo = BRApi.Database.CreateApplicationDbConnInfo(si)
52
53                                  'Execute the SQL query
54                                  dt = BRApi.Database.ExecuteSql(dbConnApp, sql.ToString, True)
55                              End Using
56                              'check to ensure we are dealing with a real and populated data table
57                              If ((Not dt Is Nothing) And (dt.rows.count > 0)) Then
58                                  'make a copy of the data table in order to amend it
59                                  Dim dtCopy As DataTable = dt.Copy()
60                                  'return a new data table plus three new fields to convert the workflow unique ID, cube root profile ID, and entity ID to meaningful names
61                                  Return Me.GetFinalDT(si, globals, api, args, dtCopy)
62                              End If
63                          End If
64                  End Select
65                  Return Nothing
66              Catch ex As Exception
67                  Throw ErrorHandler.LogWrite(si, New XFException(si, ex))
68              End Try
69          End Function
70  #Region "FinalDT"
71          'function used to add new fields to the original data table
72          Private Function GetFinalDT(ByVal si As SessionInfo, ByVal globals As BRGlobals, ByVal api As Object, ByVal args As DashboardDataSetArgs, ByVal dtCopy As DataTable) As Object
73              Try
74                  'add new fields to the copied data table regarding the entity name, workflow name, and cube root profile name
75                  dtCopy.columns.Add("EntityName", GetType(String))
76                  dtCopy.columns.Add("WorkflowName", GetType(String))
77                  dtCopy.columns.Add("CubeRootProfileName", GetType(String))
78                  'loop through the data table rows and populate the new fields
79                  For Each varRow As DataRow In dtCopy.rows
80                      varRow("EntityName") = BRApi.Finance.Members.ReadMemberNoCache(si, dimTypeId.Entity, varRow("EntityMemberID")).Name
81                      varRow("WorkflowName") = BRApi.Workflow.Metadata.GetProfile(si, ConvertHelper.ToGuid(varRow("WorkflowProfileKey"))).Name
82                      varRow("CubeRootProfileName") = BRApi.Workflow.Metadata.GetProfile(si, ConvertHelper.ToGuid(varRow("CubeRootProfileKey"))).Name
83                  Next
84                  'Create new data view to sort the entity field
85                  Dim varDataView As New DataView(dtCopy)
86                  varDataView.Sort = "EntityName Asc"
87                  'return the sorted data view as a data table
88                  Return varDataView.ToTable()
89              Catch ex As Exception
90                  Throw ErrorHandler.LogWrite(si, New XFException(si, ex))
91              End Try
92          End Function
93  #End Region
94      End Class
    End Namespace
```

Figure 8.33

In the code example above, our dashboard dataset rule implements the following principles, which can be used to tailor a custom dataset:

1. Build a starting data table or dataset by executing a SQL or method query.

2. Make a copy of the data table so that you can use coding to massage the data and create additional fields.

3. Add the required additional new fields (columns) to the data table.

4. Loop through the data table rows and populate values for the newly added fields.

   Oftentimes, this step leverages OneStream BRAPIs to convert specific field values for each row, which will then be used to populate values for the newly added fields.

5. Leverage the DataView object to perform custom sorting, filtering, etc.

241

6. Return the final data table or dataset, which will effectively be your customized dataset.

7. Leverage reporting techniques to only display the relevant result fields in a report, grid, etc., to the end-user.

Furthermore, it is worth noting that it is not required to leverage the starting point results of a SQL query or method query, and a dataset can instead be created completely from scratch by creating rows and columns on-the-fly in your business rule. Please refer to the code below for an example snippet of how to create a data table that consists of a set of rows and columns from scratch on-the-fly.

```vb
Case Is = DashboardDataSetFunctionType.GetDataSet
    If args.DataSetName.XFEqualsIgnoreCase("OnTheFlyDT") Then
        'create an empty data table
        Dim dt As New DataTable()
        'create a new data column
        Dim newCol As New DataColumn("Car", GetType(String))
        'add the column to the data table
        dt.Columns.Add(newCol)
        'start creating 3 new rows and populate a value for the car field
        Dim newRow1 As DataRow = dt.NewRow()
        newRow1("Car") = "Ford Mustang GT350"
        dt.Rows.Add(newRow1)
        Dim newRow2 As DataRow = dt.NewRow()
        newRow2("Car") = "Ford Mustang GT500"
        dt.Rows.Add(newRow2)
        Dim newRow3 As DataRow = dt.NewRow()
        newRow3("Car") = "Ford Mustang Boss 302"
        dt.Rows.Add(newRow3)
        'after adding the three rows and one column to the table, return it
        Return dt
    End If
```

Figure 8.34

Lastly, you'll want to consider that the data returned in a dashboard dataset rule is cached in memory, meaning the query will perform more efficiently – versus when running a SQL query written directly in a data adapter. The performance benefits of your custom dataset/data table being cached in memory, via a dashboard dataset rule, should not be overlooked as a report that can be cached in memory will perform and scale across an end-user community much more efficiently in a OneStream environment.

Designing Dashboard XFBR String Rules

As I previously mentioned, dashboard XFBR string rules can and will be used everywhere throughout your application. I suggest writing one customer-specific rule that contains all functions as a starting point. You can name it whatever you like, but the standard recommendation uses the customer name (or a shortened version) followed by _ParamHelper. Many different Solution Exchange solutions use that naming convention, so it would help you maintain consistency. Once the rule has been created, I like to have the main function call the helper functions that I create in a region further down in the rule. This method keeps the rule tidy and organized, and an administrator can easily decipher and modify it if necessary.

```
75   Public Function Main(ByVal si As SessionInfo, ByVal globals As BRGlobals, ByVal api As Object, ByVal args As
76       Try
77           Dim plpHelper As New OneStream.BusinessRule.DashboardExtender.PLP_SolutionHelper.MainClass
78           If Not plpHelper.ValidateWorkflowPOVInitialization(si) Then Return Nothing
79
80           If args.FunctionName.XFEqualsIgnoreCase("GetContentDescription") Then
81               'Get an alternate description for the supplied dashboard name
82               Return Me.GetContentDescription(si, globals, api, args)
83
84           Else If args.FunctionName.XFEqualsIgnoreCase("GetActivityClassName") Then
85               Return Me.GetActivityClassName(si, globals, api, args)
86
87           Else If args.FunctionName.XFEqualsIgnoreCase("GetRegisterItemNames") Then
88               Return Me.GetRegisterItemNames(si, globals, api, args)
89
90           Else If args.FunctionName.XFEqualsIgnoreCase("GetCalcPlanFullName") Then
91               Return Me.GetCalcPlanFullName(si, globals, api, args)
92
93           Else If args.FunctionName.XFEqualsIgnoreCase("GetColFmt") Then
94               Return Me.GetColFmt(si, globals, api, args)
95
96           Else If args.FunctionName.XFEqualsIgnoreCase("GetStatusList") Then
97               Return Me.GetStatusList(si, globals, api, args)
98
99           Else If (args.FunctionName.XFEqualsIgnoreCase("GetWFProfileColVisible")) Then
100              Return Me.GetWFProfileColVisible(si, globals, api, args)
101
102          Else If (args.FunctionName.XFEqualsIgnoreCase("GetWFProfileCriteria")) Then
103              Return Me.GetWFProfileCriteria(si, globals, api, args)
104
105          Else If (args.FunctionName.XFEqualsIgnoreCase("GetRegCriteria")) Then
106              Return Me.GetRegCriteria(si, globals, api, args)
107
108          Else If args.FunctionName.XFEqualsIgnoreCase("GetDeleteMessage") Then
109              Return Me.GetDeleteMessage(si, globals, api, args)
110
111          Else If args.FunctionName.XFEqualsIgnoreCase("GetIsUserInGroup") Then

139
140  #Region "Standard Helper Functions"
141
142      Public Function GetContentDescription(ByVal si As SessionInfo, ByVal globals As BRGlobals, ByVal api As Object, ByVal args As Dash
143          Try
144              'Get the clean description for the content title
145              Dim dashboardName As String = args.NameValuePairs.XFGetValue("SelectedDashboard", "[No Selection]")
146              Dim dashboardDesc As String = BRApi.Database.LookupRowFieldValue(si, "App", "Dashboard", "Name = '" & dashboardName & "'",
147
148              'Make sure there is a description for the dashboard
149              If String.IsNullOrEmpty(dashboardDesc) Then
150                  Return "** Description Not Set for Dashboard: ** " & dashboardName
151              Else
152                  Return dashboardDesc
153              End If
154
155          Catch ex As Exception
156              Throw ErrorHandler.LogWrite(si, New XFException(si, ex))
157          End Try
158      End Function
159
160      Public Function GetActivityClassName(ByVal si As SessionInfo, ByVal globals As BRGlobals, ByVal api As Object, ByVal args As Dashb
161          Try
162
163              Dim classID As String = args.NameValuePairs.XFGetValue("ClassID")
164              Return BRApi.Database.LookupRowFieldValue(si, "App", "XFW_PLP_ActivityClass", "ClassID = '" & classID & "'", "Name", "No S
```

Figure 8.35

It also helps to write in a comment as to how to call the rule from the component. This ensures that the rule name, function name, and any variables are passed to the rule correctly.

You can use these two coding tips in *all* business rules if you prefer the layout. It eliminates the need for the administrator to sift through lines and lines of code to find a specific section.

Designing Dashboard Extender Rules

When designing a Dashboard Extender business rule, you'll need to consider the requirements of when you need the rule to execute. As we discussed earlier, common trigger points for a Dashboard Extender rule include the execution of the rule via a button click, combo box click, load dashboard event, or SQL table editor component save event.

In this section, we'll review two specific use cases of a Dashboard Extender business rule and discuss the design considerations you'll need to be aware of. In addition, this section will include incredibly useful code snippets that will assist you throughout your rules journey. These code snippets will include examples of setting and refreshing a workflow status, navigating to another workflow, displaying a custom message to a user, and passing values to parameters nested in a dashboard.

In the first example, we'll review a commonly used technique to set default values for dashboard components, such as a combo box or list box component that is nested within the main frame dashboard. When creating custom dashboards – such as a dashboard form that uses combo box or list box components – it is very common for a client to ask for specific default values to be inserted into the components when a user runs the dashboard.

To meet this requirement, we can design a Dashboard Extender rule that fires upon the main dashboard initializing, and use an extremely handy XFLoadDashboardTaskResult object to enable us to set a parameter value within the main dashboard. In the snippet found in the example below, we'll query the user's Workflow POV profile, and pass in the first entity assigned to the workflow as the default value for an entity parameter (combo box) that is nested in the dashboard called WFProfileAssignedEntities. This will ensure that when a user runs the main dashboard, a Workflow Profile assigned entity is passed as a default value to the combo box used to facilitate an entity selection.

```vbnet
Select Case args.FunctionType

    Case Is = DashboardExtenderFunctionType.LoadDashboard
        If (args.FunctionName.XFEqualsIgnoreCase("OnLoadMainDashboard")) Then
            'execute when a dashboard is attempting to render (initializing)
            'And before the dashboard attempts To Get the parameter values For params nested In the dashboard
            If args.LoadDashboardTaskInfo.Reason = LoadDashboardReasonType.Initialize And _
                args.LoadDashboardTaskInfo.Action = LoadDashboardActionType.BeforeFirstGetParameters Then
                'Initialize ability to set default param values in a dashboard
                Dim loadDashboardTaskResult As New XFLoadDashboardTaskResult()
                loadDashboardTaskResult.ChangeCustomSubstVarsInDashboard = True
                'Grab the default value to pass into the dashboard
                'Retrieve a List of WF profile assigned Entities based on the POV WF
                Dim entityList As List(Of WorkflowProfileEntityInfo) = BRApi.Workflow.Metadata.GetProfileEntities(si, si.WorkflowClusterPk.ProfileKey)
                'declare a default value variable - the default value will revert to an empty string if there are no entities assigned to the user's POV WF
                Dim defaultVal As String = String.Empty
                'check to make sure there are workflow assigned entities, if so, set the default value equal to the first entity assigned in the WF
                If entityList.Count > 0 Then
                    defaultVal = entityList(0).EntityName.ToString
                End If
                'Modify the workflow profile entity parameter to pass in the default value at run time
                loadDashboardTaskResult.ModifiedCustomSubstVars.Add("WFProfileAssignedEntities", defaultVal)
                Return loadDashboardTaskResult
            End If
        End If
End Select
```

Figure 8.36

Once the Dashboard Extender rule is designed and written, the rule should then be applied directly on the main dashboard, like the figure below. The implementation of the rule on the main dashboard enables the Dashboard Extender rule to fire when it renders.

⊟ Action (Primary Dashboard Only)	
Server Task	
Load Dashboard Server Task	Execute Dashboard Extender Business Rule (Once)
Load Dashboard Server Task Arguments	{SetDefaultParamValue}{OnLoadMainDashboard}{}

Figure 8.37

Next, we'll review a Dashboard Extender implementation example that involves calling a Dashboard Extender business rule directly from a dashboard button component (the most common use case of this type of business rule).

As mentioned earlier in this chapter, having the knowledge to design and implement a Dashboard Extender business rule can vastly bolster your dashboarding skills in OneStream. After reading this section, you should be equipped with an understanding and an example of how to design a dashboard component, such as a button, to execute a Dashboard Extender business rule. This rule will enable you to perform dynamic and powerful actions such as setting a workflow's status, presenting a custom message, and navigating to a specific page or workflow in OneStream.

In the code below, you'll see a code snippet for a use case that facilitates a click action in a dashboard that completes a workflow's Workspace, displays a custom message to the user, and takes the user to the next workflow step (an input forms step).

Once you've created the Dashboard Extender rule, you can attach it directly to a dashboard component. In our example, it's on a button component, as the below examples show.

```
If args.FunctionName.XFEqualsIgnoreCase("CompleteWorkflow") Then
    Dim selectionChangedTaskResult As New XFSelectionChangedTaskResult()
    'Used to complete a workflow's workspace step
    BRApi.Workflow.Status.SetWorkflowStatus(si, si.WorkflowClusterPk, StepClassificationTypes.Workspace, WorkflowStatusTypes.Completed, "Workspace C
    'Need to start the input forms step in order to navigate to this step when we navigate back to the current workflow
    Brapi.Workflow.Status.SetWorkflowStatus(si, si.WorkflowClusterPk, StepClassificationTypes.InputForms, WorkflowStatusTypes.InProcess, "Start Form
    'Used to update the workflow status automatically
    selectionChangedTaskResult.WorkflowWasChangedByBusinessRule = True
    'Used to show a custom message box to the user upon the button click
    selectionChangedTaskResult.ShowMessageBox = True
    selectionChangedTaskResult.Message = "Workspace Completed."
    'Used to navigate to user's current workflow step
    selectionChangedTaskResult.ChangeSelectionChangedNavigationInDashboard = True
    selectionChangedTaskResult.ModifiedSelectionChangedNavigationInfo.SelectionChangedNavigationType = XFSelectionChangedNavigationType.OpenPage
    Dim navPath As String = "XFPage=Workflow"
    selectionChangedTaskResult.ModifiedSelectionChangedNavigationInfo.SelectionChangedNavigationArgs = navPath
    Return selectionChangedTaskResult
```

Server Task	
Selection Changed Server Task	Execute Dashboard Extender Business Rule (General Server)
Selection Changed Server Task Arguments	{WorkspaceLogic}{CompleteWorkflow}{}

Figure 8.38

In the figure below, a user is presented with a Workspace step and a simple dashboard with a Complete Workflow button. Note that the workflow has an additional input forms step to navigate to, after the Workspace step has been completed.

Figure 8.39

Upon clicking the Complete Workflow button, the Dashboard Extender rule triggers, updating the Workspace to a completed status, and brings the user to the input forms step to start working on their next workflow tasks.

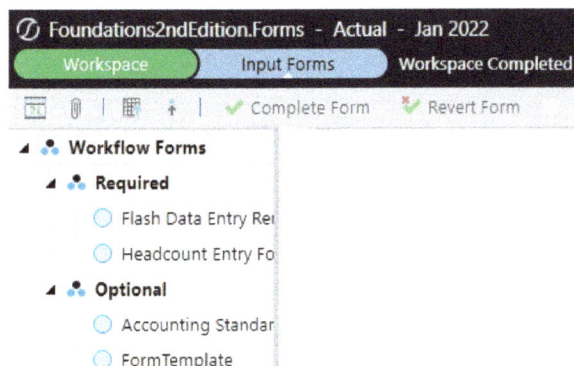

Figure 8.40

This type of advanced button-click functionality is all made possible thanks to the brilliance of Dashboard Extender business rules!

Designing Extensibility Rules

In my opinion, extensibility rules are an often misunderstood and underutilized type of business rule in OneStream; they offer a lot of power and convenience in the platform. For starters, let's talk about the convenience of these business rules.

As we mentioned earlier in this chapter, extensibility rules can be split into two different categories: an Extender rule and an Event Handler rule. We'll begin this section by discussing the role and convenience Extender rules have in the platform.

Typically, any time you are looking to automate a workflow, data extraction, or email notification process in OneStream, an Extender rule will be the best tool to facilitate said efforts. Data management jobs and Extender rules work closely together to facilitate automation solutions in the platform. Having the option to call an Extender rule directly from a data management job is ultimately a huge point of convenience because triggering the logic found in your business rule becomes a simple exercise of configuring a data management job.

Secondly, to further add to an Extender rule's execution convenience and capabilities, an Extender rule is the only type of business rule that can be triggered directly from the business rule UI.

This ultimately results in an exceptional point of convenience when designing and testing your logic, as you don't need to set up a dashboard button or data management job specifically to trigger the rule. In the figure shown below, I've emphasized the Execute Extender play button that enables you to trigger an Extender rule directly from the business rule page.

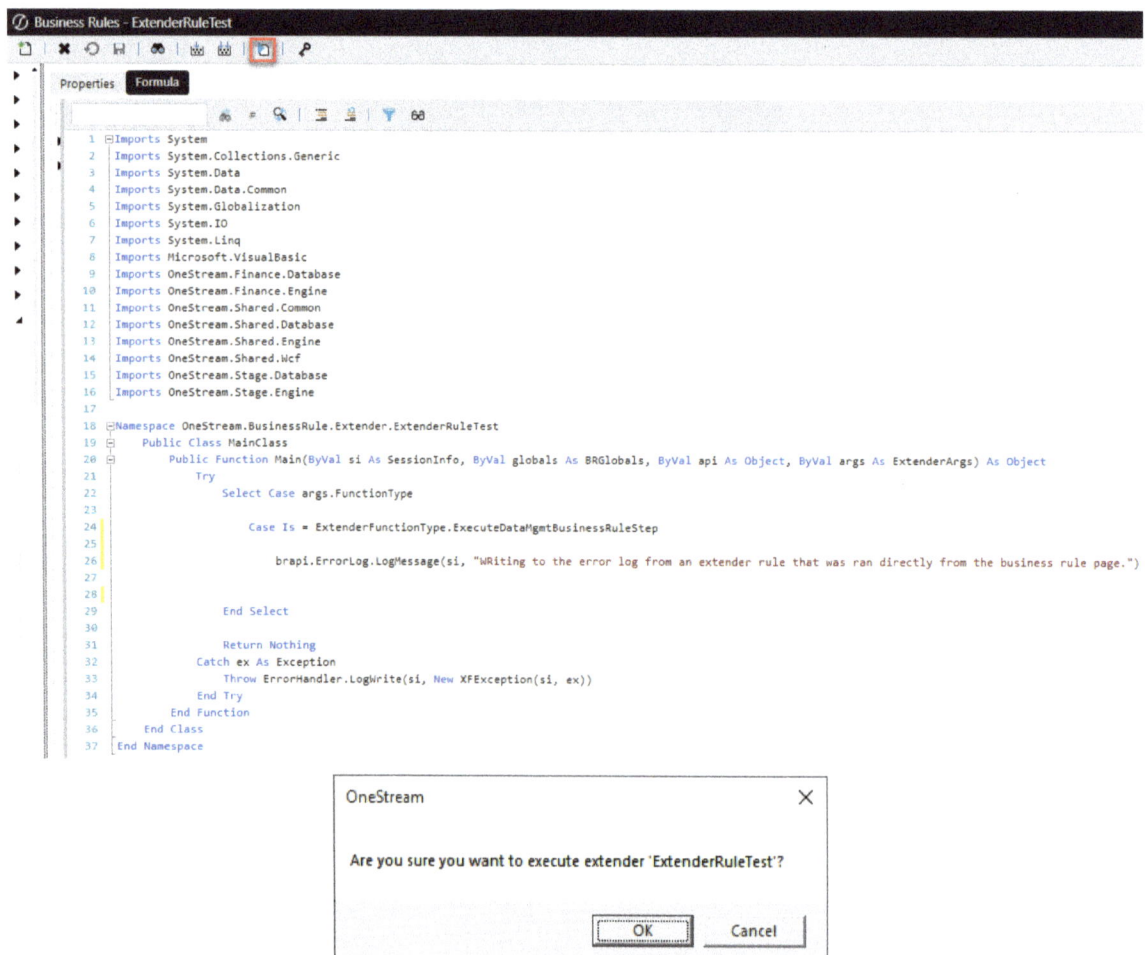

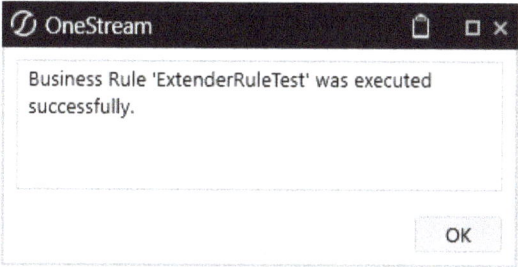

Figure 8.41

I oftentimes kindly refer to an Extender business rule as a rule writer's personal playground. If you're not using an Extender rule to explore and test OneStream's BRAPIs and coding capabilities, I highly encourage you to start doing so!

A quick tip when it comes to designing an Extender business rule is to place your code within the following case statements:

```
Select Case args.FunctionType

    'unknown case statement allows the logic to be triggered directly from the business rule page
    'Execute data mgmt business rule step allows the logic to be triggered from a data management job
    Case Is = ExtenderFunctionType.Unknown, ExtenderFunctionType.ExecuteDataMgmtBusinessRuleStep
        'do something...
End Select
```

Figure 8.42

The unknown `ExtenderFunctionType` case statement enables your code to be executed directly from the business rule (as previously mentioned), while the `ExecuteDataMgmtBusinessRuleStep` case enables your logic to be executable from a data management job. I highly recommend that you design your Extender rule logic within both of the case statements, as per the code above, to enable your business rule logic to be executable from the business rule page and from a data management job.

Next up on our extensibility rules discussion is the rule category called Event Handlers. As mentioned earlier in this chapter, an Event Handler business rule is a specific type of extensibility rule that allows you to use specific events that occur in OneStream to accentuate, block, or trigger other processes within the application.

When designing an Event Handler business rule, you'll want to consider that each specific Event Handler business rule type can only be implemented *once* in an application, and the name of the Event Handler rule cannot be adjusted or updated. For example, let's say we have a requirement to trigger an email to an administrator user upon a workflow certify event. The specific type of Event Handler business rule we would use would be called a **Data Quality Event Handler**; notice that you cannot edit the rule name.

Figure 8.43

This is an important detail to note, as you will want to be conscious of situations where you may upload an XML file that contains an Event Handler business rule. Because the business rule name cannot be changed, one must be mindful when migrating this type of rule across applications. Before uploading an XML rules file, double-check both the source and target applications to determine if this rule exists in both of them. If they do exist in both applications, the XML load file will overwrite any code and properties of the business rule in the target application. Let's say that again... if you have an existing Event Handler business rule and you load an XML that contains the *same* Event Handler business rule, it REPLACES the existing rule. If you're migrating only a section of the rule, you'll want to copy/paste the code into your existing rule rather than using load/extract functionality.

Lastly, although Event Handler business rules are an extremely powerful tool in OneStream, they can be dangerous from a performance perspective if used inefficiently. When designing an Event Handler business rule, always be sure you are cognizant of when the rule will trigger. Your goal should be to limit and control when the rule will fire to ensure the rule does not fire unnecessarily and will only be triggered when absolutely necessary, as per the business process requirements.

A great way to precisely control when the logic in an Event Handler rule fires is to implement If conditions in the business rule, much like we do (and preach) in finance rules and stored calculations.

Oftentimes, an Event Handler is used to intercept and supplement specific workflow actions, such as a workflow lock, unlock, import, validate, load cube, certify, or un-certify an event. Typically, the events you are attempting to listen for and supplement are only required for a specific workflow, scenario, and/or time period. For instance, you might have the requirement to supplement an import event for the Actual scenario and for specific workflows. In the code below, we have a small snippet of a Transformation Event Handler rule listening for the EndValidateTransform sub-event that uses If conditions to control the logic to only execute if the event's workflow scenario is set to Actual and if the Workflow Profile name ends with _Load.

```
Case Is = BREventOperationType.Transformation.ValTrans.EndValidateTransform

    If args.IsBeforeEvent = False Then
        'get information about the validated workflow
        Dim validateWFInfo As WorkflowUnitPk = DirectCast(args.Inputs(1), WorkflowUnitPk)
        'only process custom logic if the workflow was validated for the Actual scenario
        If brapi.Finance.Members.GetMemberName(si, dimTypeId.Scenario, validateWFInfo.ScenarioKey).XFEqualsIgnoreCase("Actual") Then
            'ensure the logic also only fires for import workflows that end with "_load"
            If BRApi.Workflow.Metadata.GetProfile(si, validateWFInfo.ProfileKey).Name.EndsWith("_Load", True, CultureInfo.InvariantCulture) Then
```

Figure 8.44

An important tip when it comes to Event Handler rules is to leverage the **DirectCast** syntax, used in the code above, to cast an input of a particular sub-event to ultimately enable you to derive information about the event. Common use cases of this include deriving the Workflow Profile, scenario, and time information from a workflow-related sub-event as well as deriving transformation information, such as source ID, record count, username, and start time, related to an import or validate sub-event.

To determine the valid inputs of a particular sub-event, leverage the API guide to view a visual of all the inputs that you can cast to derive specific information about the event. Check out the figure below for an example of the inputs available for the EndValidateTransform sub-event within a Transformation Event Handler rule.

EndValidateTransform		Transformation
Is Before Event: **False**	Can Cancel: **False**	Number of Inputs: **4**

Input Name
args.inputs(0). OneStream.Shared.Wcf.ValidationTransformationProcessInfo
args.inputs(1). OneStream.Shared.Wcf.WorkflowUnitPk
args.inputs(2). System.Boolean
args.inputs(3). System.Guid

Figure 8.45

The OneStream API guide, which can be found by clicking the Help button from within your application and searching 'API Guide', should be considered your best friend when designing Event Handler rules. The guide comes complete with an entire section dedicated to event listing, and can be used to understand what sub-events and inputs are available within a particular Event Handler business rule.

Lastly, in an Event Handler rule, it is strongly recommended to avoid leveraging a user's session info object to access workflow information such as the user's current Workflow Profile, scenario, and time. Tying an Event Handler rule to a user's Workflow POV is generally not a good practice. This logic and concept can cause issues if using batch processes or process automation. In both examples, the user's session info Workflow POV may not be a reliable source in determining the workflow information relevant to a particular event. Instead, use the casting technique shown in the figures above to derive workflow information about a particular sub-event; this technique will always be reliable in determining the workflow information an event was triggered for.

Less Common Rule Tips

Wow. You've almost made it through a very meaty chapter. At this point, I'll tell you that there isn't a lot you CAN'T do with business rules – being a double negative – business rules can do so much, it can be overwhelming. I'll cover a few lesser-known capabilities of business rules prior to wrapping up, so you can keep them in your back pocket should the need arise.

The first 'more common' of the 'lesser-known' capabilities is updating metadata via a business rule.

Let's say that your customer has no existing internal process to notify the OneStream administrator when or if a new member is added to one of their ERPs, and a member needs to be added to OneStream. Lame, but we can handle it. You can write a business rule within your Transformation Event Handler to add the missing member to OneStream if it doesn't exist, but it has its limitations. First, business rules aren't smart – they just do what they're told. So, yes, it can add the member with a member name and description (given those two fields are present upon import). That's where its intelligence really ends. It doesn't know the hierarchy (or hierarchies) to which it belongs. It doesn't know what its aggregation weight should be. It doesn't know the member's account type or any defaults or constraints. It doesn't know what all of the text field settings should be. And, in the case of entity, it doesn't know the most important properties of local currency, percent consolidation/ownership, and security groups. All that being said, you might be asking why anyone wants this in their application due to its limitations.

The main reason is to allow end-users to temporarily continue through their workflow process. The transformation will complete successfully; they'll be able to load data to the cube and continue with their forms and journals. The data at the top won't be correct until the administrator has a chance to go into the dimension library and move the new member(s) to their home(s), assign the correct properties, and add any necessary text fields. But at least the administrator isn't holding up the end-user.

Secondly, the **Globals** technique is like the PED of business rules – they optimize processing times when applied properly but can be devastating should you abuse them. The high-level explanation of global objects is that they're set at the beginning of a calculation, consolidation, etc., and they're retained in memory throughout the process – readily available for referencing from most types of business rules. As you can imagine, if you're constantly referencing the same table or data throughout your business rule, querying it each time can take considerably longer than querying it once and then referencing it throughout the rule. These are commonly used when some type of SQL tables and queries are involved with calculations within OneStream. You can write a SQL query and assign the resulting table to a global object. Then, throughout the rule, reference the global object rather than having to query for each calculation.

Finally, I'll leave you with a few easy pointers as you venture out on your own to write some of these business rules. If you haven't already done it, go out to the Solution Exchange and download **Snippet Editor**. Seriously, put this down and do it now. I'll wait…

Once imported into your application, you can reference numerous, well, snippets of common code. They appear in the middle window when you have a business rule open. When you select one, it gives you the code that you copy/paste into your rule and change what you need to make it work within your application. I've been working with OneStream since 2013 and still use them when I can't remember the proper syntax.

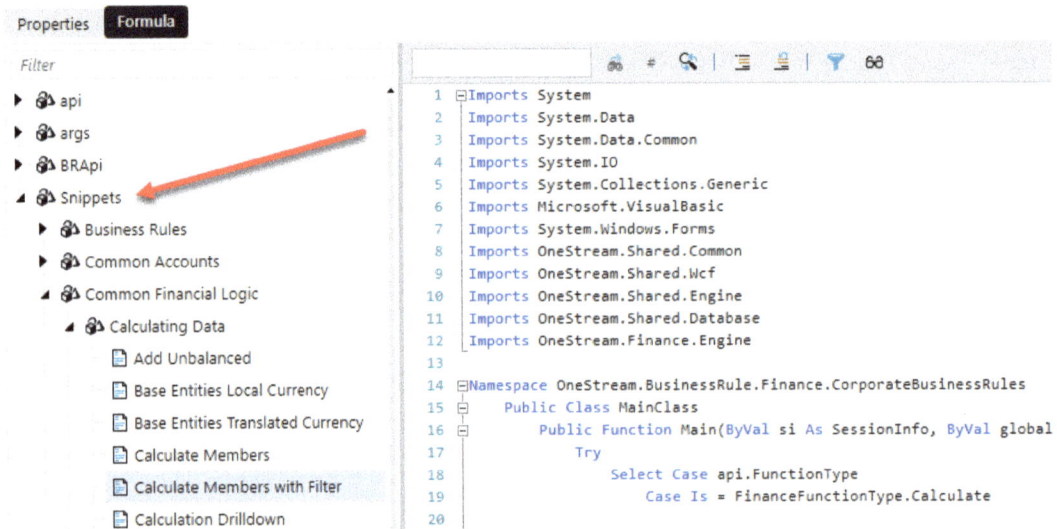

Figure 8.46

In turn, use the **IntelliSense**! As you're typing out the code, it will give you options in a dropdown that you can select (or hit tab if you're a keyboard shortcut person like me), and it completes the next section of the code for you.

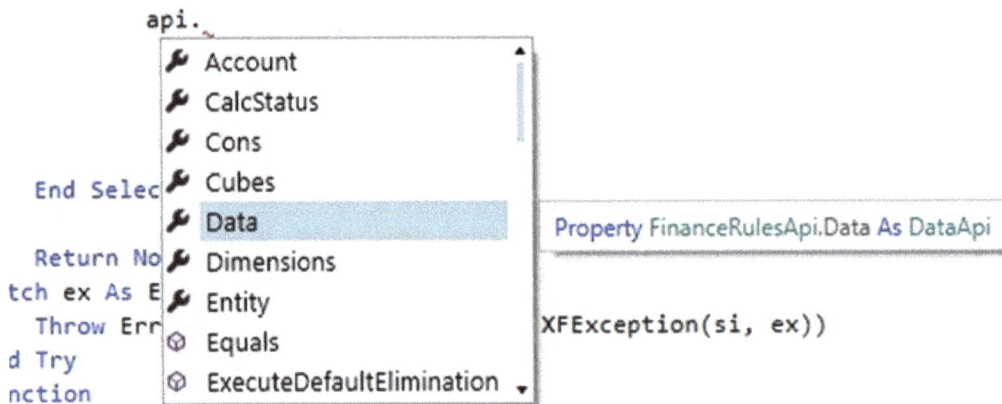

Figure 8.47

Additionally, it shows you all of the valid variations of the code. For example, I want to write a calculate statement, and the IntelliSense shows me that I have three options for the properties. I can page through them using the up or down arrows and select the one I want.

```
api.Data.Calculate()
    ▲ 1 of 3 ▼  ⓘ  Sub DataApi.Calculate(formula As String, Optional accountFilter As String, Optional flowFilter As String, Optional originFilter As
                    String, Optional icFilter As String, Optional ud1Filter As String, Optional ud2Filter As String, Optional ud3Filter As String, Optional
                    ud4Filter As String, Optional ud5Filter As String, Optional ud6Filter As String, Optional ud7Filter As String, Optional ud8Filter As
                    String, Optional onEvalDataBuffer As EvalDataBufferDelegate, Optional userState As Object, Optional isDurableCalculatedData As Boolean)

api.Data.Calculate()
    ▲ 2 of 3 ▼  ⓘ  Sub DataApi.Calculate(formula As String, onEvalDataBuffer As EvalDataBufferDelegate, Optional userState As Object)

        api.Data.Calculate()
            ▲ 3 of 3 ▼  ⓘ  Sub DataApi.Calculate(formula As String, isDurableCalculatedData As Boolean)
```

Figure 8.48

To add to this tip, if you find yourself modifying code that already exists, a quick way to get the IntelliSense to show up is to type a comma where it would expect a comma. For example, you need to modify this statement with some filters.

```
api.Data.Calculate("S#[" & curScenario & "]:F#EndBal:O#Import = S#[" & sourceScenario & "]:F#EndBal:O#Top")
```

Figure 8.49

You know that the filters come after the formula, but don't know the order in which they're listed. In the next-to-last character in the line – after the double quote and closing parenthesis – enter a comma, and the IntelliSense will show up.

```
api.Data.Calculate("S#[" & curScenario & "]:F#EndBal:O#Import = S#[" & sourceScenario & "]:F#EndBal:O#Top",,,,,)
    ▲ 1 of 3 ▼  ⓘ  Sub DataApi.Calculate(formula As String, Optional accountFilter As String, Optional flowFilter As String, Optional originFilter As
                    String, Optional icFilter As String, Optional ud1Filter As String, Optional ud2Filter As String, Optional ud3Filter As String, Optional
                    ud4Filter As String, Optional ud5Filter As String, Optional ud6Filter As String, Optional ud7Filter As String, Optional ud8Filter As
                    String, Optional onEvalDataBuffer As EvalDataBufferDelegate, Optional userState As Object, Optional isDurableCalculatedData As Boolean)
```

Figure 8.50

You may need to use the arrows to get to the syntax that you want, but it prevents you from having to re-type out the entire line just to get some guidance.

Conclusion

Congratulations! You've officially taken a drink from the OneStream firehose! Hopefully, this chapter gave you a solid foundation on, and introduction into, our business rules. Not only did you learn the fundamentals of how to write them, but when you can and should use them, a glimpse into OneStream's rule engine, and general guidance for effective rule writing. It's not the sexiest chapter to come back and re-read during your next implementation, but it's definitely one to keep earmarked.

Epilogue

(Nick Kroppe) One of my favorite memories at OneStream was back in 2015 when the Maersk team visited the newly-built Rochester headquarters for the first time. After a hard day at work, we decided to challenge our jetlagged Danish friends to a friendly game of dodgeball. Well, our friendly game of dodgeball quickly turned into more – next thing I know, I found myself winding up, pulling a Tom Brady and absolutely nailing Kasper and Peter Svendsen in the head with a dodgeball.

Mid-throw, I quickly realized my demise as it dawned on me that I had just headshot two of our colleagues from our biggest and most important customer. At the time, I was as junior in the company as you could get, and I nervously looked over at my boss – Peter Fugere – for his reaction. I thought I was going to be fired, lol, but luckily our Danish friends (and Peter) laughed it off, and we capped off a great night getting dinner and drinks in Clarkston, MI.

(Chul Smith) In 2013, I was an independent Consultant staffed on my first OneStream project. I worked at a customer with Eric Davidson, Shawn Stalker, Matt Baranowski, Tony Dimitrie, and Ricardo Rasche. I remember testing out some functionality and thought it could be improved. Those guys told me to email Tom, so… ermmm… okay… I did, and we exchanged a few emails. Later that night (at 2 am), he said that he had recoded the software and it would be in the next patch.

9
Security

Originally written by Jody Di Giovanni, updated by Bobby Doyon

In this chapter, we will discuss the areas that you can secure within the OneStream application, and general best practices around setting them up. You will also learn how to ensure that data and objects within the application are secured at the right level, at the right time, and for the right user.

You may find, while reading this chapter as well as other sections of the book, that there are various ways to go about securing data and objects, and there is not always a right or wrong way. But there can be times when doing it one way (versus another) that can make administering the application harder down the road!

Integrating security into your design and – at the very least – having a 'security check' in place to determine how you will implement security as the build progresses, as well as processes as they get introduced into the application, should make applying security a natural part of the implementation.

Often, keeping a OneStream security design modest is all that is needed to successfully give all types of users the access they need. This can be done effectively and keep the OneStream administrator's job of managing security, low maintenance.

Yes, there are business cases that lend themselves to complex security designs and OneStream can accommodate these models as well; however, understanding *where* and *when* to secure an object, role, and access to data, is the key to flexibility when designing future phases and administrative ease. It is so much easier to add security later, than unravel and rework it because you applied too much out of the gate. Of course, new requirements in the future may require even more complex security layers to accomplish the end goal.

What this chapter will not cover is the security design around our Specialty or Solution Exchange solutions. We will touch on items to bear in mind when designing security for OneStream and how it relates to the platform and Solution Exchange solution interaction, but the focus for this chapter is to canvas as much of the core functionality as it relates to the platform itself.

In addition, this chapter is not intended to be a 'how-to' guide, although you will find examples are provided. These examples are for illustrating use cases and supporting the thought processes behind the design for each of them. For a more comprehensive guide to applying OneStream security and terminology, please reference the *Design and Reference Guide*.

By the end of this chapter, you should have a greater understanding of how to design and apply OneStream security with ease. You will be able to refer to the application and understand how OneStream security flows throughout the product. We will discuss business cases with examples of common types of users and how we apply the different types of access to grant them the access they need. By the end, you will have a good understanding of the application and system security roles and how they can be applied to different objects throughout the application. In addition, you will see how creating groups that are directly applicable to the application's metadata, when combined with the correct security role access, will not only grant users the desired access, but will also aid in developing a template for adding on to your security model.

Along with this, you will take away some tips and tricks for not only setting up security but also for passing on to your administrators so that they can properly pick up and carry on. Look for references to other sections that relate to the specific handling of security under their respective topics in this chapter as well.

Framework and Environments

Before we begin to look at security design considerations, and how we can achieve the desired end results, we first need to understand where security lives.

OneStream's application security is held in its own SQL database **framework**. This database is shared by all applications that are in a single OneStream environment. Ideally, customers will have separate environments for production, QA and development, and – in this case – there would be a separate framework database for each of them. You can copy and refresh the security databases when necessary, if security testing is required. Non-production environments may be for admins only and, therefore, only a handful of users should have access to them.

As part of the OneStream SAAS offering, clients are provided with two environments. These have separate framework databases and can be secured as mentioned above. Requirements for additional environments can be reviewed and added at the client's request.

Should a company have only one environment with multiple applications for development efforts, then we can secure the applications to a restricted group of users, application by application. Similarly, there may also be multiple production applications in a production environment that are just for a subset of users. In such cases, we would secure the individual applications as well. This is made possible by applying security to the **OpenApplication** security role. Security roles like this one will be talked about in more detail as we move through the chapter. You can refer to Figure 9.2 for a full listing of application security roles.

A Heads-up as you Read through this Chapter

Here are a couple of quick tips and terms as you read through the sections in this chapter.

If you are starting with a fresh application, there are going to be default settings related to security, and two are important to take into consideration so you don't spend time trying to work around them! One is the user called **administrator**. You will notice that you can only disable this user – you cannot delete it. You will likely not want to use it or assign it to any groups.

Something else to be aware of is the out-of-the-box **administrator group**. We will discuss how you can have varying levels of administrators (admins, super-users, etc.) depending on the roles they play in the application. However, there are certain key functions of the administrator group, and the biggest is that *this group controls security in an application*. Essentially, the administrator group bypasses all security settings in the application, and you cannot change this. This often requires discussion and consideration on planning projects that include sensitive employee data.

Outside of this role, you can have lower levels of administrator access; however, this one is pre-defined, so bear this in mind when adding users to this group! We will cover the various layers of application security and how it all works together to enable the user to perform the tasks they are supposed to. Application and system security roles are unique and will have specific references on how they correlate to the access we are trying to achieve.

Applying security on dimensions varies across the dimension library, with entity having the most flexibility for applying multiple types and groups. The Entity dimension is also where we signal the cube to look for **data cell access** (often referred to as 'slice') security. Scenario will allow for separate levels of security as well, although (most often) the workflow is leveraged for *restricting* data loads to a scenario. The remaining dimensions have a setting for **display access**, which should *not* be confused with the actual restriction of data in that dimension. It will merely restrict the ability of a user to see the dimension member in a member list.

Workflow channels, which are tied to the workflow and are generally used for phased submissions (but which can also be used as a way of applying security) are also applied on the dimensions. Both display access and workflow channels are for functional purposes and should not be used as a level of security, as we would think about in our overall design.

Application Security

As we move through the flow of security in this chapter, it makes most sense to start with how we create, increase, and decrease the access a user will ultimately have. Figure 9.1, below, shows how the user passes through checkpoints as they attempt to do something in the application. If, at any one of these checkpoints, they are not in the appropriate group that allows them to complete that action, they cannot move on to the next area.

The security groups that are assigned to each of these respective areas work together to ultimately allow a user to complete some sort of action. This could be anything, from viewing a report, loading data into an entity or entities, building out a set of report books and emailing them out, or managing objects within the application itself (and anything in between!). Let's think of how this works.

A user can be in one or many groups. The group(s) that this user is in will first need to be assigned to the application they are trying to log into. Provided they are in a group that allows them to open that application, they can move on.

Next, cube access is verified. Again, if one of the groups that the user is assigned to is at least in the access group of the cube (or cubes) they are accessing, they can move on. With this step and with any other, if they are not, the process stops.

If the user is attempting to access data, we move through the full example below with scenario, entity, and data cell access, or 'slice' security access groups, in order for them to complete their tasks. Keep in mind that there are many more objects that will have been verified in the application security roles for them to carry out different tasks in the application. As mentioned above, you will be determining and assigning groups to these areas.

When working through the design of the application and determining where the data sits, you will be asking how the data is getting there. These are examples of two separate *groups* that will be relevant for this dataset. One group is the data loaders, and the other is the data consumers. We will look at how and where you need to think about securing this data.

Another question you need to think about is when users need to access the data. For the data loader, it is obvious that they need to first access the application and then load it. However, for the user that is consuming the data, when are they consuming it, and to what level? Once it is in the cube? Do they need to drill down on it? Are we limiting any part of that data, or can they see the full dataset as it was loaded?

You must assign users to groups and will find that there are times when nesting groups in groups will promote ease of administration. In other areas of the application, however, you will not want to overcomplicate your security design with several levels of nesting. We will walk through some examples of what past implementations have shown us to be proven winners, and how others can pose future implications when you are adding additional phases or users. The key is not to have your administrator or administrators – down the line – inherit an overly complicated process when it comes to explaining access to auditors, or changing how users get access to something should business needs change.

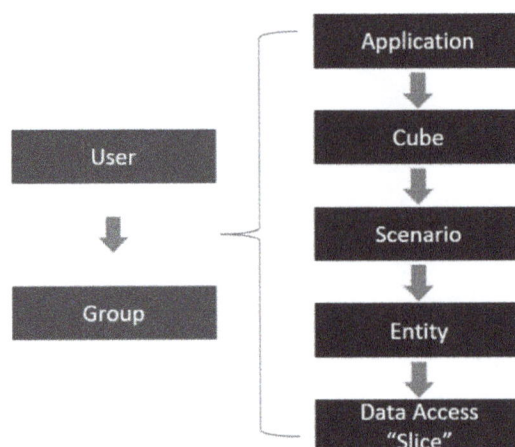

Figure 9.1

Security Roles

As mentioned earlier, to get anywhere in the application, a user must first be in the correct role(s). Again, when thinking about the different types of users in the application, you will want to determine who will oversee the different functions in the application. Some companies have view-only users, data loaders, and administrators. Others may have contributors that are in-between, plus roles that require individuals to load exchange rates, update transformation rules, maintain reports, etc., but they are not administrators. Some refer to these types of users as 'super-users'. However we choose to label them, we can segregate users and their functions by creating groups and assigning these groups to application security roles. As you can see, OneStream allows us to recognize different roles within organizations and apply access accordingly. Furthermore, we can apply role-based access by application. In addition to the application security roles in OneStream, there are **system security roles**. These roles will determine who can access and manage security-related objects and logs. We will cover this towards the end of this topic.

Application Security Roles

Application security roles address everything from who can access the application itself, to modifying data, to un-certifying and unlocking workflows, to accessing and modifying artifacts.

We will go through some of the best practices related to application security roles, plus some business cases that show how to secure certain roles at a more granular level. One thing that I can't stress enough is not to get too crazy about securing everything and everyone. Often, you will find that if you map out the functions (roles) of the users and what they are accessing (and when), you can streamline and simplify your security model.

Knowing what you are ultimately trying to secure is key as well. And while it may not be evident upfront, assigning the 'everyone' access group to a role isn't a blanket statement that they have that level of access for that object across the application. Role access should work together with specific object access that is relative to the area that users are working with at that given time. Furthermore, object access should work with any additional access related to metadata that the user is associated with. We will get into a few working examples of this when we look at workflow security, as well as other common user access requests.

Within security roles, there are two sections. In Figure 9.2, we see that when a new application is created, everything will default to the administrator security group, apart from two roles. These exceptions are for less common activities where we want to make the ability to administer these activities deliberate and by a select group. Therefore, they default to **nobody**.

⊟ Application Security Roles

Role	Group
AdministerApplication	Administrators
AdministerDatabase	Nobody
AdministerApplicationWorkspaceAssemblies	Administrators
AnalyticsApi	Nobody
OpenApplication	Everyone
ModifyData	Everyone
ViewAllData	Everyone
CreateAuditAttachments	Administrators
CreateFootnoteAttachments	Administrators
CertifyAndLockDescendants	Administrators
UnlockAndUncertifyAncestors	Administrators
PreserveImportData	Administrators
RestoreImportData	Administrators
UnlockWorkflowUnit	Administrators
ViewSourceDataAudit	Everyone
EncryptBusinessRules	Administrators
ManageApplicationProperties	Administrators
ManageMetadata	Everyone
ManageFXRates	Everyone
LockFXRates	Administrators
UnlockFXRates	Administrators
ManageData	Everyone
ManageSmartIntegration	Administrators
ManageCubeViews	Everyone
ManageDataSources	Everyone
ManageTransformationRules	Everyone
ManageConfirmationRules	Everyone
ManageCertificationQuestions	Everyone
ManageWorkflowChannels	Administrators
ManageWorkflowProfiles	Administrators
ManageJournalTemplates	Everyone
ManageFormTemplates	Everyone
ManageApplicationWorkspaces	Administrators
ManageApplicationDatabaseFiles	Administrators
ManageSmartLinks	Administrators
ManageTaskScheduler	Administrators
TaskScheduler	Administrators

Security Roles allow management of the listed objects

User Interface Roles allow access to listed objects

⊟ Application User Interface Roles

Role	Group
ApplicationLoadExtractPage	Administrators
ApplicationPropertiesPage	Administrators
ApplicationSecurityRolesPage	Administrators
OnePlacePane	Everyone
BookAdminPage	Administrators
BusinessRulesPage	Everyone
CertificationQuestionsPage	Administrators
ClientUpdaterPage	Administrators
ConfirmationRulesPage	Administrators
CubeAdminPage	Administrators
CubeViewsPage	Administrators
WorkspaceAdminPage	Administrators
DataManagementAdminPage	Administrators
TaskSchedulerPage	Administrators
DataSourcesPage	Administrators
DimensionLibraryPage	Administrators
FxRatesPage	Administrators
FormTemplatesPage	Administrators
JournalTemplatesPage	Administrators
SpreadsheetPage	Everyone
TextEditor	Administrators
TimeDimProfilesPage	Administrators
TransformationRulesPage	Everyone
WorkflowChannelsPage	Administrators
WorkflowProfilesPage	Administrators

Figure 9.2

On the left, you see the **application security roles**. These are roles that allow for access to manage or action something within that item or object (e.g., data, FX rates, dashboards, etc.). On the right are the **application interface roles**. These are roles that allow access to the object but prevent the management or action of anything within that role. Recognizing how we can give users visibility to objects in the application – while still restricting management access – will be key in any line of questioning as to who will need to view items versus who will need to update them.

System Security Roles

System security roles are typically reserved for your administrators. Should the application have varying levels of admins, system security roles are applied to the groups that administrators with the highest level of access are in.

While lesser levels may be assigned to **interface roles**, the ability to manage roles should generally be reserved for your administrator functions. For example, within the system security roles, you can limit the number of users that are able to administer security; however, you can still allow others to report on security. By creating a group that allows access to the system pane, you can then assign additional groups, based on role, to the pages shown below, should you want folks outside of your administrator function to view information about users and processes related to the application. This includes, but is not limited to, activity and error logs, access to the underlying database tables, etc.

Below, in Figure 9.3, is an example of assigned settings for the system security roles in an application.

System Security Roles	
AdministerSystemWorkspaceAssemblies	Administrators
ManageSystemWorkspaces	Administrators
ManageSystemDatabaseFiles	Administrators
ManageFileShare	Administrators
ManageFileShareContents	Administrators
AccessFileShareContents	Administrators
RetrieveFileShareContents	Administrators
EncryptSystemBusinessRules	Nobody
ViewAllLogonActivity	Administrators
ViewAllErrorLog	Administrators
ViewAllTaskActivity	Administrators
ManageSystemSecurityUsers	Administrators
ManageSystemSecurityGroups	Administrators
ManageSystemSecurityRoles	Administrators
ManageSystemConfiguration	Administrators
AccessAsNonInteractiveUser	Administrators
AdministerNonInteractiveUser	Administrators
ManageIdentityProviders	Administrators
System User Interface Roles	
SystemAdministrationLogon	Administrators
SystemPane	Administrators
ApplicationAdminPage	Administrators
SecurityAdminPage	Administrators
SmartIntegrationConnectorAdminPage	Administrators
SystemBusinessRulesPage	Administrators
SystemConfigurationPage	Administrators
SystemWorkspaceAdminPage	Administrators
DatabasePage	Administrators
FileExplorerPage	Administrators
SystemLoadExtractPage	Administrators
EnvironmentPage	Administrators
ErrorLogPage	Administrators
LogonActivityPage	Administrators
TaskActivityPage	Administrators
TimeDimensionsPage	Administrators

Figure 9.3

As we get further into this chapter, we won't be focusing on designing for the system security roles, as these are usually reserved for the application administrators. In the cases where they are extended beyond this group, the configuration involved is not coordinated with the cube or data within it, so there is flexibility when updating or editing this type of access after the initial design.

Securing Metadata

There are different methods of applying security to entities. Depending on how granular security needs to be, an organization may need to apply security at the entity level, as a 1:1 relationship with a security group. This means that for every entity, a security group would be created and assigned to the **read data group** and another created and assigned to the **read and write data group**.

OneStream also allows for a second read data group and second read and write data group, where necessary. When this level of granularity is not necessary, entities may be grouped and secured at a parent level. For example, if we are thinking of OneStream's GolfStream Reference application, and we wanted to manage the security by product line parent, we may see one read group for

V_Clubs and one read and write data group for M_Clubs, where these groups would be applied to all the Clubs entities in the hierarchy.

With either approach, you will see how we apply the write access via the workflow, but it all starts with the entity security groups. To illustrate entity security and how it will work together with our roles, mentioned above, and workflow security and functionality, we will talk through several use cases below. We will also discuss how we need to look at the security on the scenario as well as 'slice', ensuring that there are no restrictions on any of the intersections that the user is looking to report on or write data to. All these items will come into play as you are designing your security model and the types of users that will be created in the application.

Common Types of Users

In this section, we are going to discuss some of the more common types of users that most companies will have. We will review what roles and additional security rights to consider when creating the groups that will eventually be assigned to these types of users. What should also be apparent by the end of this section is how we can leverage the same groups for *different* users when access is the same for some areas, and then deviate and apply different, additional roles when more rights are granted. In some cases, we will apply **'slice' security** when we need to take away partial access to data already granted.

Administrators

Administrators are the team of individuals who are going to own the application. They can flip all the switches, see everything in the application, and modify data as well.

Due to this all-powerful role, you will want to discuss with the business what this means now and in future phases. Designing security for phase one may only mean focusing on Actuals or a financial consolidations project. In this case, having an administrator role with access to the full application is not out of the ordinary. Furthermore, having several administrators in this group may be justified, depending on the size of the organization and other considerations when it comes to administering a larger application.

Fast forward to a future phase, or flip this design around, and say phase one was for planning. In this second case, the business may have a different view on who can have this powerful role, especially when sensitive data is involved. Let's think about the design considerations for both situations and why the administrator function would want to be narrowed down depending on the type of data collection.

In scenario number one, let's imagine we will have an administrators' group with access to everything. In other words, they will have full access to administer both the application and security. Let's also assume, for this design, that the group of administrators will be handling all the 'administrator-type' tasks. Pretty simple, right? If this is the goal, then the **AdministerApplication** role in your application security roles (refer to Figure 9.2) would be set to Administrators. There will be other application security roles that you will likely leave at the administrator group level as well, due to this very simplistic model. The same would apply for your **system security roles** (Figure 9.3). Where the application applies to the administrator group in the system security roles by default, as well as the system user interface roles, you could leave as is. The users that are defined as administrators would then be in your administrator group, and nothing more would need to be done for them to have full access to the application and system, including security functions.

Now let's imagine the design for administrators is not quite as simple as our first example, and we are going to want an administrator group – just like above – for a select few to handle security, and another application admin group to assist in the management of metadata and FX rates. I'm sure you are already looking back to the application security roles and determining what we can apply security on. The answer to that is *just about everything*!

Application roles can be applied by defining who can 'manage' and who can 'access'. Referring to Figure 9.2, and the roles on the right (which, if you are in the software, are in the top section), we can see who controls the management of objects or processes. By setting a role in the top section to a security group [R_ApplicationAdmin], for our roles ManageMetadata, ManageFXRates,

`LockFXRates` and `UnlockFXRates` we are saying that users in this group will have the ability to add/delete/edit metadata and add/edit/lock/unlock exchange rates in the application.

However, just giving them access to manage is not sufficient. They must have access to the page, which is in the application user interface role. Designing for this is key, as you may want users outside of any admin function to access this page in a view-only state, while not being able to change the values. If this is the case, we want to have a separate group on it. This separate group can then be nested in the `R_ApplicationAdmin` group, leaving the interface role open to a separate audience with view-only access. I want to illustrate this because, in this example, we are showing how two application roles are working together to provide the application admin with access to a page *and* manage; later on, we can assign the page access to a different type of user.

Let's examine how our administrator access looks in this second design, and how we are still leaving the door open for groups of users down the road who would be allowed to have view-only access to a page. In Figure 9.4, you can see how we have applied specific security groups to the roles we discussed above. The administrators group has been assigned to most of the others, except for other common roles that are left open to other groups, which we will expand on later in other design discussions.

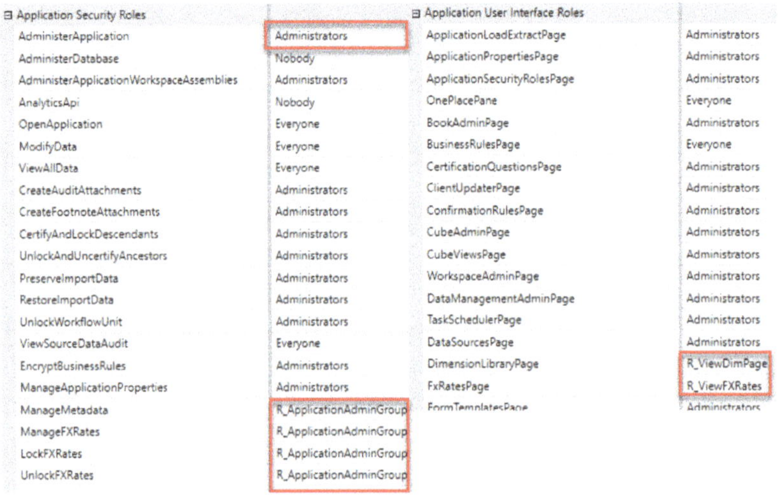

Figure 9.4

In Figure 9.5, we are showing how the roles work together to provide the intended level of access when the user is added to the right combination of groups. In our example, we could have assigned the user to the individual groups; however, the roles need to work *together*. So, assigning a group to another group made sense, as one would not work without the other.

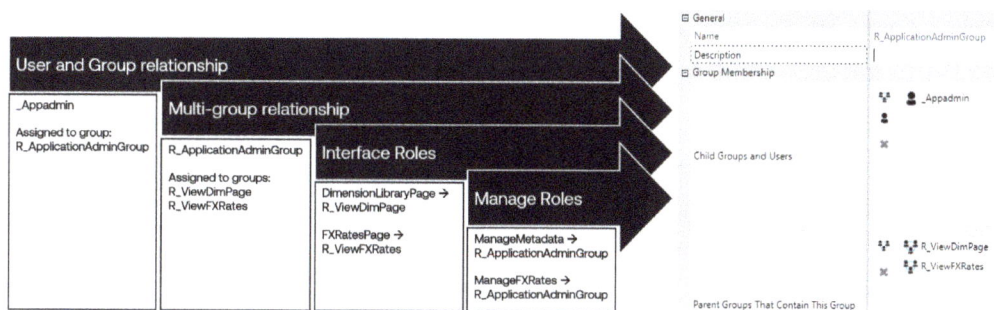

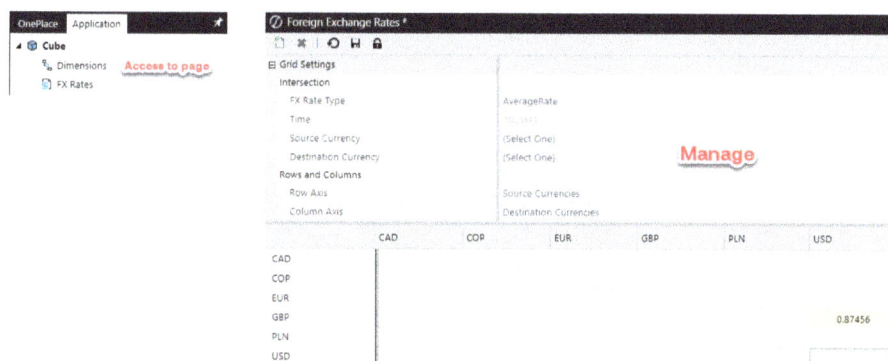

Figure 9.5

Now, what happens when you work with sensitive data relating to your employees? While I won't get too deep into our Solution Exchange solutions, in this case I am thinking of People Planning and the register detail in it. This is a worthwhile topic that needs to be planned for.

We talk about the administrator group and how it automatically has the ability to add/delete/edit everything to do with security. In theory, this means that even if we change all of the roles in the application that ordinarily default to administrator when a new application is created to another administrator-type group, this administrator group would still have overriding authority. Not to mention, somebody needs to be in it! The reality is that we know there is a need to secure the register detail and – in some cases – this will mean that the administrators' group needs to be able to do their jobs while still being excluded from having visibility to this information.

In order to do this, we use custom Event Handlers and BRAPI calls. When getting into design considerations for Solution Exchange solutions, this is one of many, many considerations and items to plan for when thinking about how security will come into play for a given solution.

App admins and super-users can look different from one organization to the next. The key to allowing them to have access to the functions they need in the application – while not creating a tangled web when it comes to their access – is to map this out as with anything else you are designing.

Determine if there is a role that can define their function or if there will need to be additional security placed after. If you find that there are a lot of restrictions being placed after the fact, you may be starting in the wrong spot. While the user might be responsible for admin-type functions, maybe they need access to specific datasets first, with increased application access second. If this is the case, look to the object access and different settings that can be found within their key function, before jumping through hoops to create a unique role.

View All Users

Not to be confused with view-only users who have view-only access to specific datasets, most applications will have a set of users that have view access *to all data*.

View all users may have additional rights that give them more access to data (e.g., modify), or certification rights in a workflow, or maybe super-user responsibility, but the idea is that they have no limits to access the data they can view in the cubes in the application.

It is important not to overthink or overcomplicate view all access. This can easily be accomplished by creating one security group and assigning that group to an out-of-the-box security role. The security role is self-administered so that when new entities, scenarios, etc. are added, this security group, and the users assigned to it, will also be granted access.

When planning for view all users, the only way you can restrict access to this user *navigating* to an entity in a Member Filter is by setting the display access to Nobody. However, this *will not* stop them from accessing the data in the entity should they type in the entity name in an **xfgetcell** or in a prompt that asks for a freeform entry.

It should also be noted that view all users will *not* be restricted by **data cell access security**.

The main point is, once a user is in the `ViewAllData` group, you cannot restrict the data they can view. You can, however, grant more rights to specific datasets via the workflow, for example. The topics of display access and data cell access security will be discussed in more detail later.

In Figure 9.6, we see our `_ViewAllUser` with view access to all entities in the displayed report on the right. Again, we can layer on additional access for this particular access, based on their function; however, we cannot limit view access to specific intersections of data because we granted access via the ViewAllData role.

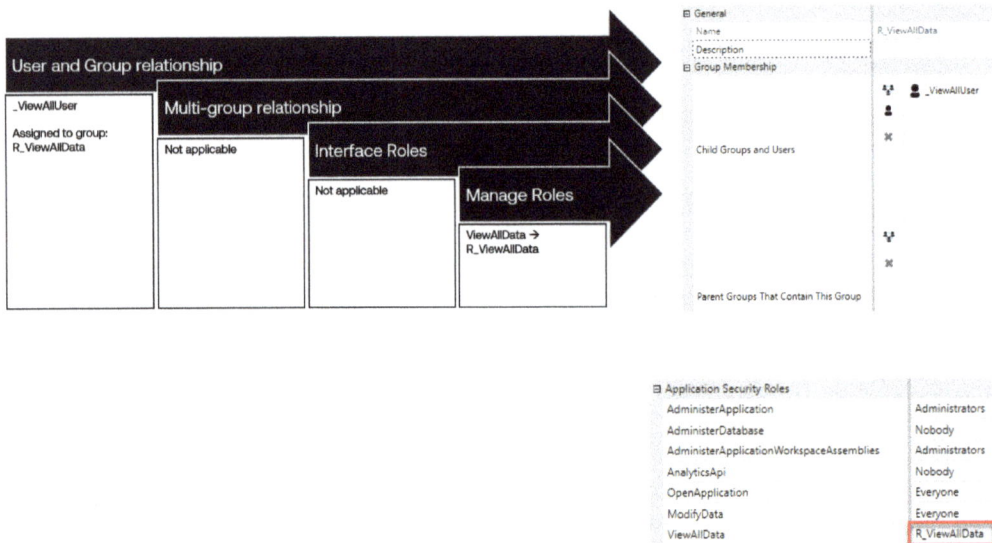

Figure 9.6

Data Loaders

Data loading is tied heavily to our workflow setup, and I will therefore reference Chapter 7: Workflow for best practices on design when it comes to the specific workflow functionality. In addition to the workflow, the user will need to be assigned to group(s) that are permitted the correct level of access to everything they are trying to write to. This includes cube, scenario, entity, account, flow, and all User Defined dimensions that are used in the cube. Some of these dimensions may be set to Everyone (e.g. cube and scenario). Account, flow, and the UDs – while not having the ability to assign a security group to the dimension member itself – may have 'slice' security attached. Or, as mentioned before, workflow channels may be in use in the case of account or UD, whereby access to specific workflow channels needs to be checked to load to them. On the latter, these should be considered for functions related to workflow processes, and not for security design.

When thinking about your design for security around data loading, there are a few considerations to keep in mind so that there is no unnecessary work being done. As with earlier examples, regarding administrators and view-only users, it is easiest to talk through design considerations and best practices with a couple of examples. These examples will show how security can be controlled mostly through the workflow when a couple of key concepts are followed.

Let's get started by thinking about your data collection. The workflow setup should drive a lot of how your security setup looks here. If you are having data submitted by many locations, and those locations translate into workflows, we will likely be securing at the workflow level.

Within each workflow, there may be different levels of security for the varying roles that a workflow allows for. Right now, we are looking at the data loader. Our first use case is for a data loader that needs to load data for two entities which are part of the same workflow. This data loader is not going to have the final word when it comes to signing or certifying their workflow.

We first start by thinking about what we are giving the data loader access to, and how OneStream will check the access to ensure they are authorized to pass through all the security checkpoints.

Our design and requirements will serve as a process flow for how security will pass through these checkpoints. Again, our goal for this data loader and our other basic data loaders will be to get into the application, access their workflow, import, validate, and load the cube. While there are configuration steps in the data collection process that will be covered in the Workflow and Data Integration sections – Chapters 7 and 6, respectively – we are going to cover what the application is looking for this user to have, in order to get to and pass through these gates to achieve success.

On the right in Figure 9.7, you will see the process that the application is passing the user through, and we need, therefore, to ensure that the appropriate access is assigned to the groups that the user will be in. On the left are examples of how this was achieved in this business case. Of course, this is not the only way this can be accomplished. For example, groups do not have to be assigned to other groups; however, where it makes sense and the parent/child group relationship will always make sense, group them together so that when a change is needed, or a new user with similar access is added, you can provision them with ease and little administration.

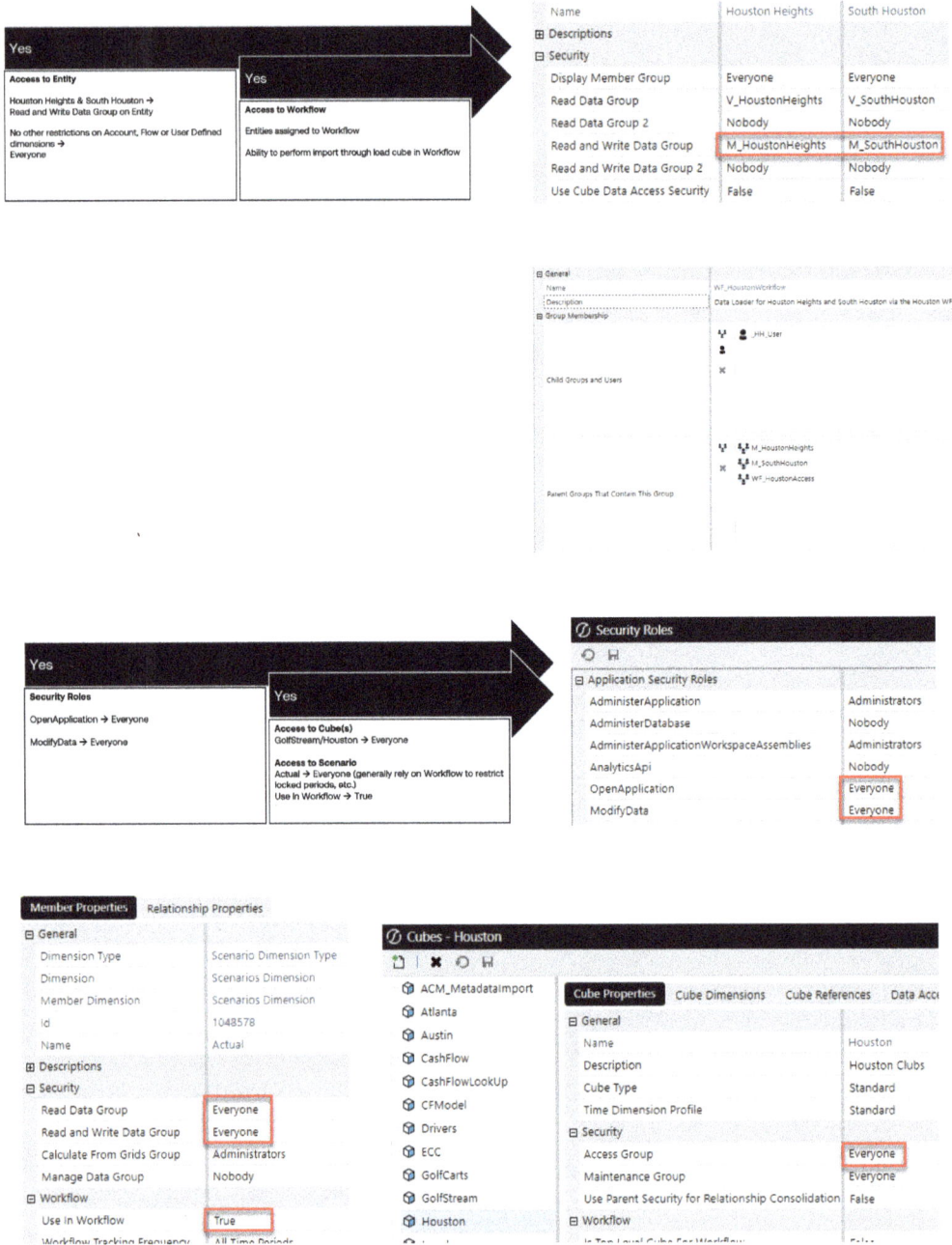

Name	Houston Heights	South Houston
⊞ Descriptions		
⊟ Security		
Display Member Group	Everyone	Everyone
Read Data Group	V_HoustonHeights	V_SouthHouston
Read Data Group 2	Nobody	Nobody
Read and Write Data Group	M_HoustonHeights	M_SouthHouston
Read and Write Data Group 2	Nobody	Nobody
Use Cube Data Access Security	False	False

Yes

Access to Entity

Houston Heights & South Houston →
Read and Write Data Group on Entity

No other restrictions on Account, Flow or User Defined dimensions →
Everyone

Yes

Access to Workflow

Entities assigned to Workflow

Ability to perform import through load cube in Workflow

⊟ General
Name
Description — WF_HoustonWorkflow
Data Loader for Houston Heights and South Houston via the Houston WF
⊟ Group Membership

Child Groups and Users — _HH_User

M_HoustonHeights
M_SouthHouston
WF_HoustonAccess

Parent Groups That Contain This Group

Yes

Security Roles

OpenApplication → Everyone

ModifyData → Everyone

Yes

Access to Cube(s)
GolfStream/Houston → Everyone

Access to Scenario
Actual → Everyone (generally rely on Workflow to restrict locked periods, etc.)
Use in Workflow → True

Security Roles	
⊟ Application Security Roles	
AdministerApplication	Administrators
AdministerDatabase	Nobody
AdministerApplicationWorkspaceAssemblies	Administrators
AnalyticsApi	Nobody
OpenApplication	Everyone
ModifyData	Everyone

Member Properties   Relationship Properties

⊟ General	
Dimension Type	Scenario Dimension Type
Dimension	Scenarios Dimension
Member Dimension	Scenarios Dimension
Id	1048578
Name	Actual
⊞ Descriptions	
⊟ Security	
Read Data Group	Everyone
Read and Write Data Group	Everyone
Calculate From Grids Group	Administrators
Manage Data Group	Nobody
⊟ Workflow	
Use In Workflow	True
Workflow Tracking Frequency	All Time Periods

Cubes - Houston

ACM_MetadataImport
Atlanta
Austin
CashFlow
CashFlowLookUp
CFModel
Drivers
ECC
GolfCarts
GolfStream
Houston

Cube Properties   Cube Dimensions   Cube References   Data Acc

⊟ General	
Name	Houston
Description	Houston Clubs
Cube Type	Standard
Time Dimension Profile	Standard
⊟ Security	
Access Group	Everyone
Maintenance Group	Everyone
Use Parent Security for Relationship Consolidation	False
⊟ Workflow	
Is Top Level Cube For Workflow	False

Figure 9.7

We can take a closer look, in Figure 9.8, at how a user and groups are configured in relation to the workflow. The user is assigned to a single group, WF_HoustonWorkflow. The access to 1. modify the entities and 2. access the workflow are then nested by assigning them to the WF_HoustonWorkflow group.

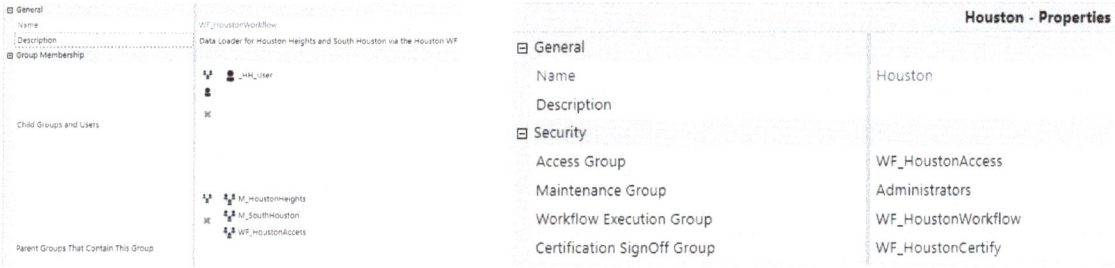

Figure 9.8

Figure 9.9 shows what the successful data loader looks like in this case. We see the user was able to complete the steps that allowed them to import, validate, and load data to the cube. In Figure 9.10, this same user was *prevented* from certifying the workflow (greyed out buttons).

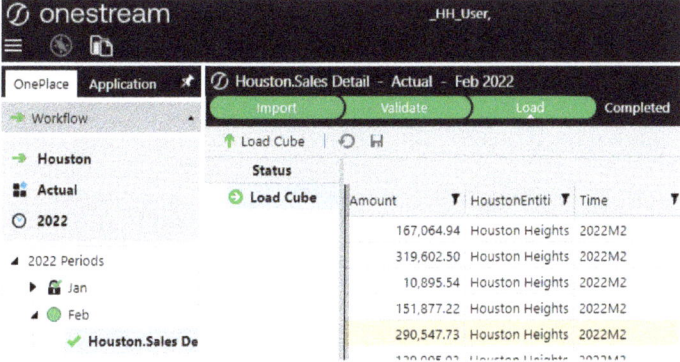

Figure 9.9

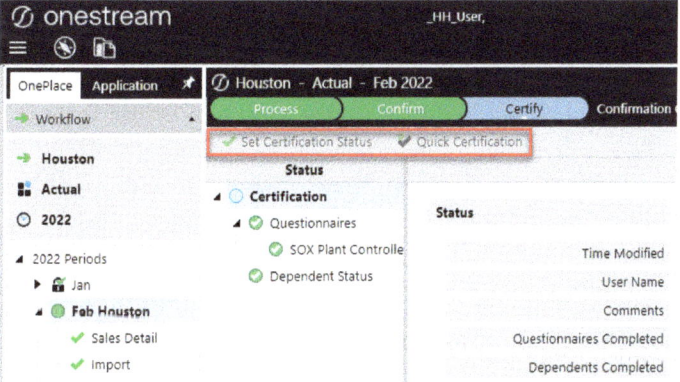

Figure 9.10

This is a good time to pause and talk about the **ModifyData** role. You will note that it is set to Everyone in this example. This is not an error nor an oversight. Although this may strike you as odd, this can be set to everyone, providing the items above are in place. There will be additional considerations that need to be determined with different application designs, but due to the way that OneStream checks the access that the user has across the application, you should be able to rely on the security checkpoints in place.

These checkpoints will be related to the Data Unit and workflow. We also look at 'slice' security, when applicable. To quickly illustrate, we can look at two users that are attempting to load data to the same entity, HoustonHeights. The first one is our example above, where we have all of the roles and proper access working harmoniously together in order to allow the user to achieve the final goal of loading data into the cube for HoustonHeights, yet not being able to certify the workflow parent [Houston].

Now let's look at a second user, `_SH_Houston`, and apply security for the entities (`HoustonHeights` and `SouthHouston`) and review the workflow security (Figure 9.11).

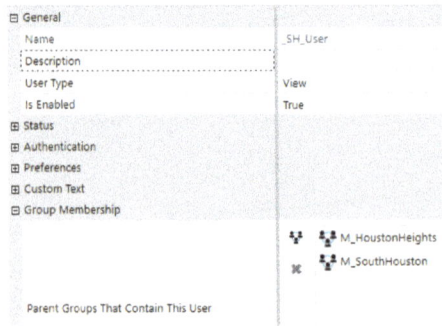

Figure 9.11

Observe in Figure 9.12 that this user cannot access the workflow to import the data. They can only see the cube root, no workflows underneath. This is because we did not add the workflow group to their ID.

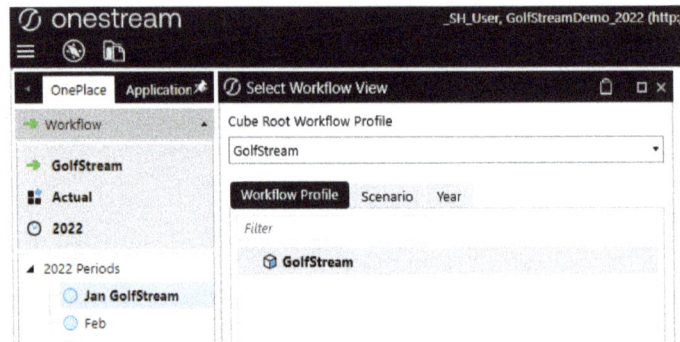

Figure 9.12

In this case, the user could still access reporting and other items in the application; however, we are using this example to point out the function of the workflow group. Let's circle back on reporting in just a moment.

Another example of security not aligning in an efficient manner would be when the workflow group is added, but the entity access for modification does not align with the assigned entities in the workflow. In this next example, we will add the workflow to the user's profile, but this time, we will omit the `M_HoustonHeights` group from the `WF_HoustonWorkflow` group. You will see that the user can access the workflow, and import the file containing the data related to the `HoustonHeights` entity, but will get an error when trying to validate against that entity.

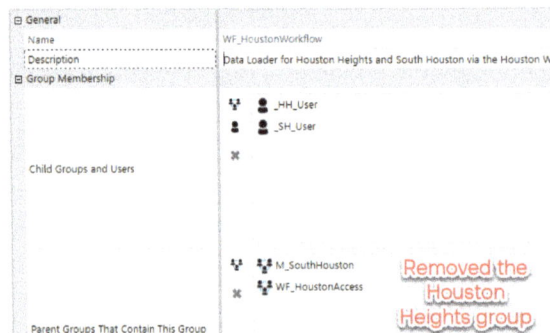

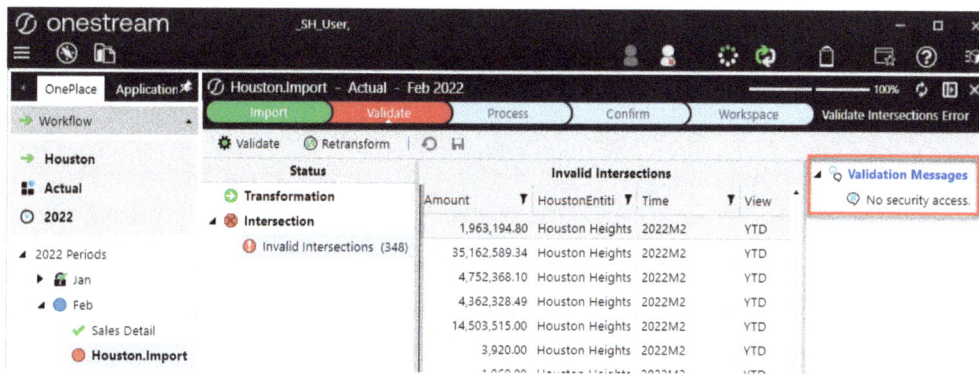

Figure 9.13

If you look at Figure 9.13, we have removed the entity group associated with Houston Heights read and write (M_HoustonHeights) from the WF_HoustonWorkflow parent/child relationship. By doing this, the result is the error shown in the bottom half of the illustration.

Data Loaders with Varying Access

Now that we have talked about designing for a simple data loader, and how we can leverage a single workflow group to nest the additional groups that will give the user access to the workflow and modify access to the entities, let's circle back on what else we may (or may not) need this data loader to do.

The use case has now expanded for this user to view the data for another location, which is Frankfurt. However, we don't want the user to see *all* the data for Frankfurt. Only the balance sheet data should be visible; the P&L data should be restricted. This will require the use of data cell access security, or 'slice' security. Since this is only viewing the data and not loading, we will not address this via the workflow. We can grant the view access to the entity with the read data group assigned in the Entity dimension. We will then leverage a security group that is assigned to our 'slice' security to restrict access on the P&L.

It is important to note that we cannot grant limited access to Frankfurt by going straight to the 'slice' security. Data cell access can only work on the premise that a user has first been granted access to an entity and its data in security. Next, we can decrease levels of access to an intersection, or subset of data, and from there have the ability to increase levels or access to intersections, or subsets of data, all stemming from the original access. Refer to Figure 9.14 to see how the access works together between the Entity dimension, data cell access, and security, and how we assign this to the user.

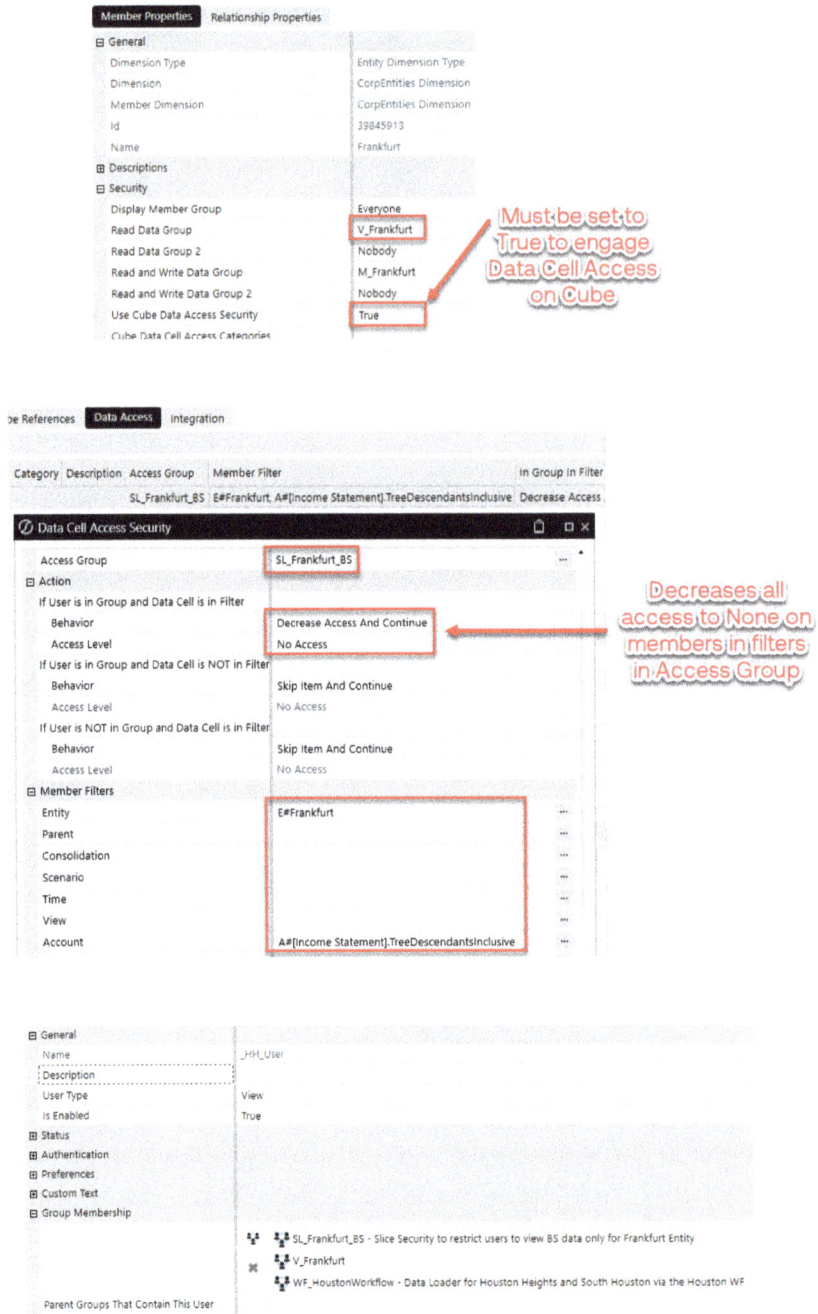

Figure 9.14

Here is what our user is seeing with the addition of the `V_Frankfurt` group in Figure 9.15 (top) and then with the addition of the `SL_Frankfurt_BS` 'slice' group added (bottom).

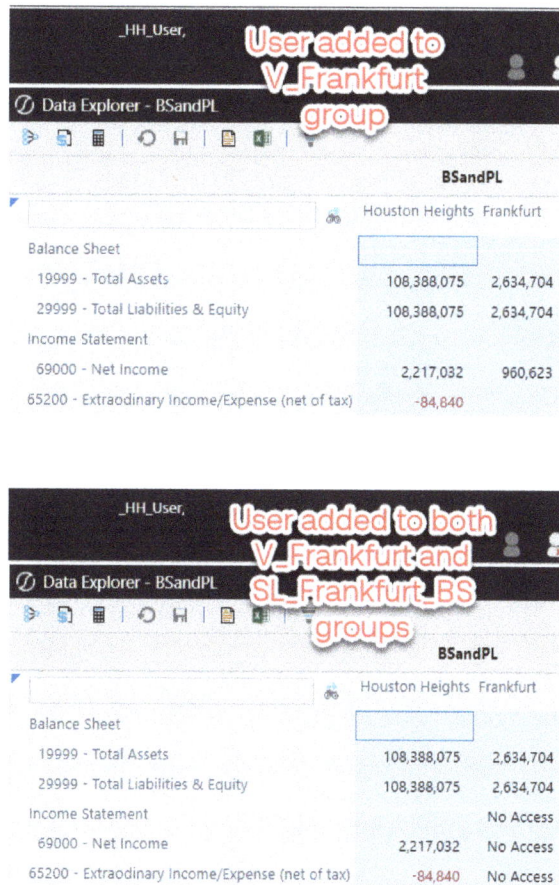

Figure 9.15

Let's continue with this use case and layer on additional access as it relates to application roles.

Think back to when we were discussing the difference between allowing lower-level administrators the ability to manage, lock/unlock the FX rates, and how we were keeping page access separate from the ability to update the rates. This use case will help demonstrate why designing for this is a good reason for keeping your options open. We want to allow this user to access the FX rates page, but we want to ensure that they cannot update the rates when they are unlocked. In addition to this, we want to give the user access to the Spreadsheet module within OneStream. We will want to allow this user and all users access to Spreadsheet.

These two items are easily accomplished because we did not go crazy when we started designing our application security by creating security groups for every role and assigning them one for one. We are creating and designing based on our processes and types of users, how they access the data, and when and where they access the data.

As a refresher, Figure 9.16 shows us the FXRatesPage role is set to the security group, R_ViewFXRates. In addition, the SpreadsheetPage is open to Everyone.

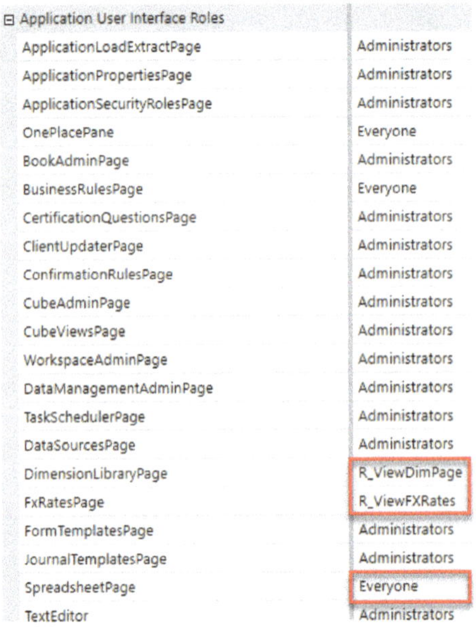

Figure 9.16

If we add our user to the R_ViewFXRates group, we will achieve the expanded access we are looking for, which can be seen by the user if they click on the Application tab. Figure 9.17 shows that _HH_User is now added to the group assigned to the ViewFXRates interface role. Refreshing the app under this user ID reveals that they can now see the FX Rates icon, as well as the Spreadsheet icon on the Application tab.

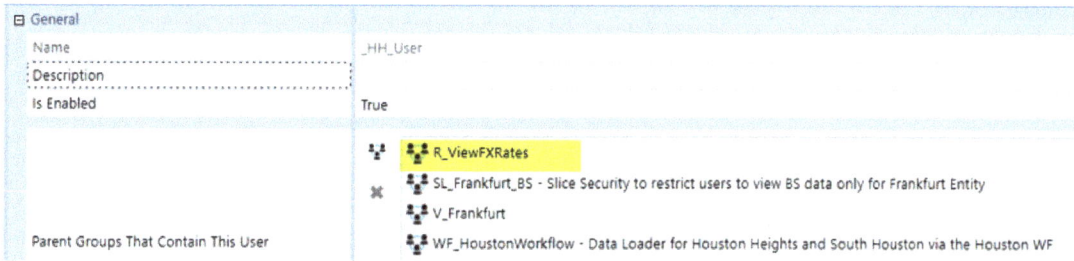

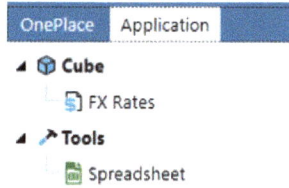

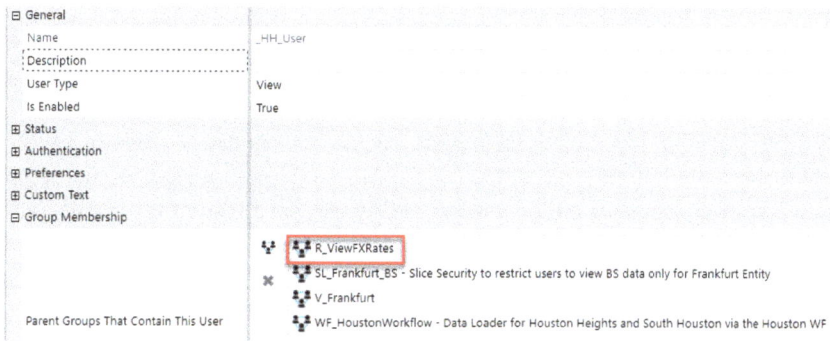

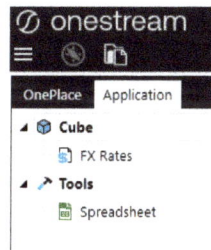

Figure 9.17

Another example of data loaders with varying access includes journal posting, reviewing, and approving. A common client requirement is to segregate these duties and prevent users from being able to self-post or self-approve their own journal entries. This security can be controlled using the workflow security properties shown in Figure 9.18 below.

Figure 9.18

To recap, we started out with a use case for a data loader that needed to import, validate, and load data for a single workflow that had two entities assigned to it. We needed to ensure that they could not certify this workflow parent. We then extended this use case so that the user would be able to view the data of another entity but be restricted to a certain set of accounts. We also added additional role-based access that would allow the user to access Spreadsheet, and view-only access to the FX rates page from the Application tab. Lastly, we added role-based access that would prevent a journal creator from posting or approving their own journal entries.

To close out our design, and the requirements for our data loaders, our use case should also have shown you how we can have groups assigned to various types of users for the different functions they perform. The groups, when combined with other groups, give you the flexibility to not only give access to different datasets in the application, but to the different roles that users play as well.

View Users with Workflow Responsibility

Now that we have covered our view all users, data loaders, and data loaders with additional view access, let's touch on varying degrees of access within the workflow.

If you read Chapter 7: Workflow, I would venture to guess that you have an appreciation of just how powerful the workflow is in OneStream, and how it will guide the user through processes – as well as where you may want them to enter the application.

Workflow has many layers and many places where you will have the opportunity to introduce different components of the application. Most of these processes and components can be secured individually; however, it is strongly recommended that you understand how all of them work together before you start creating and applying security on each of them (similar to how we discussed roles). *Over-securing* areas in the workflow can create a web that is sometimes hard to follow and, most times, cumbersome and unnecessary. If the design of the workflow considers how users actually access the processes they relate to (and the data involved), then security should be applied when it is required.

Our use case this time will be our Houston Approver. They will not need to load the data for either entity that is loaded in this workflow, but will need to certify the workflow parent after reviewing the figures. Let's think about what this user is going to need to have access to, regarding review and execution.

They will need the same level of *access* to the workflow, but a different level of *execution*. Our previous group of users loaded data; this user is certifying. In the workflow, we have a separate security setting for this. We also don't need this user to change any numbers in the entity; therefore, we don't need them to have edit rights to the entities, only view.

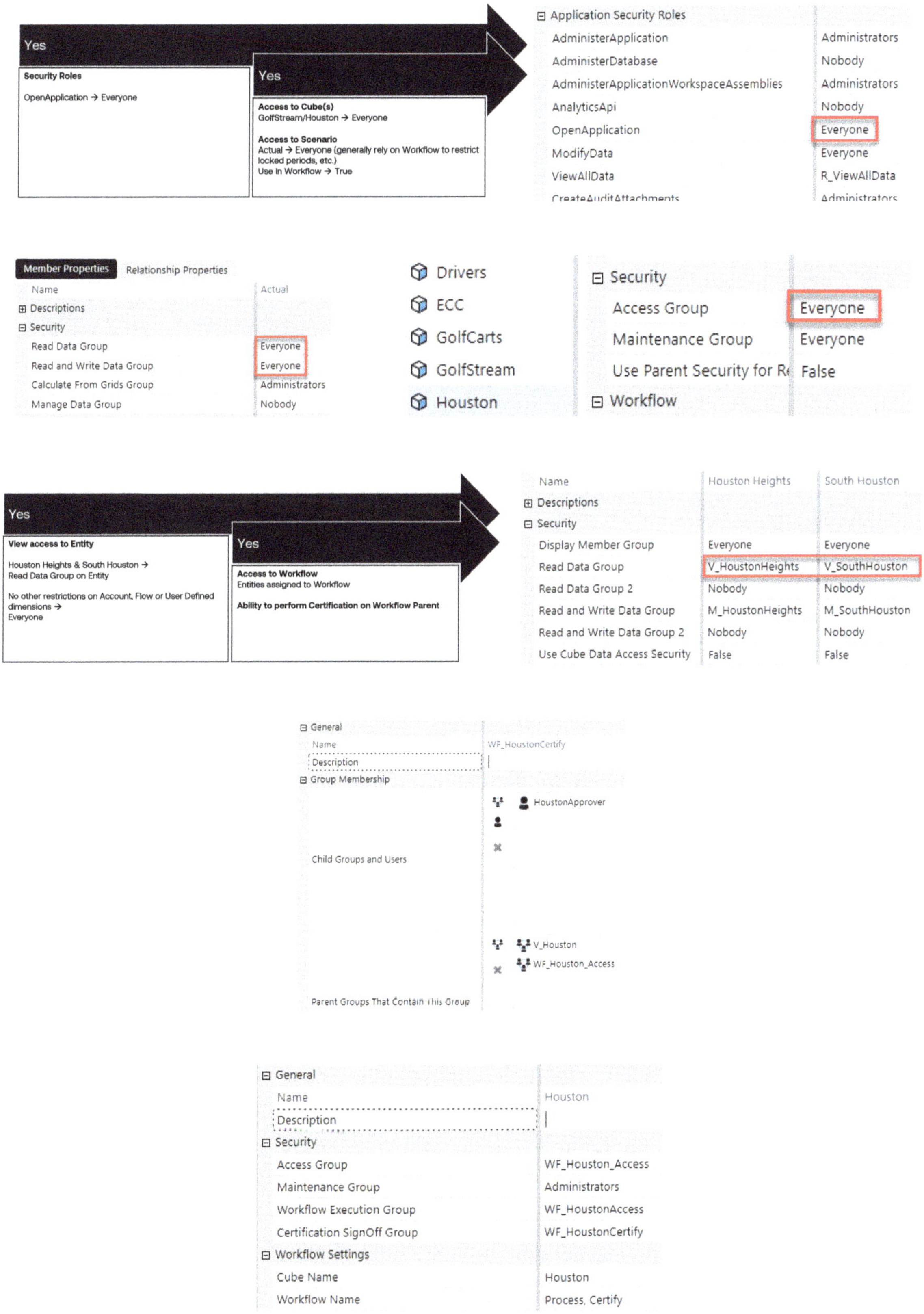

Figure 9.19

As you can see in Figure 9.19, similar to our data loaders, everything from the roles to the cube and scenario access, right down to the dimension and workflow security – *everything* has to work together to give this user the right amount of access to perform their work.

You can see in Figure 9.20 that `HoustonApprover` is not allowed to import/change data but is allowed to view the appropriate entities' data and certify the workflow.

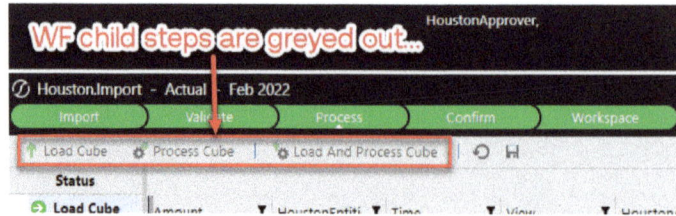

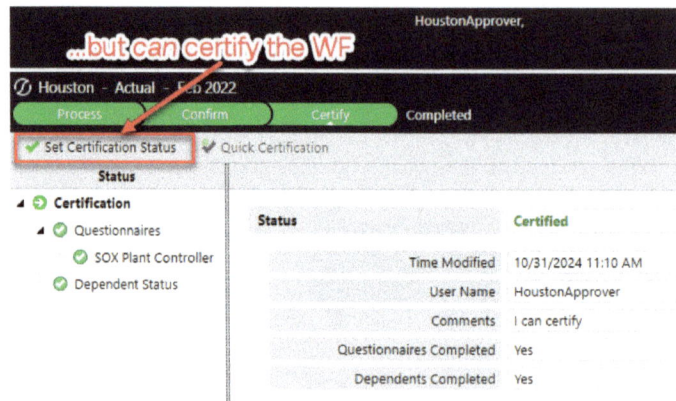

Figure 9.20

Let's expand on this use case and say that `HoustonApprover` is to have access to view all data in the application, but must still be restricted on the workflow responsibilities. If you remember back to the view all data design considerations, we will simply expand on this user's permissions by adding the security group that is already assigned to our `ViewAllData` application security role. Once we add the `HoustonApprover` to the group for the `ViewAllData` role, via the security group `R_ViewAllData`, we see in Figure 9.21 that the user can now see data in the Frankfurt entity when we rerun the same report.

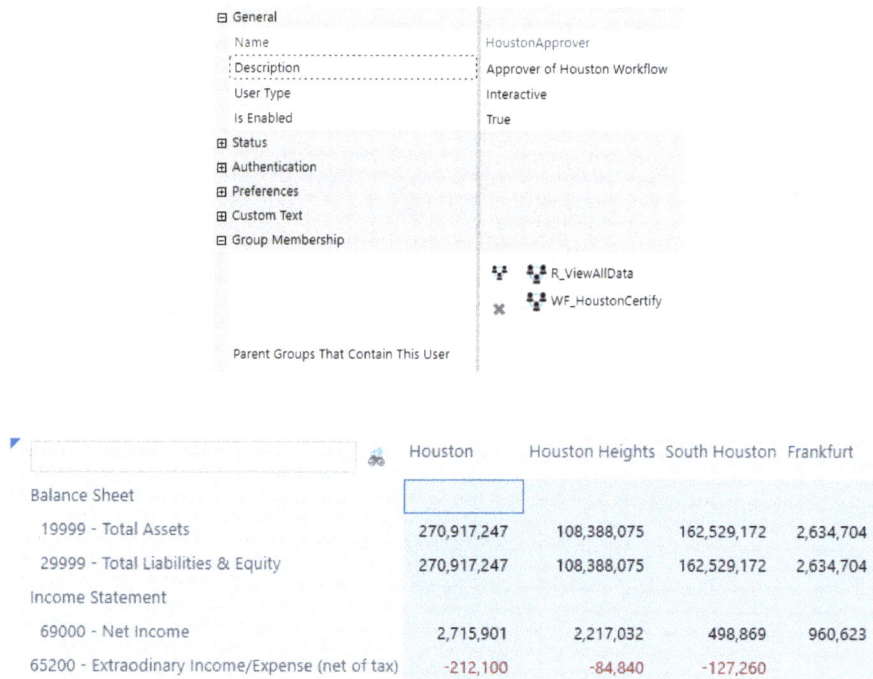

Figure 9.21

Thinking back to how we continued to expand on our requirements for our data loader, and when we gave them view access to Frankfurt, we circled back and restricted that access to balance sheet-only accounts. What happens if our requirement was the same for the Houston certifier? Could we simply add the same data cell access or 'slice' security group on?

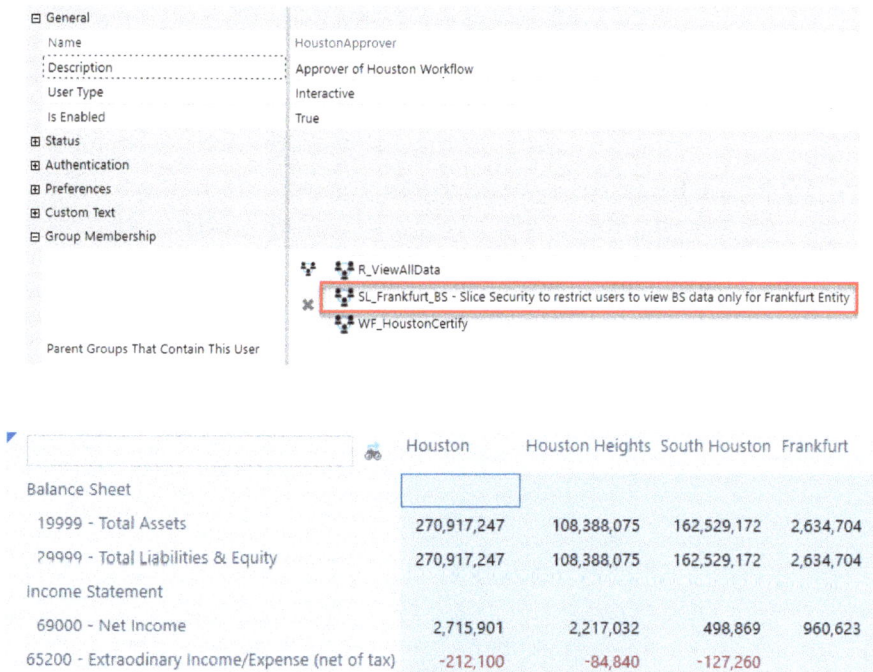

Figure 9.22

Figure 9.22 reveals that by adding the HoustonApprover to the SL_Frankfurt_BS group, it does nothing in the way of decreasing their access to the P&L accounts. Due to this user being in a group that is assigned to a role that gives them view all access to all data in the application, data cell access will not apply. For this requirement to be honored, we would have to independently

275

build out the entity access as it relates to view for all of the entities, grant it to the user, and then decrease it based on the dimensions we want to restrict.

Relationship Security

For some companies, the user's access to the relationship members on the Consolidation dimension is determined by their rights to the current entity's immediate parent. To put this in context, each entity in OneStream has the consolidation members in Figure 9.23 associated with it. The ones inside the box are the relationship members for the parent entity in that view.

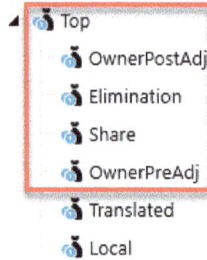

Figure 9.23

If we now need to design our security with a requirement to base our user's rights on the access the user has with the parent, we will need to apply a setting on the Cube Properties for each cube we want to enable this setting on.

Based on the access we want to give the user, we then need to consider the access they *not only* have to their entity(s), but we also need to consider their parents and the access we are granting with regard to those relationships.

Let's go back to our data loader use case and pick up where we left off. This user only had access to the two entities they could load – Houston Heights and South Houston – with additional, restricted access to Frankfurt. Our requirement is to control the viewing of the consolidation members based on the access this user has to the parent/child relationship between Houston and its children.

In Figure 9.24, you can see how there are no restrictions on the cons members before we make any changes. Next, we will make the change to the cube setting to **use parent security for relationship consolidation**. Once we do this, and without changing any security for this user, their access to the cons members is impacted. They no longer have access to anything outside of local and translated, which are determined by the user's rights to the entity itself.

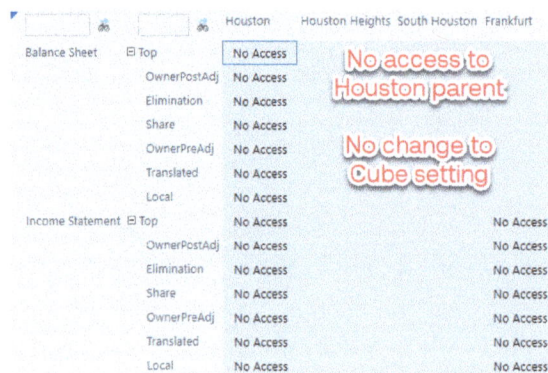

Figure 9.24

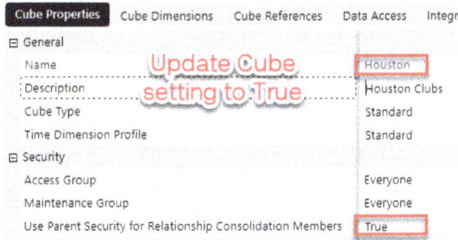

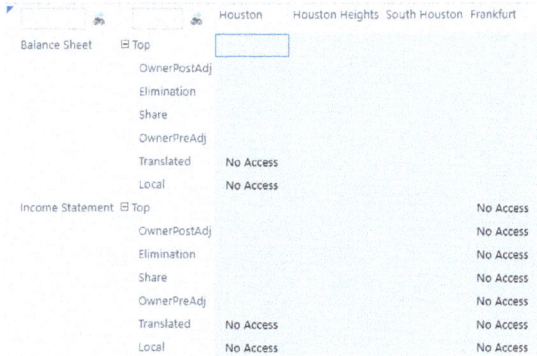

Figure 9.25

Since our requirement was to have no restrictions for this particular user, we will want to add view access to the parent. We will do this by adding them to the V_Houston group. You will see the access change after making this change (Figure 9.26).

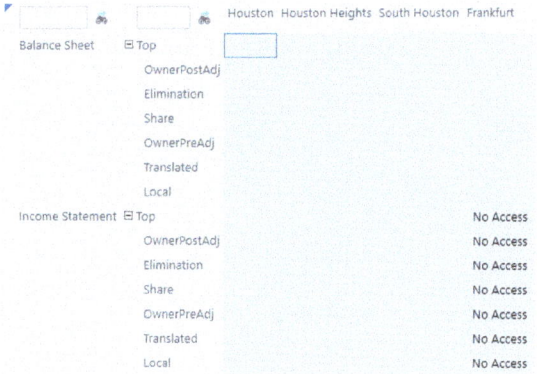

Figure 9.26

Relationship security can vary from one hierarchy to the next, or from one user to the next. However, as mentioned above, it is a cube setting. Once you turn it on, it then becomes a design consideration for all users outside of administrators and those in the ViewAllData role.

The relationship in each hierarchy will need to be reviewed, and if access to all levels of the Consolidation dimension will need to be accessible to a user, they will need to have view(s) to the immediate parent in each hierarchy that this is relevant for. If you are looking to put in this functionality and you don't want a subset of users to have access to the data of the parent, but need to have the data available at all levels of the Consolidation dimension for the base entity, 'slice' security will need to be introduced.

Access to Reporting for Users

We discussed how data loaders and WF certifiers come in through the workflow, and generally speaking, the reports that will be made available to them through OnePlace, as shown below (Figure 9.27).

We can also present Cube Views and dashboards to the user when they are related to specific steps within the workflow process, by creating and assigning profiles. The creation of the profiles is covered in Chapter 10: Reporting.

Once the profiles are created, they can be assigned in data quality settings in the workflow configuration to better assist the user in their end-to-end process. We also walked through a use case where a user may not have any workflow responsibilities. However, these users will need to report on data. We can still present Cube Views and dashboards to these users in OnePlace and not have a workflow assignment (Figure 9.27).

One thing to keep in mind is *not* to have any WF references in the reports presented to *these* users, or they will not run properly. Keeping your reports dynamic and flexible, based on the user, while still being able to adhere to the user's security permissions is feasible by referencing Cube POV references or parameters utilizing member lists from the dimension library.

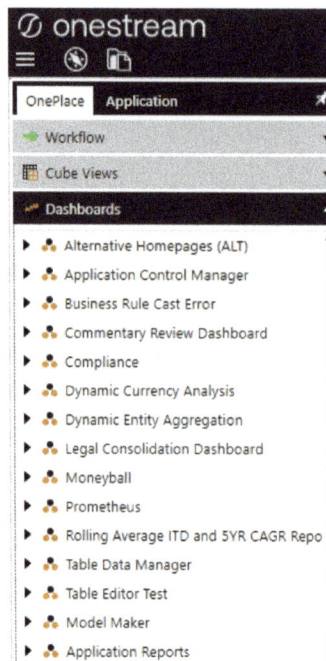

Figure 9.27

We mentioned above that data loaders, as well as non-data loaders, can access reports in the form of Cube Views and dashboards. When it comes to securing and administering dashboards, you need to think about **dashboard groups,** which are then assigned to dashboard profiles.

Both dashboard profiles and dashboard groups have access groups to which you can assign security access. The profiles are how you will ultimately get the dashboards in front of your users.

You can create many profiles and add the same groups over and over, across multiple profiles, in order to create unique dashboard profile groups, which will then be assigned to your user groups or, in some cases, be left open to everyone. You can individually manage the groups under the profiles, but bear in mind the groups are unique to the application, not to the profile you assign them to.

In addition to the security, dashboard profiles can be specified where they will be visible in the application. While there will be more information on this in Chapter 10: Reporting, it is worth mentioning here since this is a functional way to secure where you are displaying them. Figure

9.28 shows an example of a dashboard group related to a dashboard profile and the visibility and security associated with it.

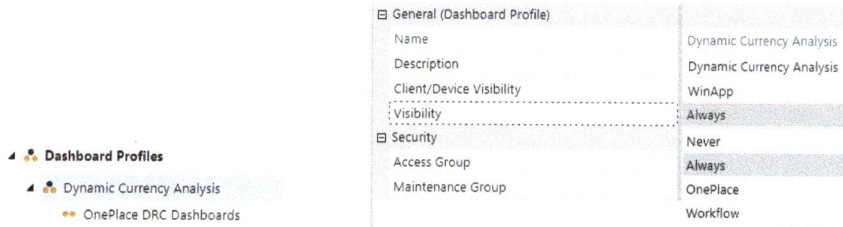

General (Dashboard Profile)	
Name	Dynamic Currency Analysis
Description	Dynamic Currency Analysis
Client/Device Visibility	WinApp
Visibility	Always
Security	Never
Access Group	Always
Maintenance Group	OnePlace
	Workflow

Dashboard Profiles
 Dynamic Currency Analysis
  OnePlace DRC Dashboards

Figure 9.28

Like how the dashboard groups and profiles are secured and presented to the user, Cube Views will have the same relationship.

Cube View groups will be assigned to Cube View Profiles, and the access group is assigned on the profile. Cube View Profiles, like dashboard profiles, also have visibility selection; however, it varies since Cube Views and dashboards can be presented in different areas of the application (Figure 9.28). Another difference is that on the Cube View itself, there is another setting that can be changed to determine if the Cube View will be visible in profiles. This is a True/False setting, shown in Figure 9.29 and Figure 9.30, and changing it to False will remove it from the user's view in OnePlace and in the workflow presentation.

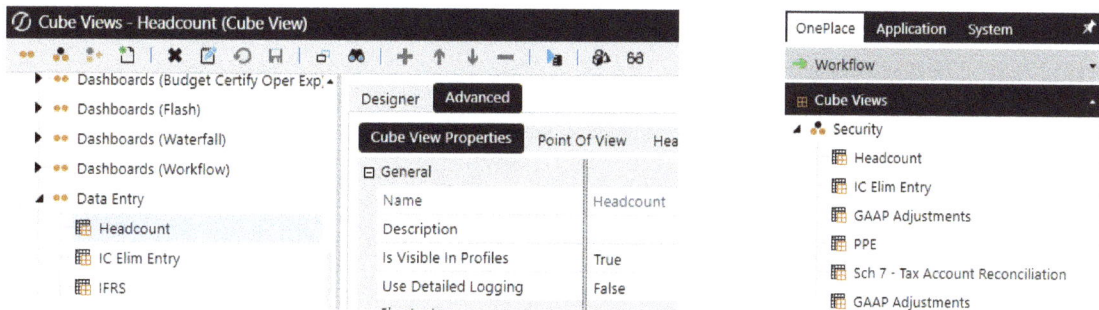

Figure 9.29

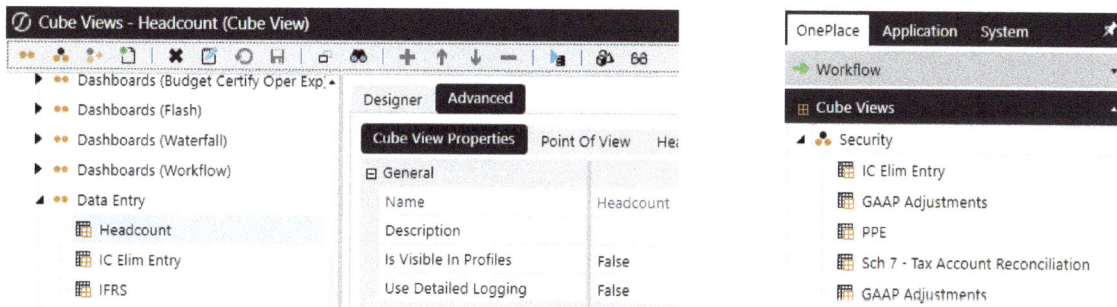

Figure 9.30

On top of ensuring the correct security is set for accessing Cube Views and dashboards, both have **maintenance group security** that needs to be addressed on the profiles. Typically, this is an administrative or super-user function since reporting is an area of the application that needs to be heavily supervised when it comes to what the reports are producing.

Another area to address in Cube Views is allowing or restricting the ability to calculate or consolidate from a grid. Most times, we have users run Cube Views to display data, not to calculate. However, there are some instances where administrators use the grid view output from a

Cube View to run an on-the-fly calculation or consolidation. In these cases, you generally design Cube Views just for the administrators, with this functionality turned on. For the general population and any Cube Views being run for reporting purposes, you would turn this off to limit the number of calculations being run. This last piece of this type of access that allows the user to calculate or ultimately update data will tie back to the scenario they are in and goes back to one of our earlier checks on the scenario security settings.

To help tie all this together, refer to the illustrations below to show the object access on a Cube View group, security restrictions on a Cube View, and the security settings on the Actuals scenario (Figure 9.31). Here, you see how to restrict access on functionality; however, we need to realize that there is a need for a data loader to have their data consolidated for their workflow if they are loading multiple entities, or perhaps consolidating a certain parent when their piece of the organization is complete. This can be accomplished via the workflow and is, more or less, behind the scenes. Please refer to the configuration of calculation definitions in the Design and Reference Guide, as this is the best place to achieve this for a data loader.

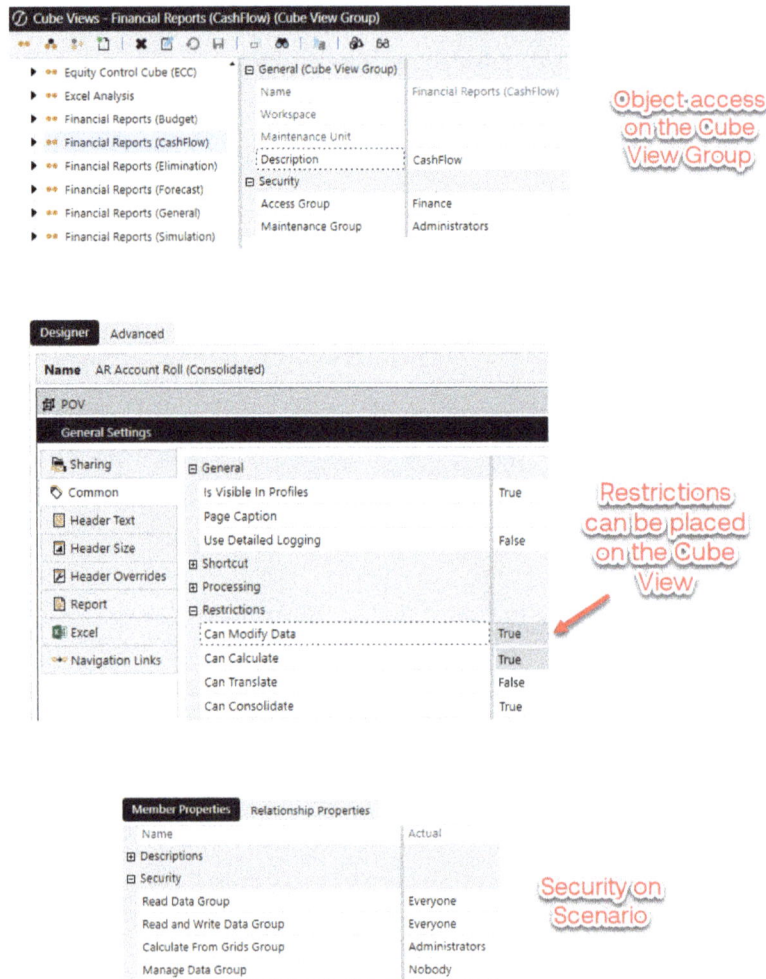

Figure 9.31

Additional Items to Note

We have discussed various types of users and security considerations that should be discussed as you are building out your application. As with most things in this software, there are multiple ways to go about designing how the different components of your application will look. Security is no exception!

I have gone through common user types in order to speak to the different areas of the software and how security applies to them. There are a few key areas where – depending on what you are securing or when you are securing it – you may find that applying access in the ways I have described is better achieved in a rule. A good example of this is 'slice' security. It is possible to apply data cell access via 'no input rules'. Refer to Chapter 8: Rules, for an example of how to do this.

In addition, if you have large amounts of transactional data and your design has taken you in the direction of using an Analytic Blend model with underlying blend tables, you will still be using OneStream's security related to the workflow. However, from there, you are restricting the data users see (related to what they are able to *view*, based on the relationship blend data they are presented with). There is more information on this in Chapter 12: Analytic Blend.

There are also ways to limit the information presented to users by leveraging text field properties in workflows. Using these, in conjunction with references to dimensions, you can limit the information that is on a form, for example. This can limit the need to create additional security groups for 'slice' security, if the form supports this type of reference and the workflow is configured correctly as well.

If you have a need to restrict the scenarios that are available to your users in the workflow, be sure to design and build out your application with the workflow suffixes in mind. These are settings on the individual cubes under Cube Properties. These are very important and need to be set at the beginning of an implementation and, most importantly, before any data is loaded to the scenarios. Please refer to Chapter 7: Workflow for a more in-depth explanation on this topic.

In summary, the above are configuration items that can secure access to data, without the need to over-apply security. It is important to understand what functionality is available in the workflow, reporting, rules, and all additional components of the software, so that the design and build of the application is configured in a way that the security is applied with those same considerations in mind.

A Deeper Dive into Data Access on Cubes

Circling back on 'slice', data cell access can only work on the premise that a user has already been granted access to an entity, and its data, before access is decreased to an intersection; from there, there is the option to increase levels of access to different intersections or subsets of data.

Earlier, we discussed how to decrease access on an intersection where access was already given. Sometimes, we find that we grant access via our conventional security model, then we need to take away access in large chunks before giving back specific intersections across the cube(s) in an application. This is where the order of 'slice' security becomes very important. When you know you will need to design for this type of security, plan for it carefully because the order in which you apply it, decrease it, increase it, etc., will ultimately determine if it is meeting the organization's needs.

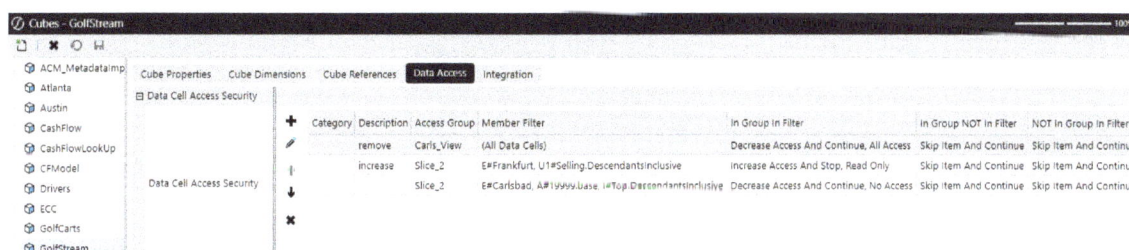

Figure 9.32

In Figure 9.32, we see three lines of data cell access 'slice'. Slice_2 group is being applied to both the second and third lines; however, the users in this group will never make it to the third line. This is because we apply this access in order, and by what the filter is telling the application to do. In this case, the filter on the second line is saying if the user is In Group In Filter, Increase Access and Stop, Read Only. The Stop action tells us not to look for any additional 'slice' security for this user. This is where the order and the actions in the filter are very important. Also, note again that the dimensions that you are designing slice around, need to be applied on *all* of the cubes where those dimensions exist.

Data cell conditional input should not be confused with 'slice' security, as you are not designing this with specific users in mind; this impacts EVERYONE. Data cell conditional input is generally used when you need to set conditions around input for a particular intersection. Quite often, we see *time* introduced here. As with most historical input, data is loaded into accounts or unique dimensions that are used for past reporting and are no longer valid for input. Once data tie out exercises are complete, you can then restrict access to accounts, flows, etc., that are no longer in use.

Conclusion

By now, I hope I have convinced you that you should be planning your security model as you plan out your processes (including workflow), metadata model, reporting, and – of course – types of users. Certainly, there are more items to design security around, but these are the essentials as we think about contributors, consumers, and admins.

By going through the use cases in this chapter, I hope I have illustrated how the different types of security are applied – and work together – so that there is no need to over-apply security in an application. By designing security in a consistent manner, the handoff of security to your administrators should be relatively easy. Consistent naming conventions, which you may have picked up on (above), along with keeping to a reliable methodology, will be key. Remember to look for security-specific references in other chapters for more detailed design guidance relative to each of those areas.

Epilogue

It's not often you can say a company has an 'all hands on deck' mentality and can back it up. Throughout my years here at OneStream, I can honestly say that I have been a part of, and witnessed many times more, where this has been the case. A gentleman in this picture has been known to say in many meetings, "We aren't perfect, but we will work together to make it right." Here is my crew, and while none of us have worked in the same department together, we have worked numerous times on the same project to ensure that we maintain our mission of being 100% referenceable!

10
Reporting

Originally written by Jacqui Slone and Chul Smith, updated by Chul Smith

Getting data loaded into a flashy new system doesn't really mean anything unless you're able to consume all of that data in a meaningful, easy-to-read, and elegant manner. OneStream has an abundance of ways to present information, based on the customer-provided reporting requirements.

So, what are reporting requirements? Simply put, customers answer the question, *"When* do *which* users need to view *what* data?"*

These requirements will obviously include the monthly, quarterly, and yearly reporting packages at varying levels, depending on the audience, but they'll also include any data to be reviewed throughout the various data submission processes. In a nutshell, reporting requirements answer *when*, *who*, and *what*. Together, you need to determine the 'how and where' and recommend the best methods – there are usually more than one – to present the data, given those requirements.

Determining the Reports to Build

Prior to endorsing any reporting methods, you must determine all of the reports you need to build. To do that, I recommend building a **report inventory** of every report, big or small, that users view at any point within (or upon completion of) their data submission process.

A customer with 13 business units produces a balance sheet, income statement, and statement of cash flows for each BU, along with a fully consolidated version of each. The 13 BUs plus the consolidated version equates to 42 reports! After a bit of analysis, all of the rows and columns are the same for these reports, with the differentiator being the BU. You would know to narrow this down to three reports, with some type of mechanism to vary by BU (which will be covered later in this chapter).

In another example, a customer may have a user who enters long-term debt rollforward data into a form. That user must look at some type of report to ensure that the data entered validates to the activity of each of the accounts. You have several options to make this user's process less painful (assuming we all think manual data entry can be somewhat painful). You could present a report showing the validation, or you could build that validation directly into the form so the user can view it in real time as they enter data. Either way, these are Cube Views, and you know that they should be presented to the user while they're entering data rather than letting them get three steps further into the process to ultimately discover that they need to go back three steps to correct an error.

A final example could enable a planning user to view a full report of KPIs just as they're updating driver data in one of their forecasting models.

Include any visuals, charts, or graphs in the report inventory that will be required in annual reports, executive decks, or self-service dashboards for end-users. Many projects prioritize visuals lower on the list due to them being 'nice to have'. I would argue that visual data provides clarity to a dataset and should, therefore, be prioritized like any other element. Yes, the visual underbelly is the data itself, but I would much rather look at a trending line graph than a matrix full of numbers.

The bottom line is that *the more complete the inventory*, the better the analysis and results of what reports need to be built, how they'll be organized, and when they'll be presented to the user.

283

Evaluating Reporting Options

Now that you've got a complete listing of all reports that need to be built, you need to determine and recommend the most optimal way of presenting them to their respective audiences.

The first question to ask is, "Will the users of this report have a OneStream license and have the ability to interact with the data?" This will lead you down one of two paths: one path grants the user the control to view, navigate through, and explore data as they're trying to understand and interpret it; the other path results in a package of static, predefined reports that may generate questions upon which the user depends upon a licensed user to explain any detail external to the presented dataset.

Assuming that the user will have a license, the second question to ask is if that person will be submitting data *during* the data collection process or if they'll only be consumers of the data. This is important because it will drive out those reports that need to be presented at some point during the process. I'll explain further when we talk about Cube View groups and profiles.

Expanding on the previous section (where you determined that you have three reports), where should you build them – a Cube View or dashboard, or an Excel/Spreadsheet Quick View or retrieve? You have so many options; it's sometimes difficult to determine what's best for the customer. In the following pages, you'll read through the characteristics and capabilities of each to help you select the best solution for your use case.

Cube Views Overview

By now, you are probably familiar with Cube Views and when and where you use them. Maybe you've built some yourself and have learned (the hard way) some of the topics that will be covered in this chapter. From those of you who are tasked with building your very first Cube View, through to seasoned Cube View veterans, you'll hopefully pick up a trick or two.

Determining Cube View Build Items

You've got your report inventory, and you're ready to start building your Cube Views – but you'll need to hold your horses! You'll want to spend some additional time analyzing the inventory – just as you did when you noticed that of the 42 reports, you only really need three.

Look for similarities or consistencies in rows and columns. Maybe all of the trending reports start with the final month of the prior year and run through the current reporting month. Maybe the variance reports compare Actuals to Budget and Actuals to Forecast, but not both in one report. Maybe you notice that some variance reports have the same columns ordered differently, depending on the report. In all of those cases, you know that you'll need to build each of those column sets, but in the last case, you could challenge the customer to take this opportunity to standardize things by ensuring that columns are always in a specific order. If they're open to it, great! You've just lightened your workload.

While analyzing the columns, spend some time on the row sets, too. It's the same type of exercise. Is there a consistent, detailed account report? Is there a consistent, summarized account report? Are there KPIs or statistical reports that share the same or similar row sets?

Sometimes, consistencies and standards don't exist in the customer's current report inventory, but they're hoping that OneStream will help resolve this for them. It presents a great opportunity for you to help establish *standards* and simplify their reporting.

In addition to the rows and columns, also note the dimensions that don't change by Cube View. For example, the customer's balance sheet always looks at all departments because it doesn't make sense to them to break down by their Accounts Payable balances by department. If the department in OneStream is UD1, then you know that the total UD1 member will be used in the POV section of the Cube View. From a maintenance perspective, having the correct members set on the POV of the Cube View allows the Cube View creators to quickly know which dimensions will be listed or required in the rows and columns.

Report formatting may seem like a trivial piece of building reports when, in fact, it's generally the opposite. I've been on numerous projects where I've asked for the formatting requirements and then received the response, "Whatever is the default in OneStream is fine." Zero times has OneStream's default been fine! It's not that the default settings look horrible; it's just not how the customers want to see their data. You can customize the look and feel of the reports to suit their requirements specifically.

Headers are important because users need to understand the data they are viewing. It doesn't present well when all of the dimensions are listed out in the report name or page caption. **Footers** can be useful for page numbers, user IDs for who ran the report and when, etc. I think we all know the benefits of using footers. Consistent headers and footers across all Cube Views really give the customer their own customized standard look and feel to OneStream reports.

Another important standard for the customer to establish is the formatting of the data itself. Scaling, percentages (to how many decimals), and KPIs (to how many decimals) are all examples of those standards.

Why am I harping on at you to establish formatting standards so early in the build? Once the standards have been set, you can use dashboard parameters to format your Cube Views instead of formatting each one individually. Should the standard change at some point in the future – the customer wants to go from one decimal to two – the administrators only need to change the parameter, and it will flow through to *all of the Cube Views* where that parameter exists. No more clicking through each Cube View to update the formatting of data or headers! That will be covered later in this chapter as well.

Your customer has **scaled reports,** and they perhaps need everything to foot and cross-foot, so there's a rounding component. Believe it or not, this topic creates heartburn on many projects. The debate centers around whether you should store rounding data in the database or just in the Cube View. OneStream strongly recommends that you build *rounding into the Cube View.* If the customer insists on storing these amounts in the database, bogus members will be required to store the data. Complex business rules or Member Formulas will be required to calculate the rounding data. Both of these will impact overall application performance and potentially create hundreds or thousands of data points that hold no value. Additionally, any changes to the metadata structures will impact both the rounding members and the business rules. On a past project, a customer asked me to "bless" the rounding rules, but I was unable to do so since I strongly opposed the decision. Customers looking to stray from OneStream's recommended approach happens occasionally, but when it does, the customer needs to know, acknowledge, and accept that it's not a recommended practice.

The reporting options presented earlier in this chapter will somewhat drive where your Cube View build will reside within Workspaces. A Workspace is a framework for building software using software, creating a robust environment for developing products on the platform. It simplifies the development process and extends development capabilities for solution creators.

Workspaces store maintenance units and facilitate community development by providing an isolated environment for developers to segregate and organize solution objects. Maintenance units are stored, created, and maintained in Workspaces, which vary by dashboard project need and application.

If you determine that a unique Workspace isn't necessary for your Cube Views, they will reside on the Workspace called Default. In addition to Workspaces, you can create unique maintenance units to further organize your Cube View groups.

The decision to create separate Workspaces and/or maintenance units isn't critical to get completely nailed down at this point in your build. Cube Views can always be copied to a Workspace or maintenance unit should you realize that it would be beneficial at some later point during the build. I would advise that any time you copy a Cube View to a new location, you take the necessary steps to sunset the old Cube View. This ensures that your Cube View library doesn't balloon and begin to create confusion among administrators (and super users).

Establishing Cube View Components to Setup

OK, so you've now determined build items – row/column sets, POVs for each Cube View, formatting, rounding, and navigation links. Let the build begin!

Within your default Workspace and maintenance unit, start by creating **Cube View groups** that will contain your row and column sets. Sometimes, there are only two – one for rows and one for columns. But you may want to break these up depending on the different types of row and column sets. You want to avoid duplicating identical sets since it will not only potentially confuse the administrators but also increase the maintenance when changes are needed.

A second type of Cube View group will contain those Cube Views that will be presented during the data submission process (versus those that are run once all data is final). These groups are then added to Cube View Profiles where necessary.

Cube View Profiles can be defined as groupings of Cube View groups. You add these to Workflow Profiles to present groups of Cube Views to the user during their data submission process. For example, upon a sub-consolidation, the user wants to review the results for some key reports. Those Cube Views are maintained in one or more Cube View groups, but you add those groups to a Cube View Profile and attach it to the Workflow Profile step. Those Cube Views then appear in the Analysis section during the process (See Figure 10.1). This is why it's important to know which Cube Views will be run upon completion of the data submission process, and which ones will be presented during the process. I'll cover this in more detail in the next section: Organizing Groups and Profiles.

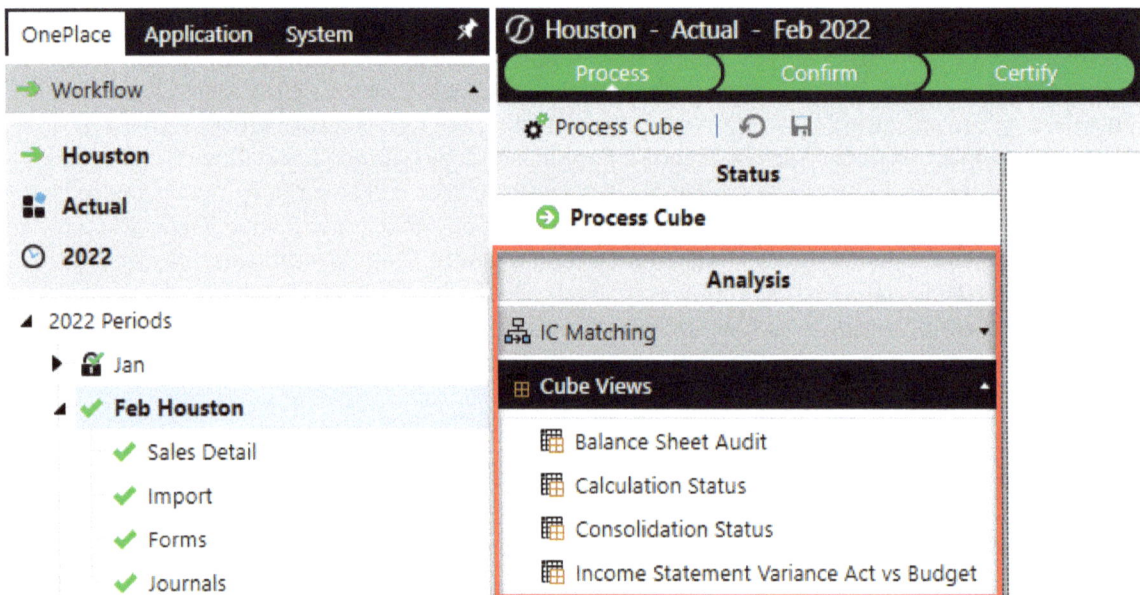

Figure 10.1

You'll also set up non-Cube View components that will aid you in building the Cube Views as dynamically as possible. As mentioned previously, you may want to create a customer-specific maintenance unit (and/or Workspace) that will contain the Cube View parameters that you identified during the report inventory analysis.

Again, two common uses for parameters are the pop-up prompts that the users select when they run the Cube View, plus the formatting text for Cube Views. You can put them both into the same maintenance unit/Workspace or create separate ones for each. Again, it's important that you've already established a logical naming convention for the parameters, the maintenance units, and Workspaces to ease navigation and maintenance.

The next couple of items were presented in the Business Rules Chapter but should be mentioned here as they'll likely be used extensively throughout the Cube View build. As a refresher, I'm speaking of **XFBR** and **member list business rules**. These provide an additional advanced mechanism for Cube View builders to create dynamic Cube Views. For example, take a customer column set that contains two columns – one for the current forecast and one for the prior forecast. The current forecast is anchored on the workflow. The Cube View should know what the prior forecast is, based on the current forecast – in other words, the user shouldn't have to specify both the current and prior forecasts; OneStream should be able to logically know the prior forecast based on the current forecast selected. This is where the XFBR business rule comes into play. You call the rule from column two and send the current forecast to the rule as a variable. The rule takes that variable (current forecast) and – based on the logic – will return the prior forecast.

In addition to XFBR business rules, you'll likely use a member list business rule to return the members you want to show up in a Cube View. An example of this would be if you're writing a Top 20 customers report. Maybe you want to list them out by sales in descending order. You would write the member list rule and, again, call it from the Cube View. It would run the logic in the rule and return your customers in descending order.

The thing to remember about these rules is that they run and return cube dimensionality. They don't run any data calculations; they tell the Cube View the dimension members from which to pull data, not the data itself. Should you need data calculations, you have a couple of options – **Cube View math** or **UD8 dynamic calculation members**. Which one is better, and when do you use each?

Before answering these questions, I'll define each of them. Cube View math takes one row or column and adds, subtracts, etc., from another row or column. For example, column one contains Actual data, and column two contains Budget data. Your variance (column three) could be set up with Cube View math that subtracts Actual from Budget. An example of it being used in rows might be taking an expense line in the P&L and dividing it by the total sales line to produce a percentage of sales line.

Alternatively, UD8 dynamic calculations can also handle both of the above examples. Most applications 'reserve' UD8 to hold these dynamic reporting members. The administrators create these members and write Member Formulas on each. The resulting data calculates every time the member is called in a Cube View rather than storing it in the database. As previously mentioned, dynamic calculations take any dimensions that aren't found in the Member Formula from the Cube View from which they're called. Going back to my variance example, you could set up an Actual to Budget variance UD8 dynamic calculation, and the Member Formula would subtract Actual from Budget. You could do the same with the percentage of sales example. You use these UD8 members on their respective rows or columns instead of None.

Back to the initial question, "Which one is better, and when do you use each?" Cube View math is straightforward and easy to read/write in the Cube View – no coding knowledge required! One downside of having to write it into each row or column set is that you could be writing this multiple times depending on the number of templates or Cube Views that require that calculation. This increases the risk that the calculation differs amongst them. It also increases maintenance should the calculation change. Additionally, all pieces of the calculation must exist in the Cube View in order to use Cube View math. I've seen many decks and reports that present KPIs without the underlying data from which they're derived. Using Cube View math to write a report like this would mean adding columns (as this cannot be done with rows) with the data used for the calculation and suppressing them, so they're hidden on the resulting report. By doing this, you've got columns of data that will never be shown but are necessary to provide the resulting calculation. This can confuse administrators and super-users who need to make future modifications to the Cube View. More importantly, it could negatively impact the performance of the rendering of the Cube View.

On the other hand, UD8 members contain Member Formulas, and you just need to add them to any Cube View. This method ensures consistency across all Cube Views using it. The administrators can also add a Member Formula for drilldown that provides end-users with the ability to see each component of the calculation should they drill down on the calculation. There's always a downside and – here – the administrators need to have some basic coding skills.

I lean towards using dynamic calculations from the start due to the benefits I previously mentioned. However, the use case and customer requirements can drive me to use Cube View math. I make three high-level assessments that help clarify this:

1. Do multiple reports present the calculation?

2. Are all of the components that comprise the calculation also presented in the report?

3. What does the report layout look like?

The first two points make sense, but what do I mean by point three? Take, for example, a report with Actuals in one column and the P&L accounts in the rows. In column two, the customer wants to show the percentage of sales on every row. Cube View math would be difficult in this case because the calculation differs on every row.

A second example (again taking a report with Actuals in one column and the P&L accounts in the rows) might present gross profit percent at the very top. You could use Cube View math or a dynamic calculation since either one easily produces the calculation.

An additional reporting question to ask the customer is if they want to display dimension descriptions on their reports in multiple languages – OneStream calls these **culture codes**. The maintenance impact requires the administrators to ensure that all members, Cube Views, and any parameters contain descriptions for all enabled cultures. It may also impact business rules or other elements that reference the member description rather than the name. This can be cumbersome but can be done given the requirement. OneStream recommends matching the Windows Regional Settings of the users' primary computers to what you set up in the OneStream configuration. The OneStream Cloud Team will need to modify the server settings on the application server configuration file for the culture codes to work properly. The culture codes do not apply to any native OneStream menu items, which means that users will still see them in English regardless of the culture code assigned.

To review, the components you will likely use during your Cube View build are Cube View groups, Cube View Profiles, a dashboard maintenance unit (and/or Workspace) that will contain parameters, an XFBR rule, and possibly some dynamic calculation members in UD8 or any other dimensions. You can set up all of these components as you build your Cube Views rather than building them all upfront. They're just things to keep in mind as you go through your build.

Organizing Groups and Profiles

As I mentioned earlier, Cube Views are organized into Cube View groups and Cube View Profiles. This section goes into more detail about how to think about the organization of the groups and profiles.

The two main drivers of how you set these up are usage and security. Earlier, I mentioned that you should set up one group for your row templates, and a second group for your column templates. This allows the Cube View administrator and any super-users who will be creating Cube Views to easily find them. This is one example of addressing the usage of the Cube Views in the group – they're all row or column templates that will be shared among other Cube Views.

Another group should contain the Cube Views that only the administrators will access – again, usage. Additional groups that fall into the usage category are groups that will contain Cube Views used during the data submission process. Depending on your workflow design, you may need more than one group for these Cube Views. It's also helpful to set up groups that will contain Cube Views in development or old Cube Views that are no longer used.

An additional factor to note is if the Cube View is specific to a particular dashboard or Workspace. The Workspace allows administrators to build sets of dashboards within an isolated environment, allowing developers to segregate and organize solution objects. This eases the migration process between applications. The administrator can extract an entire Workspace and import it into another application with confidence that all objects referenced within it have been included in the migration.

Finally, you should set up a group that contains standard reports that *all* business units will use once *all* data has been submitted. It may be helpful to set up additional groups by business unit (if each has a group of super-users who will build Cube Views specifically for their business unit) for data entry forms, for dashboard-specific Cube Views, for foreign entities, and for corporate-only reports.

Regarding security, each of these groups can be secured to grant access (who can view the Cube View) and maintenance (who can modify the Cube View). It's important to determine those two security groups because Cube Views *cannot* be secured by individual Cube View, only by Cube View group. For example, you don't want Business Unit B's super-users modifying Business Unit A's Cube Views. You also don't want any business unit super-users modifying any of the corporate or standard Cube Views. These would all need to be in separate Cube View groups. Another example would be having a group of standard/corporate Cube Views that the customer wants to allow only administrators to manage.

Once your Cube View groups have been set up and contain respective Cube Views, Cube View Profiles bring them together for use throughout the workflow. Maybe Business Unit C only uses the standard reports – you'd set up their profile and add the standard reports group to it. Business Unit A has their own group, but they also need to view the standard reports – you'd set up their profile and add the standard reports group and Business Unit A group to it. You can see that this allows for mixing and matching groups into profiles, so every business unit is able to run the reports specific to them rather than having to navigate through a massive list of Cube Views to find the few that apply to them.

Like groups, security can be applied to profiles. There's also a visibility property on profiles.

This allows administrators to hide the Cube Views within the profile from different places in OneStream (always visible, never visible, visible only in OnePlace, dashboards, Excel, forms or workflow, or a combination of any of these). This property applies to the entire profile, not specific Cube View groups or Cube Views. You may want to hide all Cube Views on the OnePlace Cube View pane and, in that case, would exclude OnePlace in the visibility property.

Exploring High-Level Advanced Cube View Properties

You have some advanced Cube View properties available to use, if applicable. These don't necessarily need to be identified prior to the build but will assist all users should you decide to use them. I'll highlight three of the most useful and common properties.

Navigation links allow users to navigate directly from one Cube View or report to another Cube View, report, or dashboard. For example, the customer wants to start with one of their high-level BU P&Ls, and from the sales line they want to see more detail by UD1 – you can build both Cube Views and create a link so a user can generate the detailed Cube View directly from the high-level Cube View. It's a way to provide some 'drill' capability in a more reporting-friendly way to both licensed and non-licensed users. Again, these are commonly used when users need to quickly jump from one report or dashboard to another.

List parameters in Cube Views are a handy tool to allow users to select from a dropdown menu to enter data that doesn't relate to any of the metadata. For example, the customer wants the data submitter to control whether a specific rule should run during the calculation of an entity. Perhaps they only want the rule to run prior to reviewing the results of that entity but not every time throughout the process. You need a mechanism to trigger (or flag) the rule to run. Since OneStream only stores data at specific metadata intersections, you're unable to store text like "run" or "don't run". Instead, the data could be a 1 for "run" or a 0 for "don't run". This can be confusing and not intuitive for a user to remember, especially in cases where the main data submitter is out of the office and the backup person needs to complete the step. This is where the list parameter comes into play. The administrators can set up a parameter that presents the two options from which the user can select. In the background, the data that's stored is a 1 or 0 based on the user selection (See Figure 10.2).

Figure 10.2

The last component to keep in mind is **Cube View Extender rules** that were covered in the Rules Chapter. A number of use cases would include advanced formatting or varying images and moving/removing headers or footers by entity or Cube View.

Basic Build Principles

This section focuses on common Cube View build principles. These aren't hard and fast rules, just more information for you to help make educated assessments and address your specific business requirements accordingly.

It's important to determine a standard **Cube View anchor**. This subject isn't as heavy as it may sound. Basically, anchoring is determining a common or standard way for your users to run reports. Different customers have different preferences, but if you mix and match anchors among Cube Views, it adds complexity and can introduce confusion for end-users. For example, in Cube View 1, the user knows they need to change their POV to see a specific dataset, while in Cube View 2 the user knows they need to change their Workflow Profile to see a specific dataset. Consistent anchors allow the user to navigate to their dataset regardless of the Cube View they're running.

The three main anchors are setting the POV to reference the workflow, the user's individual POV (right-hand pane), or a parameter that produces a pop-up window for the user to make dimension selections at runtime. There are benefits and pitfalls to each one.

Setting the anchor on the workflow allows Cube Views to use it as a reference for scenario, time, and possibly entity. The idea is that because the user selects a workflow to complete their work, the Cube Views they're running will likely relate to that workflow. By anchoring them on workflow, the users won't need to select these scenarios, times, or entities because OneStream knows they're *already* in the workflow. The downside of this is that if they're not in a month-end situation, and want to run a Cube View for a past time period, they would first need to change their workflow in order to see data for that particular time. At a minimum, any Cube Views used for data input should be anchored on workflow.

Setting the anchor on the user's POV allows the user to open their POV pane to select any dimensions for which they want to see data. Yes, it's simple enough to open that pane to ensure it's correct when they're completing their work; however, it can cause confusion if their POV is set to a time period for which they're not completing their work. So, you go back to anchor all data input forms on workflow. Now you've got some Cube Views anchored on workflow (data entry forms) and some Cube Views anchored on POV (reports or schedules), users will need to remember this should they need to go back to a prior period to view a data entry form.

Using parameters to prompt the user for dimensions at runtime is also commonly used. I would not recommend pairing this with anchoring on the POV. As a user running a Cube View with a prompt, I select the dimensions for which I want to see data. If any dimensions are left out of the prompt, I need to now go to my POV to select them. It doesn't make a lot of sense to require the user to select dimensions via two methods for the same Cube View.

I generally use a combination of anchoring on workflow with runtime parameters. This way, the user avoids ever having to go to their POV to select anything. I've found that users pick up navigation and running Cube Views much more quickly than if the customer prefers to use the POV pane.

> **Tip**: Speaking of POV, leave all dimensions that have been defined in the rows or columns as blank in the Cube View POV pane. This provides administrators or super-users with a very quick visual of what dimensions are going to need to be defined in the rows and columns. If you decide to accept my 'avoid the POV pane' suggestion, none of the row or column Member Filters should contain POV.

I shouldn't need to mention this next subject, but I will for the sake of completeness. *Build your Cube Views as dynamically as possible*. Granted, there are occasional exceptions where a handful may need to be hardcoded, but document them and ensure that the administrators know exactly which ones will require additional maintenance.

Sometimes, you'll build a Cube View, and it takes a while to render. The hot dog that rolled off the grill isn't the only situation where you apply the five-second rule. If a Cube View takes longer than five seconds to render, it's a good idea to see if you can improve performance by moving some dimensions around, slightly redesigning it, or breaking it into a number of smaller Cube Views and using navigation links to lead the end-user through them.

You've heard the term Data Unit several times throughout this book. The Data Unit doesn't only drive efficiencies in business rules, it also drives efficiency in rendering Cube Views. You want to minimize having Data Unit dimensions in the rows if possible. Challenge customers when you see this during your report analysis – maybe they'll be open to a slightly different layout: breaking some larger reports into several smaller reports, or using parameters that will return a smaller dataset that still satisfies the reporting requirement. It's not wrong to have Data Unit dimensions in the rows and, again, if the Cube View runs in under five seconds, you're fine.

A second culprit of poor Cube View performance is the nesting of multiple dimensions in the rows or columns. Granted, OneStream allows you to do it, and does it well with Cube View paging (for data explorer only). It really depends more on the design of the Cube View and the volume of the dimensions you're nesting.

If you're trying to return four nested dimensions of only 20 members, that's going to return a row set of 160,000 lines. Again, suggest some alternatives to try to minimize that. If the customer insists that the report needs to contain all 160,000 lines, I suggest you challenge them to show it to you. Any dialogue generally presents an opportunity to discuss the requirement and figure out a way to meet it in a different way.

A Cube View follows a very specific priority when it reads the dimensions for which to return data. It looks at the row, then the column, then the Cube View POV, and finally at the user's POV found in the right-hand POV pane. The minute it finds a particular dimension, it will use it. For example, if you've got a UD1 listed in the columns and in the Cube View POV, it will use the UD1 found in the column, not the Cube View POV. Similarly, if an account is specified in the row and column, it will use the account found in the row.

When you have dynamic calculations working in both the rows and the columns, you'll face a situation at the intersection of the two – so which one wins? Based on my statements above, the row formula – whether it's a dynamic calculation member or Cube View math – wins. This is where the row and column overrides come into play. The rows and columns contain several override properties by row. Using the row override in the column will use the column formulas for the specified rows. Finally, using the column overrides in the rows will use the specified formulas for the specified columns.

I try to minimize the use of overrides just for the fact that they're not immediately visible to any administrator; that person would need to specifically look for them on the Overrides tab. Ultimately, the priority is as follows:

1. Column overrides (found on rows)
2. Row overrides (found on columns)
3. Row Member Filters
4. Column Member Filters

Chapter 10

5. Cube View POV Members
6. User's POV Members (in the POV pane)

Simple conditional formatting is native to the application. Cube View Extender business rules are available for more complex conditional formatting. An example would be changing the logo found on the reports depending on the entity for which the report runs. More information about Cube View Extender rules can be found in the Rules section of the book.

Finally, native OneStream substitution variables allow Cube View builders to make their Cube Views dynamic. A full list of these can be found in the **Member Filter Builder** on the Variables tab (see Figure 10.3).

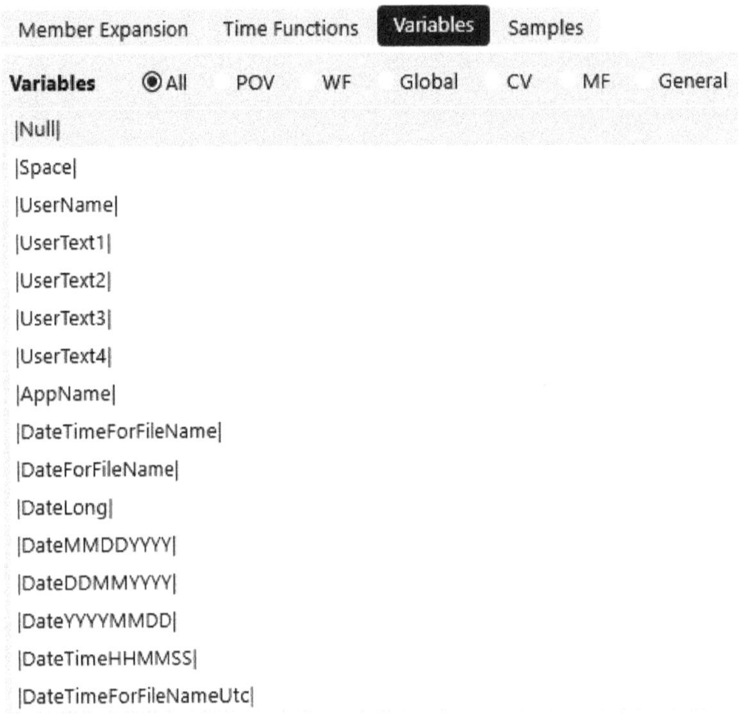

Member Expansion	Time Functions	Variables	Samples				
Variables	◉ All	POV	WF	Global	CV	MF	General

|Null|
|Space|
|UserName|
|UserText1|
|UserText2|
|UserText3|
|UserText4|
|AppName|
|DateTimeForFileName|
|DateForFileName|
|DateLong|
|DateMMDDYYYY|
|DateDDMMYYYY|
|DateYYYYMMDD|
|DateTimeHHMMSS|
|DateTimeForFileNameUtc|

Figure 10.3

The radio buttons allow users to quickly find the variable based on POV, workflow (WF), the Global POV (Global), Cube View (CV), Member Filter (MF), and substitution variables unrelated to the above (General). Common uses include headers, footers, and custom names for rows or columns.

Cube View Performance

I recommended a few common remedies for improving Cube View performance, but you've also got one last wildcard in the arsenal, just in case you've exhausted them: **application server configuration**. The OneStream Cloud team would need to change these settings.

There are a number of settings that can be changed to optimize the responsiveness of Cube Views (see Figure 10.4). This is across the entire environment, so if there are development, test, and production applications in one environment, it will affect all three applications.

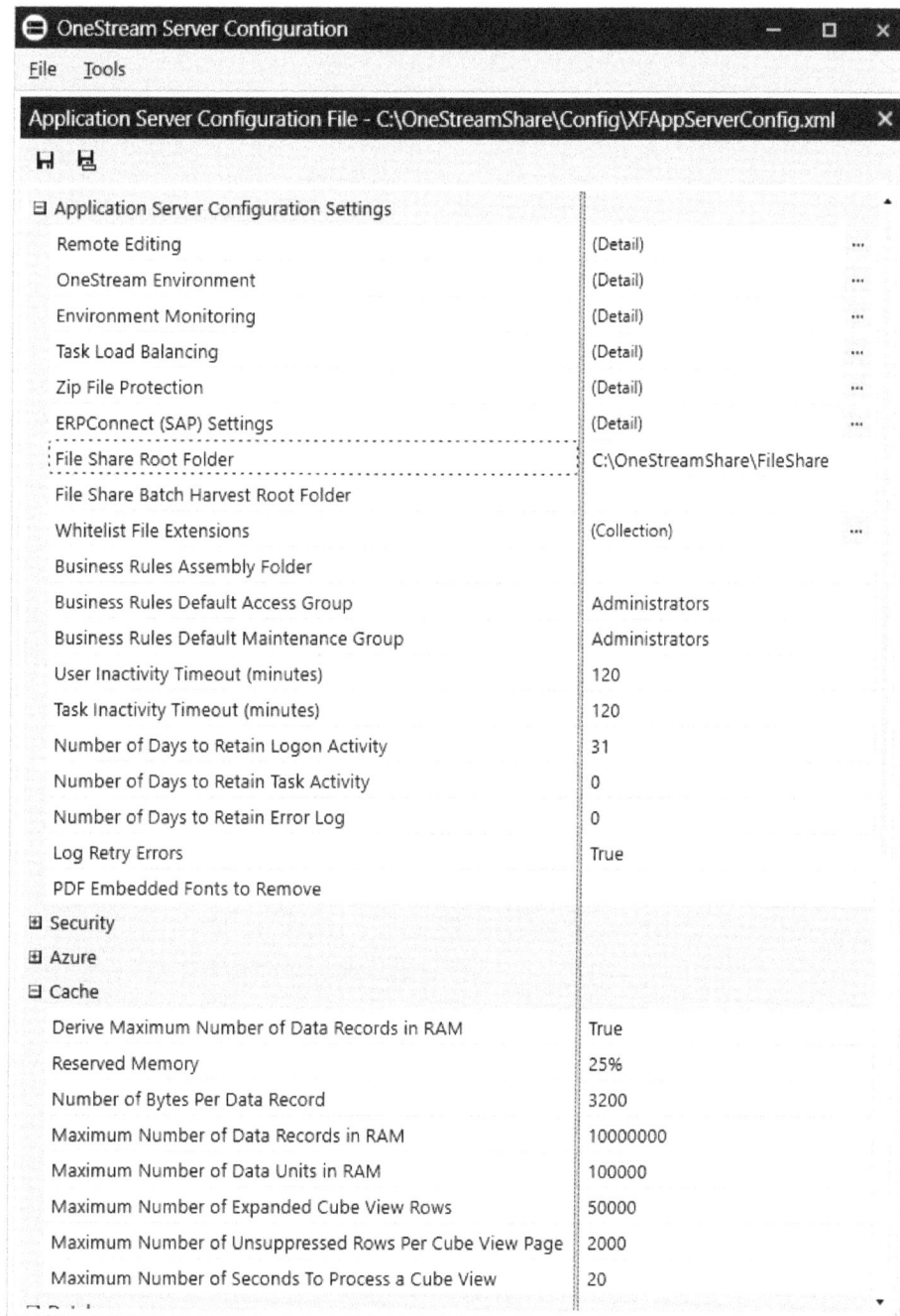

Figure 10.4

Dashboards Overview

OneStream dashboards are multifaceted and go beyond static data analysis. Dashboards provide additional functionality that far exceeds that of a Cube View or spreadsheet report. While those reports are very common in every application, dashboards provide additional reporting layers and functionality.

Dashboards use **data adapters** to generate higher-volume, custom datasets, and components to display the data and provide controlled user interactions. Parameters help make the overall user experience more dynamic in nature, and the dashboard layout displays everything in a comprehensible and user-friendly format.

In their simplest form, dashboards can house a variety of reports, allowing a user to tab through each one while doing analysis in OnePlace or a workflow. Dashboards are used to help administrators with application management, whether it is displaying audit information, workflow status, or running a series of automated tasks. On a more advanced level, dashboards provide detailed analytics using sophisticated data queries and calculations to drive results.

Given the vast possibilities that dashboards offer, and their 'choose your own adventure' capabilities, it is the responsibility of the dashboard designer to truly understand business needs, user requirements, and all contributing factors prior to building. The sections in this chapter highlight the pertinent information one needs when designing a dashboard, the logical way in which a dashboard should be constructed, and vital considerations that occur throughout the design and build.

Determine Dashboard Purpose and Build Items

Dashboards might not always be the first obvious choice when reviewing your reporting options. This is why building a report inventory (as discussed at the beginning of the chapter) is so important. Your inventory should include some detail about the report's objectives, user interaction, and anticipated outcomes.

Common reporting objectives that make dashboards a good contender:

1. **Data location** – the required data is stored outside the financial model or in an external database. This could also include multiple data sources where you need to blend different datasets.

2. **Multiple reports** – this includes taking a series of standalone reports and organizing them into one dashboard or displaying multiple reports in one dashboard view.

3. **User Actions** – this includes a high level of user interaction, such as filtering and drilling across multiple reports or modifying and calculating data.

Now that you've decided to use dashboards as a reporting tool and have an understanding of the dashboard's objectives, it's time to start drilling down into the requirements and nitty-gritty details. All dashboards begin with meticulous planning and a detailed blueprint. The more detailed you are, the better your dashboard-building experience will be.

Data Consumption

Your dashboard's reporting objectives are directly related to data consumption, which is the way in which a user interacts with a dashboard and its data. This is the basis upon which your design and build decisions are made. Based on your report objectives, define the intended audience and what they need to do, view, or understand from the content presented on the dashboard.

Static Analysis

Static reports require minimal (if any) user interaction and have a 'what you see is what you get' display. These are ideal for gathering a collection of reports and viewing them in one dashboard, as displayed in Figure 10.5. This could be used to create a financial report package for management analysis or assigned to a workflow task for accessible reporting needs. Users can easily analyze this data and navigate from one report to the next, but they cannot change or manipulate the view.

	Actual	BudgetV2	Variance
Operating Sales	23,907,690	11,290,849	12,616,841
Returns & Allowances	1,225,538	1,126,496	-99,042
Net Sales	22,682,152	10,164,353	12,517,799
Operating Cost of Goods Sold	10,843,753	9,966,058	-877,695
Cost of Goods Sold	10,843,753	9,966,058	-877,695
Gross Income	11,838,399	198,295	11,640,104
Total Employee Compensation	8,597,809	7,902,979	-694,830

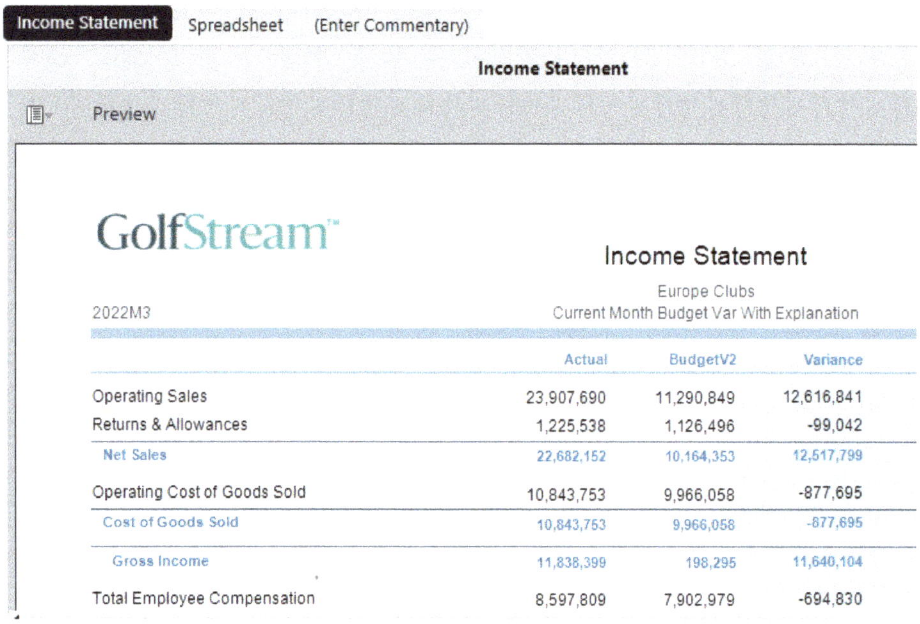

Figure 10.5

Interactive Analytics

Interactive analytics take static analysis a step further by giving users the ability to slice the underlying dataset into a variety of customized views. For example, the dashboard in Figure 10.6 allows users to modify rows and columns, drill down, and apply filters based on how they want to see the data.

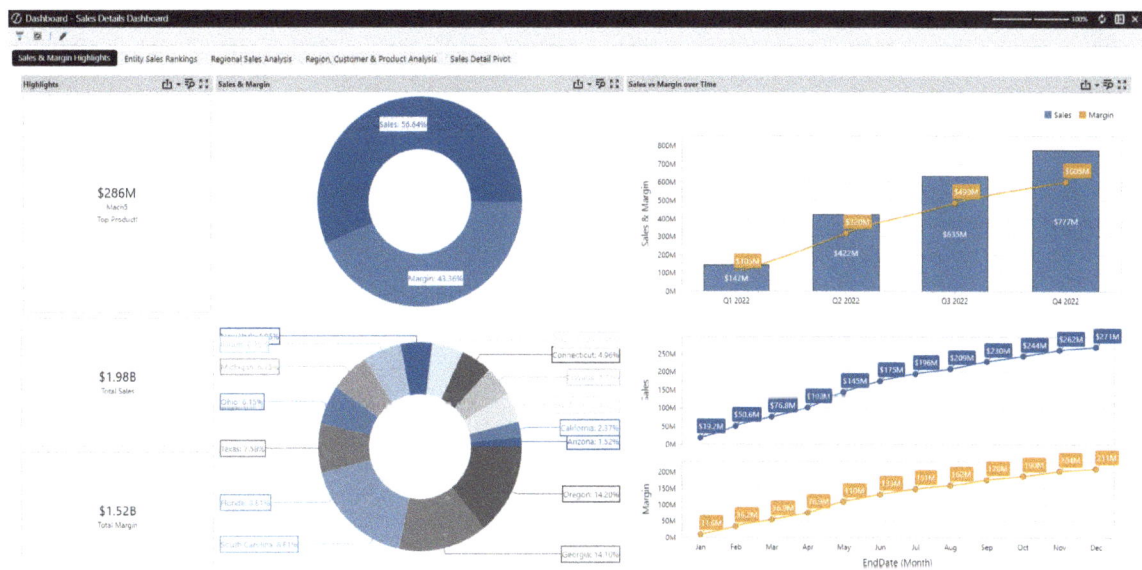

Figure 10.6

The dashboard in Figure 10.7 is another example of interactive analytics where the dashboard dynamically changes views based on user selection. The entity selection drives different Cube View results, and the selected Cube View data cell drives different source detail results.

Figure 10.7

Functional Interaction and Analysis

Functional analytics incorporate interactive analysis with actual business processes and tasks. You can provide a controlled way for users to modify and calculate data, run a series of system tasks, or navigate to other areas in the application. The dashboard in Figure 10.8 is an allocation form that allows the user to control multiple POV members, enter data, calculate it, and see the calculated results.

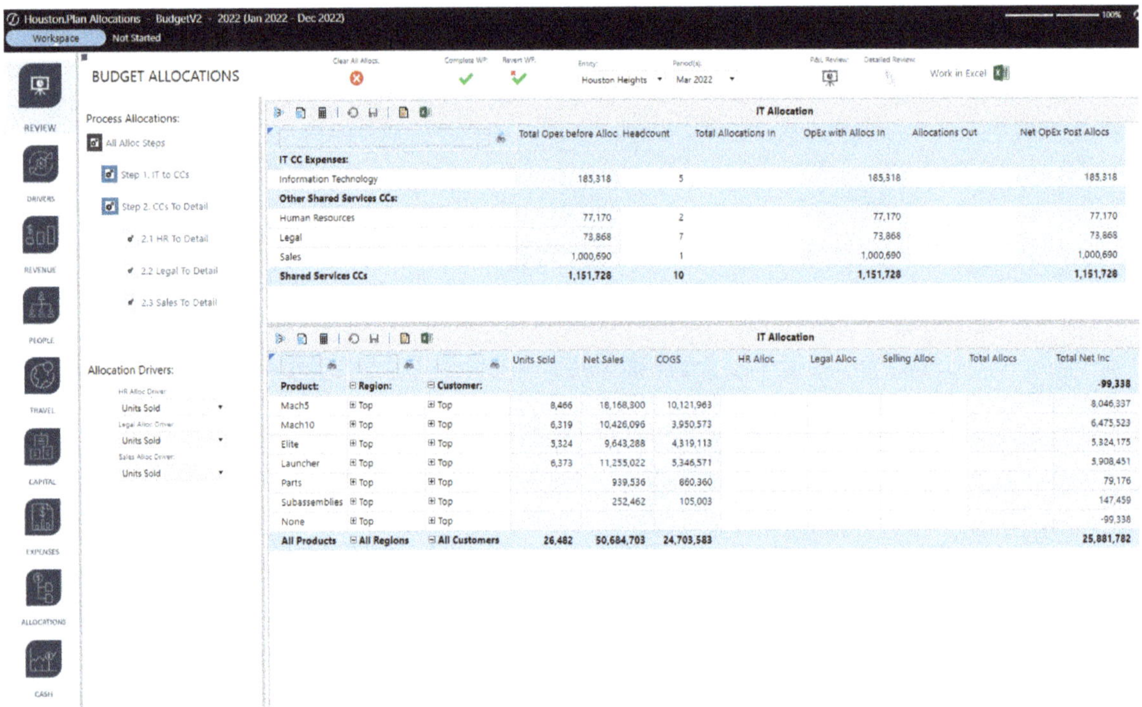

Figure 10.8

Data Requirements

Now that you have an idea of the kind of dashboard you need, it is time to take a deep dive into your data requirements. When analyzing data requirements, the first thing you need to understand is where the source data is stored. Dashboards can have multiple datasets derived from both internal and external data sources.

Data that is stored in the application or system database is considered internal. This includes data from the cube, the Stage, Analytic Blend, custom SQL tables, a Solution Exchange Solution, and status and audit information.

> **Tip:** Some internal queries require you to know if the data is application or system-related and the table(s) where this data is stored. Refer to the Database screen (see Figure 10.9) located on the System Tab for a read-only view of how the application and system tables are organized and the data fields in each table.

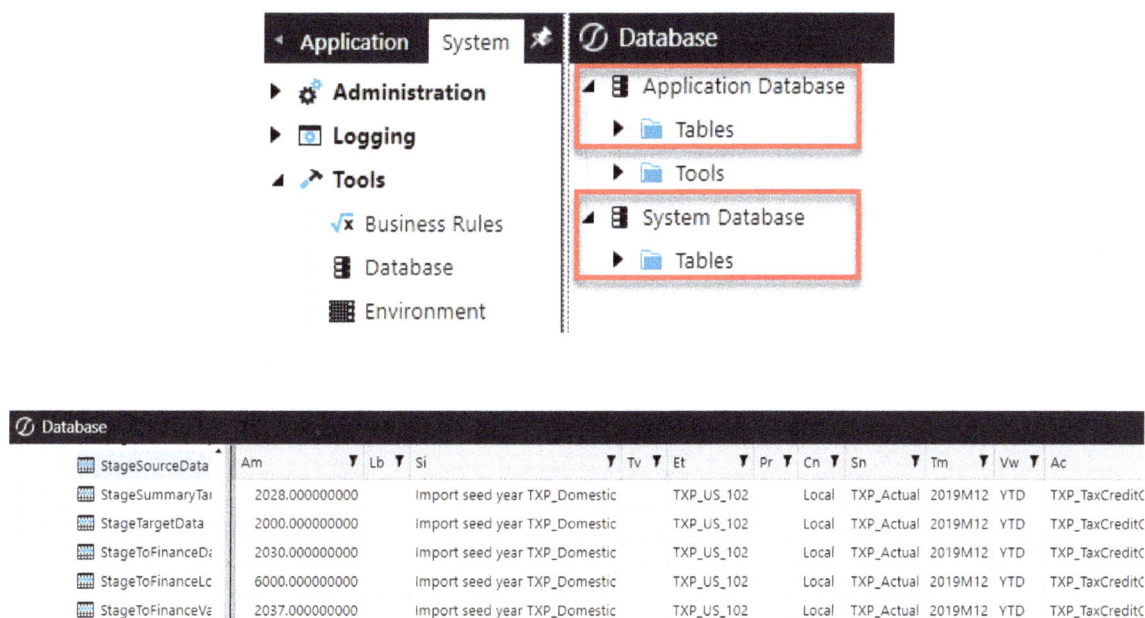

StageSourceData	Am	Lb	Si	Tv	Et	Pr	Cn	Sn	Tm	Vw	Ac
StageSummaryTai	2028.000000000		Import seed year TXP_Domestic		TXP_US_102		Local	TXP_Actual	2019M12	YTD	TXP_TaxCreditC
StageTargetData	2000.000000000		Import seed year TXP_Domestic		TXP_US_102		Local	TXP_Actual	2019M12	YTD	TXP_TaxCreditC
StageToFinanceDá	2030.000000000		Import seed year TXP_Domestic		TXP_US_102		Local	TXP_Actual	2019M12	YTD	TXP_TaxCreditC
StageToFinanceLc	6000.000000000		Import seed year TXP_Domestic		TXP_US_102		Local	TXP_Actual	2019M12	YTD	TXP_TaxCreditC
StageToFinanceVá	2037.000000000		Import seed year TXP_Domestic		TXP_US_102		Local	TXP_Actual	2019M12	YTD	TXP_TaxCreditC

Figure 10.9

Using data from an external source means the data is not stored in the application and is, therefore, dynamically queried from an external database each time the report is rendered. For example, you may want to use data from an external ERP system where the results directly relate to the application's data and provide a greater level of detail. By contrast, you may want to look at a more operational dataset stored in a blend database. The results may not directly relate to your financial data but could impact data assumptions or trends and change the way a user interacts with stored financial data.

External data queries require additional setup outside of the application. This includes creating a unique connection string via the **database configuration utility** and an external database connection via the **application server configuration file**. Refer to the OneStream Installation and Configuration Guide for more details on the setup of an external database connection.

Using multiple datasets is a typical requirement, and dashboards do not limit you to just one source. You can use data blending to query data from various sources such as Analytic Blend, custom tables, or cube and Stage to do analysis all in one dashboard. Data blending establishes relationships between the datasets to provide a greater level of granularity. For example, the dashboard from Figure 10.7, in the previous section, is displaying two distinct datasets: one from the cube and one from the Stage. The business rule in Figure 10.10, below, displays how the dashboard's data query was written using a dashboard dataset business rule and then called from a method query data adapter.

```
Case Is = DashboardDataSetFunctionType.GetDataSetNames
    'Dim names As New List(Of String)()
    'names.Add("MyDataSet")
    'Return names

Case Is = DashboardDataSetFunctionType.GetDataSet
    'Define Data Set Name to use for the Business Rule
    If args.DataSetName.XFEqualsIgnoreCase("GetFilteredNameValueList") Then

        Using dbConnFW As DBConnInfo = BRApi.Database.CreateFrameworkDbConnInfo(si)
            Using dbConnApp As DBConnInfo = BRApi.Database.CreateApplicationDbConnInfo(si)
                'Variable to get the user selection from a parameter
                'to pass into a SQL query
                Dim acctName As String = args.NameValuePairs.XFGetValue("AccountName", Guid.Empty.ToString)
                'Dim wfProfile As String = args.NameValuePairs.XFGetValue("WFProfileKey", Guid.Empty.ToString)
                Dim entityName As String = args.NameValuePairs.XFGetValue("EntityName", Guid.Empty.ToString)
                'Dim wfScenario As String = args.NameValuePairs.XFGetValue("|WFScenarioId|", Guid.Empty.ToString)
                Dim timeName As String = args.NameValuePairs.XFGetValue("TimeName", Guid.Empty.ToString)

                'Get the member formula changes within the time span and return results
                Return Me.GetSQLTable(dbConnApp, acctName, entityName, timeName)
'Create the data table to return
Dim sql As New Text.StringBuilder

    sql.Append("SELECT ")
    sql.Append("a.ac as Account, a.Lb as Description, a.ConvertedAmount as Amount ")
    sql.Append("From ")
    sql.Append("vStageSourceAndTargetDataWithAttributes a ")
    sql.Append("Where a.TmT = '" & timeName & "' ")
    sql.Append("And a.AcT = '" & acctName & "' ")
    sql.Append("And a.EtT = '" & entityName & "' ")
    sql.Append("And a.wsk = 1048578 ")
    sql.Append("UNION ")
    sql.Append("SELECT 'TOTAL' as Account, '' as Description, sum(a.ConvertedAmount) as Amount ")
    sql.Append("FROM ")
    sql.Append("vStageSourceAndTargetDataWithAttributes a ")
    sql.Append("WHERE a.TmT = '" & timeName & "' ")
    sql.Append("AND a.AcT = '" & acctName & "' ")
    sql.Append("AND a.EtT = '" & entityName & "' ")
    sql.Append("AND a.Wsk = 1048578 ")
    sql.Append("ORDER By Account ")


    Using dtSQLTable As DataTable = BRAPi.Database.ExecuteSql(dbConnApp, sql.ToString, False)
        Return dtSQLTable
    End Using
```

General (Data Adapter)	
Name	2a2_StageQuery
Workspace	Default
Maintenance Unit	Balance Sheet Analysis (BA)
Description	
Processing	
Data Source	
Command Type	Method
Method Type	BusinessRule
Method Query	{Blend_HelperQueries}{GetFilteredNameValueList}{AccountName=|ClickAccount|,EntityName=|ClickEntity|,TimeName=|ClickTime|}
Results Table Name	DataBlend

Figure 10.10

Dashboard dataset business rules are designed to provide more flexibility by combining SQL and VB.Net or C# into a customized data query, cache the dataset in memory for better performance, and – in some cases – are more user-friendly overwriting a SQL query directly into a SQL data adapter. This is OneStream's recommended approach for writing custom data queries in dashboards.

Dashboard datasets are used in conjunction with **method query** data adapters. Method queries provide another layer of flexibility as each predefined **method type** provides a set of variables and data results. This is helpful when building reports with custom datasets, and the required syntax and results can be tested during the data adapter build. Refer to the OneStream Design and Reference Guide for more details on method query syntax.

Any time you are querying data, internal or external, it is important to understand the data volume and how this could impact overall dashboard performance and usability.

Here are a few things to consider while analyzing the size of the dataset(s):

- How much data do you have in your data query results?
- Will this dataset grow over time?
- Are aggregations or calculations required to get the data results you need?
- Are there data dependencies, and does one dataset drive the results of another?
- Is the environment capable of managing high data volumes, and do you foresee any performance impacts?

This information is crucial to the overall functionality of the dashboard, which is why it should be done before you start building. If you worked ahead and discovered the original plan doesn't support the data requirements, it's not too late to go back to the drawing board.

Data Display and Layouts

Now that you've thoroughly assessed the data characteristics and how the user must interact with the data, it's time to plot out how all the pieces will work together.

If you have perused the various areas of a Workspace, dashboard maintenance unit, or have already built a dashboard, you probably noticed there is an extensive collection of components as well as a variety of layouts. As you begin planning out the kind of components to use and how the dashboard's layout should display these components, decide how each piece of the dashboard influences, modifies or affects another part of the dashboard and how this impacts the data. Determine the order of operations, the actions involved, and the anticipated results when the action is executed. This not only helps establish the components and layout(s) you need, it also provides some insight into the additional objects you may have to build outside of the dashboard.

If it's more flexibility you need, you can throw in some parameters and strategically placed business rules and – for a little flair – top it off with images, logos, and color palettes. This is where you and/or the group requesting the dashboard may need some willpower. It is very easy to get caught up in everything a dashboard can do, but that does not mean your dashboard has to do everything.

The dashboard in Figure 10.11 is the functional interactive example from earlier in the chapter. This was designed based on a functional interactive process. Each of the highlighted components control a part of that process and has control over other areas of the dashboard. For example, when a user selects an entity or changes the period in the combo box, the data in both grids update with the chosen entity's dimensionality and data. The user can then select their allocation drivers, enter data, and process their allocations as needed. In addition to choosing the right components, the way they are presented to a user should complement the objective and easily guide them through each step without errors or performance issues.

Chapter 10

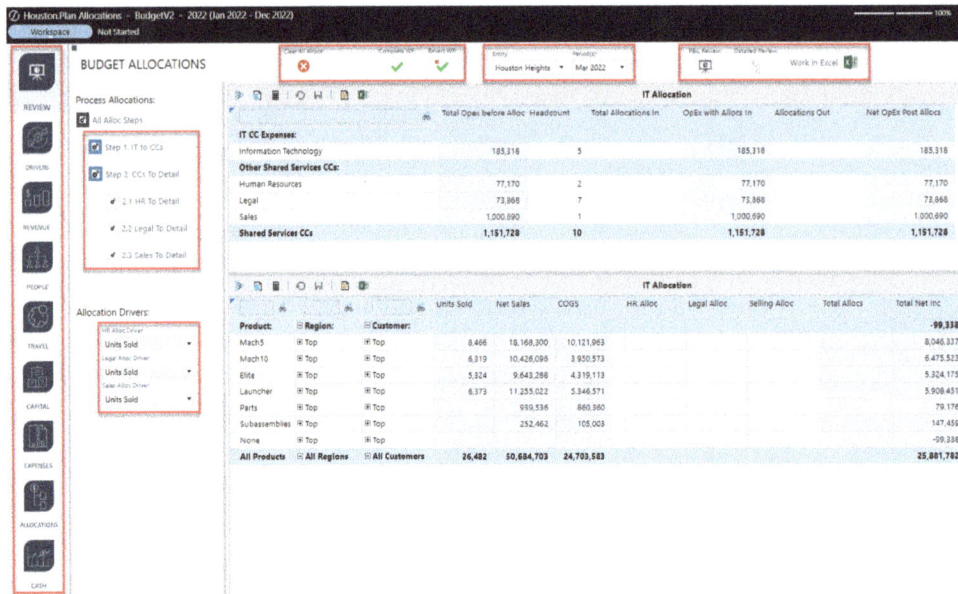

Figure 10.11

All dashboards have a specific layout, and like components, there are a variety of dashboard layout types that have different purposes and, for some, different display settings. The layout is the foundation upon which dashboard objects are arranged, and while it tends to formulate near the end of the design phase, it is actually the first thing you should build. Some dashboard layouts will only require minimal construction due to their data and/or user interaction requirements. These are more simplistic in nature because there aren't any dependencies across each dataset (as displayed in Figure 10.5 previously).

Multi-dashboard layouts require embedding a series of dashboards into one main one to create what essentially looks like a single cohesive dashboard. This kind of layout is common in dashboards that require an abundance of user interactions and, used correctly, can help with overall dashboard performance and tend to be more functional.

Designed and constructed properly, components and layouts can help control or avoid performance issues. However, if they do not support the data requirements or how the actions are arranged, you may run into some issues. When analyzing performance impacts, assess the query execution time, the amount of data loading, and the amount of data rendering. Some components, such as the large pivot grid, are designed for extremely high data volumes. The large pivot grid is used for interactive analytics and can manage millions of data records.

These 'simplistic' layout-tabbed dashboards can be easily constructed; however, the amount of data in each tab could cause issues when running a dashboard or when trying to navigate from tab to tab. Each report running independently might have little to no performance issues, but once you begin adding more data per tab, this could result in a slower analysis experience.

These types of performance issues will require some additional thought and design considerations. How can you minimize the number of data refreshes? This may be solved by embedding another dashboard into the main dashboard and specifying which one should be refreshed after a user interaction.

How can you display a large dataset in a dashboard that is meant to be more functional? This may be solved by using a list box component to align with displaying data in rows; however, it only shows slices of data to the user at one time, rather than everything at once.

Keep these benchmarks in mind as you confirm your approach:

1. **Administrative maintenance** – how much maintenance is required?

2. **Usability** – can users easily navigate through the dashboard(s), and is it intuitive?

3. **Performance** – is this the most performant design, and is it consistent with the growth of the dataset? Is there an alternative approach that provides better performance?

4. **Presentation** – is the content presented in a way that allows users to easily consume it and achieve their reporting/process goals?

These are the things you do not want to sacrifice, nor justifications as to why the dashboard isn't laid out exactly how it was requested or using a different process to get to the anticipated results.

Dashboard Build Principles

Workspaces were defined earlier, but how do you know if you want to create one specific to the dashboards that you're building? The benefits are best explained by the OneStream User and Reference Guide:

1. Isolation between Workspaces, which allows developers to work on the same solution or dashboard in a sandbox-like environment.

2. Greater flexibility among developers and other team members when testing, making changes, and planning.

3. Maintenance units, along with their objects, can have the same names in separate Workspaces and do not need to be renamed. This reduces the likelihood of naming conflicts, especially when importing and exporting objects from other applications or sources.

4. You can selectively share Workspace objects such as embedded dashboards, parameters, file resources, and string resources with other Workspaces. This lets you reuse objects rather than copying them.

5. Workspace objects can have the same names in different Workspaces.

6. Sets the foundation for future functionality and ongoing development.

7. Product packaging mechanism for creating, deploying, and migrating solutions.

From there, the main objects for your dashboard will be stored in a dashboard maintenance unit. The dashboard maintenance Unit (DMU) is a toolbox that organizes objects such as data adapters, files, parameters, and components, and which can store multiple dashboard groups and dashboards.

Begin by building the dashboard(s), and their layouts, and embed the dashboards where applicable. Once the layout is complete, begin building the dashboard items in a logical order; assign them to their respective dashboard locations and test them. This ensures each item is behaving as expected, and any issue is identified and resolved before moving on to the next section. The best option for building an embedded dashboard structure and layout is to start with one that already exists, copy it to a new maintenance unit and/or Workspace, and update it accordingly. Even if there are minimal similarities, starting with something of a shell beats the other option, which is starting from scratch.

Establish a universal naming convention. Naming conventions apply to multiple objects in OneStream, and dashboards are no exception. Developing this early on will not only make it easier for those who are building a dashboard but will also make maintenance easier if performed by a different group. The more sophisticated the design and layout, the more defined and consistent a naming convention should be. An effective naming convention will show how each object is related, whether it is assigned, embedded, or referenced in some way, and give a clear path to how any dashboard was built.

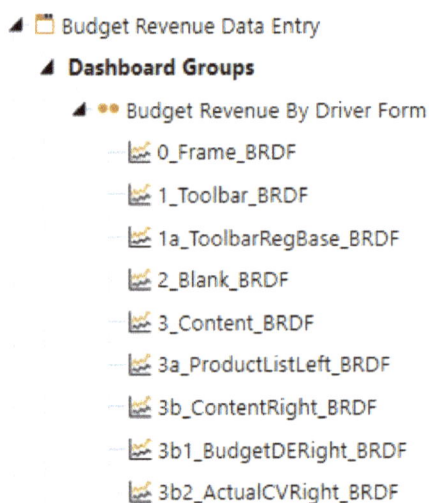

```
▲ ☐ Budget Revenue Data Entry
   ▲ Dashboard Groups
      ▲ •• Budget Revenue By Driver Form
         📈 0_Frame_BRDF
         📈 1_Toolbar_BRDF
         📈 1a_ToolbarRegBase_BRDF
         📈 2_Blank_BRDF
         📈 3_Content_BRDF
         📈 3a_ProductListLeft_BRDF
         📈 3b_ContentRight_BRDF
         📈 3b1_BudgetDERight_BRDF
         📈 3b2_ActualCVRight_BRDF
```

Figure 10.12

The naming convention in Figure 10.12 is only an example. Using a simple number/letter system, it is easy to identify the component and its respective dashboard, as well as how the dashboards are embedded. The `0_Frame_BRDF` dashboard encompasses everything and can be run to get a complete picture of how the entire dashboard looks and operates. The other dashboard prefixes indicate how these are embedded, making it easy to understand where modifications need to be done. Apply these same conventions to the other dashboard objects, such as components and parameters, to show their relationship to each other and to which dashboard they should be assigned.

In some cases, you might already have established dashboard maintenance units with universal parameters. These can be referenced by other dashboard objects or in other areas of OneStream, but if they relate specifically to one dashboard project, it is best to store them in the respective maintenance unit and have them follow your standard naming convention.

Keep in mind that the DMU does not always store everything associated with dashboards. Items such as data management sequences, Cube Views, and business rules are commonly used with dashboards, but can be stored, maintained, and extracted separately if they weren't saved in the DMU or Workspace of a particular dashboard. Files used for button images or headers may be stored in the application's file explorer or another DMU, and parameters might also be stored in another DMU. These add up quickly, which is very important from a maintenance and migration perspective. Include this in the project documentation along with the impacts and/or dependencies one might have on an object in the overall dashboard project.

Conclusion

As you can see, reporting requirements and report design all stem from the data and business processes performed in the application. Developing a report inventory provides clarity in your report build plan, and the more you can identify, the better. Establishing these requirements early on in the project will help prepare you in selecting the best reporting mechanism to use, and the most effective way to meet the needs of the user.

Epilogue (Jacqui Slone)

The Splash User Conference has always been a major focal point at OneStream. It showcases unique talent and expertise, and – year after year – it displays our overall success. The Splash bar is set higher and higher every year, and several OneStream teams work tirelessly to execute a show-stopping event. In the months leading up to the conference, it's easy to get wrapped up in the stress and chaos of it all. In the blink of an eye, the countdown goes from 12 months to two days, and then the plane lands and it's go-time. The months and months of preparing for Splash are done, and it's time to see the finished product in real time with a live audience. Every Splash happens so fast; there isn't time to stop and think about how tired you are, how much your feet hurt, how your OneStream shirt fits, or even how hungover you might be. Chicago Splash will forever stand out in my mind because – as I walked into the Navy Pier for the keynote – it made me stop and marvel at what OneStream had become. I have always been overwhelmed with gratitude for the OneStreamers who work so hard, and I'm thankful to work with such a great group of people. In that moment, standing in the Navy Pier, I remember thinking, "Look at what we did."

11

Excel and Spreadsheet Reporting

Originally written by Nick Blazosky, updated by Nick Blazosky

If you've made it this far in the book, congratulations! You are well on your way to creating your very own OneStream application. By now, you should have a fair amount of shape to your application. Dimensions, business rules, workflow, Cube Views, and – hopefully – some data to start tying everything together.

But even the best-designed applications, with the most sophisticated rules and a voluminous dataset, are not fully ready unless that data can be represented in a meaningful and concise way to your finance and business end-users. In many cases, despite the plethora of other reporting options, folks in finance like to create reports in Excel.

You could have taken 30 data sources in 100 different currencies and consolidated and translated them, but without having a way to view this data in the format your business partners want to see it, you might as well be speaking to them in a foreign language. It may seem silly – you did the hard work – why am I stuck in a meeting talking about the shade of blue on this report? You said blue, right? How was I supposed to know you meant cobalt?!

Back on one of my many field consulting engagements, I remember working for weeks on a specific calculation, creating a 35-step waterfall allocation of Budget data to replicate a downstream general ledger allocation. After the meticulous validation of every step, I remember finally reaching the point where I was pencils down, and I proudly announced that my work was complete in one of our team's calls. Well, that was short-lived, as I was asked to show my work.

I stumbled around in the guts of a financial business rule, various logs, and finally a simple report – showing that my starting amount equaled my ending amount – showcased the fact that my rule was successfully allocating data on these 35 steps! The client, understandably, was not impressed. The academic part of the exercise may have been completed, but without the proper report, it had zero value. The data was not digestible by the folks who I was building this for – the folks who were consequently signing off on my hours for the project.

If you have ever been in that situation, or you are new to CPM or the OneStream ecosystem, this chapter is for you. In fact, I wouldn't be surprised if you reviewed this chapter at some point before reaching this point in the book. The concepts we are going to describe are paramount for not only your business partners to get data out of OneStream but are equally helpful in your own efforts to validate data along the way.

I've also written this chapter to be helpful for those who, frankly, may not care or will not be doing the heavy lifting with regards to complex rules, FX translations, workflow, and all the other hard stuff you need to get the application up and running. Business partners and consumers of OneStream data, this chapter is as equally for you as for the technical architect combing over 100 lines of VB. These ad-hoc Excel reporting skills can be mastered by all.

There is no better way to learn about a OneStream application than by having to write reports against it. In my first job out of college (I was working as a consultant for a very large telecommunications behemoth that, at the time, was based in San Antonio, TX), I had no idea what this product called Hyperion Financial Management (HFM) was, or even the problems that it solved, but I was asked to author Financial Reporting (FR) reports.

It took a few weeks, but working in a converted broom closet with nothing but Google University and some legacy reports that were printed on green and white continuous paper, complete with perforated tear edges, I finally started to grasp exactly what HFM was reporting. To all the other folks working in converted broom closets who have no idea what OneStream is, this chapter is also for you. After reading this, and with a little practice, you too will be able to create reports worthy of replacing those dot-matrix reports you were given!

Understanding When to use Excel or Spreadsheet, Cube Views, Quick Views, and Table Views

Have you ever been to the grocery store, and your wife/husband/partner/passive-aggressive roommate asked you to pick up tomato sauce? Seems like a simple thing. "I need two 8oz cans of tomato sauce for a recipe." Easy, I got this.

So, as I'm wheeling my cart down the aisle, I see all the various canned tomato products. But wait, there are a lot of varieties when it comes to canned tomato sauce. Do I want to get the HEB brand or should I shell out the extra nickel for Hunts? Wasn't it my mother's Italian friend who said she always used Contadina? Oh wait, there is this new one from Italy, and something called passata that is like tomato sauce, at least according to Siri. Too adventurous? Yeah, probably, I'll just go with the Contadina. Now, should I get the organic (are tomatoes on the dirty dozen list)? Siri, are tomatoes on the dirty dozen list? Organic, good. What about with basil, garlic, oregano? No salt!?

Soon, you notice people in the store are beginning to turn their carts around in the middle of the aisle, mothers grabbing their children by their shoulders and instructing them to go down any other aisle – Any. Other. Aisle. – even the candy aisle. Why? Because you are there juggling four 8oz cans of sauce, mumbling to yourself, and debating the merits of each. As you slowly descend into madness, you finally snap and start piling a dozen cans of tomato sauce into your basket in the hope that this will satisfy the requirement for whatever dinner consists of.

So maybe this is the extreme example; hopefully, you were better prepared at the store than I was, but the concept of *choice* presents us with an interesting paradox. We like choice, but we are always afraid that with choice, we might make the wrong decision. Which is possible because, in this case, my recipe really needed tomato paste, not sauce. You live, you learn.

When it comes to ad-hoc reporting in OneStream, you've all seen the demo and read the guide (right?!) about various ad-hoc reporting methods. But which one is for me?

We are going to approach the next section as a sort of decision matrix to help you decide which tool is right for you. The more you understand what each tool does and doesn't do, the better equipped you are going to be to make the right decision when using ad-hoc reports. Let's walk through the Excel and Spreadsheet reporting options and try to understand which is the right tool for you. We are going to start at the macro level and get more specific as we go along.

Excel or Spreadsheet?

There are two primary ways to create **ad-hoc reports**. One is through traditional Microsoft Excel using a COM-based add-in that is physically installed on your individual computer. During this chapter, we are going to refer to this as the **Excel add-in** (see Figure 11.1). The other is embedded in OneStream and looks and feels like Excel, but it's not Excel. We call this **Spreadsheet**, and it offers Excel-like functionality, delivered inside of OneStream.

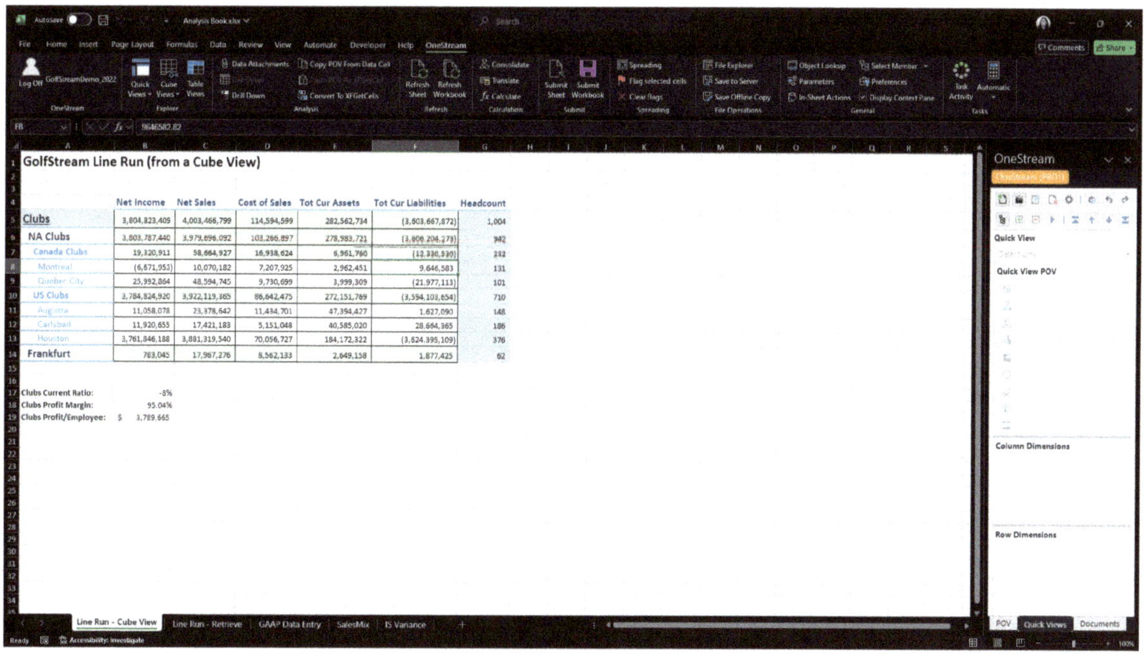

Figure 11.1

Let's talk about the Excel add-in first, and when you might consider using this. First, it's going to be a nonstarter if you, or someone in your IT department, does not have administrative rights on your computer to install the add-in. Think of your user community as well. If they don't have those rights, or your organization has a policy against these types of add-ins, then let's just say that this option is not for you.

The other thing to keep in mind about the Excel add-in is that it requires patching and updates. As you update OneStream servers with the latest version, you and your users are going to have to make updates to your individual machines and install a new version of the Excel add-in. It's a very simple update, but an update, nonetheless. For you, the administrator, and your immediate team, there is no reason you shouldn't have the traditional add-in, but when you are talking about rolling this out to 500 users, you might take a pause. Maybe I don't want to administer this for that many users. If that's the case, consider the Spreadsheet option.

Spreadsheet (Figure 11.2) is your other option for creating rich, ad-hoc reporting using OneStream data. It looks and feels like Microsoft Excel, with a few exceptions. The first two to note are that you can't run macros using Spreadsheet, and the number of shortcuts or hotkeys is slightly more limited than traditional Excel. A third consideration is that as of version 8.4, Spreadsheet's functionality via the Modern Browser Experience (MBE) is catching up to that of the Windows application. For example, it currently features limited chart types and formatting options but lacks Quick View functionality. Our product team continues ongoing Spreadsheet development for the MBE. The Spreadsheet examples shown throughout this chapter have been done in the Windows client. You can read more about the MBE at documentation.onestream.com.

The good news is that getting the OneStream Windows application is easy and doesn't require you to have administrative rights on your computer in order to install it, nor does it require a separate update. Once on the OneStream servers, or in a managed cloud environment where it's done for you, there is no need for a secondary update. It's a great option when you are looking to get the power of Excel ad-hoc into the hands of many users without worrying about crafting an IT strategy to support the roll-out of an installed COM add-in.

Table views are designed for reviewing, reporting, updating, and inserting new records into relational tables associated with the OneStream solution. The key word is *relational* tables. This is not the OneStream cube data. Think Specialty Planning data, or raw data used for the close and consolidation. Now, there are lots of ways to report or update this relational detail inside OneStream that we have discussed in previous chapters, so this is not the only way to get this detail. For example, you can use a BI viewer component that is linked to a data adapter in order to query the relational detail. This functionality is not unique, but you may find that this might be the easiest way for your end-users to internalize this relational detail. After all, it's essentially an Excel interface allowing you to query and update this data.

With table views, you must create a business rule in order to limit the query and control what actions you can take with the relational data. In other words, what tables you can query, what fields can be updated, and where you can insert new records. We are going to discuss this in more detail later.

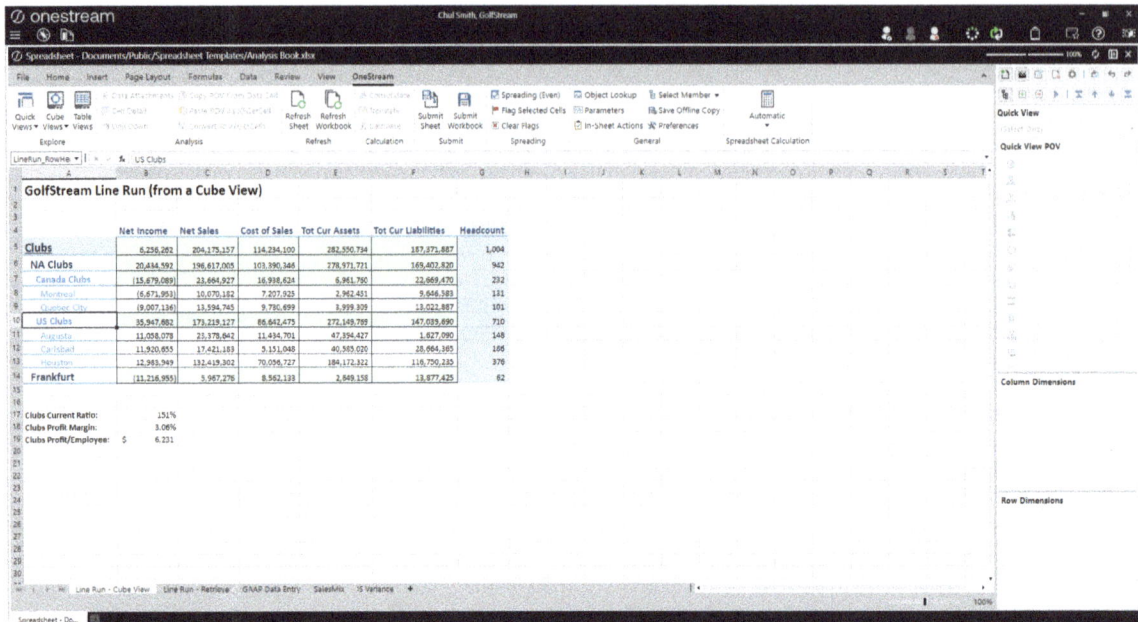

Figure 11.2

Spreadsheet files are also stored a little differently to Excel add-in files. In traditional Excel, you must save the file to a local or shared drive that you have access to. In most cases, when you create an Excel add-in file, it will be stored locally on your computer. However, since the Spreadsheet tool is embedded in the application, any file that you create can be saved locally to your machine, or can be saved directly to the OneStream server. In fact, you have a few different options when using Spreadsheet as to where you can save your file.

The **OneStream File System** is probably the most commonly used. Think of it like your C: drive on your computer, but in OneStream. It has a folder structure that is controlled by security, allowing me to save or open files in public or private folders. If you plan on using Spreadsheet, take some time to set up folders with security so people can save items there. A lesser-utilized feature – geared towards power users and administrators – is the ability to save a Spreadsheet component directly as an application or system dashboard file. This is handy if you are designing reports to be used as part of a custom dashboard, but certainly not for everyday ad-hoc use.

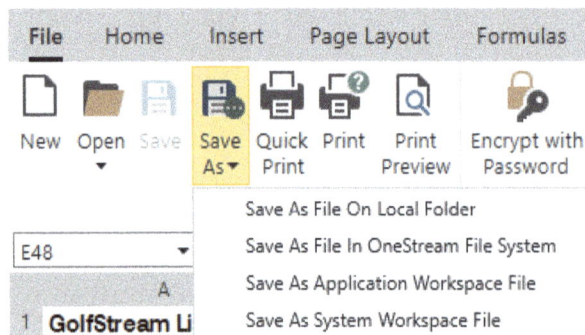

Figure 11.3

No matter where you save your files, and no matter where they were authored, files are portable between Excel and Spreadsheet. If you author a file in Spreadsheet, and then save it locally, and open it with the Excel add-in, that file will be supported. Likewise, you can start in Excel and move to Spreadsheet. I've done this numerous times and have had no issue moving between the two. I tend to be a little more comfortable using the Excel add-in, so I'll generally start designing reports there, and then move them to a Spreadsheet component.

	Excel Add-In	Spreadsheet
Quick Views	Yes	Yes
Cube Views	Yes	Yes
Table Views	Yes	Yes
Keyboard shortcuts	Yes	Some – But Not All
Supports Macros	Yes	No
Save as .XLXS file	Yes	Yes

Figure 11.4

As you can see, the choice of using Excel over Spreadsheet comes down to who, how, and what.

1. Who plans on using this? What control do they have over their local machine to install programs?

2. How do they plan on using macros? Do they live by Excel hotkey? Are they a master of Excel and only the real thing will do? If so, it is probably best to use the Excel add-in.

Cube Views, Quick Views, XFGet Cells, or Table Views?

You picked between Excel and Spreadsheet; now let's see what type of report is best for you. You have four options for ad-hoc reporting: Cube Views, Quick Views, XFGet cells, or table views.

We are going to approach this decision matrix a little bit backwards from the way we approached the decision on Excel vs. Spreadsheet. (Let's face it, you either have admin rights to install an add-in on your corporate laptop, or you don't.) For this, we need to dig into the functionality of each reporting tool, and that should help you decide what security rights we want to grant users, and what each way of retrieving data can do.

Cube Views in Excel or Spreadsheet

Cube Views, described in Chapter 10 can be leveraged in both Excel and Spreadsheet. Cube Views are one of the fundamental building blocks inside OneStream. You have learned that Cube Views are the basis for just about any report, data entry form, or dashboard you can author inside OneStream. Once you understand how to author Cube Views, you have a powerful tool at your disposal.

However, Cube Views in Excel and Spreadsheet can seem somewhat rigid, in particular for end-users who may not have the ability to update those reports. The POV, rows, columns, and even formatting are defined in the OneStream application. There is no interface in Excel or Spreadsheet that allows anyone to make changes that impact the underlying Cube View. All modifications to a Cube View need to be done in the OneStream application. This is partially because Cube Views may also be leveraged by multiple teams and multiple users. Cube Views can be used for data input forms, dashboards, or as the basis for data adapters for BI viewer components. They are not simply

Excel and Spreadsheet reporting tools. So, even though they may be available for you to use in Excel, those artifacts may be leveraged elsewhere.

Why might you consider using Cube Views for reporting? First off, it's an easy way to disseminate a large number of reports that have been pre-formatted to a poignant dataset in your application. As you will learn later, Quick Views are much more free-form, but a well-defined Cube View gets you data fast. Depending on the size and complexity of your application, it may be easy to get lost in your dimensionality. Cube Views eliminate that issue. You've *already* defined the POV, rows, and columns for your users to consume. They can simply bring the Cube View into Excel or Spreadsheet and use it for reporting. They can even use the POV of the Cube View as a jumping-off point for creating their own ad-hoc reports or Quick Views. In short, it's hard to get lost when you have a Cube View on your report. Figure 11.5 shows a Cube View in action.

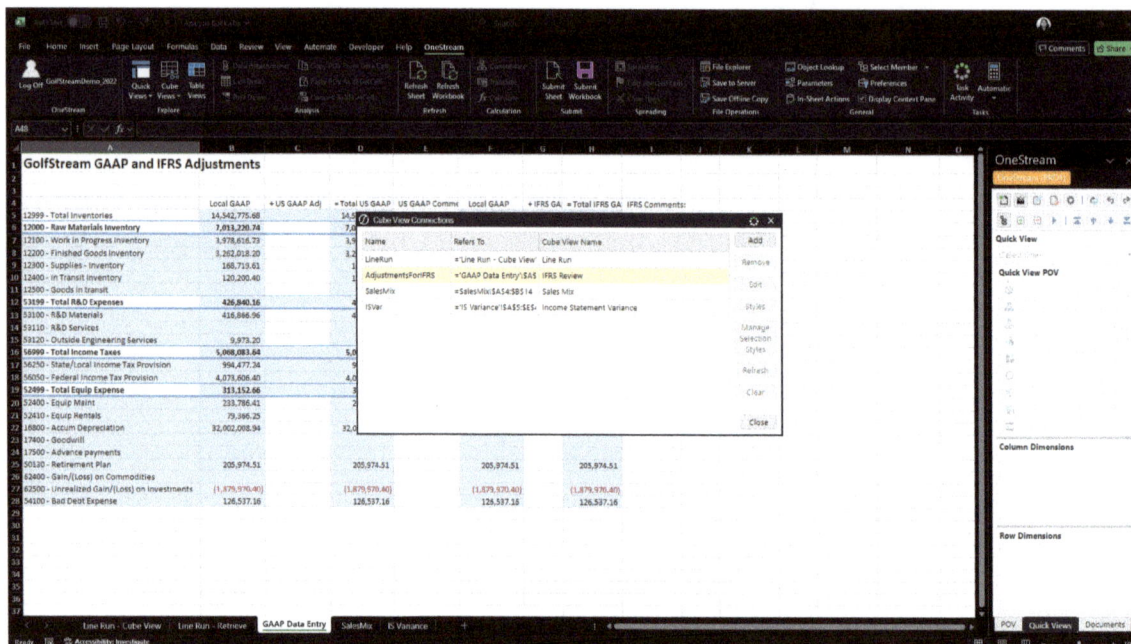

Figure 11.5

The other choice to consider, which is unique to Cube Views, is if you want to take advantage of the **retain formulas in Cube View content** feature. This feature allows you to take a Cube View and use a native Excel or Spreadsheet formula reference to derive a value that would be submitted back to OneStream. When enabled on a Cube View, this feature allows formulas in Excel or Spreadsheet to be retained on submission and retrieval instead of being replaced with the Actual value in OneStream.

The most common use case here is for an Excel- or Spreadsheet-based submission of Plan/Budget/Forecast data back to OneStream. In some cases, offline models previously built in Excel sheets may have already been created to calculate a value that needs to be submitted into OneStream. This allows those offline sheets to be connected to a OneStream Cube View, eliminating the need to 'copy and paste' values from those other workbooks in order to submit them back into OneStream. We will explore this in more detail later, but if you have a requirement for this type of submission – using formulas – Cube Views are your only option, as Quick Views does not support this.

Formatting is yet another consideration. If you plan on creating reports in Excel for a picky management team, I am going to advise you (strongly) to consider exploring Cube Views as your reporting tool of choice. And by picky, I mean if you know that the person you are going to produce this report for is going to call you into their office to discuss why the color you used doesn't conform to the corporate standard of "Customer First Blue." If you're rolling your eyes now and thinking of that exact person, I feel your pain. All I can say is that we have all been there.

One former boss of mine said that he was withdrawn from a potential promotion(!) because one of his PowerPoint presentations didn't use the new enterprise standard. Don't be that guy.

When compared to other means of reporting out data in Excel or Spreadsheet, Cube Views are the most highly formattable. When working with Quick Views, you are going to face limits with your formatting ability. It's not really meant to be for "boss quality" presentations. It's meant to be for looking into issues or variances, not sending to the CFO.

Cube Views allow you to select the font, color, background color, conditional formatting, number formatting, borders, and more. Essentially, any formatting options that you would have with any other report or dataset in Excel can be accomplished with Cube Views when you set them up.

The formatting of Cube Views in Excel and Spreadsheet is highly flexible; in addition to all the formatting options we described when you author a Cube View, they can all be overwritten with whatever formatting you want to deliver in Excel or Spreadsheet. This can go so far as having cell-specific formatting. So, if you have a Cube View and you want one number to show up in pink with bold text and in Comic Sans, you can do it (but please don't, because that sounds awful.) This is a big difference when compared to Quick Views, which are essentially limited to formatting three parts of the Quick View, which are row header, column header, and the data. With Quick Views, you – thankfully – can't highlight one data cell in pink with bold text in Comic Sans. All the data cells would have to follow that format, not just one as allowed in Cube Views. We will go into more detail about how to actually apply formatting a bit later in this chapter.

The last thing to consider – and it's a big one – is something I like to call the **asymmetrical grid** problem. Cube Views are excellent at handling asymmetry. When I set up the Cube View, I can define how many rows and columns I want, and what I want to reference in each of those rows and columns. In Quick Views, I'm stuck with one row and one column. That's not a bad thing, it can be quite beneficial from an ad-hoc perspective, but it does cause some complications on precisely formatted reports. And one of the biggest things, especially for those making the transition to OneStream from a legacy tool, is this concept of asymmetry.

What is the asymmetrical grid problem? Let's illustrate with a simple use case that you might have tried to author using a Quick View, to see where you may get into trouble and why you may want to consider a Cube View.

Let's say I'm being asked for a report where I'm looking at Actual operating income for March. That's a simple request; I can do that easily in a Quick View. It's one row and one column, and it will look something like this.

	A	B
1		Mar 2022
2	Total Operating Income	3,778,523,991

Figure 11.6

Easy, right? Let's expand the use case, and say that I want to view March compared to budgeted numbers. So now the Scenario dimension is coming out of my Point of View (POV) for the Quick View and into my columns. It's still a fairly simple report; we are still fine.

	A	B	C
1		Mar 2022	
2		Actual	BudgetV2
3	Total Operating Income	3,778,523,991	32,615,084

Figure 11.7

Let's make it a bit more sophisticated and expand the use case. We now want to have a field to show the variance between Actual and Budget. This is where Quick View can potentially start to break down on you. I have a UD8 dynamically-calculated member called `Bud Vs Act $` that I use to calculate the variance between Budget and Actuals. When I bring my UD8 dimension down to the column to show `UD8#None` and `UD8# Bud Vs Act $ (U8#None,U8#[Bud vs Act $])` I start to see some repetition in my data that I don't want for reporting purposes. This is what my report looks like now.

	A	B	C	D	E
1		Mar 2022			
2		Actual		BudgetV2	
3		None	Bud vs Act $	None	Bud vs Act $
4	Total Operating Income	3,778,523,991	(3,745,908,907)	32,615,084	(3,745,908,907)

Figure 11.8

Huh, you can see this is not really my intended result. Now, instead of looking at three columns for each period of Actual, Budget, and BudgetV2 – I'm seeing four. Why is that? This is what I call the asymmetry issue with Quick Views. Really, what I wanted was `Actuals`, `Budget`, and `Actual vs Budget`. That's it. But because I've introduced a new dimension into my Quick View analysis with two members, the Quick View will multiply by the two members that I added in. I've specified I want to see two members in my

UD8 dimension, `None` and `Bud vs Act $`; however, because I already have two scenarios and I'm adding two UD8 members in my columns, the Quick View will multiply to four columns. In this case, the Quick View has no way of knowing that I only want to see the UD8 member [`Bud vs Act $`] once. Remember, the Quick View only knows of one column set and one row set. For each column and row set, you get a one-Member Filter for each row and column. However, using Cube Views, I can achieve the desired results of simply having three columns. See Figure 11.9.

	A	B	C	D	E
1		Actual	BudgetV2		Actual
2		None	None		Bud vs Act $
3	Total Operating Income	3,778,523,991	32,615,084		(3,745,908,907)

Figure 11.9

How are we able to satisfy this in Cube Views versus a Quick View? We can have multiple columns and rows, each with their own Member Filters.

This is a simple example, but I guarantee that if you start working in Quick Views, you may run into asymmetry in some form or fashion. If you do, I'm going to advise you to move to a Cube View. There are a few tricks around how to do this in a Quick View (that we will cover in the Achieving Asymmetry in Quick View section of this chapter), but I will warn you, you are going to be writing cross-dimensional operators that sort of defeats the purpose of dragging and dropping dimension into your analysis.

Quick View also tends not to be the choice when you want to add blank columns or 'spaces' in between the analysis. Let's say I was satisfied with the way the Quick View looked (above in Figure 11.8), and I was ok with repeating data, but that I wanted to add a blank white column between Actual and Budget. I simply can't do that using a Quick View. Setting a blank white column or row between any range in a Quick View is *not possible*. You need to be thinking of a Cube View if you want to see a formatted report like the one above in Figure 11.9.

Quick View in Excel or Spreadsheet

We might have beat up Quick View a bit, especially compared to Cube Views, but they are a remarkably helpful reporting and quick analysis toolset that almost everyone uses. So, when are they useful, and when should I be considering using them?

Quick Views are best for fast analysis and are great for creating those one-off sheets that don't require the data to be highly formatted. There are three ways to create Quick Views. You can leverage an existing Cube View or Quick View to create one. You can create a Quick View from scratch, which will default your account in the rows and time in your columns. Or you can use the type-in method to define the rows and columns that you want, and select the Create Quick View button. Personally, I always try to leverage an existing report to create a Quick View instead of starting from scratch. It saves me a lot of time and frustration when searching for, and trying to define, the correct POV.

Quick Views have one row and one column. You must have at least one dimension present in each row and column. All other dimensions reside in the point of view (POV). This functions as a master view for the Quick View. You can only have one member in the POV.

A common confusion when speaking about the POV is there can be a difference between the POV and what is in the Member Filter. In Figure 11.10, the POV for Quick View is the member Actual.

Don't be confused by what is in the little funnel icon over to the right of the member. That is known as the **Member Filter**. That only impacts the Quick View when that dimension is in the row or column of a Quick View. Pay attention to what is inside the box to determine the POV. It will either show up in gray or black font. Gray means it's the default (which is determined by the user's POV), and black font indicates you have changed it.

The scenario is set to Actual for the POV, not Root.Children; that is the filter and has no impact on the POV. A filter will only impact the report when dropped into the rows or columns.

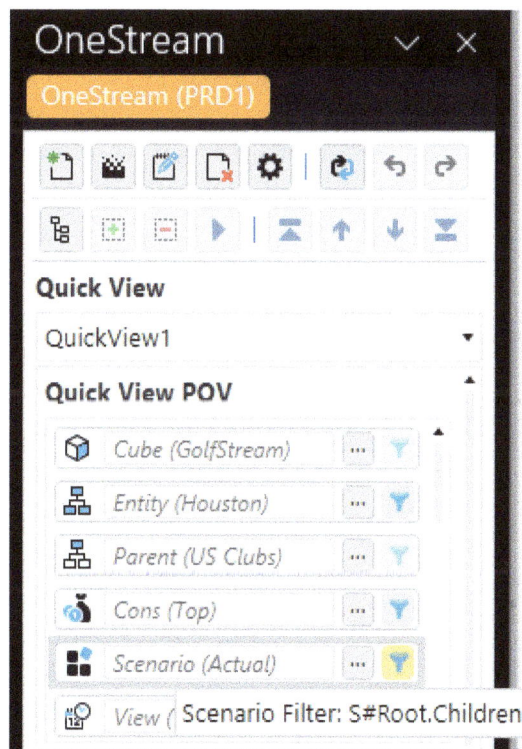

Figure 11.10

The asymmetry issue is what is probably going to be your biggest challenge when looking to use Quick Views exclusively for reports. Cube Views, as we noted above, are much better at handling asymmetry because they can have multiple independent columns and rows with their own unique selections.

The formatting of Quick Views is not as extensive as the options listed for Cube Views, but I think it's quicker and easier to create for the vast majority of reports. You are limited to formatting four areas of a Quick View, and you get to apply one format to each area. So, again, if you want to change one cell to be different than the rest, you can't.

To illustrate the four different areas you have the ability to control, I've highlighted the four different color areas in this Quick View in Figure 11.11.

- Orange – upper-left style

- Yellow – row header style

- Green – column header style

- Blue – data style

	A	B	C	D	E
1		Mar 2022			
2		Actual		BudgetV2	
3		None	Bud vs Act $	None	Bud vs Act $
4	Total Operating Income	3,778,523,991	(3,745,908,907)	32,615,084	(3,745,908,907)

Figure 11.11

Fewer options make things easier, and that is certainly true when I start to modify my Quick View. As I drag in different dimensions and expand my rows and columns, my formatting holds up. No need to go back and specify what needs to be done. My formatting simply follows suit. Figure 11.12 shows the same Quick View expanded; see how the formatting holds up even when we expand rows and columns.

If you have played around with Quick Views, you may think that your formatting options are limited to the list provided in the drop-down selection. And you are going to see some strange ones in there – like 20% - Accent1 – and wonder what those may mean. Those are cell formats that Excel and Spreadsheet have natively, and which are controlled through Styles in those products. The good news is that you can create your own styles for any workbook and use them. More on how to define those later.

	A	B	C	D	E	F	G	H	I	J	K	L	M	N
1			Jan 2022				Feb 2022				Mar 2022			
2			Actual		BudgetV2		Actual		BudgetV2		Actual		BudgetV2	
3			None	Bud vs Act $	None	Bud vs Act $	None	Bud vs Act $	None	Bud vs Act $	None	Bud vs Act $	None	Bud vs Act $
4	Total Operating Income	Top	7,405,937	913,992	8,319,929	913,992	17,774,251	3,524,186	21,298,438	3,524,186	3,778,523,991	(3,745,908,907)	32,615,084	(3,745,908,907)
5		Clubs	15,680,936	(2,101,414)	13,579,522	(2,101,414)	37,634,247	(2,224,275)	35,409,972	(2,224,275)	(63,661,371)	117,500,861	53,839,490	117,500,861
6		Parts	(106,481)	297,727	191,246	297,727	(255,554)	293,468	37,914	293,468	(425,924)	336,061	(89,863)	336,061
7		Subassemblies	16,188	28,526	44,714	28,526	38,852	29,173	68,025	29,173	64,754	22,698	87,451	22,698
8		None	(8,184,706)	2,689,152	(5,495,554)	2,689,152	(19,643,294)	5,425,820	(14,217,474)	5,425,820	3,842,546,532	(3,863,768,526)	(21,221,994)	(3,863,768,526)

Figure 11.12

The last thing to consider when deciding to use Quick Views relates to performance. Please turn on Sparse Data Suppression / Sparse Row Suppression for Quick Views. Really, this should be your default setting for ANY new Quick View. Even more so, if you have a very large Quick View that accounts for a number of deep, sparsely populated dimensions, you may run into longer than expected retrieval times. The only drawback to this feature is if you have dynamically calculated members, it will suppress them. However, you can override this on a Quick View by Quick View basis. So, it is best to keep it on and only turn it off as needed.

Quick Views, as the name implies, give your users a very fast way to create their own analysis of OneStream data. There are still several formatting options that can be deployed that are simple to maintain and manage. Certainly, you will be creating many Quick Views for analysis during your OneStream tenure, but know when to use them over Cube Views.

XFGet in Excel & Spreadsheet

XFGet functions are yet another way to get data out of OneStream using Excel and Spreadsheet. They are closer to Quick Views, as anyone with access to the Excel add-in or Spreadsheet can create formulaic retrieves using one of the many XFGet functions defined.

XFGet provides several functions that provide users with the ability to retrieve data, or certain properties about the cell, dimension, or even an FX Rate. I can also use XFGet functions to submit data back into OneStream through an XFSet function. For a handy, complete listing of all the functions available, select the Insert function button on your formula bar in Excel and filter by the category OneStreamExcelAddIn.XFFunctions. There, you will find the comprehensive list of XFGet and XFSet functions available to use, as well as formula helpers. See the following Figure.

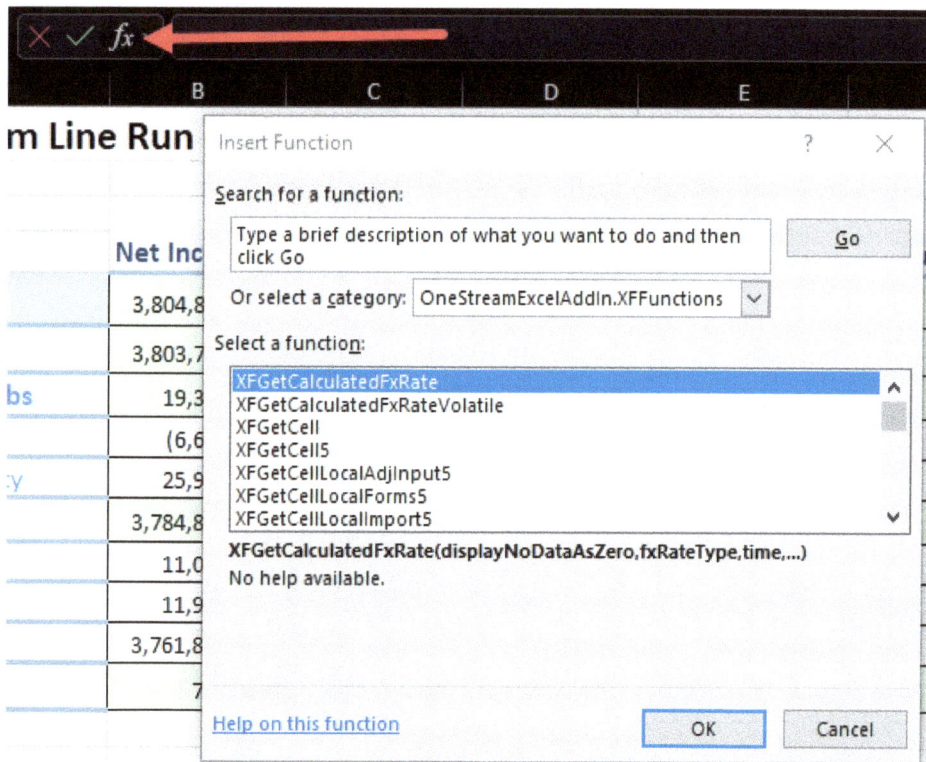

Figure 11.13

We are going to focus on XFGetCell functions because those are the most used and are the most helpful when authoring your own reports in Excel and Spreadsheet. Think of this formula like GPS coordinates. It allows me to create a precise retrieval for one intersection of data inside OneStream. You will need to define every dimension, otherwise the XFGetCell will not retrieve a value.

```
=XFGetCell(TRUE,"Houston","Houston","","USD","BudgetV2","2022M3",
"YTD","60999","None","Top","Top","Top","Top","Top","Top","None",
"None","None","PriorYearActual")
```

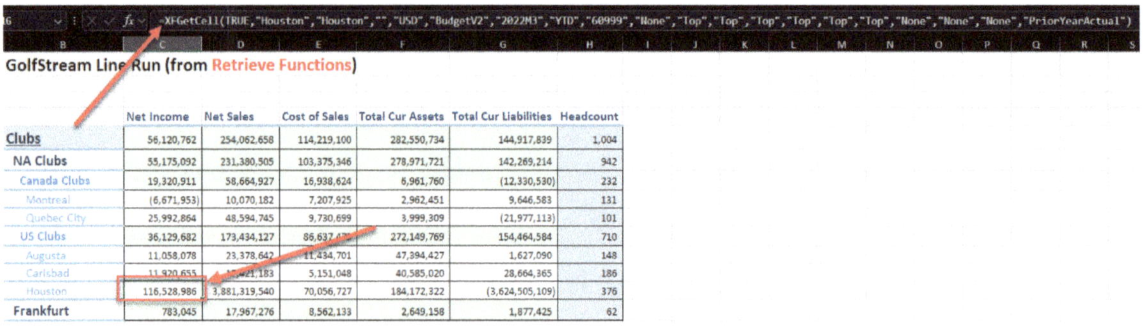

Figure 11.14

As with any formula in Excel, you can substitute cell references inside the formula instead of explicitly naming them. For example, if I have defined the Time dimension in cell C3 as `2022M3`, I can place cell `$C$3` in place of `2022M3` into the XFGetCell formula. This is handy when you have a lot of XFGetCell references on one sheet, and you want a sort of Global POV to control what you are looking at without having to update every formula.

The formatting advantages of XFGetCells are many, as they are treated like normal Excel or Spreadsheet formulas. Any formatting is available and will stick, based on the selections you make. They are just like any cell in Excel.

The XFGetCell function can also help with the asymmetrical retrieve issue we spoke about earlier that you may experience with Quick Views, especially if you are not going to have access to creating Cube Views.

Let's go back to our earlier example where we want to show three columns, not four, when comparing Actuals to Budget. A handy feature is that we can convert any Quick View into an XFGetCell using the click of a button. This function is called Convert To XFGetCells and is purpose-built for situations like this. Note that this can only be done once, and it cannot be undone. There is also no way to convert XFGetCells into Quick Views; at least for now.

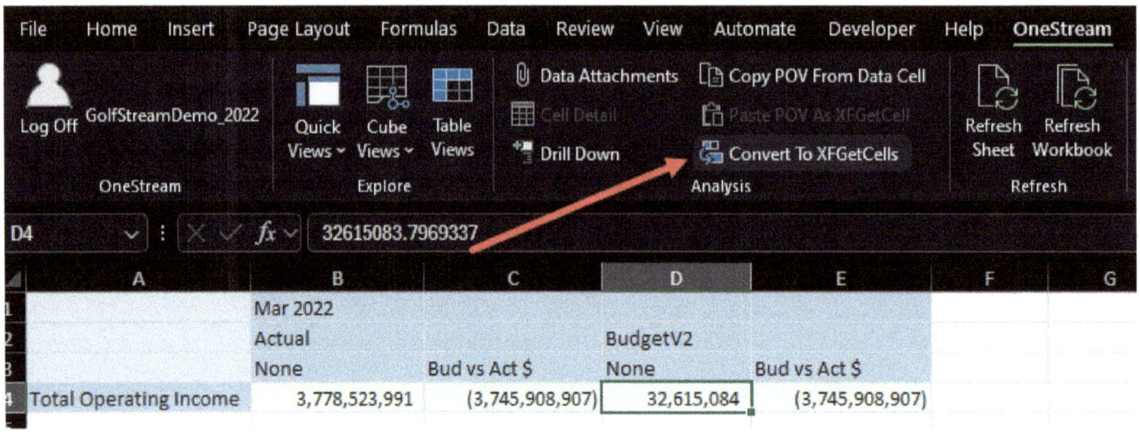

Figure 11.15

Once you convert to an XFGetCell reference, the Quick View reference is deleted, and a long formula is put in its place. The formatting that was on the Quick View is retained. There is no dependency on the rows or columns now; the cell now contains the complete reference. I am also free to delete any rows, columns, or cells, and format as I please. Figure 11.16 shows the long formula that was generated with little effort.

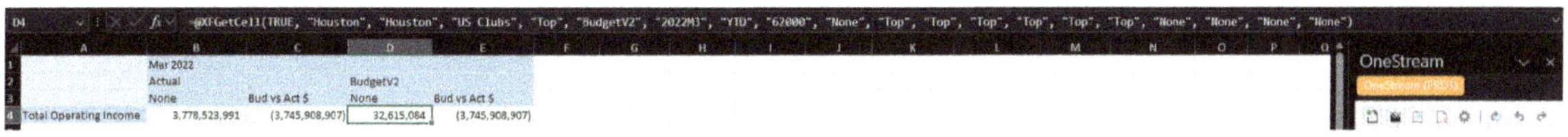

Figure 11.16

As you can see, I now have the formatted report (Figure 11.17) that I wanted, and I didn't have to create it using a Cube View.

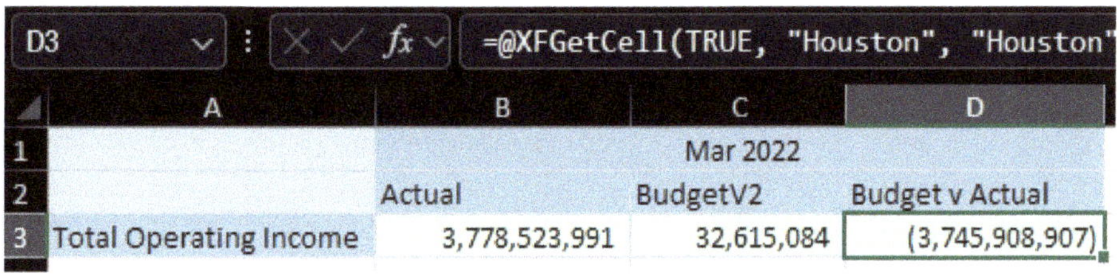

Figure 11.17

XFGetCell functions are a great option when looking for specific values, or when you have highly specific formatting requirements. Using a Quick View as a starting place is not a bad idea either, as this can cut down on the time it takes to author the report of your choosing.

As ideal as it sounds, using XFGetCells also has its considerations. The most significant deterrent is that they are static files, whether you decide to store them on a shared drive, your local drive, or the OneStream File System. This means that if mass formatting updates are needed or member hierarchies change, requiring report updates, users (or, even worse, the administrator) would need to update each individual file to reflect the changes. This can often be avoided by a smart use of Cube Views and the parameters within them.

Table Views in Spreadsheet & Excel

Table views provide the ability to read, update, and even insert records into OneStream relational tables. This is data that you might have in an Analytic Blend table, People Planning, or Thing Planning registry, or the raw source data that was used to populate the OneStream cube.

Think of it like this. Let's say we loaded in sales detail from our data warehouse by invoice, but we don't have an invoice dimension in OneStream (for very good reasons). If you were in Spreadsheet or Excel, and you wanted to see the invoice-level detail that you loaded in using our data quality engine, you can drill down to navigate to the source-level detail. This drilldown is querying the underlying raw data from my data warehouse that I loaded into OneStream, that I used to load and map up to my cube. This drilldown feature is a native feature in Excel or Spreadsheet.

For example, we have sales for the Mach5 product, for the Northeast region for the Golf Hub customer, for February. There were many invoices that made up that $431,463 sales number that we have loaded into OneStream, but we don't store all the detail at the cube level. So, we leave some of that behind in the underlying relational tables, which is a smart design move. Not everything belongs in the cube. However, we may want to look at details that we left behind in the relational layer. Enter **drilldown**. If we drill down into that result in Spreadsheet, all the way back to the source detail, we will see the raw invoice details.

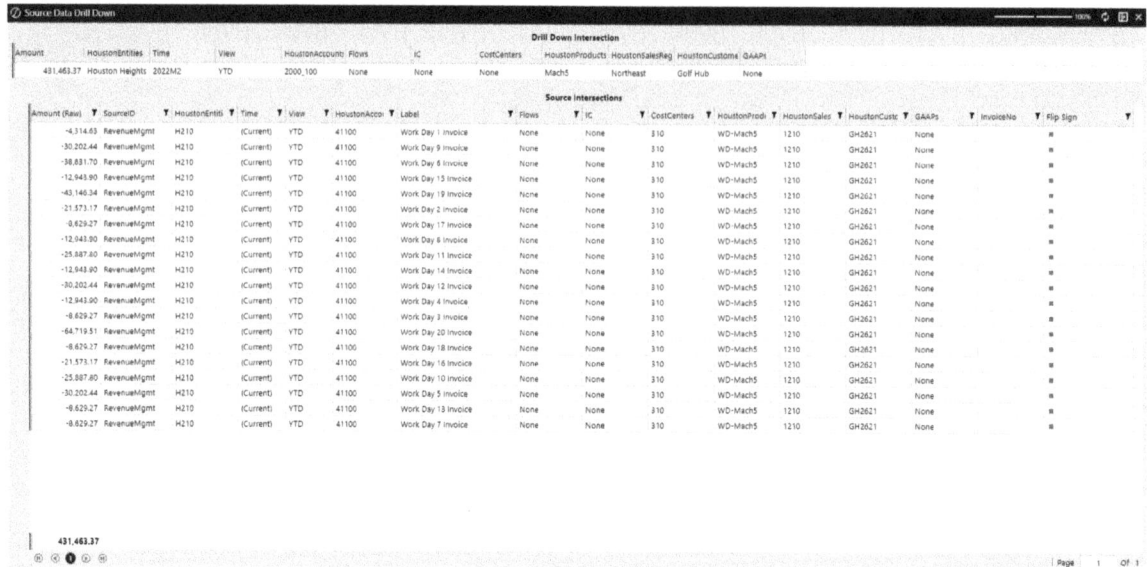

Figure 11.18

Above is a great report, but it took a little bit to drill into. Enter **table views,** which allow you to create your own query to look at the same dataset without having to drill down from the cube. Table view functions very much like a Cube View does in that it must be defined in the OneStream application first, and then be added to a Spreadsheet.

This is an example of a table view, which replicates the same query as the drilldown but is represented on the workbook and driven off parameter-driven prompts.

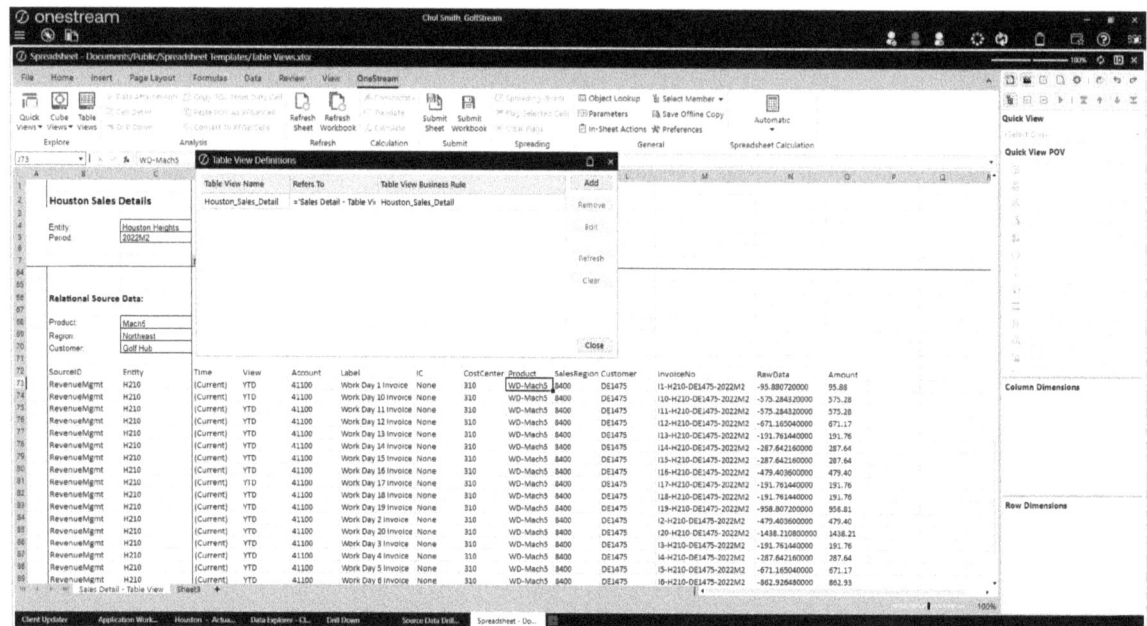

Figure 11.19

This is not the only way to query relational data inside OneStream. You can use a grid viewer or BI viewer component to report and update relational data as well. Table views is just another option and is embedded in Spreadsheet, which gives users more of that Excel-like experience to consume data.

Table views are not created on the fly. They must be set up as business rules, and users must be given access to the underlying table view rules. This is probably the most advanced option that we have discussed to date, if you want to set one of these up. You are going to need working knowledge of VB.Net or C#, SQL, and the underlying structure of the tables you plan on querying.

Upon the setup of these rules, you will also define security and whether you will allow for the editing of fields or the insertion of new records. The simplest table view is one where you simply retrieve values. They get more complex as you decide what fields can be added and what fields can be edited.

When deciding to make a table view editable, I will caution that with great power comes great responsibility. Exercise caution about what tables you are allowing people to update. I know this is not the technical reference guide, but if you plan on setting one of these up, make sure you pay attention to the Restrictions chapter. There are simply some tables that you don't want to – or can't – touch. If you are interested in writing your own table views, the most up-to-date documentation can be found in the Supplemental Design and Reference Guide on Table Views, available on the Solution Exchange or at documentation.onestream.com.

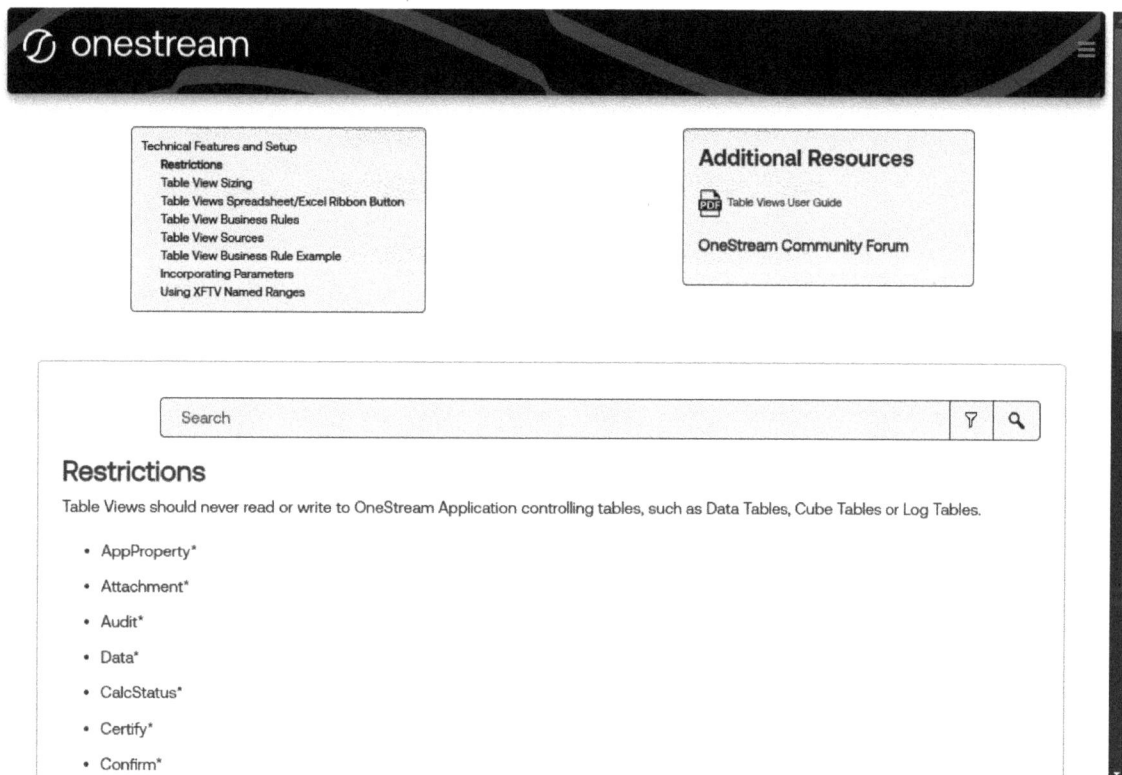

Figure 11.20

With this in mind, I find table views a great supplement for editing and inserting data into any of the Specialty Planning solutions, such as People Planning. The Spreadsheet interface provides an easy and familiar way to make updates to the relational data outside the out-of-the-box interface provided by the Specialty Planning solutions.

Like the Specialty Planning solutions in the Solution Exchange, the number of columns that I retrieve can expand and contract depending on the status that I am looking at. I can also write some clever automation when a certain action has occurred. For example, in a table view rule, I can auto-create a row of data if an active employee is marked as transferred. Or, if I mark an employee as split, I can change the status of that employee and auto-generate another record for that employee as well. I can also add more than one employee at a time, giving me the flexibility to use the comfort of the Spreadsheet interface to update this dataset. Figure 11.21 illustrates this.

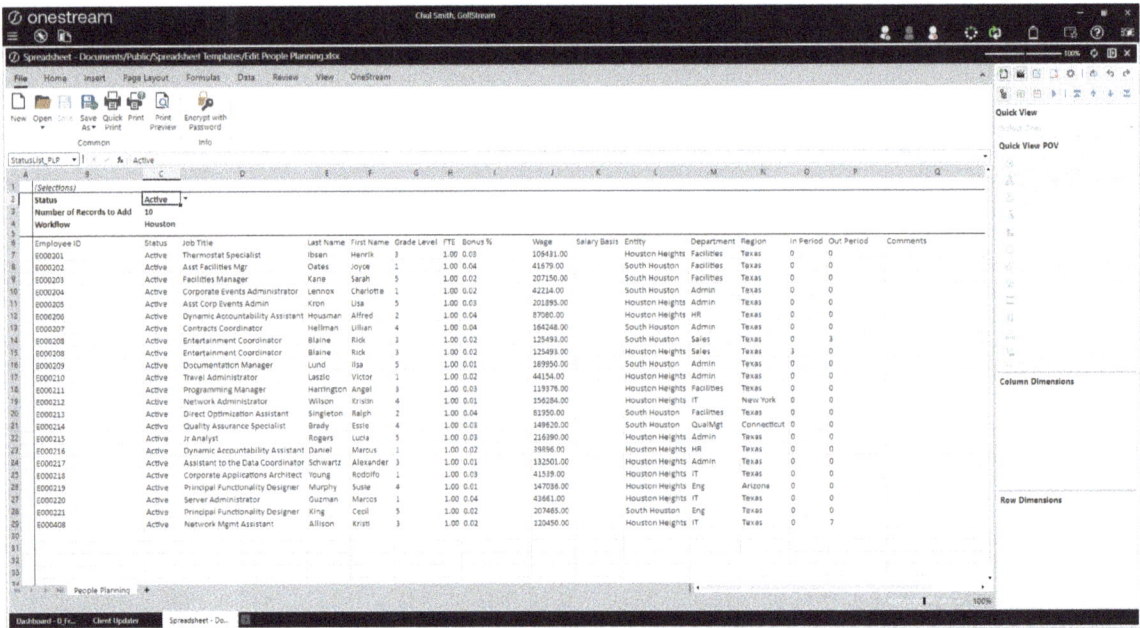

Figure 11.21

So, Which One is Right for Me?

We've gone through the plethora of reporting options for Excel and Spreadsheet. Depending on your requirements, you can choose what level of access is appropriate for your users or, after reading this, you can request access from your administrator to expand your OneStream Excel reporting options.

Using Cube Views in Excel and Spreadsheet

We've gone through what a Cube View is, and when best to use it. Let's now walk through the practicalities of getting a Cube View into Excel and Spreadsheet, formatting, submitting data, and some ways to hide any prompts you might have for parameters.

Inserting Cube Views into Excel or Spreadsheet

Getting a Cube View into Excel or Spreadsheet is a straightforward exercise. If you have a Cube View that you have created – but can't see it in Excel – you either don't have the appropriate security rights, or the Cube View does not belong to a group that is in a profile that has Visibility set for Excel.

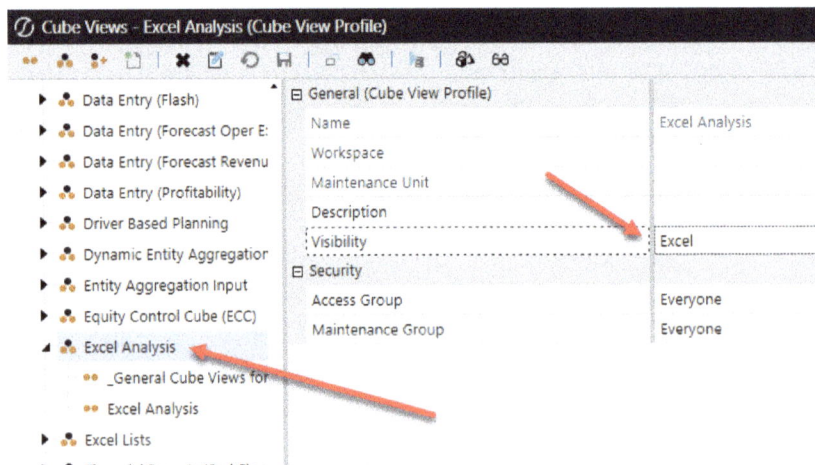

Figure 11.22

In order to add a Cube View to Excel or Spreadsheet, simply select Cube Views > Cube View Connections > Add and select the appropriate Cube View.

Here are a couple of guidelines when adding Cube Views to your workbook.

1. If you plan on having multiple Cube Views on the same worksheet, along with other content such as Quick Views or text in cell, I recommend you stick to aligning the content vertically or horizontally, but *not both*. It's really important you don't select both; you really want to choose one or the other. The dynamic nature of these items means they can change. By selecting either horizontal or vertical stacking, you ensure that content is not overwritten.

   i. If you plan on aligning the content vertically, make sure the Insert Or Delete Rows When Resizing Cube View Content is selected. Do not also select the option for columns.

   ii. If you plan on aligning the content horizontally, make sure the Insert Or Delete Columns When Resizing Cube View Content is selected. Do not also select the option for rows at the same time.

   iii. If you choose to have content both horizontally and vertically aligned, do so at your own risk. I recommend – if you select this option – that the content is static and will not expand or contract over time. That means the rows and the columns in Cube Views should have a defined member list with suppression turned off. You will also not want to enable any resizing of Cube View or Quick View content.

Figure 11.23 shows all options turned off to minimize disruption to the rest of the sheet.

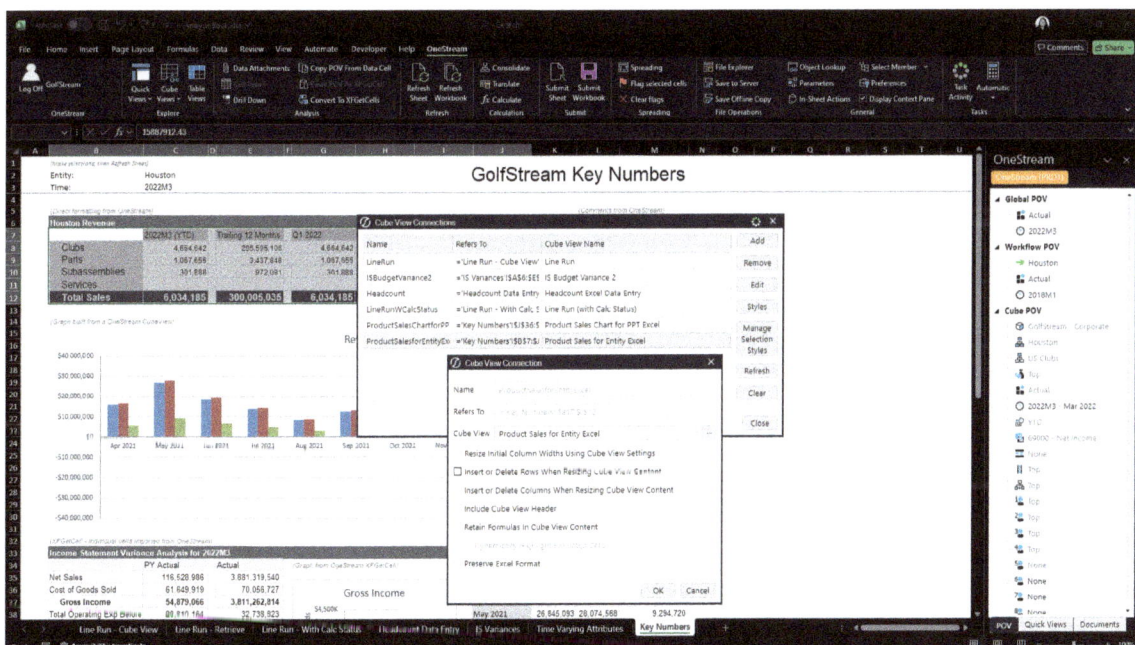

Figure 11.23

2. When inserting a Cube View, select the cell that you want to place the Cube View on. If you select cell A4, the uppermost left corner of your Cube View will start on that cell.

3. If a Cube View is added to the incorrect location on your sheet and you need to move it, you can easily move the Cube View. Simply highlight the entire cube or select the name of the Cube View in the Name Box. You will get a dark green border around the Cube View.

Chapter 11

Hover over that dark green border until you see the Move Selected Cells pointer 
Then, move the range of cells to the desired location. This trick actually works for Quick
Views as well.

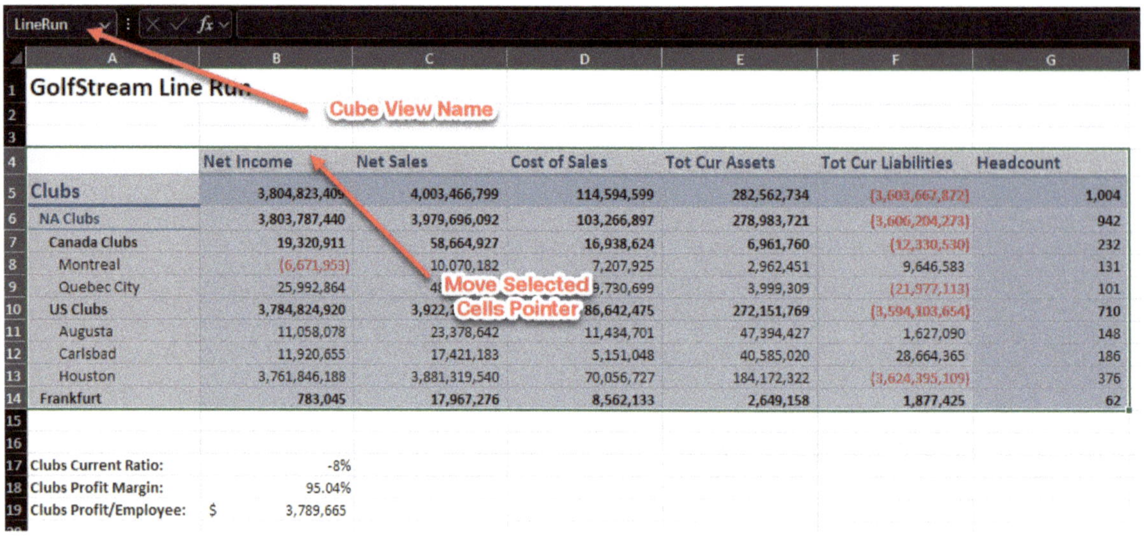

Figure 11.24

In our example, the move looks like the following.

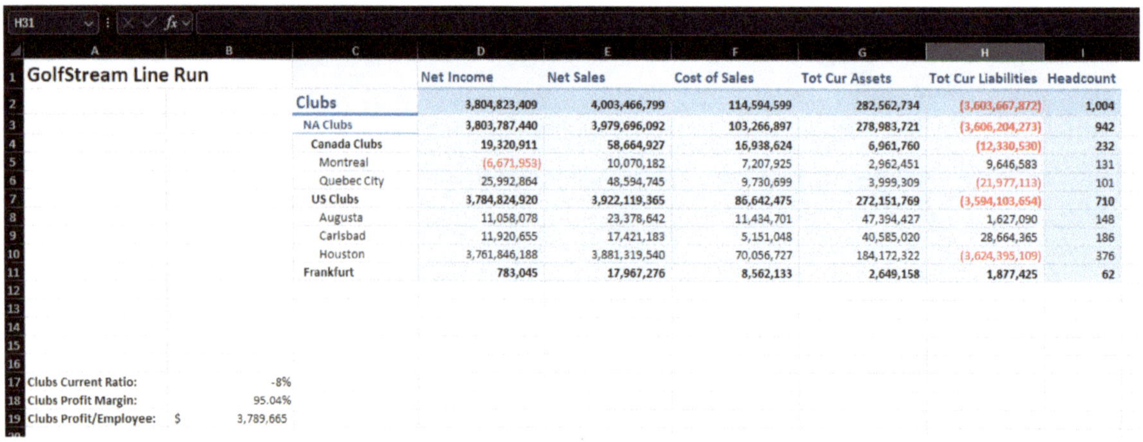

Figure 11.25

4. If you plan on sharing this workbook with someone who does not have access to

OneStream, consider turning the add-in preferences Invalidate Old Data when Workbook is
Opened to False. When the receiving party receives that Excel File, they will see values in
your Cube View or Quick View, not #Refresh in the cells.

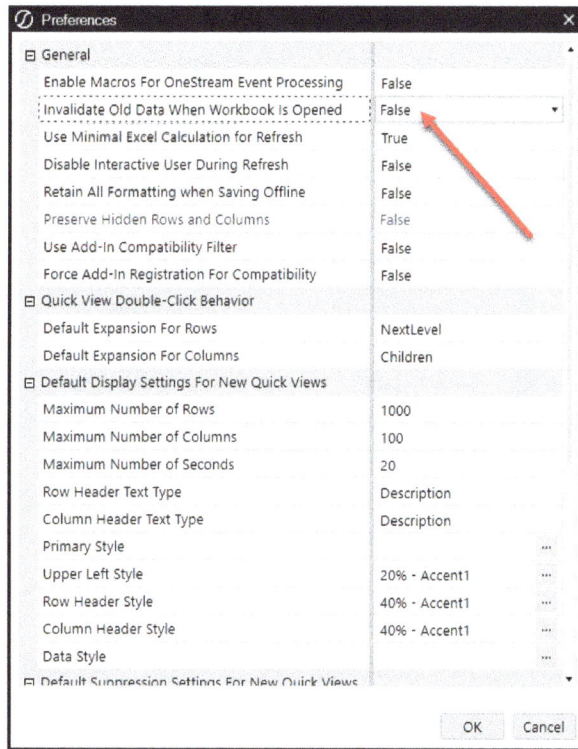

Figure 11.26

You can name the Cube View in your sheet whatever you like, provided there are no spaces in the name or special characters. If you don't select a name, one will be created for you. A unique name allows you to have the same Cube View twice in the same workbook. It is also the basis for creating name ranges automatically. The number of named ranges created will depend on the layout of the Cube View. This is important for formatting, as we shall see later.

There are a few options when inserting a Cube View; the first two are always auto-selected for you. There are two options that, by default, OneStream selects for you, but you can deselect as appropriate.

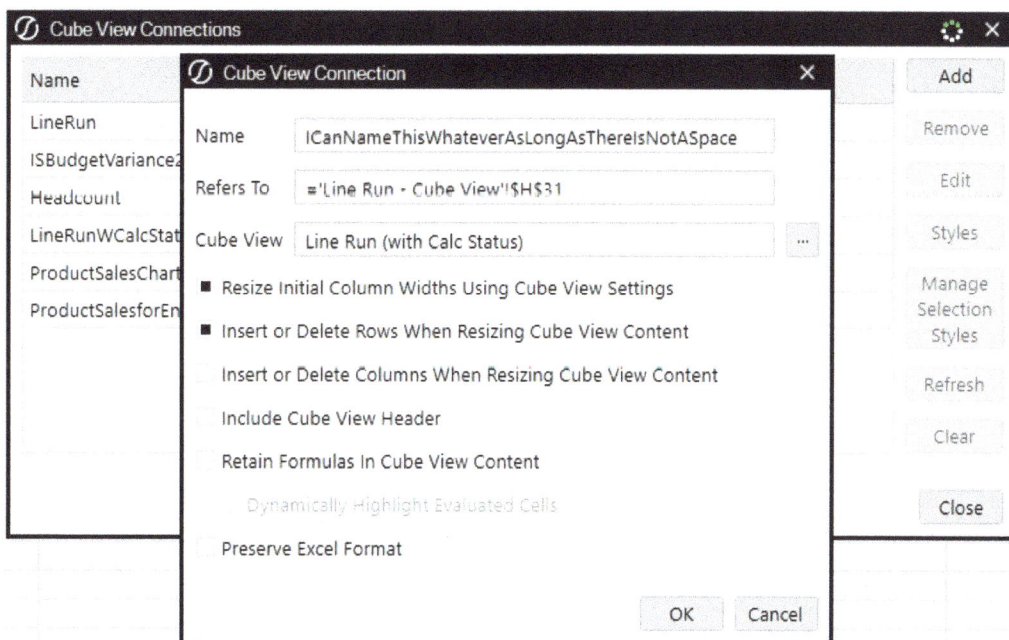

Figure 11.27

Resize Initial Column Widths Using Cube View Settings

This is auto-selected for a good reason; the column widths will expand when first adding the Cube View to the page. If not, you are going to have to resize them yourself. If you already have other objects on your sheet, and don't want them resized, you can turn this selection off. Figures 11.28 and 11.29 show the page with resize deselected, and then selected.

	A	B	C	D	E	F	G	H
1		Net Inco	Net Sale	Cost of S	Tot Cur A	Tot Cur L	Headcou	Status
2	Clubs	######	######	######	######	######	1,004	CN
3	NA Clu	######	######	######	######	######	942	CN
4	Cana	######	######	######	######	######	232	OK,MC
5	Mo	######	######	######	######	######	131	OK,MC
6	Que	######	######	######	######	######	101	OK,MC
7	US Cl	######	######	######	######	######	710	CN
8	Aug	######	######	######	######	######	148	OK,MC
9	Carl	######	######	######	######	######	186	OK,MC
10	Hou	######	######	######	######	######	376	CN
11	Frankf	######	######	######	######	######	62	OK,MC

Figure 11.28

	A	B	C	D	E	F	G	H
1		Net Income	Net Sales	Cost of Sales	Tot Cur Assets	Tot Cur Liabilitie	Headcount	Status
2	Clubs	56,120,762	254,062,658	114,219,100	282,550,734	144,917,839	1,004	CN
3	NA Clubs	55,175,092	231,380,505	103,375,346	278,971,721	142,269,214	942	CN
4	Canada Clubs	19,320,911	58,664,927	16,938,624	6,961,760	(12,330,530)	232	OK,MC
5	Montreal	(6,671,953)	10,070,182	7,207,925	2,962,451	9,646,583	131	OK,MC
6	Quebec City	25,992,864	48,594,745	9,730,699	3,999,309	(21,977,113)	101	OK,MC
7	US Clubs	36,129,682	173,434,127	86,637,475	272,149,769	154,464,584	710	CN
8	Augusta	11,058,078	23,378,642	11,434,701	47,394,427	1,627,090	148	OK,MC
9	Carlsbad	11,920,655	17,421,183	5,151,048	40,585,020	28,664,365	186	OK,MC
10	Houston	3,761,846,188	3,881,319,540	70,056,727	184,172,322	(3,624,505,109)	376	CN
11	Frankfurt	783,045	17,967,276	8,562,133	2,649,158	1,877,425	62	OK,MC

Figure 11.29

Insert or Delete Rows When Resizing Cube View Content

If you plan on stacking everything vertically on your worksheet, select this option while in the Quick View (see figure 11.30). This will auto-add or auto-delete rows as the Cube View expands and contracts. Do not select this and the Insert Or Delete Columns When Resizing Cube View Content at the same time (see figure 11.31).

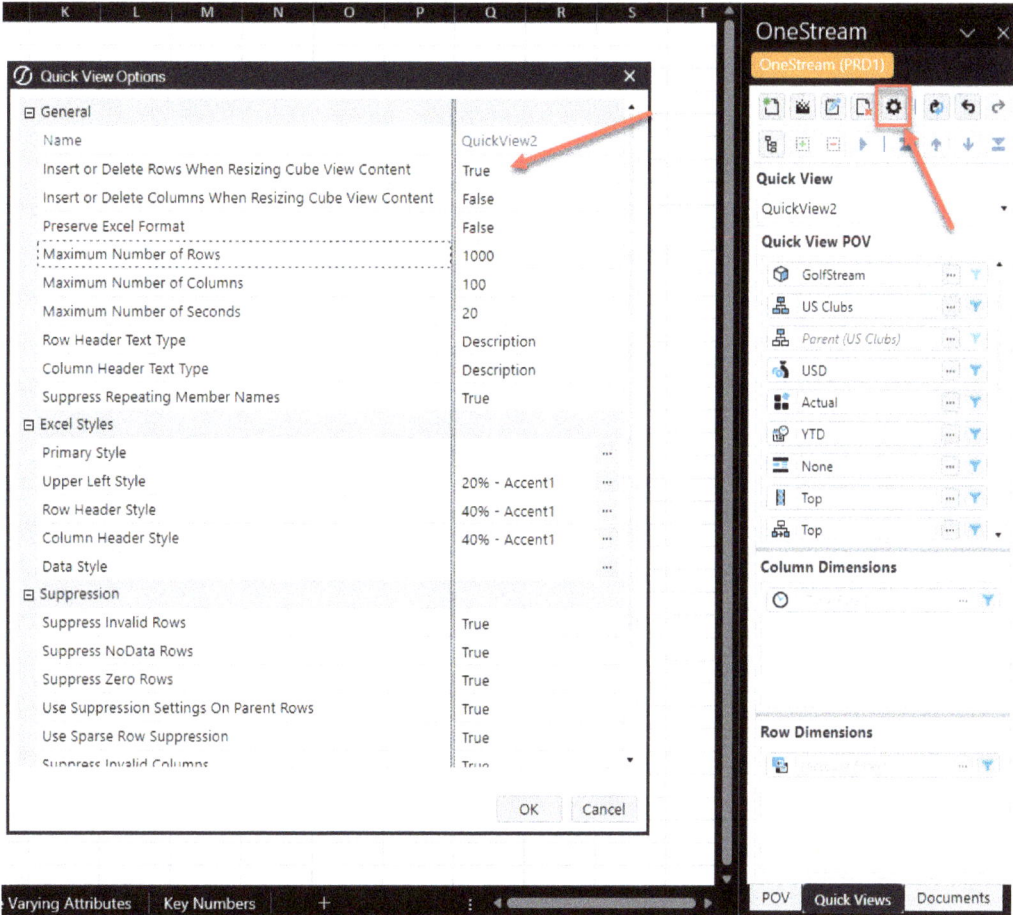

Figure 11.30

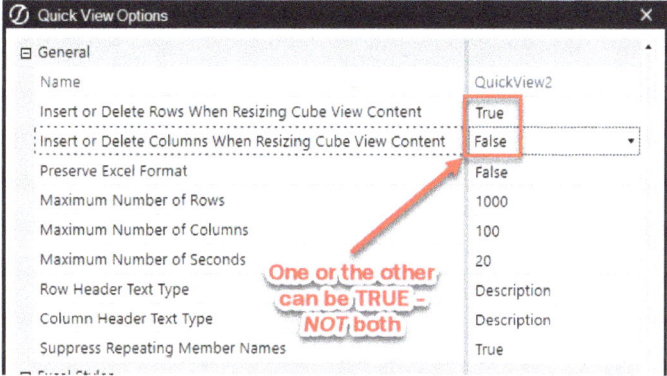

Figure 11.31

Insert or Delete Columns When Resizing Cube View Content

If you plan on stacking everything horizontally on your worksheet, select this option. This will auto-add or auto-delete columns as the Cube View expands and contracts. Do not select this and the Insert Or Delete Rows When Resizing Cube View Content at the same time.

Retain Formulas in Cube View Content

Only select this if you have a Cube View that you plan on using for data submission (using Excel formula references). Otherwise, leave it deselected; it's not necessary.

Dynamically Highlight Evaluated Cells

This option will be available if the previous option is selected. This will highlight the cell if the formula reference has changed without having to refresh the sheet. The reason this is not automatically turned on is because it can impact performance and slow down retrieval times. Use with caution on large, sparse Cube Views.

There are plenty more options, but these are the most important. Having a good understanding of these options will ultimately help you when adding Cube Views to your sheet; you'll create sheets that look good and don't conflict with other data that you have.

Cube Views Advanced Formatting Options

Once a Cube View is on your worksheet, you may want to modify the formatting that has been provided. Simply going to the Excel home page and changing the font or background color may appear to do the job, at first, but you will be disappointed to see that upon a refresh of the sheet, the formatting will disappear. The only exception to this is conditional formatting. Native Excel or Spreadsheet conditional formatting will work and stick on Cube Views without any special considerations. But if you are looking to perform other types of formatting, this section will explore how to create custom formatting and how to make it stick to a Cube View.

Order of Precedence

When deciding what style to use, you should first understand the order or precedence for each style. One selection may override a previously made selection. The default Cube View style is overwritten by anything setup at the Cube View level, called **custom Cube View format**. Conditional formatting overrides that, and so on and so forth. This handy chart below will help you understand the order of precedence for Cube View formatting.

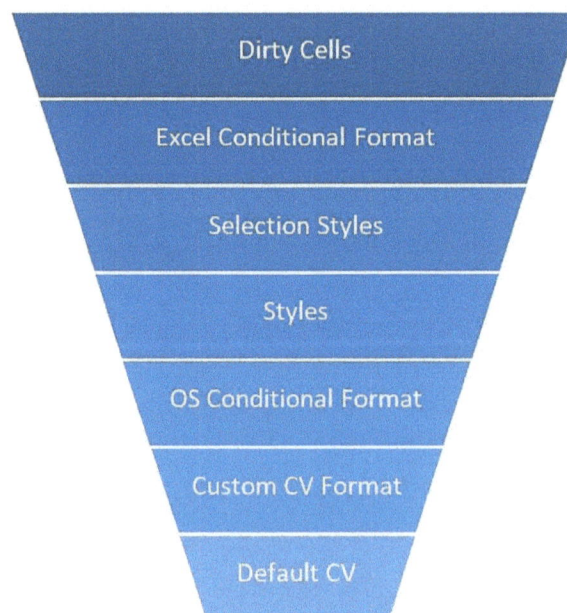

Figure 11.32

Styles, Selection Styles, Conditional Formatting

We are not going to cover the bottom three formatting styles; those are set up in the Cube View itself and were covered in the previous chapter on Cube Views.

Here, we are going to cover styles, selection styles, and Excel/Spreadsheet conditional formatting. Yes, there are two styles to define formatting for Cube Views that sound very similar – styles versus selection styles – but what's the difference, and when should you use one over the other?

Styles are defined with the Cube View connection and are limited to defining one style per named range, created in each Cube View. Name ranges are created automatically when the Cube View is brought into Excel or Spreadsheet. Because each Cube View can have multiple rows and columns when it is initially set up, the number of ranges that you have depends on how the Cube View was built.

To see the named ranges for each Cube View, go back to your Cube View connections and select Styles. You can see, in the below Figure, that the LineRun Cube View has quite a few ranges that have been created, based on the way it has been configured.

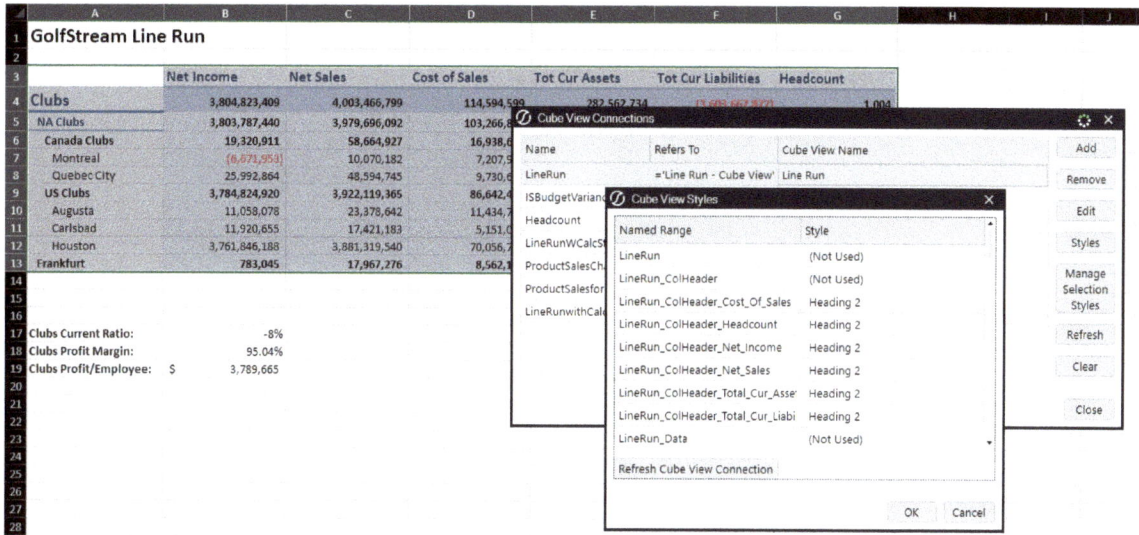

Figure 11.33

Focusing on the header, you will see that there are multiple named ranges. In this case, one for cost of sales, headcount, net income, etc. Why is that? For that answer, let's turn to the raw Cube View itself, and how it was setup. The below Figure shows the configuration of that Cube View.

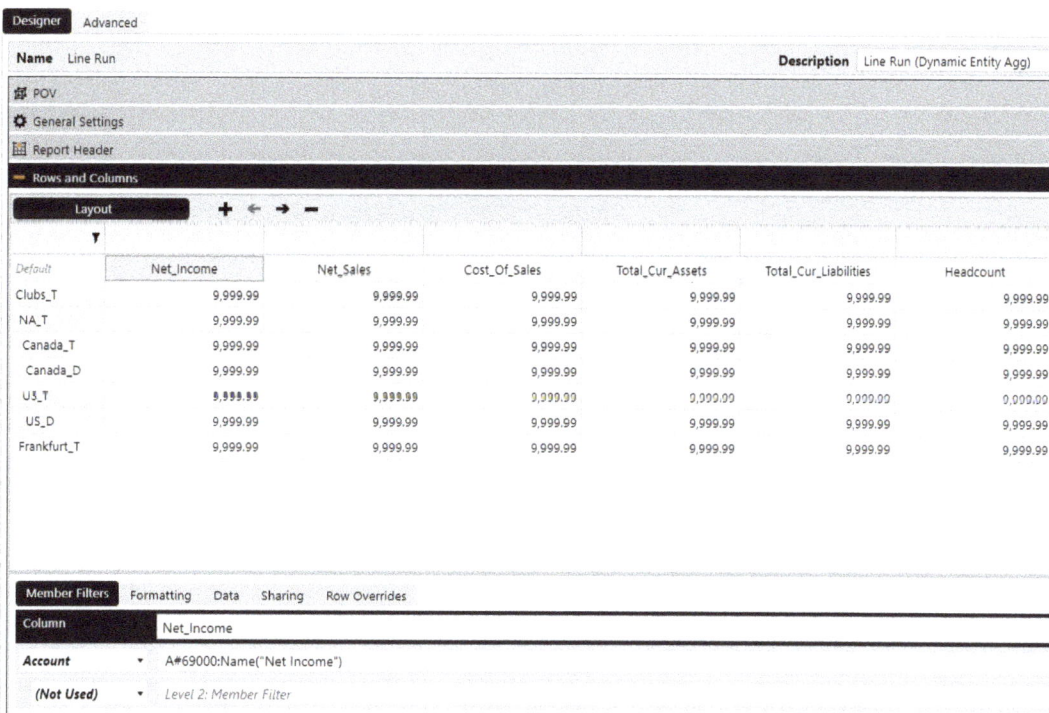

Figure 11.34

This Cube View is comprised of six columns. A range is established for each column setup in the Cube View. Does it need to be setup in this way? It depends. There are certainly good reasons to separate out different columns; remember, Cube Views are not just used for Excel reporting. Having separate columns allows the Cube View to be formatted appropriately inside the application.

Remember that each column or row in the Cube View setup can have multiple members. Taking a closer look at the Canada_D row, you can see that this one row has multiple Entity members. This is still treated as one row for named range purposes in Excel and Spreadsheet.

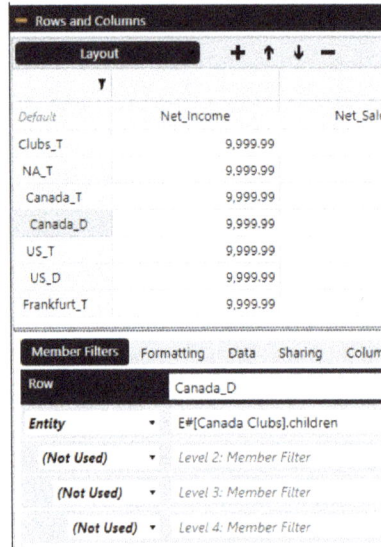

Figure 11.35

Regardless of how your Cube View is setup, and how many rows and columns it has, it's still possible to achieve your formatting goals.

Let's say my goal was to have the entire column header formatted consistently. The best way to achieve this is to set the Cube View column header to the style that I am looking for. I'm going to select the style of Total as the column header style.

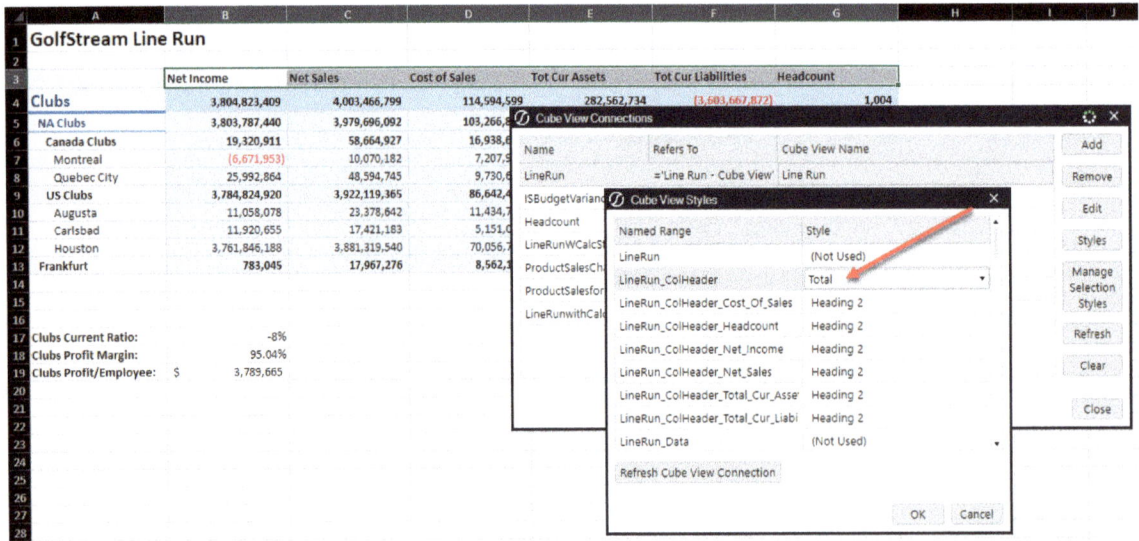

Figure 11.36

The distinct advantage of having one format for all the column headers is that if additional rows or columns are added, you don't need to worry about reformatting your sheet; they will simply follow suit.

As an example, let's say the Cube View is modified to include an additional column for operating expenses. That addition as a new column will follow the custom format for the column we defined.

Overrides are allowed, and if you define specific formatting for one range, it will not use the default setting; it will use what is defined. In the below example, I've set `Net Income` to a red background color called `Bad`. Specific formatting styles always override what has been set for the column, row, or data range.

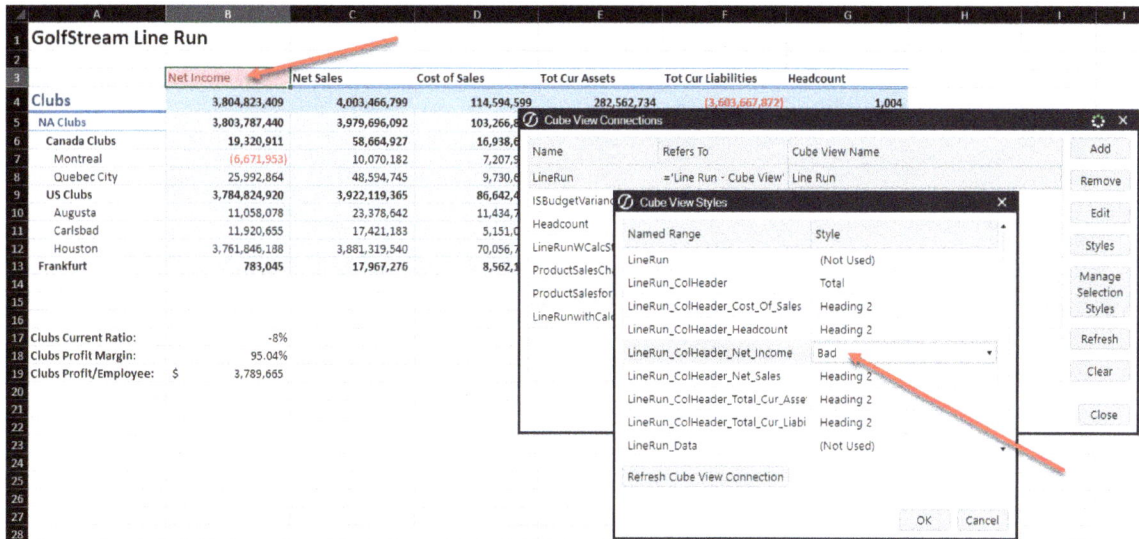

Figure 11.37

If you found styles a bit overwhelming, or simply don't like the idea of having to use named ranges to set up formatting, there is another option. **Selection styles** was introduced to give you more flexibility to define a range of formatting, much like you would in native Excel, without regard to the named ranges established. Selection styles override regular styles, so if you've tried styles and just can't get the desired result, give selection styles a try.

Another advantage of selection styles is that you can format the Cube View using native Excel or Spreadsheet functions, and then define that as a custom style. Take, for example, the following Cube View. The `Services` line of business does not have any data for this period as it was a discontinued line of business.

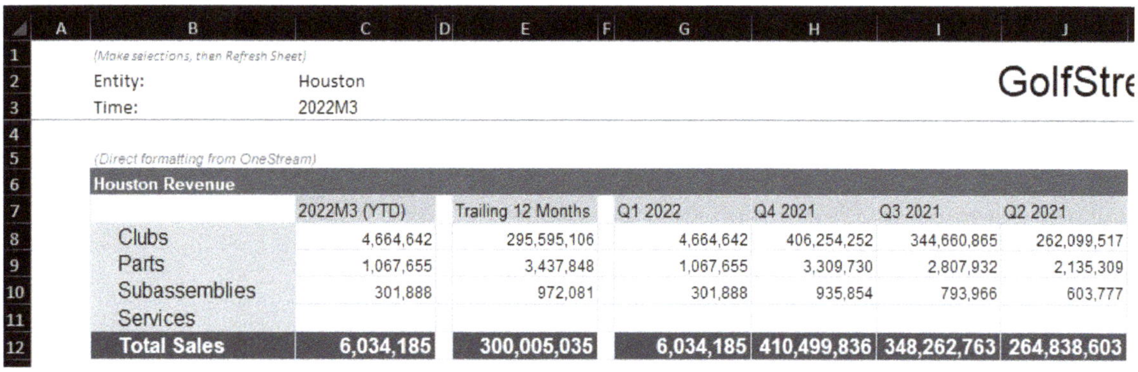

Figure 11.38

For this report, I want to highlight the `Services` LOB line in orange to indicate that it is no longer active. By simply going to the font color and defining this as orange, I can create the desired impact. But remember that if I click refresh on the sheet, the formatting will disappear. I need to associate it with the Cube View via selection styles.

While you have those cells highlighted, navigate to Cube View > Selection Styles.

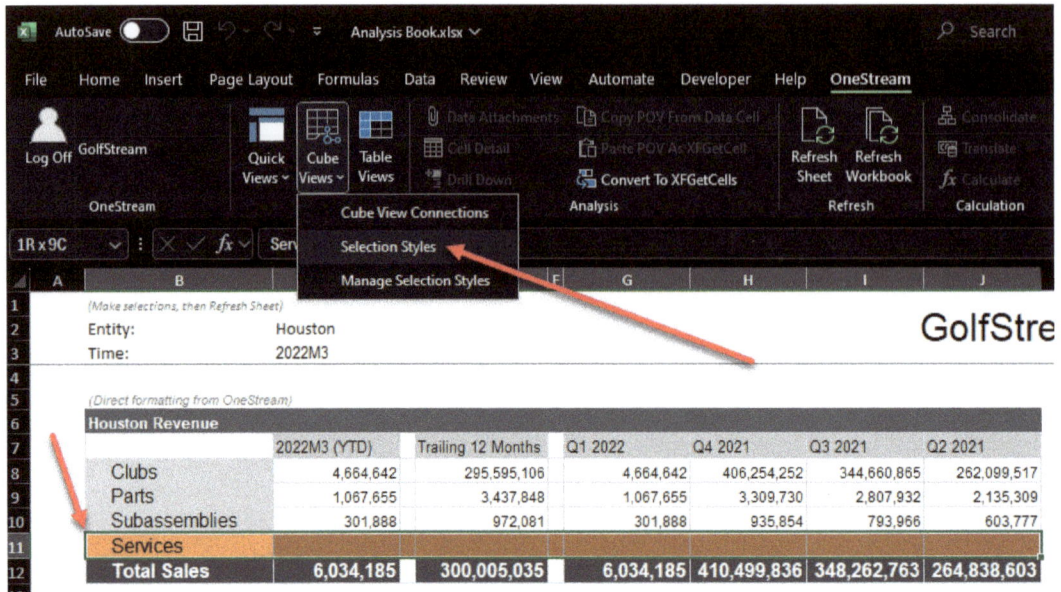

Figure 11.39

Provide a name for this selection style. I'm going to call this the `Discontinued LOB`. The style name is going to be saved locally to this workbook only; it is not stored in OneStream.

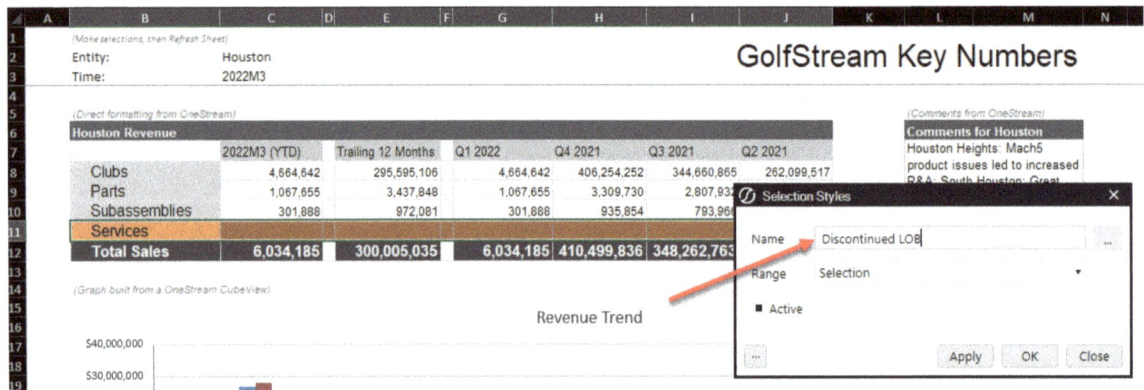

Figure 11.40

I encourage you to read more about selection styles in the Design and Reference Guide, as they will go into other scenarios about de-activating a selection style and how to manage them (which we will not cover here today). However, here are a few tips and tricks that I've learned about selection styles, which are not documented.

1. If you add in cells above or below the `Services` LOB line, those new lines will receive the formatting from the Cube View, not the new selection styles you defined. It's very handy, as changing metadata and placement of items on specific rows will not impact the selection style.

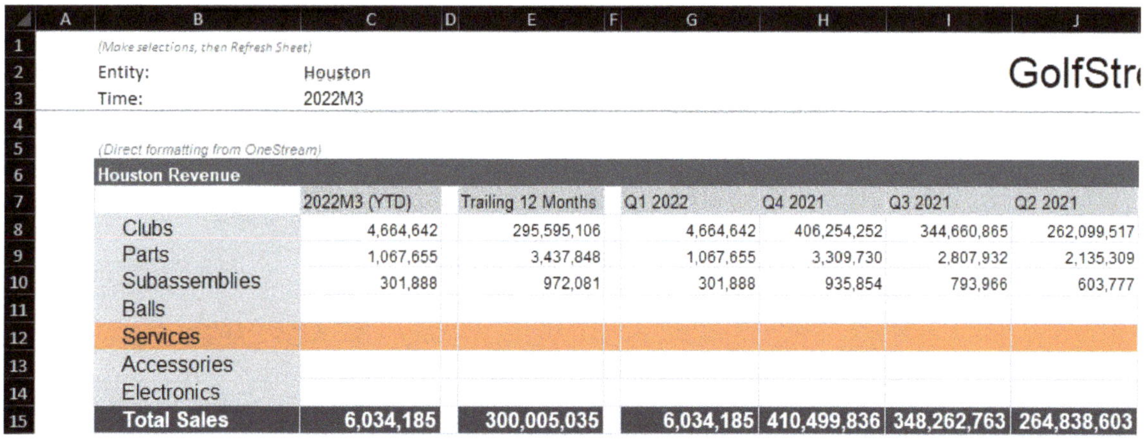

Figure 11.41

2. The creation of a selection style creates a native Excel or Spreadsheet style. Navigating back to the home screen, you will see that anything created via the means of selection styles shows up as a native style. This provides users with additional editing capabilities to define fonts, borders, or refine sizes. Instead of creating a selection style in the way we described above, you can simply define native Excel or Spreadsheet styles and use them in selection styles.

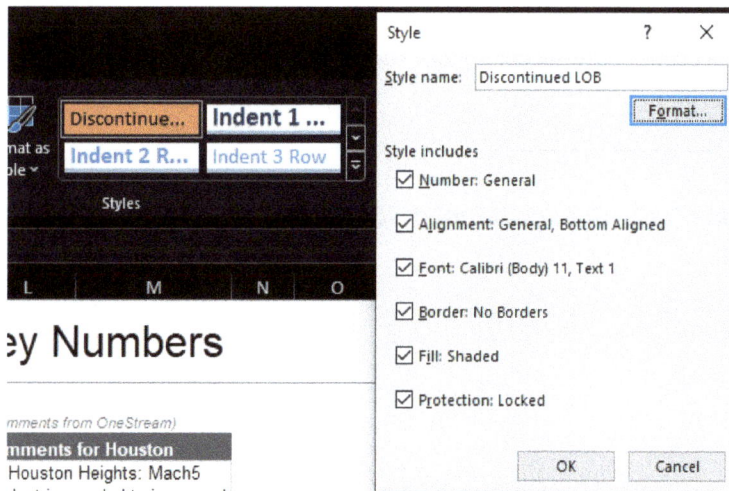

Figure 11.42

3. The selection style, or any style, cannot be a mix of different styles. For example, you cannot have one selection style to have the columns in bold text, but the dataset to be in regular text. When defining and setting selection styles, they must be consistent. No mixing and matching!

The final option for formatting Cube Views is the easiest and will take up the least amount of space. This is native Excel or Spreadsheet conditional formatting.

There is no special magic; no ranges you need to understand. Assuming you are using 6.0 or later of OneStream, conditional formatting simply works and will stick to your Cube View using the native functions. Enjoy the gift; it's that simple.

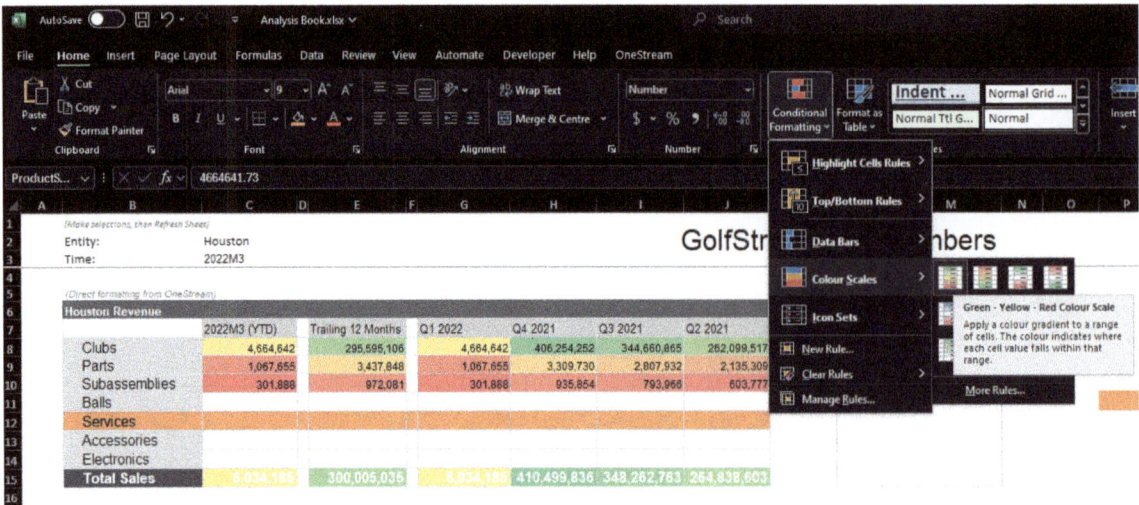

Figure 11.43

Hiding Parameter Prompts

Many Cube Views that you may leverage in Excel or Spreadsheet may contain parameters for either the POV, row, or columns – to help refine the dataset you are retrieving. When your sheet contains parameters in a Cube View, and you view it in either Excel or Spreadsheet, you will receive a prompt asking you to define the parameter.

This can be annoying and burdensome when refreshing a workbook with many parameters embedded in it. How can I remove the prompt but still define what I would like the parameter to be?

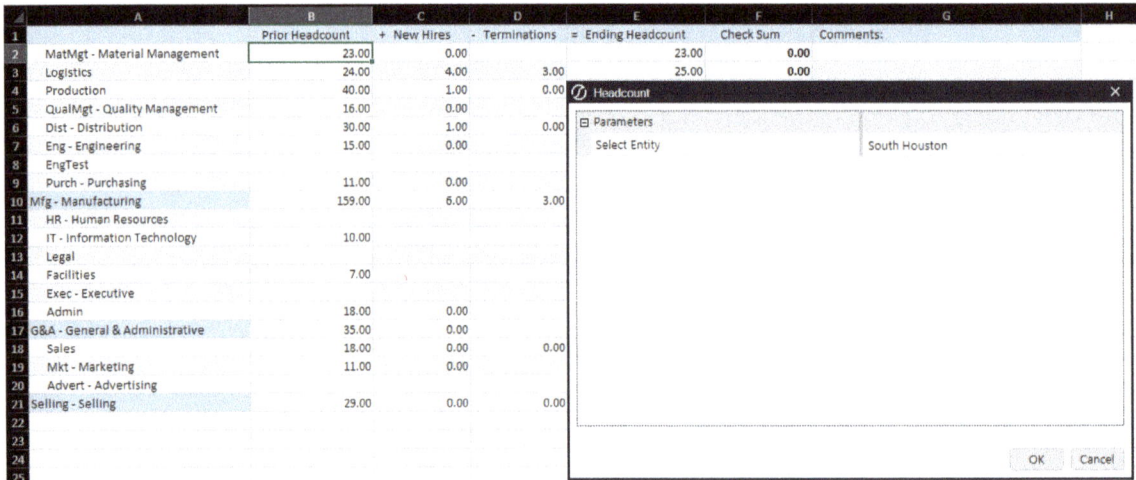

Figure 11.44

There is a simple solution. A Cube View in Excel or Spreadsheet evaluates values in the **name manager** when you refresh your Cube View. If you define the parameter as a name, you can avoid having a prompt for the parameter.

The only caveat I must make is that you *must know* what the name of the parameter is. For the above Cube View, in Figure 11.44, related to headcount data entry, we need to open the OneStream application to understand the name of the parameter that is prompting me for the entity. Remember, the parameter may be in the rows, columns, or POV.

In this case, the parameter is in the POV under the Entity members and is called
`|!WfProfile_Assigned_Entities!|`. There is another parameter for time, but that is based on the WF, so we don't need to be concerned with that.

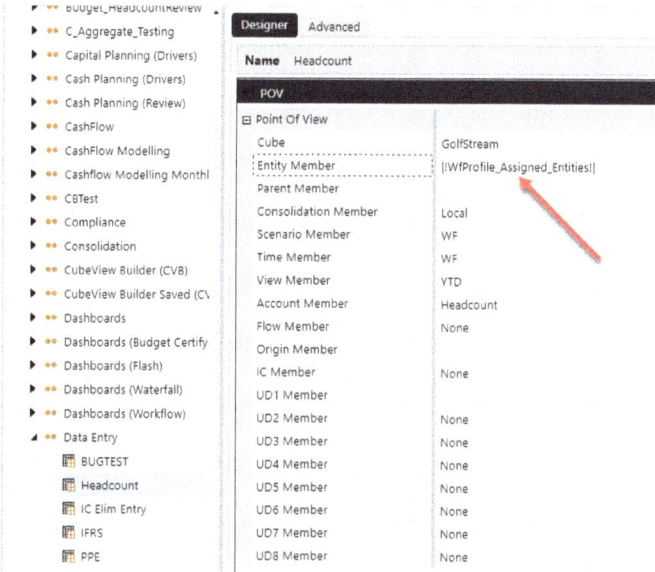

Figure 11.45

Copy the name of the parameter defined in the Cube View. Disregard the leading and trailing pipe `|` and exclamation point `!`. In Excel or Spreadsheet, set a cell equal to the value you wish to replace with the parameter. Select Define Name > New Name and set the parameter equal to the new name.

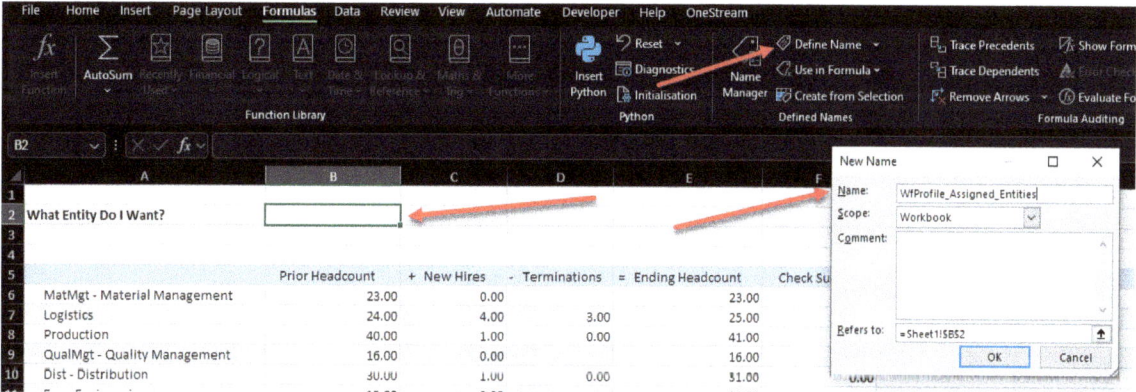

Figure 11.46

Upon refreshing the sheet, you will no longer be prompted to select the value for the parameter.

In many instances, you may want to have a list of available values that match any parameter that is being prompted for on the page. It's a little extra work, but it will pay dividends, especially if you plan on distributing this workbook to a larger audience, or if this parameter is tied to metadata that will grow over time.

First, track down the underlying value of the parameter in the dashboard and what members it references. The parameter was `|!WfProfile_Assigned_Entities!|` The values of that parameter are found in dashboards, not Cube Views.

I recommend using the search button 👓 in order to track it down. Once you do, you can see the Member Filter for this parameter, which in this case is `E#Houston.Base`

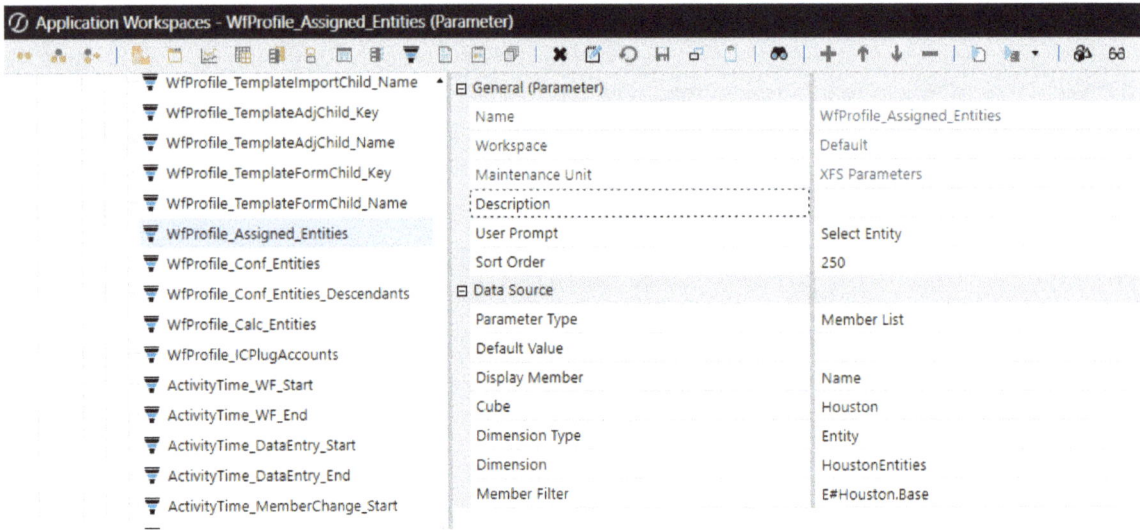

Figure 11.47

Next, create a new Cube View, where only the rows match the Member Filter defined in the parameter.

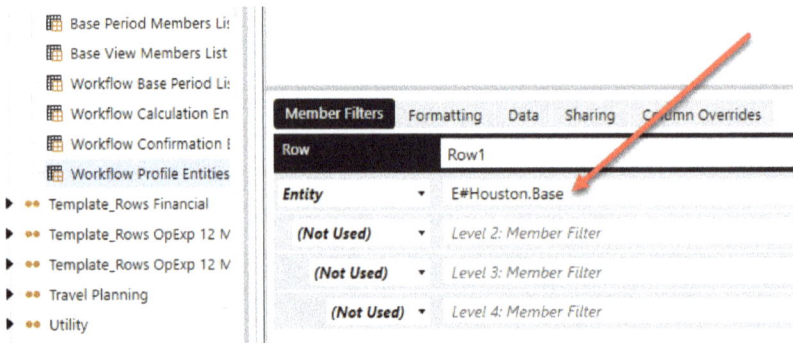

Figure 11.48

The Cube View can then be added to a new worksheet. Here, I've titled this `Lists`. The rows show the same values as the parameter prompt.

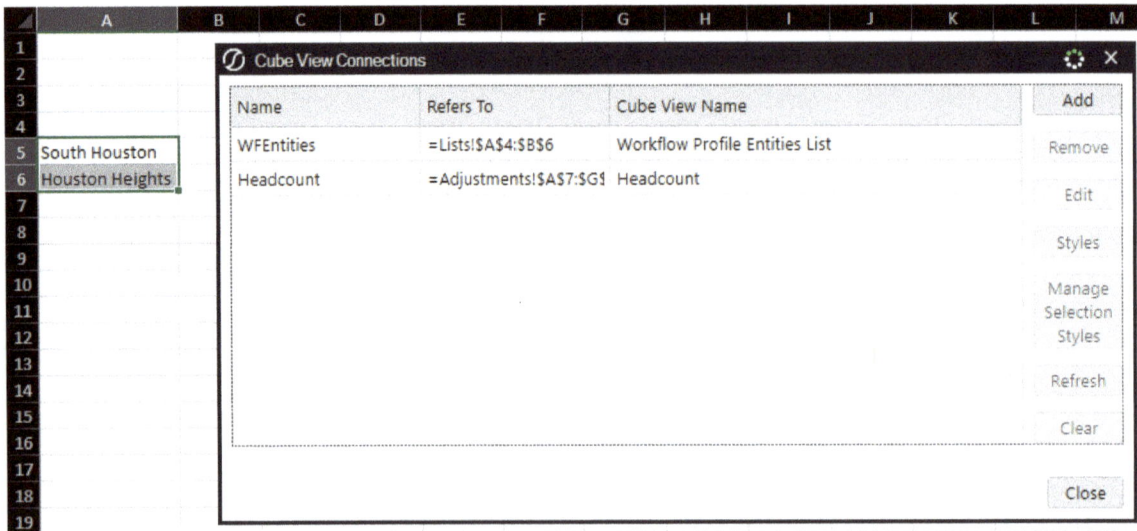

Figure 11.49

In Excel, select the cell where you have defined the name. Change the cell to perform a list validation against the newly inserted Cube View, as shown in Figure 11.50.

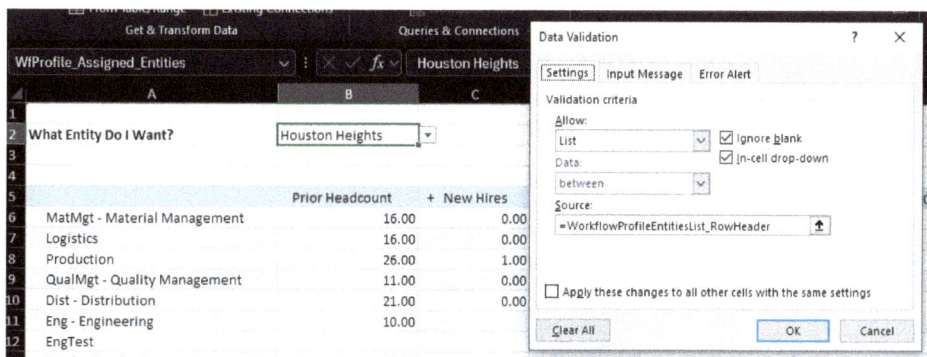

Figure 11.50

Now, you will be able to select from a list to define the parameter you wish to retrieve.

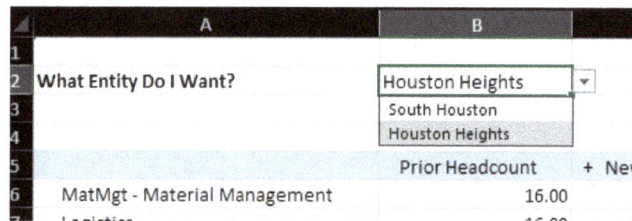

Figure 11.51

The advantage of this method is that the sheet becomes much more dynamic. As metadata changes, so will the Cube View used for the reference. As an example, if five more entities are listed under Houston, they will show up in the drop-down on your sheet to retrieve data against.

Creating Quick Views in Excel and Spreadsheet

Personally, this is my favorite topic to do with the OneStream platform. There is nothing more satisfying than being able to quickly look at data and explore financial results than with a Quick View. It's something that almost everyone who touches OneStream will use at some point in time. It's simple enough for the new analyst who just joined out of college to understand, yet has the sophistication that the controller can use to quickly answer questions about data without having to bring in the OneStream experts.

Important Preferences and The Importance of Workflow

Consider this the precursor to your knowledge of Quick Views. It's imperative that you set your preferences before creating Quick Views, as this can save you a lot of frustration later. Even if you have worked with Quick Views before, I implore you to review this section to understand how and why you should care about these preferences. Preferences are set by the individual user and are localized. The preferences you have in Excel or Spreadsheet are yours.

Global preferences define worksheet-level behavior and are the starting place for all new Quick Views you create. This is your baseline, the way you want to start with all your new Quick Views. That means if you have suppression turned on for invalid rows, every Quick View you create will default to that preference. Global preferences can be overwritten. These are called Quick View options, which are tied to each Quick View you create and can be changed independently of your global preferences.

It should be noted that changing your global preferences will not impact any existing Quick Views you have already created except for **double-click behavior**. The key word here is *existing* Quick Views. I've seen this so many times when someone is trying to change suppression, and they wonder why it doesn't work. Ten out of ten times, it's because they are changing the global preferences and not the Quick View-specific preferences under **Quick View options**. And remember, each Quick View can have its own unique preferences. It's not an 'all or nothing' type of situation. In a sheet with many Quick Views, you can have different styles and different suppressions set up between them.

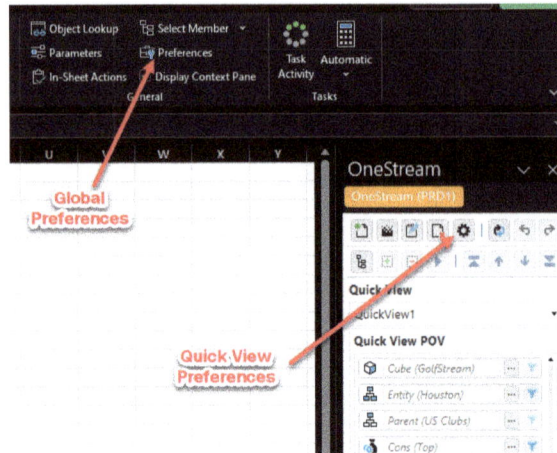

Figure 11.52

Let's talk about global preferences first. Those are found under OneStream > Administration > Preferences.

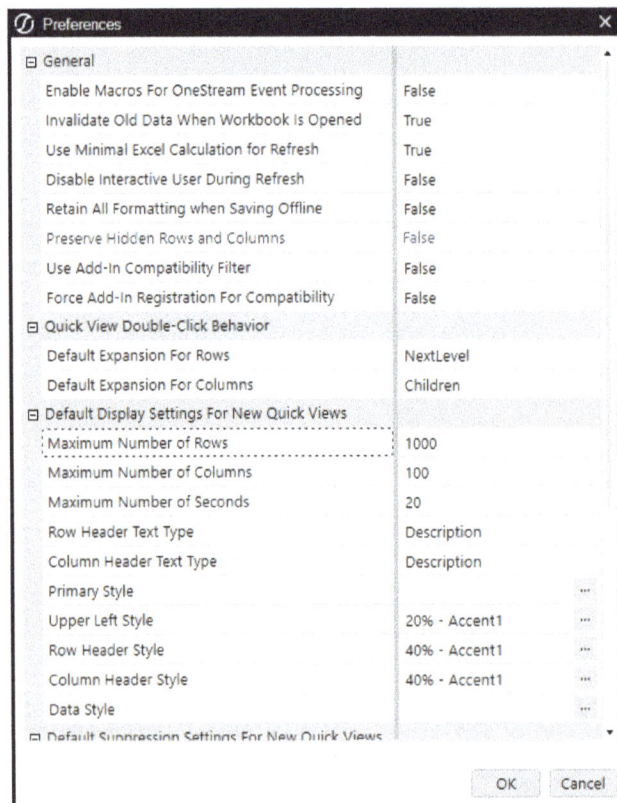

Figure 11.53

Important General Preferences

Invalidate Old Data When Workbook is Opened – this is important if you are distributing Excel files with Cube View or Quick View data to users who do not have access to OneStream or the add-in. If selected, when those users open the book, it will show `#Refresh`, not the Actual data values. So don't select it if you plan on passing this along to a boss who doesn't plan on refreshing the sheet.

Where this does come in handy is when there is frequently changing data. By forcing you to refresh your sheet, it ensures that the data you see on your sheet is up-to-date. Think of it as a good reminder to make sure you have the latest and greatest dataset.

Retain all Formatting when Saving Offline – I highly recommend you set this to `true`. An offline copy can lose all the formatting work you put into it, so keep it on.

Quick View Double-Click Behavior

These settings are global for all Quick Views you have on your Excel or Spreadsheet file. My only caution on these is to *know your hierarchies*. If they are cliff-like, and they are very sparse or large, I would stay away from the descendants or base as you could be in store for lengthy retrieval times.

Default Expansion for Rows – I prefer mine set to `NextLevel`.

Default Expansion for Columns – I prefer mine set to `Children`.

Default Display Settings for New Quick Views

The number of rows and columns is set to a suggested number of 1000 and 10 for your protection, in case you do accidentally drill into a very deep hierarchy. Modify at your own discretion or consider using a Cube View, which at the time of writing had a **sparse data suppression** feature that greatly improved performance when retrieving large datasets. That has not been extended to Quick Views yet.

Row/Column Header Text – based on your preference, but remember that even if you select `Description` or `Short Description`, you cannot type those in when changing selections.

Style – For a detailed discussion, see Figure 11.11 in this chapter.

Default Suppression Settings for New Quick Views

Suppression settings are described in detail in the Design and Reference Guide.

Warning: if you turn suppression on, this can cause a great deal of confusion. If you are new to Quick Views, don't turn on suppression right away. It will make it seem as if there is no data or members in your list. Start to turn suppression on when you get a little more comfortable.

Creating a Quick View from a Data Explorer

If you are new to Quick Views, there is no better way to get started on your ad-hoc analysis journey. This feature was introduced to overly simplify the creation of a Quick View.

Simply open a data explorer grid or anything with a Cube View embedded in it. Right mouse click on the cell and select Create Quick View Using the POV From Selected Cell. You will have the option to render it in Excel or Spreadsheet and your analysis journey begins. The most advantageous thing is that you don't need to worry about setting a POV as it will inherit it from an existing report that is well-formed, making this a foolproof method for creating a Quick View with data. It really is that simple, and you have the fine folks on the platform to thank for that handy enhancement.

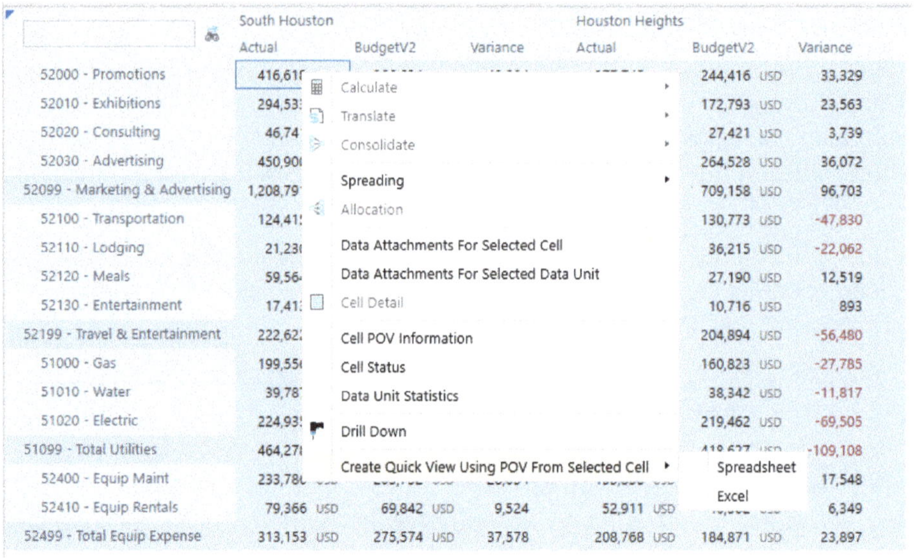

Figure 11.54

With little effort, you can start slicing and dicing any number using that one action. Analysis in a few clicks.

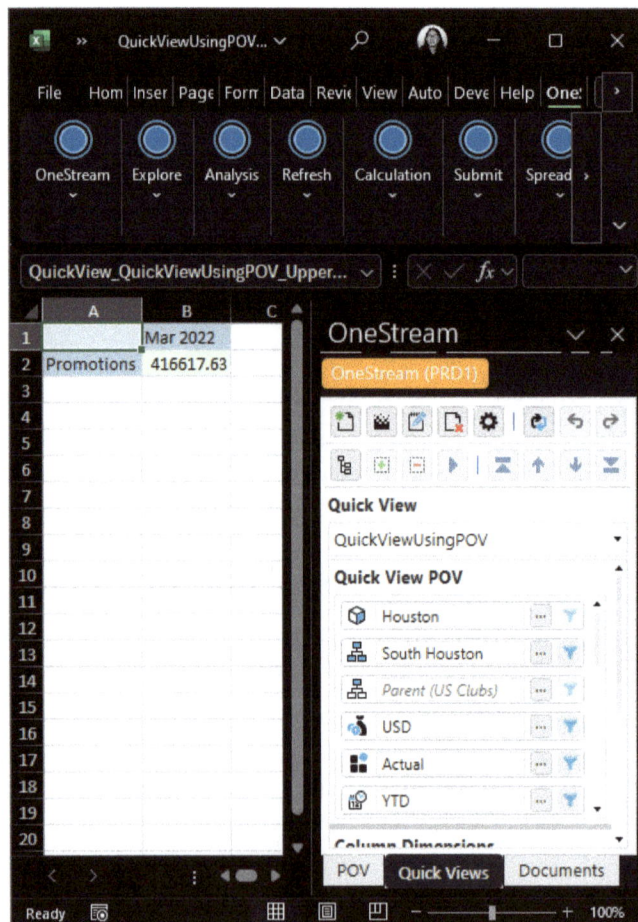

Figure 11.55

If you have a great idea like this, be sure to log it in IdeaStream, which you can access via the OneStream Community page (community.onestreamsoftware.com.) The OneStream development team really pays attention to this, and it is partially how they prioritize new features. If you have never been, be sure to check it out and vote up the ideas you find interesting. During Splash 2023, in Washington D.C., at the regular Excel presentation, Gidon Albert suggested a new feature to have drill down available on XFGet cells and asked the room to vote it up on IdeaStream. Well, Gidon asked and the community responded, and the development team listened. By Splash 2024, the drill down on XFGet cells was a welcome addition to the platform. So, get out there and have a look at the current suggestions and add your own!

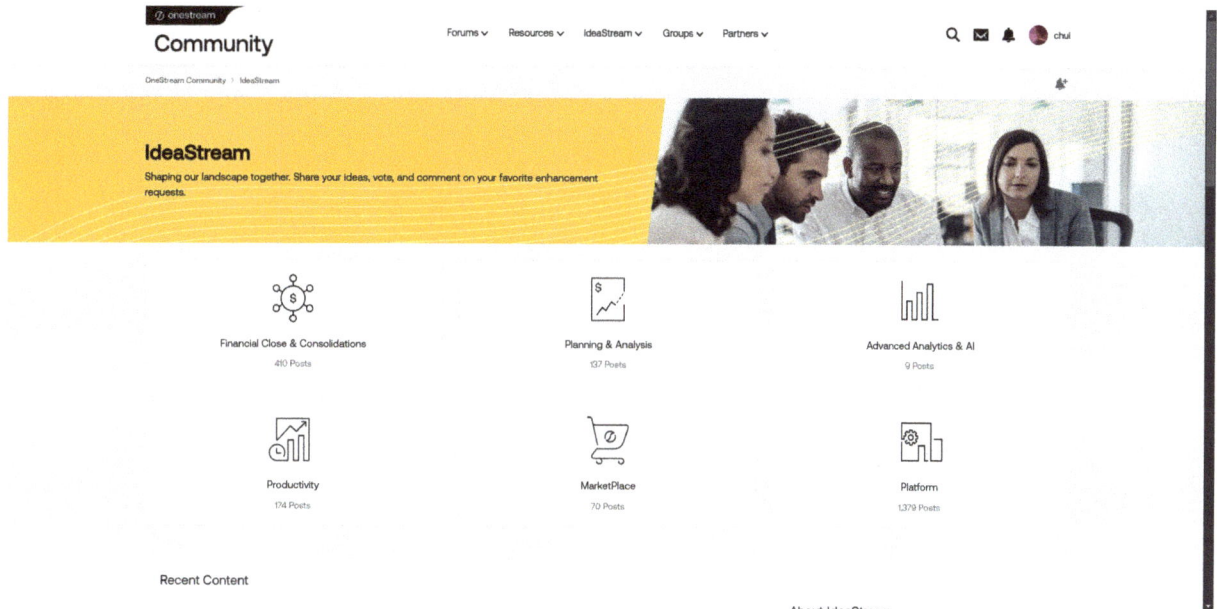

Figure 11.56

Creating a Quick View from Scratch

There are a few different ways to create a Quick View from scratch.

The most common way is to go to the OneStream Menu and select Quick Views > Create Quick View.

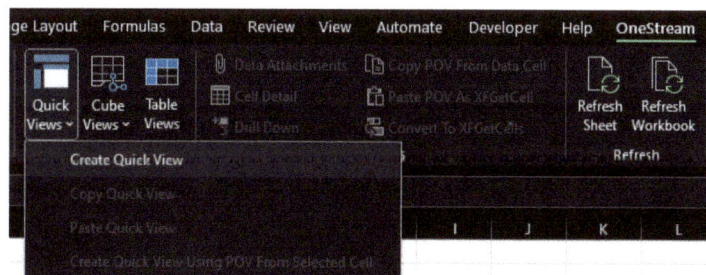

Figure 11.57

The Quick View will give you an option to name it, or it will default to `QuickView1`. As you add additional Quick Views, OneStream will auto-index the number so you don't end up with the same name for multiple Quick Views.

As per our discussion with Cube Views, if you are planning on having multiple Quick Views on the same sheet, it is best to decide if you plan on stacking them horizontally or vertically. It is not recommended to do both, as this can create conflicts.

If you plan on stacking vertically, keep the default Insert or Delete Rows when Resizing Cube View Content. Otherwise, if you plan on organizing horizontally, select the column action. It is not recommended to select both.

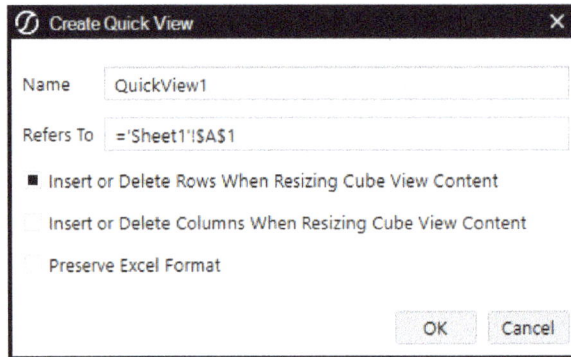

Figure 11.58

The Quick View will appear on your sheet. By default, time will always appear in the column, and account will always appear in the rows.

The Importance of the POV

When you first create a Quick View, your individual user POV is going to dictate the Quick View POV. If you are unsure as to what your POV is, open the tab titled POV. This is the same POV you will have when you log into the OneStream application. It can change as you navigate to different workflows, so be cognizant of what your POV is on a Quick View.

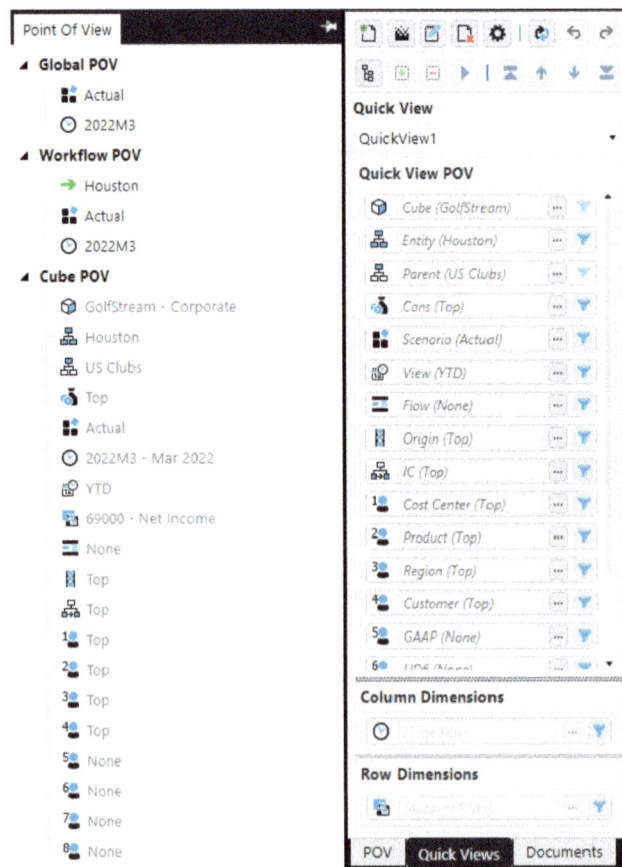

Figure 11.59

As you change your POV – either in the application or in Excel – the Quick View POV will follow suit unless you explicitly change it.

Notice the color of the POV in the Quick View. It's shaded in gray and indicates what dimension it is. This means that you are using the POV. For example, in the above Figure, you can see that my POV for the Scenario dimension is set to Actual because it is displayed in gray and lists the dimension prior to the member. In order to override the POV, you can change it by selecting the ellipses (…) next to the name, or by typing in the member name directly. This removes the dimension name and will display your selection in black text. This indicates that you have overwritten the POV with your own selections, and those selections are decoupled from the user's POV.

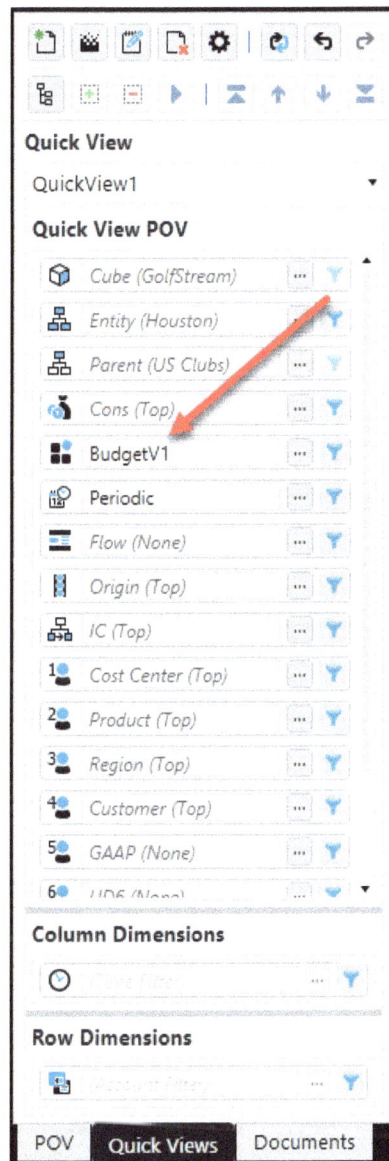

Figure 11.60

The other important distinction is my POV member versus my Member Filter. This is another gotcha, and I can see why. It's a little confusing, especially when I start to drag and drop dimensions from my POV to my grid in either the rows or columns.

Remember, the POV member is explicitly listed in the box and is either using the user's POV or is overwritten and displayed in black text. The Member Filter is different to the POV. The filter is what is in that little funnel to the right of the POV, as you can see in the below graphic. When you create a Quick View, you have no control over what members are placed in the Member Filter by default. This is something the OneStream platform controls; you cannot set it. By default, the Member Filter on all dimensions is going to be set to `Root.Children`. The only exception is the View dimension, which contains the members `YTD` and `Periodic`.

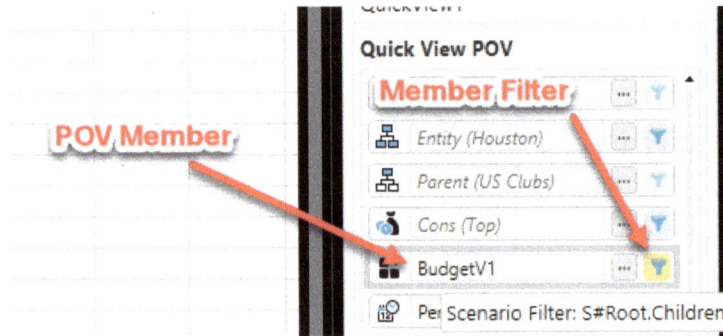

Figure 11.61

When the dimension is in the POV, the Member Filter has no impact on the Quick View. I want to reiterate this: no impact! Likewise, when the dimension is in the column or row, the POV has no bearing on what is shown in either the column or the row.

In the above example, you can see that I have `BudgetV1` set as my POV, and the filter is set to `S#Root.Children`. Let's explore what happens when I move this down to my Column dimension.

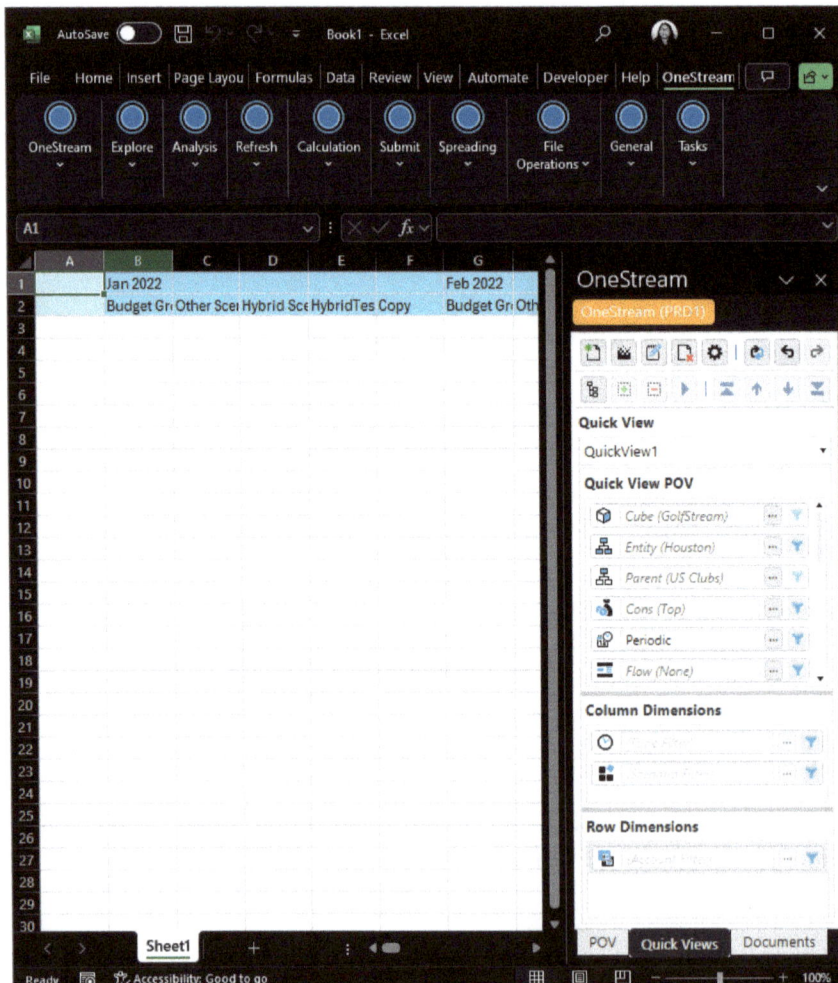

Figure 11.62

Notice that the Member Filter takes over. It is showing me the children under the root Scenario dimension, not `BudgetV1` that I set it to in the POV.

If I inverse the move, and return the Scenario dimension back to the POV, notice that it will revert to the single POV member `BudgetV1` and will still retain the filter that I had in place.

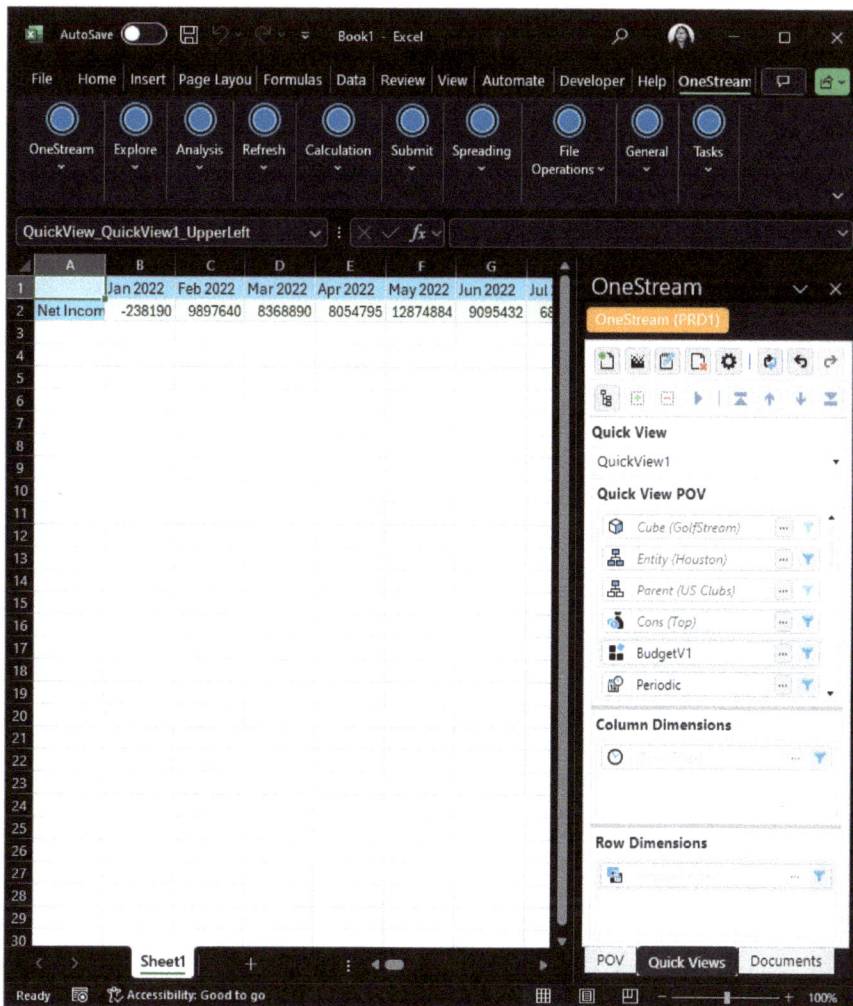

Figure 11.63

The bottom line is *don't get confused or frustrated*. Just know the difference between the POV member and what is in your Member Filter.

Another Way to Create a Quick View from Scratch

If you are a bit more adventurous and really know your OneStream metadata, there is another way to create a Quick View from scratch. You can simply type in the POV you wish to create. You are, however, limited to only using the member name, not the description. This is because OneStream allows you to use the same description across multiple members in the same hierarchy. You must also prefix each dimension because you can have duplicate member names across different dimensions. In other words, don't just type in `2022M3`; for example, it must be `T#2022M3` to specify it is part of the Time dimension. I've included this handy chart on dimensional prefixing.

Chapter 11

Dimension Prefixing		
A# - Account	I# - IC (Intercompany)	T# - Time
C# - Consolidation	O# - Origin	UD1# - UD8# - Custom Dimensions (these also work! U1# - U8#)
E# - Entity	P# - Parent	V# - View
F# - Flow	S# - Scenario	

Figure 11.64

The advantage of this method for the power user is that you can define many members at once, including expansion operators. And if you don't remember what a member is called, use the Select Member button to browse out for the member in the hierarchy. An active Cube View is not required to use this function.

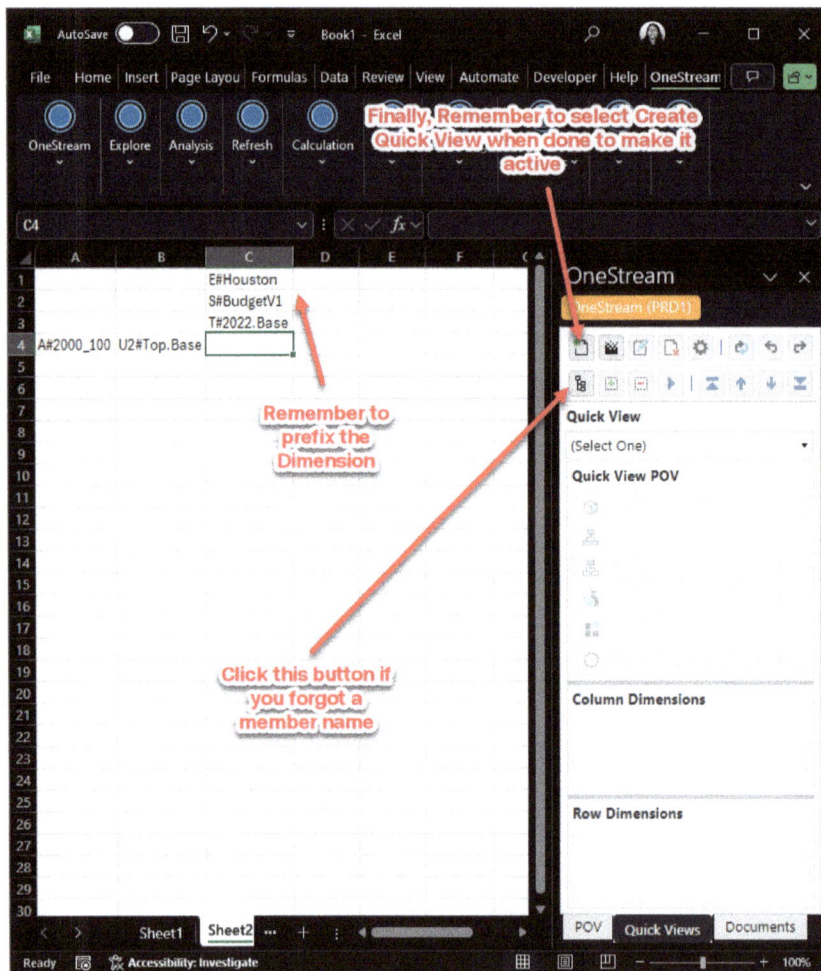

Figure 11.65

Once you have defined all the dimensions and expansion operators, highlight the range of cells and select Create Quick View. Any dimension not defined will show up in your Quick View POV and

344

will inherit the POV from the user. The report below in Figure 11.66 is the result of what I typed in Figure 11.65.

		Houston BudgetV1												
		Jan 2022	Feb 2022	Mar 2022	Apr 2022	May 2022	Jun 2022	Jul 2022	Aug 2022	Sep 2022	Oct 2022	Nov 2022	Dec 2022
Third Party S	Mach5	3511848.707	9258511	14047396	18676652	26498497	31925899	35916637	38311079	41982557	44696259	47888849	49485144
	Mach10	2636720.599	6951354	10546882	14022560	19895255	23970187	26966461	28764225	31520796	33558262	35955281	37153790
	Elite	2463018.73	6493413	9852075	13098781	18584596	22391079	25189964	26869295	29444269	31347511	33586619	34706173
	Launcher	2861354.126	7543570	11445417	15217201	21590217	26012310	29263849	31214772	34206188	36417234	39018465	40319081
	Hybrid LT	1331677.07	3510785	5326708	7082101	10048109	12106155	13619425	14527386	15919594	16948617	18159233	18764541
	Hybrid XF	1598012.489	4212942	6392050	8498521	12057731	14527386	16343310	17432864	19103513	20338341	21791079	22517449
	Hybrid SL	799006.2388	2106471	3196025	4249260	6028865	7263693	8171655	8716432	9551756	10169170	10895540	11258724
	Iron LT	1331677.07	3510785	5326708	7082101	10048109	12106155	13619425	14527386	15919594	16948617	18159233	18764541
	Iron XF	1967158.294	5186145	7868633	10461705	14843103	17883257	20118664	21459909	23516483	25036560	26824886	27719049
	Iron SL	799006.2388	2106471	3196025	4249260	6028865	7263693	8171655	8716432	9551756	10169170	10895540	11258724
	Wedge LT	1065341.658	2808628	4261367	5665681	8038487	9684924	10895540	11621909	12735675	13558894	14527386	15011632
	Wedge XF	2130683.313	5617256	8522733	11331361	16076974	19369848	21791079	23243818	25471351	27117788	29054772	30023265
	Wedges SL	1331677.085	3510785	5326708	7082101	10048109	12106155	13619425	14527386	15919594	16948617	18159233	18764541
	Soft Touch	1099439.728	2898523	4397759	5847020	8295772	9994907	11244270	11993888	13143302	13992869	14992360	15492105
	Choker	266335.4166	702157	1065342	1416420	2009622	2421231	2723885	2905477	3183919	3389723	3631847	3752908
	Ice Man	266335.4166	702157	1065342	1416420	2009622	2421231	2723885	2905477	3183919	3389723	3631847	3752908
	Thunder	969024.947	2554702	3876100	5153451	7311734	8809318	9910482	10571181	11584253	12333045	13213977	13654442
	Ultimate XL	1157127.965	3050610	4628512	6153817	8731056	10519345	11834263	12623214	13832939	14727083	15779018	16304985
	Fat Boy	532670.8244	1404314	2130683	2832840	4019243	4842462	5447770	5810954	6367838	6779447	7263693	7505816

Figure 11.66

Creating a Quick View from a Cube View or Existing Quick View

If you are new to Quick Views, this is also a good way to get started. You leverage existing Cube Views or Quick Views for your own analysis (although arguably the easiest way is to create a Quick View from a data explorer grid.)

Under the Quick View menu, you will see an option called Create Quick View using the POV of the selected cell. Let's create a new Quick View from the one we just authored in Figure 11.65. The Fat Boy product needs some examining, and I want to have my own Quick View in order to drill into some details. Simply select the cell and go to Quick View > Create Quick View Using POV From Selected Cell.

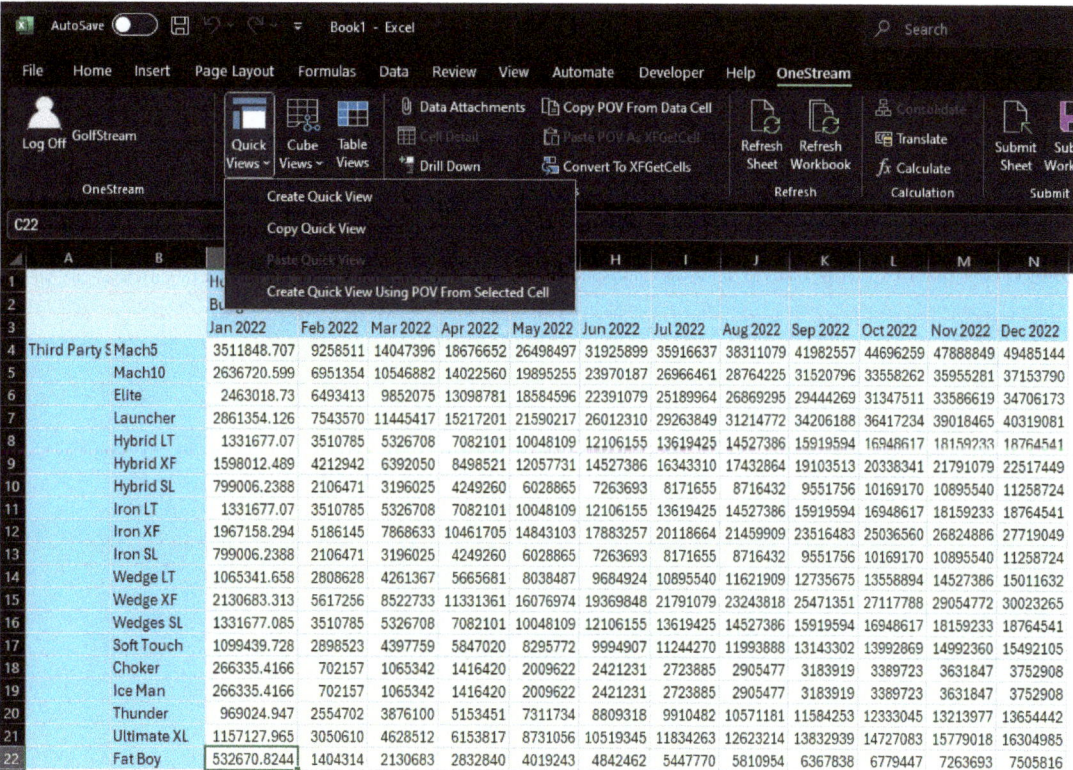

Figure 11.67

The resulting Quick View will have an overwritten POV, as indicated by the black text in the Quick View POV. The Quick View will also have account defined in the row, and time in the column. Note that the POV for this new Quick View is not set to the POV; it is set based on the intersection of the Quick View it was authored from, which is why the POV will be in all-black font.

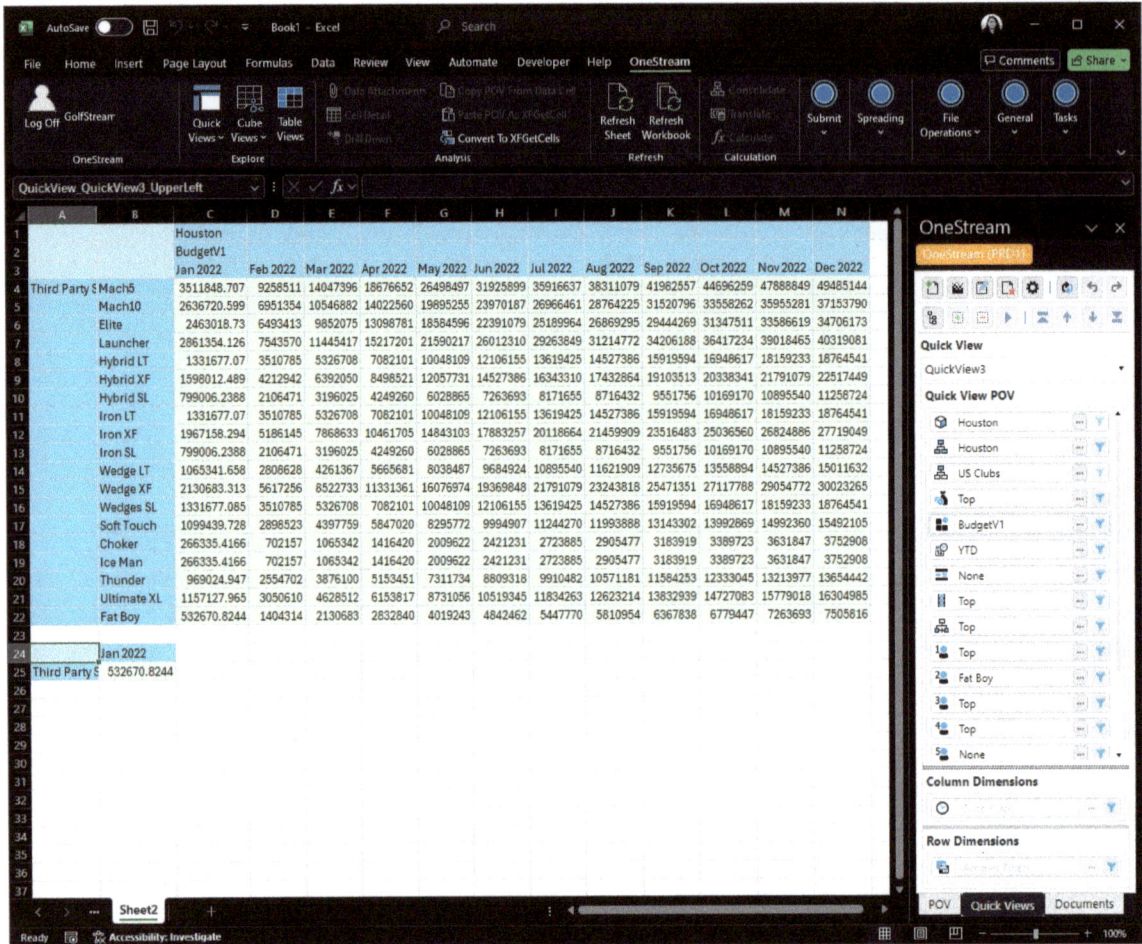

Figure 11.68

Achieving Asymmetry in Quick Views

The final topic on Quick Views is working around asymmetry. We discussed asymmetry at the beginning of the chapter and recommended Cube Views to combat this due to the unlimited nature of the number of rows and columns you can add to them. In some cases, Quick Views could be used to represent asymmetry using cross-dimensional member references.

Let's say we have a requirement to see one product aligned to one account. For example, we want to see third-party sales for the Mach5 product and Returns and allowance for the Hybrid LT product. In other words, two rows.

Quick Views present a unique challenge as we only have one real row and column to work with. And there is no way to explicitly limit the products to an account when introducing two dimensions to a row.

This is the traditional result of our efforts using a Quick View.

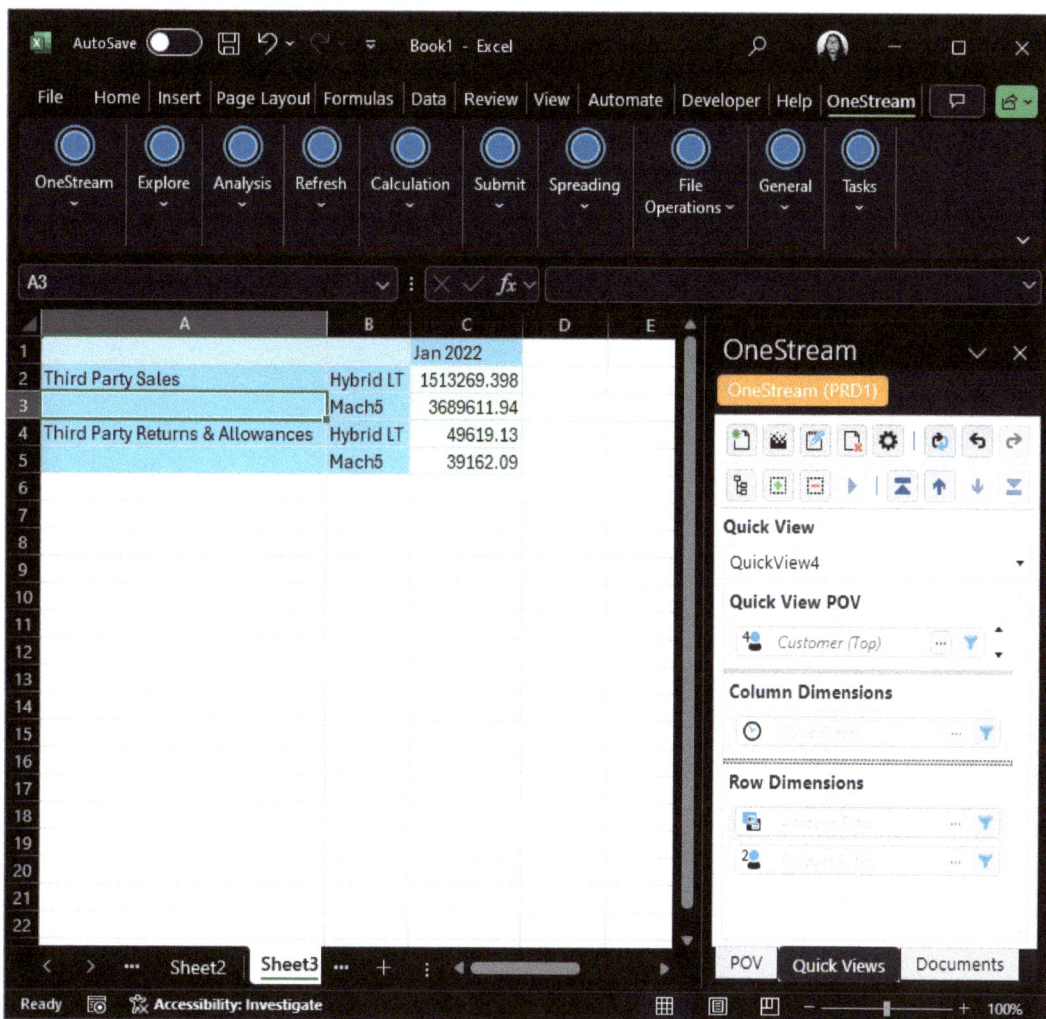

Figure 11.69

But there is another way. Instead of formally introducing the UD2 dimension into the row, I can leverage a little scripting to call out the corresponding partner member I want to see with the account.

Place the Product Filter back into the POV. Open the Account Filter and use the colon symbol to join third-party sales (A#2000_100) with the Product dimension Mach 5 (UD2#Mach5). The resulting concatenation overrides the POV and allows you to use just one row to represent a very succinct data point. This is sometimes referred to as cross-dimensional member operators.

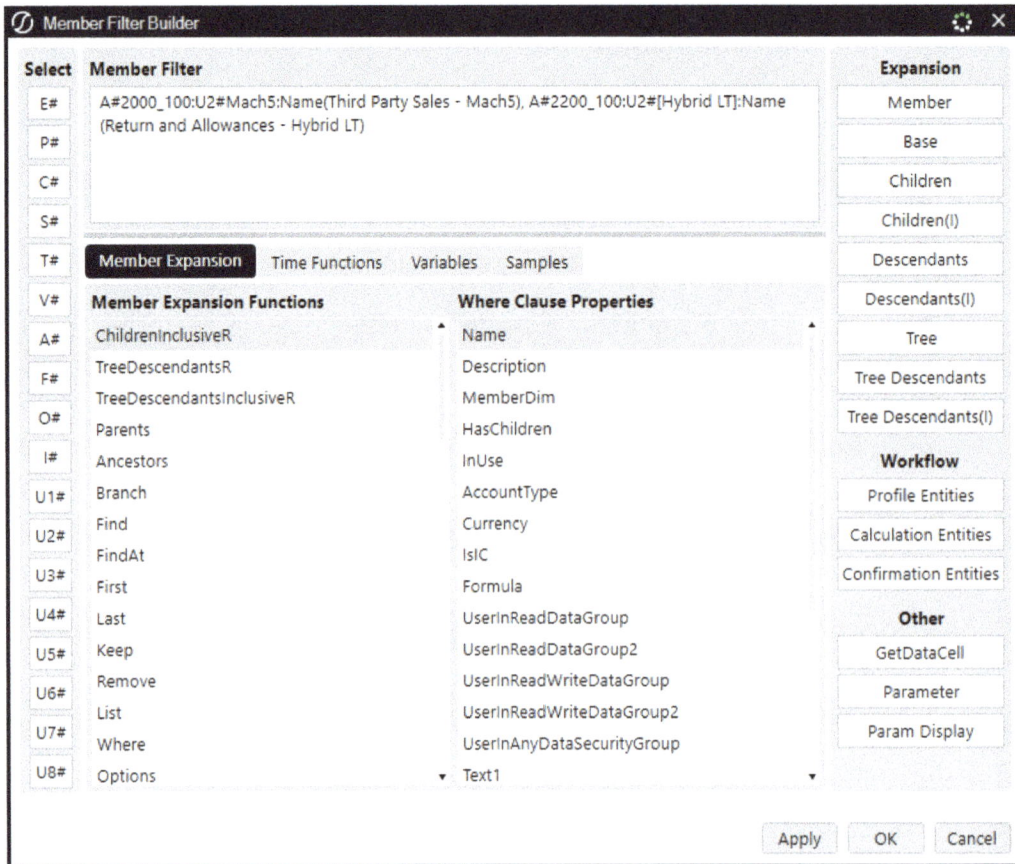

Figure 11.70

I do recommend using the Name function (after) to give the row a precise name. Without it, it will only show the account name.

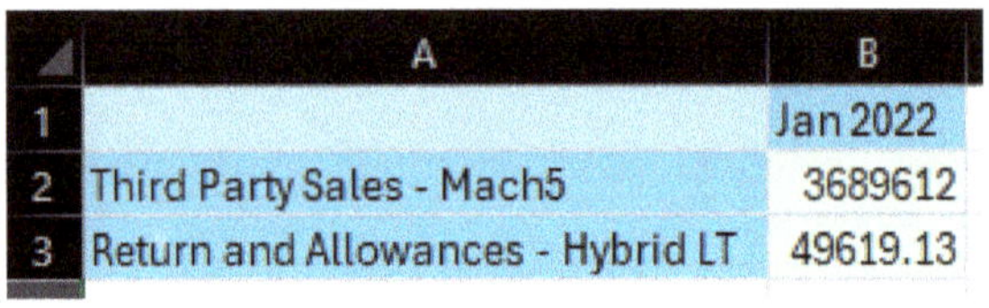

Figure 11.71

Conclusion

You made it to the end on Excel and Spreadsheet!

We've spent a lot of time reviewing the plethora of options available to you from a reporting perspective in Excel and Spreadsheet. After reading the chapter, my sincere hope is that you have the tools you need in order to use Cube Views and Quick Views in a meaningful way that will satisfy the requirements of your customer or organization. This chapter is the culmination of years working in the OneStream ad-hoc toolset, and coming from other Excel add-ins. I hope you enjoyed reading this as much as I enjoyed writing it.

Epilogue

This was from Presidents Club 2020 in Cancun, Mexico, with my favorite people at OneStream Software. It's the first time that my wife got to meet Roy and Diane, and our last trip and last meal before the COVID-19 lockdown took effect. We were blissfully unaware of the year that would unfold in front of us. I'm glad we had that time together before the whole world shut down.

From left to right: Katy & Tucker Pease, Allie (my lovely wife) & Nick Blazosky, Diane Terrusa & Roy Googin.

12

Analytic Blend

Originally written by Andy Moore, Sam Richards, and Terry Shea, updated by Chul Smith

In the world of business, finance teams have traditionally focused their efforts on closing the books of record data and forward-looking plans. This focus begs the following question: have you ever wondered what insights exist between the past and the future when considering what affects your today, tomorrow, or later this week?

Previously, companies would approach this question by attempting to gather datasets in Excel, or a data warehouse tool stacked with a BI reporting tool for their data visualizations. But the question presents many business challenges in today's world of data analytics because of latencies in the data; these latencies prevent proactive and actionable decision-making.

Just think. Your business must pull data from multiple sources and books of record, maintain data governance throughout the whole process, and – all the while – you have this goal of making actionable decisions that will help the business grow and prosper. By the time the business can complete all these steps, the financial data is already stale, and you are still trying to react!

Consider this. What would it take today for your business to combine Actuals, driver-based planning, and relational invoice-level data all in one place to make real-time decisions? Let's stop waiting to absorb the problem your business has traditionally reacted to, and gain insights into your data by leveraging OneStream's **Analytic Services**; it can enable you to produce the necessary financial indicators that allow your business to be proactive in understanding the challenges that you face today. In OneStream, we call this **financial signaling**!

Financial signals (see Figure 12.1) leverages the power of OneStream's extensible platform to create a single, unified reporting system that blends governed financial information with detailed operational and transactional data, all in one place.

Traditionally, you have always waited until the end of the month to look back at how you performed against your current targets. However, with **Analytic Blend** (one component of Analytic Services), you no longer need to wait until month's end. Using real-time daily and weekly analyses, finance teams can steer the business rather than react to it. Think of taking a road trip and getting from one city to another. You plan your general route and punch it into the GPS. While on your way, you encounter an accident that puts you behind schedule to your destination. Do you stay on the originally planned route and suffer through the delay, or do you search for an alternate route that gets you there with a minimal setback? Being able to quickly pivot requires access to timely, mid-month information.

Every business today knows what drives their business, but the access to indicators that show whether it is supplier information, customer churn, or bookings and billings has never been previously available alongside your Actuals and currently planned targets on a daily, weekly, or monthly basis. Essentially, the ability to gain the necessary insights into these sources of value is immense because it reduces the guesswork involved in business strategy. Why get stuck in traffic when you can lead with speed?

Figure 12.1

Now that OneStream has introduced financial signaling via Analytic Services, we'll be discussing how you can design your Analytics Reporting Center of Excellence to provide the operational insights needed to guide your business.

Analytic Services vs Analytic Blend

What is Analytic Services?

We have established that there's a need to help finance leaders who are looking to become better business partners by using analytics on top of their current financial models, but what really is Analytic Services, and how is it going to help you? What should finance leaders consider when implementing it? These are just some of the questions you should be able to answer as you approach any data analytics implementation.

Analytic Services is the concept of aligning your different datasets into a consumable, unified reporting view on a dashboard. This data can reside in OneStream within a cube model, a Solution Exchange model, a transactional/operational model that needs light-to-moderate financial intelligence added (via Analytic Blend), or data that lives outside OneStream (given there's a connection between OneStream and the source database).

The **BI Blend** engine within OneStream is similar to the consolidation engine or Stage engine that allows OneStream to provide the light-to-moderate financial intelligence piece to the overall Analytic Blend model (as shown in Figure 12.2).

This financial intelligence is provided through mapping, aggregation, simple currency conversion, and derivative rules, among others. There are seven engines in total that make up the OneStream platform:

1. BI Blend
2. Finance
3. Stage
4. Workflow
5. Data Quality
6. Data Management
7. Presentation and BRAPI

Out of those seven engines, the ones that we are focused on – that define Analytic Services – are the finance, Stage, presentation, and BI Blend engines. To summarize, Analytic Services is the combination of the core book of record, planning, daily/weekly signaling, and financially intelligent transactional analytics into a single platform.

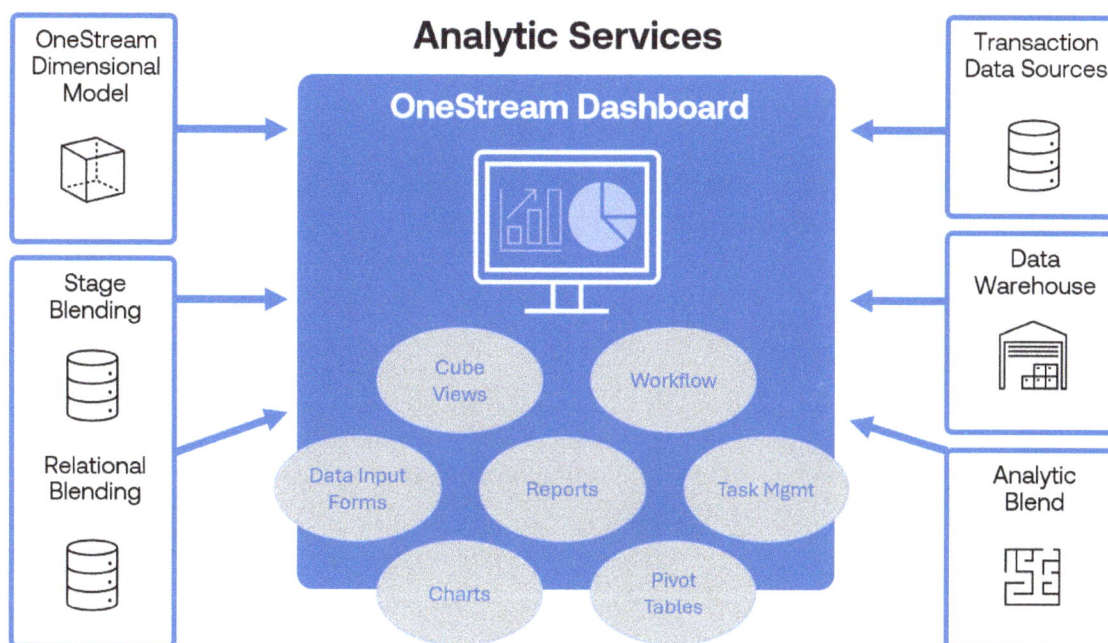

Figure 12.2

What is Analytic Blend?

Analytic Blend (formerly BI Blend) is not a replacement for traditional BI reporting tools. Instead, it should be viewed as a "read-only" aggregated storage model, designed to handle the reporting of larger datasets that do not fit within the traditional OneStream cube.

These types of reporting requirements typically reside in data warehouses or lakes that have no auditability, control, or telemetry. How does a business rationalize data that scales to heights that do not fit within their data warehouse, and how do they standardize reporting at the key levels required to create financial signaling? By leveraging OneStream's extensibility and data governance tools, described in earlier chapters, OneStream's BI Blend engine uses **operational telemetry** to transform and unveil your financial signals.

Operational telemetry within the OneStream platform is the process of applying financial intelligence to your transactional datasets using accounts, hierarchies, dimensionality, mappings, and rich calculations within one singular OneStream financial model. The resulting telemetry data is aggregated and stored within column-indexed tables in OneStream, and then brought into unified data visualization dashboards to guide and support the business in real-time decision-making: daily, weekly, and monthly.

These views provide finance leaders with the ability to measure their operational insights at the frequency required to be proactive within today's economy. With the ability to adjust plan targets ahead of the month-end close, finance teams are able to adjust and steer the business appropriately, acting swiftly on timely vital information.

In summary, Analytic Blend is *not* a BI reporting tool replacement, but adding financial intelligence to your operational datasets can provide benefits such as:

- Faster decision-making, supported by high-frequency operational data

    o   Track daily business trends

    o   Add financial intelligence to operational data

- o Manage financial performance daily
- o Drive monthly financials based on daily operational insight
- Powerful analytics through unified visualizations
    - o Visualize finance data
    - o Visualize operational data
    - o Combine in one visualization
- Securely visualize and analyze your latest financial data
    - o Immediate access to the latest financial data
    - o Leverage OneStream security as a query filter
    - o Data latency eliminated
    - o Data quality guaranteed and auditable

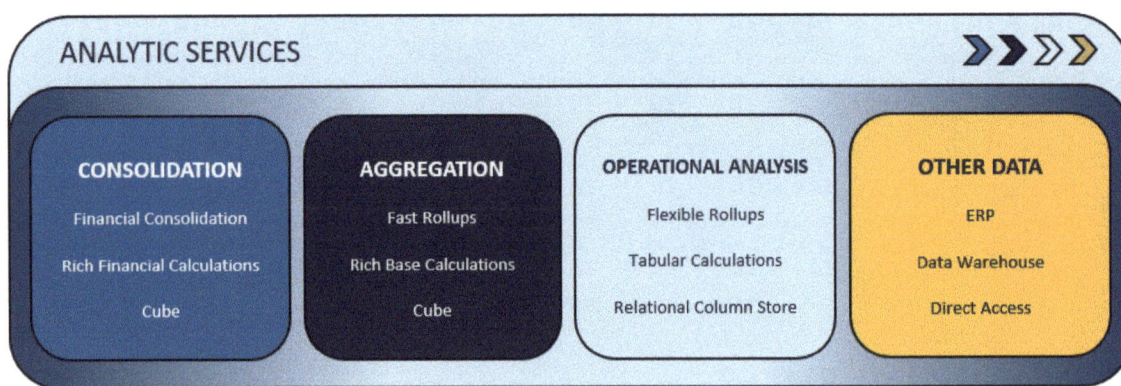

Figure 12.3

To achieve these benefits, we must first understand how Analytic Blend came to solve the business challenges your finance leaders face. Throughout this chapter, we will be discussing the two realms of finance that have been on a converging path, and to do this, we do not focus on trying to close your general ledger every day when implementing Analytic Blend. Instead, we shall focus on defining what business problem you want to solve, and what transactional dataset you will require to solve it. Then, we focus on applying your current financial intelligence from your financial close consolidation or planning processes in OneStream, and integrating it with the specific transactional datasets – so you can understand the vitals that drive working capital, sales opportunities, or revenue from customer sales.

The History Behind Analytic Blend

Why Do We Need It?

The OneStream platform simplifies and unifies your financial close and consolidation, planning, forecasting, data quality, and reporting. It is used today – around the world – from small to mid-sized companies and global enterprises to handle complex financial reporting requirements.

OneStream solves traditional problems like shortening the close, delivering more timely and accurate reporting packages, streamlining financial processes, and eliminating redundant legacy CPM applications. While this has worked for many organizations, we are seeing a shift in the Office of Finance that focuses on finance teams' efforts around operational planning and BI to support financial decisions. They want to pull data more frequently, and load more transactional volume types of data with the ability to execute overnight as a batch process or on-demand throughout the day. Waiting until month-end is no longer acceptable for businesses to operate effectively, especially in high-stress economic environments. These higher frequency datasets scale in volume quickly, become stale the moment you turn your head, and require refreshes at the snap of your fingers.

OneStream knew this high rate of change and demand would not fit the traditional OneStream cube and would require data governance and financial intelligence that delivered the robust reporting needed to make sense of these more transient transactional datasets.

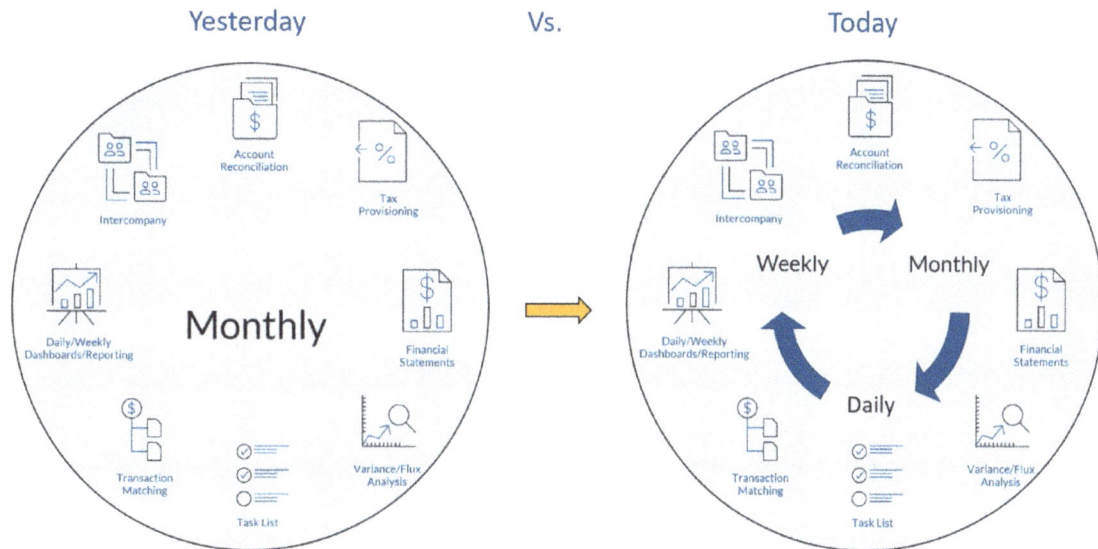

Figure 12.4

Based on Figure 12.4, above, OneStream provides the ability to aggregate quickly, and apply financial intelligence-leveraging hierarchies, which already exist to align the results among *daily, weekly, and monthly* time frequencies. It was very evident that to deliver unified views of information, two sides of the house – 1. ERP, which runs day-to-day business activities, and 2. CPM, which manages businesses monthly – needed to be combined into one unified model using 'data blending'.

Data blending in Analytic Blend provides:

- **Insights** within your financial ERPs, warehouses, and OneStream.
- **Agility** – vertically and horizontally within your business.
- **Alignment** across the organization at the reporting points which are key to the business.

Analytic Blend

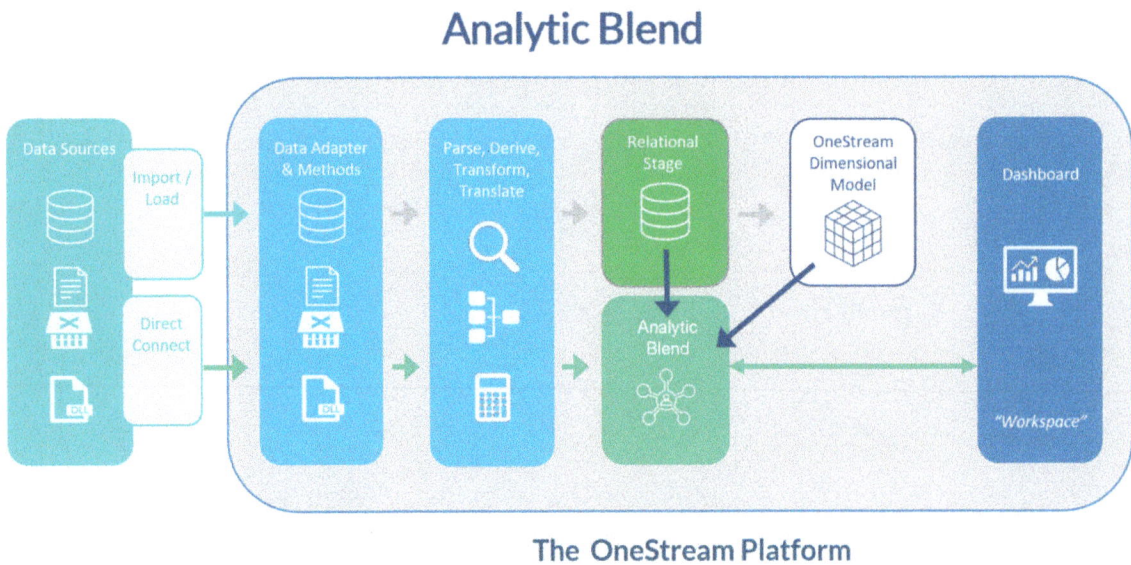

The OneStream Platform

Figure 12.5

In order to accomplish the unified views above, OneStream leverages its BI Blend engine (shown in Figure 12.5), which sits within OneStream's Stage engine. The BI Blend engine leverages new Stage cache functionality that allows it to rationalize and process large transactional datasets 'in memory' and write the results out to SQL-based column store indexed tables.

Once the data is written, it is considered 'read-only' and can be dropped and recreated as frequently as the end-user would like it to be – making it scalable in every aspect. The engine leverages existing mappings and hierarchies, as shown in Figure 12.6, to apply operational telemetry, resulting in a financially intelligent dataset for reporting. The BI Blend engine uses the cube hierarchies' parent members to evaluate *all* the base members within that hierarchy underneath it, to derive and aggregate the parent levels to the finalized column store index table. During this process, Analytic Blend also utilizes key properties within the cube to perform direct method translations, based on the cube's defined reporting currency.

Transaction Analysis

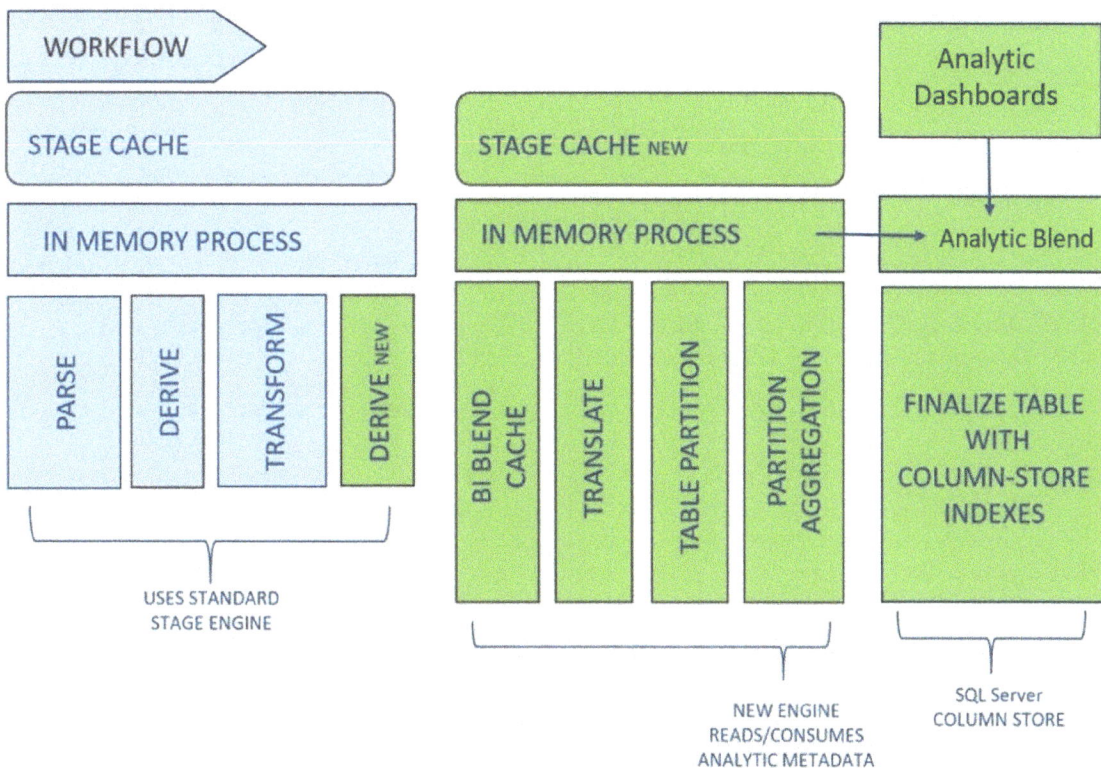

Figure 12.6

When Should We Use It?

With this model, OneStream is combining relational, Stage, cube, and source transactional data in one platform and financial model. This allows you to let the data reside where it belongs and prevents businesses from compromising their current processes inside a traditional cube-based model.

During discovery, determine if OneStream is adding value to the data set. If the answer is no, it may be best to let OneStream query the data from its source rather than taking the time to import those records into the application. Our goal is never to replicate an entire cube or an entire ERP book of record dataset within Analytic Blend. Traditional cube-based models are more structured by nature, but Analytic Blend can leverage these structures to connect your structures to your source system transactional data, such as invoice data related to customers or vendors.

Any time you find yourself in a design, and the dimension you are discussing is related to customers, for example, you should stop and consider if you are compromising the goals of the cube-based financial model. You likely have thousands of customers that change frequently in both relevancy and data volumes. It is important, in situations like this, to consider tools like Analytic Blend to achieve your reporting goals.

Analytic Blend is efficient and performant with large transactional datasets not just because it processes the data 'in memory' in a cached state, but because it also allows you to aggregate data via **Blend Units** dynamically or based on your definition! Within the BI Blend engine, OneStream lets you determine what dimension should drive performance and be assigned as the Blend Unit. The engine processes and aggregates all data by the Blend Unit, which is one of the first design considerations when undertaking implementations. This is conceptually similar to the cube-based model, where parallelism and performance are increased by adding more threads. The more members you must aggregate means that dimension should be the Blend Unit. With Blend, any dimension can be defined as a Blend Unit, not just entity-like in the cube-based model. The aggregation process works like this:

- The Blend Unit is defined, based on how data will be consumed and aggregated.

- The engine aggregates the Blend Unit first and creates a page for each parent and base member in the defined Blend Unit dimension.

- Next, the Blend Unit pages are aggregated for all other dimensions in parallel by the Blend Unit.

Cases where Analytic Blend should be considered are:

- **BI Reporting** – to provide the ability to add rationalized reporting against source data.

- **Multiple BI Tools** – to eliminate the maintenance of multiple systems, and the challenge of security. OneStream is a single source.

- **Attributes** – to incorporate attribute reporting, such as invoices or projects with aggregated reporting against the cube dimensions.

- **Aggregation and Reporting** – column store index, stored parent data

- **Transient Data** – create report, drop, rebuild

- **Aggregation** – bypass consolidation overhead for fast reporting, similar to other high-performance aggregate storage solutions

- **Intermediate Data Source** – where Blend is used as a high-performance pre-processor to source data to the cube. Lots of customers are pushing to load more transactional-level detail to Stage so, when that detail exceeds the norm, Blend can be used to eliminate compromising situations that may arise, related to complete mapping or transient metadata.

Let's review and summarize the dos and don'ts of Analytic Blend.

We've established Analytic Blend is not a BI replacement reporting tool and that we shouldn't look to replicate entire ERP datasets or traditional problems that a cube-based model would solve. Okay, but what else specifically should we consider? Analytic Blend is first and foremost a read-only analytic modeling tool that leverages our cube dimensions for aggregations at specific parent levels. Blend data is written and stored outside the cube in the application database tables as a SQL-based column store index. It creates unified views for slice and dice insights, has some financial intelligence, and allows you to drop and recreate on the fly – making it very susceptible to handling incremental metadata use cases where point-in-time reporting (as well as up-to-the-minute reporting) needs to be accomplished.

Static point-in-time reporting is accomplished using our **star schema** functionality. When using star schema functionality, you can align your results with our **leveled hierarchy** feature. Analytic Blend provides basic direct method translation to your reporting currency as well as additional attribute-level reporting through the attribute dimensions within the cube, and within our existing Stage engine. Lastly, it provides rich calculations via derivative transformation rules that behave differently to traditional derivative rules and have comparable data buffer concepts to OneStream's finance rules. Other cube and metadata settings used by Analytic Blend include the **account type**, which helps manage hierarchy aggregation, **entity currency** for simple rate translation, and **workflow tracking** and **input frequencies**, which help drive the table creation within Analytic Blend.

What does it not do? And where should you determine whether to use a more traditional cube-based model? Analytic Blend never writes data to the cube and doesn't handle complex translation, consolidation, or elimination logic. If your data requires this type of logic, you should consider a traditional cube-based approach. More specifically, the Analytic Blend solution does not use Member Formulas or rules from the application cube, relationship properties such as percent consolidation, percent ownership, or aggregation weight, which supports any type of complex consolidation or custom elimination logic. Simple translation using the cube's reporting currency is mentioned above, but the solution would not be used to handle any type of custom translation logic or periodic value translation methods that would typically be found in a consolidation cube model.

Analytic Blend Data Model Types

Within Analytic Blend use cases, there are defining model types or characteristics that help identify when it should be used. We will go into these models in more detail later in the data source section, but these model types include:

- **Multidimensional Hybrid Model** – Highest financial intelligence model type with rich calculations, multidimensional reporting, and security requirements.

- **Financial & Operational Model** – Medium financial intelligence model type with medium- to low-level calculations, table-level security, table-level metadata geared towards dropping and recreating each time, basic drill reporting, or pivot analytics.

- **Excel or Outlier Model** – Very flexible to be financially intelligent (or not). Not multidimensional, lower volume based on Excel files that rely on human intervention, basic drill reporting, or pivot analytics.

- **Relational Model** – No financial intelligence, table-level security requirements, basic pivot analysis requirements, basic drill reporting, or pivot analytics.

- **Operational Telemetry Model** – These are true deviations from the standard financial cube or hybrid model, above, and will be close to real-time analysis and signaling.

Analytic Blend Design Considerations

When designing Analytic Blend, you first want to consider the following questions to define your use case. This is important because you want to continuously confirm that Analytic Blend is the right fit for your use case. The key questions are highlighted below:

- What's the analytic reporting use case we want to accomplish? Consider where in Figure 12.7 your data is coming from.

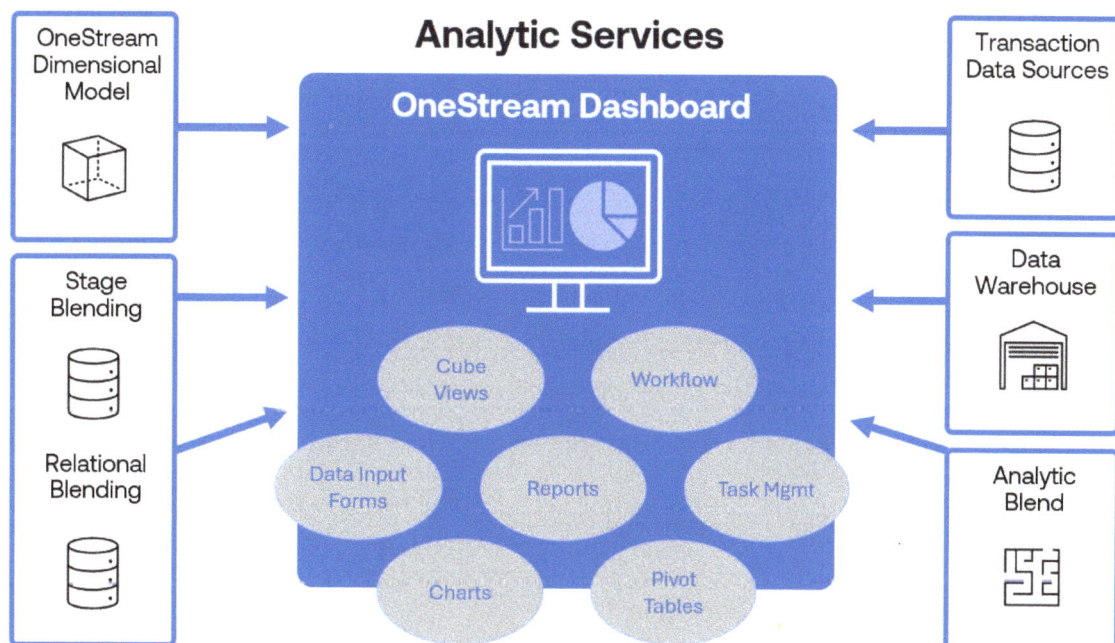

Figure 12.7

- Are we consuming or creating?

  o See Figure 12.8 below; this helps identify if the model type will be a true operational BI, multidimensional hybrid, or consolidation cube-based model type.

- How will this be integrated into reporting processes?

- Who is the main consumer of this information?
- How will this information be delivered for consumption?

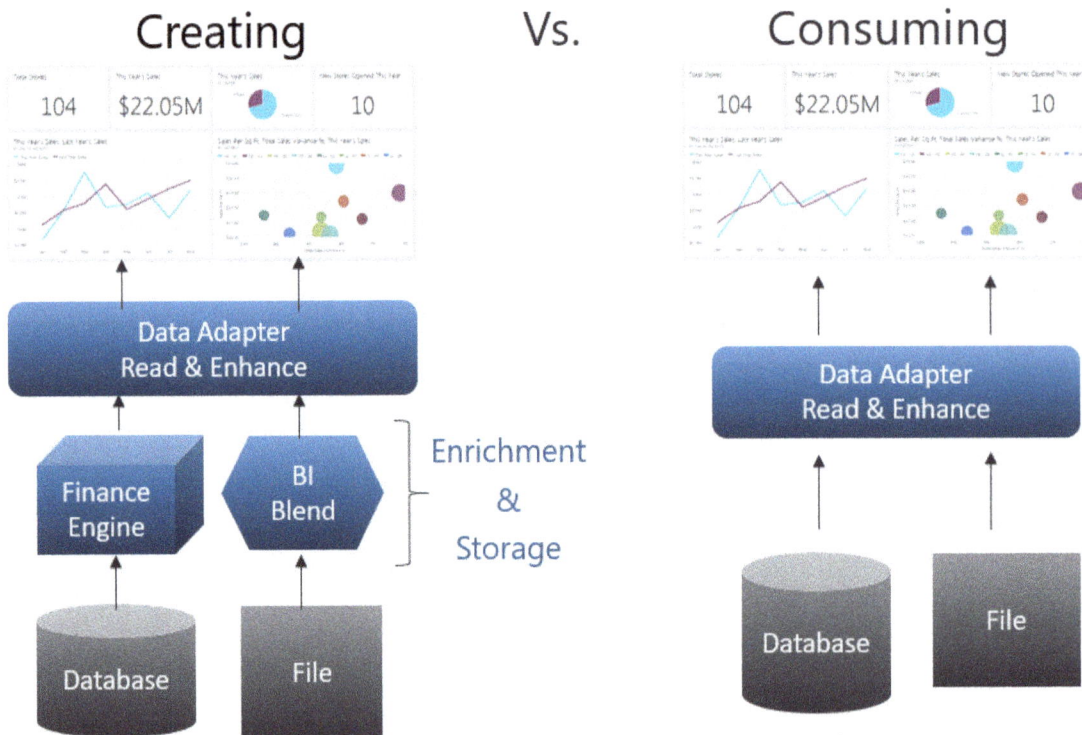

Figure 12.8

Key design implementation concepts are as follows:

- Design starts with end-reporting in mind and ends with reporting!
- Define your data source inventory
  - Spreadsheets, financial & operational reports, KPI/OKRs, access, transactional
- Define the new data view you want to achieve in your analytics implementation
  - Are they financial or operational KPIs, or both?
- What's our data integration strategy for our data source inventory?
  - Are we using BRs, FDX connectors, or SQL adapters?
  - Are we automating the integration via an overnight batch process, and on-demand during the day?
- Will it be a central or an inline workflow process?
  - Have we defined all the necessary dimension mapping rules that exist in the cube on which to do aggregations?
- Data creation – calculations, translations, and aggregations
  - Are all the appropriate time-based or user-defined measures defined? For example, quarterly KPIs or trailing metrics
  - Do we require a specific Analytic Blend Scenario Type to be used to hold a dimension the financial model may not need, but which Blend needs to provide aggregated reporting at certain parent levels?
  - Will attribute dimensions be used for aggregated reporting, and if so, are they defined in the cube or Stage?

- Have we thought about how we want to prepare the data views?

    o Will we be using dataset business rules, SQL data adapters, or the Analytic Blend adapter components?

- Finally, how are we planning to present the information to the end-user, and do we have multiple end-user audiences relative to the data we are collecting?

Analytic Blend Data Sources and Integration

One of the key items with Analytic Blend is the ability to get data out of OneStream (or out of another data warehouse) without having to use a typical connector to bring it into Stage or the cube. This feature came out with the 5.3 release, and it's called **FDX queries**; FDX stands for Fast Data Extract.

There are approximately nine different FDX queries that can be used for different reasons, such as a data source for a load, or to create a table to use in reporting for Analytic Blend. For example, say your business has a bunch of dynamically calculated data, as well as stored data, that you want to display on a dashboard. You could use the `BRApi.Import.Data.FDXExecuteCubeView` call to run the Cube View, via a business rule, that has all of the data you want to put in a table. One benefit to this approach is that since it is a rule, you could layer on another extract to create a custom view of the data to use in a report component within Analytic Blend.

In the next two sections, I am going to go over the most common FDX queries and example use cases.

- `BRApi.Import.Data.FDXExecuteCubeView` – as described above, this call is used to extract Cube View data and put it into a table to be used for Analytic Blend.

- `BRApi.Import.Data.FDXExecuteCubeViewTimePivot` – this call is very similar to the previous call, with the exception of the time pivot. What that is going to do is take the Time dimension and pivot it from being in one column to each month having its own column. This type of call comes in handy if you are trying to take and add months to a table, since all you need to do is add them to the end.

- `BRApi.Import.Data.FDXExecuteDataUnit` – this call is really handy when you are trying to extract stored data out of the system. For example, before this call was created, the only way to do something similar was to create a data management job that would extract the data for you. This call also has the added benefit of being able to run using multi-threading, hence the "fast" in FDX. I would use this call if I had stored data that a client was editing, and then wanted to extract it for analysis in an analytic component within a dashboard. You could have the button run the rule that extracts the data and renders below.

- `BRApi.Import.Data.FDXExecuteDataUnitTimePivot` – this call is the same call as above, except with the time pivot that we previously covered.

- `BRApi.Import.Data.FDXExecuteStageTargetTimePivot` – this call is really similar to the Execute Data Unit query, except for the fact that we are pulling data from Stage instead of from the cube. If you transformed data from multiple workflows, then you would be able to leverage this call to extract that data from the Stage table (all with a single call). This rule is beneficial when you have data that needs to be transformed but not aggregated; you can use the Stage engine to do transformation on the source data, then use this extract – with the combination of Analytic Blend – to create reporting off the transformed Stage data.

- `BRApi.Import.Data.FDXExecuteWarehouseTimePivot` – all of the previous calls were focused on pulling data out of OneStream, whether it be in the cube or in Stage. This call is where you can use similar logic to pull data from an external warehouse or ancillary table that might not be directly in OneStream. You could leverage this call to join ancillary tables with external sources, and even use another FDX query to bring in cube data to report on. You can see how the leveraging of these FDX queries really opens OneStream up to a whole new level of reporting capabilities.

Deployment/Execution Methods

When you are deploying your solution, one thing to consider is how you want the user to interact with the data loads. Several different integration options (covered previously) will come into play when you weigh how best to deploy it. This section details considerations when generating data that is being reported on. If you are consuming directly from an external source, or a source that doesn't need the end-user to generate the data, then the workflow-related section doesn't apply.

Workflow-Related

Since you are leveraging a data source like Analytic Blend that uses the workflow, your two main options are a **central load** or a **distributed load**.

The central load is setup so that an admin or a central user controls when the Analytic Blend tables are created. The distributed load (or inline load) is where you mix the Analytic Blend load into the user's workflow where they are completing the other task.

Two of the main things to consider when deciding on a central or decentralized workflow would be the end-users of the report, and how often the load needs to be performed. For example, if you are leveraging this for a planning process, and your Analytic Blend load needs to be loaded daily, but the planning process is only done monthly, you could use a central load since it doesn't follow the pattern of the normal end-user process.

Non-Workflow-Related

Another data source that you may be using with Analytic Blend is for leveraging databases to create views or tables to report directly from. This type of integration may require a rule to generate the table or view. If this is the case, then you need to either have a button that triggers the rule, or you need an event such as a load. For example, if you had an Analytic Blend report that leveraged cube data merged with another table to give you more detail, you might leverage an Event Handler rule to create the view once the load was complete. If the load was an Analytic Blend load (mentioned before), then you could leverage the below transformation Event Handler to have the view created after the load.

`BREventOperationType.Transformation.BiBlend.FinalizeBiBlendTable`

Automate or On-Demand

The next thing to consider in your deployment is whether you are going to have the load 'on-demand' only; this means that an end-user triggers the process to create the table or view, or you are going to automate it. If you are going to automate it, you would follow our standard **batch harvest process** to load the Analytic Blend workflow. If you are not leveraging the Analytic Blend process, then you could use Task Scheduler to call the data management sequence, which fires the extensibility rule to create your tables or views.

`BRApi.Utilities.ExecuteFileHarvestBatchParallel`

Reporting, User Interaction, and Visualizations

End Audience and User Interaction

The first thing that you want to think about when it comes to Analytic Blend's reporting capabilities is the audience, and how it is going to be used. For example, if you want to leverage this data in a report that needs to be used in a book, then you need to be aware that not all components can currently be used in books or extensible documents; for example, analytic dashboards cannot currently be used in books. If you are building a standard month-end report, you might not want to allow the user to make format changes. If you are building a report for analysis, then you want to give users all the flexibility that's needed to really understand the information they're viewing.

Data Sources for Reporting

Now that you have your workflow set up, and you have the data on which you want to build your reports in OneStream, it is time to decide how OneStream will retrieve it. There are several different methods that allow OneStream to consume the data. They fall into several different big buckets, based on the data type you are trying to consume.

- **Relational Model** – With a relational data model, OneStream will simply consume relational data. You will be more likely to use a data adapter with an external connection via a SQL data adapter, or a BI Blend Command Type found in the data adapters in the dashboarding section.

- **Excel Model** – Here, OneStream consumes an Excel file instead of a database. This type of data source is very helpful for data that is not housed in a source system and is not large. There are some considerations when using Excel as your data source; you are confined to the limitations of Excel, the file must be unzipped and read each time it is processed, and you have a big potential for user error because the file is kept up to date manually.

- **Multidimensional Hybrid** – This type of data source has the highest financial intelligence because you are leveraging OneStream and its multidimensional capabilities to structure your data. Since we are using OneStream's dimensional model, you will have to take the data model size into consideration and know that – on the larger data models – you might have some performance tuning and hardware requirements.

  The data that you usually analyze here is a periodic snapshot of your data in OneStream and can be gathered in different ways. The main consideration is the amount of data you are extracting. For solutions where a small data set is required, you can build a Cube View and use that as the source. On the other hand, for more complex or high data volume solutions, you might need business rules to extract the data or run multiple Cube Views in parallel. If you find yourself in this situation, I advise using an FDX query. There are two types of extracts: the **FDX Data Unit extract** and the **FDX Cube View extract**. The main difference is that with Cube Views, you can extract dynamic data; with the Data Unit query, you cannot. There are also two variations of each of these rules where you can have the data display in a pivot, based on the Time dimension.

  ```
  BRApi.Import.Data.FdxExecuteCubeView
  ```

  ```
  BRApi.Import.Data.FdxExecuteDataUnit
  ```

- **Financial & Operational Model** – This type of data source is really where you try to get an indicator as to how the business is doing on a daily basis. This type of data usually doesn't have a lot of meaning without adding some financial intelligence to it. For example, you might have sales data that you want to map to a given entity and then join with another attribute from another table to aggregate up – to see how the business is tracking against the plan. This type of data model and data source can be complex when leveraging SQL data adapters, connections to data warehouses, and FDX queries. When using this data source, consider when the individual parts are refreshed; is it overnight for some and throughout the day for others? You will want to consider performance when looking at how often each process runs; because of the resource requirements, you will control this process centrally.

BI Viewer or Large Data Pivot Grid Components

Now that we have all of the background considerations in place, we can start to get into the more exciting (in my opinion, at least) stuff. How do we want to turn our information into a masterpiece? The two main ways to consume data in the Analytic Blend methodology are through **BI Viewer** or a **large data pivot grid** component. One of the key factors that will push you toward a large data pivot grid (over a BI Viewer) is the volume of data.

- **Large Data Pivot Grid** – The large data pivot grid is all about large amounts of data. And that is because it can leverage **paging**. In other words, OneStream does not try to render all of the data at once. Large data pivot grids pull directly from a table and can filter down the data in some basic manner, as seen below in Figure 12.9.

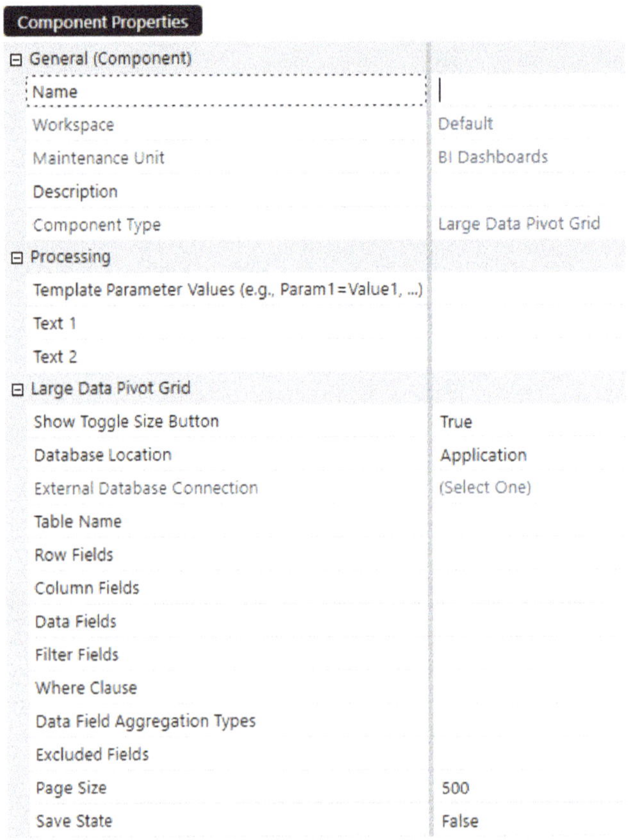

Component Properties	
General (Component)	
Name	
Workspace	Default
Maintenance Unit	BI Dashboards
Description	
Component Type	Large Data Pivot Grid
Processing	
Template Parameter Values (e.g., Param1=Value1, ...)	
Text 1	
Text 2	
Large Data Pivot Grid	
Show Toggle Size Button	True
Database Location	Application
External Database Connection	(Select One)
Table Name	
Row Fields	
Column Fields	
Data Fields	
Filter Fields	
Where Clause	
Data Field Aggregation Types	
Excluded Fields	
Page Size	500
Save State	False

Figure 12.9

In the large data pivot grid section, you will see that you can connect directly to a table only. You can choose between an application table, Analytic Blend database table, or an external database table. The next sections will show what a user will see when they open it, so you need to ask what you want to display in the rows, columns, data, and filter fields.

You can have more than one table column in each field and need to separate them with a comma. The next three options control whether you are showing all data in the table or not. You can leverage the `where` clause to filter down the results, data aggregation, or the excluded fields so a user cannot see those fields from the original table.

The next property is the paging size; this is an important field when it comes to performance. The higher you have the paging size number, the more rows that the large data pivot grid will allow to appear (up to a maximum of 3,000 rows).

The last option is the save state, which allows the user to update the default settings and keep their preferred look to the grid. Below, you will see an example of a user's view of a large data pivot grid that they've customized and saved.

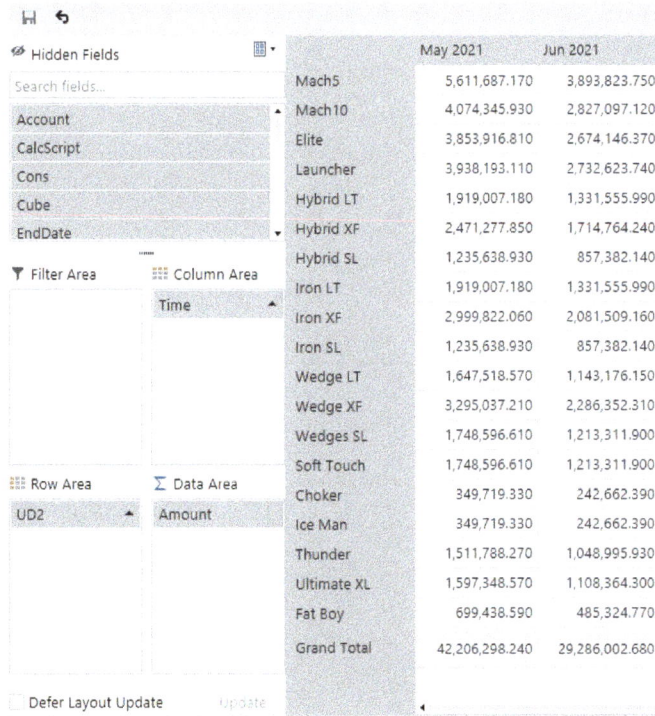

Figure 12.10

- **BI Viewer** – The BI Viewer component is where you can get the most visualizations and interactions with an end-user. BI Viewer has many different reporting options in it. It has charts, graphs, pivot tables, grid reports, and filter items. One big difference between the large pivot grid and BI Viewer is that the BI Viewer (as mentioned) does not have the ability to do paging.

  The BI Viewer does, however, have one big capability that the large pivot does not. It has the ability to do simple calculations on the data from your data source. You can do gross margin percent calculations and calculate the time between the current day and a date in the table. You can also do some simple logic statements as well, like `If` statements, as well as others. For a full list, go into the BI Viewer tool and – in the fields on your data source – right-click and add in a calculation. This will open all the options that you have in the calculation builder. Below is an example of what you can create for your end-users.

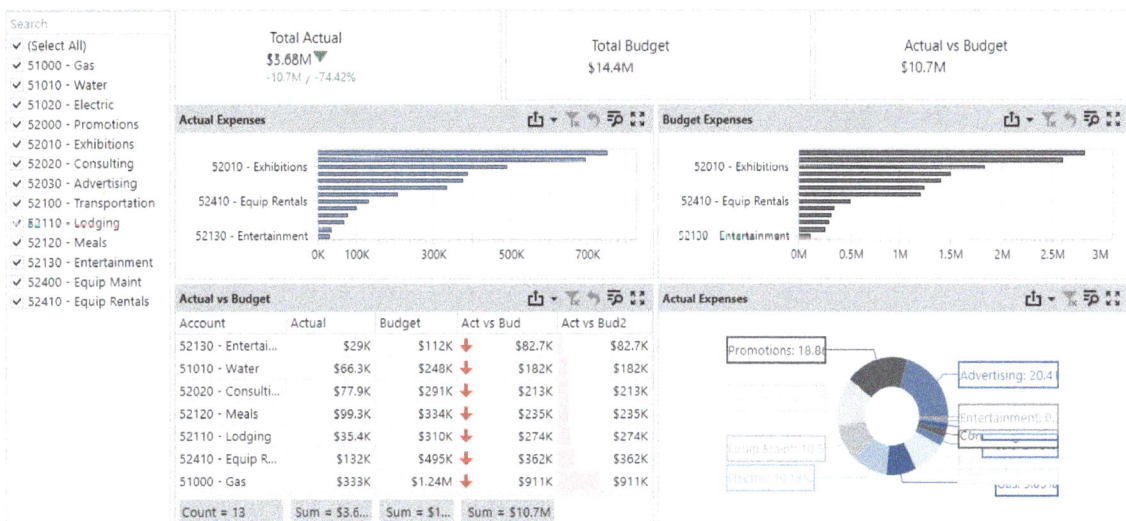

Figure 12.11

Analytic Blend-Specific Functionality

When you are considering Analytic Blend as part of your solution, there are some overall general items to consider.

- **Calculations** – The Blend Unit is a setting on the initial setup that tells OneStream how to divide the load into pages to process. This is important because it affects performance. Should you try to process all the data in one Blend Unit, you can't leverage multi-threading. It will also affect your ability to run calculations on the data that you are loading. For example, when you are leveraging blend data buffers in derivative rules, you can only run calculations on the page that you are processing. Therefore, if you choose the wrong Blend Unit, and try to run a calculation on two different pages, it will not work. You will notice in my previous comment that you can reference a blend data buffer in the derivative rule calculation; this is an added feature to Analytic Blend loads that you cannot do in normal derivative rules that process on the typical Stage load.

- **Star Schema** – Here, you can have Analytic Blend produce a star schema when you generate the loads. OneStream produces several different tables when this option is selected and will produce a set of tables that show all of the aggregating dimensions (or just the ones that you have designated in the star schema). Next, it will produce a view of the data joined with the dimension tables that include the basic metadata columns, based on your settings in the workflow setup.

Figure 12.12

- **Leveled Hierarchy** – The leveled hierarchy is a feature that is only available when you use a star schema. It gives you the ability to produce a hierarchy in your reporting tool instead of using a flat list. This feature works by creating additional columns in the table to tell you where the data exists. Currently, this feature is not available on the Account dimension. Parent members will be stored as **XF stored** at lower levels, and base members are marked as **XF leveled**. Please see the illustration below for a visual of this.

Figure 12.13

- **Performance** – There are several things to consider in terms of performance when leveraging Analytic Blend. The first is that you will want to have a dedicated server for Analytic Blend. This is because the process will utilize *all* the memory that is available when it is processing data, in order to get through it as fast as possible. With any dedicated server, you will want to think about the number of aggregations and calculations you are running. If you have a lot of aggregation, then you will be producing a lot of rows, which means that you need a larger server with more RAM and a higher processor speed for it to process in a timely manner. You will want to make sure that the amount of data that you are trying to process doesn't exceed the 2GB in-memory .NET limitation. Lastly, you will want to consider when to run your **shrink**. This is a setting that shrinks the database after it has been run, in order to clean up the resulting fragmentation from Analytic Blend creating and dropping the tables every time it is run. The best practice is to make sure that you are not running the shrink in parallel, as it runs across the entire database. Also, make sure it is on the last job in the batch or as part of an overnight process. A good way to check for data explosion is to look at the processing log on the workflow, which has the detail of the load. This will give you the ability to see who is running the load, when it runs, as well as what the data looks like before and after aggregations.

Conclusion

In conclusion, you should by now start to see how Analytic Blend can really open the path toward a whole new level of reporting inside OneStream.

In reading this chapter, we have given you the tools to design a solution using some of the key concepts of Analytic Blend. If your solution is trying to utilize transactional data for directional reporting or taking and combining OneStream data with external data to give you more flexibility on the overall data model, you can see how it is possible in OneStream. In our ever-changing world, using Analytic Blend can deliver information to the key decision-makers that they need when making truly informed decisions.

Epilogue

There is always time for fun at OneStream. We truly all work hard and play hard.

13

Introduction to the Solution Exchange

Originally written by Shawn Stalker, updated by Shawn Stalker & Chul Smith

What is the Solution Exchange?

The **Solution Exchange** is the distribution mechanism for OneStream Platform software and solutions. It allows users to download pre-created solutions to add extra functionality to an existing version of the OneStream application. The platform section contains all currently supported OneStream Platform installation packages. Think of it like an app store for your phone, which also allows you to download new versions of your phone's operating system.

The solutions within have been developed by OneStream's Solution Network team, varying OneStream partners or the greater OneStream community. Partner-developed solutions are supported by the respective solution provider. Due to the various developers, our focus in this chapter will remain on the OneStream-developed solutions.

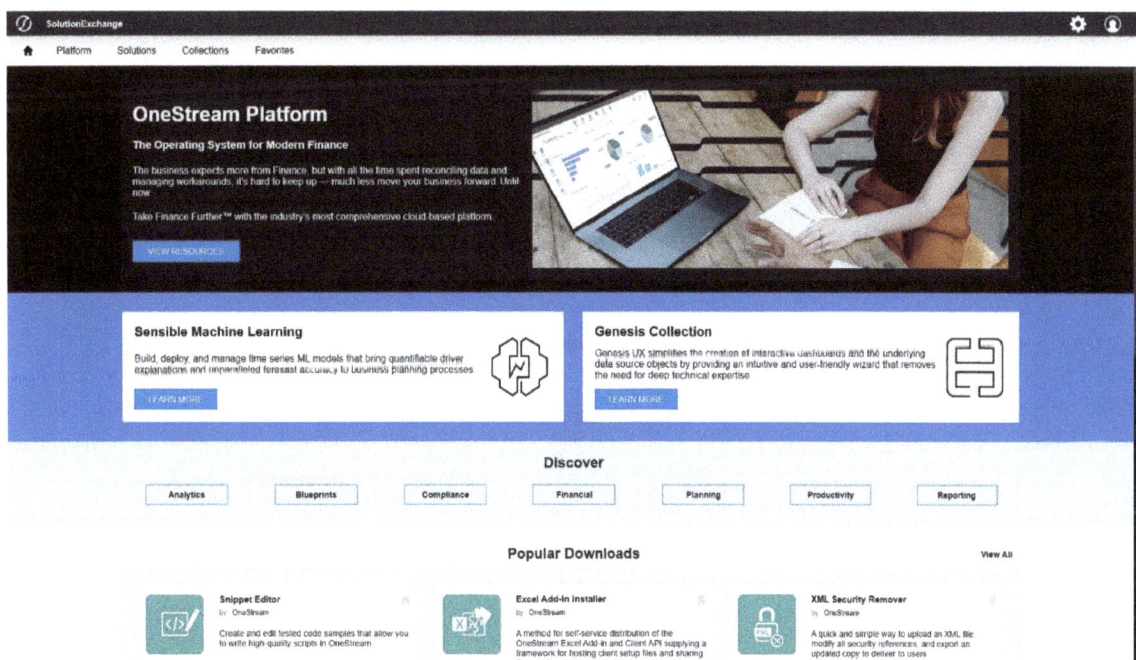

Figure 13.1

369

First, a short history lesson…

History of the Solution Exchange

At the very first OneStream user conference (August 2013), we discussed our vision for OneStream during the keynote presentation. At that point, we already had the basis for our first solution and knew that we were on to something. In the keynote presentation, the founders discussed their journey with OneStream using old cell phones to showcase the transition in technology through the years – along with how they came to start OneStream. The smartphone was the perfect analogy for where OneStream was going. Do you need a separate cell phone, flashlight, camera, and GPS? No! And the same should go for financial software. You should no longer need to buy separate financial consolidation, planning, and account reconciliation solutions. It should be a smart system – all in one package – just like a smartphone.

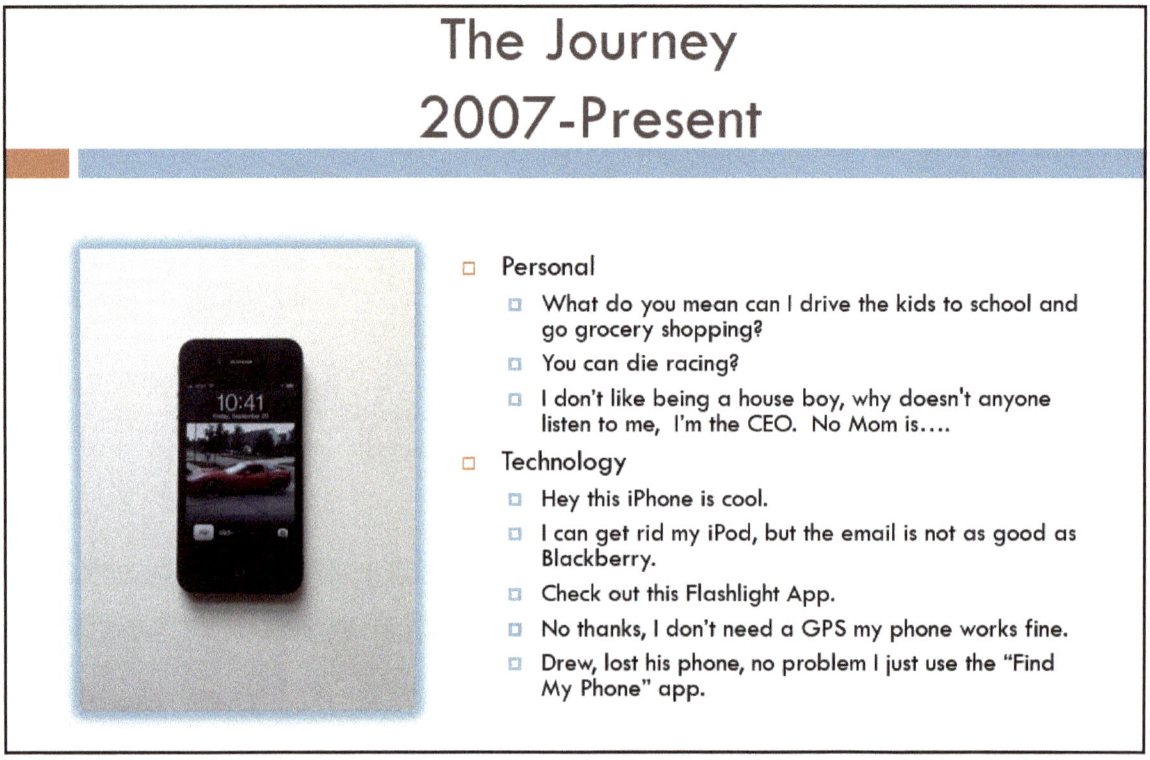

Figure 13.2

In the spring of 2014, at the second OneStream Splash user conference, OneStream released the first incarnation of the **Solution Exchange**. It was originally called the OneStream Fish Market based on the company's original fish logo, and allowed users to access OneStream software, solutions, and online video training, as well as link to OneStream support. By the spring of 2016, OneStream had updated its logo, and with it came a rebranding of the Fish Market as the OneStream MarketPlace. In the spring of 2023, the Solution Exchange was launched. This expansion extended the availability of solution offerings from others within the OneStream community. PartnerPlace and OpenPlace were created for this reason, while **MarketPlace** continued to provide the OneStream-developed solutions. Two years later, the Solution Exchange simplified its model by removing the three "Places", providing a single location where consultants and administrators can search and download these solutions as well as various platform versions. Figure 13.3 shows the origins of Solution Exchange.

Figure 13.3

When I started at OneStream in early 2013, I was working on a project for one of our first customers. This customer had already implemented Actual reporting and was now adding in their Forecast process. Part of their original Actuals **reporting implementation** had been a custom reporting dashboard that allowed users to select their scenario, time period, entity, and report from predefined dropdowns. Those selections would generate the reports and display them to the user.

One of the items I was tasked with adding was support for their Forecast data to the custom reporting dashboard. As I had never worked with OneStream dashboards before, I had to basically disassemble the code to figure out how it all worked. It turned out that their Forecast involved more than just adding a new Scenario Type; they were looking to forecast at a much more detailed level. Many of the items on the dashboard that were already working for Actuals would need to be refactored in order to support the new Forecast.

The final version of this custom reporting dashboard turned out to be something that we thought would be useful for more than just one customer. It could be used by all our customers and expand OneStream's value with minimal effort. With some additional features and documentation, the Guided Reporting (GRT) solution was born.

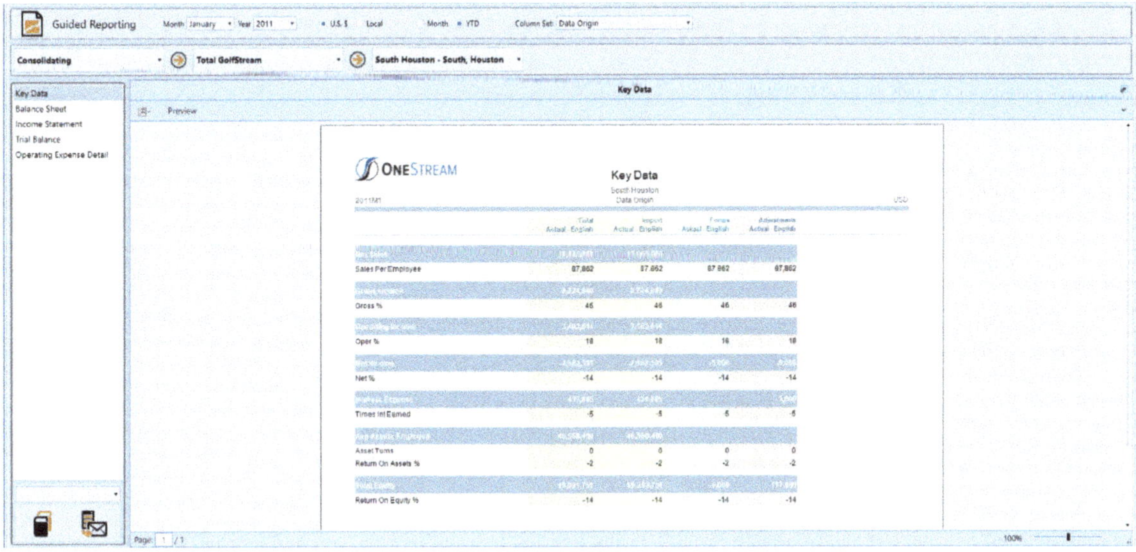

Figure 13.4

OneStream as a Development Environment

The original intent behind the dashboard and business rule toolset in OneStream was for reporting and workflow customization. Users would be able to create forms to enter data and have dropdowns that allowed selections to be entered into the form. This was also the thought process for the custom reporting solution that we originally implemented. During the process of creating the Guided Reporting solution, we came to the realization that what we had was not just going to be used for reporting and customization. This was a platform for developing OneStream solutions. We had created a *full development environment*, enabling developers to write software on our software.

One Platform To Rule Them All

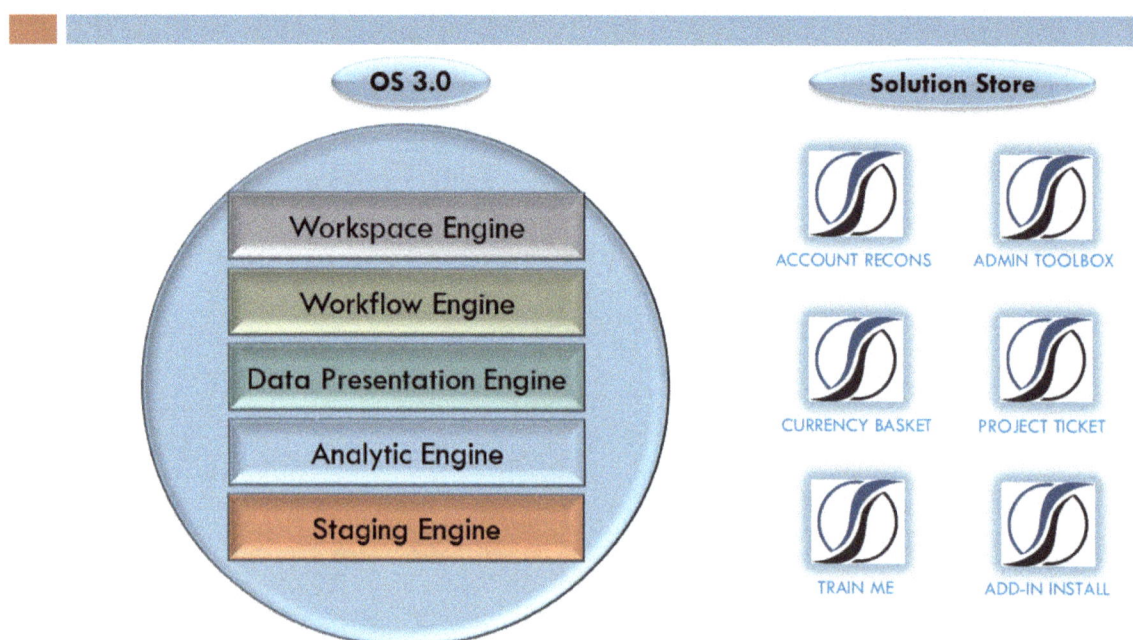

Figure 13.5

There was everything needed for OneStream to be a true development platform… just as envisioned at the first conference. There was an interface for creating UI with our application dashboards, a truly integrated development environment (IDE) with our business rule editor, and access to all of OneStream's BRAPIs. In addition, we had full access to all the OneStream engines, as well as security.

The Solution Exchange itself is a great example of OneStream's platform concept. Once we started creating solutions, we knew that we would need a store/distribution method for getting the solutions to our user base, and when we started thinking about building a website for hosting a store, we quickly concluded that OneStream itself would be the perfect method for hosting it. OneStream already has built-in security that can be accessed through the BRAPI, and we could even run other solutions in the MarketPlace as part of the MarketPlace.

On the very first version of the MarketPlace, we also included a solution that could be used online. The section for training videos was the Train Me (TRM) solution, which was used to provide access to OneStream-created video content. This was used to provide video instructions on how to use OneStream and the MarketPlace itself. Additionally, we added a section called Online Solutions into the MarketPlace that contained dashboard accelerators and samples. These allowed users to create starting points for their own solutions. We had turned the MarketPlace itself into a solution that not only allowed solutions to be downloaded but which also allowed users to create their own custom solutions.

Solution Exchange vs. Platform Development

There are two distinct development teams within OneStream: the **Platform** team and the **Solution Network team** (previously called the MarketPlace team). When I started with the company, only the platform team existed. As the company was so small, there was no official quality testing team; everyone in the company participated in testing new releases. At the time, this worked well; the early releases were small.

By the end of 2013, I had moved from working on customer implementations to the development team. At this point, I was running the testing for platform releases as well as working on developing the Fish Market and its solutions. This was the beginning of a separate development team that focused on solution development.

Time to Market

The platform development team focused on adding new features, and many of the new platform features would be in process for more than one release. Feature code would be added but not available (or visible in the product) until the new feature was fully complete sometime in the future. Typically, the release cycle for the platform code would be three to four months for these feature releases.

What we found with the MarketPlace solutions was that many of the early solutions were much smaller in scale compared to the platform. With built-in access to the platform infrastructure, we could develop solutions much quicker than the major platform features could be implemented. Solutions to compete with major products in the financial arena could be created and released in less than six months.

Tip of the Spear

MarketPlace solutions became a weapon used by the team to win deals. As the MarketPlace team was able to create new solutions so rapidly, we easily created the new features and functionality needed for prospective deals. The MarketPlace team was beginning to focus on creating these new products in order to expand OneStream markets.

A great example of this is the Account Reconciliation solution, which is now found within OneStream Financial Close (OFC). We already had customers' books of record for their financial data. If we could reconcile that back to their source systems, we could have a fully functioning account reconciliation system quickly. Why should a financial systems user buy a reconciliation suite and then need to take their *existing verified data* and load it into another separate system to reconcile it? It's the same way with your smartphone; you don't have two separate contact lists – one for texts and one for phone calls – you have *one contact list* that links to both.

In the spring of 2016, we started working on the initial build using the validated data that we already have in our workflow process as the source for allowing users to reconcile that data back to their source. Account reconciliation was another market opportunity that just seemed to be a natural fit for what we already did. In four months, we had a working prototype that we could demo to get feedback. One of the very first demos was to a group in the office for initial admin training.

In that group was a customer who was in the process of looking for account reconciliation software; they had already made a preliminary selection for a competing product. After demonstrating the solution to the class, the customer was ready to put the competing product on hold and wait for it to be completed. This allowed us to validate that we were on track with our thought processes, and showed how an agile team could quickly create a solution able to compete with products from billion-dollar competitors.

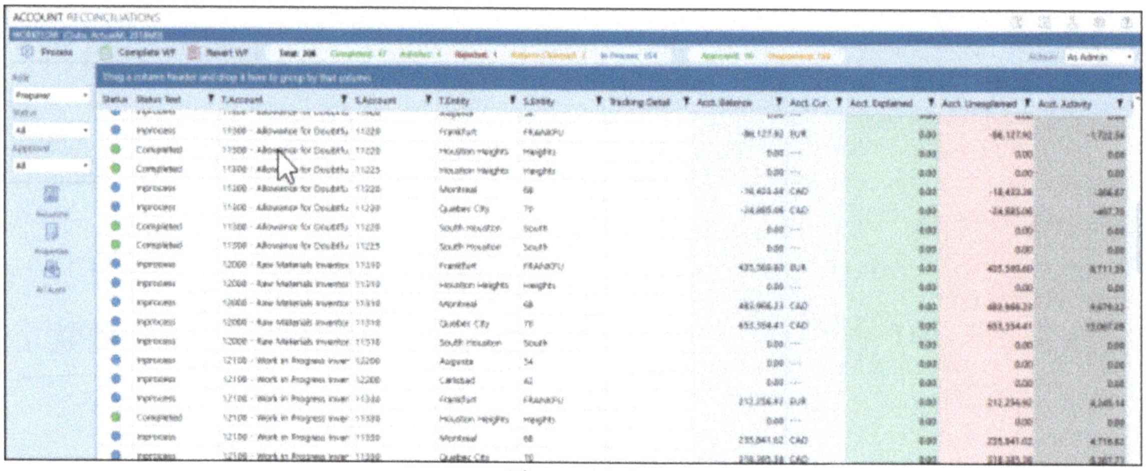

Figure 13.6

Solution Exchange Ties to Platform Releases

Since OneStream-developed solutions in the Solution Exchange are created using the platform as the basis, solutions are tied to platform versions. As the platform team adds new features, we can take advantage of these new tools and components to expand the functionality of our solutions. This allows us to focus on adding valuable new features and solutions without having to develop the toolset as well.

As the platform is our development environment, the Solution Exchange is a customer of the platform team. We request new features just as an external customer would; we go through a similar triage process as well. The main benefit is that – since we are part of the same company – we have more input into updates to the development tools than companies that use external development tools.

The downside of this is that every solution that is released is tied to a minimum version of the platform. Every time the Solution Exchange uses a new component or BRAPI added by the platform, we can only use that solution on servers running that same version of the platform or higher. This is due to the new component/BRAPI only existing in that new platform version. The solution may not work properly and may even fail to import on an older version of the platform, depending on the new components being utilized in the solution.

The labeling we use to identify each Solution Exchange release represents the linkage with the platform versions. A normal solution would have the following version: PV620-SV100. This represents platform version 6.2.0, solution version 100. That means that this solution will only work with platform version 6.2.0 and greater, and that this is the first version (100 version) of the 6.2.0 release.

Development Process

Outside of release schedules and development time, the Solution Network and platform development teams are really very similar. Both are structured such that they have multiple sprint teams that each focus on an area of the product or a solution. Each sprint team is made up of developers, quality testers, document writers, and product management. The teams work together to create quality products.

The Solution Network and platform development teams are customer-driven, focusing on making products that meet both customers' and partners' needs. Every week we have a team made up of a variety of stakeholders in the company (support, services, customer success, partner management, etc.) that reviews all open requests that have been entered in our defect/enhancement tracking system. Each item is reviewed during this triage meeting to determine the next steps.

The requests come in from either support requests or via IdeaStream. IdeaStream has its own section on the OneStream Community website that allows users to submit enhancement ideas. Additionally users can browse other submitted requests and upvote them. This allows us to identify what items customers find the most valuable so that we can prioritize those requests during our triage meetings.

During these meetings, the attendees can bring up any other open item or rejected enhancement for discussion. This request may come from a partner or customer who is looking to get guidance on when a new enhancement will be coming, or maybe someone stating the reasoning behind a rejected item to show its value to the community. Many times, a feature that was dismissed is reopened and added after a solution has evolved and new use cases come to light.

Any bugs are assigned to a **quality assurance** tester to replicate. If the issue is replicated, then the QA works with development to determine if there is a workaround that can be given to the customer as an interim solution. If the issue cannot be replicated, the QA works with support to help determine if the issue is a configuration issue or if the QA team needs additional customer files to replicate the problem. In the end, if the issue is a bug that requires a code change to resolve, it is approved and assigned to a release.

Any enhancement or new feature requests that come in are discussed with the team to determine if the request is a very specific use case (that does not apply to the majority of customers) or if this is a needed component that we did not originally define when the solution was created. If we think that a request only applies to a very specific use case, product management works with our subject matter experts to verify the customer request and determine if the request can be handled in a more innovative manner than was originally defined in the request.

Enhancement requests come in from both customers and partners, and sometimes from partners on behalf of a customer. In many cases, partners have modified or customized a solution to add functionality that a customer is looking for in a solution, instead of putting in a request to OneStream. In most cases, this should be avoided as it causes problems with support for the solution going forward. When new versions of a solution are released, customers with modified solutions will find themselves needing to attempt to make the same changes again in the newer versions. In some cases, the code can be changed so much that the original modification may no longer work, leaving the customer stranded.

When partners get requests from a customer to modify a OneStream-developed solution, or do this to meet a customer requirement, they should *reach out to OneStream support first*. This allows the development and product management teams to view the request and propose alternate solutions, whether that be a design change, or potentially a temporary code workaround that can be implemented in a full feature in a future release. This avoids customers feeling upset about their solutions not working properly, and their requests get to help make the solutions that much better.

What's in the Platform Section?

The platform side of the **Solution Exchange** is the download site for the OneStream Platform software. It contains download links that allow users to download any of the currently supported versions of the platform, as well as all related content.

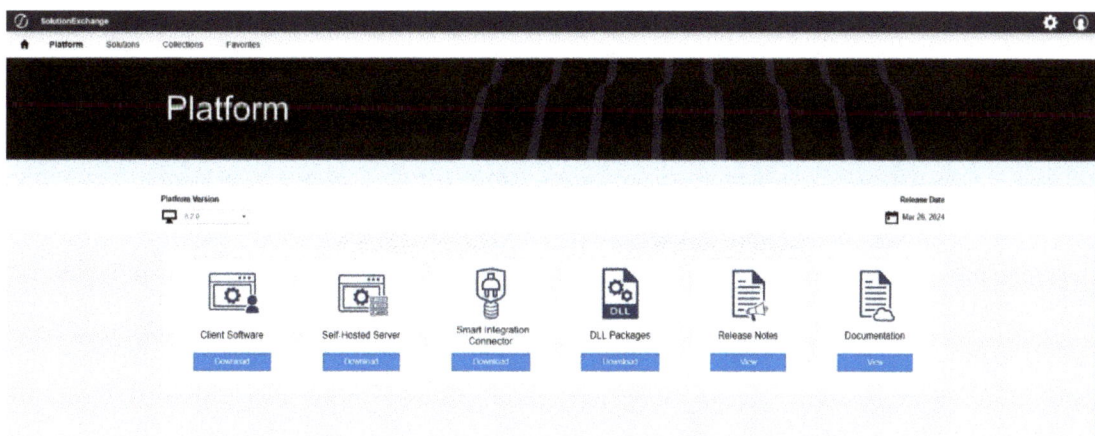

Figure 13.7

On the Platform page, there are six tiles for downloading platform installation software, as well as reports and reference material.

- **Client Software** – contains installation files for the Excel add-in, OneStream Studio Report Builder, OneStream Desktop, and the silent install packages for automating the installation of client tools.

- **Self-Hosted Server** – contains the installation files for the OneStream servers. Additionally, this contains all documents related to installing on-premise.

- **Smart Integration Connector** – contains the installation package for OneStream Smart Integration Connector.

- **DLL Packages** – contains the ERPConnect DLL, used when connecting to SAP.

- **Release Notes** – document detailing new and changed items for the selected release.

- **Documentation** – links to OneStream documentation for the current platform version available including the Design & Reference Guide, Platform Guides, Solution Guides, System Guides, etc.

What's in the Solution section?

The Solution area in the Solution Exchange holds, as you would expect, all the available solutions for download. They are broken into categories such as Financial Close, Advanced Analytics, and Planning.

Full **solutions** are the primary focus of the Solution Network development team. These solutions can be described as separate software products. They can involve a consulting engagement with an implementation team and application design. While they may use or access financial data from within OneStream, the main functionality of any solution is completely separate from the platform, and is accessed through custom screens that have been created specifically for *that* solution.

Financial Close (OFC) is a good example of this. Even though it is free within the Solution Exchange, it's a full product with its own dedicated development team. It has even been the main reason for purchasing OneStream when customers want to implement OFC before implementing budgeting or Actual consolidations. This solution can be compared to some of the main products from our competitors (that sell for millions of dollars).

While solutions can be complex and require a full implementation and design, many are simple tools that add useful functionality to OneStream. For example, the Cloud Admin Tools (CAT) solution's main purpose is to provide users with the ability to maintain their cloud users and applications on their own… without intervention from the OneStream Cloud support team. This solution can be downloaded from the Solution Exchange and installed in a customer environment with no support or implementation.

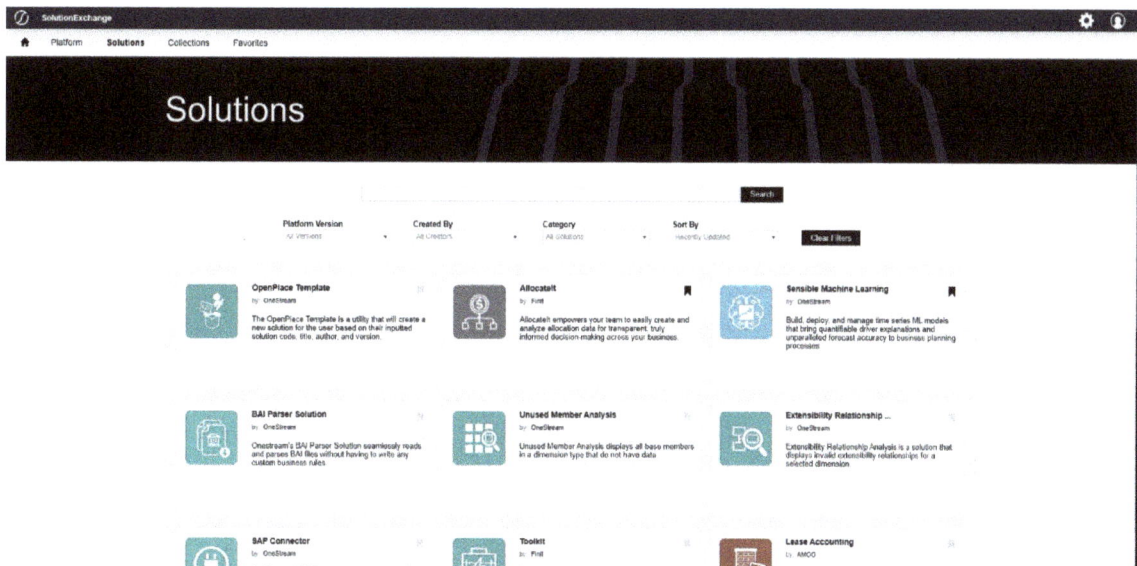

Figure 13.8

What Makes up a Solution?

Solutions are made up of multiple OneStream components. The two main components that make a solution are dashboards and business rules. These two items make up the user interface and logic behind the solution. Occasionally, other components such as Cube Views, metadata, extender rules, or data management tasks are included.

When you download a solution from the Solution Exchange, you get a zip file that includes the Solution ID (e.g., – OFC, ACM, etc.) and the solution version information. Inside this zip are all the files that make up the solution. Most solutions can be directly imported into an application, and any solution will be ready to setup and configure. There are a few that also contain other files in the main zip, and the zip file cannot be imported directly into an application. Users should read the installation instructions shown in the Solution Exchange prior to installing a solution for the first time.

With solutions where the downloaded zip file can be imported directly, the only contents are XML files. The components are named based on the objects from OneStream that they contain. For example, a file named ExtensibilityRules.xml will contain extensibility business rules, and DataManagement.xml will contain data management steps and sequences. The heart of the solution is usually going to be ApplicationDashboards.xml, as this contains the dashboard maintenance unit and the three main **dashboard types** that interact with dashboards (dashboard dataset, dashboard extender, and dashboard XFBR string rules).

Workspaces

Workspaces are the framework for building OneStream solutions. They store maintenance units and facilitate development by providing an isolated environment for developers to segregate and organize solution objects. Workspaces provide an isolated environment in which solution developers and creators can develop multiple solutions to solve complex business processes. Each Workspace can be made up of multiple maintenance units, so multiple solutions can be housed in the same Workspace. Additionally, this allows users to have multiple instances of a solution in different Workspaces without causing object naming conflicts.

Dashboards

Dashboards – and the components that they include – are the visual interface for solutions. The dashboards are arranged to hold components and other dashboards. All these items are contained in one Workspace, and each solution is made up of one Workspace. The Workspace contains maintenance units, dashboards, Cube Views, components (buttons, combo boxes, grids, reports, etc.), data adapters, assemblies, parameters, and files.

Chapter 13

Dashboard Organization and Naming

All dashboard objects that are within a maintenance unit are required by OneStream to have a unique name. Solution dashboard naming is specifically designed to aid in the layout of the user interface, as well as ensure object naming uniqueness. When designing dashboards and dashboard groups for a solution, we have standardized object naming.

Dashboard groups are named based on the screen content. Each dashboard group is a self-contained screen, as all the dashboards that are displayed on the screen are included in the one dashboard group. Each group has a suffixed extension on the name that includes the solution abbreviation in parentheses, for example, One Place (UTM). In larger solutions (e.g., when there are a lot of groups), this is extended to include an additional character to denote the type of group or component.

- Administration groups should have their abbreviation end in an A.

- Analysis groups should have their abbreviation end in a Y.

- Help groups should have their abbreviation end in an H.

- Settings groups should have their abbreviation end in a T.

- Setup groups should have their abbreviation end in an S.

- View groups should have their abbreviation end in a V.

See below for several examples.

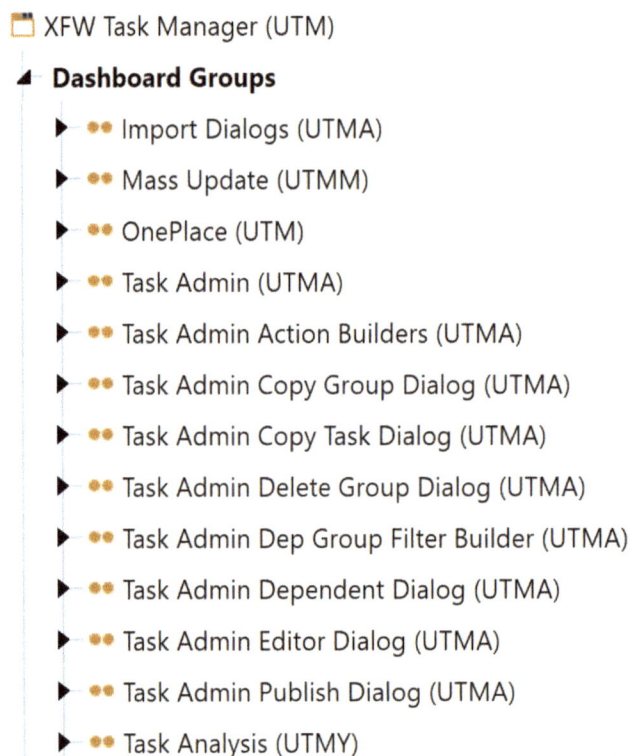

XFW Task Manager (UTM)

Dashboard Groups

- Import Dialogs (UTMA)
- Mass Update (UTMM)
- OnePlace (UTM)
- Task Admin (UTMA)
- Task Admin Action Builders (UTMA)
- Task Admin Copy Group Dialog (UTMA)
- Task Admin Copy Task Dialog (UTMA)
- Task Admin Delete Group Dialog (UTMA)
- Task Admin Dep Group Filter Builder (UTMA)
- Task Admin Dependent Dialog (UTMA)
- Task Admin Editor Dialog (UTMA)
- Task Admin Publish Dialog (UTMA)
- Task Analysis (UTMY)

Figure 13.9

Dashboard names are designed to keep related dashboards together and related to their placement in the container dashboard. Standard dashboard naming is broken into three parts – prefix, main, and suffix – each separated by an underscore.

The prefix section is used to organize the visual layout on the application dashboard administration screen. The top-level dashboard in a group is prefixed with a 0 to ensure it is displayed at the top of the dashboard group, as this is normally the dashboard that is referenced by other dashboards. Dashboards within dashboards should be listed as #a and #a#, again to keep things together. The

378

main section is meant to be a meaningful description of the object – what the dashboard is going to display. This may range from "Header" to "Toolbar" to "Content". The suffixed section is simply the same suffix used on the containing dashboard group. See the example below:

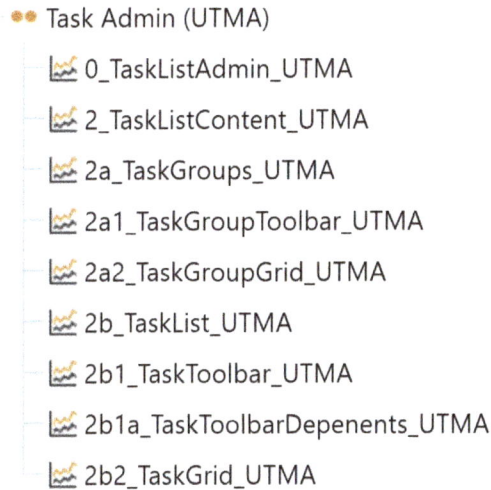

- ●● Task Admin (UTMA)
  - 0_TaskListAdmin_UTMA
  - 2_TaskListContent_UTMA
  - 2a_TaskGroups_UTMA
  - 2a1_TaskGroupToolbar_UTMA
  - 2a2_TaskGroupGrid_UTMA
  - 2b_TaskList_UTMA
  - 2b1_TaskToolbar_UTMA
  - 2b1a_TaskToolbarDepenents_UTMA
  - 2b2_TaskGrid_UTMA

Figure 13.10

Component Naming

Components also have standard naming in order to ensure the same unique object naming. Each object is prefixed with a standard three-letter abbreviation (denoting the object type) and suffixed with the three or four-letter solution abbreviation, separated by underscores. Originally, we used the prefix to add the ability to sort all components of the same type together in the application dashboard screen for a given solution. The need for this was removed, however, when the platform team added grouping for the component types. Nonetheless, the prefix is still used when adding components to a dashboard as well, as it's a good identifier for objects when looking at the object tree in design mode.

Component Types

BI Viewer – biv	File Viewer – fvw	Report – rpt
Book Viewer – bvw	Gantt Viewer – gtv	Sankey Diagram – san
Button – btn	Grid – grd	Spreadsheet – spr
Chart – cht	Image – img	State Indicator – sid
Check Box – chk	Label – lbl	Supplied Parameter – spp
Combo Box – cbx	Large Data Pivot – lpg	Table Editor – ted
Cube View – cvw	List Box – lbx	Text Box – txt
Data Explorer – dex	Map – map	Text Editor – txe
Data Explorer Report – der	Member Tree – mtr	Text Viewer – txv
Date Selector – dat	Password Box – pwd	Tree View – trv
Embedded Dashboard – emd	Radio Button Group – rbg	Web Content – web

Figure 13.11

Business Rules

Business rules are the main logic behind solutions; they provide all the actions that happen in a dashboard. When you process recs in Account Reconciliation or a task is completed in Task Manager (UTM), it's a function in one of the business rules that is doing the heavy lifting. There are three main types of business rules that are used in solutions: **dashboard dataset, dashboard extender,** and **dashboard XFBR string**. Each of these business rule types has specific functions, but they are coded so that they can talk to each other. This allows us to create core functions in one rule and share the use of those functions with the other business rules.

Dashboard Dataset

Dashboard dataset rules are used to create datasets and return them back to the calling component or function. The main uses in solutions are for reporting and populating component lists. For example, combo box and list box controls have a bound parameter that provides the list of data that each component will display. The parameters can either be defined manually by typing in a hard-coded list, running a SQL query against a database, or processing a dashboard dataset function. The function may simply be to run a different SQL query, but the benefit is that you can control it *programmatically*. This allows you to change the query *dynamically* based on user input.

The standard naming format we use for this type of business rule in solutions is XXX_HelperQueries (where XXX = the selected solution code, as described above).

Common dashboard dataset uses:

- Combine different types of data for a report.
- Build programmatic data queries (e.g., analytic plus SQL).
- Conditionally build data query reports.
- Conditionally build data query for parameters.
- Create data to display in advanced components (map advanced charts, etc.).

Dashboard Extender

Dashboard Extender rules are used to extend the functionality of dashboards and components. This is the primary business logic for the solution. When we want to click on a dashboard component – and have it do something (update a value, process data, etc.) – a Dashboard Extender is utilized.

Functions are defined in Dashboard Extender rules, and these functions are then assigned to the dashboard component in the **server task** property. When the button is clicked, or a grid is saved, then the function that was assigned to the specific component is run. This allows us to control how the dashboards function. Additionally, Dashboard Extender rules are often applied to launching dashboards, allowing us to set specific values when a dashboard is opened. The standard naming format we use for this type of business rule in solutions is XXX_SolutionHelper (where XXX = the selected solution code, as described above).

Common Dashboard Extender uses:

- Execute a task when the user clicks a button.

- Perform a task and show a message to the user.

- Perform a custom calculation.

- Upload a file from the end-user's machine.

- Include page state to store parameters and values about a specific dashboard page instance.

Dashboard XFBR String

Dashboard XFBR string rules are used to process conditional dashboard parameters. Most dashboard components have properties that only allow selections from a predefined value list. However, when the value list is stored, it saves as a text value. This type of rule allows us to replace the stored text value with a conditional rule. For example, on many solutions, we have a settings button that should only be visible to administrators. However, button components have the property IsVisible where we can only enter True or False. In this situation, we can replace the True / False with a rule that checks if the user is an administrator; if they are, then it returns True. When the dashboard is rendered, the rule gets processed and returns the result. The button receives that result and is displayed or hidden based on user security. The standard naming format we use for this type of business rule in solutions is XXX_ParamHelper (where XXX = the selected solution code as described above).

References to Other Business Rules

Most solutions utilize common functions that are defined in a Dashboard Extender business rule. The public functions defined in the shared business rule can be referenced and executed from other business rules. These *shared functions* create a set of standard helper functions and centralize maintenance of this shared logic.

In order to create a reference from one business rule to another, navigate to the rule calling the shared function and add a declaration in the Referenced Assemblies field of the Properties tab. The syntax used in the referenced assemblies field requires a BR\ prefix and the business rule name to reference (e.g., BR\RCM_SolutionHelper). Once added, an instance of the shared rule is declared in the calling function. This instance can be used to call any public function defined in the shared rule.

```
Dim rcmHelper As New OneStream.BusinessRule.DashboardExtender.RCM_SolutionHelper.MainClass
Return rcmHelper.GetAccountMemberList(si)
```

Solution Exchange Access

When new customers join OneStream, they go through an onboarding process with the customer enablement team. This process involves identifying two or three users who will be provisioned for access in the Solution Exchange. Typically, the **import/export** functionality (used to import solutions) is secured to administrators within customer environments. As such, the users granted access are typically administrators for the company, although any user in the company can be granted access. The customer enablement team will provide user login information for each user that is provisioned.

The Solution Exchange can be accessed from the OneStream Software webpage (www.OneStream.com) by clicking on the Solution Exchange link (see Figure 13.12).

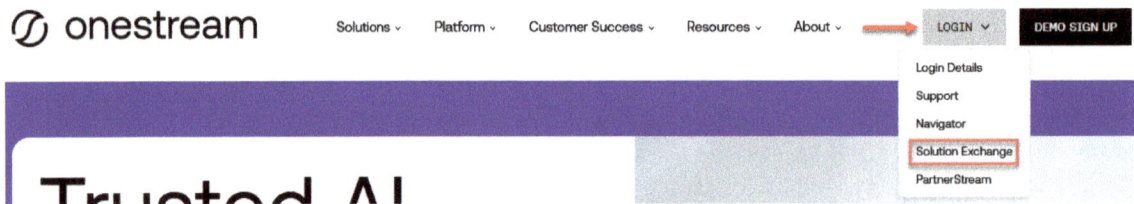

Figure 13.12

Environment Considerations

Before beginning the installation of any solution, it is important to decide whether to build directly in the *production* OneStream application, or in a separate *development* OneStream application. The primary advantage of building in a production application is that you will not have to migrate the resulting work from a development application. However, there are intrinsic risks when making design changes to an application that is being used in a production capacity, and this is *seldom advised*. As a best practice, use a development OneStream application to build complex solutions.

If you do implement in a development environment, you will need to migrate the implemented solution to production before going live. Implementation and migration advice for each solution are included in the instruction documentation. Users need to read the instructions and carefully consider any impact prior to implementing in development or production environments.

Another major consideration, when implementing a solution, is the impact on the environment infrastructure. Solutions from the Exchange can put additional strain on servers due to processing. As the solutions normally utilize general server processing, you need to be aware that infrastructure requirements may need to be revisited in order to ensure a performant system. You also need to consider who will be using the solution when evaluating infrastructure, as many solutions in the Exchange are used by a different set of users to those originally defined. For example, the people who perform account reconciliation may not necessarily be the same users performing the financial close. This can mean that there are additional concurrent users in the system, potentially requiring a review of your infrastructure.

Upgrading and Maintaining Solutions

OneStream-developed solutions are regularly updated with enhancements and bug fixes. Our product management team defines the new features being added with each new release. To get these new features and bug fixes, users must download the new version from the Solution Exchange and install it into their environment. From the solution download screen, users can view the release notes for each available version of a solution. Each release note document shows the changes that are included in the release, as well as a deployment section that details the instructions for installing the new version.

Occasionally, the instructions will require an uninstall of the previous UI prior to installation. This is normally due to object naming changes in the dashboard objects. When solutions are installed, they do not load as a replacement; they load via merge. So, if a dashboard or control is renamed in an updated release, and if the old version of the solution was not removed prior to installation, the originally named object in your application will be left where it is. This can lead to problems in the future if the old object is added in a later release.

After installing the new version of the solution, users are shown the standard setup screen when the solution is run for the first time. Normally, when a solution is installed for the first time, the table creation button simply creates the required tables. When a solution is upgraded, however, the new version may require changes to existing tables or the addition of new custom tables. If this is the case, the table creation button will detect the prior installation and will update the table accordingly.

New installations of solutions also require users to specify multiple settings prior to use. OneStream-developed solutions store these solutions in parameters. These parameters are overwritten when an upgrade is imported. To reduce the need to apply the prior settings after every update, we also save settings to a custom table when the settings are updated. After any schema update, these settings are restored to the dashboard parameters to remove the need to re-enter them again.

Adding Multiple Applications

Occasionally, users need to install multiple copies of the same solution. This is normally done in order to limit access to specific portions of OneStream data. As many solutions integrate through workflows, and restrict access using workflow security, solutions need to integrate through multiple workflows and not share data between them. Since all dashboards, components, and business rules are required to be unique, users cannot normally install multiple versions of the same solution.

To handle this situation, we created the MarketPlace Solution Tools (MST) solution. This solution allows users to make multiple copies of a solution. The solution takes every object in a solution zip file and renames them with a numerical extension, creating a *new unique name* for each object. To use MST, users upload the solution zip to be copied, select the instance number to be used, and then click copy to create the new instance. The new zip that is created can be imported into an application, and the solution will not conflict with the original solution.

> **Note:** Each instance of a solution must be set up and configured separately. Additionally, when new updates for a solution are released, users must go through the same MST copy process to create updates for each instance.

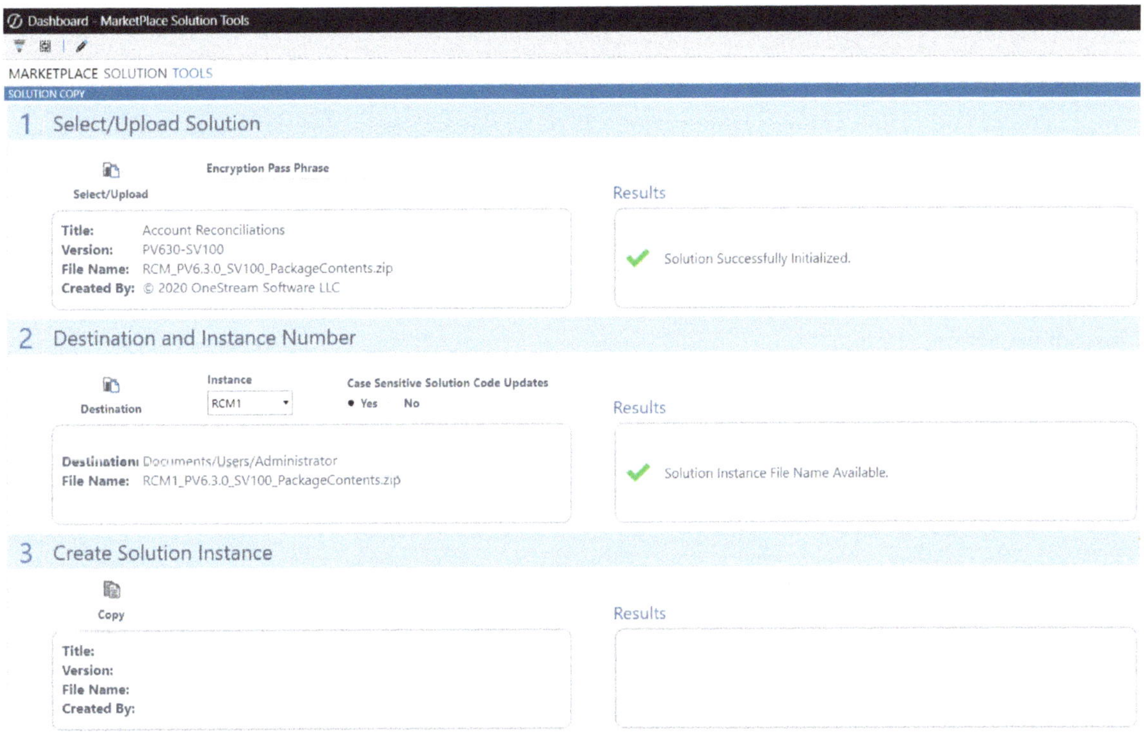

Figure 13.13

Starting with platform release 5.0.1, the ability to encrypt business rules was added. New solutions released for the first time (and a few older solutions) are being encrypted in order to prevent changes from being made to business logic. This was done in order to ensure that solutions are maintainable for all users. If a user was to make changes to a business rule, they could potentially alter the output of the solution in a negative manner. As customers rely on these results – in the same way that they rely on financial data – it is of the utmost importance that solutions provide the results as envisaged and designed by the Solution Network team. For these encrypted solutions, if a copy is desired, users can contact support to have instances provided.

Customizing Solutions

Modifying Solution Exchange Solutions

A few cautions and considerations regarding the modification of solutions:

- Major changes to business rules or custom tables within a solution will not be supported through normal channels as the resulting solution(s) are significantly different from the core solution(s).

> **Note:** For Partner-developed solutions, you must check with the solution developer or its documentation to determine if customizations are supported.

- If changes are made to any dashboard object or business rule, consider renaming it or copying it to a new object first. This is important because if there is an upgrade to a solution in the future, and the customer applies the upgrade, this will overlay and wipe out the changes. This also applies when updating any of the standard reports and dashboards.

- If modifications are made to a solution, upgrading to later versions will be more complex, depending on the degree of customization. Simple changes, such as changing a logo or colors on a dashboard, do not impact upgrades significantly. Making changes to the custom database tables and business rules – which should be avoided – will make an upgrade even more complicated.

Custom Event Handler

With the addition of encryption to business rules, we knew that we needed to provide a mechanism to allow some customizations. To support this, we added custom event models to encrypted solutions to select OneStream-developed solutions. Some solutions interact with the platform and cloud environment at such a deep level that we do not allow any changes to the code, in order to protect the OneStream environment (e.g., Cloud Admin Tools). The solutions that do enable custom event models have information in their help documentation that details how to enable custom events.

The custom event model is a separate custom event business rule that references the solution's main Dashboard Extender rule. It allows users to add custom processes before and after select events. For example, you can add an event that sends an email after a specified button is clicked, or which validates data in a grid prior to a save.

Integration

Most Solution Exchange solutions require some integration with the OneStream environment in order to work properly. In most cases, it is simply adding a custom workflow and pointing to a dashboard in the solution. This allows the solutions to use built-in workflow security to limit access and provides users with a guided experience that they are used to in OneStream's data loading process.

In account reconciliation, for example, the setup involves creating a new scenario and assigning it to an unused Scenario Type (Model in the reference below). This is the scenario that will be used to process account reconciliations. Creating a new Scenario Type allows users to re-use existing workflows and simply update the Scenario Type security to limit the users that can access it. From the Workflow Profiles screen, the administrator selects the workflows to be used with RCM, sets the Workflow Name to Workspace, and assigns 0_Frame_RCM_OnePlace as the Workspace Dashboard Name.

Figure 13.14

> **Note:** Each solution will include detailed instructions on the steps needed to integrate said solution into OneStream.

Testing

Each solution that is released by the Solution Network team is tested by a team of Quality Assurance engineers. Each development team works to create high-quality code, but – as with other software – this needs to be tested to ensure a quality product. We test not only that the new feature works the way the ticket says it should, but we also test for negative use cases where the developer may not be expecting a user to enter an incorrect value or select a certain combination of options. We're looking to cover all the bases to ensure that users can rely on our software right out-of-the-box.

Even though each solution goes through quality testing during development, we recommend that users install any update on a development server prior to installing it in production. This allows users to verify results within their own environment before making a change that cannot (potentially) be rolled back. For non-OneStream-developed solutions, testing is left to the provider of the solution. OneStream does not test or certify these solutions. The solutions are code scanned to ensure that they comply with development guidelines but the developers of the solutions are responsible for functionality.

Solution Exchange Enablement

In addition to developing the roadmap for the Solution Network team and providing guidance on new feature development, the product management team is responsible for product enablement. For each release, the product management team creates the marketing and knowledge transfer for a given solution. This enablement ranges from release notification emails to webcasts and online videos.

After a solution has been released on the Solution Exchange, the product management team sends out a release notification internally to all employees so that everyone is aware of the new product or update. Brand-new solutions are demonstrated internally to ensure that all teams have all the information they need to support and market the new product. After the internal teams have been notified, they notify customers and partners of the release. For the initial release of a solution, an email is sent to all customers detailing the solution and its uses. Solution releases that are only updates of existing solutions are only sent to users who have previously downloaded the solution. Notification emails include key new features and a copy of the release notes.

The product management team also creates Academy videos for major solutions. These videos show how solutions work, as well as setup and design considerations. OneStream Academy delivers the information needed on-demand, which enables the OneStream community to learn via a self-serve approach. The OneStream Academy is available free of charge for those OneStream administrators and implementation consultants who attend the Application Build or the Power User Reporting Class.

Key Takeaways

The customization of solutions should be avoided, and the custom event model should be utilized whenever possible. Prior to making changes, please reach out to support to determine if there is a better design/method to achieve the desired result. If not, support can enter an enhancement to update the solution to try to meet your requirements. Users get more reliable, maintainable solutions, and new features get to be shared with the entire community.

Always consider your existing environment when implementing a new solution. Adding a new solution can have an impact on the amount of data being processed as well as the number of concurrent users. This may require additional server resources or additional OneStream licensing. The OneStream support and cloud teams can help with this type of request.

The MarketPlace Solution Tool (MST) provides an efficient way to copy an existing OneStream-developed solution; it enables multiple solution instances to coexist in a single OneStream Application. This provides the flexibility for different business units (within the same OneStream application) to segregate and secure their data.

> **Note:** If a solution has been encrypted and thus cannot be copied, the OneStream support team can provide additional copies of a solution.

Epilogue

One of the things I love about having joined OneStream early on is all the celebrations that truly represent this group of people.

In my second year with OneStream, we closed our first million-dollar deal near the end of December. This was, of course, a reason to celebrate. A $20B international company having the faith to buy financial software from a startup located in a small office in suburban Michigan even more so. So, in true OneStream fashion, we head to our local bar. However, we don't celebrate with Champagne; we instead opt for black velvet (Guinness and Champagne).

14

Performance Tuning

Originally written by Jeff Jones and Tony Dimitrie, updated by Jeff Jones

Introduction

One of the questions that always comes up as part of a OneStream implementation – after the appropriate design has been implemented and processes have been put into place for the workflow – is "How can I improve performance?"

There are many different areas within OneStream that can be tweaked to improve performance or fine-tune the platform to improve the performance of a *particular* process; the following chapter will discuss the architecture of the OneStream platform with performance tuning in mind.

Understanding Application Server Roles

OneStream's architecture supports multiple application servers, which are the heart of the system and designed to handle specific activities. Application servers can be configured to support processor-intensive consolidation tasks, data-intensive Stage activities, or general navigation and reporting activities. The role that each server plays in the environment architecture will have a different impact on the hardware that is available to the application server.

- **General application server** – processes user navigation clicks, Cube View execution, dashboard execution, report execution. These tasks are mostly single-threaded in nature and are not intensive on the CPU of the server.

- **Stage application server** – processes Stage activity in the Stage engine (load and transform, journals, forms, Analytic Blend processing). These tasks are multi-threaded in nature and are processor-intensive.

- **Consolidation application server** – processes all consolidation activity in the finance engine (process cube, consolidate, translate, calculate). These tasks are multi-threaded in nature and are processor-intensive.

- **Data management server** – processes all data management sequences in the system. Tasks are multi-threaded in nature and are processor-intensive.

After understanding the roles of the application servers in the environment, you can then begin to understand how each server will be affected by tasks performed in the application.

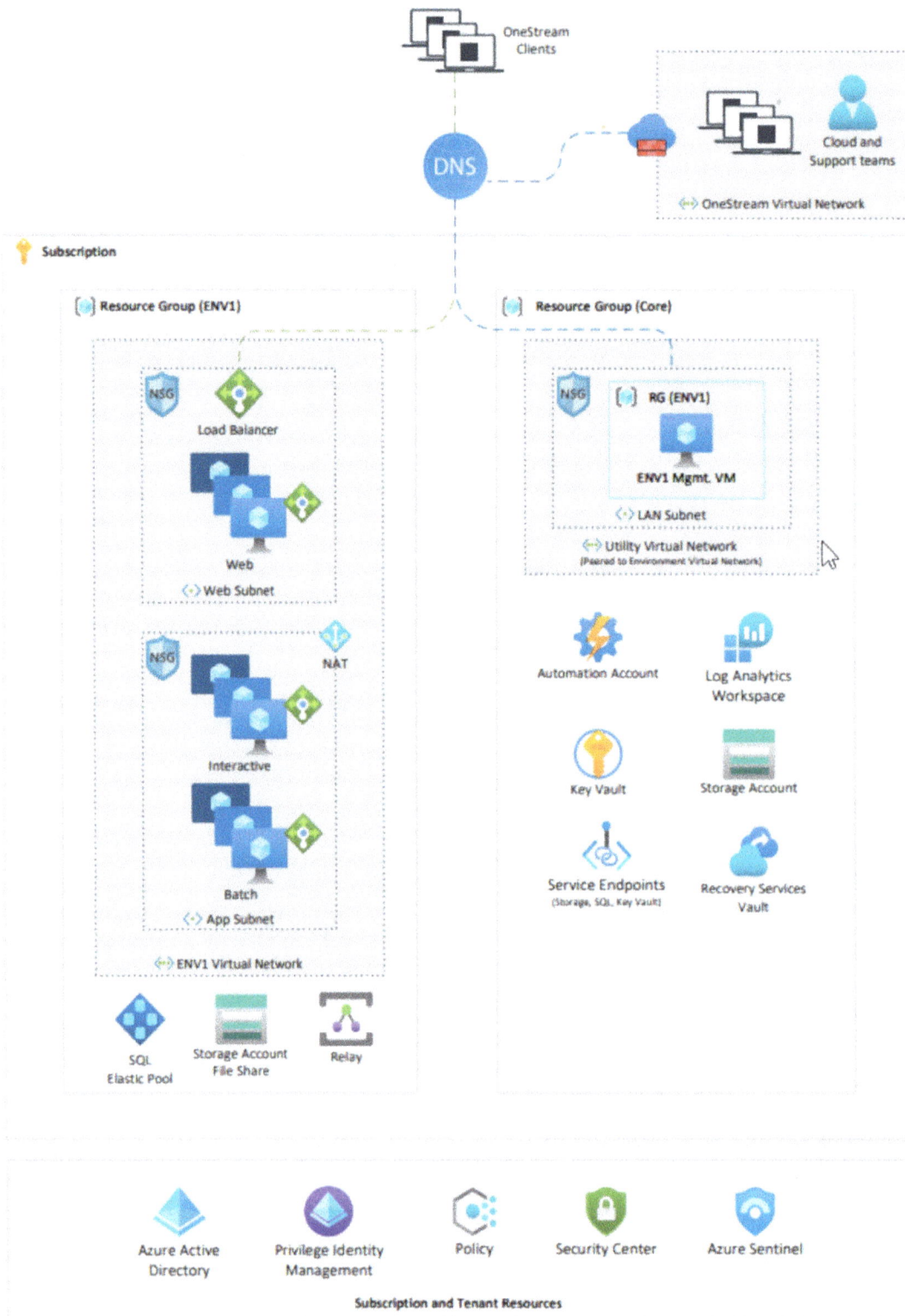

Figure 14.1

The above diagram shows the infrastructure setup for a OneStream SaaS environment in Azure:

- **Interactive application server scale sets** – processes user navigation clicks, Cube View execution, dashboard execution, report execution. These tasks are mostly single-threaded in nature and are not intensive on the CPU of the server.

- **Batch application server scale sets** – processes Stage activity in the Stage engine (load and transform, journals, forms, Analytic Blend processing), process consolidation activity (process cube, consolidate, translate, calculate), as well as data management. These tasks are multi-threaded in nature and are processor-intensive.

Stage Application Server Performance

Within the Stage engine in OneStream, there are a few steps that are performed to initially process data that is brought into the staging area. During the initial process of "load and transform," there are multiple sub-steps that are performed, including parsing the source data, executing transformation rules, deleting data from the Stage tables, and posting data to the Stage tables. Each of these steps can be individually performance-tuned to improve the overall task time.

Adjusting Workflow Cache Page Size

When importing source data into the Stage engine in OneStream, data is brought into a data table in memory on the Stage application server for processing. The size of the data table is based on the cache page size settings that are defined within the import input channel of the workflow. The settings define how large the pages are for multi-threading during the load and transform process.

The cache page settings define the size of the cached pages and the maximum number of cached pages in memory. If you are importing a smaller number of records into the Stage engine (for example, 200,000), the default settings (20,000 cache page size, and 200 cache pages in memory limit) will be sufficient, as this will allow for up to a total of 4 million records to be processed in RAM on the application server. In this example, the workflow settings would generate 10 data pages in memory.

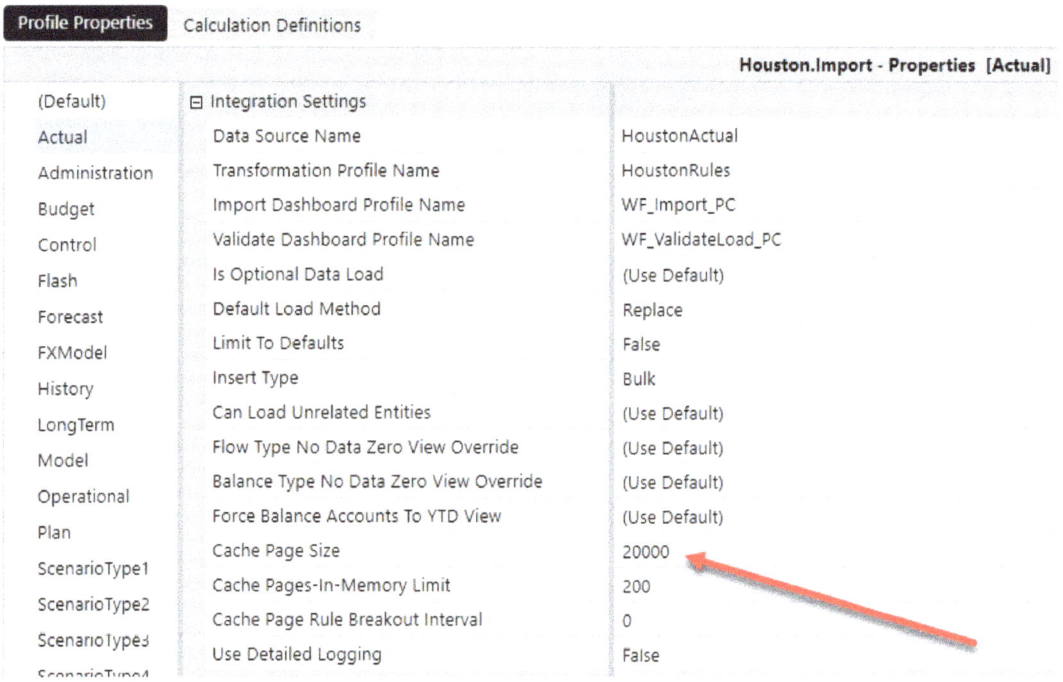

Figure 14.2

If the cache page size is set to a small number, such as 2,000, and the cache pages in memory limit is increased to 2,000 – which will still allow for 4 million records to process in memory (2,000 x 2,000) – it will actually cause a decrease in performance as the number of pages to process in memory will be much larger. There will also be an opportunity for **SQL Server deadlock issues** to occur, which will reduce the efficiency of the process. Below is an example of the task steps that can be viewed when importing a data file.

	Step Type	Description	Duration	Thread Id	Processing Information	Start Time
⚠	InitializeTransformer	WP#Houston.Import:S#Actual:T#2022M3	0.00:00:00.196	116	Page Size=2,000, Pages Limit=2,000, Parallel Xform=16, Pa	10/31/2024
⚠	ParseText	WP#Houston.Import:S#Actual:T#2022M3	0.00:00:00.046	116	File=Houston-Trial_Balance-2022-03_XFe1b473c1db794da	10/31/2024
⚠	EvaluateDataCache	WP#Houston.Import:S#Actual:T#2022M3	0.00:00:00.001	116	Data Pages=1, Data Rows=888, Data Keys=1, Invalid Data	10/31/2024
⚠	ExecuteDerivativeRules	WP#Houston.Import:S#Actual:T#2022M3	0.00:00:00.011	116	Source: Rule Groups=1, Rules=11	10/31/2024
⚠	ExecuteTransformationRules	WP#Houston.Import:S#Actual:T#2022M3	0.00:00:00.026	116	Thread Batch Count=16	10/31/2024
⚠	DeleteData	WP#Houston.Import:S#Actual:T#2022M3	0.00:00:00.035	116	Thread Batch Count=5	10/31/2024
⚠	DeleteRuleHistory	WP#Houston.Import:S#Actual:T#2022M3	0.00:00:00.007	116		10/31/2024
⚠	PostCacheData	WP#Houston.Import:S#Actual:T#2022M3	0.00:00:00.135	116	Thread Batch Count=8	10/31/2024
⚠	PostSummaryData	WP#Houston.Import:S#Actual:T#2022M3	0.00:00:00.045	116	Summarized Rows (Stage Server)=721, Thread Batch Coun	10/31/2024
⚠	PostRuleHistory	WP#Houston.Import:S#Actual:T#2022M3	0.00:00:00.008	116		10/31/2024
⚠	PostFileArchives	WP#Houston.Import:S#Actual:T#2022M3	0.00:00:00.007	116		10/31/2024

Figure 14.3

For **large source datasets** (2 million source data records), the Workflow Profile cache page size and maximum number of cache pages in memory should be adjusted to accommodate the full data record set; they should provide large enough cache pages for efficient processing on the application server. For example, if processing a 2 million record source dataset, the Workflow Profile cache page size should be adjusted to 100,000 and the cache pages in memory limit set to 200 allowing for up to 20 million records in memory.

If the cache page size is not large enough to accommodate the source data record set, the process will begin to write the data records out to temp files on the disk on the application server for processing, which is inefficient and will result in much longer processing times.

The cache page settings should be configured where the cache page size and number of pages will always accommodate the largest file size that would be imported into the Workflow Profile.

Understanding Transformation Rule Performance

The performance of the execution of transformation rules in the load and transform process is dependent on the types of transformation rules used within the transformation rule profile assigned to the Workflow Profile. Each type of transformation rule will have an associated processing cost associated with it. Each of the transformation rule processing types that are available have been broken up by cost, below.

Low Processing Cost Transformation Rule Types

These transformation rule types require a simple update and pass through to the database.

Map One to One

- Source Value → Target Value
- Table Join/Update Query

Map Composite

- `A#[199?-???*]:E#[Texas]`
- Performs a pattern match based on the first condition, and then verifies the second dimension condition. In this example, it would pattern match on the account `?` and then would check for the results that contain `Texas`

Map Range

- `Range xxxx,yyyy` → Target
- Executes an UPDATE SQL Statement with a BETWEEN clause as the main criteria.

Map List

- `List (xx,yy,xx)` → Target
- Executes an UPDATE SQL Statement with an `IN(xx,yy,zz)` clause as the main criteria.

Map Mask (One Sided *)

- `Mask 12*` → Target
- Executes an UPDATE SQL Statement with a (`Like %`) clause as the main criteria.

Map Mask (* to *)

- `*` → `*`
- Executes an UPDATE SQL Statement that passes the source value as the target value.

Low/Medium Process Cost Transformation Rule Types

This rule type requires a simple update and passes through to the database. However, masking queries must use table scans, which can hurt performance on large record volumes.

Map Mask (One Sided ?)

- `Mask 12??56` → Target
- Executes an UPDATE SQL statement with a (`Like 12??56`) clause as the main criteria. This forces the data server to use a pattern match, which can be slow on large record volumes.

A performance tip for this rule type is to keep the total number of placeholders (`?`) to a minimum. The more placeholders in each statement, the longer it will take the database server to process the mask rule.

Transformation Rule Types with very high processing costs

These rule types are required to return a record set with all dimension fields back to the Stage application server in order to perform the conditional mapping process. This causes a large amount of data transfer and memory utilization to be performed.

Map Range (Conditional)

- `Range xxxx,yyyy` → #Script
- Executes a SQL statement that pulls ALL dimension fields from a worktable with a `BETWEEN` clause as the main criteria, and passes the records back to the application server. This is required for conditional processing. After conditional processing is complete, individual update statements are sent to the database server as part of a record set update process.

Map List (Conditional)

- `List (xx,yy,zz)` → #Script
- Executes a SQL Statement that pulls ALL dimension fields from worktable with a `IN(xx,yy,zz)` clause as the main criteria and passes records back to the application server. This is required for conditional processing. After conditional processing is complete, individual update statements are set to the database server as part of a record set update process.

Map Mask (Two-Sided – Source Values used to Derive Target Values)

- `Mask 12*` → Target*

- Executes a SQL Statement that pulls only the fields for the specified dimension using a LIKE clause as the main criteria and passes the records back to the application server. This is required in order to use the source value to derive the target value. After conditional processing is complete, individual UPDATE statements are sent to the database server as part of a record set update process.

Map Mask (Conditional)

- `Mask 12*` → #Script

- Executes a SQL Statement that pulls ALL dimension fields from worktable with a LIKE clause as the main criteria and passes the records back to the application server. This is required for conditional processing. After conditional processing is complete, individual UPDATE statements are sent to the data server as part of a record set update process.

Derivative

- Executes a SQL statement that pulls ALL dimension fields from worktable with a LIKE clause as the main criteria and passes the records back to the application server. This is required for the application server to derive the calculated rows. After the calculate value process is complete, the new records are inserted into the worktables on a one-by-one basis.

The following performance tips can be implemented for the transformation rule types with high processing costs to assist with performance when possible.

Map Range (Conditional)

- Keep conditional ranges restrictive. Rather than using one large range (0000 to 9999), break the range up into multiple smaller rule blocks (0000 to 1000), (1001 to 2000), etc. This will keep memory utilization optimal, and the rules will process faster.

Map List (Conditional)

- Keep List restrictive. Rather than using one large list that could return a large volume of records, break the list into multiple smaller lists. This will keep memory utilization optimal, and the rules will process faster.

Map Mask (Two-Sided – Source Values used to Derive Target Values) and (Conditional)

- Keep Mask criteria restrictive. Never use a * without any other criteria in the rule definition. This can cause a very large volume of records to be brought back to the application server. Use criteria such as (1*, 2*, 3* or A*, B*, C*) to limit each query to a small chunk of what you need to map. This will keep memory utilization optimal, and the rules will process faster.

The execution of transformation rules during the "load and transform" step of the Workflow process is heavily multi-threaded and can be processor-intensive on the application server. During this process, it is normal to see the CPU on the application server increase in utilization as the system will use 16 threads for processing (all the processing occurs on the application server).

Increasing Delete Performance

Once the data has been successfully parsed, and transformation rules have been successfully applied to transform the source data to the appropriate target members, any data that had existed previously for the workflow Data Unit needs to be deleted from the Stage tables.

With large datasets, this step of the load and transform operation will need to remove a large amount of data from the Stage table. If this step of the process is taking a large amount of time to complete, there are a few available load options within OneStream that can assist with performance improvement.

Replace Background (All Time, All Source IDs)

Replaces all Workflow Units (individual period within the selected year and scenario combination for a particular Workflow Profile) in the selected workflow view and all source IDs in a background thread while the new file parses or connector execution is running. The delete is performed while the parse is performed.

> **Note:** This load method must always be used to delete ALL source IDs. If the workflow uses multiple source IDs for partial replacement during a load, this method cannot be used.

This method can be used for monthly input frequencies.

Replace (All Time)

Replaces all Workflow Units in the selected workflow view (if multi-period). Forces a replacement of all time values in a multi-period workflow view.

Understanding Load Cube and Consolidation Performance

Once the data has been successfully loaded and transformed and validated, the data is then loaded to the cube. The load cube step of the Stage workflow process moves the data from the Stage tables in the application database into the data record tables in the cube. The first time the cube is loaded for a workflow/scenario/time combination, the process will perform database record **inserts** into the following three database tables in the application database:

- Calc Status Table (CalcStatus)
- Time Stamp Table (DataUnitCacheTimeStamp)
- Data Record Table (DataRecordxxxx or BinaryDataxxx)

Any subsequent load cube operations that are performed for the same workflow/scenario/time combination will be more efficient than the initial load cube, as the process will perform database updates on these tables versus inserts, which will be more efficient at the database level.

Analytic Blend Considerations

Analytic Blend is used to report on large volumes of transactional data that are not appropriate to store in the traditional financial cube. To analyze data by invoice, a standard cube would require metadata to store the data records. In a short period of time, most of the invoice metadata would become superfluous because of the transactional nature of the data.

Analytic Blend processing occurs on the Stage application servers in the environment by default; however, by utilizing the Blend settings on the workflow, it can be assigned to run on a specific application server or group of servers. There are two main ways to execute the processing of Analytic Blend within OneStream.

Overnight Batch Jobs

- Run via data management to populate the Blend database table with transactional data for reporting.

- Appropriate for large Analytic Blend implementations (millions of records generated).

Interactive Workflow

- Analytic Blend runs interactively by the user via in-line workflow tasks. Users access the workflow as they normally do, and execute load and transform to populate the Blend database table.

- Appropriate for small Analytic Blend tasks.

It is important to design the Analytic Blend process to be run appropriately, based on the volumes of data that will be processed. If there is a large data warehouse that contains the transactional detail information that populates the Blend tables, this should be scheduled to run as a data management job *nightly* to populate the tables for the end-users to report on the next day.

Consolidation Application Server Performance

Consolidation application servers are the heart of the financial engine in the OneStream environment. When a consolidation is executed within OneStream, the engine will multi-thread the operation as much as possible to obtain optimal performance and execute the process as efficiently as possible. In order to achieve this, the server will use all the CPUs available to it to multi-thread the calculations being performed at the base-level entities and continue up the entity hierarchy to the top-level parents. It is normal behavior for the CPU utilization on the server to reach 99% during the consolidation operation, as it is using all the resources available to multi-thread the process efficiently. As the consolidation reaches the upper-level parents in the entity hierarchy, the CPU utilization will begin to decrease as there is less opportunity for multi-threading (since the data is consolidated to the top-level parent).

Understanding Consolidation Application Server Performance

Within a OneStream application, there are numerous things that can affect the performance of the consolidation.

- Formulas within the application (cube business rules, Member Formulas)
- Metadata structure

    o Deep hierarchies drive up consolidation times due to the large number of intermediate parent entities.

    o Parallelism is limited on parent entities; faster processors allow for parent calculations to complete faster.

- Data Unit size (cube, entity, parent, cons, scenario, time, view)

Tools Available

When a consolidation operation is running slower than would be expected, there are a few tools available to diagnose what could be contributing to the slow performance.

- **Long-running formulas debug option** within the application server configuration file. A formula that is running for 3 to 5 seconds or more is something that should be investigated; this is a very long amount of time for a formula to compute.

    o This setting allows the system to write to the error log any formulas that – when the consolidation is run – take longer than the numeric value specified to complete processing.

- Located in the `XFAppServerConfig.xml` file under the multi-threading settings section of the configuration file.

- Requires IISRESET on all application servers for change to take effect.

```
<NumSecondsBeforeLoggingSlowFormulas>5</NumSecondsBefore
LoggingSlowFormulas>
```

- **Application analysis reports** are available in the standard application reports (available on Solution Exchange).

  - Reports provide analysis of the dimension statistics, formula statistics, data statistics, and Data Unit statistics. These reports are discussed in further detail later in this chapter.

OneStream System Diagnostics Solution

The **OneStream System Diagnostics (OSD)** Solution Exchange solution is available for system administrators to examine application metrics and application data volumes. It allows the administrator to capture snapshots of the application at a period of time and perform an analysis of key application metrics and data volumes.

OneStream System Diagnostics (OSD)

OneStream System Diagnostics is broken up into four main pages and an Overview page:

1. Environment Analysis

2. Application Analysis

3. Task Analysis

4. Live Monitoring

The Environment Analysis page creates snapshots of the environment hardware state by gathering the information from the environment monitoring features in the software. The snapshots provide details on the application servers and database server.

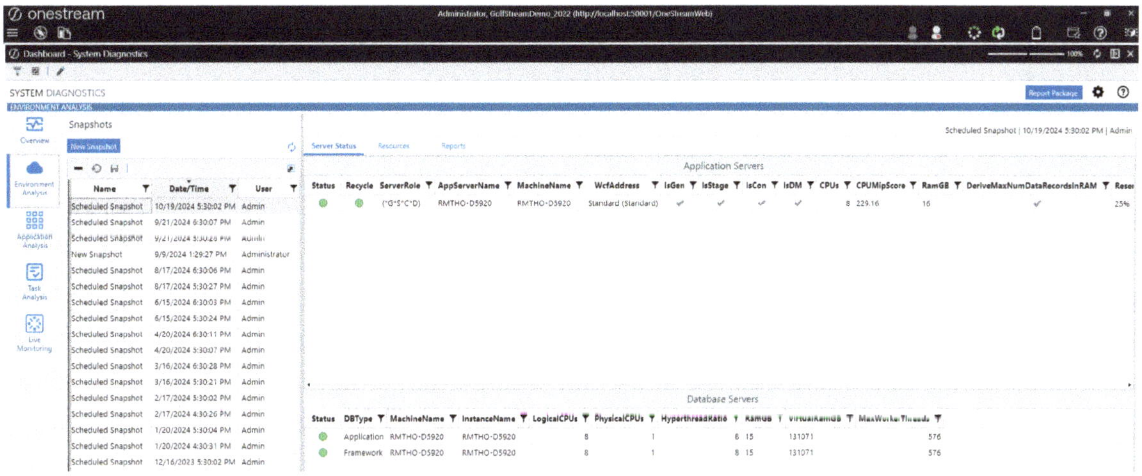

Figure 14.4

The application servers table lists each of the application servers contained in the environment as well as additional information.

- Role assignment

- Number of CPUs

- RAM

- Application server configuration file settings (parallelism, reserved memory setting, etc.)
  - CPUMipScore
    - This is important to note as it shows how fast the CPUs are on the server. The higher the MIP recorded score, the faster the processors in the environment. Fast processors are best for consolidation and data management server roles in the environment.

The database servers table lists the database server that is currently being used for the application and framework databases in the environment, and corresponding resources.

The Resources button within the page will perform a resource validation that displays a traffic light report, based on calculations performed in the solution. This is a great tool to verify that the environment has the appropriate number of general application servers and consolidation servers based on historical metrics of supporting 4.5 concurrent users per CPU before including any deflators due to large Data Units and shared server roles.

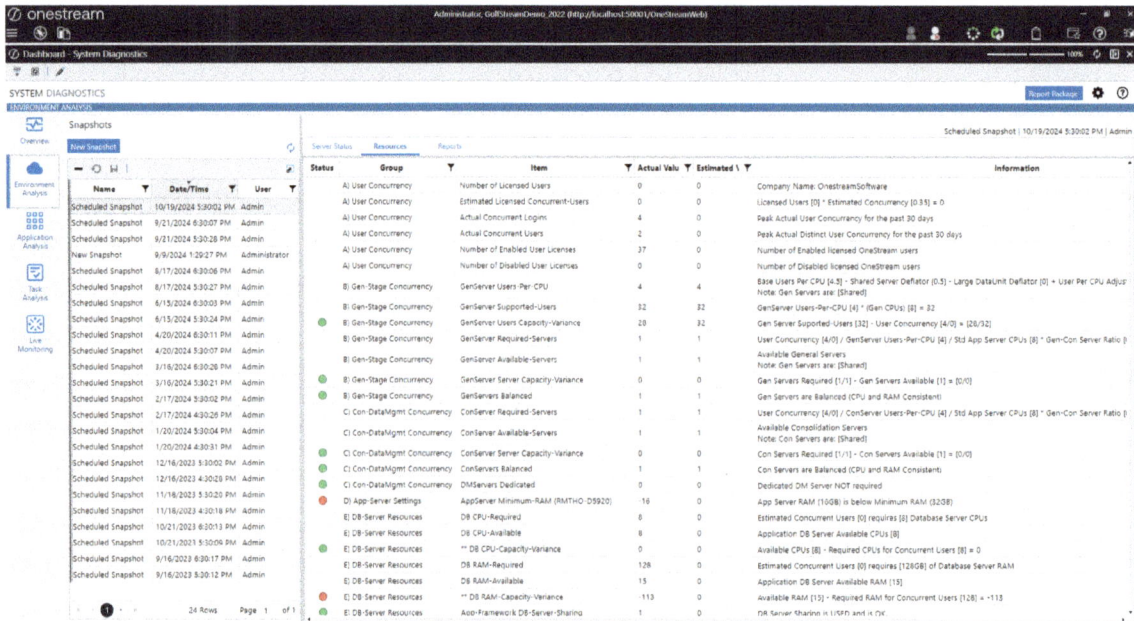

Figure 14.5

There are also some additional analysis reports that are available for viewing within the environment analysis page:

- Database Sizes
  - Displays a listing of each of the databases that are contained within the Azure SQL elastic pool and the corresponding disk space allocated and used by each database in the elastic pool. This allows you to visualize the amount of disk space currently used in the elastic pool and what free space is available.

- Memory Manager report
  - This report displays how often the IIS memory manager executes in the environment to remove the oldest Data Units from the analytic cache in the environment. If the memory manager is executing at a high rate on a daily basis, this is an indication that the servers require additional RAM resources to handle the analytic model and data volumes being processed. An example of these entries can be seen in the OneStream error log below:

Summary: The Data Cache Memory Manager removed Data Units from the cache. Initially there were 2,399 Data Units and 7,984,332 records, and the largest Data Unit contained 357,552 records. Afterwards there were 896 Data Units and 2,475,821 records, and the largest Data Unit contained 168,664 records.

- Resources validation
  - Displays the same detail found in the resources tab in a PDF report format.
- Server detail
  - Provides a detailed report of each server in the environment and its corresponding application server role and settings.
- Server startup
  - Provides a report of the number of IIS restarts that have been performed each day for each server in the environment. The software is designed to restart IIS once every 24 hours.
- The Application Analysis page allows the user to create application snapshots by gathering information maintained by the selected application and its database tables. The page displays application metrics, data volume statistics, and reports. The page also allows administrators to compare snapshots between applications and from different time periods to see changes in the application.

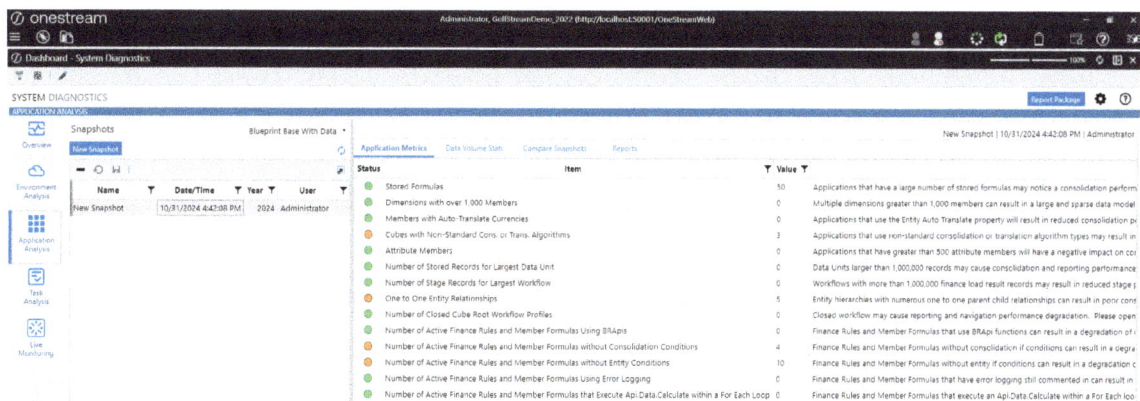

Figure 14.6

- Application metrics
  - Displays the application metrics that are considered key stakeholder drivers for the performance of an application. Clicking on a row will show additional details on the item selected.

Stored Formulas

Stored Formulas

Drag a column header and drop it here to group by that column

DimName	StoredFormulaCount	DimTypeName
AllAccounts	2	Account
SummaryAccounts	3	Account
Flows	24	Flow
ReportingMetrics	21	UD8

Figure 14.7

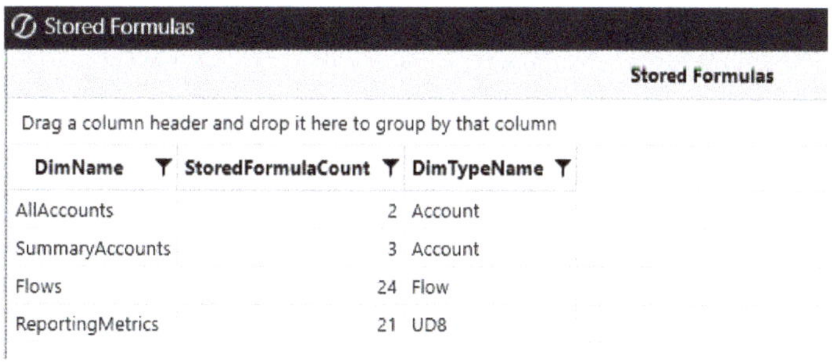

- Data Volume Stats
  - Provides detailed information on data volumes within the application database. Data volumes are broken out into cube data volume, Stage data volume, register data volumes (planning), and Blend data volumes. This page allows the OneStream administrator to visually see where data is stored in the application.

Scheduled Snapshot | 9/16/2023 6:33:31 PM | Admin

Application Metrics   **Data Volume Stats**   Compare Snapshots   Reports

Cube Data Volumes   Stage Data Volumes   Register Data Volumes   BiBlend Data Volumes

Cube	Scenario	Consolidation	Entity	Year	DataRowCount	DataCellCount	RealCellCount	ZeroCellCount	NoDataCellCount	DerivedCellCount
Houston	FcastM2	USD	Houston	2023	7,109	85,308	6,963	146	0	78,199
Houston	FcastM3	USD	Houston	2023	7,109	85,308	13,930	288	0	71,090
Houston	FcastM4	USD	Houston	2023	6,782	81,384	19,908	438	0	61,038
Houston	FcastM3	USD	South Houston	2023	5,173	62,076	10,065	281	0	51,730
Houston	FcastM4	USD	South Houston	2023	5,173	62,076	15,423	96	0	46,557
Houston	FcastM2	USD	South Houston	2023	5,173	62,076	5,140	33	0	56,903
Houston	FcastM3	USD	Houston Heights	2023	2,585	31,020	4,816	354	0	25,850
Houston	FcastM2	USD	Houston Heights	2023	2,585	31,020	2,439	146	0	28,435
Houston	FcastM4	USD	Houston Heights	2023	2,258	27,096	6,339	435	0	20,322
GolfStream	FcastM2	USD	Total GolfStream	2023	1,882	22,584	1,700	182	0	20,702

Figure 14.8

- Compare Snapshots
  - Allows the OneStream administrator to compare any two application snapshot metrics side by side. This is useful to see if there were changes to metadata or rules that were completed recently that could affect performance.

Scheduled Snapshot | 9/16/2023 6:33:31 PM | Admin

Application Metrics   Data Volume Stats   **Compare Snapshots**   Reports

Select Snapshot for Comparison:

Blueprint Base With Data   New Snapshot - Oct 31 2024 4:42PM

Statistic	Original	Original Status	Comparison	Comparison Status	Difference
Stored Formulas	497	🟢	50	🟢	447
Dimensions with over 1,000 Members	0	🟢	0	🟢	0
Members with Auto-Translate Currencies	50	🟢	0	🔴	50
Cubes with Non-Standard Cons. or Trans. Algorithms	4	🟠	3	🟠	1
Attribute Members	76	🟢	0	🟠	76
Number of Stored Records for Largest Data Unit	7109	🟢	0	🟢	7109
Number of Stage Records for Largest Workflow	0	🟢	0	🟢	0
One to One Entity Relationships	26	🟠	5	🔴	21
Number of Active Finance Rules and Member Formulas Using BRApis	27	🟢	0	🔴	27
Number of Closed Cube Root Workflow Profiles	0	🟢	0	🟢	0
Number of Active Finance Rules and Member Formulas without Consolidation Conditions	119	🟠	4	🔴	115
Number of Active Finance Rules and Member Formulas without Entity Conditions	113	🟠	10	🔴	103
Number of Active Finance Rules and Member Formulas Using Error Logging	7	🟢	0	🔴	7
Number of Active Finance Rules and Member Formulas that Execute Api.Data.Calculate within a For Each Loop	8	🟢	0	🔴	8

Figure 14.9

- Reports
  - Provides a list of reports that outline any Solution Exchange solutions installed in the application, database table size, list of long-running formulas from the error log (if long-running formula switch is enabled).
  - Provides a snapshot summary report that includes the application metrics and data volume stats in a single PDF summary report. Data Units larger than 1,000,000 records may cause consolidation and reporting performance degradation. Consider using extensibility to reduce the size of Data Units. In addition, consider leveraging the aggregation feature when processing abnormally large data sets when possible. Lastly, consider using hybrid scenarios when encountering reporting performance issues related to large Data Units.

The Task Analysis page facilitates research tasks by concurrency, statistics, and overall counts. This is very useful for viewing daily logins to the environment by module (Windows app, Excel, API) to view true concurrency in the system over a period of time.

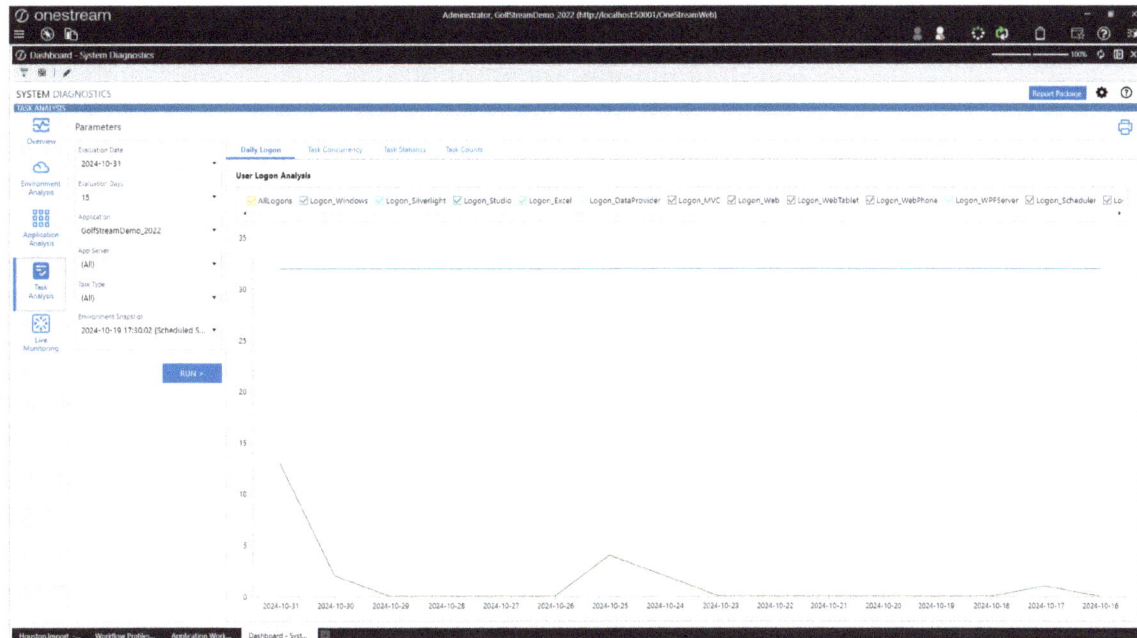

Figure 14.10

The graph displays a line to show the estimated user concurrency and also the maximum supported user concurrency. They can be used as a guide against the total user logons to verify that there are enough general application servers in the environment to support the user community.

The **Task Concurrency** module will display charts showing the number of tasks that were run on a day, by task type, and then allow for drilldown into the graphs to view the data by hour and minute, as well as the individual task in task activity.

Task Statistics display daily runtime statistics by type (Max, Min, Avg) for the task type selected. This data can be filtered by application servers and by applications.

Task Counts display the total number of daily tasks that were run for a particular task type. For example, if the user selects Cube View, it will display the total number of Cube View tasks run for a day and display how many were completed, failed, or cancelled.

The **Live Monitoring Module** provides environment and task health data over a given timeframe. The user is able to set a duration of time to monitor the system and an interval in seconds where the system will capture pre-defined environment metrics and then display them in a traffic light report. This process is performed via a data management job in the solution to capture the metrics, before writing the results to a report with explanations.

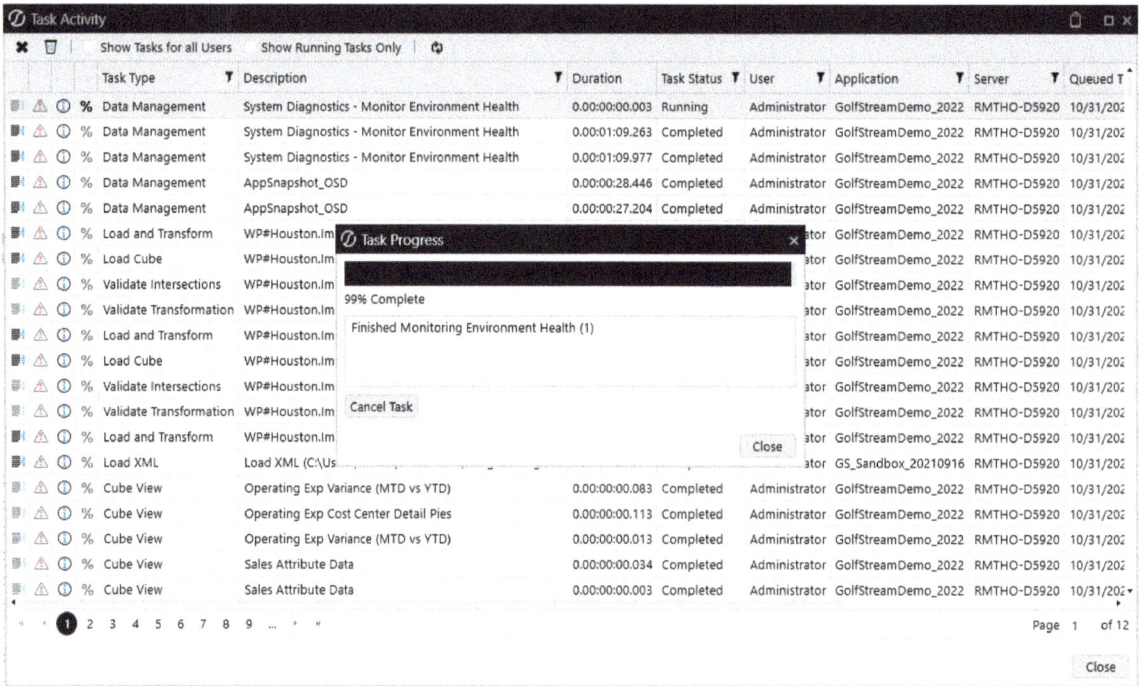

Figure 14.11

When the data management job is complete, the results can be viewed in the Analysis report, which displays the results captured and highlights any items that are critical to address in the environment.

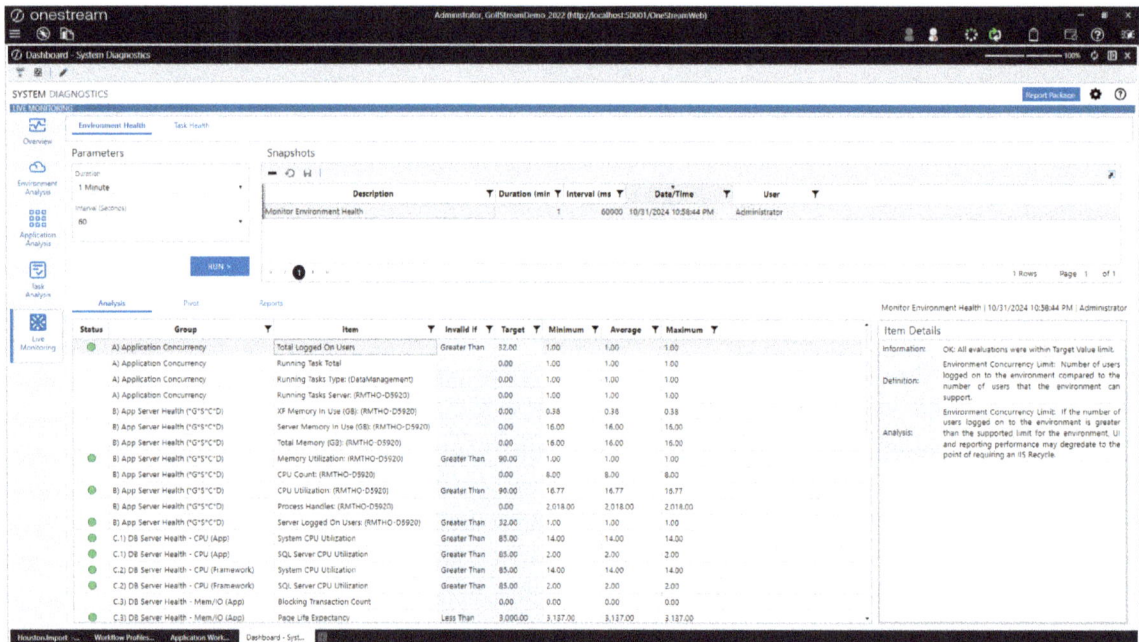

Figure 14.12

The Live Monitoring module also offers a means to monitor a particular task type and identify the task as unhealthy if it is running for a long period of time (identifying environment resources at that period of time). This can be useful when a process is not responding, and if there is a particular environment resource that is under pressure, which needs to be addressed accordingly.

Solution Exchange Solutions (What Application Servers Are Used?)

With the ability to use Solution Exchange solutions to further extend the OneStream platform, it is important to understand what application servers are used for processing in these solutions. For example, what servers are used to perform a calculation in the Specialty Planning solutions?

Specialty Planning

Specialty Planning solutions are a group of similar applications created around a common OneStream relational blending framework. Each has been configured to focus on a single Specialty Planning subject, including People Planning, Cash Planning, Capital Planning, Thing Planning, and Sales Planning.

Specialty Planning solutions will use the general application servers for navigation within the solution dashboards, but many of the buttons within the register are configured to execute on the data management servers within an environment. For example, the Calculate Plan button – which executes the calculation plans for the items in the register – will execute the process on a data management server in the environment. Since this is a heavily multi-threaded process and can be longer-running, the button within the solution is configured to run this on a data management server rather than a general application server. If you find that the calculation executes on a general application server in the environment, this can be modified within the button dashboard component for the solution within the action items Selection Changed Server Task.

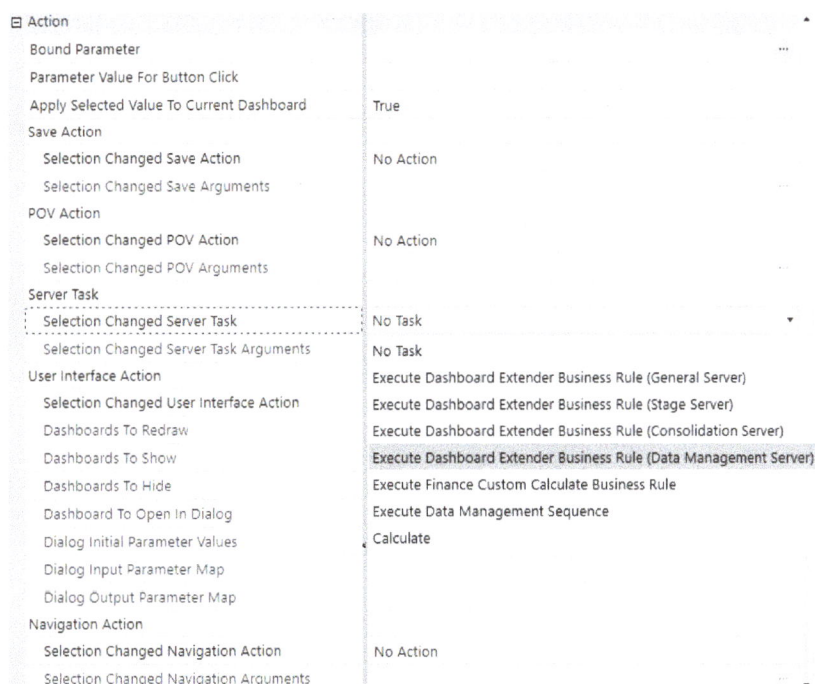

Action	
Bound Parameter	...
Parameter Value For Button Click	
Apply Selected Value To Current Dashboard	True
Save Action	
Selection Changed Save Action	No Action
Selection Changed Save Arguments	...
POV Action	
Selection Changed POV Action	No Action
Selection Changed POV Arguments	...
Server Task	
Selection Changed Server Task	No Task
Selection Changed Server Task Arguments	No Task
User Interface Action	Execute Dashboard Extender Business Rule (General Server)
Selection Changed User Interface Action	Execute Dashboard Extender Business Rule (Stage Server)
Dashboards To Redraw	Execute Dashboard Extender Business Rule (Consolidation Server)
Dashboards To Show	Execute Dashboard Extender Business Rule (Data Management Server)
Dashboards To Hide	Execute Finance Custom Calculate Business Rule
Dashboard To Open In Dialog	Execute Data Management Sequence
Dialog Initial Parameter Values	Calculate
Dialog Input Parameter Map	
Dialog Output Parameter Map	
Navigation Action	
Selection Changed Navigation Action	No Action
Selection Changed Navigation Arguments	...

Figure 14.13

This can be useful for dashboard design inside of the platform to define what server type is used to execute a process for a button.

Managing Changes in a OneStream Environment

Deploying changes to a production environment should be avoided during times of high load and high application activity. Changes to the following types of application artifacts – *especially* – should not be performed against a production environment experiencing heavy activity:

- Business rules, whether they contain global functions or not
- Confirmation rules
- Metadata, especially when using Member Formulas

Applying changes like this while the production system is under a high level of activity may have a negative impact on servers and have the potential to cause running processes to produce an error.

Standard environments are recommended to schedule production changes during slow periods or non-work hours. Large environment managers should also consider the use of the Solution Exchange solution **Process Blocker**, which allows for a pause of critical processes to perform maintenance on the system, without having to shut down the entire application. Process Blocker allows current tasks to be completed, while any new requests are queued, allowing the changes to be applied safely and effectively. Once these changes are in place, it is recommended to significantly limit the ability for users to make such changes during high volume times.

It is key that servers get a chance to recycle for good system memory health.

For active, global environments with data management sequences regularly being executed, a recycle of IIS is recommended every 24 hours for these OneStream app servers, which is default for customers.

Application Design Impacts Performance

In this section, we will discuss how factors related to application design impact the environment's performance.

For example, let's say you have an environment built to support up to 75 users. This is the equivalent of using a small charcoal grill. As a consultant, knowing that a small charcoal grill is being used means that the requirements, design, and build will be limited. The small charcoal grill has constrained options. So having decided on the meal to make, there will be limitations as well. For instance, the designer won't be able to cook sausages, baked potatoes, and grilled vegetables all at the same time.

What's the problem with the constraints of the grill? Well, firstly, it takes a significant time to warm up as the charcoal burns and turns gray. Next, you are unable to fine-control the heat to cook the food quicker. Finally, the small charcoal grill is not conducive to cooking a lot of items at one time! There are considerations on what needs to be cooked when. This can be considered a queueing process. Potatoes first, sausages next, and finally grilled vegetables last? Because potatoes take the longest to cook? Or is the order different because there are more sausages to cook, and the baked potatoes are cut into tiny pieces so they can cook faster? Basically, lots of considerations to think about, and the various factors represent the same conundrum that designers and implementers have when designing and building an application with environment performance in mind.

Financial Data Model

Building a well-designed financial model is crucial for environment performance. This is the foundation of every data collection process that will be developed now and into the future. As mentioned previously, data model size and Data Unit size are other factors that impact environment performance. These factors contribute to the physics of data modeling. Awareness of data modeling physics is the key for any high-performing data model within the application and the environment. The goal of the financial data model is to meet customer requirements by partitioning the metadata and data into manageable consumable chunks that are relevant to audiences. Let's look at how data model size and Data Unit size affect performance.

Data Model Size

Cube, dimensions, and dimension metadata members create the data model. Dimension metadata members and hierarchies are often determined at the time of the project. The customer normally has some vehicle for reporting their data (whether it was in a former solution or something as simple as Excel).

The metadata could include dimensions such as Entity or Account, or any other User Defined dimension such as Cost Center, Department, Region, State, or Data Type. What usually isn't decided during requirements are **cubes** and **extensibility**. They are hugely important during design because they create the data partitioning for best performance. As mentioned in previous chapters, all designs should start with extensibility. For data modeling design on cubes and extensibility, please refer to Chapter 3: Design.

Why is data partitioning so important? **Data partitioning** provides operational flexibility and improves performance. This is because the unit of work is broken up into data chunks that are more manageable and operationally relevant. Cube data is stored in data record tables by year. From there, any calculation or consolidation processing is broken down further by unit of work. The unit of work is processed by the **Data Unit**, which consists of cube, entity, parent, consolidation, scenario, and time. The remaining dimensions and dimension members exponentially create the data model and the potential cube cells that can be created.

Let's look at a diagram of how physics plays a role between the data model and performance.

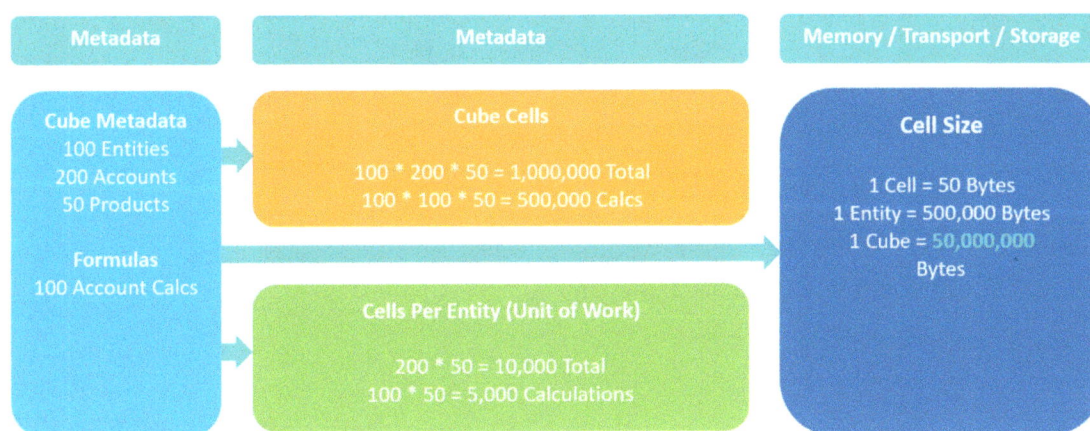

Figure 14.14

This example demonstrates a very basic data model. The metadata consists of cube, entities, accounts, and products. Remember that the unit of work is determined by the Data Unit. Cube and entity are part of the Data Unit along with parent, consolidation, scenario, and time, while accounts and products are not. The data model has 200 accounts and 50 products. Out of the 200 accounts, we have 100 accounts that are calculated. That is a ratio of 50% of our accounts calculating data. In turn, for every cube/entity/parent/cons/scenario/time *combination*, we will have 200 accounts and 50 products. What does this mean for the total number of cube cells and unit(s) of work?

Cube Cells Created from Data Model

1. 100 entities * 200 accounts * 50 products = 1,000,000 total cube cells

2. 100 entities * 100 calc accounts * 50 products = 500,000 total cube cells from calculations

Cube Cells per Entity (Unit of Work)

1. One entity unit of work = 200 accounts * 50 products = 10,000 total cells per entity

2. One entity unit of work = 100 account calculations * 50 products = 5,000 total cells from calculations

Once the data model is determined, how does this tie back to performance? We know that breaking up the unit of work is important for performance, but what's behind the scenes?

Determining the number of cells is key, but what does the cell size look like, and what is the cost to store and transport the cell data in a single cube? Using our diagram and example from Figure 14.14:

Chapter 14

Cell Size for Memory, Transport, and Storage

1. One cell = 50 bytes

2. One entity = 10,000 total cells * 50 bytes = 500,000 bytes

3. One cube = 1,000,000 total cells * 50 bytes = 50,000,000 bytes

This is a simple example of a data model and the resources needed to store and transport cell data. In reality, most data models are much larger. Data models come in all sorts of shapes and sizes where additional dimensions are used and/or dimension member counts are larger to accommodate requirements. The more dimensions and dimension members outside the Data Unit used in a data model, the more consideration is needed to determine potential cube cells and units of work per entity.

Another impact on performance – in terms of the design of the data model – is the **entity hierarchy**. The **consolidation server** really loves an entity hierarchy with lots of base entities and fewer parent entities. This is because of the multi-threaded processing of the unit of work. Base entities can be processed in parallel and leverage the CPU threading on the consolidation server.

In Figure 14.15, the entity hierarchy has five base entities that roll up to one parent entity.

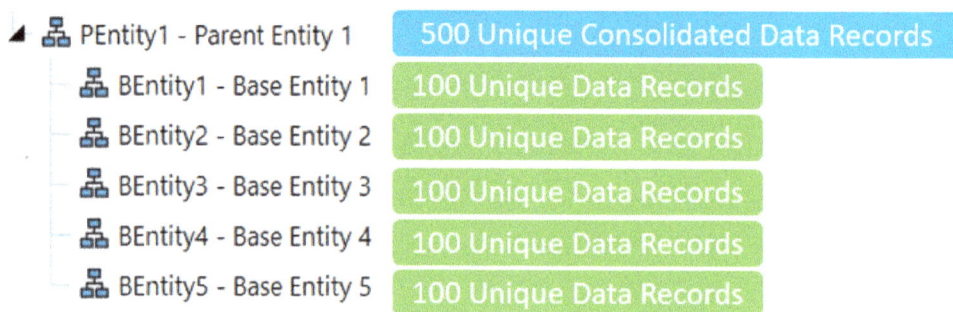

Figure 14.15

From a performance perspective, the consolidation server will efficiently process the base entities as they can be processed in parallel and consolidate to only one parent. During the consolidation process, the CPUs on the consolidation server will sit at around the 90-95% mark. This is good. The CPUs are using their multi-threading capabilities to split the unit of work across all CPUs on the consolidation server.

During this time, the database server is also working as data is being written/updated within the server. However, it's not as hard as with the consolidation servers. It is much easier to update data records that already exist in the database table, in comparison to inserting new data records into the database table. CPUs on the database server will sit at around 40%. This is normal behavior. The consolidation servers are the robust servers, and these are the servers built to take the brunt of the consolidation process.

Also, there is a possibility that the data records for each base entity are unique and don't share common data record intersections. This is considered a **non-aggregating pattern**. Therefore, during the consolidation, PEntity1 cannot aggregate the data records from its base entities to combine into a single data record. The final consolidation at PEntity1 will consist of 500 unique data records.

In Figure 14.16, the entity hierarchy has more of a one-to-one ratio between base and parent entities. For every parent entity, one base entity rolls up to it. This is a one-to-one relationship; five base entities and six parent entities in this hierarchy.

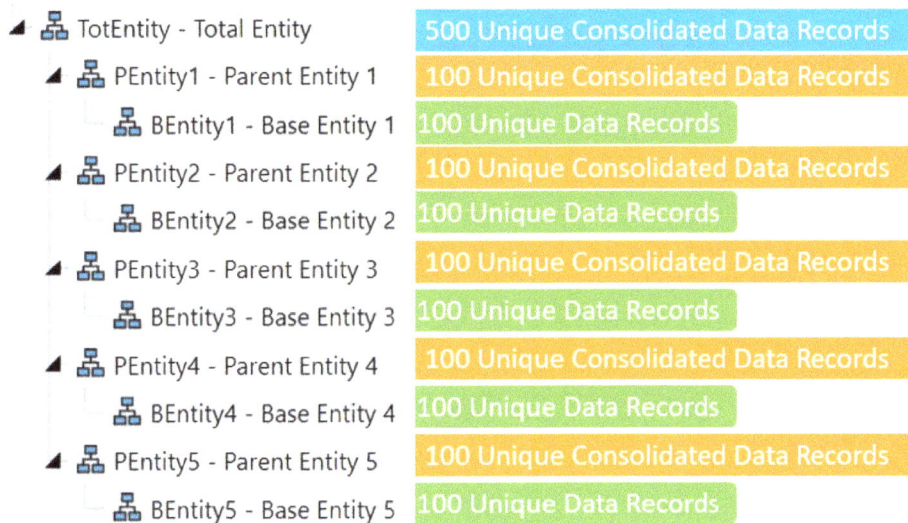

▲ 🖧 TotEntity - Total Entity ┃500 Unique Consolidated Data Records┃
　　▲ 🖧 PEntity1 - Parent Entity 1 ┃100 Unique Consolidated Data Records┃
　　　　🖧 BEntity1 - Base Entity 1 ┃100 Unique Data Records┃
　　▲ 🖧 PEntity2 - Parent Entity 2 ┃100 Unique Consolidated Data Records┃
　　　　🖧 BEntity2 - Base Entity 2 ┃100 Unique Data Records┃
　　▲ 🖧 PEntity3 - Parent Entity 3 ┃100 Unique Consolidated Data Records┃
　　　　🖧 BEntity3 - Base Entity 3 ┃100 Unique Data Records┃
　　▲ 🖧 PEntity4 - Parent Entity 4 ┃100 Unique Consolidated Data Records┃
　　　　🖧 BEntity4 - Base Entity 4 ┃100 Unique Data Records┃
　　▲ 🖧 PEntity5 - Parent Entity 5 ┃100 Unique Consolidated Data Records┃
　　　　🖧 BEntity5 - Base Entity 5 ┃100 Unique Data Records┃

Figure 14.16

But what happens in terms of performance? Introducing the additional parent levels with the one-to-one relationship will change the way both the consolidation and database servers work. In addition, extra work is happening at all the PEntity-level parents, as they are essentially replicating the same data records as child entities data.

The extra work (consolidating the same data as child entities) is done in a more single-threaded manner, creating increased performance times. In this scenario, the CPUs on the consolidation servers will perform at a 40-50% level, and the database server will perform at an 80-90% level.

The roles are now reversed compared to an entity hierarchy with fewer parents. The database server is now taking the brunt of all the work, since there is a lot of writing of data to all the parents. Again, this is in a single-threaded manner. This hierarchy has six parents to have to write to, versus one parent in the other entity hierarchy. In addition, the data records are in a non-aggregating pattern, so the top parent entity cannot optimize data storage to common data records. At the end of the consolidation, the cube-stored data record count is 1,500 in this hierarchy, compared to 1,000 cube data records in the previous illustration.

One last data model concept to consider – in terms of performance – is turning on the **stored share** option through the **consolidation algorithm type** on the cube. As a default, share is dynamically calculated on the fly using (Translated + OwnerPreAdj * % of Consolidation). When the stored share option is turned on, the same logic is executed but is now stored in the DataRecordXXXX tables.

When the consolidation runs, the consolidation and database servers perform differently when the storing of the share data records is executed. The same behavior happens if the entity hierarchy has a one-to-one relationship between parent and base entities. The consolidation server will process at 40-50%, while the database server will process at 80-90%. There are a lot more data records to now write to the DataRecordXXXX tables, and this process is not able to take full advantage of the CPUs on the consolidation server. Share is now stored and is the base for elimination data records. By default, elimination data records are always stored in the database table.

To summarize, data partitioning is vital for optimal performance. The data model is primarily the key to partitioning the unit of work and providing optimal performance. Cube and entity are drivers for total cube cells and unit(s) of work. Together, they combine to partition data efficiently for calculations, consolidations, reporting, and operational relevance. The data model also has a direct relationship with data volumes, which will be covered in the next section.

Data Records and Data Unit Size

In the previous section, the relationship between the data model and performance was discussed. In this section, the impact of data records and Data Unit sizes on performance will be discussed.

Before jumping into data records and Data Unit sizes, let's look at the foundation tables in which the data records are stored.

Prior to loading data into a cube, the source data goes through a transformation process. During the transformation process, the source data is mapped and validated against dimension members determined as part of the data model. When source data is first imported, the source data resides in tables within the staging engine. As the data gets transformed and prepared for the cube, this is the opportunity to aggregate the source detail data to target summarized data through the mapping process.

Once the data is prepared for the cube and the cube is loaded, the data resides in two tables: `StageToFinanceLoadResult`, which is a table associated with the staging engine, and the `DataRecordXXXX` table, which is a table associated with the finance engine. The `XXXX` in the `DataRecord` table indicates the year. This is a data partitioning technique that is inherent within the infrastructure. Data is stored by year.

Anatomy of DataRecordXXXX Table

The `DataRecordXXXX` table can be identified as the consolidation tables for any data collection process, whether it is Actual, Budget, Planning, etc. Data records are stored in these tables from either import, forms, journals, the result of calculations, stored share, or eliminations. The table contains 46 columns that hold dimension member IDs, data cell values, and data cell status. The first seven columns are related to concepts that were discussed as part of the data model. These columns are associated with partitioning and Data Unit dimensions.

PartitionId	CubeId	EntityId	ParentId	ConsId	ScenarioId	YearId
0	0	35651584	-1	176	1048578	2022
0	0	35651584	-1	176	1048578	2022

Figure 14.17

CubeId

The `CubeId` is a unique Id assigned to the cube upon cube creation. The `CubeId` has a direct relationship with `EntityId` and `PartitionId`, and is part of the Data Unit.

EntityId

The `EntityId` is a unique Id assigned to each Entity member upon Entity member creation. The `EntityId` has a direct relationship with the `CubeId` and `PartitionId` and is part of the Data Unit.

ParentId

The `ParentId` is a unique Id assigned to each parent member. The `ParentId` will populate with a valid parent during the consolidation process when the direct entity/parent relationship is executed. `ParentId` is part of the Data Unit.

ConsId

The `ConsId` is a unique Id assigned to each cons member. The `ConsId` is specific to each cons member and is static. For instance, `ConsId 176` is USD. The `ConsId` is part of the Data Unit.

ScenarioId

The `ScenarioId` is a unique Id assigned to each scenario member upon scenario member creation. The `ScenarioId` is part of the Data Unit.

YearId

The `YearId` is a unique assigned Id based on the year associated to the `DataRecordXXXX` table. The `YearId` is part of the Data Unit.

PartitionId

The `PartitionId` is a unique Id to divide the unit of work into chunks. The `PartitionId` has a direct relationship with the `EntityId`. Every Entity member is assigned to a specific `PartitionId` within the `DataRecordXXXX` table. Within the `EntityId` and `PartitionId` relationship, different `CubeId`s exist.

PartitionId ▼	CubeId ▼	EntityId ▼
0	0	35651584
0	0	35651584
0	10	35651584
0	10	35651584

Figure 14.18

In the above illustration (Figure 14.18), the entity exists in multiple cubes, which were created through the data model. `CubeId 0` will be the top-level cube, while `CubeId 10` is the cube where the entity resides.

In addition to the Data Unit and partition columns, there are 12 monthly data value columns and 12 monthly cell status columns.

M1Value	M1Status	M2Value	M2Status	M3Value	M3Status	M4Value	M4Status	M5Value	M5Status
21598181.670000000	65	22048143.790000000	65	22498105.910000000	65	18898408.964400000	65	19798333.200800000	65
21598181.670000000	65	22048143.790000000	65	22498105.910000000	65	18898408.964400000	65	19798333.200800000	65

Figure 14.19

Value Columns

Every `DataRecordXXXX` table contains 12 monthly value columns M1-M12. These store the data cell values for a specific data record by month. For every data record, there are 12 data cell value columns.

Status Columns

Every `DataRecordXXXX` table contains 12 monthly status columns M1-M12. These store the data cell statuses for specific data records by month. For every data record, there are 12 data cell status columns. Common statuses for base entities are:

1. `65` which indicates `Cell Amount <> 0.00`, `Is Real Data = True`, `Is Derived Data = False`, and `Storage Type = Calculation`

2. `33` which indicates `Cell Amount <> 0.00`, `Is Real Data = True`, `Is DerivedData = False`, and `Storage Type = Input`

3. `18` which indicates `Cell Amount = 0.00`, `Is Real Data = False`, `Is Derived Data = True`, and `Storage Type = StoredButNoActivity`

4. For a parent entity, a common status is `97`, which indicates a parent with data, `Is RealData = True`, `Is Derived = False`, `Storage Type = Consolidation`

Now that some of the key columns for the `DataRecordXXXX` table have been explained, data records and data volumes can be discussed.

A data record is a record that consists of a combination of 18 different dimension members. Data records can be created in many forms. Data records can be created as the result of mapping source data in the staging engine and loading into the `DataRecordXXXX` tables. Data records can be submitted through forms or journals.

In addition, data records can be created as a result of calculations or consolidations. Data records are stored for eliminations as well as when **stored share** is used in the data model design. Stored share is typically created dynamically, and not stored. However, if stored share is turned on, the data records for share will be stored in the `DataRecordXXXX` table.

For every unique data record created in the DataRecord table, there are 12 value columns, one for each month. That means there are 12 data cells per data record in the DataRecord table. The first month that data is loaded into the `DataRecordXXXX` table takes a little time. The reason is that this is the first month when data records are inserted into the table. For all subsequent months, the data cell value is updated on the data record for that month. This technique allows for faster loading to the cube since data records are being updated versus inserted. In addition, the number of data records is controlled as there is no unique data record by month.

As illustrated below (Figure 14.20), one entity contains 1,000 data records through import, calculation, forms, journals, and elimination. Each one of those data records contains 12 data cell values. Using simple multiplication, the total data cells for this entity is 12,000.

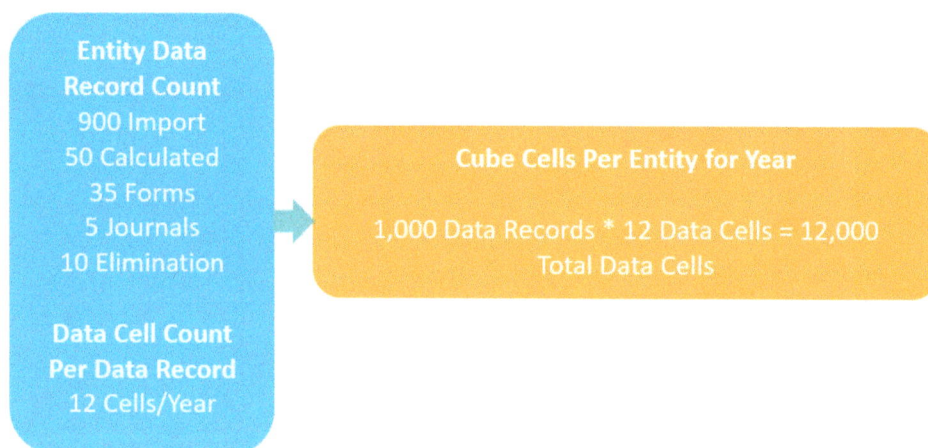

Figure 14.20

As part of the project, it is highly recommended to review the **Application Analysis Dashboard** found in the OneStream Diagnostics Solution Exchange solution. This dashboard highlights key metrics that support Data Unit records, Data Unit sizes, and the optimization of formulas.

- **Formula statistics** – provides visibility into all the Member Formulas and dynamic calculations by dimension and the impact on the CPU usage. This is very useful when identifying member calculations in conjunction with CPU usage.

- **Data statistics** – provides insight into cube records broken out by scenario and origin. In addition, the report identifies how many data records were imported through the workflow. The **explosion factor** is a ratio metric that identifies the percentage of data records created in the import origin as a result of calculations. Experience has shown that the lower the explosion factor, the better the performance.

- **Data Unit statistics** – provides insight into data records by the Data Unit. This is the most impactful report for understanding the data records at base entities, and data records at parent entities. The data records can be shown by local currency, translated currency, and elimination. If using the stored share option, there will be data records shown for share as well. *This report should be used as part of all implementations.*

Why is all this important? Because data record volumes and data cell count have significant impacts on performance. Optimally, for a well-performing full-year consolidation, the top-of-the-house consolidation entity should be at approximately 250,000 total data records in a cube. This equates to 3,000,000 total data cells for the year. During a full-year consolidation, 3,000,000 data cells will be processed. Once the data records start to reach beyond this point, physics and technology play a bigger role in performance. This is where hardware comes into play.

As the data record count grows past 250,000 total data records at the top entity, adjusting the hardware can prove useful in optimizing the consolidation servers. The optimization of a consolidation server can be done in a few ways:

1. Adding more processors

2. Increase multi-threading capabilities

3. The addition of faster CPUs

By adding more processors and/or increasing multi-threading capabilities, there is an opportunity to improve parallel processing. This means that more base-level entities can be processed at once, and each unit of work is performed faster. The downside is that the consolidation server is working faster than the database server and creates even more database pressure, which limits scalability. The database server would need to be addressed for more resources to be applied.

At some point, however, there is a point of diminishing returns. It doesn't matter how many CPUs or multi-threading get added or increased. The data record volume is just too great to power through the parent entities. This could even happen at a base entity if the base entity contains ~90% of the overall data records, for example. At the parent entity level, there are fewer multi-threading options and more single-threaded processes. Therefore, threading on the CPUs becomes less effective and is now dependent on the CPU processors and processor speed. Faster processors have a big impact on large parent entities. A minimum CPU clock speed of 3.7 GHz – 4.0 GHz is preferred.

As much as faster processors sound fantastic, there are some limitations. In cloud environments, physically replacing the CPUs with faster processors is not possible. The CPU and CPU processors are provided by the cloud providers and the data center. As a consultant, this may require a discussion after the data model and data record volumes are determined, and the question to be asked is, "Does the customer deem consolidation performance acceptable?" If data record volumes exceed 250,000 total data records at any parent entity, or at the top entity, and consolidation performance time is not where the customer would like, then it spawns the conversation to determine if the customer is at the proper SaaS level.

This example started out as a small charcoal grill. After having defined all requirements and completing the design and build, you may realize that a bigger cooking vessel is needed to cook everything on the menu.

Conclusion

This chapter outlined some of the tools that are available for properly tuning a OneStream application to meet your customers' needs. Tuning opportunities exist for each component of OneStream; they help ensure that the overall processing times of end-users' daily workflows are as optimal as possible.

Epilogue (Jeff Jones)

My first user conference was in May of 2015, at Splash, in Boston, MA.

This was the first time that I was able to personally experience talking with the OneStream customer and partner community, and I really felt the enthusiasm people had for this platform.

The customer and partner community was so enthusiastic about the software – and where it was headed – and about the service that was provided. The last event of the user conference was at the Heart and Soul of Boston, Fenway Park. Peter Fugere and I were able to go onto the field at Fenway before the Red Sox and Rangers game, and OneStream Software was welcomed by the Red Sox on the video board at the ballpark. Being a HUGE baseball fan, this is something that I will never forget!

Epilogue (Tony Dimitrie)

When I first joined OneStream back in 2011, we had six of us jammed up in one big suite, broken out into two offices and a 'main lobby'. Welcome to OneStream! The photo (right) shows my desk when I was in the office. This lovely desk and hutch set was part of the new renovation of OneStream.

I became good friends with UPS and the FedEx delivery folks. This is also where I found out that John Von Allmen hates peanut butter, razzed Jacqui Slone with Little River Band, enjoyed Friday afternoon mimosas, and put Jody Di Giovanni in a corner. Literally, we tucked her away in the corner when she joined. Nobody puts Jody in the corner. Little known facts.

When I was not at my desk or at a customer, I spent time in the conference room (left) either on calls or delivering training for our first offering of the Administrator Build Class.

We could only hold eight students in the class. You can't see it in this picture, but the bathroom is right next to the conference table where the trainer trains.

The biggest decision to make during training was what we should NOT have for lunch. The walk of shame to the bathroom was real.

When training wasn't happening, we would use the conference room for our weekly OneStream meeting. During this time, we would dial into the Free Conference meeting number, where Eric Davidson would dance to the erotic, dulcet tones of the hold music.

This third image (right) shows *the* place to warm up on a cold Michigan winter day – the IT room. This room served a dual purpose – the location for our physical server, and the hottest place on earth.

I look at these pictures, and I can't believe where we are today. These pictures serve as some of the greatest memories of my lifetime, and I would never trade these experiences for anything. I am so fortunate to have gone through this journey with all my brothers and sisters. I thank everyone in this book because these are the people who I grew up with, and I love them all like family. Did you know Peter Fugere is kind of a big deal?

Index

Index

Index

Index

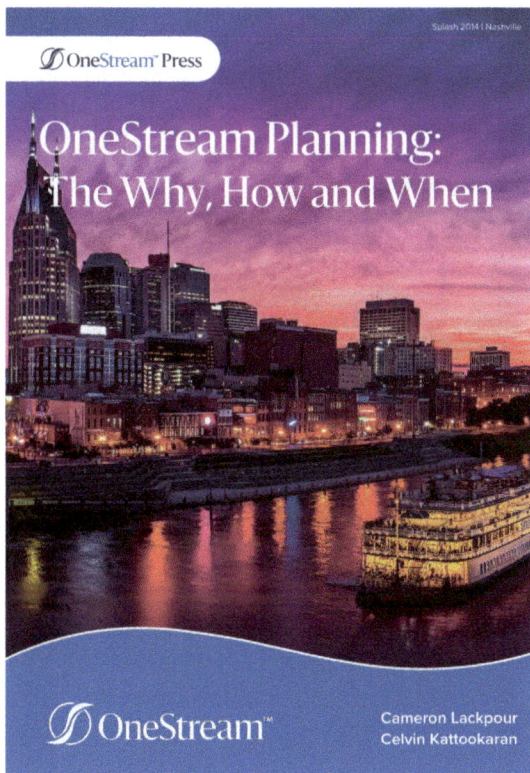

OneStream Planning: The Why, How and When

OneStream is a world-class Intelligent Finance Platform that handles the complex planning, consolidation, reporting and other requirements of mid-sized to large enterprises. Whether in retail, financial services, manufacturing or other industries, the OneStream platform provides the means to integrate multiple data sources and utilize a wide range of tools and methodologies to improve business processes and performance. Through OneStream, organizations benefit from unified, real-time, enterprise-wide planning and forecasting.

Aimed at OneStream Planning practitioners, administrators, implementors, and power users alike, as well as Financial close and consolidations practitioners, *OneStream Planning: The Why, How and When* is the first standalone book in the performance management space to cover the power and potential of Planning in OneStream. Drawing from real-world deployments, the book is rooted in easily understood business use cases, and explains approaches (with code) through a comprehensive exploration of the solution. All this is offered within a framework of top functional and technical practice as informed by the authors' decades-long consulting and application development experiences.

- Which should I do – Import or Direct Load, Consolidate or Aggregate?
- How do Data Buffers really work; what is Eval and why should I care? Which approach is fastest and does it really matter?
- Why Multiyear Scenarios should never be Yearly
- Can Thing Planning run in the Spreadsheet? (It can.)
- Combining REST API and Analytic Blend
- Slice Security down to the very tiniest slice
- Pivot Grid or Large Pivot Grid, that is the question
- A book filled with clear use cases
- Exhaustively tested and verified solutions, and extensive source code
- Undocumented features and functionality covered, along with functional and technical good practices

OneStream Finance Rules and Calculations Handbook

Hundreds of companies have turned to OneStream to solve complex planning, consolidation and operational reporting needs. OneStream's unique ability to provide a multitude of solutions across dozens of industries is largely due to its dynamic Finance Engine which provides the capability to add industry- and company-specific business intelligence to data. Employing the full power of the Finance Engine allows companies to extend the platform and fully exploit the power of their investment.

Aimed at everyone from novices to seasoned veterans, this handbook—by OneStream Distinguished Architect Jon Golembiewski—will break down the Finance Engine and outline how to write Finance Business Rules and Calculations. Its insights will help propel OneStream applications to the next level.

- Fundamentals of the Finance Engine
- Detailed breakdown of the Cube and Data
- A look under the hood of the Api.Data.Calculate function
- Techniques for tackling complex calculation requirements
- How to use the Custom Calculate function to make calculations dynamic
- How to write calculations for optimal performance
- How to troubleshoot calculations
- How to solve and avoid common errors and pitfalls
- Real-world calculation examples with detailed explanations
- A full application with all referenced code examples is available to download

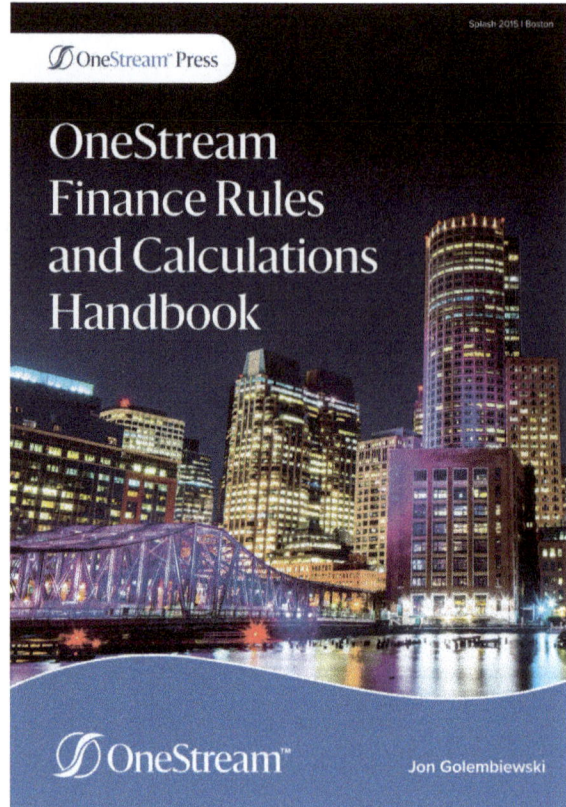

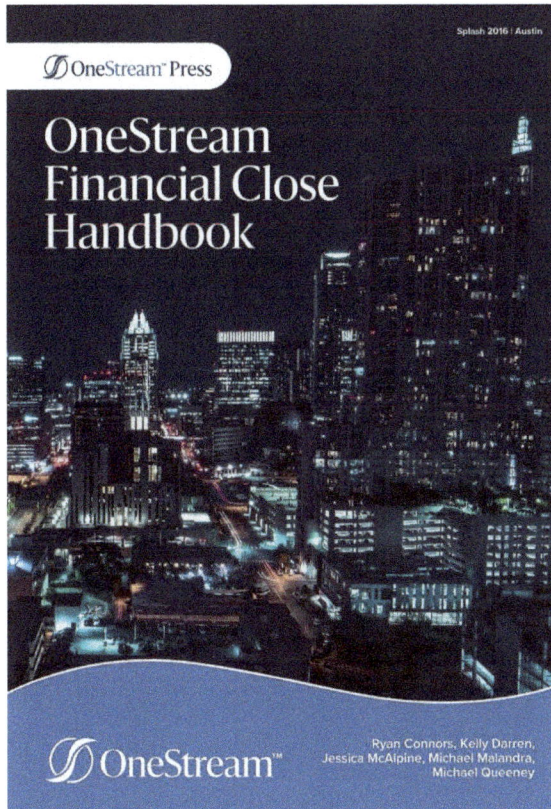

OneStream Financial Close Handbook

OneStream provides a market-leading Intelligent Finance Platform that reduces the complexity of financial operations. It unifies corporate performance management (CPM) processes such as planning, financial close & consolidation, reporting and analytics through a single, extensible solution.

The OneStream Financial Close Handbook – written by expert authors – is a practical book for implementors, administrators, and end-users, that dives into the Financial Close with a specific focus on the Account Reconciliations and Transaction Matching solutions.

The Account Reconciliations solution is a complete package that plugs into the Financial Close Workflow to leverage data that already resides within the consolidation application, whilst Transaction Matching helps accounting teams automate the collection and matching of large numbers of transactions across multiple sources.

With these solutions, OneStream Financial Close delivers the four key pillars of a good reconciliation process: Visibility, Standardization, Efficiency and Control.

In this book:

- Get a better understanding of the Financial Close process, and how OneStream delivers a streamlined, automated solution.
- Learn how to implement Account Reconciliations through detailed project phases, and accompanying case studies.
- Get to grips with the administration of Account Reconciliations, including settings, security, and auditing.
- Deep dive into the Account Reconciliation Solution from the End User's perspective, including how to prepare a Reconciliation, the sign-off and approval process, and overall reporting and monitoring capabilities.
- Learn what Transaction Matching is, plus how to build, test, and implement OneStream's highly automated system.
- Understand how to administer Transaction Matching through global options, access control, match sets, data sets, rules, and more!

OneStream Advanced Reporting and Dashboards

OneStream is a world-class Intelligent Finance Platform that empowers organizations to have confidence in their data and make decisions that maximize business impact. It is used by enterprises all over the world to streamline financial close, consolidation, planning, reporting and analysis, and drive effective business decisions – all based on near real-time data.

The user experience is the point of contact with the platform, and while OneStream comes with a powerful standard UI, one of its greatest strengths is its ability to create bespoke reports and custom dashboards. Like our customers, each OneStream application is unique – whether you're a novice or have experience with CPM solutions, OneStream provides the flexibility to tailor a solution to meet your needs. Concepts discussed in this book are intended to help you understand the unlimited possibilities of designing your ultimate user experience.

Written for administrators, dashboard and report designers, plus end users, and filled with background knowledge and step-by-step guides, this book deep dives into Cube Views, dashboards, reporting, and highlights the tools and tricks that will take user experiences to a new level. We examine how leveraging the full power of the OneStream Platform will help you move beyond the standard interface, align your end-user experiences with your business and process requirements, promote user adoption through efficiency and ease of use, and truly maximize the value of your OneStream implementation.

By the end of this book, you will have a deep understanding of the components that drive the user experience and how and when to use them. You'll walk away with a plethora of tools and ideas to incorporate into your application to deliver your very own user experience.

In this book, we will:

- Design and build Cube Views, based on data entry and reporting needs.
- Discuss the use of Cube View extender business rules to expose advanced formatting capabilities.
- Explore how navigation links and drill to dashboard functionality provide intuitive analysis.
- Identify the benefits of configuring personalized home pages to ensure user adoption.
- Create working role-based dashboards inspired by real-world customer requirements.

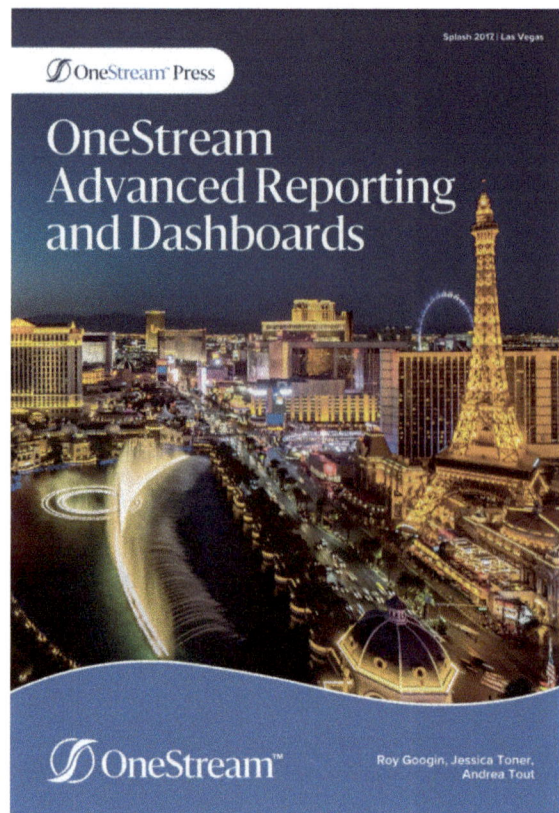

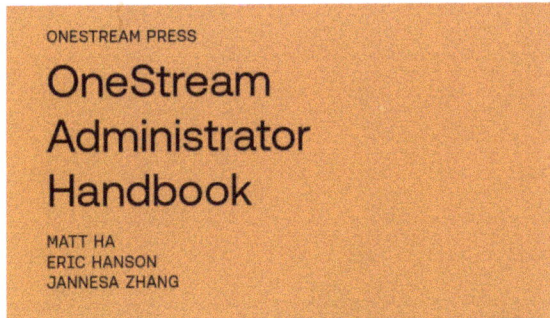

OneStream Administrator Handbook

ONESTREAM PRESS

OneStream Administrator Handbook

MATT HA
ERIC HANSON
JANNESA ZHANG

ⓘ onestream

Administrators are integral to the day-by-day operations and overall wellbeing of a company's financial ecosystem. Although each OneStream application is unique, the challenges that administrators face when managing the OneStream platform remain similar when it comes to processes and troubleshooting.

Whether you are a novice or seasoned administrator, this book examines key concepts to help you understand and manage the financial and data processes of your OneStream application. Written for administrators, this book is filled with technical and functional contexts – whether syntax-related to business rules or general accounting concepts – and dives into practical examples and use cases that provide guidance and insights into commonly encountered themes.

By the end of this book, you will have a deep understanding and appreciation of the capabilities that the OneStream platform offers, and have the tools needed to tackle the wide variety of administrative actions that may surface. In this book, we will cover:

- Components within OneStream, such as application properties, metadata, and workflow
- Data troubleshooting for missing or off data, whether that is related to integration setup, workflow setup, calculation adjustments in business rules, or more.
- Translations involving cube and metadata settings, plus the loading and viewing of FX rates.
- The security framework, and all the nooks and crannies that can be secured within OneStream.
- Constraining and locking data through systems-level and process-level controls.
- Considerations – as companies mature – for the updating of new or existing business processes.

www.ingramcontent.com/pod-product-compliance
Lightning Source LLC
Chambersburg PA
CBHW041621220326
41598CB00046BA/7426